W9-BHY-683

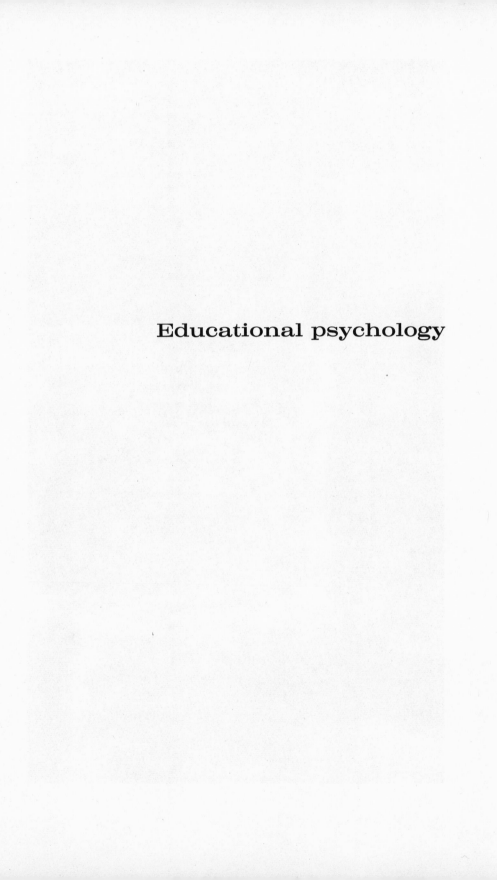

Educational psychology

The Century Psychology Series

Richard M. Elliott (1887–1969)
Kenneth MacCorquodale
Gardner Lindzey
Kenneth E. Clark
Editors

Educational psychology
Instruction and behavioral change

Francis J. Di Vesta
The Pennsylvania State University

George G. Thompson
The Ohio State University

APPLETON-CENTURY-CROFTS
Educational Division
New York **MEREDITH CORPORATION**

To Evy and Ginny

Contents

Preface

Although this is technically a new edition of our *Educational Psychology*, published first in 1959, the present volume presents almost completely new content. This edition bears only a very modest similarity to its predecessor in design, scope, or manner of presentation. There are several reasons for this essential discontinuity between the two editions. For example, during the intervening decade there have been substantial, and in some instances dramatic, changes in the manifest and socially inferred needs of pupils, teachers, and parents. Progressive racial integration within the public schools and federally subsidized educational programs for some of the children of culturally and economically underprivileged parents are among the more important of the many *social changes* that have altered classroom teachers' duties and responsibilities. Moreover, *scientific progress* during the last ten years has highlighted the significance of a somewhat different set of psychological variables, and has in many instances forced a considerable restructuring of psychological theories. Cognition, adaptation, attention, and imagery are no longer *verboten* topics for discussion in respectable circles of scientific psychology. Short-term memory, operational processes in thinking, and organizational factors in recall have been, and continue to be, studied assiduously. The psychological relevance and implications of psycholinguistics and computer-simulation models are also being investigated with profit in a great many research centers. These theoretical modifications and empirical advances are solidly integrated into the content of the present volume. In addition, the findings of numerous investigations of creativity, intelligence, verbal mediation, and learning to learn are also generously sampled and conceptually reflected in this new interpretation of what we believe to be the most relevant and useful information that psychology can offer teachers and other educational personnel.

In writing the present work we conscientiously did our best to integrate psychological development into the various discussions of learning and behavioral change, to interweave current curricular and instructional reforms and emphases within the network of psychological principles and theories that have initiated and sustained these educational innovations and reforms, and to incorporate much of the material on measurement and evaluation into related presentations of substantive content. It is our belief that these integrations will greatly enhance the teachability and usefulness of this volume.

Throughout this project we did our best to maintain a functional orientation toward teachers' many opportunities and responsibilities for influencing the lives of their pupils. We have consistently emphasized the teacher's many pedagogical roles—as a quasi-scientist, as a quasi-clinician and therapist, as a highly informed and concerned guide and tutor, as an evaluator of the economics of behavioral change, and as a warm and supportive comforter of discouraged and disheartened pupils. It is our opinion that master teachers play all of these roles, drawing as best they can on their knowledge of the social sciences and utilizing whenever possible the artistic skills of pedagogy that they have accumulated over the years. It is our conviction that the contents of the present volume can serve as a reliable and useful guide to the rudiments of what is now known about the scientific method, the contributions that psychology can make to effective teaching, the complex interactions of development and learning that go into psychological adaptation, and antecedents of learning and behavioral change, the structure and dynamics of personality and character development, and the measurement of individual abilities and achievements.

In this writing we have presented supplementary materials of special interest set off from the main text by a green border. It is our hope that these summaries of research, theoretical points of view, and philosophical stances will stimulate reflection and colloquy among students who may use this volume as a textbook in their introduction to educational psychology. We believe that students should have the privilege of confrontation with the basic issues as they are viewed by our most productive and respected theoreticians and investigators.

In our selection of research studies to support psychological generalizations and to illustrate scientific principles we attempted a representative sampling—choosing some classic but mostly recent reports, presenting some correlational but a much greater number of experimental findings, citing some findings obtained from animal studies but the larger bulk from research with children and adolescents. We have also sampled freely from diverse theoretical orientations, in the belief that no single one is adequate for meeting the teacher's needs and that the availability of some educated hunches, however fragmentary, is generally better than no knowledge. We have frequently reminded the reader that the findings of psychological research only very infrequently provide directly translatable information on what can be done to optimize learning and psychological adaptation within the classroom. Rather, the findings of psychological research at best usually have only implications for modifying the teaching arts. In all instances we have tried to enumerate and illustrate these implications, rather than leaving the burden of interpretation to the reader. This does not mean that we have exhausted all such implications in our discussion. This would entail a degree of professional perfection not claimed or possessed by the authors. The reader is left with plenty of conceptual room to consider additional, as well as different, implications for improving educational procedures.

The substantive content of the present edition is concerned with the teaching of all pupils from kindergarten through the twelfth grade. Whenever possible we have sampled research studies that proportionately represent these various levels of psychological and physical maturity. As noted earlier, we have tried to interweave developmental and learning variables in our discussions of the antecedents of behavioral change.

Underlying the general philosophical orientation of this book is a fair measure of concern for the education of pupils from backgrounds that may prove to be disadvantageous in the majority of our present school settings. Included for consideration are children from such groups as the barrio Mexican-Americans; ghetto-bound Puerto Ricans, blacks, Orientals; and whites from the poverty-stricken areas of Appalachia. While there has been much written about the educational needs of children from these groups, not much is known about how these educational needs can best be met. Nevertheless, wherever possible we have introduced materials which we hope will aid the teacher in making tentative decisions about such important matters. Some of this material is based on research evidence, while other parts are based only on writings by informed observers.

Decisions regarding these pressing social issues cannot be made in the absence of sociological, philosophical, and moral (value) considerations. Solutions for current problems require attention to the school's role in promoting values related to the reduction of prejudice and discrimination, to its role in educating ethnic groups to understand their history, and to its role in helping pupils to take pride in their particular cultural heritage. Nor can decisions about educative processes be made in the absence of concern for mental health and human relations. The school must be a friendly yet challenging place in which pupils and teachers are freed of oppressive administrative requirements; in which they can pursue personal and imaginative paths to the accomplishment of routine objectives; and where there is freedom and flexibility, at least on occasion, to contemplate the present and future significance of a current event. As a consequence of our concern for these matters such related substantive materials comprise an important part of this book.

In developing this work we have carefully guarded the expenditure of space, insisting that every sentence, table, chart, and figure make an important contribution to the total effort. Although psychologists are notoriously dull writers, as are the majority of their scientific brethren, we like to believe that the present volume is above average in readability because we made the extra try in that direction and received some expert assistance from our editors. To the latter we express sincere appreciation. We have dedicated this work to our wives who have helped in many ways to bring this writing project to a mutually satisfying conclusion. They have guided us successfully through the recent childrearing days of our lives, frequently protecting our sanctuary during periods set aside for work on "the book," often attending PTA meetings in our behalf, frequently interpreting school problems to us in ways quite foreign to our psychological perspectives, and never hesitating to use their feminine intuitions to seeming advantage when we were in deep water without a psychological principle to cling to. For these and many other favors that permitted the completion of this project we are grateful.

F. J. D.

G. G. T.

Part I

Psychological foundations of education

Some zealous chauvinists in the behavioral and social sciences have stated from time to time that psychology is *the* basic science of education. Being, we hope, of temperate disposition and mindful of the flaws and shortcomings of our infant science, we prefer the more modest claim that psychology is the science most directly relevant to what goes on *within the classroom.* It is our firm conviction that a knowledge of the research findings and theories of psychology can be helpful to teachers and other educational personnel. In the next two chapters we attempt to show how psychologists function as scientists and how their activities influence the many dimensions of modern education.

1

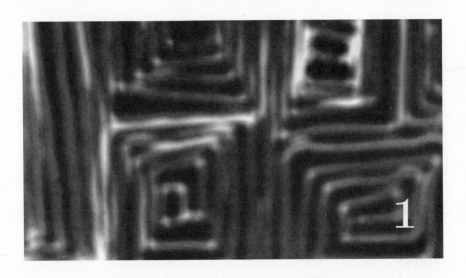

Contributions of psychology to education: A science and its applications

It is obvious to all that teaching had become a highly refined art and education an intricately structured institution many centuries before psychology split off from philosophy and became a distinct area of scientific inquiry. The arts and crafts have always preceded formal science and related technologies in all domains of knowledge. For example, the Romans built magnificent bridges and aqueducts, some of which are still in daily use after two thousand years, long before those experimental and rational elaborations of physics that now undergird civil and architectural engineering. The applied arts with their bench marks and rule-of-thumb principles have always preceded the experimental, analytic, and theoretical operations on which modern science has been constructed. When the artisan is socially and economically pressed to work faster or produce a superior product, he often conjures up a way of accomplishing the assignment even though he remains ignorant of its conceptual origins. The artist's thinking " . . . more frequently proceeds to its terminus by a leap than does thinking in the closed system or in experimental science" (Bartlett, 1958). Despite the advantage of such leaps in thinking, there are limits to the artisan's resources for problem-solving, natural restrictions which can be pushed back only by the systematized knowledge of science.

The successful teacher may appropriately ask why he should be concerned with the behavioral sciences, since his currently used princi-

3

ples and methods appear to be adequate, or even superior. Such a question needs to be answered and, fortunately for science, history offers a reply that usually satisfies the culturally informed majority. The technical arts, restricted as they are to concerns about the here-and-now's of daily experience, typically approach an upper limit of perfection that defines the asymptote of man's ingenuity for valid generalizing without the aid of specially constructed observational, logical, and conceptual tools. Eventually, even the most skillful and successful of artisans can profit from the added freedom that science provides for the manipulation of the as-if's of man's creative imagination. Logic and mathematics have supplied the scientist with a powerful but permissive set of rules for the knowledge game, as well as a relatively unambiguous language for retracing the game or describing his conceptual adventure to others.

The tools fashioned by science help man to stretch the limits of his creative imagination, and thereby permit him alternative views of the "obvious." For example, consider the tremendous advance in the engineering art of harnessing and transporting electrical energy made possible by the mathematician's imaginary numbers (e.g., $\sqrt{-1}$). Or, as a more general example, consider the great advantage in the ability to use the precise language of science by a master artisan for more definitive communications with less experienced apprentices. The latter can follow the master artisan's dicta with a degree of precision that makes the reproduction of the artisan's technical achievement a satisfying commonplace. When the concepts, methods, and metric principles of a science are available in teachable form, the apprentice need no longer journey to study under the guidance of the master; he can learn from the writings of many masters, some of whom lived in other centuries.

The foregoing is not to imply that scientific knowledge arranges for its own dissemination or application—this is far from true. Finding effective ways of applying the findings of science toward an improvement of man's control over his environment and his relationship thereto taxes the best of man's inventive and technical resources. The difficulties involved in discovering appropriate and socially acceptable methods for applying what is scientifically known seem especially compounded in the behavioral sciences. The modification of educational practices in a democracy where the majority's approval for change must be secured and maintained requires a large measure of human ingenuity and planning. The availability of scientific knowledge is only a beginning, the first lap of the course leading to an improvement in the human condition.*

*Consult Appendix C for a discussion of psychology as a science and as an applied discipline.

In something as complex as a school system, we need another level of research strategy, which I shall call *the strategy of innovation*. The best of equipment may be idle, the best of resources remain unused, the best of techniques sabotaged, if there is not care in introducing the new methods or new materials to all concerned. Once the pure-science principles have been established and the applications validated in practice schoolrooms, the more widespread adoption is by no means guaranteed or, if the adoption is forced, there is no assurance that the desired results will be forthcoming. Abstractly, the steps of innovation are clear enough: Provide (*a*) a sound research-based program, validated in tryout, (*b*) the program packaged in such a way as to be available, as in good textbooks, supplementary readings in the form of pamphlets, films, programs for teaching machines, and guides for the teachers, (*c*) testing materials by which it can be ascertained if the objectives of the program have indeed been realized, with appropriate normative data on these evaluative instruments, (*d*) in-service training of the teacher to overcome the teacher's resistance to something new and to gain his enthusiastic acceptance of the program as something valuable as well as to train him in its use, and (*e*) support for the program from the community, school boards, parents, and others concerned with the schools. (From Hilgard, 1964, pp. 413–414. With permission of author and publisher.)

What Teachers Expect from Psychology

Teachers seek answers to such questions as "What can the pupil learn?" "What tasks are required of the pupil?" "How must the classroom setting be manipulated to accomplish specific objectives?" "What considerations must be made of individual differences?"

Theories of learning and theories of teaching fortunately provide a basis for answers that, at least, are better than folklore and, at best, have important implications for the activities involved in teaching. It would be most desirable to have one theory of learning or teaching which contains implications for all objectives. Unfortunately we have no such theory at the present stage of psychological knowledge. Some theories and facts about learning will be more useful for producing change in the psychomotor skills area, others will be more useful for understanding learning of the cognitive behaviors, and still others will be more useful for modifying the affective components of behavior. These theories direct the psychologist toward what the pupil can learn and what variables must be considered by the teacher if certain clearly defined changes in the pupil's behavior are to be produced.

Some psychologists have focused on finding relationships between existing differences in pupil characteristics on the one hand, and some measure of his behavior in a classroom task on the other. We might learn, for example, that intelligence is related to achievement, or that interests are not highly related to achievement. Such facts could be useful for prediction and diagnosis. If we know something about the pupil's performance on a test we can often predict (within certain probability limits) what his performance in some classroom assignment is likely to be.

Although this kind of data aids in identifying what to expect of a pupil, it is not too helpful in identifying methods for facilitating learning, except by inference. From a practical standpoint, the teacher is very much concerned with what can be done to help the pupil learn. This is implied in the question "But, *how* do I teach?" frequently asked by students who are preparing to teach. This question is answered in more than a superficial manner from knowledge about specific techniques that have proved helpful in teaching. Knowing how to organize a class register before going into class, how to make lesson plans, how to assign study tasks, how to lead discussions, how to lecture, and how to use demonstrations can be most helpful guides to the beginning teacher.

A hierarchical model of learning applied to instruction

A number of theorists have worked with the idea that there are several types of learning, each with its own laws. One of the most traditional classifications is the distinction between classical and instrumental conditioning based on the principles of association and reward, respectively. Tolman (1949) was among the first to accept several types of learning including the acquisition of value or secondary reward properties, attitudes, concepts, patterns of readinesses for learning drive discriminations, and psychomotor skills.

More recently, Gagné (1965) has also developed a model proposing several types of learning. Although he was influenced by earlier theories the new model differs from them in several important respects: First, there are eight kinds of learning proposed rather than the fewer numbers suggested in earlier theories. Second, the kinds of learning are arranged from simple to complex. Third, the model is hierarchical in the sense that proficiency in one type of learning is assumed to depend upon proficiency in those types fundamental to it, and, in turn, facilitates mastery of those above it. Fourth, Gagné suggests that the higher order processes within rule or principle learning can be hierarchically organized. Fifth, there is an attempt to apply this hierarchical organization of learning types to planning for learning, managing learning, instructing, and selecting media for use in teaching.

The hierarchical model based on a description by Gagné (1965, pp. 58–61) with an example of a learning structure for the basic skills of reading (Gagné, 1965, p. 201, Figure 16) is shown in Figure 1-1.

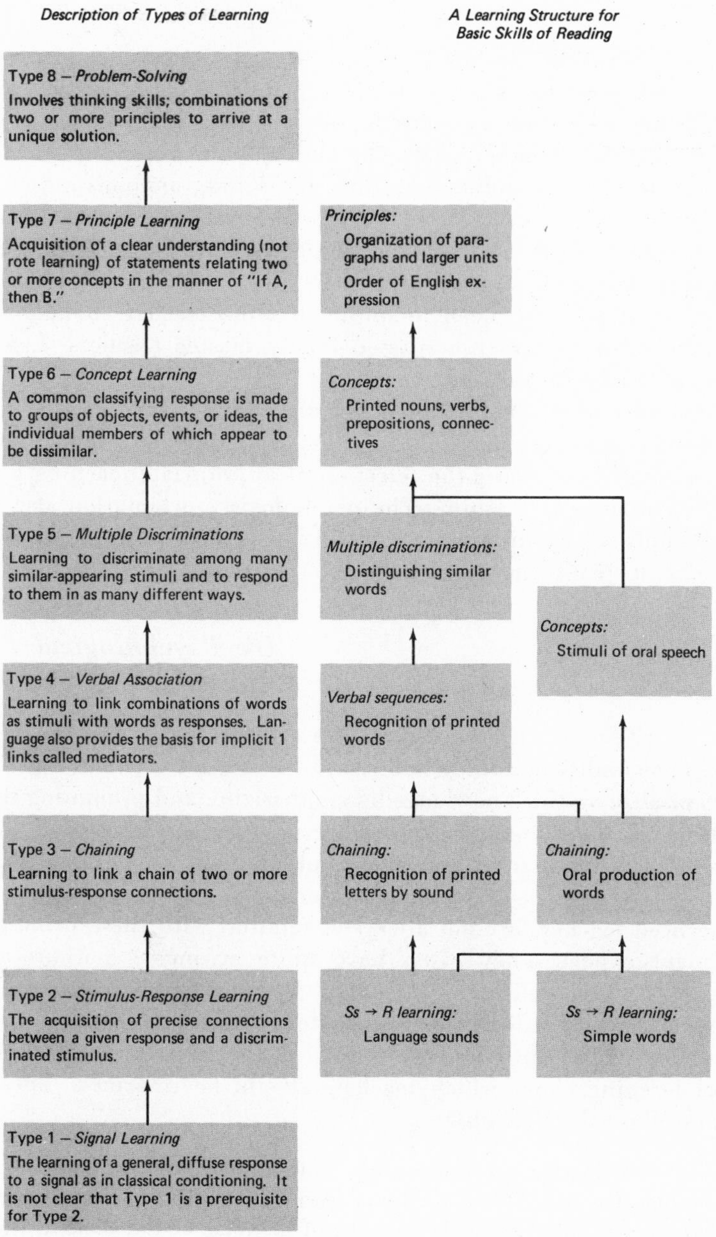

Type 8 — *Problem-Solving*

Involves thinking skills; combinations of two or more principles to arrive at a unique solution.

Type 7 — *Principle Learning*

Acquisition of a clear understanding (not rote learning) of statements relating two or more concepts in the manner of "If A, then B."

Principles:

Organization of paragraphs and larger units

Order of English expression

Type 6 — *Concept Learning*

A common classifying response is made to groups of objects, events, or ideas, the individual members of which appear to be dissimilar.

Concepts:

Printed nouns, verbs, prepositions, connectives

Type 5 — *Multiple Discriminations*

Learning to discriminate among many similar-appearing stimuli and to respond to them in as many different ways.

Multiple discriminations:

Distinguishing similar words

Concepts:

Stimuli of oral speech

Type 4 — *Verbal Association*

Learning to link combinations of words as stimuli with words as responses. Language also provides the basis for implicit 1 links called mediators.

Verbal sequences:

Recognition of printed words

Type 3 — *Chaining*

Learning to link a chain of two or more stimulus-response connections.

Chaining:

Recognition of printed letters by sound

Chaining:

Oral production of words

Type 2 — *Stimulus-Response Learning*

The acquisition of precise connections between a given response and a discriminated stimulus.

$Ss \rightarrow R$ *learning:*

Language sounds

$Ss \rightarrow R$ *learning:*

Simple words

Type 1 — *Signal Learning*

The learning of a general, diffuse response to a signal as in classical conditioning. It is not clear that Type 1 is a prerequisite for Type 2.

Figure 1-1. A hierarchical model of learning and a parallel learning structure for basic skills of reading. Each type of learning requires as a prerequisite the learning described below it. (Based on Gagné, 1965, pp. 58–61, 201, and Figure 16. With permission of author and publisher.)

However, knowing only these techniques does not provide the teacher with useful and durable principles for the improvement of teaching with added experience. Here a knowledge of learning theories and learning principles can play an important role. The latter provide a basis for understanding why certain teaching methods are effective and they provide a background for new innovations. Teaching is an art, in large part, because it depends upon the adaptation of techniques to each pupil in each class by a specific teacher.

We do not mean to imply that the teacher should ignore completely the information passed on by master teachers. Lawfulness in these methods that have been used over several decades can be discovered. One of the major tasks confronting every teacher is to find, in the vast literature of psychology, those principles and laws that hold the promise of governing the selection of appropriate teaching methods for the guidance of learning. The psychologist's orientation also focuses on the optimal conditions for effecting behavioral change. Thus, in a real sense, his concerns significantly overlap those of the teacher.

Are Psychological Principles
Self-Evident to the Teacher?

Teaching can be viewed as a complement to the learning process. If the conditions that benefit learning are known, then the teacher can capitalize on this knowledge by emphasizing and promoting these conditions in the classroom. Thus, it would be expected that all teachers should be familiar with principles of learning.

It may be surprising to some readers that mature and experienced teachers are not always as familiar with these principles as one might expect. They often have quite erroneous notions about how pupils learn, and their teaching is sometimes guided by uncritical acceptance of half-truths. In one study, Weber (1965) had his graduate students in a course on theories of learning identify some characteristics of learning about which teachers should be informed. These students agreed on the following:

(1) Motivation is necessary. Unless learners desire to learn, learning is not likely to occur. (2) Transfer of learning is not likely to occur automatically. Experiences must be made meaningful in terms of the goals of the learner if transfer is to occur. (3) Mere repetition, exercise, or drill by itself is not necessarily conducive to learning. They often appear to be sufficient conditions because learners see that these activities are related to their goals. (4) Learning is not merely a matter of change. While learning is often variable, it is usually related to goals or purposes of learners rather than to purposes of teachers. (5) Responses are modified by their consequences; plans of action that lead learners toward their goals are more likely to be learned; those that

divert learners from their goals are less likely to be learned. (6) Learning is, in part, a process of discriminating one situation or one plan of action from another in meaningful patterns which are related to learners' goals. (Weber, 1965, p. 433. With permission of author and publisher.)

After the foregoing summary was made, these graduate students interviewed a total of 156 teachers in 22 schools. The question asked was simply, "What is your understanding of the learning process; how, in your opinion, do children learn?" Their replies are summarized in Table 1-1. It is interesting to note how many teachers felt that difficulties in learning were, for the most part, the responsibility of the child. Where there was awareness of the responsibilities of the teacher, the notions of the learning process were incomplete or erroneous. The fact that one third of the teachers were oblivious to (or didn't care about) the way children learn (see item with rank of 3 in Table 1-1) seems to be a serious weakness in the attitude of some teachers toward the psychological foundations of their profession.

Table 1-1. The beliefs of 156 teachers about children's learning.

Rank	Category	No. of Replies	Percent of Teachers Giving this Reply
1	Children learn through drill and repetition.	73	47
2	Children learn by imitating others.	59	38
3	Do not know; had not thought about it.	51	33
4	Children learn by hard work.	40	26
5	Children learn by following directions of teachers.	33	21
6	Children learn by trial and error.	27	17
7	Children learn by maturation.	19	12
8	Miscellaneous.	11	7

SOURCE: Weber, 1965, p. 434. With permission of author and publisher.

Similar misconceptions about learning and teaching were found among teachers by Burton (1944) in a study conducted much earlier. The teachers in his study thought that: (1) Learning is very much the same as memorizing. (2) Learning is strictly an intellectual matter. (3) Facts and verbalisms are sufficient outcomes of teaching. (4) Transfer is automatic. (5) Attitudes and emotional reactions are of secondary importance.

These and other matters are discussed in some detail in this book. For the present, it may be sufficient to say that it is the teacher's responsibility to have an accurate understanding of the learning process. Furthermore, research findings related to the educational process must be critically examined before they are used to direct teaching methods.

The Relationship of Teaching to Theories of Behavioral Change

Gage (1964) has analyzed one contribution that might be made to the teaching process from the psychology of learning. The general ideas of his analysis are summarized in this section. He indicates that teaching is not necessarily dependent on any one theory. It is more likely to be idiosyncratically related to several theories, each in quite a different way. Cognitive theories, for example, imply that knowledges are learned more readily and retained for a longer period if the tasks are structured. Concepts are taught through emphasis on constancies, groupings, and ways of perceiving visual and auditory stimuli among instances of a concept-class.

Structure, meaning, discovery, and creativity have become important concepts for understanding the development of cognitive behaviors during the past decade. The value of these terms as constructs to guide laboratory experimentation, or as ideas that can be communicated to the teacher, must still be determined. Nevertheless, such theories help to identify variables that might be considered when course content is presented. (In Figure 1-1 is displayed an example of how one description of learning is used to analyze the structure for teaching basic skills in reading.) The teacher will organize the pupil's tasks, or the organization will be discovered by the pupil. Methods of instruction should make provision for structure if pupils are to learn effectively. When teaching ideas one must consider the structure of the material that is to be taught; either a structure is imposed on the material, or it is left to the student to grasp the structure through his own study.

Other theories seem important for developing classroom climate. Again, the notion of "climate" is not clearly defined. The term commonly refers to a favorable working relationship between teacher and pupil and to the amount of support provided by the teacher when the pupil succeeds or fails at a task. The ratio of successes to failures, and the feelings of acceptance or rejection are potential indicators of the "climate" of a classroom. As a result the pupil's attitude toward his work, his motivations, and his feelings of avoidance or approach toward classroom work may be affected. These consequences are affective in nature. They involve the emotions or "feeling-tone" associated with school. Classroom climate, then, is necessarily dependent upon the patterns of rewards and punishments, often verbally provided by the teacher; and by the pupil's associations of success and failure with the typical classroom situation that he is in. The first is involved in instrumental learning and the second in classical learning.

The principles guiding emotional learning point to different factors than those indicated by cognitive theories. Classical learning is generally recognized as a potent process in learning emotional reactions (Bijou & Baer, 1961; Bugelski, 1964). Disapproval, a negative consequence of behavior, may cause the child to blush. The presentation of an unexpected favorable consequence may produce such physiological reactions as goose pimples, flushing of the face, and breathing faster, all of which are associated with the experience of being "thrilled." The removal or withdrawal of an expected favorable consequence from a pupil can cause him to become angry. If he is threatened by the removal of some favorable consequence he may become fearful.

Sometimes the pupil is required to make a choice between two favorable alternatives (e.g., going to a party or going to a ball game) or between two unfavorable alternatives (e.g., studying or failing a course). Under these circumstances a casual observer might say that the person is "torn" by conflict. Decisions of the sort described are often accompanied by the physiological reactions associated with emotions and, if they are typical of everyday activity in a class, they will contribute to classroom climate.

The categories of "rejecting," "indulging," "dominating," "democratic," "autocratic," and so forth, are also used to describe teacher behaviors associated with classroom climate. However, these terms may not be as functionally useful as observations based on the principles of conditioned learning (Bijou & Baer, 1961, p. 20). It may be more useful instead to concentrate upon the kinds (favorable or unfavorable) of stimuli a teacher provides in attempting to strengthen some behaviors of the pupil, to weaken others, and to leave still other behaviors unaffected.

It can be seen that structure is important for cognitive learning. Rewards and punishments as consequences of behavior may affect emotional learning. Other learnings are facilitated by gradually "shaping" patterns of behavior through differential reinforcement of relevant responses. Shaping implies that each succeeding response gradually approximates the terminal objective. However, shaping procedures are time consuming and require a great deal of painstaking effort. The question here is whether there is a more effective procedure that might be used by the teacher in controlling the pupil's behavior.

One alternative to the shaping procedure is to base teaching methods for some objectives on theories of identification and imitation (Bandura & Walters, 1963). The teacher might teach handwriting by asking the child to imitate the way a letter or word is written. Imitation can be an effective requirement for a range of activities from learning to articulate to learning attitudes. Much can be learned, for example, by imitating a good demonstration of the backhand stroke in tennis. Many social behaviors appear to be learned by imitating others. Adolescents adopt the dress, the mannerisms, and the language of their peers. The acquisition of these behaviors must seem almost automatic to the casual observer. To the psychologist, they provoke an inquiry of the process of learning by imitation and of the factors affecting the imitation of the behavior of others.

One important variable in the imitation process appears to be the role of the person imitated, that is, the "model." The teacher is a potential model in the classroom. Especially important for such modeling to occur is the relationship between the teacher and the pupil. For example, the pupil is more likely to imitate a rewarding model than one who is not rewarding. Another concern is with the variables affecting the selection of a teacher as a model; that is, a model with whom the pupil can identify. An effective model is one who is perceived as prestigious in his chosen field, as successful, and whose behavior is capable of being imitated. Thus, a degree of identification is involved if learning by the process of imitation is to be successful. Given the appropriate conditions, psychomotor skills and attitudes are probably learned efficiently through teaching methods (e.g., demonstrations) that capitalize on imitation of a successful model. There is still much to be learned about the implications of this theory for teaching. Nevertheless, one implication is that sound and efficient teaching methods for some objectives, at least, must be related to the interpersonal relationships that exist in the classroom.

Regardless of the theory within which the psychologist conducts his investigation, he is concerned with the factors that contribute to behavior change. The teacher is also concerned with behavior change and with the factors that control it. The difference between the interests of the two professional groups is that the psychologist directs his efforts to the explanation of the processes of learning and teaching while the teacher is more concerned with the way in which the principles may be engineered to fit a given teaching situation. If the teacher is to be successful in this function he must have a thorough and critical grasp of the understandings to be gained from experimental evidence and theory, of the distinctions between learning theories, and of the principles of learning that have been verified within these theories. With continual translation from learning principles to the practices of teaching, the teacher will be able to adapt successfully to idiosyncratic teaching problems as they occur and to provide innovations where required.

Summary

Teaching was a highly refined art long before psychology became a science. Nevertheless, within its relatively short history as a science, psychology has brought about many changes in educational practices.

Science permits and supports advances that cannot be produced by artisans and technicians in its absence, because science frees the human imagination to manipulate the "might be's" and "as if's" of abstraction and combine them into fruitful models and theories. It should be noted, however, that scientific knowledge is not enough by itself to influence human affairs; creative and innovative practitioners are needed to put scientific findings into practice.

There are many ways of viewing such a complex task as teaching. Mere description of routine activities or even of fragmental segments of the teacher's day-to-day behavior are among the possibilities. The lore of the teacher is another possibility. While tradition is valuable where consistent results are obtained, the procedures passed down from generation to generation generally tend to be incomplete. Teachers themselves are often unaware of the factors affecting learning or of the reasons why one teaching method seems better than another, though they deal in these commodities daily. Whatever principles emanate from such analyses, they are not likely to have the depth and durability so necessary for guiding the learning process from one year to the next, from one subject matter area to another, or from one teacher to another.

Contributions to an understanding of teaching and learning must come from several vantage points. All must be critically examined and evaluated for whatever implications they may have for education.

Psychological theories that emphasize organization of ideas, structuring of the subject matter, discovery, and the like appear to be especially suited for teaching concepts and other knowledges involved in thinking. Some theories emphasize the consequences of the pupil's behavior, the teacher's relationship to the pupil, and the pupil's successes and failures. These theories are helpful in the understanding of the emotional tone of the classroom, and in the acquisition of behaviors through shaping processes. Other theories emphasize how one learns by imitation of a model. The identification of variables involved in social imitation are relevant to the teaching and learning of skills and attitudes.

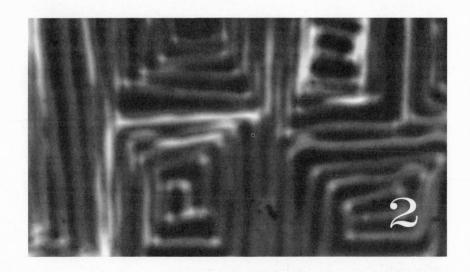

Psychology focuses on optimal conditions for behavioral change: Some influences on education

As psychology plays a more important role in education, new avenues of research are opened and innovations are initiated, critically examined, and modified. There are several fronts on which interchanges between psychological findings and educational practice promise to influence the structure and dynamics of the curriculum in the not-too-distant future. Among the areas now being intensively examined are creativity, discovery methods, meaning, cultural deprivation, and grouping practices. The subject-matter areas of social studies, mathematics, and reading are undergoing similar investigation.

Included in this chapter are some examples of the current attack on educational problems, with some illustrations of new directions in educational procedures. In a real sense they may be considered part of what appears to be a genuine revolution in education. These should not be taken as the only illustrations of changes occurring within the educational system. There are many other subtle means by which the total process is being changed. Not the least important modification is that teachers themselves are becoming more proficient in applying the principles of learning, and of psychology in general, to their teaching practices on a day-to-day basis. Since the problems of adapting to individual differences have led to some comparatively striking changes, these problems are presented for the purpose of highlighting current trends.

14

The reader should bear in mind that the importance of psychological findings varies from one area of teaching to another, and that many of the issues involved in these new practices have not been resolved. The highlighted sections warrant critical examination, but will require further investigation before definite answers become available.

Sensory Deprivation, Cultural Deprivation, and Preschool Experiences

This area of research has implications for education from the preschool level through the early elementary grades. Psychological research has suggested that sensory restriction leads to disordered cognitive functioning (Hebb, 1949). This effect has been experimentally investigated, for example, by severely confining adult human subjects for a period of time. Visual stimulation is restricted by requiring the subject to wear translucent goggles or by confining him in a lightproof room. Auditory stimulation is reduced by the use of continual white noise (a background of noise comprised of all the frequencies sampled from the audible range of sound) or by placement in floating soundproof rooms. Tactile stimulation is restricted by heavy gauntlet-type gloves. Social stimulation is restricted by isolation from other persons.

These restrictions produce a temporarily impoverished environment. As a consequence of such confinement, adult experimental subjects are stunted in their ability to cope with the environment. After eight hours of confinement the subjects experienced hallucinations and unreasonable fears. On tests following confinement, perceptual aberrations persisted for as long as one hour: triangles seemed to change shape, straight lines appeared to move, and arrowheads seemed larger or smaller to the subjects, as illustrated in Figure 2-1. In addition, they were unable to count for more than 20 or 30 consecutive digits (Freedman, Grunebaum, & Greenblatt, 1961). In another study (Vernon, McGill, Gulick & Candland, 1961) deprivation of up to 72 hours produced deleterious effects on motor skills and color perception as illustrated in Figure 2-2. Other evidence from studies with lower animals has shown that rats raised in a "stimulating" environment (cages with figures on the walls) learn more efficiently than those raised in plain cages (Gibson & Walk, 1956; Forgus, 1954).

Some psychological theorists have postulated that there are critical periods in development during which stimulation is essential for normal development. Unless certain forms of stimulation are provided during such a period the detrimental effects of deprivation on ability to learn may become irreversible (Bloom, 1964). In the early years of growth, continued experience with a varied environment appears to be

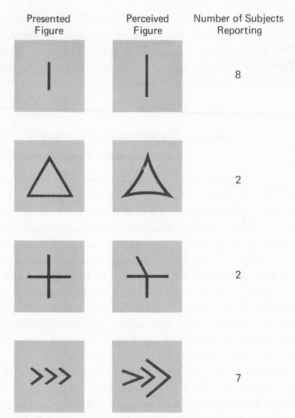

Figure 2-1. Examples of figures used in perception test and of perceptual aberrations after 8 hours of confinement. (From Freedman, Grunebaum, & Greenblatt, p. 65. In Solomon, 1961. With permission of authors and publishers.)

essential for the normal development of an individual's capacities. Without this experience, the development of exploratory behavior, perceptual ability, ability to draw inferences, and ability to apply learned techniques to new problems (nonspecific transfer) may be permanently arrested.

The educational analogue to the critical period for sensory stimulation is to be found in the research literature on cultural deprivation, which focuses upon the substantial group of children from homes in lower socioeconomic areas. Such homes are often characterized by divorce, parents with minimal education, large family size, slum conditions, ethnic discrimination, or poverty, all of which play a part in limiting the amount or quality of stimulation that is provided for growing children.

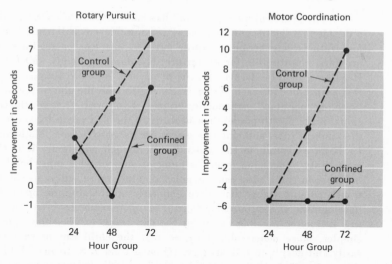

Figure 2-2. Performance on motor tasks of a normal group of subjects compared with performance of a group confined for periods of 24, 48, and 72 hours. Improvement scores are based on tests before and after confinement for the confined group and on tests comparably spaced for the control group. (From Vernon, McGill, Gulick, & Candland, p. 49. In Solomon, 1961. With permission of authors and publishers.)

Readiness and the need for early educational opportunities

... early opportunities for development have loomed ... large in our recent understanding of human mental growth. The importance of early experience is only dimly sensed today. The evidence from animal studies indicates that virtually irreversible deficits can be produced in mammals by depriving them of opportunities that challenge their nascent capacities. In the last few years there have been reports showing the crippling effect of deprived human environments, as well as indications that "replacement therapies" can be of considerable success, even at an age on the edge of adolescence. The principal deficits appear to be linguistic in the broadest sense—the lack of opportunity to share in dialogue, to have occasion for paraphrase, to internalize speech as a vehicle of thought. None of these matters are well understood, save that the principle discussed earlier seems to be operative, that, unless certain basic skills are mastered, later, more elaborated ones become increasingly out of reach. It is in the light of this fact that we can understand the increasing difference of intelligence with age between such culturally deprived groups as rural Southern Negroes and more culturally privileged whites. In time, and with sufficient failure, the gap is reinforced to irreversibility by a sense of defeat. . . .

The "curriculum revolution" has made it plain even after only a decade that the idea of "readiness" is a mischievous half-truth. It is a half-truth largely because it turns out that one *teaches* readiness or provides opportunities for its nurture; one does not simply wait for it. Readiness, in these terms, consists of mastery of those simpler skills that permit one to reach higher skills. ... To take the aim of the new, "second-generation" mathematics project, if you wish, to teach the calculus in the eighth grade, then begin it in the first grade by teaching the kinds of ideas and skills necessary for its mastery later. Mathematics is no exception to the general rule, though admittedly it is the most easily understood from the point of view of what must be clear before something else can be grasped. Since most subjects can be translated into forms that place emphasis upon doing, or upon the development of appropriate imagery, or upon symbolic-verbal encoding, it is often possible to render the end result to be achieved in a simpler, more manageable form so that the child can move more easily and deeply to full mastery. (Quoted from J. S. Bruner, Education as Social Invention. *Saturday Review*, 1966, February 19, p. 72. With permission of author and publisher.)

Children from homes of lower socioeconomic status often have little experience with the cultural patterns necessary for successful performance in school (Deutsch, 1964b). Based on a description by Silberman (1964) what this means can be seen in very concrete terms as follows: In such environments the lack of privacy increases the noise level so that children tend to screen out incoming sounds and learn *not* to attend. Adults do not have the inclination or competence to correct the child's mistakes in syntax and grammar. Unfamiliarity with language rules makes listening difficult since the child cannot fill in words that are missed. Commands and directions are given in monosyllabic words —"get this" or "do that," with the consequence that the teacher's complete sentences are not understood. Since objects are not named at home, but simply referred to as "things," many abstractions and conceptual distinctions made in school are meaningless. Experiences with books, colors, object-naming, numbers, music, art, and occupations so familiar to the child from homes of middle socioeconomic status, are often unknown to the disadvantaged child. Ownership of a private room, toys, paints, bicycles, and so on are rarely enjoyed privileges. The social stimulation provided by an interested parent or sibling may be a desired activity but infrequently encountered. Membership in clubs, Boy Scouts, church, and other groups is similarly uncommon. These deprivations seriously impair the younger child's readiness—i.e., his attempts to participate in the learning tasks required by the school all too frequently meet with failure. As a result of continual failure, an initially neutral attitude toward school changes to an aversive one. Such attitudes do much to hinder efficient learning. It is little wonder, then, that these children have difficulty in reading, arithmetic, and many of the other elementary processes taught in the elementary school. Unfortunately, these weaknesses continue to persist so that the differences between the child in the middle socioeconomic class and the child in the lower socioeconomic class increase in magnitude with increasing grade level.

Other laboratory findings also contribute to an understanding of the effects of deprivation. In one study, 20-month-old children who had been exposed to the word "doll" in many contexts showed greater ability to discriminate "doll" from other objects than did those children with more restricted experience. When children were allowed to handle a doll they learned to discriminate "doll" in a learning task with greater facility than those children who were only permitted visual experience (Jensen, 1963b). In another study (John, 1963), fifth-grade lower class children had more difficulty than middle class children in verbalizing their reasons for categorizing objects. Additional research (Jensen, 1963a, 1965) suggests that lower class and middle class children are equally proficient at rote memorization but that middle class children are superior in learning to link pairs of words where conceptualization is of more importance. Lack of tutoring and corrective feedback in the homes of the lower class children thus seems to retard abstract and integrative learning.

One attempt to remedy the intellectually debilitating effects of early deprivation of experience has been to provide preschool children with special opportunities for sensory and cognitive experiences thought to be lacking in the home environment (Deutsch, 1964a). The new curricula are organized to teach the child those verbal and perceptual skills necessary for learning to read, to label, to discriminate sounds, to experience toys and other objects, to identify colors, and other similar, almost inconceivably elementary experiences. The benefits of these experiences include the development of a sense of self-confidence and a motivation to learn. Thus, the disadvantaged child is given special opportunities for early psychological development that are normally afforded the middle class child in the home and the nursery school. It should be noted that programs for the disadvantaged child are not merely downward extensions of the typical nursery school or kindergarten curricula.

A preschool program for disadvantaged children based on verbal processes

Preschool programs differ in their underlying assumptions. Bereiter and Engelmann (1966), for example, forthrightly reject the idea that sensory deprivation is a major factor in the intellectual and academic deficiencies of lower class children on the basis of their interpretation of the research evidence. A summary of their position is as follows: Lack of concrete experience appears to be of little importance in the inability of disadvantaged children to profit from academic experience. Rather, the evidence seems to suggest that cultural deprivation is equated with language deprivation, and is related to *what* the child has or has not learned instead of the amount of stimulation he has received. Lower class children can use language within their social milieu to implement their needs but they have not acquired the kind of language facility necessary to control their own behavior, to communicate information, to reason, or to engage in other cognitive processes required for success in school. Part of this difficulty rests on the possibility that these children learn sentences as "giant words." As a consequence they fail to capitalize on the full potentiality of the nuances of language for understanding their immediate environment and they do not have the flexibility required for the full development of language skills or for the use of language in learning. Fundamental to language deprivation is the difference in language codes, that is, the translations of language by the culture (Bernstein, 1967). When such differences exist, as they do between the lower and middle-class, social control and communication become complicated.

With the identification of a source of intellectual inadequacy in the lower class child, Bereiter and Engelmann proceeded to develop a preschool educational program which concentrates heavily on verbal processes and direct instruction. As they say, "The curriculum starts at the rock-bottom foundation of language" (p. 168). Initially, the child is taught how to point at, identify, and name an object (e.g., "This is a _____. This is not a _____.") and how to modify statements (e.g., "This _____ is _____.") Once the elementary skills are acquired the child moves to more complicated levels where similar comparisons are made among groups of objects. Instruction may occur in the context of reading, arithmetic, music, science, or any other substantive area. In the course of these experiences the pupil learns to perceive, to identify, to name, and to compare objects. He learns the rudiments of empirical investigation, of the art of questioning, of organizing experiences, and of logical reasoning.

Changes in Grouping Practice: The Nongraded Plan in the Elementary School

Individual differences among pupils are often regarded as merely a nuisance by the teacher. Heterogeneity in intelligence, achievement, interests, chronological age or other "readiness" variables makes it necessary to vary teaching methods, tasks, and teaching materials, often beyond the capabilities of a single teacher. Accordingly, schools have always used some method of grouping in an attempt to arrive at more homogeneous groups of children. Age grading is the traditional method used by schools for grouping purposes. The assumption is that pupils of a given age will perform in similar ways, have similar needs, and can be taught by similar methods. One need not teach for long to realize the fallacy in this idea. Within a given age group there may be a range of several years in the children's abilities to read or do arithmetic.

As a result of the latter observation, school personnel have attempted to group children within a class on other bases. Intelligence and achievement levels were once popular criteria for grouping. Thus, the problems in teaching a group of pupils with high (or low) intelligence test scores, or a group of high (or low) achievers in arithmetic were supposedly eliminated. This belief was soon found to be invalid. Among pupils in any "homogeneous" group based on a single criterion, there was wide variability on motivational or other criteria. Pupils in a homogeneous group based on high achievement in arithmetic differ widely in reading achievement. Similar differences occur in the achievement of pupils grouped according to intelligence.

In addition to these grouping practices, some schools adopted a nonpromotion policy in their attempts to achieve homogeneity within the classroom. But again, the arguments in favor of this method were exploded. It was found that nonpromoted pupils do not perform better than their promoted counterparts. Nonpromotion typically involves a cycle of failure, discouragement, decrease in interest, and increase in aggression. The development of adequate personal and social adjustments are often disrupted by such practices.

Thus, when only one criterion is used to eliminate individual differences, the group remains heterogeneous on other criteria. Furthermore, these methods disregard another related fact: the growth rate of abilities for an individual pupil may vary from time to time and is not consistent for all abilities (see Figure 2-3). As a consequence of these observations, educators and educational psychologists (Goodlad & Anderson, 1963) have intensively studied the nongraded plan; a "grouping" procedure that has met with more success than its predecessors. The nongraded plan conveniently combines the best features of the many prior bases for grouping: promotion, acceleration, and enrichment policies. The single classroom is still the basic unit. The child proceeds through the first four grades without ever being identified with a single grade. A given child may move ahead rapidly in reading but may spend more time at a lower level in arithmetic. Groupings may be based on interests, on progress with fundamental learning skills, or on achievement. At other times, especially where a variety of interests are important for a project or discussion, there may be planned heterogeneity. On occasion, some groups will proceed with little attention from the teacher, others will receive a great deal more guidance in planning their work. Specialized grouping may be used to capitalize on interests and abilities of individual teachers. A pupil may be working at several

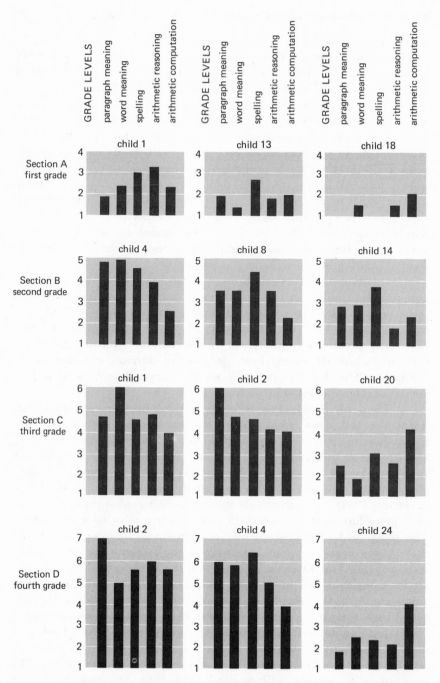

Figure 2-3. Achievement profiles for twelve children from four grades, each section showing three children from the same grade level. (From Goodlad & Anderson, 1963, p. 16. With permission of authors and publisher.)

GIFTED LEARNERS

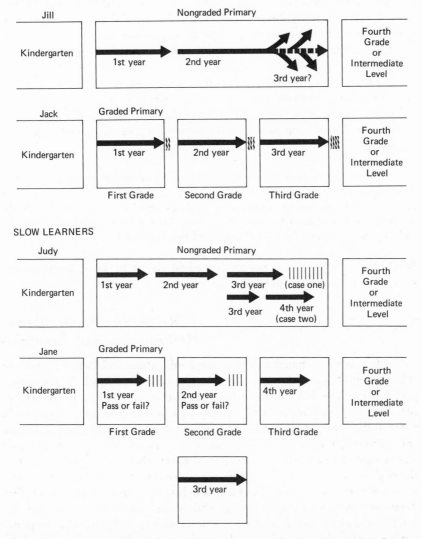

Figure 2-4. A comparison of the progress of two gifted and two slow learners in the graded and nongraded school. Each arrow represents a year's academic progress. (From Goodlad & Anderson, 1963, pp. 144 and 146. With permission of authors and publisher.)

different levels at the same time. Flexibility is of central importance in this plan as shown in Figure 2-4.

Even where school systems do not permit the use of the non-graded plan, it still has important implications for the classroom teacher. Until more individualized instructional techniques are avail-

able, some form of homogeneous grouping seems desirable. Such grouping may vary according to the tasks to be accomplished and to the
growth rates of individual pupils. On occasion the teacher may even
want to form heterogeneous groups to capitalize on the existence of
different interests or to increase motivation through friendly competitive efforts.

For remedial purposes, the groupings may be based on deficiencies in reading, arithmetic, or other subject-matter areas. A grouping of
pupils who excel in an area might be made for enrichment experiences.
Goodlad and Anderson (1963) have commented on the nongraded plan
as follows:

> This point of view is based on a theory of continual progress. . . . The
> child spurts ahead in one area and lags behind in others. . . . Slow progress is
> provided for by permitting longer time to do given blocks of work. . . . Bright
> children are encouraged to move ahead regardless of grade level of the work;
> with no fear of encroaching on the work of the next teacher.

While they speak of the nongraded plan, the same considerations are
worthy of the attention of every teacher.

Responsive Environment, Mathematics, and Readiness

It was once thought that selected educational objectives could be
achieved only when the pupil reached a given age level. There was a
search for the optimal age at which reading could be taught, for example. The period identified by one investigation was the mental age of six
years and six months (Morphett & Washburne, 1931); almost a "magical" number and one easily remembered, perhaps too well! Arithmetic
was relegated to the elementary school curriculum, and mathematics to
the high school. Foreign language was restricted to the high school and
was only rarely taught at grade levels below the junior high school. The
dominant view was that learning ability was correlated with the age
level of the child. What could be assimilated was believed to be dependent upon the child, almost to the exclusion of the control exerted by
teaching method, educational setting, and tasks with which the pupil
was confronted.

The psychologist's primary concern is not what *should* be taught
but what *can* be taught at a given age level. As a result of this sort of
inquiry several new notions are being tested about the level at which
teaching of certain subjects can occur. One of these innovations has
resulted from Moore's (1966) invention of the Responsive Environment
Laboratory. The child, as young as three or four years of age, learns to

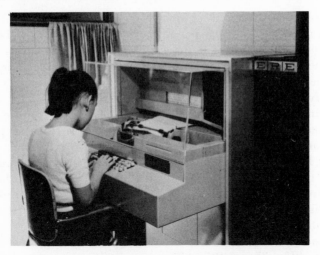

Figure 2-5. Picture of a "talking" typewriter from Edison (Courtesy of O. K. Moore.)

read by a technique employing the application of psychological principles from several theories of learning. Briefly, the keyboard of a typewriter is learned first. The pupil matches his fingernails, which are painted different colors, with the typewriter keys. The keyboard is color-coded to match the colors of the appropriate fingers. When the key is depressed the child listens for feedback from a teacher or tape-recording to indicate the letter of the alphabet that has been typed. Associations linking finger, typewriter key, voiced symbol, and visual recognition of the letter are soon formed. The child then gradually learns to copy individual letters that are presented visually. At this point the typewriter is adjusted to permit operation only when the correct letter is typed. Both visual and oral confirmation are used when the child is correct. That is, when he types the letter "t," he sees the letter, "t," says "t," or hears it enunciated by the teacher. Later the child learns to type the words from both visual and oral directives. Training on the typewriter is also interspersed with training in handwriting.

The original "responsive environment laboratory" was somewhat primitive by comparison with later developments. An ordinary typewriter was used. Directions, presentation, and oral confirmation were given by a teacher. At present, the procedure is almost completely automated and is controlled by electronic devices. The child is allowed to use the machine for as short or long a period of time as he wishes. He is free of the usual classroom pressures. Learning to read even by very young children or by mentally retarded children of the age of the normal first grader usually proceeds in a dramatic fashion.

A somewhat different approach has been used to study what can be taught in mathematics by such investigators as Beberman (1958) and Davis (1966). The emphasis in these studies is on the "discovery" of concepts, generalizations, and procedures employed in mathematics by the pupil. The teaching method leads the pupil through the steps necessary to identify the principles in a mathematical operation. In this way pupils gain the idea that knowledge has a logical basis. They do not rely on the mere exercise of formulas. In a sense, these teaching processes are similar to those identified as prompting in the research on programmed learning (discussed later in this chapter). With prompting, however, the pupil learns first a generalization, or other information about the task to be learned, and then learns how it is applied and where it is applied. With the discovery method, the pupil becomes familiar with examples, and relationships among examples, and then draws conclusions about these relationships in answers to questions of "What?" "How?" and "Why?"

There is at present much debate among educational psychologists about the value of discovery methods and even about the question of whether discovery is a useful or misleading construct. However, as used by the mathematicians, the general procedure has led to successful attempts to teach identity of sets and discrimination of triangles, quadrilaterals, and polygons with kindergarten and first-grade children (Suppes, 1964). The work of the investigators in this field has permitted children to pursue mathematics previously regarded as beyond the usual abilities of elementary school pupils. Children in the first grade are encouraged to progress from intuitive solutions of problems to the formulation of logical principles. Similar changes are also occurring in the teaching of such subject-matter areas as social studies (Bruner, 1961).

The foregoing examples are presented to illustrate the point that newer definitions of readiness go beyond attributing the ability or deficiencies in learning to the "nature" of the child. They reemphasize the view that behavioral change is, at least in part, dependent upon teaching methods. Thus, the view that *the pupil does not learn with present teaching methods*, must be given as much consideration as the view that *the pupil does not learn because he has inadequate ability*. As discussed elsewhere in this book, this is not an indictment, but rather a reexamination of other facets of the classic nature-nurture controversy. It highlights the psychologist's concern with what can be taught to the child, as reflected in Bruner's hypothesis that " . . . any subject can be taught effectively in some intellectually honest form to any child at any stage in development. . . ." (Bruner, 1961, p. 33).

A rational and flexible approach to individual differences is further implied in the following:

. . . instruction . . . need not follow . . . the natural course of cognitive development in the child. It can also lead intellectual development by providing challenging but useful and usable opportunities for the child to forge ahead in his development. Experience has shown that it is worth the effort to provide the growing child with problems that tempt him into next stages of development. . . . young children learn almost anything that adults do if it can be given to them in terms they understand. Giving the material to them in terms they understand, interestingly enough, turns out to involve knowing the mathematics oneself, and the better one knows it, the better it can be taught. [When mathematicians are told that] fourth-grade students can go a long way into "set theory" a few of them reply: "Of course." Most of them are startled. The latter ones are completely wrong in assuming that "set theory" is intrinsically difficult. Of course it may be that nothing is intrinsically difficult. We just have to wait until the proper point of view and corresponding language for presenting it are revealed. Given particular subject matter of a particular concept, it is easy to ask trivial questions or to lead the child to ask trivial questions. It is also easy to ask impossibly difficult questions. The trick is to find the medium questions that can be answered and that take you somewhere. (From Bruner, 1961, pp. 39–40. With permission of author and publisher.)

It should, of course, be emphasized that what the pupil *should* learn is quite another matter, one that depends upon continuous examination and clarification of societal goals.

Technology of Teaching

Over 35 years ago Pressey (1932) wrote his "Contributions toward the coming industrial revolution in education." He developed some simple machines for self-teaching, and used them in educational psychology classes. The apparatus primarily replaced other testing procedures. The student obtained immediate knowledge of results and correction of errors on multiple-choice questions. Unfortunately, the idea did not catch on. The testing function was handled in other preferred ways.

About 20 years later, there was a revitalization of interest in the methods by which teaching could be automatically guided and monitored. Since materials were presented by mechanical devices this method was given the name "teaching machine." The title called attention to the apparatus rather than to the principles involved or to the "heart" of the procedure, that is, the programming of the subject matter to be taught.

The reexamination of self-teaching methods for more automated guidance of learning exercises was translated by Hively (1959) into the following tutorial activities to parallel Skinner's analysis of behavior:

1. Eliminate distracting and extraneous stimuli, insofar as possible, to create a favorable setting for study.

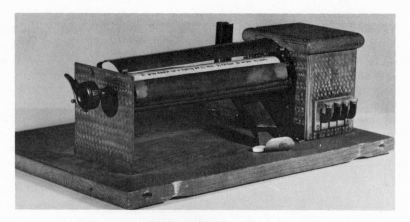

Figure 2-6. Some early forms of self-instructional devices. (Top: Department of Photography, Ohio State University. Bottom: from Kendler, 1968, Figure 18.11, p. 657. With permission of author and publisher.)

2. Remove conditions of negative reinforcement so as to avoid the interfering effects of anxiety and timidity on learning.

3. Identify effective reinforcers by observing the pupil's behavior carefully and by gaining his respect and confidence. Note especially those consequences that increase the frequency of a behavior and those that decrease the frequency of a behavior.

4. Rewards can be administered by knowledge of results, relating subject matter to the student's interests, and dispensing (or withholding) attention or approval. Thus, rewards can include all secondary, or learned, reinforcers and are not limited to "tangible" rewards.

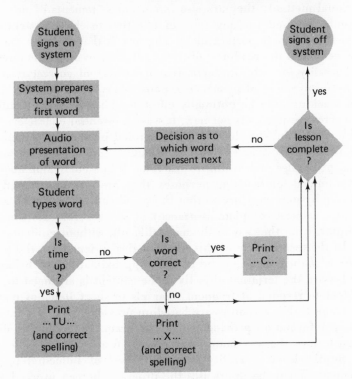

Figure 2-7. The computer device for self-instruction shown above "pronounces" a word and then presents it, both pictorially and in written form, to the student. The student touches his light pen to the screen to tell the computer that he can read the word. The lower part of the figure diagrams the steps in the process. (From R. C. Atkinson & H. A. Wilson. Computer-assisted instruction. Science, *1968, 162, 73–77.)*

5. The tutorial analogy to successive approximations is the presentation of a sequence of successively challenging problems that are within the pupil's grasp.

6. The accurate presentation of rewards and of the timing of rewards is essential. Behavioral outcomes may not be those desired because the dispensation of rewards is often uncontrolled by the teacher. Apathy may result from infrequent rewards. Misinformation may be the result of slipshod contingencies of reward. Misbehavior can occur if reinforcements from the pupil's peers conflict with those administered by the teacher. Anxiety, avoidance, and resentment result from the use of negative reinforcers. All of these unfavorable outcomes interfere with learning and with the teacher's control of learning.

7. The skills and knowledge acquired are maintained by systematic review.

Although these principles have guided the research in self-instructional methods, they are also important statements of principles that should be used for any type of effective teaching. Attention is called to three very important ideas. The first is that effective teaching must be geared to the readiness of the pupil. The second calls attention to the necessity for reinforcement (confirmation) of correct responses and nonreinforcement of incorrect responses—i.e., feedback and correction—if teaching is to be optimally effective. The automatic confirmation of correct responses is not new. It was an essential characteristic of Pressey's approach. The third process, implied in the last principle, is that of programming, and is one of Skinner's major contributions in applying principles of learning to teaching. When curricular materials are programmed for teaching purposes, they are serially ordered in a careful step-by-step sequence so that the pupil can proceed with a high probability (almost complete assurance) of success from the simple to the complex, from the easy to the more difficult, without guidance from others. In the terminology of this psychological orientation, the pupil's behavior is *shaped*, through the gradual approximations of behavioral change toward the terminal objective. The content is arranged to allow the student to respond at frequent intervals to short items of material called "frames." His responses are based on previously learned information or on information provided in the program. Programming directs attention toward the way material is presented and adapts the content to the pupil's level of ability or to his level of immediately prior achievement. When the pupil uses the program, he can proceed at his own pace within the limits of his own resources and capacities. Many devices are being used for presenting instructional programs. They range from a simple scrambled textbook or programmed textbook all the way to complex electronic machines involving computer networks.

As suggested above, the main contribution of this technique is

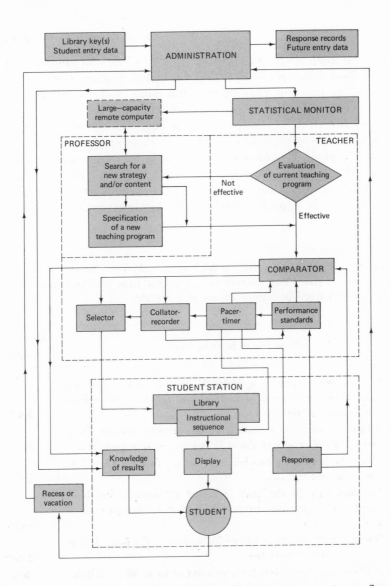

Figure 2-8. A flow chart for the instructional process via a System for Organizing Content to Review and Teach Educational Subjects (SOCRATES) in which a computer is used as the central processor. The system provides the student with information, gets a response from him, analyzes the response, compares it with responses made by other students and also with the expected response. Feedback, appropriate to the student's personality and response, is then provided. These steps may be traced by the reader if he starts at "Display." Note that a program is identified on the basis of student characteristics in relation to course objectives prior to the student's interaction with the system. If an adequate program is unavailable in the system, the student is instructed to see his teacher for further direction. (From L. W. Stolurow, 1968, Figure 3, p. 40. With permission of author and publisher.)

not in the mechanical device or machine by which the program is presented. Most important of all is that this technical innovation has forced educators to program learning activities more carefully and in greater detail. The programmer must consider what the pupil is doing, and what he is capable of doing, at various points in the learning process. No other teaching procedure places so great an emphasis on the readiness of the pupil. Programming has led to a renewed recognition that if the pupil is to learn, the conditions of learning must be controlled by the teacher (programmer). As a result, the common practice of placing the blame on the pupil becomes an indefensible excuse for teaching failures.

Figure 2-9. Part of a program in high school physics. The machine presents one item at a time. The student completes the item and then uncovers the corresponding word or phrase shown at the right.

Sentence to be completed	Word to be supplied
1. The important parts of a flashlight are the battery and the bulb. When we "turn on" a flashlight, we close a switch which connects the battery with the ____.	bulb
2. When we turn on a flashlight, an electric current flows through the fine wire in the ____ and causes it to grow hot.	bulb
3. When the hot wire glows brightly, we say that it gives off or sends out heat and ____.	light
4. The fine wire in the bulb is called a filament. The bulb "lights up" when the filament is heated by the passage of a(n) ____ current.	electric
5. When a weak battery produces little current, the fine wire, or ____, does not get very hot.	filament
6. A filament which is *less* hot sends out or gives off ____ light.	less
7. "Emit" means "send out." The amount of light sent out, or "emitted," by a filament depends on how ____ the filament is.	hot
8. The higher the temperature of the filament the ____ the light emitted by it.	brighter, stronger
9. If a flashlight battery is weak, the ____ in the bulb may still glow, but with only a dull red color.	filament
10. The light from a very hot filament is colored yellow or white. The light from a filament which is not very hot is colored ____.	red

Source: *Cumulative Record* by B. F. Skinner. New York: Appleton-Century-Crofts, Inc., 1961. (Enlarged ed.) P. 168, Table 2.

Self-instructional procedures have been extended to the point where the programs are stored in computers located in central areas. The programs are elaborate and permit extensive branching, that is, students may proceed through the sequence of course materials in different ways. Depending on their backgrounds, they may start at different points. As they proceed through the program, provision is made for students to make up deficiencies that might hamper later progress. Another direction allows them to obtain enrichment experiences. Information that is already known can be skipped. The computers with stored programs can be made available to response stations throughout the nation. At the time of this writing, programs stored in computers in New York are used directly for experimental studies, by students working from response terminals in Pennsylvania, California, Michigan, and Florida.

An experimental program in computer-based mathematics instruction

Several years of research in learning theory convinced Suppes that one of the most important (and also most neglected) principles of learning is the existence of differences in individual rates of learning. "Single-minded concentration on individual differences," he feels, "could result in the greatest improvement in subject-matter learning." Computer technology seems one way in which such improvement can be brought about. Since each student works independently of the progress of the other students, he can proceed at his own pace. Computer-based teaching machines can also provide immediate reinforcement and correction, giving a reasonably close imitation of a teaching situation in which a tutor works with one individual student. In addition, a computer facility permits a deeper analysis of transfer phenomena as the child moves from one mathematical concept to another.

During the last three years, members of the Computer-based Mathematics Instruction project have developed experimental programs (in mathematical logic) for grades 1, 4, and 6. . . .

The first-grade program consists of approximately 50 sections, each introducing a new "concept." Problems to be solved follow each section. . . . As the child proceeds through the material, review problems test his knowledge of the previous concepts. If he responds correctly to half of the problems, he will continue through the review to the next concept; if he fails more than half the questions, the computer will register these data and on the next day present him with an intensive review of the particular concepts. In this way the child is continually tested on his retention of previously learned subject matter.

The instructional units of the fourth-grade material consist of a number of learning blocks, each of which contains a major topic [such as addition, subtraction, operations on numbers, or commutative, associative, and distributive laws] and several problems to be worked by the student. . . . Failure to meet specified criteria results in return to remedial material.

The sixth-grade lessons, based on the previously developed sequence in mathematical logic, make full use of the versatility of computer-based teaching machines. Since such a facility allows immediate evaluation of response data and accepts any valid step in a proof, it is possible to present new stimulus items that are contingent upon the student's immediately preceding performance.

The student in this course is first presented with logical symbols, which are interpreted for him. He is then asked to view the symbols as concrete objects and, using arbitrary rules of derivation introduced one at a time, to manipulate the symbols as he would pieces on a game board. At the next stage he learns to regard the "pieces" as carriers of the possible truth values of "true" or "false"; through a number of steps he is shown that the rules initially introduced as arbitrary never allow the derivation of a false conclusion from true premises. Subsequent lessons inform him about the methods of conditional proof, indirect proof, and biconditional replacement. Finally, they acquaint the student with the formal concepts of arguments and consistency or inconsistency of sets of premises. A discussion on the development of a logical system concludes the course. (Goodlad, Von Stoephasius, & Klein, 1966, pp. 37–38. With permission of author and publisher.)

Self-instructional devices have also recently been extended to simpler levels by Pressey (1965) for application to teaching with immediate implications for the classroom teacher. He draws on a study by Milton (1962): Students in the first course in psychology never met after the first few weeks in class, but simply took weekly tests on each week's assignment. These people did a little better than, or at least as good as, those who met regularly for two lectures and one quiz section each week. In addition, more students in the nontaught section bought supplementary reading matter and later elected another course in psychology.

On the basis of these results, Pressey suggests that the individuals in the nontaught section might have learned even more effectively if they had a frequent (at least weekly) opportunity to use a self-scoring autoinstructional test. These devices are simple 3- by 5-inch cards with rows of small black dots to represent numbered or lettered test-item alternatives. The student then erases the dot in each row that represents the alternative he judges to be correct for a particular question. If it is right he will find an "R" after the dot overprint is erased. If his answer is wrong, there is no R under the overprint and he must try other alternatives until he finds the correct answer. It can be seen that, as with other self-instructional procedures, the student is provided with immediate feedback.

In one study this technique was used in regular classes as check tests and study aids, integrated with classroom and textbook study activities. Student grades on midterm and final examinations were raised. The procedure has also been used to guide superior students in their study for credit by examination and in independent instructional laboratories. It clearly permits students to proceed more rapidly in their study.

In this example, the principles of programmed learning were translated into a self-instructional device that can be incorporated with little effort or cost into daily classroom use. Pressey calls this "teach-test" or the "adjunct autoelucidation technique." As a teaching aid, it provides a basis for facilitating effective study, for enrichment, or for acceleration within a course. It may be noted that this procedure is not very different from Pressey's original contribution to programmed learning. Over the years, the technology of programmed learning has broadened to allow for a simple integration with everyday teaching, on the one hand, and yet permit the development of the complex computer-assisted-instruction methodology, on the other. Both developments are directed toward helping the teacher adjust to individual differences.

The New Linguistics and the Language Curriculum

Currently, there is a quiet but certain reform going on in the English curriculum. As was the case with mathematics, it is now recognized that the course content in English grammar is patterned after eighteenth century models. Traditional pedagogical grammar teaches the routine segmentation of a sentence into its constituent parts and classification of those parts into categories called parts of speech (Lees, 1963). The grammar is organized around the acquisition of:

1. A lexicon, that is, a store of words, or, if you prefer, a dictionary.
2. A set of paradigms, e.g., commonly accepted methods for the conjugation of nouns, verbs, and other parts of speech.
3. A small set of formulae, for example, the preposition plus noun (P + N) formula into which any preposition or noun can be "plugged" to attain a prepositional phrase.
4. A set of examples to illustrate the kinds of well-formed sentences that can be constructed.

A view now held by the modern linguists is that given the fact of an indefinite set of sentences in the language, the four components of traditional grammar are inadequate to generate *all* combinations in the language. What the speaker must do is to study the examples in the fourth step. Then, by analogy, he is able to construct the new and indefinite set of other examples in the language. Typically, the degree of learning depends as much on the insight of the learner as on what is taught. Nevertheless, the traditional grammar *does* enable the person to use and understand the language although the procedure is cumbersome, ambiguous, and inefficient.

The new grammar, called the transformational generative grammar, on the other hand, has as its goal the *formalization of the rules* which the person infers by analogy from the examples of well-formed sentences in the traditional grammar. That is, the goal of the transformational grammar is to say precisely what it is that a human speaker knows when it can be said of him that he knows the language. The linguist attempts to make explicit the sources of the intuitions the native speaker has about his language, or, in other words, to make explicit the rules of grammar.

The process used by the linguist is illustrated below by analysis of the sentence "John picked up the ball" and its possible modifications (transformations) through the application of a rule. Consider the original sentence:

> John picked up the ball;

and its modification,

> John picked the ball up.

Consider, also, the sentence:

> John picked up it;

and its possible modification,

> John picked it up.

The reader will note that the variations involve the verb + particle (pick + up) construction and whether the object of the sentence is a noun or a pronoun. In addition, it can be observed that sentences 1, 2, and 4 "sound right" and the third sentence does not although the speaker may find it difficult to provide a reason. (This is an example of linguistic intuition.) Additional observations are also made by the linguist (Chomsky, 1957, 1965). For one thing, the first sentence sounds correct whether the particle follows the verb (sentence 1) or the noun (sentence 2) phrase, that is to say, the sentence sounds correct in either the modified or unmodified state. However, when a pronoun is substituted for the noun phrase the third sentence does not sound right unless the particle follows the pronoun as in its modification (sentence 4). On the basis of such logical and systematic analyses, the modern linguist infers the following rule or rules employed in the intuitive transformation (that is, modification) of sentences with the characteristics described above: For sentences with the verb + particle construction, the particle *must* be brought out to the end of the sentence if the object of the verb is a *pronoun*, that is, the rule to use the verb + pronoun + particle (picked + it + up) construction is *obligatory*. However, if the object of the verb is a *noun, either* the verb + particle + noun phrase, or the verb + noun phrase + particle construction can be used, that is, the rule one uses in the transformation (or modification) is *optional*. (The reader may want to transform other strings of words with verb + particle constructions to see how general this rule really is, e.g., try transforming the sentence, *the police brought in the criminal*; or, *the boy called up the girl*; or, *the cat drove away the birds*.) This, of course, is only one example of the many situations for which the transformational generative grammar attempts to establish explicit rules. It serves, however, to illustrate how a sophisticated theory attempts to state the rules for rewriting sentences so as to correspond to intuitive judgments about well-formed sentences.

The intuitions about language, to which continual reference has been made, are learned at a very early age. Children of six are far removed from the repetitive-speech stage of language development so characteristic of the two- or three-year-old child. Thus, the child of six does have a grammar, as well as other mechanisms for producing sentences. So universal is this fact, and considering the extremely complex nature of such learning, Lenneberg (1967), among other theorists, has suggested the possibility that the human brain has a special innate capability for using the rules that generate sentences, although many psychologists do not accept this idea.

There is the hope of some (e.g., Thomas, 1965) that a knowledge of the new transformational grammar will help the teacher to explain, and the pupil to understand, the nature of language and, perhaps, to provide some appreciation of literature with its richness of grammatical forms. When it is known more specifically what is involved in the human speaker's intuitions about his language the teacher may find it easier to interpret and evaluate the pupil's performance in the language and to provide feedback to the pupil about his mistakes and successes. Deepened insights into the nature of language should lead to increased efficiency in the presentation of subject matter.

The new look in the study of language is being styled by the work of educators, psychologists, linguists, anthropologists, and sociologists. It promises to have an influence on the teaching of the language arts no less dramatic than the revolution in mathematics. Whether this promise is fulfilled remains to be seen. In the meantime there will necessarily be much experimentation to determine the effectiveness of even the possibilities of this innovation to follow the critical analyses currently being conducted concerning the relationships of the new grammar to the teaching of English.

Two thoughts on the teaching of grammar

One view:

. . . On the basis of the aims we have and the facts we know, the author [Thomas] makes the following proposal:

> *The English language arts should be firmly based on the axiom that the vast majority of children intuitively know the fundamental structure of their language before they begin their formal education.*

This is the most important axiom, but there are several corollaries that are only slightly less important:

1. A child should study *language* rather than grammar.
2. The ideal form of study is *discovery* rather than memorization.
3. The end result of the discovery procedure should be increased *self-confidence*.
4. Self-confidence is best developed through *sequentially ordered instruction*.

(From Thomas, 1965, p. 209. With permission of author and publisher.)

Another view:

. . . I consider the major importance of grammatical studies to lie in the areas of the so-called behavioral sciences and not in supposed applications to the pedagogy of rhetoric. While it is obvious that every well-informed teacher of our school children ought at best to be familiar with the latest results in this area of linguistic science, it is not at all clear to me that the study or teaching of English grammar is very helpful in training children to write better or to appreciate literature. I would guess rather that there is only one way to provide that training—namely, with massive supervised reading and writing.

. . . in the near future materials will become available for the schools to explain in simple terms many of the results and insights of the most recent research in English syntax and phonology, and . . . these materials will stress our best understanding of human linguistic capacity and behavior.

If English grammar is to be taught at all in the secondary schools, then there is little if any justification for teaching it in conjunction with rhetoric or literature; rather such a study of language belongs in the area of science and general education along with psychology and anthropology. (From Lees, 1963, p. 345. With permission of author and publisher. As Professor Lees has indicated in private correspondence, "since our publication date of 1963 our ideas in transformational grammar have very markedly matured and developed." The full educational implications of these advances must await empirical study.)

Summary

The range of direct influence of psychological knowledge on teaching seems vast in perspective. It is currently affecting preschool education, the individualization of instruction, and the curriculum revolution, to name but a few "frontiers" of education.

Research on sensory deprivation can be thought of as an early step in understanding the direction compensatory education must take, although the influence, in this movement, of the Montessori method and other similar innovations must not be denied. Attention to the educational needs of the culturally disadvantaged has led to the recognition that readiness is not an innate quality but is a requirement for learning that can be taught and learned. Currently, the theory of sensory deprivation is being challenged by some investigators who believe that cultural deprivation is synonymous with language deprivation. Accordingly, some preschool programs for the culturally disadvantaged are based heavily on language development.

The influence of psychology on adapting teaching to individual differences can be exemplified by grouping practices and by the nongraded school. Any grouping practice, such as age grading, which attempts to attain homogeneity on one factor has revealed heterogeneity among pupils on other factors. If only one basis is to be used for grouping, it probably should be reading ability. The nongraded school permits the child to progress at his own pace at whatever point he may have reached in the curriculum. Deficiencies are met by remedial teaching; rapid progress permits opportunity to provide the pupil with enrichment experiences. The deeper insights into individual differences have also led to other practices such as team teaching as a method for taking differences among pupils into account.

The technology of teaching shows signs of coming of age. While far from maturity it is beginning to have a major influence on education. At the preschool level are such innovations as the responsive environments with their emphasis on successful discovery of correct responses by the pupil. Closely related are the developments in programmed learning (which actually began much before the responsive-environment approach) and computer-based instruction with their emphasis on highly programmed sequences, active response requirements, and continual feedback and correction. Programmed learning in the form of programmed textbooks, teaching machines, and various electronic devices have invaded classrooms from kindergarten through college. The language laboratory is another technological advance that has gained a firm place in most school systems. What were formerly simple audiovisual aids have now changed so radically that their complexity is properly reflected in such descriptive terminology as the multimedia approach. Though it is very unlikely that any of this parade of technological innovations will ever replace the teacher, nevertheless, used with appropriate understanding of their underlying principles, these devices can be of great assistance to the teacher.

The psychologist's role in education is further exemplified in the revolution taking place in curriculum development. Only two curriculum areas were briefly described in this chapter. The reform in mathematics was presented because it is so well underway and its influence is felt at every grade level. The elements of advanced mathematics are now taught even in the primary grades with the outcome of improved understanding of, and better attitudes toward, mathematical reasoning. The reform in English was described because it is now on the threshold of change and its direction is less clear than that of mathematics at the time this is being written. Nevertheless, traditional grammar is clearly being challenged by the new transformational generative grammar. In the new grammar the linguist is attempting a precise analysis of the rules underlying the development of sentences and their modification. The psychologist's role will be to determine how these rules are learned and the effect of these rules on other behavior. Although the total influence this innovation will have on the curriculum is difficult to predict, it will certainly result in a pronounced change not only in teaching English but in our understanding of behavior as well.

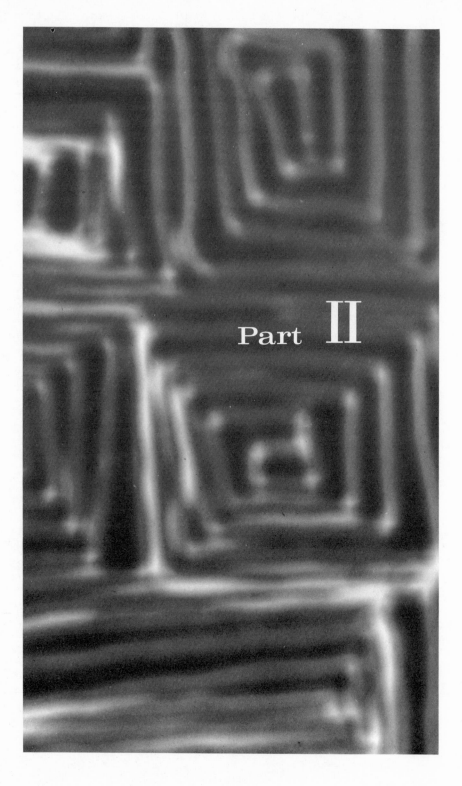

Part II

An overview of psychological growth, adjustment, and educative processes

The following three chapters were especially designed to present the reader a broad panoramic view of the processes involved in education, as they are defined and interpreted by psychologists. The key concepts of development, learning, adjustment, and adaptation are emphasized as the psychological dimensions of special relevance to behavioral elaboration and change. The many educative roles of parents, peers, and teachers are identified and discussed, as are the significant subcultures that provide the stage settings for the educational drama. Some of the psychological needs, goals, frustrations, and coping skills of those involved in the social interactions that constitute formal education are discussed.

Why this overview? It is well known that under some conditions of psychological set all of us "fail to see the forest for the trees." Research has shown that this response tendency is greatly augmented when we are rewarded only for emphasizing details and are given no encouragement or guidance to integrate such particulars into more comprehensive conceptions. It is hoped that the present overview will help the reader to appreciate and to remember the total scope of the educational undertaking, as it is viewed by psychologists. It is important that this interpretation of the grand scene be kept in mind as the reader ponders the significance of the many research findings and theories presented in the later chapters of this book.

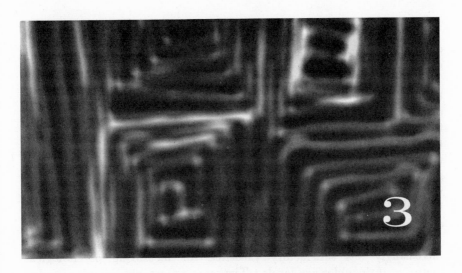

3

An overview of psychological development during the first two decades of life

Heraclitus, an early Greek philosopher, once concluded that "you can't step into the same stream twice." This generalization provides an apt summation of the conceptual difficulties involved in trying to understand and predict the future behavior and psychological status of the *growing* organism. There is a sort of indeterminacy, or Heisenberg effect, in studying the individual organism at any age, i.e., our making an observation frequently interferes with what is being observed and thereby leaves the organism different than it was before. The effects of this methodological difficulty are minor, however, when compared with the rapid changes in behavior that occur on the basis of natural growth processes and which become cumulative over time.

A few days of growth during early infancy can bring about a profound change in human behavior. New responses may appear in a remarkably short period of time; other well-established responses may disappear just as suddenly (McGraw, 1943). Although such dramatic shifts are not commonly observed in the behavior of the school-age child, abrupt changes in children's and adolescents' interests, skills, and learning aptitudes do sometimes surprise parents and teachers. Fortunately for the informed and observant teacher, some of these changes are correlated with normal psychological growth, therefore the teacher

45

can be prepared for their appearance and plan needed revisions and elaboration in curricula.

In the "old days" before the advent of the psychologist with his theories and measuring devices, chronological age was used almost exclusively by parents and educators as a crude, rule-of-thumb yardstick for estimating the developmental status and learning potential of the child and adolescent. For example, six was the age to start school, fourteen was the age to enter high school, or sixteen was the age to quit school and get a job. Standards have changed and the frequently inaccurate, or misleading, use of chronological age is no longer as common, however most communities still admit beginning pupils to their school systems on an inflexible basis of year, month, and even day of birth. (See Figure 3-1 for an illustration of why chronological age becomes an increasingly less satisfactory yardstick for measuring psychological maturity at the older age levels.) The more progressive schools of today

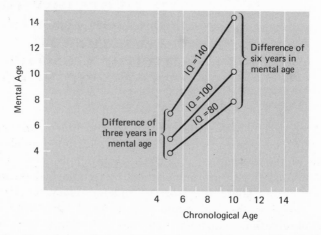

Figure 3-1. Mental growth functions of three pupils with IQs of 80, 100, and 140. Note that the absolute differences in the mental age of these pupils are increasing with age. In kindergarten their mental ages are 4, 5, and 7 (not too dissimilar for a flexible educational program), but by the fifth grade their mental ages will probably approximate 8, 10, and 14 years (a wide span of learning aptitudes for most curricula).

are likely to use some combination of chronological age, learning aptitude as evaluated by psychological and educational tests, and physical and social-emotional maturity as appraised by examination and interview to provide basic information about a prospective pupil's developmental maturity as it relates to available curricula and teaching procedures. Then one or more members of the educational staff will use this information to arrive at a *judgment* of the most appropriate time for a particular pupil to enter school for the first time, or to be introduced to later learning experiences within the school system. In high quality educational programs such judgments are likely to be based not only on information about the pupil but also on a systematic philosophy of the proper functions of particular school programs and the availability of specialized school personnel, e.g., promotion of academic skills, guidance for healthy and happy living, teaching of social skills, and so on in a rationally balanced program.

Since information about the pupil's present status and most probable rates of future psychological growth in its several dimensions gets put to use only on the basis of some educator's evaluation and best judgment, it is important that teachers be knowledgeable about the most reliable research findings and the most promising theories related to psychological growth. This chapter is a survey of the high points of what has become a vast professional literature on this topic during the last half century.*

Theories of Psychological Growth

Speculating about how children grow and how they can best be nurtured and guided toward happy, successful, and responsible patterns of living has been popular among philosophers, physicians, and other learned men during all the recorded periods of civilization. (See Kessen, 1965, for some amusing and informative excerpts from representative writings.) Opinions have ranged all the way from a belief in the primacy of racial and individual inheritance (e.g., G. Stanley Hall's recapitulation proposal, 1904) to a conviction of John Locke, the great English philosopher, that the child's mind begins as a *tabula rasa*, or a blank slate upon which nature writes (Locke, 1690). The last 50 years of research in psychology and in genetics has produced findings that support an interaction theory of inherited and acquired bases of human development. (See Anatasi, 1958, for a scholarly discussion of this point of view.) The vast majority of contemporary theorists in psychology and the allied behavioral sciences now conceptualize the child as a striving organism, selecting as well as responding to environmentally available stimuli. It is now known that the developing human organism is not completely dominated by its environment, because some responses appear according to an internally controlled series of maturational, or genetically controlled, variables virtually independent of external conditions (e.g., the emergence of the human smile, as described by Spitz, 1946). On the other hand, it is now equally well known that the absence of, or distortion of, certain usually and conventionally available condi-

*For extended reviews of research findings and theories about psychological development, the following books are suggested: Baldwin, 1967; Carmichael, 1954; Hoffman & Hoffman, 1964, 1966; Horrocks, 1969; Powell, 1963; Thompson, 1962.

tions of stimulation and nurturance can have pervasive and profound effects on psychological development (e.g., an infant's depression in response to separation from the mother, as described by Bowlby, 1966). The deleterious effects of dietary protein deficiencies on the mental development of the young child have also been well documented in the research literature on nutrition. Whether or not marginal deficiencies in nutritional states have similar adverse effects remains hypothetical.

The nervous system stands supreme among the federation of organs which together constitute the human individual. Its supremacy consists in the function of maintaining and furthering the integrity of the body and its behavior. By virtue of this function nature has safeguarded it with certain distinctive growth characteristics. Among all the organs of the body the nervous system manifests a high degree of autonomy in paradoxical union with a high degree of impressionability. It is remarkably resistant to adversity. It withstands much deprivation. When other organs of the body starve, it does not starve as much as they do. This relative invulnerability gives it a certain stability in the somatic competition between organ systems. It tends to grow in obedience to inborn determiners, whether saddled with handicap or favored with opportunity. It responds to opportunity and capitalizes [on] it; but its supreme function is the optimum integration of the individual in all circumstances.

All things considered, the inevitableness and surety of maturation are the most impressive characteristic [sic] of early development. It is the hereditary ballast which conserves and stabilizes the growth of each individual infant. It is indigenous in its impulsion; but we may well be grateful for this degree of determinism. If it did not exist the infant would be a victim of a flaccid malleability which is sometimes romantically ascribed to him. His mind, his spirit, his personality would fall a ready prey to disease, to starvation, to malnutrition, and worst of all to misguided management. As it is, the inborn tendency toward optimum development is so inveterate that he benefits liberally from what is good in our practice, and suffers less than he logically should from our unenlightenment. Only if we give respect to this inner core of inheritance can we respect the important individual differences which distinguish infants as well as men. (From Gesell, 1928, pp. 377–378. With permission of Macmillan and Co.)

The Continuous versus the Discontinuous View of Psychological Growth

Physics, that highly respected and much emulated patriarch of the empirical sciences, has gradually accepted a theoretical compromise recognizing that *some events* can best be understood and predicted when they are conceptualized as continuous processes, while *other events* can be most fruitfully regarded as discontinuous states which may merge over time to give a semblance of continuity but which are really identifiably separate. The physicist's principle of complementarity, that describes this conceptual compromise, is an explicit admission in our most highly developed science that it is sometimes to man's advantage to view the same phenomena differently for different purposes. The need for multiple views and alternative conceptions seems especially strong in a relatively new science like psychology that deals with the complex interacting functions of living organisms.

The complementarity principle of physics also appears to apply to some dimensions of psychological growth. For example, some aspects of human development appear to change over time in a smooth, continuous manner, others appear to change by quantal increments, and still others appear to be changes in organization that transform the descriptive qualities of the phenomena under observation.

The continuous view of psychological growth is popular with the lay majority because it is so obvious that the infant gradually grows physically toward childhood and the child gradually grows physically toward maturity. The latter span is a little troublesome for this viewpoint because of the preadolescent spurt in physical height, but the layman can rationalize this as "the exception that proves the rule." By analogy to physical growth, many developmental psychologists have assumed that the various dimensions of psychological growth change over time in a continuous manner, although most psychologists have usually recognized the existence of spurts and regressions in these continuous processes (for example, see Figure 3-2).

The discontinuous view has been most often expressed by psychological theorists as "stages" or "critical periods" during the developmental years during which the organization of behavior differs or is subject to different types of environmental influence. Building a credible case for stages or critical periods is always difficult because it necessarily involves the making of inferences about developmental processes not subject to direct observation. We have selected for comment three theorists who have approached this matter in somewhat related but still distinctly different ways. Freud, Hebb, and Piaget have all postulated the existence of discontinuities in the developmental period, but here any strong similarity among their theoretical propositions ends. Our comments are largely restricted to each theorist's postulates or suggestions that have important implications for education. Some of the details of each theorist's position are presented in the later chapters of this book.

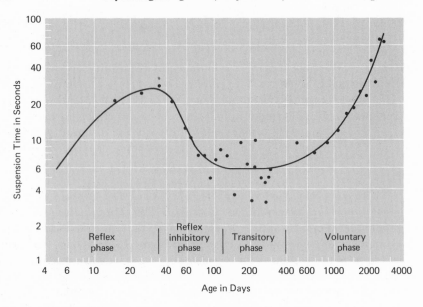

Figure 3-2.   Suspension time for a group of children as a function of chronological age (both variables on logarithmic scales), showing the stages in this motor response with characteristic rates of growth and decline. (From McGraw, 1943, with permission of the Columbia University Press.)

Freud's Stages of Psychosexual Development

One of Freud's most influential proposals related to the important influence of early childhood experiences such as feeding, toilet training, and handling on the later character, temperament, and personality of the individual. His basic conception of the psychosexual stages is schematically represented in Table 3-1. During the primacy of a particular stage the human personality is thought to be subject to the effects of unique experiences that will permeate certain dimensions of his later life. For example, if the infant is permitted very little nursing satisfaction, his later life will be characterized by strong oral erotic tendencies: excessive eating or drinking, oral stimulation like thumbsucking or lip licking, and more symbolic types of oral gratifications like talking.

Thus, one of Freud's keenest insights was the observation that deprivation and conflict during the early stages of human life have permanent effects on the individual's wants, desires, and interests, and on his preferred behaviors for satisfying these needs. Freud concluded that something of the infantile remains in all of us for all time, although it may be deeply buried and in highly transformed guise. The teacher who remembers and appreciates this seemingly simple but actually very profound wisdom has a better chance of understanding pupils, colleagues,

Table 3-1. **A schematic illustration of Freud's hypothesized periods and stages in psychosexual development.**

A. Libidinal Localization (erotogenic zones)	B. Aim, or Mode of Pleasure-Finding	C. Libidinal Object-Finding		

INFANCY PERIOD

		Auto-eroticism	*Narcissism*	*Allo-eroticism*
Pregenital Period	*Infantile Sexuality*			
1. Oral Stage				
a. early oral	Sucking, swallowing (incorporating)	at first objectless		Oral object-choice
b. late oral	Biting, devouring (destroying, annihilating)		Primary Narcissism	Oral-sadistic object-choice
2. Anal Stage				
a. early anal	Expelling (rejecting) (destroying) — looking, exhibiting, handling, inflicting pain			Anal and anal-sadistic object-choice
b. late anal	Retaining (controlling) (possessing) — submitting to pain			
Early Genital Period (phallic stage)	Touching, rubbing, exhibiting and looking at genitalia, investigating, comparing, questioning, phantasying (tender affection)			Parent object-choice Oedipus-phantasies

LATENCY PERIOD

No new zone	Repression Reaction-formation Sublimation Affectional trends	Further decline of auto-eroticism	Diminished Narcissism	Development of social feelings

ADOLESCENT OR PUBERTAL PERIOD

Late Genital Period				
Revival of zone sensitivity of infancy period	Reactivation of modes or aims of infancy period	Revival of auto-eroticism	Fresh wave of Narcissism	Revival of Oedipus object-choice
Later, functioning of vaginal zone	Emergence of adult mode of pleasure-finding			Homosexual object-choice
				Heterosexual object-choice

and himself, simply because everyone does respond emotionally at certain times in a manner characteristic of him at an earlier time in his development. At such times an individual must be understood and reacted to as if he were, indeed, much less mature. In addition, this conception of stages and their pervasive influence on later motivation can serve as a continuous reminder that pupils with widely different social backgrounds can be expected to have comparably different interests and aspirations.*

Hebb's Psychoneurological Theory

Hebb's theory sort of splits the difference between the two perspectives of continuity and discontinuity as the preferred description of psychological development. He comes closer than most theorists in developmental psychology to the complementarity view proposed by contemporary physicists. Something akin to the stage concept is useful to Hebb in describing what has gone before and what will come later at any point where one may wish to section the developmental span. The principal postulate in Hebb's theory as it relates to developmental processes is that early experiences produce psychoneurological organizations that make later experiences less potent influences on organization, or in some instances powerless impacts as far as reorganization is concerned. Early learning, as contrasted with later, is conceptualized as prepotent in effects because of its priority in organizing cell assemblies and phase sequences which are more available and flexible in the early stages of experience.†

If instinct is a poor theoretical conception we must abandon it for technical purposes, but we must not forget the problems of behavior to which in the past it has been applied. Man everywhere has a fondness for the sound of his own voice, singing and listening to songs, telling elaborate tales for their own sake (some of them being true), or talking when there is no need of communication. Man everywhere uses tools, organizes social groups, avoids darkness in strange places. All cultures are said to have developed string games, related to the childhood game of cat's cradle. The taboos of incest or of food use, the belief in spirits good or evil, the tendency to ornament the body in particular ways and to impose strong sanctions against ornamenting it in other ways—all these are things which, in their details, are subject to the influence of special learning, but which in one form or another spring up in every society of which we have knowledge. In detail,

*See Hall, 1954, for a highly readable and succinct summary of Freud's psychoanalytic theory. Consult Blum, 1953, for details of the various psychoanalytic views of character development.
†See Hebb (1945, 1949, 1959) for details of this interesting and influential theory.

therefore, they are not species-predictable; but in a larger sense they are very much so. The fact that the specific way in which the hair may be worn varies from culture to culture, or from one time to another in the same culture, does not change the fact that all cultures at all times have such rules, and that they play an important part in the behavior of man in the presence of his fellows. We cannot predict the content of folk tales in a culture encountered for the first time; but we can safely predict that there will be folk tales, learned and passed on from generation to generation. A false opposition of the "instinctive" to the "learned" has tended in the past to prevent us from seeing these common features of human behavior and from recognizing that they must result, much as the instinctive behavior of rodent and carnivore does, from (a) the way we are made, and (b) the universal features of the human environment. (From Hebb, 1966, p. 160. With permission of author and W. B. Saunders Co.)

Hebb's theory has spawned a whole series of investigations of variations in early experience as antecedents of later behavior and flexibility of behavioral modification. The influence of this theory on education is just beginning to be noticeable as we become more sensitive to the potential ill effects of an impoverished social-emotional environment during the preschool years on the later educability of the child. In their experiments with rats (see Figure 3-3), Krech and associates (1960,

Figure 3-3. Some of the equipment used to provide an enriched intellectual environment for laboratory rats. Animals with experience in this situation developed a larger amount of cortical tissue than litter mates raised in the usual laboratory cages. (From Bennett, Diamond, Krech, & Rosenzweig, 1964. With permission.)

1964) have concluded that an intellectually stimulating environment produces superior cortical growth and greater learning ability. Whether or not data can be obtained to support a similar generalization for children, psychologists are generally persuaded that man's potential for acquiring skills and utilizing creative reasoning to his own advantage is undoubtedly far greater than has been traditionally conceived in educational programs.

Piaget's Theory of Cognitive Stages

This creative theorist, resourceful investigator, and prolific writer is truly an interactionist as well as a proponent of progressive levels of cognitive organization during the developmental period. Piaget reminds us in all of his writings that the child and adolescent not only *assimilate* information from their surroundings but they also *accommodate* to this information, and thus the organizational base for future assimilation is always progressively changing. This continuous interaction between assimilation and accommodation comprises adaptation, a concept very similar to the adjustment notion of modern behaviorism. These are the linear, continuous growth processes that periodically summate to move an individual child from one level of cognitive organization to another. Piaget perceives the growing child as going through the series of stages shown in Table 3-2. During each stage the child reaches a relative state of equilibrium in his resources for adaptation. However this is eventually terminated by an increasing disequilibrium that in time moves the developing child along to a new and more advanced stage of psychological organization.

The general descriptive parameters of Piaget's conception of psychological development have been successfully identified by many scientific observers around the world. Whether or not his explanations of the dynamics of development will prove to be useful models for guiding research remains an open question, but certainly his observations and speculations are currently having a substantial impact on educational curricula and methodology. For example, Piaget's observation that nonmetric mathematical concepts precede metric ones in the child's cognitive growth has led to much educational research on the feasibility of teaching some geometrical concepts during kindergarten and first grade. Or, Piaget's notion that the child from about six to twelve years of age is restricted to concrete operations has stimulated educational experimentation on the possibility of introducing pupils during the elementary grades to some complex concepts usually reserved for junior or senior high school pupils. The reasoning has been that once suitable and appropriate concrete operations can be found, or invented, to support and carry the logical processes through to their conclusion, then the concrete operational skills of the elementary school pupil will enable

Table 3-2.   Stages of mental development in Piaget's theory.

Approximate Chronological-Age Interval	*Distinguishing Mental Operations*
	Sensori-Motor Group Structures
Birth	0–1 month—reflex exercises
	1–4½ months—primary circular reactions (motor habits and perception)
	4½–9 months—secondary circular reactions (intentional acts and prehension)
	9–11/12 months—object constancy and grasp of means-ends relations
	11/12–18 months—*invention* of *new* means (sensori-motor intelligence)
18 months	18 months—internalization of sensori-motor schemata and achievement of *reversible actions* permitting detours
	Concrete Operation "Groupement" Structures
18 months *Formation* 7 years	1½–7 years—period of formation of the beginnings of *representative* intelligence, made possible by the emergence of *symbolic* functions which differentiate significants from significates—events *represented* by symbols in play, drawing, and language.
7 years *Equilibration and Concrete Operations* 11 years	7–11 years—*mental* actions are grouped in *reversible systems* but still attached to their contents (concrete quality). Reversibility of mental operations enables child to understand certain invariances as they relate to concrete operations, e.g., conservations of liquids, lengths, surfaces, and so on. Concrete operations serve as basis for later emergence of formal operations.
	Combined "Group" and "Lattice" Formal Structures
11 years	11–14 years—the capability emerges of deducing from hypotheses, thereby reasoning is freed from concrete facts; ability to "suppose" appears, to take an "if then" attitude not directly related to personal experience.
15 years	14–15 years—equilibrium achieved on formal mental structures that integrate partial groupements into structured whole; hypotheses in *formal operational* form can be handled simultaneously, e.g., as of the lattice type in combinational analyses.

him to grasp and use almost any conceptual schema. He can learn and understand anything that can be veridically reduced to concrete models. Whether or not this assertion is really valid is again an open question, but it has definitely piqued the educator's curiosity, and he is busily engaged in experimentation that may do much to change standard teaching practices over the next two decades. Of course, the fact that some series of operations *can* be taught to first-grade pupils does not necessarily imply that it is the most appropriate learning experience and therefore *should* be taught at that time. The latter is the more difficult question that often takes generations to answer and then provides the answer only for a particular culture at a given time in its history.

All behaviour presupposes, apart from maturation factors, an acquisition through experience, either in the form of exercise or as direct acquisition. Experience and environment are everywhere presupposed. There are, however, in the development of the child two kinds of experience which are always more or less intermixed, but which can easily be distinguished on analysis. These two sorts of experience give two kinds of knowledge or two kinds of methods of acquiring knowledge. There is first the experience which I will call "physical experience" or "experience derived from the physical environment" which is experience in the accepted sense of the term—it is what everybody thinks of, while forgetting on the other hand the second category of which I will speak later.

Experience derived from the physical environment furnishes knowledge taken from objects and gives rise to what one might call an abstraction derived from the object: certain qualities of the object may serve as signals for associations or for conditionings.

I will give just one example: the concept of heaviness and lightness. Evidently, it is by experimenting with objects that the child, before he is able to speak, at the sensorimotor level, notices that there are heavy objects and light objects. Then this knowledge gives rise to associations. He discovers that heavy objects are generally larger and larger objects are generally heavier. You all know the illusion of weight. When you see two boxes of equal weight but of different volume you always expect the larger to be the heavier; this results from an effect of contrast. The illusion does not exist among the mentally deficient nor among very young children. It is produced partly by a weight-volume association. This type of knowledge is acquired by abstractions derived from the object.

There is, however, a second kind of experience which I should like to stress. Experimentation here is also carried out on objects and can be carried out only by manipulating objects. But in this case the knowledge is not drawn from the object and the abstraction does not derive from it. The abstraction is derived from the actions themselves which are performed on the object, which is something quite different.

I shall give only one example, which is very nice from the symbolic point of view. One of my friends, a mathematician, ascribes his first interest in mathematics to an experiment he made as a child. I should like to emphasize again the fact that everything, even mathematical knowledge, presupposes experience; such knowledge is not innate; it presupposes an experimental construction, an acquisition, learning, but this learning is of a particular kind. It is an abstraction derived not from the object but from the action. To come to my friend's experiment: as a child—I don't know how old he was—he clearly remembers counting pebbles. He had ten in front of him and he put them in a straight line. He began counting: one, two, three ... up to ten. Then he counted from the other end: one, two ... etc., and he was very surprised to get to ten. Then he mixed them up, he permuted and he began counting them again and again he got up to ten. This was a miracle to him. He tried every way and always arrived at ten. This is a result which he could not yet deduce in advance although later on he became a great mathematician. It was the experiment that taught him that the cardinal sum is independent of the order. But how did he experiment? With pebbles, yes, certainly. He could have done it with bits of wood, and if he had been an atomic baby with electrons—although they would have been rather more difficult to count. Anyway the object does not matter.

Where did he get his knowledge from? Two ideas come in here: the idea of order and the idea of the cardinal sum. The order is not inherent in the pebbles; you can put them in any kind of order. It is action which introduces a definite order into the arrangement of pebbles. In the same way, the sum is not inherent in the pebbles; the pebbles have no property of being ten. The sum is again a product of an adding operation, of an actual action. These two ideas of order and sum are not properties of the object. The object always conforms to the action, on the macrophysical scale at any rate. But it is not from the object that the knowledge is drawn. Here it is drawn from an abstraction based on the action. [From comments by Piaget. In Tanner & Inhelder (Eds.), 1954, Vol. II, pp. 58–59. With permission of the International Universities Press, Inc.]

A Theory of Maturation and Readiness

The concept of maturation was borrowed from biology so long ago that it is considered the property of all who may find it useful. It has probably been used more effectively in the past by Gesell (1928) and McGraw (1943).

Although the several billions of neurons that make up the central nervous system of man are all physically present at the normal time of birth, they are largely physically immature: myelin sheaths either absent or scantily present in efferent fibers, little elaboration of laterals on axones and dendrites, and so on. McGraw has postulated that the vast majority of the neurons in the human cortex are nonfunctional at the time of birth. She has further hypothesized that when these cortical neurons mature with increasing age, they modify the behavior of the infant in several ways: certain patterns of response are inhibited (see Figure 3-4), other patterns of behavior are initiated (for example, the

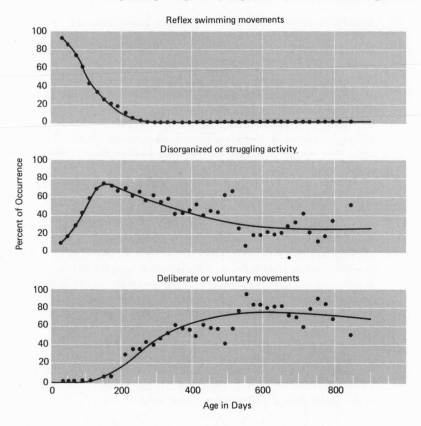

Figure 3-4. The aquatic behavior of infants during the first two years and four months of life. Note the three phases attributed by McGraw to cortical maturation. (From McGraw, 1943. With permission.)

human smile), and still other patterns of response become differentiated, generalized, and complexly interrelated in the ways that undergird the distinctly human dimensions of intelligence.

The maturation of the neurons in the cerebral cortex may thus be regarded as setting certain limits for "what is possible" by way of influencing the individual child at a particular time in his development. As may be seen, of course, environmental influence of a particular type may be neurophysiologically possible at times when the appropriate stimulation is absent. Maturation may be sufficiently advanced to support a given learning experience, but the young learner may not have had the necessary prior experiences to respond positively to the educational assignment. Maturational status in conjunction with the necessary prior experience defines the educational concept of *readiness*. For example, a first-grade pupil's state of readiness for reading instruction determines whether or not the pupil can master the skills and utilize the concepts embedded in the learning exercises at a rate sufficiently high to maintain his interest and to make it worthwhile for him socially and economically at that point in the school's curriculum. It is, of course, obvious that readiness cannot be defined without a specification of teaching methods and instructional materials. Many of the currently new programs in arithmetic, reading, and science have stemmed from a fresh look at readiness within the new perspective of automated and computerized presentations of learning opportunities, in conjunction with more ingenious methods of partitioning, arranging, and illustrating the curricular content.

> Just as the human brain develops anatomically from the brainstem upward to the diencephalon and mesencephalon, to the cerebral hemispheres, and finally to the telencephalon, so also does brain function ascend during individual development from the centers of the brainstem upward. This determines the neurological behavior of the successive developmental stages. One level after the other becomes capable of functioning and assumes direction of brain function with the always indispensable older layers as a foundation.
>
> Only the ontogenetically and phylogenetically older centers of the brainstem have begun to function in the newborn infant, the cerebral hemispheres being still inactive; thus, the total brain is composed of an older, already functioning layer and a younger stratum not yet capable of activity. Foerster (1913) named the newborn infant a "pallidum creature" after his highest functioning brain structure.
>
> As even Aristotle recognized, the older layers are included in the younger layers. The younger layers are placed above the older but cannot work without them, whereas the lower layers can function very well without the higher, as embryology and phylogenesis prove. The higher layers are able to inhibit and to guide the lower. Many a function which a lower layer may fulfill is taken over and performed better by a higher layer. In addition, new functions are added. But at each stage the function of the brain remains a uniform whole. (From Peiper, 1963, p. 580. With permission of Consultants Bureau Enterprises, Inc.)

Some General Principles
of Psychological Growth

On the basis of the available research findings it is possible to formulate some fairly general principles of psychological growth. Although the following discussion does not exhaustively review all such principles, it does encompass those that have major implications for education. These principles can serve as helpful guides to understanding and guiding psychological growth during the first decades of life.

Some behavior patterns appear spontaneously when the human organism reaches a certain level of maturity

Since these behaviors appear under all known cultural conditions, they appear to be independent of environmental conditions within the normal range of infant, child, and adolescent care. Some of the more obvious of these behaviors involve motor responses to what are postulated to be innate releasing mechanisms within the organism (Lorenz, 1960), for example, the emergence of the true human smile in the infant around five or six weeks of age (Spitz, 1946). Convincing evidence for the hypothesis of an innate releasing mechanism when one notes that true smiling appears at approximately the same time among the responses of the congenitally blind infant. The most dramatic evidence has been obtained with infrahuman subjects in studies of imprinting. For example, as shown in Figure 3-5, the age interval during which infant animals can become socially "attached" to moving objects is fairly sharply limited.

As another interesting example, consider the differential timing of the innate releasing mechanisms that determine the onset of puberty in the sexes (see Figure 3-6). The changes in behavior associated with

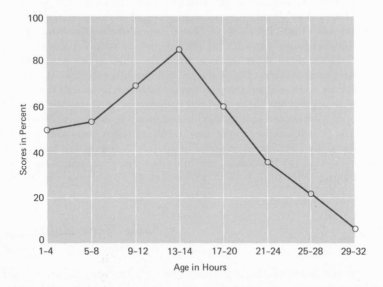

Figure 3-5. Ducklings tend to follow the first visible, moving object (usually the mother, but it can be any moving stimulus). As shown here, the critical developmental period during which ducklings show this imprinting ranges from the time of hatching to about 32 hours of age. (From Hess, 1959. With permission of the American Association for the Advancement of Science.)

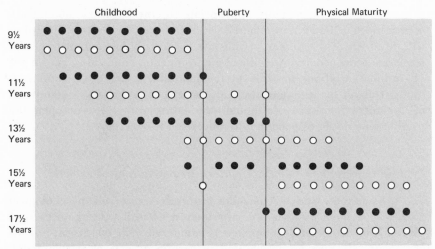

Each Black Dot represents 10 percent of all boys of given age measured.
Each White Dot represents 10 percent of all girls of given age measured.

*Figure 3-6. Variations in ages at which children mature sexually. Note espe-
cially the earlier maturation of girls. (From Alice V. Keliher.* Life and growth.
New York: D. Appleton-Century Co., 1938. With permission.)

this differential timing are well known: girls become interested in heter-
osexual companionship at an earlier age than boys, late maturers among
either sex are less advanced in social development, and so on.

These are only a few of the more obvious behaviors that appear
rather abruptly when an individual reaches a given level of inner
maturity. Psychologists have theorized and obtained some evidence for a
good many other emergents "from within" throughout the developmental period: varieties of emotional response like sympathy and anxiety,[*]
dreams and fantasy behavior, social responsiveness, and many others.

The foregoing should not be interpreted as testing the limits of
possible environmental controls over behaviors that have been associated with the hypothesis of innate releasing mechanisms. All of the
human and animal subjects in the studies cited were given *normal* care,
within a rather broad but still limited range dictated by the benevolent
and humanitarian sensibilities of experimenters. So-called instinctive
behaviors in lower animals *can* often be modified when normal environmental conditions are drastically modified. This has caused some psychologists (for example, Beach, 1955) to reject the instinct concept and
call for a detailed ontogenetic analysis of behavioral change. Such

---

[*]Again the most spectacular evidence comes from animal studies. For example,
the chimpanzee reared from infancy under controlled laboratory conditions remains
only mildly curious about a toy snake until suddenly one day in his development
(and thereafter) the snake's appearance terrifies him (Hebb, 1945).

recommendation seems more appropriate for investigations of infrahuman subjects where environmental conditions can be severely altered at
will. Students of the human organism must usually be content to accept
a relative homogeneity of civilized environmental conditions, except for
(1) minor variations possible in the laboratory, (2) those conditions
brought about by wars and their aftermath, or perhaps (3) conditions
in "primitive" cultures (although the latter always leaves open the
troublesome doubt of genetic differences).

Each individual has a distinct pattern of psychological growth

As parents and teachers are generally aware, the psychological
growth of a given pupil is typically uneven when his status on each of
several dimensions of development is compared with the average of his
age group. He may be accelerated in certain aspects of development,
average in some, and retarded in others: His state of readiness for learning experiences at any point in time is the resultant of a complex interaction of cognitive abilities, skills, interests, and maturational potentials
for further behavioral change. The typical uneven patterning of some of
these dimensions of psychological and physical resources is illustrated
in Figure 3-7.

The relatively uneven growth pattern of the usual boy or girl
makes the task of appraising a pupil's competencies and aptitudes a
difficult one. It cannot be assumed, for example, that a pupil who is
above average in intelligence is also above average in motor skills,
because there is practically no correlation between these two types of
growth (Peterson, 1930). The pupil who is poorest in handwriting may
be the best within the classroom in reading, arithmetic, or some other
subject-matter achievement, because handwriting correlates to only a
negligible degree with other kinds of academic progress. Pupils with
competence levels below average in arithmetic may be superior in the
language arts—this particular relationship being especially characteristic of girls (McCarthy, 1930).

The foregoing should not be interpreted as implying that there
are no positive or substantial correlations between different types of
development. Rather, since these relationships are often very modest in
magnitude, one must be extremely cautious in making inferences about
growth status when the relevant data are not in hand. To be sure, as was
shown many years ago, the intellectually gifted child tends to be average
or above in all growth functions (Terman & Oden, 1947). Good things *do*
tend to go together in nature, however one must always remember the
caution implied by the verb "tend," because there are notable exceptions to this generalization.

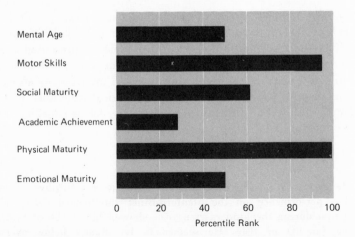

Figure 3-7. A profile of the maturity of one pupil in several areas of development. Note that his mental age is at the 50th percentile which indicates that he is average when compared with his same-aged peers in this dimension of development.

It may also be well to remind ourselves at this point of the falseness of some other once commonly drawn generalizations that are related to the frequent lack of correlation among growth patterns. Each of the following *corrections* to superstition, prejudice, and legend can be documented by the findings of many research studies:

The lefthanded child suffers no related handicaps, except those attributed by the prejudiced viewer.

The intellectually retarded child does not eventually "catch up" with his peers, despite wishful thinking to the contrary.

The child who is retarded in many dimensions of development does not always have the saving grace of possessing some superior talent.

The child who "stutters" does nothing more than repeat some sounds and words more frequently than the average of his peers.

During the preadolescent growth spurt in physical height there is not a correlated spurt in mental growth.

The child who is accelerated in many dimensions of development is not necessarily retarded in some dimensions—there is no such poetic justice in nature to humble the bold and the brave!

The teacher must rely on unprejudiced observation, the results of available tests, and the opinions of specialists to help him appraise the many facets of pupil growth. Research has shown no shortcuts; rather it has demonstrated that many of the differences among pupils in rates and levels of development are extremely subtle and difficult to appraise.

Since success in most of the learning exercises presented to pupils is dependent on *many* different psychological functions, lack of maturity in any one of these processes will prevent pupil progress. As an example of this intricate interaction of many psychological functions, which are dependent on different dimensions of maturity, let us consider the case of Henry B. who had difficulty learning to read.

Henry was an attractive boy slightly above average in physical development. His performance on the Stanford-Binet Intelligence Scale, administered to him during the kindergarten year, showed him to be of average intelligence (an IQ of 104). He seemed to be slightly below average in emotional maturity as evidenced by his difficulty in giving up the security of his mother and home environment, and by his dependence on the kindergarten teacher for signs of approval. He tended to be an observer rather than a participant during informal play periods, although he seemed pleased to play with his classmates when invited. His personal folder showed that he was the only child of indulgent parents, both in their early forties at the time of Henry's birth. Mrs. B. indicated that Henry had suffered many illnesses during his preschool period and that they had not permitted him to engage very much in informal play with neighborhood children. Despite these deprivations, Henry's motor development appears to be somewhat above average. At the end of the kindergarten year his teacher described him as "apprehensive and socially shy, but of average intellectual ability."

When Henry entered first grade his teacher noted his continuing tendency to become anxious and tense in new situations and during informal play periods. When formal reading instruction was begun in the second half of the year, Henry seemed interested but easily distracted by the performances of other pupils. He appeared to learn new words easily but was unable to remember them the next day. His reading vocabulary fell behind and he became listless and apathetic during reading instruction. He became even more socially withdrawn. Upon the teacher's request Henry was examined and observed by the school psychologist. The latter interviewed Henry's parents and recommended a program of action designed toward lessening Henry's feelings of inadequacy in social situations involving other children. That summer Henry participated in a special play group supervised by youth leaders from the local Y.M.C.A. He learned to swim, play many new games, and generally enjoy himself during informal play periods. His apprehensive and anxious responses declined in frequency as he matured socially. His parents reported, "Henry seems more like a *real* boy."

The next year with the aid of a tutor Henry rapidly made up his deficit in reading skill. He joined play groups spontaneously and seemed to be a genuinely happy and relaxed second-grade boy.

Needless to say, from our limited information about Henry B. we cannot identify the exact locus of his immaturity. We can only infer that his " readiness" for reading (a complex function of maturation and experience) was deficient. And his inability to learn to read was not his only important handicap. It seems probable that the school psychologist anticipated that Henry was "ready" to expand his social skills and acquire new securities in the big world outside his home. Was social and emotional immaturity the stumbling block in his efforts to master the reading skill? Perhaps. Certainly we know that the anxiety and distraction of failure in one area of personal adjustment can interfere with learning and adjustment in other spheres. However, it is also possible that sheer maturation and learning experience over a stretch of time permitted Henry to profit from both types of educational experience, and that social adjustment and reading skill were not causally related in his case. In any event, the psychologist's recommendations might have been very different for another pupil with similar difficulties but a different pattern of maturation and experiences.

There is a complex interaction between maturation and experience that results in "readiness" for learning and adjustment

The child and the adolescent are responding to both internal and external environmental conditions. Convincing research findings are now available to demonstrate that some types of behavior can be permanently depressed if the organism is deprived of certain kinds of interaction with the environment (for example, Dennis & Najarian, 1957). Other research findings show that "enriching" the environment beyond what is usually provided under mildly deprived conditions can enhance the organism's ability to learn certain behaviors (Rheingold, 1956). Still other investigations have demonstrated that the timing of opportunities for experience (when they are available during the developmental period) can make a crucial difference in their influences on behavior and later development (Hess, 1959).

The internal environment for central nervous system activity, that portion of the human organism that mediates the behaviors for which education is most directly relevant, can also be permanently modified by manipulations of external environmental conditions (for example, Levine's studies of the effects of early handling, 1958). The most exciting demonstration to date with the human organism is the acquisition of nutritional and biochemical controls over a deficiency that produces one kind of mental retardation, phenylketonuria. Happily for society this condition of the internal environment can be prevented by manipulations in the external environment (Bower & Jeavons, 1963).

Many of the most interesting and suggestive research findings on the effects of the interactions of maturation and experience have been obtained in studies of infrahuman subjects. Whether there are as many, or more, "critical periods" during the developmental periods of childhood and adolescence in man is an open question. Most theorists postulate that the developmental organization of humans is more flexible, therefore one might expect fewer critical times for maturation-experience interactions. On the other hand, because of its complexity, the psychoneurological organization of the child or adolescent is extremely influential on the *selection* of experiences, which would emphasize the significance and pervasiveness of those critical periods that do exist.

Psychological Growth in Extended Perspective

The classroom teacher and other educational personnel are frequently so immersed in their work assignments that they may forget to view human development from a broad view extended over years rather than days, weeks, or months. Just because a given pupil is not progressing satisfactorily toward some particular educational achievement doesn't necessarily mean that he will drop out of school at the legally permissible age, that his parents are going to be unhappy about his scholarly progress, that he will be a failure in adult life, or a good many other pessimistic predictions that can be made.

The findings of follow-up studies of individuals who failed one or more courses at different times in their school careers makes one extremely cautious about inferring that academic failure usually leads to maladjustment or outright indigence in adult life.* History relates the story again and again of individuals who did unsatisfactory work in one or more academic subject areas but subsequently went on to make satisfactory, or even superior, contributions to society during adult life. Even persons classified as mentally retarded and academic failures often adjust and contribute to society sufficiently well to be self-supporting and responsible citizens (Baller, 1967). The substantial success of these individuals in taking care of themselves, holding steady jobs, supporting and caring for families, and meeting the standards of community life makes one appreciate the resilience and resourcefulness of the human organism over the long haul.

*See Kagan & Moss (1962), Anderson (1959), and Jones (1967) for follow-up studies that show continuity but also a large measure of flexible change in human behavior tendencies and disposition during the developmental years.

All the world's a stage,
And all the men and women merely players.
They have their exits and their entrances;
And one man in his time plays many parts,
His acts being seven ages. At first the infant,
Mewling and puking in the nurse's arms.
Then the whining schoolboy, with his satchel,
And shining morning face, creeping like snail
Unwillingly to school. And then the lover,
Sighing like furnace, with a woful ballad
Made to his mistress' eyebrow. Then a soldier,
Full of strange oaths, and bearded like the pard,
Jealous in honour, sudden and quick in quarrel,
Seeking the bubble reputation
Even in the cannon's mouth. And then the justice,
In fair round belly with good capon lin'd,
With eyes severe, and beard of formal cut,
Full of wise saws and modern instances;
And so he plays his part. The sixth age shifts
Into the lean and slipper'd pantaloon,
With spectacles on nose and pouch on side,
His youthful hose well sav'd a world too wide
For his shrunk shank; and his big manly voice,
Turning again toward childish treble, pipes
And whistles in his sound. Last scene of all,
That ends this strange eventful history,
Is second childishness and mere oblivion,
Sans teeth, sans eyes, sans taste, sans everything.
(From William Shakespeare, *As You Like It*, Act II, Scene VII.)

These cautions should not be interpreted as absolving the teacher of his responsibility to do his best to guide pupils toward the highest possible levels of scholarly competence. Rather they are reminders that each pupil has many nonacademic coping abilities that may very adequately carry him through a socially useful and personally rewarding life despite a record of unsatisfactory progress in school. Whenever he consistently fails to stimulate a particular pupil's interest or guide him to expected levels of skill and competence, the teacher may properly be perplexed and even discouraged, but he should not be demoralized. It is helpful for teachers to "back off" occasionally so that they can get a broader perspective of an individual pupil's total development. It is easy to become so overwhelmed by the vagaries of a pupil's day-to-day behavior that one forgets the continuity, flexibility, resourcefulness, and self-healing properties of the human organism. There is also the tendency for the teacher to forget that he is involved in only one segment, albeit an extremely important one, of the pupil's total development. The tenth-grade boy of average intellectual ability who is almost certainly headed for an apprenticeship in his father's skilled trade may not have enough need for a knowledge of Latin II in later life to merit the teacher's apprehension over his lack of interest and progress in this required part of the school's curriculum. Teachers in a culture that requires school attendance by statute until the pupil reaches his sixteenth birthday must be more than tutors of academic knowledge and skills. Their knowledge and appreciation of a pupil's total life adjustment, a significant portion of which comes under their supervision in the modern school, will be enhanced in most cases by their attempting to gain a broad and extended perspective of the pupil's long-term development.

Summary

The *growing* infant, child, or adolescent is difficult to understand because his behavior is being continuously influenced by an internal (as inferred) as well as an external (as directly observed) environment. Behaviors appear and sometimes disappear as a function of both internal and external stimulation and support. The most influential theories of human development, like those of such theorists as Freud, Hebb, and Piaget, postulate the existence of stages or critical periods in human development, intervals during which psychological tendencies to response and their organization are especially likely to lead to certain kinds of interaction with the external environment. Research has shown that environmental deprivation during certain periods of development can have pervasive, and sometimes catastrophic, effects on later development and potentiality for behavioral change. Other studies have yielded promising findings that the course of human development can be positively influenced by manipulating some aspects of the internal as well as the external environment. Maturation of the neurons in the cerebral cortex sets certain limits of "what is possible" by way of influencing the child or adolescent at a particular time in his development. Maturational status in conjunction and interaction with the necessary prior experience defines the educational concept of readiness. For example, readiness for reading instruction is defined by whether or not the pupil has matured and interacted with his environment sufficiently to master the skills embedded in the learning exercises at a rate high enough to maintain his interest and to make instruction socially and economically worthwhile in the school's curriculum. There are some general principles of development that can be extremely helpful to teachers' understanding of their pupils. Psychological research findings have demonstrated the untenability of some older beliefs about human development; knowledge of the falsity of these unscientifically derived generalizations may prevent the teacher from jeopardizing the welfare of some of his pupils. The teacher in today's schools is more than a mere tutor of academic knowledge and skills. In their total roles as preceptors of youths, teachers can usually become maximally influential by taking a broad and time-extended perspective of each pupil's long-term development.

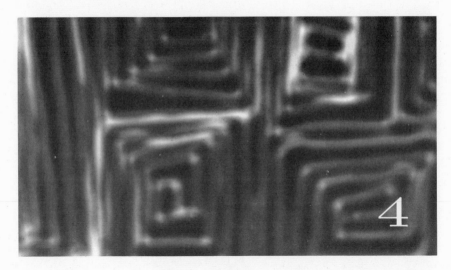

Parents and teachers as mediators of social and cultural influence

Psychologists are now generally agreed that developmental processes are based on the complex interactions of hereditary tendencies and environmental conditions. It is, therefore, only for the convenience of discussion that the two sets of variables are considered in separate chapters. Geneticists have shown that some genetic predispositions become manifest in their influence only under certain environmental conditions. Psychologists have similarly shown that some behavior tendencies, ones that are usually associated with the normal development of a given species and therefore inferred to be under genetic control, can be greatly altered by varying the customary environment in a systematic and substantial manner during the developmental period.

Psychologists and sociologists have collected many different kinds of data which support the hypothesis that institutions and broad social classifications, such as social class, can have strong influences on child-rearing beliefs and practices (Miller & Swanson, 1958). The latter in turn set the stage for much that happens in psychological development. Cultural anthropologists in their studies of widely differing cultures, ranging from the "primitive" to a variegated "civilized," have suggested that child-rearing procedures can have very subtle effects on children, as well as the more obvious consequences that may easily be seen by untutored theorists. The findings of the behavioral and social scientists remind us that many social and cultural forces impinge on the growing child and adolescent, often in concert, but sometimes at cross purposes, in today's rapidly evolving societies.

It seems that both the reality and the autonomy of the concept of culture could better be validated if culture were treated, from an operational point of view, in the same way as the geneticist and demographer treat the closely allied concept of "isolate." What is called a "culture" is a fragment of humanity which, from the point of view of the research at hand and of the scale on which the latter is carried out, presents significant discontinuities in relation to the rest of humanity. If our aim is to ascertain significant discontinuities between, let us say, North America and Europe, then we are dealing with two different cultures; but should we become concerned with significant discontinuities between New York and Chicago, we would be allowed to speak of these two groups as different cultural "units." Since these discontinuities can be reduced to *invariants,* which is the goal of structural analysis, we see that culture may, at the same time, correspond to an objective reality and be a function of the kind of research undertaken. Accordingly, the same set of individuals may be considered to be parts of many different cultural contexts: universal, continental, national, regional, local, etc., as well as familial, occupational, religious, political, etc. This is true as a limit; however, anthropologists usually reserve the term "culture" to designate a *group* of discontinuities which is significant on several of these levels at the same time. That it can never be valid for all levels does not prevent the concept of "culture" from being as fundamental for the anthropologist as that of "isolate" for the demographer. Both belong to the same epistemological family. On a question such as that of the positivistic character of a concept, the anthropologist can rely on a physicist's judgment; it is Niels Bohr who states that "the traditional differences of human cultures in many ways resemble the different equivalent modes in which physical experience can be described." (From Lévi-Strauss, p. 288. With permission.)

Parental Influences on Child and Adolescent

Most theorists in the social sciences agree in assigning major influence to the home environment in molding psychological growth and behavior during the early years of life. Through early nurturing, through selective reinforcements, both positive and negative, and through precepts, expectations and demonstrations, parents set the stage and initiate the dramatic action-and-dialogue of the growing child's personality and character.

Even as early as infancy the socialization picture in the home includes a good many features that may easily be overlooked by the casual observer. For example, the following interactions and mutual influences between parents and infant are continuously present: (1) infant responds to stimuli arising from social objects (at first largely parents and other members of immediate family), (2) infant initiates social contacts, (3) infant's social behavior is modified by responses of others to him, and (4) infant's social responses modify the behavior of others in his group. The latter of these influences, listed by Rheingold (1966), is often overlooked. Anyone who carelessly assumes that brothers and sisters are reared in the same environment just because it happens to be the same home is obviously forgetting for the moment that different children do many things to create and maintain different environments for themselves.

It is the wise teacher who realizes and remembers that his influence on a pupil must build on what has gone before, even as far back as infancy. With perseverance and good fortune the teacher may add a little of personal and social value here and there, apply a few correctives, extend a few horizons to include more of what is possible, but all the time he is forced to recognize that his contributions are likely to be rejected and his well-intentioned good works undone if they conflict seriously with parental expectations and pressures.

The evolving family

Because there are so many changes occurring almost daily in the hard sciences that support modern electronics, atomic reactions, and the other wonders of our time, it is easy to forget that social institutions are also evolving in continuous adjustment to these changes. The family is an institution that has evolved with almost unbelievable rapidity during the last few decades. Problems involved in child rearing have become less easy to specify and their solutions more elusive. As noted by Clausen (1966), it seemed much simpler a generation ago to define an effective family. The recognition of social modeling, needs for achievement and affiliation, social cohesiveness, and so on has made the task appropriately more difficult. Moreover, being in the midst of rapid social change makes it hard to identify stable landmarks by which to identify evolving goals and means-ends relationships.

The following summation by Miller and Swanson (1958) succinctly describes some of the more important social forces in family evolution:

A comprehensive history of child care is yet to be written, but it certainly will show that the "best" way to raise a child is infinitely complicated by the rate of change in modern society. In a very real sense, each generation of Americans has come to a new world and has lived to see much of it outmoded. Child training is always a problem in such a society because it always occurs under changing conditions. Like its environment it is in flux. There has always been a new generation—new in its problems and skills, and tastes and theoretical vogues. It is unlikely that this changing will end in our time. The state of cold war that transforms many traditions to those more compatible with a nation ever under arms, ever watchful, ever concerned about its strength and resilience and solidarity, cannot fail to shape the training of children. Whether we make history or adapt to it, we are always in and of it, and an understanding of behavior cannot escape the conditions of time and place in which it appears. (From Miller & Swanson, 1958, p. 236. With permission.)

Some dynamics of parental influence

From the very beginning of life and throughout the dependency period children need the emotional support of stable parental affection and concern. Although there may be acceptable and just-as-good substitutes for parents (Harlow & Harlow, 1965; Rabin, 1965), the full range of consequents of such substitutions is still in debate. Certainly some kinds of consistent adult contacts and care are necessary to sustain normal development and avoid the mental disturbances and various kinds of retardation and deviation characteristically observed in children deprived of their quota of maternal care (Bowlby, 1966; Goldfarb, 1944).

Ego and super-ego development are thus inextricably bound up with the child's primary human relationships; only when these are continuous and satisfactory can his ego and super-ego develop. In dealing here with the embryology of the human mind one is struck by a similarity with the embryological development of the human body, during the course of which undifferentiated tissues respond to the influence of chemical organizers. If growth is to proceed smoothly, the tissues must be exposed to the influence of the appropriate organizer at certain critical periods. In the same way, if mental development is to proceed smoothly, it would appear to be necessary for the undifferentiated psyche to be exposed during certain critical periods to the influence of the psychic organizer—the mother. For this reason, in considering the disorders to which ego and super-ego are liable, it is imperative to have regard to the phases of development of the child's capacity for human relationships. These are many and, naturally, merge into one another. In broad outline the following are the most important.

(a) The phase during which the infant is in course of establishing a relation with a clearly identified person—his mother; this is normally achieved by five or six months of age.

(b) The phase during which he needs her as an ever-present companion; this usually continues until about his third birthday.

(c) The phase during which he is becoming able to maintain a relationship with her in absentia. During the fourth and fifth years such a relationship can only be maintained in favourable circumstances and for a few days or weeks at a time; after seven or eight the relationship can be maintained, though not without strain, for periods of a year or more.

The process whereby he simultaneously develops his own ego and super-ego and the capacity to maintain relationships in absentia is variously described as a process of identification, internalization, or introjection, since the functions of ego and super-ego are incorporated within the self in the pattern set by the parents. (From Bowlby, 1952, pp. 53–54. With permission of Schocken Books and World Health Organization.)

Poor and inadequate mothering practices appear to be passed insidiously from one generation to the next. For example, the Harlows (1962) found that "inadequately" mothered infant monkeys almost inevitably become reluctant and inadequate mothers when they reach maturity and have offspring of their own. "Like mirrors locked face to face," the children of one generation reflect the errors and shortcomings of the just preceding one in matters of childrearing.

From the many research studies that have attempted to identify the essential variables involved in favorable mothering experiences have come some fairly consistent findings that obviously have implications for child care and educational programs at all levels of human development. Involvement, or concern by human caretakers over the child or adolescent in his efforts to cope with acculturative demands, seems essential. Painful contacts with concerned adults are better than neglect or abandonment. A sharp word or a slap is better than lack of care. This may help to explain why pupils prefer and profit from interactions with teachers who appear to use all of the "wrong" approaches, with the exception that they are intensely concerned about each pupil. Such teachers may be authoritarian, sarcastic, punitive, threatening, and unreasonable, and still be preferred by pupils over teachers who use all of the other "best" educational methods and procedures but without personal concern or involvement.

Another essential component of mothering, one that also has important implications for education, is love and affection. Physicians and nurses have long recognized the importance of tender loving care to good health, and even to survival. The hospital charts in pediatric wards often carry prescriptions for TLC as well as for physical medications. Love does indeed "make the world go around," and there is nothing more important in parental care. In one of the most carefully conducted investigations of child rearing, tender loving care was sampled by the complex variable of maternal warmth, and this proved to be a pervasive quality in all dimensions of mothering. Some of the possible reasons why this is so are suggested in the following summary:

There is no clear evidence in our findings to explain why warmth should have such widespread influence. We can speculate, on the basis of our general theory of the learning process, about the possibility that it may play several roles. A warm mother spends more time with her child. She offers him more rewards, technically speaking, and gives him more guidance. He develops stronger expectancies of her reciprocal affection, and thus is more highly motivated to learn how to behave as she wants him to. He becomes more susceptible to control by her, for he has more to gain and more to lose. It seems likely, too, that he gets proportionately more satisfaction and less frustration from his growing desire for affection. (From Sears, Maccoby, & Levin, 1957, pp. 483–484. With permission of Harper, Row, and Co.)

All of these qualities in *warmth* can be related to the teaching relationship. Teachers can be warmly affectionate toward their pupils and thereby become socially powerful agents for reinforcing their best efforts toward academic achievement and personal maturity. Although the teacher cannot meet all of the love demands normally satisfied in psychologically adequate homes or make up for all the forms of damage sustained from neglectful or rejecting parents, he nevertheless can be concerned and attempt to be at all times warmly affectionate toward his pupils. His success in projecting these very basic qualities of the human relationship will determine in large measure his success as a teacher in the best sense of this professional role.

School Influences on Child and Adolescent

It is easy for the classroom teacher to remember that he is charged with teaching some group of skills or area of knowledge such as a foreign language or mathematics. The curriculum, textbooks, expectations of parents and pupils, and daily lesson exercises all remind him of his primary functions in education. During the press of these types of duties it is not always as easy, however, for the teacher to remember that he is simultaneously teaching much more than these skills or backgrounds to knowledge—whether he chooses to do so or not.

Learning to learn

The paradox of the human condition is expressed more in education than elsewhere in human culture, because learning to learn has been and continues to be *Homo sapiens'* most formidable evolutionary task. Although it is true that mammals, as compared to birds and fishes, have to learn so much that it is difficult to say by the time we get to chimpanzees what behavior is inborn and what is learned, the learning task has become so enormous for man that today learning—

education—along with survival, constitutes a major preoccupation. In all the fighting over education we are simply saying that we are not yet satisfied—after about a million years of struggling to become human—that we have mastered the fundamental human task, learning. It must also be clear that we will never quite learn how to learn, for since *Homo sapiens* is self-changing, and since the *more* culture changes the *faster* it changes, man's methods and rate of learning will never quite keep pace with his need to learn. This is the heart of the problem of "cultural lag," for each fundamental scientific discovery presents man with an incalculable number of problems which he cannot foresee. Who, for example, would have anticipated that the discoveries of Einstein would have presented us with the social problems of the nuclear age, or that information theory would have produced unemployment and displacement in world markets? (From Henry 1963, pp. 283–284. With permission of author and publisher.)

The modern teacher is called upon to assume many social and professional roles: imparter of information, guider of developing skills, disciplinarian, comforter (especially as a temporary mother substitute for the very young who are leaving home for the first period of sustained time), counselor (especially to the older adolescents who often prefer the teacher to either parent as an adult confidante), critic, ideal, defender, or just about any role that an adult may assume in his, or her, interactions with children and adolescents. The teacher is frequently thrust into playing roles for which he has little inclination or sympathy. He may even resist or deny that these functions ever should be performed by members of the teaching profession. Despite such disinclinations and protestations, the teacher is often elected to serve, because the social situation calls for the participation of an adult, and the teacher is the only one available.

Over and above planning and guiding classroom learning exercises and the unintentional services demanded by the social situation, the dedicated and conscientious teacher also consciously attempts to be influential in ways that extend beyond the traditional concept of teaching. These additional efforts usually promote noncurricular or extracurricular skills and interests, or emphasize certain standards of behavior and moral conduct. They may be semiconsciously produced exemplars through which the teacher hopes to teach basic lessons about human conduct, or they may be completely unconscious and artless guides for acculturation embodied in the teacher's representation of some of the best qualities of civilized and educated man.

What we need in education is a genuine faith in the existence of moral principles which are capable of effective application. We believe, so far as the mass of children are concerned, that if we keep at them long enough we can teach reading and writing and figuring. We are practically, even if unconsciously, skeptical as to the possibility of anything like the same assurance in morals. We believe in moral laws and rules, to be sure, but they are in the air. They are so *very* "moral" that they have no working contact with the average affairs of everyday life. These moral principles need to be brought down to the ground through their statement in social and in psychological terms. We need to see that moral principles are not arbitrary, that they are not "transcendental"; that the term "moral" does not designate a special region or portion of life. We need to translate the moral into the conditions and forces of our community life, and into the impulses and habits of the individual.

All the rest is mint, anise, and cummin. The one thing needful is that we recognize that moral principles are real in the same sense in which other forces are real; that they are inherent in community life, and in the working structure of the individual. If we can secure a genuine faith in this fact, we shall have secured the condition which alone is necessary to get from our educational system all the effectiveness there is in it. The teacher who operates in this faith will find every subject, every method of instruction, every incident of school life pregnant with moral possibility. (From Dewey, 1909, pp. 57–58. With permission of the publisher.)

The teacher's expectations

How teachers interact with their pupils depends in large measure on what they believe is expected of them in their various roles as teachers. Some of these expectations are pretty generally understood and accepted by all, while others are restricted to subcultures or related to the personalities of individual teachers.

In one investigation of 284 teachers-in-training the following moderately intercorrelated role expectations were identified by two different factor analyses (Sorenson, Husek, & Yu, 1963):

Advisor and information giver: the teacher adopts a role of recommending particular courses of action judged to be most desirable for his pupils. He also gives information without advising on alternative courses of action in certain areas of behavior.

Counselor: the teacher tries to foster independent thinking and decision-making in his pupils; also attempts to understand basic causal factors underlying his pupil's behavior.

Disciplinarian: the teacher enforces the rules and regulations, largely by using punishment and threats of punishment; represents authority in the classroom.

Motivator: the teacher sets up situations that he believes will stimulate certain pupil actions, then uses rewards to reinforce these behaviors when they occur.

Referrer: the teacher utilizes the help of other persons and agencies (counselor, special teacher, school psychologist, special class) to deal with pupil problems that seem beyond the teacher's own skills and knowledge.

The foregoing is merely a listing of some of the commonly shared role expectations of teachers. It is not exhaustive, nor does it predict how these roles may be differentially emphasized in a given teacher's expectations nor in his decisions about learning-teaching processes. Despite these limitations in scope, however, these findings show something of the kinds of role conflicts that may confront classroom teachers.

For example, the early and now near-classic study by Wickman (1928) and the follow-up studies by Griffith (1952), Schrupp and Gjerde (1953), and Stouffer (1952) all demonstrate that teachers are more concerned than mental health workers with the following kinds of behavior problems found among pupils: discipline problems, authority relationships, and sexual attitudes and practices. In contrast, clinicians and other mental health workers are more concerned than teachers with various behavioral indicators of social withdrawal and emotional conflicts. These findings have been generally supported by a very recent study by Tolor, Scarpetti, and Lane (1967). These investigators have suggested that these differences may be due to the differences in role expectations between teachers and mental health workers. Teachers *are* more concerned with aggressive and emotionally expressive behaviors, but then these behaviors are viewed as falling within a domain of education and control for which they have important responsibilities. The teacher knows that if he cannot maintain order within the classroom, he is likely to lose his position. Happily, the mental health worker is not so threatened, and can become more realistically concerned with other kinds of undesirable behavior disorders found among pupils (cf. Beilen, 1959).

The teacher's attitudes and values

Over and above what teachers believe others expect of them, teachers are guided and influenced, as all of us are, by their relatively stable and integrated belief systems. Their basic attitudes and values, growing out of these belief systems, determine the structure and tenor of their interactions with pupils, in and out of the classroom. Although a knowledge of the teacher's attitudes and values may not be a highly significant predictor of the minutiae of his classroom behavior, such information is likely to have value in predicting behavior patterns over the long run, at times of stress and strain, and in terms of the subtle dimensions of classroom atmosphere and tone. For example, as observed by Medley and Mitzel (1959), some approaches to measuring teacher effectiveness (such as pupils' reactions and supervisors' ratings) tend to reflect the teacher's ability to get along with pupils, while other approaches (such as teachers' self-ratings and pupils' gains in educational skills) appear to reflect the teacher's abilities to motivate and stimulate pupils toward learning academic skills as prescribed by the formal curriculum.

The teacher's attitudes and values are undoubtedly related to his classroom activities and style of teaching, but it is by no means easy to untangle this complex of interrelatedness. Of all the techniques employed in such efforts, the Minnesota Teacher Attitude Inventory (MTAI) has probably been most frequently employed. Developed by Cook, Leeds, and Callis (1951) this questionnaire solicits teachers' degree of endorsement or nonendorsement of such generalizations as: "As a rule teachers are too lenient with their pupils," "Children just can't be trusted," "There is too great an emphasis upon 'keeping order' in the classroom," and so on through 150 evaluative statements.

One research study of the attitudes tapped by the MTAI has yielded instructive findings. Horn and Morrison (1956) obtained data that suggested the presence of at least five factors, only modestly interrelated, basic to this particular complex of teachers' attitudes.

Factor I: a bipolar factor, ranging from traditionalistic to modern attitudes about classroom control—strict enforcement of rules and many restrictions versus pupil-centered, maximum freedom, and play-it-by-ear orientations.

Factor II: a bipolar factor, ranging from favorable to unfavorable opinions and evaluations of pupils—the unfavorable expressing a general pessimism about children's abilities and behavior inclinations, as well as a general dislike for them.

Factor III: a punitive and rejecting factor, reflecting a concern that all misbehavior be punished and that the punishment "fit the crime."

Factor IV: an expression of inability to "get inside" and truly "understand" the child.

Factor V: not a very reliable factor, but one suggesting a belief that individuals are truly "blithe, free spirits"—a sort of laissez-faire orientation toward child guidance in the Rousseau tradition.

These diverse attitudes toward children and the teaching act interact with many other dimensions of individual personality and social setting to affect teachers' interactions with their pupils, but it would be difficult to believe that they do not have an influence on the learning and future welfare of pupils.

Teachers also have diverse values with respect to the teaching profession, which in turn influence their classroom attitudes and pupil interactions. Why do individuals become teachers? There must be many antecedent conditions in personality, culture, and happenstance. One investigator (Mori, 1965) has identified a structure of motivations diagrammed in Figure 4-1.

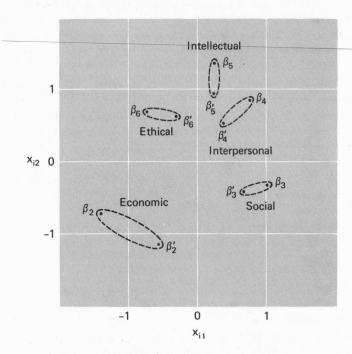

Figure 4-1. Two-dimensional plot of major motivations for becoming a teacher. (From Mori, 1965, p. 182. With permission.)

These communities of motivations were inferred to be the outcomes of perceived occupational values of teaching interacting with individual needs for becoming a teacher. Some individuals enter the teaching profession because of the prospects for continuing intellectual stimulation, others are seeking economic security although admittedly a modest level of income, others desire a routinized series of satisfying social interactions, and so on. It is easy to see that an individual's values toward the teaching profession will color his interactions with pupils. Are they the center of his professional universe or merely a means to personal ends or even a necessary nuisance to be endured as other ends are sought? A teacher-in-training would do well to ponder such questions, because his own happiness as well as the success and happiness of pupils across the generations may well be involved in the kinds of motivations that have led him into the teacher-training program.

Pupils' reactions to the school environment

How pupils respond to the school environment is very much dependent on antecedent experiences in the home (McClelland, 1953) and in socioeconomic subculture (Coleman, 1966). These prior experiences, all of which may be relevant to school progress and adjustment, fall into many different classes of behavior and their interactions. The most subtle and perhaps the most important class of antecedent experiences involves motivational variables such as interest, level of aspiration, need for achievement, and so on. Since these concepts and related research findings are discussed at length in a later chapter of this book, only their importance is noted here as a background for considering how pupils react to school attendance.

> The schools do differ, however, in their relation to the various racial and ethnic groups. The average white student's achievement seems to be less affected by the strength or weakness of his school's facilities, curriculums, and teachers than is the average minority pupil's. To put it another way, the achievement of minority pupils depends more on the schools they attend than does the achievement of majority pupils. Thus, 20 percent of the achievement of Negroes in the South is associated with the particular schools they go to, whereas only 10 percent of the achievement of whites in the South is. Except for Oriental Americans, this general result is found for all minorities.
>
> The inference might then be made that improving the school of a minority pupil may increase his achievement more than would improving the school of a white child increase his. Similarly, the average minority pupil's achievement may suffer more in a school of low quality than might the average white pupil's. In short, whites, and to a lesser extent Oriental Americans, are less affected one way or the other by the quality of their schools than are minority pupils. This indicates that it is for the most disadvantaged children that improvements in school quality will make the most difference in achievement.* (From Coleman, 1966, p. 22. With permission of author and publisher.)

As the reader can probably remember from his personal experiences, the business of being in school has its ups and downs, spurts of splendid progress interspersed with steady but often intellectually dull progress, and a sprinkling of failures. This is the picture for the average to superior pupil, the one who usually proceeds as far as his abilities and other intellectual resources will carry him. Unhappily for teachers, there is also that substantial group of pupils whose background and

---

*The several conclusions presented in this widely quoted report by Coleman and colleagues were based on nonexperimental data and should be regarded only as reasonable hypotheses, subject to verification by further research studies.

abilities do not qualify them to remain interested in or make satisfactory progress in the available school curriculum.

The findings of one research study that compared the attitudes and feelings of adolescent boys and girls who were satisfied versus those dissatisfied with their classroom experience are interesting and instructive. These groups of boys and girls who were matched on intellectual ability and general achievement differed in the important ways shown in Table 4-1. As may be seen, the dissatisfied girls felt more ignorant,

Table 4-1. Number of subjects choosing negative adjectives when asked to describe typical classroom feelings. Boys and girls in satisfied and dissatisfied groups were matched on intellectual ability and general achievement.

Adjective	Boys			Girls		
	Dissatisfied (N = 27)	Satisfied (N = 25)	Chi Square	Dissatisfied (N = 20)	Satisfied (N = 20)	Chi Square
Inadequate	19	16	ns	17	7	10.42**
Ignorant	19	13	ns	15	3	14.54**
Dull	25	16	6.36*	16	9	5.60*
Bored	24	13	8.61**	20	13	8.48**
Restless	20	15	ns	19	9	11.90**
Uncertain	20	21	ns	17	13	ns
Angry	15	4	8.76**	13	4	8.29**
Unnoticed	19	5	13.25**	7	4	ns
Unhelped	18	8	6.24*	9	6	ns
Misunderstood	16	5	8.31**	5	2	ns
Rejected	12	3	6.66**	4	0	ns
Restrained	17	2	16.91**	9	3	4.29*

* Significant at the .05 level.
** Significant at the .01 level.
SOURCE: Jackson & Getzels, 1959, p. 298. With permission of authors and publisher.

inadequate, uncertain, dull, angry, bored, and restless than the girls who were generally satisfied with their classroom experiences. The dissatisfied boys felt more bored, dull, angry, unnoticed, unhelped, misunderstood, and rejected than those boys generally satisfied in their classrooms. Both boys and girls in the dissatisfied group felt significantly more restrained than the satisfied group by their classroom experiences. Some of these attitudes and feelings are probably temporary dissatisfactions with particular school subjects or teachers, however others are more pervasive and likely to be carried over in time because they relate to the pupil's feelings of adequacy and worthwhileness, not only as a scholar but also as a person. What teachers can do to counteract such negative feelings is discussed throughout the present book. Psychological research and theory have convinced the majority of educators that there are many avenues to success as a scholar and as a person and that helping those who stumble or fall by the wayside is never a simple undertaking. Although there are no simple rule-of-thumb guides or tricks of the teaching trade on which one can rely for helping troubled pupils, the authors of this book are convinced that there are some validated psychological principles that can be helpful.

Neighborhood and Community Influences on the Pupil

Even before the child leaves his home to embark on the long educational journey required in our culture, he has already been strongly influenced by social forces in his neighborhood and community. Many of these influences have been indirectly effected through the interpretations of the larger environment by parents, siblings, neighbors, and older playmates. Other influences have been based on the child's firsthand excursions with the family: going shopping, attending recreational events, and so on. How the child will form his first impressions of the larger community is now known to be significantly related to his parents' perceptions (Ainsworth, 1966).

The child asks questions to which parents respond in a variety of ways. Some parents typically tell the child to stop bothering them. This may eventuate in a stunted curiosity about all types of events and a general apathy toward involvement in any kinds of learning experiences (Hess & Shipman, 1967). Other parents may characteristically avoid answers, or even replies, to certain kinds of questions, as for example, questions about sex, about members of certain racial or religious groups, or about other taboo topics. All such experiences sharpen the child's psychological set with all the related empathic sensitivities.

The child comes to feel and understand something of what it means to be a pupil, a black, a Jew, a day laborer's child, or to hold membership in some other identifiable group well in advance of actual discrimination in the larger community. The impacts of these early psychological sets are discussed in many places in the present book.

The Teacher as a General Cultural Influence

It is easy for a casual observer to overlook or to underestimate the effects of the omnipresent general culture. Being continuously immersed in it, he has difficulty imagining what life might be like under other conditions. It is a great temptation to assume that almost everything about one's own subculture, or about the Western culture in general is good and desirable, and therefore worthy of emulation by all of the world's inhabitants. The truly educated man finally overcomes this provincial perspective, however, and acquires a cosmopolitan appreciation that his home culture is not necessarily the most advanced on all fronts in the long march toward civilized living. He also comes to an understanding that one can learn much of human value from the diverse cultural matrices of other geographical, racial, and national groupings. In the broad and very best interpretation of education the teacher's proper role in these matters is clear. He is responsible for being a cultural influence—an emissary from the world's accumulation of knowledge and, hopefully, wisdom.

> Although it is both appropriate and necessary for many kinds of studies to treat cultural forms and symbols as a distinctly phenomenological system, there is actually, as opposed to conceptually, no part of a culture which is clearly separable from the social structure of groups, large and small, and the psychological systems of individuals. Culture exists, and is observable, only in the behavior, attitudes, motives, and perceptions of "reality" which individuals show, in the interaction systems individuals develop, and in the products which individuals, singly or collectively, create. Conversely, there is no aspect of human behavior which is not influenced to some degree, either directly or indirectly, by culture. Basic values are a particularly pervasive cultural factor of influence. (From Kluckhohn & Strodtbeck, 1961, p. 364. With permission of authors and publisher.)

In some culturally impoverished communities the teacher may be one of only a few individuals who can offer his pupils a view of the alternatives that are available in civilized living. Such a teacher may be the only resource available to the pupil in his effort to evaluate his own aspirations for a more satisfying pattern of living than the one he commonly observes in the community. To be sure, the teacher's opportunities and responsibilities in this realm will vary from community to community, depending on such factors as the educational level of the parents and their breadth of experience. Regardless of the community, however, the successful teacher, by the very virtue of his being a liberally educated person, should be able to offer his pupils new vistas, to help them question the necessary appropriateness of the usual and traditional, and to incite them in a continuing struggle against superstition and prejudice.

Will the teacher be successful in such attempts to broaden his pupils' cultural perspectives and appreciations? The answer to this question will vary with many conditions, one of which is heavily determined by the teacher's understanding of the concepts and principles presented in the present book and similar volumes in the social and behavioral sciences. It will require all of the teacher's understanding and skills to be successful in this sometimes professionally risky part of his teaching mission. Parents may resent their children's being exposed to what they consider "foreign" ideas unless they also understand the advantages of a liberal education. If the teacher's offerings are too far removed from the familiar, without some provision for avoiding abrupt transitions and cultural shock, pupils may reject the teacher as some kind of a "kook" and thereby discount all that he says and does. An anticipation of these and related hazards may persuade the teacher to play it safe or retreat at the first sign of opposition or controversy. Either of these courses of action will make the teacher less effective as an educator in the full sense of this important professional responsibility.

Summary

The contents of this chapter have been restricted to the social and cultural influences of parents and teachers. A broader orientation, although ultimately desirable, would take the reader into the findings and theories of sociology and cultural anthropology. It may be the reader's privilege at some point in his, or her, educational experience to explore the offerings of these social disciplines. The present orientation is directed to the psychological influences of parents and teachers on young boys and girls. The intent has been to survey the larger cultural picture before discussing the details in subsequent chapters of this book.

It has been suggested that the family is in rapid transition to a new form and new functions. There is a hint that the teacher may in some instances be required to assume some of the parental roles for troubled children. Some of the dimensions of interpersonal relations have been identified and their relative importance weighed. The teacher is considered as a person who has his own needs as well as his responsibilities. His expectations and his multiple social roles have been compared and contrasted. An attempt has been made to sketch in some of the important teacher functions that are often neglected under the press of overcrowding and overwork in the classroom. The thesis has been presented that the teacher is potentially a highly significant social and cultural influence on the pupil's progress toward a *liberal* education.

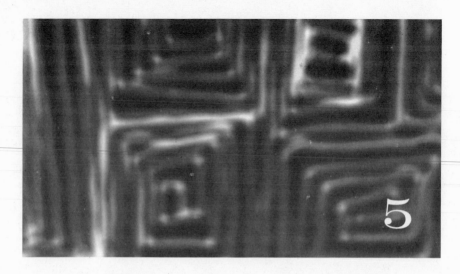

Modes of psychological adjustment and adaptation

There was a time, and not so long ago, when many psychologists likened the human organism to a relatively passive, homeostatic agent. According to this view, an individual would become quiescent once his tissue and tissue-related needs were all satisfied. Recent research has shown that this was far too simple an analogy to encompass the range and versatility of the human spirit. We know that man is not a passive recipient of stimulation from the external environment; rather, he operates on his environment, as well as being influenced by it. He seeks not merely to adjust to his world but to master it. He displays curiosity, he investigates, he creates, he takes risks for their own sake, and in many other ways goes beyond the mere maintenance of his customary relationships to things and other organisms. A quest for varied experiences is, therefore, an important dimension of "psychological adjustment," and this search seems especially strong during the first two decades of life (Berlyne, 1960).

It seems conceptually useful to consider the relatively short-term interactions between organism and environment under the rubric of *adjustment*, while reserving the concept of *adaptation* for the long-term, more clearly developmental, changes in the organism's responsiveness to, and actions directed toward, environmental events. Modes of adjustment are correlated with developing modes of adapatation, but the usual magnitudes of such correlations are not extremely high (Kagan & Moss, 1962). It therefore appears desirable to speak of the pupil's adjustment, with its associated structure and dynamics, as of a given moment, and at the same time be mindful of his capacities and abilities for adaptive change with further experience and development.

Modes of Psychological Adjustment

Every organism strives to satisfy its needs by seeking appropriate relationships with a variety of preferred environmental conditions. The physiologist speaks of *homeostatic processes* whereby the organism normally maintains a stable internal state in its interactions with the external world. For example, the human organism by perspiring cools itself and by shivering warms itself, both homeostatic processes which aid in maintaining a constant internal temperature (Cannon, 1923). The psychologist has developed a somewhat similar concept called *psychological adjustment* whereby the organism tries to satisfy its native and acquired needs by varying patterns of behavior (Shaffer & Shoben, 1956).

The pupil attempts to satisfy his many needs by directing his behavior toward preferred goals. His need to be socially dominant may lead him to social interaction with another individual whom he has previously been successful in dominating. His need for social recognition may draw him to another person who usually praises his accomplishments. Some of his responses are successful and he *learns* to direct himself in similar directions on subsequent occasions. Some of his need strivings end in failure and then he must attack the problem anew, seeking an alternate route to the preferred goal or an old established path to a substitute goal. And of course, some of his need strivings are continuously frustrated and he must adjust to the frustration conditions—at least at his particular level of adaptation.

Pupils differ in all components of the psychological adjustment process. For example, they vary in the strength of their various needs. One pupil may have a very strong need for social interaction with his classmates and a relatively low need strength for academic achievement. This preference may be reversed in another pupil. In addition, even when it can be inferred that two pupils have approximately equal need for academic achievement, one may seek to excel in arithmetic while another neglects this subject in favor of social studies. In other words, pupils may select different goals to satisfy the same needs. And of course they differ in the aptitude and talent they can command for reaching preferred goals.

Pupils also vary in the ways in which they respond to frustration. Some display much more flexibility and ingenuity than others in modifying a previously successful pattern of behavior which is no longer appropriate. Pupils of equal measured intelligence may differ greatly in their capacity for varying responses in a problem situation. One pupil will rigidly adhere to an unsuccessful approach with only minor variations in his attack. Another more creative pupil will systematically try out what appears to him to be a whole series of reasonable approaches to the problem (Torrance, 1962). And, of course, it is this pupil who has the greater chance for success in the long run.

The interior spiritual life of man is a web of many strands. They do not all grow together by uniform extension. I have tried to illustrate this truth by considering the normal unfolding of the capacities of a child in somewhat favorable circumstances but otherwise with fair average capacities. Perhaps I have misconstrued the usual phenomena. It is very likely that I have so failed, for the evidence is complex and difficult. But do not let any failure in this respect prejudice the main point which I am here to enforce. It is that the development of mentality exhibits itself as a rhythm involving an interweaving of cycles, the whole process being dominated by a greater cycle of the same general character as its minor eddies. Furthermore, this rhythm exhibits certain ascertainable general laws which are valid for most pupils, and the quality of our teaching should be so adapted as to suit the stage in the rhythm to which our pupils have advanced. The problem of a curriculum is not so much the succession of subjects; for all subjects should in essence be begun with the dawn of mentality. The truly important order is the order of quality which the educational procedure should assume. (From Whitehead, 1950, pp. 43–44. With permission.)

There are also tremendous differences among pupils in their responses to chronic or prolonged frustration. The varied behavior patterns of small children when confronted with a "closed" playground are shown in an interesting way in Figure 5-1. As may be seen, some of the children continue to attack the problem in a most direct fashion: efforts to climb the fence, force open the gate, or pry under the fence. One child modifies his approach by soliciting aid from a nearby adult. Another child accepts without disturbance the less desirable goal of

Figure 5-1. When faced with frustration, children respond differently, depending on their individual patterns of psychological adjustment.

playing with rocks, thereby substituting one play activity for another. And a few of the children give up the struggle with their play needs still unsatisfied: one pouts, and another withdraws into sleep. With increasing age, boys and girls show an ever greater variability in response to prolonged frustration. Verbal defenses like rationalization (the "sour-grapes" defense) and projection of blame become more prevalent. The patterns of adjustment most commonly employed by a pupil define important features of his style of living. In summary, pupils have different need strengths, different preferred goals for satisfying their needs, different aptitudes and competencies for reaching desired goals, and different ways of responding to temporary and to prolonged or chronic frustrations. When the foregoing are combined with different environmental opportunities and deprivations the immense complexity of pupil adjustment becomes obvious.

An equally important component of psychological adjustment involves the pupil's self-evaluations. How does he regard himself? It is well known that individuals are very often unrealistic and biased in their self-appraisals. The very tall boy may consider his height a handicap, whereas a shorter boy may long to be taller. The girl with blond hair genuinely believes that only brunettes are interesting to the opposite sex. The star football player imagines that everyone considers him "dumb" just because he is big and has athletic skill.

Even when pupils have real handicaps they may be perceived and evaluated in a number of different ways. There are many biographical records of individuals who overcame their original handicaps by various programs of self-improvement. Others have developed special skills to offset or compensate for their deficiencies. A handicap may be interpreted as a challenge or accepted as a signal of defeat. There are also the depressing biographies of individuals who became overwhelmed by "imagined" deficiencies or who led psychologically "warped" lives to prove to the world (and more importantly to themselves) that they were masterful men of destiny even though they were physically undersized or deficient in some other human attribute. In the history of the Western world the careers of Napoleon and Hitler come easily to mind.

Pupils have different needs

It seems rather certain that all human infants are born with pretty much the same basic needs. However, even the most casual observer of human behavior must conclude that from these few basic needs the child can move in many different directions as far as his demands on the environment are concerned. One child may develop a very strong need to relate himself to others in a dependent fashion, whereas another child of equal age and similar parentage may develop a strong need for social independence. One adolescent youth may display strong needs for cognizance—that is, for understanding things, with little apparent need for more tangible achievements which might be more widely recognized and approved by his fellows. And another pupil's behavior may reflect just the opposite hierarchy of need strengths.

An accurate evaluation of the relative need strengths of a given pupil is an important step toward understanding him, and constitutes the most effective point of departure for influencing his behavior. Let us consider a situation that illustrates the importance of need strength as an influence on human behavior. Terman (1947) in his now famous study of the adult life achievements of boys and girls who had very high intelligence (IQs above 140) found that some few of them failed to extend their education through university and professional schools. They seemed content to accept unskilled or semi-skilled employment in adult life. An examination of their backgrounds and interests revealed the relatively low strength of their need for achievement. They were just as intelligent as the boys and girls who became doctors, lawyers, dentists, and professors, but they were not as ambitious for these or any similar kinds of achievement. They also seemed just as happy and content with their low-level careers as the professional individuals with their more highly rated accomplishments. The teacher cannot, and probably should not, attempt to force such pupils to work toward achievements for which they have only a low level of need. But we may ask whether he can influence them to "raise their sights," to strive toward more socially significant goals. What are some of the factors that promote a high need for achievement?

McClelland and his research associates (1953) have studied the origins of the need for achievement in a number of experimental settings. The following excerpt is a summary of their observations and inferences about the development of a need for achievement:

The data we have to date strongly support the hypothesis that achievement motives develop in cultures and in families where there is an emphasis on the independent development of the individual. In contrast, low achievement motivation is associated with families in which the child is more dependent on his parents and subordinate in importance to them. In both types of homes there may be plenty of love and affection, but in the homes of the "highs" the son is more apt to "talk back" without deep feelings of guilt and to go off on his own rather than submit to the standards imposed on him by his parents. The contrast should not be thought of too simply in terms of the autocratic-democratic dimension, currently so popular in psychological literature. The parents of the "highs" may be quite dictatorial, particularly when the son is young before he has learned to act successfully by himself; but if they are, they still act as if the child exists as an individual worth developing in his own right rather than as a subordinate part of a larger, "solidary" family unit to which he owes loyalty over and above his own individual interests. In the latter type of home from which the "lows" are most apt to come, the son must subordinate his interests for the sake of the family or even more extremely, he may not even develop a conception of himself as an individual having interests more important than his obligations to the family unit. Thus when, as an adult the "low" is faced with the problem of going against a group all by himself as in Asch's experiment, he often cannot do it. It is inconceivable. (From McClelland, *et al.*, 1953, pp. 328–329. With permission.)

Pupils strive toward different goals

Even when two pupils are experiencing the same need at comparable levels of need intensity they may still strive toward very different goals. Two hungry boys may seek very different kinds of food to satisfy their needs. Or in response to more complex social needs like the need for achievement or the need to be recognized as outstanding the same two boys may direct their activities in very different directions.

What are the dynamic processes that determine a youth's demand for a particular type of goal object? The explanation offered by the reinforcement theorists is attractive because it is relatively simple and at the same time extremely useful (Spence, 1951). According to this conception there is a preferential ordering of response tendencies in any individual when he is experiencing a given need. That is, there is a hierarchy of response tendencies with a first most probable (and "preferred") pattern of behaving, a second most probable, and so on. If the most preferred pattern of response is not reinforced, i.e., does not meet with success, then the second most probable response is initiated. When there is continuing frustration of goal approaches, we observe a falling back in response patterns to those very low in the pupil's hierarchy. For example, the pupil who is repeatedly frustrated in his goal strivings toward achievement-recognition may eventually display a mischievous or defiant pattern of response which demands recognition of even this as a kind of "accomplishment." This response tendency is usually very low in the hierarchies of well-socialized boys and girls because it typically results in some form of punishment. However, pushed to the limits, most pupils will demand recognition whatever the consequences, i.e., whatever else may come along with it.

How do youth come to prefer different goals for the satisfaction of the same need? The pupil's hierarchy of preferred patterns of response is established by the learning principles discussed at some length in the later chapters of this book. In brief, each pupil has a unique history of successes and failures, of rewards and punishments, connected with his efforts to satisfy a given need. Youth from diverse social and cultural backgrounds learn to prefer different goals. Response patterns that have repeatedly satisfied needs move very high in the habit hierarchy and will be repeated again and again, even under conditions of frustration and failure.

Another interesting feature of goal-directed behavior involves individual differences in the *quality* of the goal required to satisfy a given need. For example, some pupils are satisfied and happy with a mediocre achievement, while others demand a high level of performance. This aspect of goal setting is what Lewin (1944) called "level of aspiration." He and his students have shown that the quality of goals demanded by a boy or girl increases with age. For example, a preschool child may be pleased and satisfied to stand directly over the post in a game of ring toss and simply drop the rings over the pin. Older children force themselves to stand back at ever increasing distance in order that they may experience feelings of success about their accomplishments. A few children seek goals which are so difficult and idealistic that they are almost certain to fail. Other children accept goals that are so ridiculously easy that they are certain of success. The most desirable goals for a pupil's continuing development would seem to be those that offer a reasonable challenge to ever increasing levels of achievement. There is good reason to believe that the teacher is a most important influence on the pupil's goal-setting tendencies. For example, Sears (1940) has shown, in a now classic study, that pupils who experience prolonged academic failure become either apathetic or very unrealistic in their levels of aspiration. Even adults with records of outstanding achievement may become depressed at their failure to reach still higher but actually unreasonable goals. It would appear that the teacher should help individual pupils to strive for goals commensurate with their abilities, so that they experience both considerable success and some degree of failure, which will stimulate them toward the acquisition of more skills and knowledge. A wise use of social approval and disapproval with aids toward pupil self-evaluation would seem to be the best teaching procedure.

What integrates our energies is the pursuit of some goal. When the goal is attained, the energy is dispersed. A person centered on becoming what he wants to become is far more integrated than one who has reached his goal—and has no place to go. To reach a goal we have to overcome distractions, discords, and obstacles. The effort involved welds unity.

Goethe saw that it was Faust's relentless search for objectives, particularly for the life-goal he set himself ("a free people on a free soil"), that was his salvation. Mephisto made a wager with Faust that he could so beguile him that Faust would no longer struggle for com-pleteness but would surrender to some tempting state of self-satisfaction along the way. Had Faust yielded to the illusion that he had found his objective, he would have been damned. In the end he was saved because he ceaselessly strove for the goal he never attained.

Like all great epics, Goethe's Faust gives us a profound insight into human nature; in this case into the conditions under which unifi-cation of personality is achieved. The psychologist Jung recognizes the same situation in his definition of *self*. According to Jung the *self* is not something we have, but something we are throughout our life span endeavoring to achieve. It is in this special sense that "self" confers unity. (From Allport, 1961, p. 380. With permission.)

Pupils respond differently to frustration

All goal strivings are liable to be frustrated at one time or another. Pupils often set impossibly high goals for themselves. Or they may not transfer appropriate knowledge from past experience in their efforts to reach a particular goal. Or they may be prohibited from attaining a given goal by personal limitations in skills or knowledge. Also they are sometimes too restricted by the mandates and cautions of adults to be able to reach their desired goals. Whatever the restricting conditions may be, frustration is an inevitable problem of human adjustment with which every pupil must cope at some time in one manner or another. It is important for the teacher to know the charac-teristic way in which each pupil responds to frustrations.

Failure to reach a desired goal means that that pupil has: (1) uti-lized an inappropriate response from his established hierarchy of behavior patterns, or (2) does not have the response available from his repertory of habits formed through previous experiences. In order to overcome the frustrating conditions of an inappropriate response the pupil must be able to vary his interpretation of the problem, or his manner of attacking it, in such a way as to insure effective behavior. Some pupils have great difficulty in shifting from an unsuccessful pat-tern of responding. They rigidly repeat the inappropriate approach and become increasingly emotional over their failure to reach the goal. This type of behavior seems especially characteristic of pupils under the fol-lowing conditions: (1) when the inappropriate response has been "over-learned" or overpracticed in a perceptually similar situation, (2) when the pupil has an exceptionally strong need to reach the goal, and (3) when the pupil is anxious or apprehensive about his personal adequacy in solving the problem (Tolman, 1949).

Frustration imposed by the pupil's lack of appropriate experi-ence is a more familiar educational problem. Teachers are generally more sensitive to the differences among pupils in reacting to such an adjustment problem. Some pupils typically expend large amounts of time and energy in acquiring whatever skills are needed for success, while others seem reluctant to strive for the necessary skill to master any problem. The former seem eager to meet the challenges of frustrating barriers. Indeed, it has been shown that some individuals prefer more difficult goals even when to a disinterested observer they seem identical in worthwhileness with more accessible goals (Child, 1946). On the other hand, there are pupils who appear to be demoralized by almost any type of frustrating circumstances. They give up, beg for outside help, or become so emotional that they are totally incompetent to cope with their personal problems. Rosenzweig (1945) has described such individuals as unable to tolerate frustration. They appear to lack the habits which are necessary if they are to overcome even minor obstacles in their goal strivings. It is suggested that they could profit from planned exposure to problems which are not too difficult to permit success, and which become gradually harder and more complex. It is as if they need to be immunized against the ravages of frustration by coming up against a graduated series of problems which they can solve successfully with their own resources. The net result of such a program of education is an ability to "tolerate frustration," or what the layman might simply describe as "self-confidence" when up against difficult adjustment problems.

Maladjustive responses to frustration

One of the most interesting theories concerning the consequences of frustration asserts that frustration always leads to an increased need for aggression. This conception which has been developed by a group of scientists at Yale University is known as the "frustration-aggression hypothesis" (Dollard et al., 1939). According to this point of view each frustration produces an increment in the need for aggression. These increments from successive frustrations gradually add up until an aggressive response is made; then the need is reduced. Such aggression results ordinarily in injury to an organism, or an organism surrogate (something standing for the organism as, for example, a frustrating neighbor's dog). In some instances the organism that gets injured may be oneself—like self-deprecating remarks, or even self-mutilation or suicide. However, because aggression toward oneself is immediately painful, most of an individual's aggressive tendencies are "extrapunitive"; that is, directed toward other persons or to substitutes for them.

It is commonly observed that frustration does not always produce an immediate act of aggression. This is so because any sign of aggression is often followed by some form of punishment which tends to restrain such hostile and destructive behavior. However, whenever the need for aggression mounts to a high level of intensity the pupil is alert to any opportunities where he can vent his *latent aggressive impulses* without too much threat of reprisal. Under such circumstances he may "attack" a younger child or join other classmates in making a "scapegoat" of a psychologically defenseless classmate. Or he may cast his aggressive behavior into a form that cannot be easily detected by others (teasing is a favorite form of camouflage), or he may merely daydream about overcoming his enemies (typically a most unsatisfactory release). In all these forms of aggression it is to be noted that the attack is on the person held responsible for the frustration, or something that can be identified with him.

It is also instructive to remember that the *need* for aggression builds up with each successive frustration until the aggressive impulse is somehow resolved. The latter offers an explanation for the behavior of pupils (and teachers) who "blow up" over minor irritations in the classroom. Responding to frustration with direct and unequivocal aggression is almost always maladjustive because it leads to counteraggression and hostility.

A case of chronic maladjustment as viewed over time by psychiatrists and school personnel

Psychiatric Comment

Age 7: A friendly, restless attractive little boy, in need of help; psychiatric treatment would be desirable.

Information From School

Age 7: Expelled from school for incorrigible behavior. Fights all the time, tries to attract attention in annoying ways. At a second school he continued to fight and be destructive in the classroom. His intelligence level is slightly above average.

Age 8: Is making no progress in school. Has ability but will not use it. He does such things as he wants to, and "no one on earth can guess why he wants to do it." Is destructive of his own things and of others'. Ignores the other children.

Age 10: Has been put out of school again. His achievement test scores are good.

Age 12: Again showing problems. If he does not behave, will probably be expelled.

Age 15½: He is making a relatively good adjustment for a boy who had as many negative experiences as he has had, and, although unhappy, at least he is not cracking up. There is something effeminate about him that is difficult to describe. There is a certain amount of passivity in his makeup.

Age 15½: Has made a fair adjustment this year. Has been fortunate in having an understanding principal and a teacher to whom he has felt a great deal of loyalty. Has been doing pretty good work in school—his grades have been above average. His relationship to other children has not been too good, but has been as good as at any other time and perhaps better than in some schools.

Adult Outcome

In service 3 years; several disciplinary offenses; discharged under honorable conditions; schizoid personality, manifested by autistic thinking, preoccupation with religion, and ineptitude in social situations, chronic, moderate. (From Roff, Mink, & Hinricks, 1966, pp. 424–425. With permission.)

Now let us look at a decidedly different response to frustration. Some pupils become apathetic and socially withdrawn under frustrating circumstances. This adjustment pattern is evaluated very unfavorably by mental hygienists because it signifies an orientation away from goal-directed actions. The pupil is no longer striving to satisfy his original needs, so there is now no possibility that he may acquire the skills that are required for success.

Mental hygienists are also especially concerned about pupils who adopt apathetic withdrawal as a pattern of adjustment, because such pupils frequently go unnoticed by parents and teachers. The withdrawn pupil does not disturb classroom or home routines. Even though he is personally unhappy and socially ineffective, he does not demand attention or aid in solving his problems. The experiences of success that he needs to build up his frustration tolerance, self-confidence, and feelings of personal adequacy cannot be planned by the teacher who does not detect his difficulties. As a matter of fact, he may be regarded as a "model pupil" because he never disrupts classroom procedures. His low level of accomplishment may be inaccurately diagnosed as lack of interest or a poor background in academic skills.

Still another way of responding to chronic frustration is frequently observed. The pupil develops various psychosomatic complaints and symptoms. When other adjustment mechanisms fail the pupil may become physically ill as a means of avoiding further frustrations. Psychological distress is converted into physical disorders like nausea, headaches, asthma, colitis, peptic ulcers, and so on. These are real physical disorders induced by chronic anxiety and frustration and are the subject of study in psychosomatic medicine. Whenever a teacher learns that one of his pupils is ill during the school week and completely recovered over the weekend, or is nauseated just before leaving for school, he should examine the child's relation to the curriculum, his social relationships within the classroom, and his own teaching practices, for possible sources of frustration. If the symptoms persist after he has done everything within his power to correct the adjustment conditions, he should seek aid and counsel from specialists like the school psychologist, and guidance counselor, or some member of a nearby child guidance clinic. It is strongly recommended that some action be taken because psychosomatic disorders are likely to become chronic modes of adjustment that remain to handicap the pupil throughout his entire life.

Now let us turn our attention to the conflicting social demands made on a pupil for different types of psychological adjustment. The concept of "good" pupil adjustment is relative to a given reference group. It usually has no absolute meaning, for the very same pattern of behavior may be regarded as "good" by one group of people and as undesirable by another. Since the same behavior pattern is often evaluated so very differently in various social settings, the pupil is called upon to play several roles. That is, he must be dependent in one situation and independent in another, question authority and think for himself under some social circumstances and not under others, be aggressive on the playing field and submissive in the classroom, and so on. The role of "good" scholar, which elicits teacher approval, may have to be changed to an attitude of "school is really a bore" in order to gain approval from peers.

Figure 5-2. An illustration of conflicting interpretations of an adjustment pattern.

In order to understand pupil behavior in its broad perspective the teacher must have knowledge of the many roles that get rewarded in a variety of social groupings. He must also be sensitive to a pupil's conflicts when different roles are demanded in the same social setting. When a pupil defies the teacher's authority, this may have little to do with the reasonableness of the teacher's request or the pupil's desire to please the teacher. Rather the pupil may feel called upon to maintain a role he has established for himself among his classmates. Understanding this is not to condone the defiant action, but it often does provide the teacher with leads as to how he may assist the pupil in handling his conflicting roles on later repetitions of a similar occasion.

Modes of Psychological Adaptation

At one time in the history of pedagogy the young child was viewed as a miniature adult with all the adjustive structures and dynamics of the mature personality but in less well-developed and coordinated forms. This perspective has all but faded into oblivion under the critical analysis and research findings of psychologists and the other behavioral scientists.

The next manner of looking at the growing child is one that still guides much of our educational planning. This conception of the child views him as *gradually* acquiring the personality structure and dynamics of the mature person in a more or less continuous fashion. This view recognizes the existence of individual differences in rates of psychological growth and levels of eventual attainment, but conceptualizes such differences as mainly *quantitative*. That is, although it is true that some children acquire skills and knowledge faster than others, it is the *same kinds* of behavior, processed in the *same manner*, only at a slower rate. The Binet-type intelligence tests are good examples of this approach. A four-year-old child with a mental age of eight years on one of the Binet tests of intelligence is assigned an intelligence quotient (IQ) of 200. This child is viewed as functioning intellectually in the same manner as a chronologically eight-year-old child with an earned mental age of eight years (and an assigned IQ of 100) on the same test. This theoretical approach conceptualizes experiences and skills as being pretty much interchangeable. What the child doesn't get now he can get later. The timing of experiences is not regarded as crucially important, with the exception of the early acquisition of skills (such as being able to read) which open doors to new knowledge.

At the present time this perspective is giving way to the theoretical position that psychological growth, in its adaptive mode, involves *qualitative* as well as quantitative changes. Although this approach was clearly manifest in Freud's theory of psychosexual development, its relevance to the intellectual, or cognitive, phases of human behavior has been most forcefully established by the research and theories of Piaget (1952).

Piaget's conception of psychological adaptation

In Piaget's theory of psychological development the individual is conceptualized as assimilating (or responding to) information in the surrounding environment on a developmentally selective basis. Simultaneously the individual is accommodating to these events by an increasing awareness and facility to respond to such information. As development proceeds, the individual moves through modes of adaptation during which there is a relative stability (or equilibrium) between reception and reaction to external events. Although there are many subphases within each period, the following stages are proposed as primary: sensory-motor period (birth to around eighteen months of age), preconceptual period (about two to five or six years of age), concrete operational period (approximately five to ten years of age), and formal operational period (about ten years to psychological maturity).

From the point of view of present approaches to education the concrete and formal operational periods are most important. During the concrete operational period, the five- to ten-year-old child acquires abilities (through the continuous and developmental interplay of assimilation and accommodation) to construct a consistent and reproducible reality through a series of mental operations on direct experiences. He becomes competent at *conserving* certain constructions (such as volume, mass, number, and so on) when two or more attributes are balanced against each other in simultaneous change. He can *decenter* from involving himself exclusively with one dimension of variation while other dimensions are also changing. However, despite these developmental advances, he is still pretty much bound to the here-and-now of concrete experiences. It is not until entry into the formal operational stage (at about ten years of age) that the individual can construct a reality about the possible, the "let us suppose," and the related models of logic and mathematics. For example, letting "X" stand for a variable without reference in concrete experience is beyond the operational prowess of the average five- to ten-year-old child.

Perhaps the most significant contribution of Piaget's theorizing to date lies in his emphasizing the development of new cognitive structures that encompass the old but which add new dimensions to the growing child's intellectual life. The educational implications of this theory for curricular content and organization are just starting to be explored.

Piaget's idea of cognitive *continuity* is encompassed in a series of overlapping constructions of reality where the new simply reorganizes and transforms what has gone before. This implies that there will be parallel continuity in modes of adjustment at different levels of adaptation; however, the addition of new dimensions of assimilation and accommodation at progressively more mature levels of adaptation will make for some discontinuities in a given individual's characteristic modes of psychological adjustment. The child who is not adjusting in ways satisfying to himself, parents, or significant others at one period of his psychological adaptation may do so with ease during a later period.

According to this theoretical position, boys and girls do outgrow some of their adjustment difficulties. Unfortunately this is not always the case; moreover, progress toward more mature levels of adaptation usher in new maladjustive problems for some boys and girls. The alert teacher with a good background of education and training is in an unusually strategic position to spot such maladjustive tendencies near their inception. At such times their amelioration may involve nothing more than a hint, a word of advice, or some appropriate encouragement from a concerned adult.

It is clear that if we were to look at our social arrangements as an outsider, we should infer directly from our family institutions and habits of child training that many individuals would not "put off childish things"; we should have to say that our adult activity demands traits that are interdicted in children, and that far from redoubling efforts to help children bridge this gap, adults in our culture put all the blame on the child when he fails to manifest spontaneously the new behavior, or overstepping the mark, manifests it with untoward belligerence. It is not surprising that in such a society many individuals fear to use behavior which has up to that time been under a ban, and trust instead, though at great psychic cost, to attitudes that have been exercised with approval during their formative years. In so far as we invoke a physiological scheme to account for these neurotic adjustments we are led to overlook the possibility of developing social institutions which would lessen the social cost we now pay; instead we elaborate a set of dogmas which prove inapplicable under other social conditions. (From Benedict, 1938, pp. 166–167. With permission.)

Summary

In this chapter psychological *adjustment* is viewed as a series of modes governing relatively short-term interactions between the individual and his environment. Psychological *adaptation* is employed to encompass those modes of long-term developmental transformations in the individual's responsiveness to and actions directed toward environmental events.

Psychological adjustment is conceptualized as being influenced by a series of psychological and social variables such as interests, needs, goals, reactions to frustration, and so on. Modes of adjustment are regarded as the outcomes of learning experiences at a given level of adaptive resources.

Psychological adaptation is described by the use of Piaget's concepts of assimilation and accommodation. The interplay of these developmental processes leads to periods of relative equilibrium which can be defined by their related modes of adjustment and adaptation.

It is suggested that teachers who are observant and responsive to their pupil's modes of adjustment and adaptation will be in a favorable position to understand and influence their pupil's learning experiences.

Part III

The nature
and process
of learning

At first glance, the educational enterprise seems simple enough. Teachers are employed to teach, pupils are instructed to learn, and schools are constructed to house the total program. But what really constitutes the essence of such a seemingly simple and yet admittedly so complex an undertaking?

Adaptation, the core of all educational programs, is the primary goal of all efforts of acculturation on which civilization must rely for its perpetuation and further elaboration. During the first two decades of man's life, a period especially reserved for education in most cultures, adaptation represents a dynamic interaction between maturational and experiential influences. What stimulus events are perceived by the child, how they are processed, when and in what ways they affect future commerce with the environment—all are functions of the resultant developmental structure: Each new experience leaves the pupil with a slightly modified repertory of behaviors which in turn further modifies his sensitivity and response to future encounters with his surroundings.

The knowledge that man has acquired, regarding the ways behavior is modified, permits some measure of prediction and control over performance and learning. Studies of development provide descriptive information about the limits of behavior modification. These two important factors, and their interaction, contribute to the pupils'

adaptability. They provide a basis for realizing the kind of information a teacher requires when faced with a decision about which
instructional strategy (amount and kind of experience to provide the
pupil) to use at a given time. Accordingly, we find his decisions must
involve concerns about (1) the pupils' developmental characteristics
(preparedness for learning including maturational level, previous
experience and training, personality characteristics and intellectual
aptitudes), (2) the principles by which pupils learn, remember, and
use what they know, and (3) the kinds of objectives (behavioral outcomes) to be achieved.

The several chapters in Part III contain a review and related
interpretation of the most reliable research findings on each of the
presently identified attributes of learning. The equally important
dimension of development serves as a necessary backdrop for the
entire discussion, and is used as a restricting or extending condition
for adaptive change whenever current knowledge makes it relevant.
Conditioning, learning, and problem-solving are viewed as merely
different facets of the same dimension of adaptation.

6

Psychological explanations of the learning processes: Concepts and theory

Education provides experiences that contribute to the acquisition of those behavior patterns that are necessary for successful living in one's society. The school is of course not the only influence in this process. Learning is not limited to the classroom, or to the school's objectives. Pupils learn from whatever they experience whether this happens in the home, school, on the baseball diamond, or in the corner store they use for their hangout. Some of these changes in behavior may not be of long-range benefit to the pupil. Many will be unnoticed by the teacher who, nevertheless, is aware that pupils learn much in the classroom that is in no formal assignment. For good or ill, pupils learn certain attitudes toward their own capabilities and the limitations of them; they learn good or poor work habits, and appreciations or dislikes.

The major difference between informal learning experiences and those in the classroom is that in the latter the teacher efficiently guides the direction and course of learning. In this context, the formal educational process has many facets. A few of the teacher's tasks include developing curricula, stating objectives, determining course content, assessing and adapting to individual differences, monitoring and guiding learning experiences, managing the classroom, and appraising achievement. More than a bundle of routine tricks and techniques is required in their execution. Schools within a community often vary as much and in

105

as many ways as do the pupils within a particular classroom or even in different classrooms. It is impossible to supply teachers with specific techniques for each of the hundreds of unique situations that may occur in the course of a year, much less to handle those that arise in a decade of teaching. By understanding the progress of development and the events affecting the process of learning, the teacher will be prepared to ask significant questions about the improvement of his teaching, to make sophisticated inferences and decisions in relation to these questions, to adapt to most of the novel situations as they occur and to introduce intelligent innovations whenever necessary. Our discussion in this chapter is directed toward the learning process that constitutes the very foundation that makes teaching possible.

The Components of the Pupil's Behavior

The subject matter of our observations of people and of any inferences about them and the subject matter of teaching in particular, is *behavior*. It is so omnipresent, so much the substance of our lives, that one can easily lose sight of its importance and have difficulty in identifying its components. Analyze, for example, a number of different situations for the elements of behavior common to all: an outfielder *catching* a fly; the pupil *answering* a question raised by the teacher; the *typing* of a letter from copy; or, inner-city youths standing in front of a vacated building and *scattering* when a policecar rounds the corner, or *running* towards it if there is an accident. Each of these illustrations involves an environmental event that acts upon the individual—the ball coming toward the outfielder, the question directed to the pupil, the typist's copy, and the policecar. These events occur in the individual's environment and are classified as *stimuli*. A complex of many stimuli is best described as the *situation*. The other element in the above situations is the reaction to each situation by the person or persons involved, that is, a *response* indicated by the terms "catching," "answering," "typing," "scattering," and "running."

The situations to which the pupil reacts

The pupil, like everyone else, is always surrounded by stimuli, some of which originate in his environment and others of which originate within him. Obviously, the pupil does not react to all of these stimuli simultaneously. He reacts to those that provide important cues for any behavior related to the satisfaction of whatever motives may be active within him at the moment. These are the functional or effective stimuli. Irrelevant stimuli are neglected. If he is severely threatened by school work, the internal stimuli created by anxiety become the effective stimuli and, if sufficiently intense, will dominate his behavior to disrupt further his academic performance; if he has a strong need for achievement, the class assignment will attract his attention. An important role of the teacher is so to shape the situation that the effective stimuli for the pupil are related to what is to be learned. A learning theory that emphasizes the importance of effective stimuli is described in the following:

Stimulus sampling and learning

Estes (1959) has proposed a learning model patterned after an earlier one by Guthrie (1952). Simply, this model is based on the following assumptions: (1) Learning is regarded in terms of its outcomes. The psychologist working with this model is unconcerned with stimulus-response connections or with what the learner does but only with whether the learner is successful or unsuccessful in what he accomplishes. Thus, one employing this model is concerned with "acts" such as number of correct answers in arithmetic or the number of ring-tosses in a game of quoits as opposed to a concern with the specific muscular "movements" involved in the performance of an activity. (2) In any learning environment, even for very simple learning tasks, there is a hypothetical large but finite population of stimulus elements. The basic stimulus unit is undefined but it is assumed that the stimulus complex is composed of a multitude of small events and of variation in these events. (3) On any one learning trial only a small but constant fraction of stimuli are sampled. No attempt is made to explain how stimulus sampling is made, except that it occurs on a random basis. We might suppose that it is, in part, a function of the stimuli available on any trial, the learner's attention, and the like, but such a supposition is unnecessary provided the assumption of random sampling allows correct prediction of learning phenomena. (4) The stimuli that are present (sampled) on any one trial become immediately and permanently associated with the response. In this sense, learning can be considered as a discontinuous process. Each trial contributes its share to the overall learning performance independently of the previous learning. (5) Since sampling is random the stimuli selected on one occasion (trial) have no effect on their availability during succeeding occasions, nor does the sampling of an element affect the availability of any other element. Selection is based entirely on chance. Each learning trial provides another opportunity for drawing another sample of stimuli from the population. Gradually, all stimuli will be represented, which gives the impression that learning is incremental. (6) The probability that a given response will be made in a given situation depends upon the proportion of stimulus elements

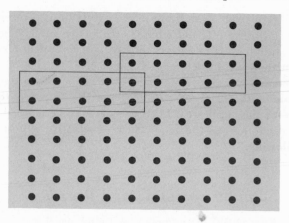

Figure 6-1. A representation based on stimulus sampling notions of learning outcomes after two learning trials. It is assumed that there are 100 stimulus elements in the population of stimuli to be associated with the behavior to be learned, and that a constant one-tenth of these will be sampled in each trial at random. Thus, on Trial 1, 10 new elements will be sampled. Though 10 elements will also be sampled on Trial 2, there is the chance that one-tenth of these will have been sampled before since sampling occurs on a random basis. After Trial 1, the probability of making the response is only 0.10; after Trial 2 the probability has increased to 0.19. (Adapted from Gregory A. Kimble & Norman Garmezy, Principles of general psychology, *3rd ed., copyright © 1968, The Ronald Press Co., New York. Figure 10.9, p. 306. With permission of author and publisher.)*

sampled from the population of stimuli relevant to learning the task at hand.

Graphic representations of the learning and forgetting processes according to the assumptions in a stimulus sampling model are displayed in Figures 6-1 and 6-2.

The ideas from this model suggest the importance of several processes; attention will increase the certainty that stimuli will be sampled. Fatigue, adaptation to a new situation, excitement, and other distractions unrelated to the learning task will drastically change the population of stimulus elements available to the learner. Frequent reviews, rehearsal, and practice provide opportunities for sampling stimuli missed on earlier trials. Transfer requires the behavior to the used in new situations, which contain new stimulus elements. Accordingly, when teaching a given behavior the material should be presented in a variety of settings. Forgetting can be counteracted only by reexposure to the stimulus population, which means reviewing learned material again and again. Cramming, at best, can only permit sampling a limited proportion of the stimulus population.

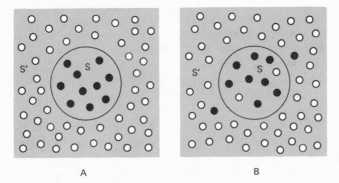

Figure 6-2. A representation of forgetting according to the stimulus sampling model. In A, the black circles represent stimuli associated with response X (e.g., pushing a lever to the left) and open circles represent stimuli associated with response Y (e.g., pushing a lever to the right) following conditioning. In B, several hours later, 20 percent of the elements associated with X have drifted from S to S' and were replaced by elements from S'. The probability of making the X response has dropped from 1.00 to 0.80. The number of elements leaving S is also a function of how different the situation is on the two days and of the person's degree of fatigue, attention, or other temporary factors. (From Hill, 1963, Figure 7, p. 178. With permission of author and publisher.)

The response: The pupil is active

Another element of all behavioral settings is the *response*—the "doing" part of the behavior. It is typically defined in terms of organized acts or behaviors such as catching a ball, typing a letter, studying, or reading.

Most responses can be indexed according to frequency, strength, or rate. The *frequency* of responses, for example, might include the number of times a pupil volunteers in class, the number of times he makes social contacts, the number of days he is absent from class, or the number of correct answers he gives in an achievement test. The *strength* of a response might be reflected in the pupil's certainty or confidence when giving an answer, his delay in making a decision, his comprehension of a passage he has read, or his dependence on a number of cues rather than on a few very important ones in performing a skill. The *rate* of responding is the relation between number of responses and time; for example, the pupil reads 50 words per minute, completes 75 out of 100 multiple-choice items correctly in an hour, or runs a mile in 10 minutes.

The labels used to identify consistent patterns of behaviors in everyday settings are inferred, whether consciously or not, from both the situation and the response. A person is said to be "afraid" if we can discover threatening stimuli in his situation *and* if he makes withdrawal responses. Note that to observe only his "running away" from a stimulus is not sufficient information to conclude that he is "afraid." He might be running for a number of reasons other than fear. Thus, running to catch a ball in the outfield requires a different interpretation than running away to avoid the threat of being hit by a thrown stick. Continual practice in analyzing behaviors by identifying both situations and responses is essential if the teacher is to become a skilled observer of behavior.

Most contemporary theories whether in the stimulus-response tradition (Guthrie, 1952; Spence, 1956; Miller, 1959; Osgood *et al.*, 1957) or of the cognitive variety (e.g., see Biggs, 1968) assume some form of an additional, mediating response to intervene between the presentation of the stimulus and the overt response as viewed by an objective observer. Generally, it must be inferred by means of special experimental methods and instrumentation. Especially important is the fact that these mediators are assumed to change or transform the characteristics of the incoming stimuli, thereby drastically altering the characteristics of the final response that might otherwise have been made. Although this topic will be described in more detail in a later chapter, it may be sufficient for the present to indicate that thinking, self-verbalizations, instructions, imagery (Paivio *et al.*, 1968), meaning, and labeling all belong to the class of mediating responses which includes attending behaviors.

Describing objectives in behavioral terms: Avoiding ambiguity

The analysis of behavior presented above is a useful guide in making observations but it also is an important understanding for developing a curriculum. Course or unit objectives are devised for directing the activity of the teacher and the pupil. They state precisely what kinds of behaviors are expected of the pupil including the kind of response, the characteristics of the responses, and under what conditions the responses are to be made. One should not confuse a course objective with a course description commonly found in college catalogs. A course description tells what a course is about. An objective tells what the student must do during the course and what he will be able to do if he successfully completes the course. Some behavioral definitions are shown in Figure 6-3.

An illustration of a poor objective will help to emphasize the importance of stating objectives in precise behavioral terms. Suppose a class of teachers was asked to prepare a unit in which their students were "to learn to appreciate mathematics." One can imagine that 40 teachers,

Figure 6-3. Illustrations of behavioral definitions of some psychological processes.

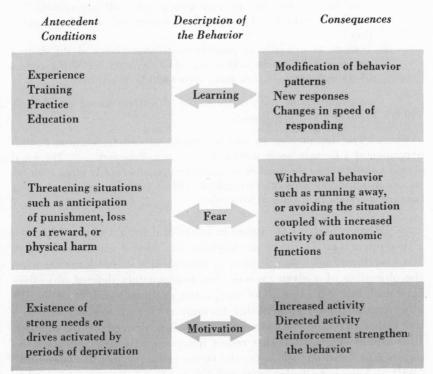

given only this statement of the objective, would prepare 40 quite different lessons. The term "appreciate" is vague and is open to a number of interpretations. It says nothing about what the learner will be doing when he completes the lesson. Do we expect the learner to take other courses in mathematics? Does the pupil spend his time playing mathematical games or solving mathematical puzzles? Do we expect him to tell others how interesting math is? Or do we want him only to achieve a grade of "A" in math? The objective may be a desirable one but it fails to tell either the student or the teacher what is expected of the learner. Other vague terms found in ambiguous course objectives are "to understand," "to enjoy," "to believe," and "to know."

The development of course objectives in behavioral terms requires the following steps according to Mager (1962):

1. Identify the *responses* or behavior expected of the student at the end of the activity. You may want the student to be able to place his fingers on the appropriate keys of the typewriter; to be able to type out several words in exercise form; to type a business letter; or to type a technical manuscript.

2. Identify the *situation* or conditions under which the behavior is to occur. Do you want the learner to type a letter of his own composition? Do you want him to make a copy of one already available? Is the letter to be typed under a time restriction or with unlimited time?

3. Indicate as precisely as possible the *characteristics* of the desired response (performance). How neat must the letter be? Will evenness of typing be scored? How many errors will be permitted?

Two examples of adequately stated objectives based on Mager's (1962) discussion are as follows:

. . . The student must be able to provide, in writing, a literal English translation of a German poem without the aid of a dictionary. . . . The pupil should be able to find the number of square feet in an irregular plane with the aid of references and slide rule. His answer will be graded on whether he uses the correct process in arriving at his answer.

When objectives are stated in behavioral form, the pupil is given a good opportunity to know just what he is to do and why he is doing it. His uncertainty otherwise is often a consequence of not knowing what the objectives of a given exercise are. Inadequately defined objectives may teach the pupil to depend upon a test or other pupils to define the objectives for him. Pupils in this dilemma are forced to study to pass a test rather than for the more intrinsic values desired by the teacher. Illustrations of questions that reflect ignorance of course objectives by pupils are: "Will our test cover the entire course or just the last unit?" "Will we have a multiple-choice or essay test?" "Will we be required to apply what we have learned or just 'parrot' back information?" "I don't see why we are doing this!" Objectives are intended to spell out your teaching aims and goals to the students. It is unfair to the pupil if you communicate, implicitly or explicitly, one expectation such as that he must "*solve* a quadratic equation," then test him on his ability to "*derive* a quadratic equation." Attention to the steps in developing objectives will help to avoid this difficulty. Nevertheless, the objectives of some teaching assignments can be stated more easily and precisely than other equally important objectives (e.g., math routines as against music appreciation).

A Look at the Learning Process

A commonly accepted definition of learning is: An enduring or permanent change in behavior as a result of experience. One kind of change in behavior can be seen when a pupil consistently behaves in a different manner to a given situation than he did previously. For example, when he sees the numbers 3 and 2 in learning addition, he consistently gives "five" as the answer. However, when he learns multiplication, the two numbers are connected with the multiplication sign and he learns to answer "six." Another kind of behavior change can be observed when the pupil uses an old response in a new situation. Simply, he may first learn to calculate percentages in an arithmetic class and then later to apply this procedure to the calculation of batting averages.

Not all changes in behavior are learning. Note that another phrase used in our definition was "as a result of experience." Some changes in behavior occur as a result of maturation. The stroking of the sole of a neonate's foot, for example, elicits the Babinski reflex characterized by a spreading upward and outward of the toes. A few months later the same stimulation causes the plantar reflex found in adults, that of curling the toes downward. Other factors (including organic deterioration, damage to the nervous system, the use of drugs, and the like) can cause changes in behavior that are often dramatic but since these changes in behavior are not the result of the kind of experience that occurs when a task is practiced, they would not be covered by this definition. The effects of fatigue, pain, and adaptation, even though experienced as part of a learning situation, are also excluded since the resulting changes in behavior are either temporary or indirect.

The definition of learning is an important one for teachers. Since the teacher's task is to promote efficient learning, the nature of his role in changing the behavior of pupils is implied. He guides students to strengthen motives related to learning, to acquire new perceptions, to adopt new behaviors, to use already learned responses in a variety of situations, or to fix responses to make them *habitually* available to the pupil. The accomplishment of these objectives will challenge the best of the teacher's skills, and even then may result in only partial success. Whiteman and Deutsch (1968), for example, describe an incident involving two East Harlem boys engaged in friendly horseplay on their way to school. In the course of the tussle one child banged the other's head with a notebook. The book promptly slipped from his hand and fell into a puddle of water. Both boys immediately stopped their scuffling, contemplated the seriousness of the calamity and the possible recovery of the notebook, then walked off arm in arm amidst gales of laughter . . . without the notebook. This seemingly trivial incident represents but one of many in the progressive alienation of the child from a school that, as a consequence of its failure to adapt to the preparation and experience of the disadvantaged child, means frustration and failure.

Furthermore, expected changes in behavior are not necessarily highly related to the course descriptions, to the fact that the class is labeled a chemistry or English class, or to the pupil's passing or failing an examination. What the pupil learns is ultimately determined by what he does in class, by the experiences provided in his reading, classroom projects, discussion, laboratory work, and the multitudinous variety of other activities in which he is engaged.

Basic explanations of learning

Despite the changes, over the years, in methods for the study of learning processes, certain conceptualizations have retained their importance. Classical conditioning, the procedure employed by Pavlov, has led to an understanding of the way environmental factors come to influence or control one's behaviors. The investigations of the law of effect, in its various forms, by such men as Thorndike (1949), Hull (1943; 1951), and Skinner (1954) indicate how behavior is related to the control of environmental events. Other theories and investigations such as those of the cognitive psychologists attempt to explain how thinking and reasoning behavior is developed and how thought processes influence other behavior.

Classical conditioning as a form of environmental control of behavior

Perhaps the most elementary explanation of the learning process was provided by what is known as classical conditioning. It was among the earliest formal explanations of learning (Pavlov, 1927; 1957). In this form of learning some stimulus is used which is initially and immediately capable of eliciting a response. In the first stages of such learning the responses are reflexive; a puff of air (stimulus) elicits a blinking response, an electric shock elicits a withdrawal response, a tap on the knee elicits the knee jerk, and food elicits salivary responses in a hungry organism. Stimuli of this sort are called *unconditioned* stimuli and the responses are called *unconditioned* responses since the behavior is already part of the organism's repertory. The behavior of the organism is changed in this kind of learning when a neutral stimulus (conditioned stimulus) regularly precedes the unconditioned stimulus. For example, though a ringing bell is ordinarily neutral and does not arouse eating responses, if it is rung each time the child smells a hamburger, and only then, his behavior eventually changes in such a way that the bell alone will be sufficient to cause salivation. Conditioned responses also tend to be *anticipatory* responses. When learned they precede (anticipate) the unconditioned response. In fact, any behavior that regularly follows a stimulus will occur with increasing rapidity after the stimulus. Thus, the bell (CS) is followed by salivation (CR) in anticipation of eating (UR) the hamburger. Words, too, have anticipatory characteristics. A young child who is taken by car each day to play on the swings will soon learn to say "swing" first, at the sight of the swing; then, when he first views the playground; later, as he sees cues enroute to the playground, and, finally, as he approaches the car before his trip. The idea of the anticipatory response, and other characteristics of classical conditioning are shown in Figure 6-4.

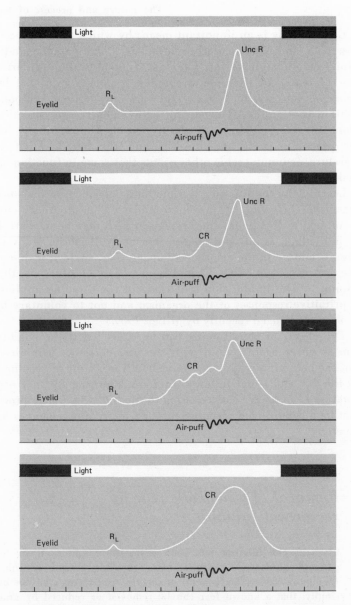

Figure 6-4. Tracings from an eyelid conditioning experiment. Over consecutive trials the conditioned response (CR) occurs nearer to the presentation of the conditioned stimulus (CS)—it becomes anticipatory. The CR in the second record is a miniature replica of the unconditioned response (UCR)—it is a fractional representation of the UCR. Finally, the eyelid closes immediately after the presentation of the CS thereby preventing the airpuff from hitting the eye—an avoidance response has been learned. (After Hilgard, 1936, Figure 4, p. 379. With permission of author and publisher.)

Conditioning is an important means by which learning occurs in the classroom, and is particularly relevant to a better understanding of the pupil's emotional behavior. The flow of blood to the capillaries and the flow of tears, for example, are reflex responses regulated by the autonomic nervous system. Initially, they are unconditioned responses to unconditioned stimuli. After pairing with embarrassing situations or situations involving feelings of guilt, provoked unwittingly by the teacher, parent, or peers, both blushing and tears may be elicited by a word, gesture, or innumerable other events that come to function as conditioned stimuli.

Learning by conditioning is sometimes described as the control of the organism's behavior by the environment. The situation (environment) automatically elicits some response which may be uncontrollable by the individual, as any person who blushes will affirm. Many of the responses produced in the emotions of anger, fear, anxiety, jealousy, and the like are subject to being elicited by a variety of situations through conditioning. (The implication that classical conditioning applies only to the primitive responses of the organism and not to voluntary behavior has been challenged recently by Miller, 1969.)

The effects of conditioning can be cancelled if the conditioned stimulus is never again paired with the unconditioned stimulus. The effect of the bell on salivation is diminished if it is rung at varying times during the day and is not followed by food. Blushing will not occur if the situation is no longer embarrassing to the individual. The process of eliminating a conditioned response through nonreinforcement is known as extinction.

Removal of a neurotic fear by reciprocal inhibition

Classical conditioning has been successfully employed in helping patients "unlearn" neurotic fears through reciprocal inhibition (Wolpe, 1958). The general principle underlying the method is, simply, that a known fear can be removed or reduced by gradually exposing the fear provoking stimuli to the patient while he is relaxed and comfortable until the entire situation is reinstated.

This procedure can be illustrated by showing how desensitization was applied to reduce a young woman's unbearable fear of cats (as described by Eysenck, 1967). Initially, an interview was carefully taken to obtain the patient's general history and to identify any unusual situations connected with the disorder. Next (in another, or other, sessions) the therapist works with the patient to reduce other

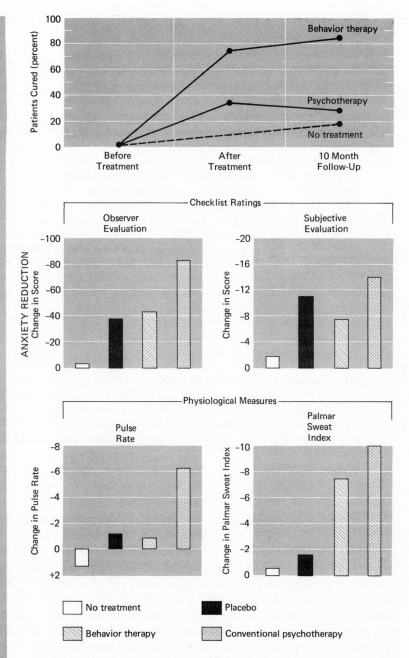

Figure 6-5. Changes in behavior as a consequence of behavior therapy compared with conventional psychotherapy, placebo treatment, and a control group. (From Eysenck. New ways in psychotherapy. From Psychology Today magazine, 1967, 1, 41–44. With permission of author and publisher.)

anxieties not connected with the major symptoms and which might interfere with the success of subsequent therapy. Thirdly, the person is taught how to relax by learning to relax one muscle then another; gradually progressing from one part of the body to other parts. This is an essential step because relaxation will be used to replace anxiety. Finally, the therapist, in discussion with the patient, identifies the situations in which the fear might be aroused and arranges them in a hierarchy of least to most threatening.

Then the reciprocal inhibition process is begun. In the first session, the patient is told to imagine, as clearly and as vividly as possible, a kitten in the arms of a small child (the least disturbing situation). This evoked some anxiety but she was able to relax under instruction from the therapist, as she was previously taught to do, while the image was retained. The use of relaxation is important in this therapeutic process because it is incompatible with anxiety, i.e., it is impossible for a person to be simultaneously anxious and relaxed. The procedure was repeated in additional sessions until the "mental picture" of the kitten in the child's arms no longer provoked fear. Then the young woman was asked to imagine the next most disturbing situation, a cat pouncing on a ball of yarn, while relaxed. When she could handle this situation without anxiety the therapist gradually moved the patient up the hierarchy of situations until, eventually, she was able to manage the most disturbing image of all, that of a large black tomcat stalking a field or curled up on her bed. At each stage the patient could cope more effectively, i.e., with less anxiety, with the sight of cats in real life than she could in previous stages. As in all classical conditioning, the unconditioned response (fear or anxiety) was replaced with the conditioned response (relaxation).

Operant learning: Control of the environment

Another basic learning process called operant or instrumental learning by Skinner (Holland & Skinner, 1961), and trial and error learning by Thorndike (1949), is based on the law of effect. The term *instrumental* indicates that the person does something (makes a response) that will help him to achieve a reward or favorable consequence. The term *operant* suggests that a given response affects some aspect of the environment; the person does something to the environment, he operates on it. In either case, the response results in desirable environmental conditions. As with classical conditioning, many of the principles of operant learnings are used (often unknowingly) by teachers, parents, and other individuals interested in promoting change in the behavior of others.

While the antecedent situation is still important in this kind of learning, it is virtually impossible to know which specific stimuli are effective for each individual. Accordingly, attention is focused on establishing a situation that will permit the pupil to make the responses that are desired. Such situations may be highly restricted as in a spelling class where the word m-a-n-u-f-a-c-t-u-r-e is presented orally and the pupil is to provide the exact response in writing. At the other extreme, the presentation may be highly flexible, as in teaching problem-solving behaviors, when it is desirable that the pupil attempt many alternative behaviors. Once the situation has been established, the teacher's attention is directed to the nature of the pupil's responses. If correct, according to the teacher's objectives, the pupil is rewarded. If the response is incorrect, the pupil fails to obtain a reward and he either tries a different response or is guided to make the correct response.

Operant learning differs from classical conditioning in several ways (Kimble, 1961). In operant learning the pupil's behavior is adaptive. His behavior produces a change in the environment that is rewarding to him and he avoids behaviors that are nonrewarding or punishing. In classical conditioning the pupil's behavior is controlled by environmental circumstances. The behavior is elicited more or less automatically rather than evoked voluntarily. In operant learning the focus of interest for the teacher is on the response of the individual while in classical learning the focus of interest is on the stimuli. Behaviors are reinforced (strengthened) by the attainment of rewards and/or favorable consequences in operant learning and by frequent presentation of the conditioned stimulus immediately following the unconditioned stimulus in classical learning. Extinction, or the elimination of a behavior pattern, follows the withholding of rewards, or the provision of other nonrewarding consequences such as punishment, in operant learning situations. Extinction in classical learning is accomplished by never again pairing the conditioned stimulus with the unconditioned stimulus.

Theories of learning and instruction

Classical and instrumental learning are descriptions of basic *techniques* by which behavior can be modified. More elaborate "theories" of behavior attempt to integrate known facts into a succinct explanatory network of learning events. The value of such theories may be judged according to their potential for predicting, controlling, and explaining behavior.

Each theory views learning somewhat differently. One class of theories emphasizes stimuli, responses, and reinforcements; another class emphasizes ideas, thinking, and reorganization; and still another emphasizes individual differences, personality, and motivational dynamics. These and other theories will be constantly referred to throughout this book. In fact, we have already presented, earlier in this chapter, a brief example of one of the newer theories, called the stimulus-sampling model. Unfortunately, no theory yet provides a complete explanation of behavior although each helps, in its own way, to explain some important aspect of behavior. The differences among the theories, in the kind of behavior emphasized and in the processes considered relevant for understanding behavioral change, together with their educational implications, are presented in some detail in Appendix D. The reader will find it helpful to identify for himself where such differences occur by reference to those summaries.

Conditions Modifying the Learning Process

A course of study printed in 1914 for a town in the Midwest contained the statement that "Nothing but drill day after day, week after week, and month after month, will fix these memory facts" (Glennon & Hunnicutt, 1952, p. 24). This was a course of study in arithmetic. It would not be difficult to imagine the schoolmaster's methods in using the "drill" theory, it would be quite simple—no concern for the pupils' boredom and rebellion, just drill. This approach has at least some merit. Growth in proficiency does require frequent contact with the activity. It neglects, on the other hand, the other important variables in learning, some of which are discussed in this chapter. The teacher using drill or other oversimplified approaches to learning may unwittingly be an ineffective teacher.

Our illustration is not one which represents a completely isolated instance. Many teachers in the past have believed in such "brute force" in teaching. They have entertained similarly incomplete ideas of the learning process: some, with regard to the use of rewards; others with regard to permissive classroom atmospheres; and still others with some currently popular fancy. They taught accordingly.

It is not difficult to see, then, why it is so important to understand the known conditions of learning and how they fit together in a "picture" of the teaching-learning process. Every teacher continually makes inferences about the teaching settings that will most effectively promote learning. He is guided by whatever "theory" he holds in making decisions about how assignments are to be made, how course work is to be sequenced, the amount and kind of pupil participation to plan for, and the frequency and purpose of testing. The psychological basis of teaching cannot be reduced to the application of a single principle or even of two or three principles. In this section we will examine instruction with a view toward attempting a more complete description of what happens when pupils learn. This should serve as a guide for making reasonable decisions to establish effective learning situations. The several principles of learning are developed in more detail in later chapters. Whatever these turn out to be, the reader will be reminded from time to time that learning occurs only as a result of some activity by the learner, even though the activity may not be accessible to direct observation, as in thinking.

The pupils' preparedness for learning

All pupils within a class do not respond with equal efficiency to a similar learning experience when they are free to pace themselves (Gagné, 1967). Each pupil progresses at his own rate toward achieving mastery (Glaser, 1968; Atkinson, 1967). Given the same task and the same conditions of learning, one pupil goes ahead rapidly and another more slowly because of differences in motivation or in aptitude (Carroll, 1963; Bloom, 1968). Or, one proceeds rapidly at first and then may slow down; while another's progress may be made more evenly. Sometimes two pupils arrive at the same goal, as in the solution of a problem in multiplication, but they reach the goal by different procedures. Similarly, differences may occur in what *can* be learned and what *is* learned. Maturational factors, acquired behavior patterns, and temporary factors related to adaptation (attention, excitement, and fatigue, for example) contribute to the pupil's ability to learn from experience in a given setting and affect the pupil's preparation for learning or, in other words, his readiness to learn.

The importance of preparation for learning can be easily seen in attempting to teach a pair of first-grade identical twins to learn to read. One of them might learn reading quickly and easily; the other might learn with considerable difficulty. Since they are identical twins, their genetic inheritance and maturational level probably have little effect on their immediate learning ability. Newman, Freeman, and Holzinger (1937), for example, found that identical twins were consistently more similar than fraternal twins on maturational measures, and identical twins reared apart were more alike than fraternal twins on all indexes except weight. Accordingly, the difference between the twins, in ability to read, was probably due to differences in their past experiences. The importance of adapting training conditions to readiness (age level) is depicted graphically in Figure 6-7.

From experimental findings (Gibson, Walk, *et al.*, 1958; Hebb, 1949; Skinner, 1959) we have come to infer that the initial periods of little or no learning in the early stages of learning at any age may, in actuality, be periods of building readiness in its many forms such as periods in which the student is maturing; in which fundamental skills necessary for current objectives are being learned; or, in which he is

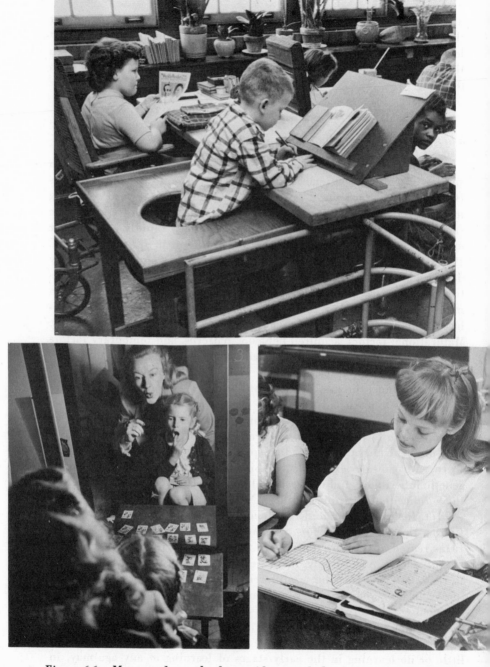

Figure 6-6. Many modern schools provide special classes for exceptional children such as those who are physically handicapped, those with hearing difficulties, or those who are gifted. (Top and bottom right: St. Louis Post-Dispatch from Black Star. Bottom left: Ross Madden from Black Star.)

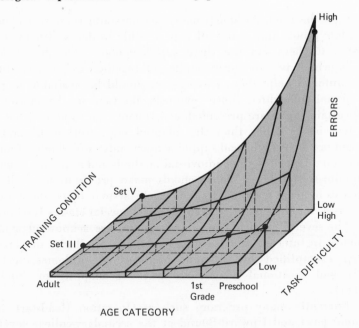

Figure 6-7. An illustrative graph showing the relationship between age, task difficulty (generalizability from previous learning) and performance scores. (From E. S. Gollin, A developmental approach to learning and cognition. In L. P. Lipsitt & C. C. Spiker (Eds.). Advances in child development and behavior, 1965, Figure 3, p. 176. New York: Academic Press. With permission of author and publisher.)

adapting to new requirements, new teachers, or new peers. At the higher educational levels, the high school and college were always very much concerned with the student's readiness. Entrance requirements were and are based on grades earned in previous courses, scores on intelligence tests, scores on interests tests, extracurricular activities, and evidence of physical health and emotional stability. Many youngsters from the ghetto and other disadvantaged areas are proving that such factors are not the only determinants of academic performance. Very often motivation can be an important factor in building readiness for further academic progress. Any one or all of these factors may be related to the individual's ability to profit from the experience in a school curriculum. They are the prerequisites to learning.

Once the pupil's ability is identified, teaching is then matched to differences in readiness levels. Typical procedures provide background experiences (such as prerequisite courses) or remedial work for pupils who are deficient, or enrichment experiences for the advanced pupil. In large classes varied bases of grouping pupils with similar readiness patterns might be used. Although many teachers aim their instruction at the middle group, this is not all it is possible to do. As Bloom (1968) indicates, teachers can use these supplementary procedures: Group study in which two or three pupils get together to go over difficult points; tutorial help, though expensive, should be available to pupils with special difficulties. Since textbooks do vary in the clarity with which certain topics are presented, assignments can sometimes be made from text books other than the adopted one; workbooks and programmed text books are good supplementary aids; and, finally, there are the perennial favorites, the audiovisual methods and academic games. At the administrative level, many schools make provision for individual differences by team teaching, by the "track" system, by establishing separate classes for the exceptional child, or by special classes for remedial work. The several curricula in school systems are acknowledgments of differences in interests and learning capacities. Similarly, the levels of training exemplified by different high school diplomas, technical schools, and vocational schools are ways of adapting to individual differences.

Currently many programs such as Operation Headstart at the preschool level and Upward-Bound at the secondary-college level, are direct attempts to remedy deficiencies in readiness. Some programs make a special point of adapting to the near panic, or culture shock, experienced by the young pupil recently arrived from Puerto Rico rather than making the pupil adapt to the program. Another program will provide male teachers, to serve as masculine models, where the majority of pupils come from father-absent homes. The damaging effects of segregation, not only on language and other academic skills but on the pupil's potentiality for self-development, are being recognized through in-service training programs to help teachers develop awareness of the emotional needs of children in biracial situations. These are but beginnings; much remains to be done. When teachers or schools choose to ignore the pupil as an individual, the effects on learning are pervasive, and usually negative.

Attention and vigilance

All theories of learning stress, at least implicitly, the importance of attention. For the teacher, too, getting the pupil's attention must be considered a part of preparing the pupil to profit from his learning experiences. The observing response is a part of attentive behavior (Wyckoff, 1952). It determines which stimuli will be effective; the incoming stimulus pattern is changed. Accordingly, the cues on which the observing response is focused will make a difference in the pupil's level of learning; often the difference between a good and a poor pupil is a matter of the one making a correct discrimination and the other making an incorrect discrimination.

What the pupil has attended to can be identified through appropriate tests, as illustrated by an example based on one of Luria's (1961) experiments. Three- and four-year-old children were required to make a choice between a picture of a red airplane on a gray background (rewarded) and a green airplane on a yellow background (not rewarded). They were always rewarded for selecting the former and never for selecting the latter. After several trials the rewarded choice was learned to the exclusion of the unrewarded one. Did the children attend to the color of the airplane or of the background? To answer this question Luria interchanged the two airplanes, thereby reversing the backgrounds, and asked the children again to make a choice. Now the children always selected the red airplane on the yellow background, never the green airplane on the gray background, even though yellow was previously part of the unrewarded stimulus, and gray was part of the rewarded stimulus. Thus it was made clear that the airplane was the dominant part of the stimulus pattern.

Teaching these same children to attend to background characteristics is analogous to teaching the pupil in a classroom to attend to certain stimuli. Luria found that pointing to the background was an inadequate procedure. The young children attended to it only after it was made meaningful through the instruction. "When the sky is yellow, the day is sunny and nice so the plane can fly; when the sky is gray, the day is rainy and dark so that the plane must not fly." In this way the background was made significant to the young child and became an object of attention.

Attention, as a general behavior, can be learned through reinforcement. In some industries, inspectors are expected to find defective products that occur only once in 10,000 items. Radar observers are expected to be continually vigilant for enemy planes though none are ever spotted at some bases. Under such circumstances people become lax or inattentive. Their attention then must be increased by external means; the inspector's by deliberate placement of a defective item into the assembly line at irregular intervals, and the radar observer's by an occasional simulated enemy flight. The procedure also enables a check on the accuracy of perception. For our purposes, however, these examples serve to illustrate techniques that increase attention.

Other determinants of attention are as follows (Reynolds, 1968):

1. Once attention to a given attribute has been established the pupil will exclude all other properties unless its connection with reinforcement is no longer reliable.

2. Discriminations are often initially established on large differences in one characteristic. If so, the introduction of a small difference in another characteristic, though important, will be ignored unless it is made relevant through meaningful experience as in Luria's experiment.

3. The simplest and most obvious way of directing (or redirecting) the pupil's attention is by instruction. Tell a pupil that an insect has three body segments and he will respond to this characteristic to the exclusion of number of legs, number of spiracles, life stages, habits, and so on. So strongly will this direction dominate his attention that other characteristics, though in view, will often go unrecognized.

4. When a pupil's learning seems to be dictated (controlled) by attention to only one characteristic, another one can be made important by presenting the two together and then "fading" the original stimulus. For example, the pupil who studies the position of the states on a map of the United States depends upon a number of cues but especially on the printed names. Once he has studied the map in complete form, he can be taught to depend on the shape of the state and its general location by removing the names (a few at a time) and requiring him to label the states for himself. Later, even the boundaries of states may be eliminated to focus attention on specific locations. Line drawings of relevant attributes of different kinds of arches, of different kinds of theater stages, or of anything else that can be depicted pictorially serve the same functions.

Attention and the disadvantaged pupil

The arousal of attention is influenced by the pupil's motivational state, and by the organization of stimuli in the pupil's social environment.

Cynthia Deutsch (1966) has applied these two premises to the education of the disadvantaged child. Of course, the prerequisite condition of attention is the pupil's motivational state. If he is fatigued, ill, or bored the teacher will have more difficulty in arousing his attention than if he is physically fit and alert. When attention is "tuned-out," so to speak, then external conditions will have little effect. Similarly, a child who has never been exposed to more than a few minutes of continual discourse, or to more than one instruction at a time in his home environment will be at a loss in school. He will be distracted by the unfamiliar demands and materials of the school.

Attentional proclivities are most important for learning when they direct the pupil toward attributes relevant to the learning objective at hand. Furthermore, as Deutsch suggests, the organization of stimuli must be consistent with the pupil's background and experience, his already learned hierarchies, since these affect the attractiveness of the stimuli. What the specific contents of these behavioral hierarchies are for children with different backgrounds, or even for children of different ages, is far from clear. However, it appears reasonable to expect that varied backgrounds do yield different stimuli. Growing up in a given subculture channels attention to certain stimuli while excluding others. It is fairly certain that the middle class child is exposed to those stimuli which are important to school learning. On the other hand, the teacher may find the disadvantaged pupil relating to what is considered an irrelevant or unimportant part of the learning task.

External manipulation of stimuli to arouse attention often defeats the purpose of teaching. Deutsch (1966), for example, notes that the format of the modern primer is an attempt to attract the young pupil's attention through its many colored pictures. These function so successfully that most children, and especially the disadvantaged children, look only at the pictures which receive little or no competition from the small, black print (the relevant stimuli). Analogous teaching practices include such devices employed by teachers as sudden change in stimuli (hitting a ruler on a desk) the introduction of novel stimuli (a "surprise" event), telling jokes, and so on. These will arouse attention temporarily, but unless they direct the student to some aspect of the teaching purpose their effects will do little more than provide a moment of relaxation from the immediate task. A more effective procedure would be to analyze beforehand the learning materials to be presented, thereby determining which stimuli are relevant. Then the child's attention can be judiciously steered to these particular stimuli by purposeful attention-getting aids rather than by the indiscriminate use of big displays, splashes of color, or movements.

These points are nicely summarized in a caution by Reynolds (1968) who says,

It is dangerous . . . to maintain that a given [pupil] cannot discriminate between two stimuli without attempts to produce the discrimination, . . . all [people] have discriminative capacities that are never fully developed because their environments never provide differential consequences of selective behavior in the presence of minimally different stimuli. The cultured palate of the wine taster, the discerning nostrils of the perfumer, the critical ear of the conductor, the sensitive fingers of the safecracker, and the educated eyes of the painter are familiar illustrations of discriminative capacities that remain relatively untapped in most human beings (pp. 49–50).*

Motivation: The arousal of behavior

Motivation, of course, is a large part of the pupil's preparedness for learning. A motivated pupil is active and energetic. Motivation thus raises the pupil's level of performance and hence the arousal of

*From G. S. Reynolds, *A primer of operant conditions*, 1968, 49–50. Glenview, Ill.: Scott, Foresman, and Co. with permission of author and publisher.

motives is said to have an energizing function (Melton, 1950). This is analogous to the "go" instruction in computer programming (Biggs, 1968)—there are several ways of viewing (coding) an environment: if no discrepancy exists for the person behavior turns elsewhere; if a discrepancy is seen then the pupil is aroused to seek more information to resolve it.

When the pupil is participating and responding there is opportunity for the teacher to vary the situation, to modify responses, to evaluate and reinforce appropriate behaviors or to provide for the extinction of inappropriate behaviors. Without motivation and the resultant increase in activity there would be no opportunity to employ these important procedures during learning. Illustrations of the effects on changes in behavior resulting from attempts to satisfy needs are in abundance. To mention a few: The *hungry* infant learns to eat with a spoon instead of his hands; the *inquisitive* and alert first-grade pupil learns to read; the *socially* needful adolescent in the inner city may learn that hostility toward the school aids the development of camaraderie with his peers.

Figure 6-8. Learning is easier for motivated than it is for uninterested pupils. (King Features Syndicate.)

At each developmental level, one of the teacher's tasks is to capitalize on the existence of dominant needs. In early adolescence pupils have strong social needs, so instruction can be oriented around social skills. In later adolescence, economic needs may be important and some classwork can be easily directed toward vocational matters. For any group of pupils regardless of nationality, religion, or race, knowing about one's origins and culture is a personally significant matter and certainly is educationally relevant.

Closely related to motivation are understandings regarding the roles of goals, incentives, feedback, and correction in learning. They are important because they provide direction to motivated behavior. The next sections are devoted to discussions of these topics.

Level of arousal and effectiveness of performance

The study of emotions is related to motivation. Emotions can be organizers of behavior thereby increasing its effectiveness, or disorganizers of behavior thereby decreasing its effectiveness. Hebb (1966) provides an interesting classification of emotions relating them to their arousal functions. Some emotions, he says, are pleasant (such as love, joy, and pride) about which the person tends to do *nothing to terminate* them and often seeks ways to cause their reinstatement. Others such as fear, anger, and jealousy are unpleasant with consequent efforts by the person to *terminate* the emotion. And other emotions (such as depression and grief) are disliked but are *interminable* by the person. These states sometimes lead to specific behavior, (e.g., fear leads to running away and anger leads to hostility) but they can also be related to general motivational states. Both motivations and emotions share the qualities that they can be organizing and energizing or disorganizing and debilitating of behavior depending on the level of their arousal (Hebb, 1966, p. 235). This relationship may be seen in Figure 6-9. This figure suggests that, in general, with low arousal, the person is not receptive to all of the important stimuli and so behavior is relatively ineffective. Lower levels of arousal are always increasingly organizing up to some moderate level, following which the person becomes highly aroused. Presumably, beyond some optimal point, he is receptive to too many stimuli, "too many messages get through and prevent the [pupil] from responding selectively to any one set of stimuli" (Hebb, 1966, p. 236). In addition, the effects of the same degree of arousal differ according to the behavior being performed. In general, the performance of a well-established simple skill is less likely to be impaired or disrupted by the disorganizing effects of high arousal than is a skill which is difficult to perform or one that is not so highly practiced. (From D. O. Hebb, *A Textbook of Psychology*, 2nd ed. Philadelphia: W. B. Saunders Co., 1966.)

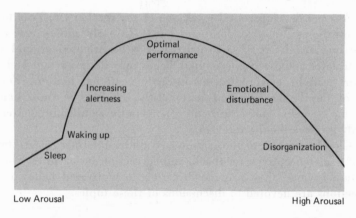

Figure 6-9. Relation of the effectiveness with which stimuli guide behavior (cue function) to the level of arousal, varying from deep sleep to disorganizing states of emotion, with maximal behavioral efficiency at an intermediate level of arousal. The shape of this curve is different for different habits. For example, in a simple long-practiced habit such as giving one's name when asked, maximal efficiency is reached with low arousal and maintained over a wide range; in a complex skill, maximum efficiency appears only with a medium degree of arousal; and in a performance such as running a race which is relatively uncomplicated but demands full mobilization of effort, the maximum efficiency appears with higher arousal. (From Hebb, 1966, pp. 235 and 238. With permission of author and publisher.)

The pupil strives toward specific goals: incentives and other indications of achievement

Goals and incentives provide direction to the more generalized energizing function of motivation. All organisms strive for a satisfying culmination to their efforts. In the lower organisms, the most evident goals are those that satisfy the homeostatic drives such as hunger and thirst. Other goals, such as satisfying one's curiosity through exploring the environment or by manipulating objects, are less obvious but are unquestionably sought after (Harlow, 1950).

Similar goals are directive factors in the behavior of pupils. Responses that result in attainment of a primary reward or goal like candy will be learned. At a later stage of development acquired (also called learned or secondary) goals become important. Also characteristic of human goals are indicators of one's competence in a field, or of achievement of some kind. All can be effective in guiding behavior. Which will be functional depends in part upon the level of development, particularly that characterized by the ability to verbalize. In learning to draw a picture, for example, the goal may be to reproduce a

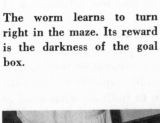

The worm learns to turn right in the maze. Its reward is the darkness of the goal box.

The kitten learns the maze pathways. His reward is food.

The monkey learns some simple mechanical skills. His rewards are the satisfactions of his curiosity and manipulation needs.

The pupil learns complex skills and ideas. His rewards include the approval of others and achievement.

Figure 6-10. One of the characteristics of all living organisms is that they modify their behavior in terms of success experiences. (Top left: Syracuse University, Physiological Psychology Laboratory. Top right: Pix. Lower left: Courtesy of Harry F. Harlow, Department of Psychology, University of Wisconsin. Lower right: Portland, Oregon, Public Schools.)

"likeness" on a plane surface from a three-dimensional scene or object in real or still life (Holland & Skinner, 1961). Or, in mathematics the pupil's goal may be the competence that follows the satisfaction of deriving a mathematical equation (Beberman, 1964).

The pupil's goals, accordingly, may be in the form of primary or secondary rewards or they may be in the more abstract forms, dependent upon his capacity to verbalize. In whatever manner they occur they function to indicate what kind of information he should seek, what is expected of him, and the *level* of this expectation (Sears, 1940). Goals, thus, may be of varying levels of precision. It is one matter to arrive at a correct solution to a mathematical problem by whatever means is convenient. It is quite another matter to arrive at a correct solution by use of a specific algebraic theorem.

The reader will recognize that the teacher's task paralleling this phase of the learning process is to clearly formulate objectives. The pupil is thus made to understand precisely the performance expected of him and why he must do it this way (Bloom *et al.*, 1956).

The learner varies his behavior: Making provisional tries

Teachers want pupils to be psychologically active in ways connected to the school's objectives. A relatively limited range of activity with well-defined behavior patterns is required for effective learning. The pupil's behavior is not confined to his overt actions; it also includes the cognitive activity otherwise called thinking, reasoning, or problem-solving. A major problem in teaching is to discover the nature of these covert behaviors. This end is accomplished by asking questions or engaging the pupil in discussion. The best way to learn what an individual "knows" is to observe whether his actions in appropriate situations reflect the response patterns he is supposed to have learned. In this regard, the teacher, like all other persons, is an "inference-maker" and an "experimenter." In particular, he observes the classroom scene, and makes inferences about the possible effects of a change in the situation on the pupil's performance. He tests his hypotheses by making the changes and then appraises the results through observation, questioning, and testing.

To say that the pupil varies his behavior is not the same as saying that he makes random trial-and-error responses. In most problem situations pupils have a repertory of alternative patterns of behavior learned through previous experiences. Certain of these will be more useful in a given situation than in others. Some pupils, for example, may scramble to the dinner table or push their way into a movie line. These are dominant responses and were learned because they have been used successfully in the past. Eventually something may change them. Social encounters may temper the dominance of these behaviors, perhaps replacing them with waiting one's turn. Thus, instead of *trial and error*, it is more accurate to speak of this process as *trial and correction*.

Language is intimately tied to making provisional tries. This is fortunate, for it permits the teacher to use shortcuts in teaching methods and it also permits him to make the new learning distinct from the old learning, if it is necessary to do so, in order to eliminate interference. Verbal instructions aid the learner in arriving at many new behaviors quickly and efficiently. Incorrect responses can often be eliminated by merely telling the pupil what to do. Nevertheless, verbal instruction alone is an insufficient condition for learning, especially motor learning. The pupil must be stimulated to respond himself. It is one thing, for example, to tell a person not to move his head while making a golf shot; it is another for the learner to translate this instruction into action. So widespread is this difficulty that a golf instructor known to one of the authors invented a gimmick to help his pupils. He has the person stand with his back to the sun so that a shadow is cast before him. Then a golf ball is placed on either side of the shadow of the student's head while he is in the stance using the driver. When the swing is made the shadow is to remain within the boundaries defined by the balls. Thus, no learning can take place without the pupil's *doing* something. His motions are limited to certain ones; he must think about them, review them, and otherwise work at the assigned task in a decidedly concrete way.

Feedback: The consequences of the learner's behavior

Much of the incentive for the pupil's activity comes from what in a broad sense may be called information about the consequences of his provisional tries, of his goal-directed behavior (Fitts, 1964). Especially important in motor learning is *intrinsic feedback* in the form of proprioceptive and kinesthetic cues that arise naturally from his own movements. This kind of feedback is not dependent upon cues from the environment. What we may call *augmented feedback*, on the other hand, is provided by some external source. The learner receives information about his progress from the teacher's remarks, test grades, and the like. Then, in addition, the pupil perceives his progress in relationship to his goals. This is *cognitive feedback* and is characterized by the reduction of a conflict incongruity, or disparity, seen between the present state of affairs, such as an unsolved problem, and the desired state of affairs, such as the solution to the problem or some other goal (see, for example, Miller, Galanter, & Pribram, 1960; or Biggs, 1968).

Fitts and Posner (1967) argue that all forms of feedback serve three functions: They provide the learner with knowledge about himself and his environment just as does information that is gathered from any other stimuli. They may act as powerful motivators to continue a task, when success is indicated, since they show progress toward a goal. Thirdly, since any of the forms of feedback typically occur in close contiguity with the behavior, they serve as reinforcers of the behavior.

The successful forms of behavior, as judged by feedback, will tend to be used with increasing frequency by the learner. Consider, as an example, the pupil in a typing class. He is encouraged to type at the rate of 35 words per minute. He finds that in using the touch system he cannot quite attain this speed. However, as he interprets the situation, he believes that if he looks occasionally at the keys (provided the keyboard is marked) then the desired rate might be met with relative ease. Upon trying this behavior he finds his interpretation is accurate. Thus, the consequences (results) of his action confirm his expectations. Peeks at the keyboard will be increased even though this practice may hinder his long-range achievement (the effectiveness of the touch system depends upon elimination of such wasteful movements as looking back and forth between the copy to be typed and the keyboard). Accordingly, it is important to monitor the pupil's behavior and provide corrective feedback information if the pupil is to avoid learning inefficient behaviors. In formal education, pupils are carefully guided through important processes so that their performance is efficient. Errors are corrected before ineffective patterns of behavior become firmly fixed.

The learner practices: Acquiring confidence and mastery in the use of new behavior patterns

A very young child who has just learned to climb in and out of his stroller will spend many minutes repeating the activity over and over again. Each attempt appears to be in the direction of improvement over the previous one. Finally, he gains enough confidence in the action so that it becomes an habitual part of his behavior that can be used efficiently and without apparent deliberation. Similarly, a golfer engages in repetitive practice when learning to drive, putt, or make an approach shot. In addition to motor skills like these which are so directly observable, the majority of human activities are composed of complex patterns of behavior. Repetition in some form is necessary, if the specific behaviors are to be tied together into a coordinated, efficient pattern. But it is also necessary if pupils are to have *confidence* in using what they have learned.

Practice is most effective when the pupil is optimally motivated. Enforced practice can lead to decline in interest, a fact which has been frequently overlooked in the use of drill. If pupils perform under conditions where they are not motivated, they may learn to avoid and dislike other parts of the situation, including the teacher and the school. They may even learn *not* to do what is practiced if the consequences are viewed as not meeting their needs.

Figure 6-11. Unmotivated practice may not result in changed behaviors.

When accompanied by appropriate motivation, by meaningful understandings of the reasons for practice, and by knowledge of progress, practice helps the pupil eliminate the incorrect responses and fix the correct ones. Contacts with *varied* activities may provide him with understanding, and thereby reduce the amount of drill-like practice required. Pupils may be encouraged to use learned responses in a variety of ways, in new and different situations, and with confidence.

What Is Learned?

Many curricular reform projects currently underway are based on the premise that the instructional procedure does make a difference in the attainment of objectives over and above that which is measured on a traditional achievement test. In mathematics, for example, there is the School Mathematics Study Group (1966); and in physics there is the Physical Science Study Committee (1965). The focus of all of these groups is on a restatement of objectives, on course content to be taught at each grade level, on the instructional methods best adapted to achieving stated objectives, and on methods of examination. The "new look" in the curriculum has resulted in the emergence of such methods as *inquiry* teaching and *discovery* methods. Controversy has arisen regarding the earliest age at which some elements of set theory (in mathematics) can and should be taught. There is a new concern for understanding the nature of scientific inquiry and its relation to the problems of mankind. The influence of psychology is manifest throughout these endeavors. However, most apparent to anyone reviewing these curricula is that they focus on the discipline, and all that it implies, rather than on specific isolated behaviors, as Goodlad, von Stoephasius, and Klein, (1966) indicate in the following:

If previous eras of curriculum development can be described as child centered or society centered, this one can be designated as subject or discipline centered. The ends and means of schooling are derived from organized bodies of knowledge. Further, the curriculum is planned by physicists, mathematicians, and historians, and students are encouraged to think like these scholars. The word "structure" has replaced "the whole child" in curriculum jargon.*

Most school objectives can be classified in psychologically meaningful ways. Each category has identifiable variables associated with the efficiency with which it is learned. These variables provide a foundation for understanding the general teaching methods used by teachers. We now turn to a brief overview of the kinds of classifications of behaviors, together with some of their characteristics, that are of most concern in developing educational objectives.

Skilled patterns of behavior

Motor patterns of response appear, on the surface, to be the simplest kind of learning. One reason may be that they are among the first behaviors to develop. The young child engages in many motor patterns such as walking, running, climbing, and jumping. In their earliest forms these activities are relatively primitive forms of behavior. They permit crude adaptations to changing environmental demands. Furthermore, they comprise the primary means by which many of our basic needs are satisfied.

Motor performance is important, in fact essential, to an industrialized civilization. Many vocations require precise motor patterns, including the work of the plumber, carpenter, machinist, electrician, and mason; professionals, such as musicians and artists, depend upon special perceptual-motor talents. For most individuals, motor skills play an important role in recreational and just plain day-to-day activities.

Fitts (1964, 1965; Fitts & Posner, 1967) describes three phases in learning skills: First, the pupil must understand the nature of the performance demanded of him. His teacher helps by demonstrating the skill to provide a criterion for the standard of performance the pupil is to achieve. When the learner first attempts the skill he attends to many cues that may be unimportant later. In learning to play a musical instrument, for example, the pupil pays much attention to visual cues about placement of his fingers on the strings of a violin or keys of a piano. Later, these cues will be ignored in favor of kinesthetic cues. During this phase the instructor provides diagnostic feedback and correction by demonstrating important cues and response characteristics.

*From J. Goodlad, R. von Stoephasius, & M. F. Klein, *The Changing School Curriculum*, 1966. Pp. 14–15. New York: Harcourt, Brace, and World, with permission of authors and publisher.

The intermediate phase is the hook-up or associative stage in which the separate habits and individual units are coordinated and integrated with one another. Wrong sequences, wrong cues, and wrong subroutine patterns are corrected or eliminated. Distributed practice, that is, practice with frequent rest periods appears to be important especially where extended (massed) practice may result in wrong responses because of fatigue. The sequence in which the parts are practiced is also an important variable. Although a complex issue, the evidence (Bahrick, 1957) suggests that where a task requires the smooth coordination of all its parts (as in playing an instrument) the task should be practiced as a whole. But the teacher should not attempt a rote application of this principle. Obviously, some tasks such as memorizing long poems or playing compositions with several movements may be too difficult for the beginner. In such cases good judgment suggests that the task should be subdivided into meaningful subunits; then each part can be practiced independently, and properly integrated with the parts already practiced.

In the final phase, practice is important for the skill to take on its autonomous character. At the end of this stage a skill runs off much as

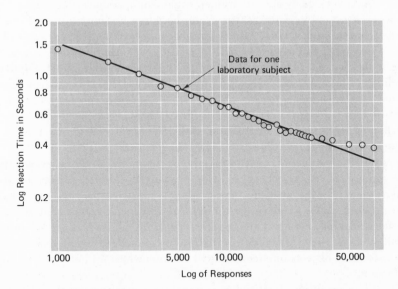

Figure 6-12. Skills continue to improve even after enormous amounts of practice. Above is shown the reduction in reaction time of one subject in using a ten-finger key-pressing task. (After R. Seibel, 1963, as quoted by E. T. Klemmer, Communication and human performance, Human factors, 1962, 4, 75–79, and reported in Fitts & Posner, 1967, Figure 3, p. 18. With the permission of M. Posner, Brooks/Cole Publishing Co., and the Human Factors Society.)

does a chain reflex. The performer, for example, a skilled typist or pian-
ist, can perform the skill with little interference from another activity
such as talking. Thus, in this stage the skill becomes independent of verbalization and conscious control; because of these characteristics it is
highly stable even under difficult conditions like stress.

Wherever skills are involved we find a learned pattern of behavior which can be repeated on any occasion. Good "form" is essential,
since it assures that similar posture is maintained from one performance
to the next with invariant kinesthetic and proprioceptive cues. Response-
produced cues provided by the latter enable the stable, coordinated
sequence of responses described as a skill. Efficiency is enhanced further
if the learner is aware of the underlying rhythmic patterns that might
be used in typing or in music. Such rhythms provide plans or cognitive
codes for implementing the motor activity. These characteristics are present in all motor activities, whether typing, writing, speaking, reading,
or driving a car, making our lives more efficient and insuring economy
of effort.

Attitudes, beliefs, and values are learned

At a very early age the human organism *approaches* certain situations at regular intervals, as, for example, when he must nurse in order
to satisfy the hunger need. Other situations are *avoided*, as, for example,
those involving the negative goals of noxious stimulation, such as touch-
ing a hot stove. Out of many similar experiences, the pupil acquires
feelings of acceptance or rejection toward "objects" in his environment.
Some are specific, *concrete* objects such as foods, cars, colors, and
people that the pupil may like or dislike. Others are more *abstract* ideas
such as those involved in religion, politics, moral codes, governments,
ethics, and loyalties. Toward these, too, pupils acquire feelings of
acceptance or rejection. Attitudes are by-products of all learning and
are the result of direct or vicarious experience with objects in the
environment. Some attitudes are extremely positive feelings of acceptance such as those we have for the ethical and social values that are the
cornerstones of society. Others are strongly negative feelings of rejection, such as those we have for lack of responsibility and dishonesty.
Toward most objects our feelings will be somewhere in between the two
extremes.

The teaching of attitudes necessitates a concern for the affective
correlates of learning. Identification with the teacher or other persons as
a favored model will facilitate the acquisition of attitudes held by that
person and conversely, a rejection of a person will be accompanied by a
rejection of his attitudes (Rosekrans, 1967; Byrne, 1961). Pleasant consequences in the form of rewards lead to favorable attitudes; unpleasant

consequences, in the form of annoyances or punishments, lead to unfavorable attitudes (Nunnally, 1968; Scott, 1959). Similarly, pleasant settings in which an event is experienced, for example as when one listens to classical music, are essential to the development of appreciations. Perhaps the most potent of techniques for influencing attitudes is that of verbal communication. The use of one adjective over another to describe an attitude-object (person or group) may make the difference between the pupil's liking or disliking that object (Bossart & Di Vesta, 1966). Regardless of the teaching method used, the pupil's affective reaction is the prime concern in attitude formation and change.

Since attitudes influence the future behavior of the pupil, society is particularly concerned with certain of them in the acculturation process. Of particular importance are the attitudes and values related to the maintenance of health, interpersonal relationships, democratic institutions, spare-time interests, and attitudes toward self. Various ethnic subcultures have quite different attitudinal requirements for their members which may appear quite irrational to some but are nevertheless important for getting along in that society (Brown, 1965). A democratic society permits values to be tested in responsible ways and many different, even seemingly contradictory, values may exist side by side.

Concepts are learned

Communication is dependent upon the use of symbols and concepts. Man uses language symbols in the forms of words to convey the abstractions we call concepts. Through such concepts and symbols we are able to experience a baseball game by listening to the radio, almost as though we were present. (Some spectators find the verbal radio account of a ball game a valuable aid to observing the game from the stands!) Much of what has occurred in previous generations is transmitted to us through the writings of historians.

Education via communication processes permits pupils to have very similar common experiences, many of which are indirectly patterned around specific language or mathematical symbols. These represent individual experiences from which the pupil has abstracted the common properties of certain classes of objects. These meanings or properties associated with a word or other symbol define his concept which may be loosely described as a "mental image" or "mental picture" of a thing, action, or idea.

When concepts are taught, emphasis is placed on experience providing for discrimination, abstraction, and transfer. In the elementary school or when older pupils are being introduced to new fields, direct experience (through such teaching techniques as demonstrations, laboratory work, and field trips) is helpful. In the later school years and for advanced topics verbal descriptions of concepts, of comparisons and contrasts, of relatedness to other events, and of applications may be all that is necessary. Indeed, this may be the only way most abstract concepts can be taught. Especially important, regardless of method, is the use of inquiry to direct the pupil's attention to perceptual similarities and differences among experiences and to relate events with those he already knows about (Suchman, 1966). The use of inquiry methods is based on the premise that the teacher provides the pupil with many experiences with the concept. Through problem situations and questioning the pupil is guided in active search for its meaning. Such teaching methods presuppose that simpler facts, associations, and understandings have been learned as a foundation for efficient use of inquiry methods (Gagné, 1965).

The social interaction in the family contributes to the development of concepts through its effect on communication. The disadvantaged child whether Puerto Rican, Mexican-American, or from the

Figure 6-13. An example of a concept task for children to test their performance of inclusion operations. A child with no understanding of inclusion relations will answer to the question "Are there more people or women?" that "there are more women because there are only two people" thinking that a comparison is to be made between the two groups. (From G. A. Kohnstamm. An evaluation of Piaget's theory. Acta Psychologica, 1963, 21, 313–315. With permission of author and publisher.)

Appalachia region, develops very different conceptualizations, verbal facility, and cognitive skills than does the child in the typical middle socioeconomic status home. Family interaction in the lower class provides little or no basis for abstraction of an idea. The child's questions, typically, receive no answer or a curt "Be quiet!" He performs tasks according to a definite role which functions well for that family but is highly restrictive. In the middle class home the child's questions provide him with the opportunity to reflect and to accommodate. He may be asked to think his way through to the answer, to relate his ideas to another dimension, and to interpret the question further. When he performs a task he may be asked to describe what he is doing, to invent alternative ways of dealing with it, or to suggest the possible effects on other people. He is continually engaged in a complex verbal communication network. Upon entering school his concepts will be vastly richer, and as a consequence his preparations for school work, as we know it today, at least, will be considerably more adequate than those of the disadvantaged child.

Concepts embody everything the pupil knows and has experienced. Since they are an important part of his cognitive structure (knowledge) they affect this behavior in many ways. Accurate concepts serve as mediators to facilitate learning by tying new learning with earlier experiences. They act as bases around which new experience can be organized. They enable the pupil to solve problems by the methods correctly employed in similar situations. Through the integration of concepts in new ways he can arrive not only at correct but also at novel solutions to problems—essentially the manner in which the inventor operates. Thus, concepts are used in communication, thinking, reasoning, and invention, in all of which there is manipulation of ideas rather than of the concrete objects or experiences themselves.

Problem-solving and thinking

Participation in school and classroom activities does not result in substantive achievement alone. In addition to the development of concepts, attitudes, and skills, the pupil may be taught some of the processes related to inventive ideation which includes problem-solving, thinking, and creativity. The identifying characteristics of these behaviors are unique experiences integrated around a relevant question, in a manner permitting a novel answer.

An important initial step for effective problem-solving is learning to learn. In other words, the pupil acquires general methods, techniques, and procedures that affect subsequent successful performance. That this can be accomplished was first demonstrated by Harry Harlow (1949, 1950). After solving several (sometimes more than a hundred) problems, his subjects showed that they had learned a strategy for successfully solving later problems. Similar processes appear in classroom situations. After long practice pupils learn ways of organizing their notes, of scheduling their time in studying, and of memorizing their assignments. These how-to processes have been found by them to work successfully. Included are the "rules of the game" for efficient work habits.

Learning how to learn, though a relatively unexplored area, is the province of many rule-of-thumb experts. The how-to-study, how-to-solve-problems, how-to-read-rapidly, and how-to-win-friends-and-influence-people manuals and courses are made available on the assumption that individuals can learn how to learn. An example of learning to learn applied to study methods is shown in the SQ4R procedure described below. These processes are so important that someday large parts of the curriculum might be process-oriented so that the pupil will learn the heuristics and strategies necessary for adjusting to the scholastic, social, leisure, and work facets of his world.

Summary of SQ4R: A procedure for effective study of a chapter*

I. *Survey*
    Determine the structure, organization, or plan of the chapter.
    Details will be remembered because of their relationship to the total picture.
    A. *Think about the title.* Guess what will be included in the chapter.
    B. *Read the introduction.* Here the main ideas are presented, the "forest" which must be seen before its details, the individual "trees," are introduced to make the thought maximally clear.
    C. *Read the summary.* Here is the relationship among the main ideas.
    D. *Read the main heads* (boldface type). Here are the main ideas. Determine where in the sequence of ideas each one fits.

II. *Question*
    Having in mind a question results in (1) a spontaneous attempt to answer it with information already at hand; (2) frustration until the question is answered; (3) a criterion against which the details can be inspected to determine relevance and importance; (4) a focal point for crystallizing a series of ideas (the answer).

---

*From D. E. P. Smith, *Learning to Learn.* New York: Harcourt, Brace and World, 1961. As adapted from Francis Robinson, *Effective Study.* Harper & Brothers, 1946. With permission of authors and publishers.

    A. Use the questions at the beginning or end of the chapter.

    B. Formulate questions by changing main heads and subheads to questions. Example: *Causes of Economic Depression.* What are the causes of economic depression? What conditions are usually present before an economic depression occurs?

III. *Read*

Read to answer the question. Move quickly. Sort out ideas and evaluate them. If content does not relate to the question, give it only a passing glance. *Read selectively.*

IV. *Recite*

Answer the question—in your own words, not the author's.

V. *"Rite"*

    A. Write the question (one sheet of paper is to contain *all* the notes for this chapter—so keep it brief).

    B. Write the answer using only key works, listings, etc., that are needed to recall the whole idea.

VI. *Review*

Increase retention and cut cramming time by 90 percent by means of immediate *and* delayed review. To do this:

    A. Read your written question(s).

    B. Try to recite the answer. If you can't, look at your notes. Five to ten minutes will suffice for a chapter.

    C. Review again after one week.

Closely related to learning how to learn is problem-solving, one of the most adaptive behaviors that pupils can learn. Problem-solving becomes doubly important in the face of the rapidly changing technological developments of our times. In view of recent revolutionary advances, our cultural heritage is not adequate to provide answers to the urgent questions challenging today's society. Interpersonal relationships are no less immune to revolutionary changes. New solutions must be found for questions emerging on all fronts. Because problem-solving or reasoning is a way of dealing with unanswered questions, it is an element much emphasized in education.

Pupils are not taught reasoning by being given a series of identical exercises (often incorrectly called problems) for which answers are required. In reality such exercises are merely slight variations of a single problem, which in arithmetic may be division, finding areas, or finding volumes; in chemistry, the balancing of equations; in physics, the routine application of a formula to determine momentum or acceleration. As important as practise is in these areas, such exercises require only assimilation into the rule or principle that leads directly to a solution. They are not "problems" for which *new* methods and solutions must be found, for which new accommodations must be made.

Problem-solving begins with unsatisfied needs. There must be a question for which the individual urgently wants a solution. The solution (or goal) is one that is not immediately attainable. Exploration is required in order that relevant prior experiences can be brought to focus on possible answers. Independent experiences are integrated so that several alternative solutions are suggested. Then the individual must identify the choice that best answers his question.

Problem-solving is not so much a different kind of learning as it is a more complex form of learning. Unlike learning how to learn, problem-solving requires more than the application of habitual responses, although these habits do influence the learner's efficiency. The integration of relevant experiences is accomplished on the basis of available concepts and skills. The outcomes, as we shall see in later chapters, are influenced by the individual's needs, and prior learnings, including concepts, skills, and attitudes.

Summary

The teacher's task is a complex integration of many activities including the statement of objectives, the determination of course content, the adaptation to individual differences, the monitoring and guidance of learning experiences, the management of the classroom, and the appraisals of achievement. These activities, changing as they are from day to day, even from moment to moment, demand a continual series of decisions based on hypotheses about what must be done, on inferences as to probable outcomes of certain procedures, and on the testing of the utility of these procedures. Thus, it is virtually impossible to list such decisions in cookbook fashion. Accordingly, it is essential that the teacher has an understanding of the fundamentals of behavior, of learning, and of educational technology if he is to make justifiable decisions and if he is to implement sound innovative practices.

Behavior is the raw material with which the teacher works. Technically, it is any detectable reaction or response to a situation. Within the behavioral situation all of the potential stimuli, often easily perceived by any observer, are called nominal or situational stimuli. However, those most closely correlated with the pupil's behavior are effective or functional stimuli. The other facet of all behavioral settings, the response, is judged indirectly by such indexes as a pupil's score on a test, the rapidity with which he gives an answer, or by his understanding of a passage. Internal responses, such as those from proprioceptive cues or from thinking, mediate much of the pupil's behavior. Our inferences about behavioral traits and other psychological phenomena are based on observations of both the situation and response.

Useful objectives are most often stated in behavioral form. Such objectives identify the response expected of a pupil at the end of a lesson, the situation in which the behavior is to occur, and the characteristics of the final performance. When objectives are explicitly formulated in accordance with these characteristics they help to specify, for both the teacher and pupil alike, the standards to be achieved as a consequence of a learning unit and the activities necessary if these expectations are to be met.

Learning has been defined as a long-term change in behavior produced by such experiences as practice or training. Learning is an intervening variable that can only be inferred from the performance of the pupil. This definition excludes changes in behavior produced by maturation or drugs or by temporary states such as fatigue or pain. The definition also implies that behavior can be changed, in accord with educational objectives, by providing carefully selected activities for the pupils to perform.

Two paradigms, fundamental to understanding learning both in and out of educational settings, are classical conditioning and operant learning. Classical conditioning, pioneered by Pavlov, emphasizes procedures for accomplishing behavioral change by manipulation of stimuli. Thus, a neutral stimulus increases in ability to elicit a response if it frequently precedes the evocation of an unconditioned stimulus for that response. Classical conditioning deals with the effects of environmental change on the production of learning that is often involuntary. It appears to be particularly important in understanding the development of emotional responses.

Operant learning procedures emphasize the instrumental characteristics of the pupil's behavior. Within this paradigm the behavior that produces a change in the environment satisfactory to the learner is the behavior that will be strengthened.

The strength of a behavior learned by classical conditioning depends, in part, on the number of times the conditioned and unconditioned stimuli are paired, on the optimal separation of the two (about one half of a second in laboratory setting), and on the intensity of either stimulus. Extinction is accomplished by the complete withdrawal of the unconditioned stimulus on all occasions in which the conditioned stimulus occurs.

The strength of an operant depends upon the number of times it is reinforced. The operant is extinguished if it never again results in a reward or reinforcement.

Motivation determines whether the pupil will respond and incentives determine which responses he will make. When making lesson plans, teachers make conscious attempts to increase the pupils' level of motivation to relate work to the pupil's dominant interests, and to capitalize on the pupils' learning, curiosity, and competence. Clearly stated goals and incentives are essential to provide direction to what both teachers and pupils are engaged in doing.

The principal purpose of any unit within a course is directed toward some terminal behavior to be achieved. The effects of motivation, readiness, attention, and reinforcement are all directed toward this end. The pupil varies his behavior in accordance with the teacher's use of teaching method. Inquiry methods allow much variation in behavior; lecture methods are more restrictive. Nevertheless, the pupil's successful provisional tries will be the primary determiners of whatever knowledge he ultimately acquires. Feedback and correction are essential if his knowledge is to be precise. At first, feedback may come from some external source, but in the educational process it must gradually be transferred to the pupil so that he can make independent realistic evaluations of his progress.

Once a behavior pattern has been acquired, the pupil must learn to use it with confidence if it is to be useful. Accordingly, teachers provide opportunity for pupils to practice a new learning in a variety of settings so that it can be stabilized and transferred to use in other courses where it is relevant, and particularly, to use in out-of-school situations.

Course content can be classified according to several end-products. When thinking about a teaching plan for a unit of work, it is worth considering whether the pupil is expected to learn a skill, a concept, an attitude, or whether some more general process such as learning to learn, problem-solving, or reasoning is the explicit focus of the lesson. Such considerations are helpful because they provide the teacher with cues regarding emphases to be placed in the specific teaching methods he will use. Skills develop in three phases: initially, pupils must understand the total process to be learned; in the intermediate phase they learn the elements that make up the skill; and in the final phase the skill is made autonomous. The teaching method parallels these phases by providing demonstration to enhance understanding, feedback and correction to facilitate associations of individual units, and finally, above all else, practice to permit coordination of all subroutines and to make the skill autonomous.

When pupils are to learn concepts the teaching method will emphasize perception of cues, discrimination, and generalization. Drill-like practice will be of much less importance than time spent on making the subject matter meaningful through concentration on its organization and structure.

If an attitude is to be taught affective components become highlighted and the teacher is sensitive to the importance of the emotional concomitants of learning, to the effect of rewards and punishments on feelings, to the potential models available in the reading material or films assigned, and to the general "climate" of the setting.

For attaining skill in problem-solving, reasoning, and creativity it is desirable that pupils respond in ways that, for them, are unique. An objective here is to allow the pupils to arrive at unusual but useful solutions, and simultaneously to develop confidence in their ability to reach such solutions independently. Thus, discovery and inquiry techniques are often emphasized as teaching methods for these end-products. They allow a greater degree of permissiveness and require more pupil responsibility in generating the content of the unit than do the traditional methods.

The reader is cautioned that this classification is not meant to be a rigid one. It is true that most learning is fundamentally governed by similar variables. Furthermore, classroom activities are rarely directed toward one end-product. Thus, in the practical situation it will be necessary to employ close approximations of the individual recommendations and, even more often, a blending of several of them.

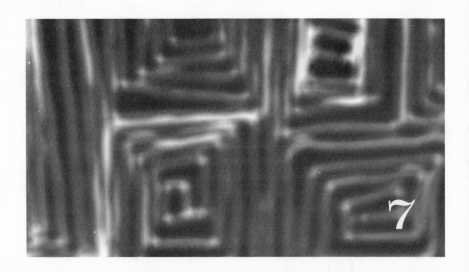

The motivated learner:
Motives and aspirations

Pupils who seem to desire to learn appear attentive, inquisitive, industrious, and productive. The arousal of these tendencies is earnestly sought after in school, because teachers know that it is the motivated pupil who attacks problems, who persists until solutions are attained, and who thereby learns.

The energies aroused by such motives direct the individual toward interaction with satisfying goal-objects. Motives may be satisfied in many ways. Three pupils, each with the same desire to be liked by others, may have quite different ways of expressing this motive. One may try to achieve all "A"s in his school work; the second may try to be the life of the party; and the third may seek superiority in extracurricular leadership. Motives thus provide direction, as well as supplying energy, for activities.

The attainment of goals by recurring patterns of behavior has an influence on further motivated activity. Successful behavior is more likely to be displayed in future similar situations. Several "successes" will tend to perpetuate a given pattern of behavior. The "A" student becomes recognized by his peers as the "Brain," the life of the party as the "Clown," and the extracurricular leader as the "Star." Each of these labels indicates that peers view these pupils as having a certain kind of distinctive stability in some of their behavior tendencies. If the pupil views the label favorably, each use of it becomes a sign that the respective behaviors have been successful. The attainment of rewards and the reaching of goals are consequently said to be *reinforcing*.

The teacher may profitably ask the following questions in considering motivation: What are the needs and drives that move the pupil to action? What goal is the pupil seeking? What is the effect on learning and subsequent behaviors when these goals are reached? Our purpose in this chapter is to provide a basis for a better understanding of the principles involved in answering these questions. Our discussion will center around the energizing, directing, and reinforcing functions of motivation.

Some Functions of Motives and Goals

The following are brief descriptions of the ways needs, drives, and motives are defined when research situations require increased precision: Needs are relatively permanent ways by which persons can be motivated and which can be satisfied by overtly identifiable or inferred goals. They can be aroused through deprivation, or through the effect of unpleasant situations in increasing emotional states (Mowrer, 1960a, 1960b). Drive refers to the increases in energy levels as a consequence of internal changes resulting from the arousal of needs (Hull, 1943). While the physiological bases and goal objects associated with physiological needs are fairly obvious, those associated with complex human needs are less easy to identify. Under most circumstances human needs are inferred from consistent patterns of goal-seeking, or avoidance behaviors characteristically associated with an emotional state (McClelland, 1955). These are called motives and are described below in more detail. Since for practical purposes the terms *needs, drives,* and *motives* imply that a lack

Figure 7-1. The stages in the motivational cycle. (From Introduction to psychology, *3rd ed., 1966, by C. Morgan, p. 66. Used with permission of author and McGraw-Hill Book Co.)*

of something leads to action (English & English, 1958), they are used synonymously in the discussion that follows.

The energizing, directing, and selecting functions of motives

Motives have three important functions in behavior (Melton, 1950; Berlyne, 1960). First, they are *energizing*. The motivated pupil is demonstrably active and his activity is maintained at relatively high levels until relevant goals or rewards are attained. While aroused motives will make the individual more *alert* in general, he will be particularly alert to those stimuli that will facilitate the satisfaction of the motive. The high school pupil who is interested in mathematics is likely to stick to his lesson in mathematics, for example, until he achieves the correct solution to all its problems. The behavior sequence may, of course, be halted by extinction when he fails to achieve success in the solution of problems, or the behavior sequence may be disrupted by the distracting influence of stronger conflicting and competing motives such as might be aroused if the boy receives a note from a pretty girl in an adjacent seat.

Secondly, motives have a *directing* function. They determine, from a repertory of many possible behaviors, a class of responses likely to be most appropriate; for example, the high school pupil goes to the cafeteria when he is hungry or to the water fountain when he is thirsty. These quite obvious examples may be extended to the cognitive processes. Organized thinking may be conceived as a set of covert verbalizations consisting of verbalizations about oneself and verbalizations about many aspects of the environment which direct the pupil to organize certain of his ideas around whatever theme is important to him at the moment. In a music class, his train of thought will be determined by ideas which are primarily musical in nature; in the history class, he will be concerned with historical explanations; and in the mathematics class, his ideas will be organized around the mathematical processes. Thus, the motive provides the pupil with *cues* directing him to the most appropriate behavior in the situation.

Thirdly, motives have a *selecting* function. Reinforcement, consequences, and feedback will determine which of a number of competing responses will be selected. Highly refined athletic skills emerge from crude general behaviors. Large, cumbersome printing by the first-grader develops into the stylized script-writing of the adult. Thinking processes are comprised of a number of choice points generally encountered in developing a theme. A number of interpretations and ideas are available at each choice point. Some of these interpretations are instrumental to the achievement of pupil goals as they are related to motives. Other of the competing responses will be irrelevant and remain unreinforced. The probability of reoccurrence of those interpretations leading to favorable consequences will be increased on future occasions. The probability of reoccurrence of those responses not reinforced will be decreased. Thus, the selecting function of motives helps to make behavior more efficient and precise.

The pupil's hierarchy of motives

A description of motivation by Maslow (1954) is helpful in understanding the variety of pupil motives, their emergence, and their interrelationships. Figure 7-2 presents a diagram of this system.

Figure 7-2. A pictorial representation of Maslow's "hierarchy of needs." As those needs at the bottom are satisfied, the ones above become proportionately more important.

The reader will notice that the diagram represents a hierarchy—the motives are shown in ascending order of emergence. Those at the bottom are of initial importance.

One should avoid the impression that there is an absolute hierarchy that applies to all pupils. An individual does not necessarily have to gain *complete* satisfaction of the motive at one level before going on to another. Maslow's hierarchy is a kind of ideal representation of the way motives emerge. Generally speaking, as gratification at one level occurs, the next level or levels become proportionately more important.

The levels in this hierarchy are highly interrelated. Activity at any one may influence needs at another level (Maslow, 1962). If the pupil lacks affection, for example, he may find that overeating is an alternative satisfaction. If status and achievement motives are not sufficiently gratified or if they are threatened, this may interfere with the digestive process.

If the functions of his motives are not understood, it is possible to work against the pupil's best interest in attempting to motivate him. Affection may be withheld by purposely rejecting the pupil or by threatening his attainment of prestige by assigning impossible tasks to accomplish. Among the outcomes of rejection will be frustration (with consequent hostility) and feelings of insecurity. Remarks such as, "The other pupils won't like you if you don't stop annoying the class," or "Your brother John can do these problems. Why can't you?" may have similar negative effects. Comments threatening loss of affection and invidious comparisons with others may lead to feelings of inferiority and to lowered levels of aspiration. By temporarily suppressing undesirable behavior these actions and comments may seem to have a positive effect on learning, discipline, and other behavior. The invariable result, however, is to threaten the pupil and increase his anxiety.

Since anxiety may itself be considered a motive (Mowrer, 1960a, 1960b; Spence, 1964) that demands satisfaction, the potential for needless conflict is apparent.* Whatever behaviors are instrumental in reducing anxiety will provide positive reinforcement. Such responses are often antagonistic to those necessary for effective learning. They include hostility toward the person responsible for the anxiety, physical withdrawal from the situation, and psychological withdrawal in the form of lack of involvement and the like. Consequently, any appearance of anxiety symptoms on future occasions is likely to produce a repetition of behaviors that results in reduction of the unpleasant state but which also conflicts with achievement.

Acquired goal preferences

The pupil's needs become increasingly stable and fixed, but individual preferences for rewards are continually changing. New ones are sought and old ones are neglected. Rewards vary in importance according to their perceived value. Pupil preferences for previously desirable goals may be altered when new ones are found to be more satisfying. Some individuals prefer certain colors in clothing, even colors that are distinctly distasteful to others. Success in dramatics may lead the individual to undertake highly ambitious roles. Thus, it appears that an

---

*Anxiety commonly refers to a vague feeling of subjective apprehension or fear that a desired goal will not be reached, often without knowing the source of the fear (English & English, 1958). However, for scientific purposes anxiety is considered a construct which is defined partially by operational definitions and by relationships among them. For an intensive treatment of this and other aspects of anxiety see Levitt (1967).

individual's hierarchy of acquired goals is influenced by the same principles that affect all learning.

These observations help to explain why children's motives are usually so variable in the different social classes (Riessman, 1962). For example, Howard L. comes from an average middle class home. He is encouraged to achieve good grades in school. "A"s on his report card bring praise from his peers and his parents. Because of his scholastic success he is permitted to engage in many extracurricular activities. He belongs to the editorial staff of the school newspaper. He is permitted entrance into club membership and school fraternities which put an emphasis on scholastic achievement. Howard is like many other pupils from the middle class. These privileges are evidence of success. The academic grades can be "exchanged" for many other rewards. Like other middle class pupils, he learns a socially adaptive fear of receiving poor grades in school, of being aggressive toward the teacher, and of fighting—or of any activity likely to jeopardize his status as a superior scholar.

Peter S., on the other hand, comes from a socially and economically disadvantaged home. When he brings his report card home, little if any attention is paid to it. He may even sign it himself. His parents rarely attend school functions or PTA meetings. If *anyone* notices that he received a good grade, it may only serve as a social stigma, particularly to his crowd or gang. Time spent in studying interferes with other neighborhood activities. In fact, it takes him from activities common to the rest of his peer group. The "A" grade has little value as social currency in this setting. In general, schools are not attuned to the experiences and problems of the underprivileged: the content of Peter's books is oriented toward the middle class. He is deficient concerning "school procedures." It is not surprising that school rewards do very little for such pupils. Like other children in the lower class, Peter learns from his gang to fear the consequences of quite different social acts than does the middle class pupil. He quickly learns from his neighborhood gang that to study homework is a disgrace. He conceals good marks. He likes to be considered a good street fighter. While the culture of the school is essentially a feminine one, his values are largely masculine. They run counter to the "eager-beaver," conformist, nonaggressive, and "make-believe" world of the book he reads in school (Riessman, 1962). Because of this discrepancy between the goals of the lower class pupils and of the school, children such as Peter often give the impression that they lack ability to achieve. Their lack of academic success can often be attributed to the fact that the teacher, either coming from the middle class or aspiring to that class, emphasizes goals and rewards important in the middle class and of less or of no importance in the lower class culture.

Acquisition of preferences by association with rewards

Preferences for many previously neutral objects are acquired, or learned, by association with rewards (Nunnally, Duchnowski, & Parker, 1965). Consequently, it is to be expected that goal preferences will change with changes in reward value. Thus, children entering adolescence are often less responsive to a pat on the head from the teacher, or other forms of adult approval, than they are to approval from their peers. For many, preference for the athlete's "letter" replaces preference for the "gold star" for academic excellence. Schroder (1956) assumed that the preference value of an object was related to the probability that it would be followed by a reinforcement. His hypothesis was examined experimentally with elementary school children. They were first asked to rank, in desirability, 20 trinkets, of the sort that can be made into a bracelet, and a cardboard square (or token). They always ranked the token at the bottom of the series for it had no real value to them. Then they were told that the token could be dropped into the slot of a machine to "buy" trinkets. The trinkets received in exchange for the tokens were always the highly valued ones. The children had either 8 or 16 trials. One group had 16 trials in which to exchange the token for a trinket but received a reward on only 8 of the trials. A second group had 8 trials and 8 rewards. The third group had 16 trials and 16 rewards. Then the objects and the token were ranked once again. The token was now found to have significantly more reinforcement value for the children in the second and third groups than for children in the first group. In the second stage of the study the preference value for the token was extinguished, i.e., the token was used in the machine but it no longer yielded a trinket. The extinction process was continued until the token returned to its original value, i.e., the last on the scale. Under these circumstances the first group maintained their preference for the token for about 40 trials whereas the second and third groups lost their preference in about 12 extinction trials.

In summary, since the children learned that the token could be exchanged for other reinforcers, it is said to have acquired reinforcing properties. The token continues to have high preference value provided it is followed by reinforcement and the preference value is maintained more effectively by schedules of partial reinforcement than by continuous reinforcement.

Thus teachers and parents alike can have enduring influences on the pupil's preferences by providing occasional association of such events as the assignment of grades, with praise or opportunities for peer approval. That such results do occur as a consequence of periodic associations of secondary reinforcers with primary reinforcement can be illustrated by the durability of the value of school grades. Students place much emphasis on these signs of achievement through high

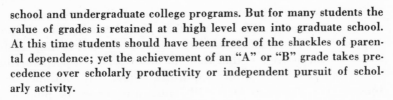

school and undergraduate college programs. But for many students the value of grades is retained at a high level even into graduate school. At this time students should have been freed of the shackles of parental dependence; yet the achievement of an "A" or "B" grade takes precedence over scholarly productivity or independent pursuit of scholarly activity.

The functional autonomy of motives

Many drives and goal preferences are learned. For example, the color white produces a fear drive in a rat after he has been shocked in a white box (Miller, 1948b). Chimps and children learn to work for tokens which can be traded for food (raisins or candy). After a period of time white color will lose its motivating and fear effects if it is never again accompanied by shock. Tokens will eventually lose their goal value if they cannot be traded for food. Sometimes several or even hundreds of trials are required before a given stimulus will no longer cause fear or serve as a reward, but extinction always occurs if the reinforcing consequences are removed.

Some human motives do not, however, disappear so surely under nonreinforcing conditions. They seem to become independent of the primary drives or rewards responsible for their development in the first place. They come to serve as ends, or goals, in themselves. They appear to be transformations of what at first were activities instrumental to achieving satisfaction of other motives; they were extrinsic but are now intrinsic; they were in the service of a drive or simple need but now serve the self-ideal. Allport (1961, pp. 226–251) called this phenomenon *functional autonomy*. Others have spoken of acquired drives and rewards (Dollard & Miller, 1950) or equivalence beliefs (Tolman, 1949a). The functional autonomy of motives is illustrated in the following examples: The human miser hoards money as a goal in itself, sometimes even hoarding it to the neglect of using it for its original instrumental purpose of buying the necessities of life. The skilled craftsman perceives exact workmanship as an end in itself. The boy who had to work endless hours to help provide for his family continues to do so in his adult years when it is no longer necessary for him to work any more than regular hours.

A critic (Bertocci, 1940) of this view suggests that functional autonomy is not a simple matter of extending the persistence of a simple physiological motive, but that certain forms of behavior become associated with many unfulfilled motives during years of experience. As a result, where the behavior of working long hours was initially associated with a basic hunger drive, it also becomes associated with many other incomplete gratifications such as social status, affiliation, and financial independence. Accordingly, it can be elicited by so many different motives in as many different occasions that the behavior only seems to be functionally autonomous. Nevertheless, the interesting feature of some human motives is that they do seem to be self-perpetuating. The needs and goals that pupils acquire in school will continue long after they are out of school. They will continue to direct the pupil's activity into, and through, the adult years. As the teacher encourages the pupil to think creatively, the pupil is learning more of its advantages. Pupils who are actively engaged in hobbies learn the many ramifications and satisfactions of the hobby. Good work habits are found by the pupil in school to bring favorable results in many endeavors outside school hours. As each little trick of skill and application to the task is used more frequently and is extended in breadth, the activity is elaborated from a simple to a more complex one. Consequently, more and more ways develop in which the activity satisfies a pupil's needs. The teacher will find it worthwhile, in efforts to provide for the acquisition of desirable motives, to include activities similar to those described in the pupil's everyday classroom experiences.

Functional autonomy—routes or goals?

In one of his later writings, Tolman (1951) questioned whether functionally autonomous goals for acquired needs are really final goals; or merely routes, means, or subgoals connected by beliefs to basic goals. This challenge of traditional beliefs should aid the reader to distinguish among the variables involved in the analysis of alternative possibilities.

Thus, a given object such as the attainment of a college degree might be . . .

A. a final goal to satisfy a related functionally autonomous acquired need, aroused by deprivation. Accordingly, academic success symbolized by the possession of a degree is direct gratification of a functionally autonomous need for academic success;

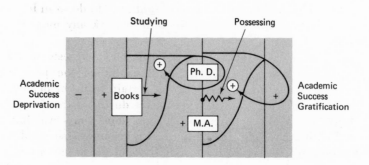

B. a route believed by the student to be required for the satisfaction of physiological needs. Accordingly, the college degree may not be a functionally autonomous goal but merely a means to an end;

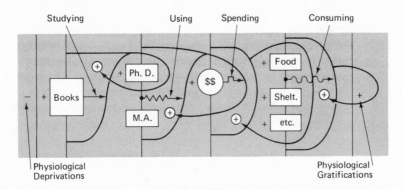

C. or a means to the satisfaction of the needs for affection and approval (this position is the one preferred by Tolman). Thus, the final goal objects are the approval responses of a model with whom one identifies, the imaged approval responses of an ideal composed from many identification figures, or the approval responses of the person as he judges himself against an ideal.

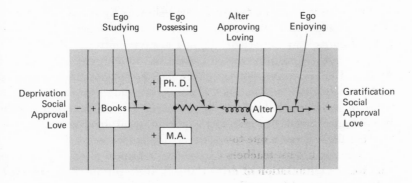

The three alternative explanations of motivated behavior represent many of the relationships among needs, beliefs about means to goals (behavior routes), and goals or purposes. Each alternative shows a basis for associating activities with needs or goals, and with other activities. However, rather than three alternative explanations of the same motivated person, the above descriptions probably represent the motivations of persons at different levels of "motivational maturity." Thus, the least mature person works for a degree only to obtain the diploma which he considers to be a passport enabling him to compete for a "better paying" position. With this goal attained he will be able to purchase the necessities of life, and, perhaps, some of the luxuries. The intermediate level represents a person who seeks a degree to prepare himself intellectually but primarily to please or to win the approval of important figures in his life who have convinced him that "it is a good thing to do." Finally, the most mature student, for whom academic success is a functionally autonomous need, works and studies to attain intellectual achievements independently and free of the influence of tangentially relevant factors. (Figures for this section are reprinted by permission of the publishers from Talcott Parsons & Edward A. Shils (Eds.). *Toward a General Theory of Action.* Cambridge, Mass.: Harvard University Press, Copyright 1951, 1962, by the President and Fellows of Harvard College.)

Exploratory and Cognitive Motives

As previously noted, several classes of motives have been identified by psychologists. Physiological drives serve behaviors that are instrumental in maintaining consistent internal balances in blood-sugar, water, temperature, and oxygen levels. The process is called *homeostasis.* Imbalance in these products causes the organism to engage in behavior leading to appropriate goal-objects for restoration of stability. But not all states of physiological disequilibrium are of motivational importance and their effects as drives are inconsistent. It is true that a thirsty organism can be taught a new behavior by rewarding it with the water it seeks. On the other hand, certain other deficiencies (for example, vitamins and minerals) do not always motivate the organism to search for their fulfillment. Nor does the human eat only when he is hungry. Under severe deprivation he may no longer suffer hunger pangs and, consequently, will not eat. Conversely, some persons will eat quantities of food much beyond the point of normal satiation. Although physiological needs are related to psychological drive states, it is apparent that there is not a one-to-one correspondence.

Nevertheless, teachers do not depend upon physiological deprivation for the stimulation of drive states in their pupils. It is expected that school will provide pupils with adequate light, comfortable temperatures, quiet surroundings in which to study, and adequate nourishment, though often they do not. Accordingly, we shall turn our attention to intrinsic sources of motivation more relevant to teaching in today's schools.

All who have observed children at play have noted that they often engage in highly repetitive activities without immediately apparent sources of motivation. A preadolescent will become excited at the opportunity to explore the unique surroundings of a long-vacant and run-down house. A child who seems to have little interest in academic school work may spend long hours at hand crafts. Even adults can be observed spending valuable time at relatively trivial activities like solving brain-teasers, and crossword puzzles. Although extrinsic sources of motivation, such as the motive for social approbation by peers or adults, can be considered as potential motivators in each of these examples, very often such behavior is stimulated by a class of intrinsic and, in some instances, innate motives.

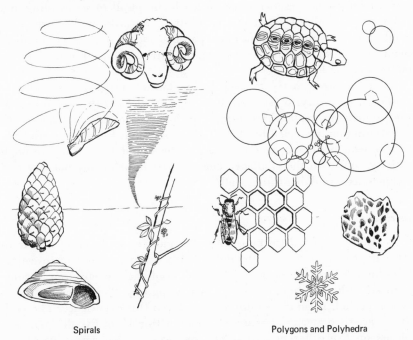

Spirals   Polygons and Polyhedra

Figure 7-3. Capitalizing on pupil interests in mathematics. The recognition of the many novel geometrical forms found in nature has been used effectively by some teachers to arouse the curiosity motive in their pupils.

Activity, exploration, and manipulation

Some of the initial research on intrinsic motives was conducted with monkeys by Harlow and his colleagues (Butler, 1953). Their investigations determined that a monkey would learn to work a mechanical puzzle in the absence of primary motives. The only apparent reward was the opportunity to perform the task. As is true for physiological drive states, the exploration motive may be satiated when the organism performs the same activity for too long a period.

To determine further the autonomy of the manipulation motive food was added as a reward. The task was not learned any faster as a consequence of this change. Instead, the food reoriented the general behavior of the animal. The intrinsic appeal of manipulation as a motive succumbed to that of using the manipulatory skills for getting the food.

At the human level, the exploration motive is more apparent in children than in adults (Murray, 1964). Perhaps this is because the eagerness of young children to manipulate objects and to be active gets directed into other channels by the time they become adults. Traditional educational practice tends to teach the pupil to see reading and other school activities as a means to attain rewards in the form of a good grade or approval from one's parents, rather than as accomplishment for its own sake. In the process, the intrinsic appeal of the subject matter may be lost.

If we were to try to prevent the loss of intrinsic motivation it would be necessary to associate learning situations with such things as the excitement created by continually changing learning settings, with the stimulation provided by the intellectual search for unique solutions to problems, with the energy release to be found in learning through activity, and with the challenge encountered in achieving mastery and competence—in doing things well.

Curiosity

Closely related to the exploration motive (and perhaps basic to it) is the curiosity motive. Mendel's (1962) study is typical of investigations in this area of research. He had kindergarten children become familiar with a group of eight toys by playing with them during a habituation period. A control group was not given this experience. The children were then given opportunity to play with each of five different sets placed on five different tables. The sets were varied according to the number of toys used in the familiarization period. The number of familiar toys were 0 (none the same as those used in the habituation period), 2, 4, 6, or 8 (all the same as in the original), depending on the set. The preferences of children in the experimental group were directly related to the number of novel stimuli. On the other hand, the children in the control group showed no significant preference for any one set.

Curiosity motivation clearly can be observed in primates and in humans at all age levels (Berlyne, 1951; Cantor & Cantor, 1964). Novelty appears to be important but motion, conflict (for example, a picture of a bird with four legs), change in color, and change in design are also important elements in arousing curiosity in experimental settings and are worthy of consideration by the teacher attempting to utilize this motive. Perhaps it is sufficient to remember at this point only that such motives *can* be aroused.

The continual use of novelty eventually fails to sustain curiosity and its value tends to wear off. This is called *habituation*. If the stimu-

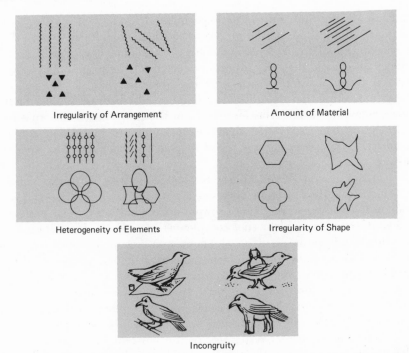

Figure 7-4. *Some stimulus materials employed in studies of arousal and curiosity. Exploratory behavior is oriented toward stimuli that have such characteristics as novelty, surprisingness, complexity, incongruity, and ambiguity. (From D. E. Berlyne & P. McDonnell, 1965, p. 156. With permission of authors and publisher.)*

lus is not presented for awhile, *recovery*, a reinstatement of the ability of the stimulus to arouse curiosity, occurs (Berlyne, 1957).

Epistemic curiosity

Our discussion of the curiosity motive thus far has emphasized the importance of *perceptual* curiosity elicited by novel stimuli. However, of equal importance in school learning is *epistemic* curiosity (which comes from the Greek word *episteme*, meaning knowledge—thus, curiosity about knowledge) elicited when a question arises that demands an answer. Berlyne (1960) demonstrated how epistemic curiosity may be intensified by methods that have implications for teaching practice. An experimental group was administered (1) a preexperimental test of questions about invertebrate animals, each having two alternatives between which a choice had to be made; (2) a list of informational statements concerning invertebrate animals that included correct answers to all questions on the preexperimental test; (3) a posttest consisting of all questions on the pretest but without the alternatives so that the answers had to be constructed by the student. The control group underwent exactly the same procedure except for the pretest. The experimental group achieved significantly higher scores than did the control group suggesting that the initial test heightened curiosity thereby facilitating retention of the facts learned from the information list. In addition, the evidence suggested that the questionnaire intensified general curiosity about invertebrates as well as curiosity about the specific answers.

Mittman and Terrell (1964) conducted another clever experiment to demonstrate the epistemic curiosity motive in children. First- and second-grade children were given a simple discrimination task to perform. A 50-dot drawing problem (not completed) of either a dog standing on its hind legs begging or of an elephant standing on its hind legs and wearing a hat was placed on a music stand near the child. The child was permitted to draw one line (connect two dots) after each correct response on the discrimination task. In the high-arousal (also called high-conflict) groups, the child was given the completed drawing by the experimenter after 29 correct responses, and in the moderate-arousal condition, after 8 correct responses. In the low-arousal group the completed drawing was given the child immediately after the initial instructions and before the discrimination task was begun so that there was no waiting (hence no conflict) for this group. The low-arousal group made significantly more errors than either of the other two groups. An interesting sidelight in this study was that a number of subjects in the high-curiosity group commented favorably about the task and were disappointed when it was finished. The low-arousal group thought the task was difficult and seemed relieved at its conclusion.

The arousal of epistemic curiosity has important implications for teachers at all grade levels from kindergarten to college. It can be accomplished by questioning, allowing students to anticipate outcomes of an experiment, or other techniques that raise intrinsic interest by questions beginning with "Why . . . ?"

Cognitive dissonance

There are many interesting experiments described by Festinger (1961, 1964) to suggest the conditions under which cognitions can have motivational effects.* His experiments indicate that under some circum-

---

*The ideas involved in the theory and research related to cognitive dissonance are intuitively appealing and cleverly analytic as are the experiments themselves. However, at least one article (Chapanis & Chapanis, 1964) has been written to challenge, on the basis of methodological flaws, many of the conclusions drawn.

Figure 7-5. As a consequence of making a difficult decision involving equally attractive alternatives some dissonance will exist and the person will attempt to reduce it. He can convince himself that the characteristics of the rejected alternative are less attractive than he initially believed or that the unattractive features of the chosen alternative are not really unattractive. Or as a consequence of making a difficult decision, he can exaggerate the attractive features of the chosen alternative and the unattractive features of the rejected alternative to reduce dissonance, and "Those who are highly rewarded for doing something that involves dissonance change their opinion less in the direction of agreeing with what they did than those who are given very little reward. . . . The critical factor here is that the reward is being used to induce a behavior that is dissonant with private opinion." (From Cognitive dissonance, *L. Festinger. Copyright © 1962 by Scientific American, Inc. All rights reserved.)*

stances the information a person receives may conflict with what he already knows or believes. When this *cognitive dissonance* occurs, the person tries to reduce the discrepancy, typically through changes in beliefs and attitudes. Conversely, the person will avoid information that increases dissonance. For example, in one study high school students were told that they were to hear an assembly speaker talk about a topic important to teenagers (e.g., voting, intermural football, or driving), who would be taking a stand in opposition to the general student view. This group was unaffected by the speech; they probably didn't listen to it or listened only to the positive arguments. Had they listened to the speech, dissonance (i.e., the discrepancy between their position and the speaker's) would have been increased, not reduced. Another group was uninformed about the lecture content and was told only to attend carefully. The attitudes of this group, who did not anticipate the content of the speech, *were* changed.

In another study high school girls were asked to prepare for an examination by studying a list of arbitrary definitions of symbols. Half of the group of girls were told that they could bring the list of symbols to the examination. Preparation for the exam was easy for this group. The remainder were told that they could not bring the list to the examination and therefore would have to memorize it. Preparation was difficult for this group. The students in both groups were also told that only half of the group, already selected in consultation with the teacher, would have to take the test. After a period of time during which the list was studied, the pupils answered a series of questions. Among the questions was an inquiry about whether the pupil felt that she, personally, would actually be among those required to take the test. In general, the subjects who engaged in the difficult preparation felt it was more likely that they would participate in the examination than did the persons in the easy preparation group.

The explanation is clear: If one engages in a task involving a great deal of effort it must be for a good reason, for a worthwhile goal. It must be in preparation, in this case, for an event likely to occur. One does not expend effort for no purpose. Conversely, the easy preparation group used little effort so their expectations were relatively uninfluenced.

What a pupil does after a decision, then, is very much affected by his earlier expectation. This principle is often employed in teaching techniques intended to raise issues or distinctions previously unrecognized by the pupil, including the use of such methods as inquiry, discovery, debate, and questioning. Especially relevant is the use of "dithering devices" (Turner, 1966), which are intended to increase the student's uncertainty (Salomon & Sieber, 1969), and thereby motivate him to seek further information. Assume, for example, that students are deliberately presented with an admittedly controversial topic, that of determinism versus free will. The students' expectation is that they will be able to arrive at an acceptable resolution. The discussion during the class period brings out a number of alternative solutions, none of which is completely acceptable or logically inevitable. The resulting situation stimulates the students to review their notes and to seek further information so that participation in the following class period will be more informed and more likely to reach a conclusion. If, on the other hand, the students believed the issue to be insoluble or inexplicable and if the ensuing discussion confirmed their expectation, the dissonance would not be aroused. Hence, they would do little more with the issue once class was dismissed. Thus, it can be seen that the influence of rewards and motives on behavior is capable of being modified considerably by cognitive events.

Competence

Our discussion of the manipulation and curiosity motives calls attention to pupils' needs that are often ignored in the classroom. The motives to be active and to explore enable the pupil to interact with his environment in ways that ultimately enhance learning. White (1959), whose discussion of the competence motive is the basis for this section, indicates that while such activities are often playful and pleasurable, they are also directed toward an increase in competence. Children often prefer to spend more time at difficult than at very easy tasks. Once the difficult tasks are mastered, there remains the challenge of still more complex ones (Walker, 1964).

These experiences teach the person how to control many features of the environment. This results in the acquisition of new knowledge. Unlike the traditional assumptions regarding drive, the motivation of these activities does not seem to come from biological imbalance or tension reduction and does not seem to require a tangible reward. Rather such activities appear to involve satisfactions derived from increased competence or effectiveness in dealing with the environment. Thus, the term *effectance* is used to label this class of motives.

These theories should not be interpreted as meaning that traditional approaches related to physiological motives are unimportant, or that they should be replaced entirely by conceptions of intrinsic motivation. Rather, they suggest that much of the child's behavior is aroused by those very motives with which the school is primarily concerned. To illustrate, one of the authors of this textbook observed a young child in the second grade on his own accord bringing pictures of the moons of other planets for the rest of the class to see. Voluntary activity of this sort is common in the early grades. Children are inquisitive. They want to participate and explore. However, in this case, the teacher abruptly informed the child that the class was studying the earth's moon and that the pictures were not relevant to the class discussion. As a result, one can imagine that the child's voluntary contributions on subsequent occasions would be effectively discouraged. Such negative practices are most prevalent in formal education where teacher-directed classrooms are the rule. There are also the practices of dogmatic insistence on quiet classrooms, rigid adherence to a prescribed curriculum, or extreme emphasis on grades and other extrinsic incentives and failure to allow for individual initiative. Such inflexibility can only stifle, at a very early school age, the very motives that teachers later find absent in their pupils.

Socially-Oriented Motives

The intrinsic motives discussed above are individualistic and relatively independent of an orientation to other people. Another class of motives involves abstract or concrete relationships between the individual and all others in his social environment. While more than 20 social motives have been identified and defined (Murray, 1938), we shall concentrate our discussion on the two that have been the subject thus far of the majority of investigations in human motivation.

Murray's list of needs

Murray's description of a theoretical analysis leading to the conceptualization of need and to a taxonomy of human needs was presented in detail in his *Explorations in Personality* (1938). An important assumption was that a state of need can be inferred from behaviors and accompanying expressions of affect, particularly of satisfaction when desired results are obtained or of disappointment when they are not. From Murray's basic list of 20 human needs, some that are relevant to understanding the pupil's (and teacher's) behavior are listed and briefly described below.

n *Achievement*   This is a need to organize objects, people, events, or ideas in such a way as to control and master them. It is important that the way of doing this be carried out smoothly, rapidly, independently, and with excellence. The pupil with strong need for achievement wants to accomplish and may try to exceed his own as well as his rival's performance. Self regard is enhanced by successfully using his abilities, especially in difficult tasks.

n *Play*   This is a need to engage in games, parties, sports, and other "fun-activities" for relaxation, diversion, and entertainment.

n *Affiliation*   The need for affiliation leads to behavior reflecting satisfaction through being near and with other people, and through working cooperatively with them, especially with those who are like oneself. The pupil with a strong affiliation need strives to please others, to win friendships, and to remain loyal once friendships are formed.

n *Autonomy*   This is the need to work independently without the constraints of convention or other influences from outside. There is a tendency to avoid activities supervised by a domineering authority. On occasion the pupil with high need for autonomy may appear impulsive, irresponsible, and unconventional.

n Deference The need for deference is reflected in behavior apparently designed to gain admiration and support of an authority, such as a teacher or other "superior"; to follow willingly his example and direction; and to cooperate with him.

n Exhibition The pupil with strong need for exhibition strives to attract attention to himself with exaggerated attempts to excite, entertain, intrigue, or shock others in an effort to make an impression and to make himself seen and heard.

n Order This need is to maintain orderly arrangements and to be well organized, neat, tidy, balanced, and precise.

n Understanding The need for understanding is a cognitive need to inquire, seek answers, speculate, analyze, and to generalize. The pupil with a strong need in this area will have interests in formulating explanations of the phenomena he observes and in obtaining solutions to problems.

(From H. A. Murray, *Explorations in personality*, 1938. New York: Oxford University Press. Summarized in Hall & Lindzey, 1957. With permission of authors and publishers.)

The achievement motive

Measures of the achievement motive (n:Ach) are obtained from the stories a subject tells when shown pictures depicting achievement situations (McClelland, *et al.*, 1953). The statements in the story are scored according to the *stated needs* (for example, "He wants to earn more money."); activity *instrumental* to attaining achievement ("They worked diligently to finish the report."); and the *anticipation of goals* indicative of success ("He is thinking of the day when he will complete college."). The need to succeed or to excel in relation to a high standard of excellence characterizes many individuals in a typical work-oriented culture. The achievement of high standards as a measure of one's competence is especially rewarding to such persons.

The mere possession of a high achievement need (n:Ach) does not automatically guarantee excellence in learning. Most investigations suggest that the need must be aroused by the challenge of an important task, by a task that affords the opportunity to compete with other people, or by setting a standard of excellence.

As one might expect, the motive to achieve is very much related to tasks in school. Individuals characterized by the hope for success are task-oriented and set realistic goals. Indeed, McClelland (1961) theorizes that people with high achievement needs tend to prefer occupations that involve them in large scale business decisions. Thus, the entrepreneur measures his competence by the magnitude of the enterprise he undertakes. Money and profits are sought as marks of achievement and not as goals in themselves. Even in Communist countries where the pursuit of profit is supposedly deprecated, the manager takes pride in the scale of his communal accomplishment.

Fear of failure also promotes achievement. However, anxiety related to the possibility of failure results in erratic behavior directed as much toward avoiding or reducing anxiety as it is to the completion of the task (Cattell, 1966; Spielberger, 1966). Persons with high defensive anxiety may exhibit symptoms of rigidity when stress is high, persisting at insoluble tasks or at trying to solve a problem with ineffectual procedures (Kogan & Wallach, 1964). Some studies have implied that pupils with characteristic traits of defensive anxiety may benefit from structured situations where short-term and intermediate-term objectives are clearly defined, from highly supportive classroom environments where there are opportunities for dependence, and from interactions with teachers and peers where the pupil's sense of accomplishment is bolstered by guidance and feedback at relatively frequent intervals (Grimes & Allinsmith, 1961).

Affiliation

Pupils who are motivated by n:Ach tend to be competitive and businesslike when working at a task. Pupils who are motivated by the affiliation motive, on the other hand, are more concerned with socially-oriented behaviors. Task-orientation is of less concern than the development of friendly and affectionate relationships. Peer and adult approval are most important to them. Activities are directed toward maintaining friendship and avoiding rejection by others. They prefer to work and study with others.

Some of the dynamics involved in affiliation motivation are illuminated in a study by Schachter (1959). The purpose of the study was to determine the conditions under which individuals seek the companionship of others. College girls who reported for a required experiment in an introductory psychology course were confronted by an elaborate electrical apparatus. The experimenter was allegedly a physician who gave them a talk about the need for more information on electric shock. High-anxiety was induced in one group by telling them that severe, painful, but probably harmless, shocks would be administered and that reactions would be recorded. Low-anxiety was induced in a second group by informing them that very mild, harmless shocks would be administered. The subjects were then told there would be a slight delay to get the apparatus ready, and then were given the alternatives of waiting individually in a small comfortable room or in a larger room where they could congregate with others. Their choice was reported on a questionnaire and the experiment was concluded (that is, the shock was never administered).

It was found in this experiment that two thirds of the women in the high-anxiety condition compared to only one third of the women in the low-anxiety condition preferred to wait in a social situation rather than remain isolated. Speculation about these results suggests that "being together" during stress probably gives the anxious person an opportunity to talk out problems and to compare his emotions with others in similar situations. If the other people are perceived to be as anxious as oneself, some relief from an unpleasant affective experience is probably achieved.

Dependence on other people was also found in this study to be related to the ordinal position (order of birth) of the person in the family. The first-born persons desired to be with others when anxious more than did the later-born. Again speculation about the reason for this result suggests that parents tend to encourage the first-born child's dependence on others in his social environment by being more solicitous about him when he is under stress. On the other hand, the later-born is not typically favored with such indulgence. In fact, he may become an object of abuse by older brothers or sisters, thus making him suspicious of the intent of others. Such early experiences with dependence training appear to influence the differential emergence of affiliation and achievement motives.

The interaction between kinds of feedback and motives

Achievement-oriented pupils prefer feedback about their performance on a task; affiliation-oriented pupils are concerned more about their interpersonal relationships. This conclusion has important implications for teaching, and was neatly demonstrated in an experiment by Elizabeth French (1958). Two groups of subjects, one with high achievement needs and another with high affiliation needs were presented a problem-solving task. The task consisted of reconstructing a story from 20 sentences or phrases, each of which was presented on individual cards. The difficult feature of the task was that the problem had to be solved in groups of four, with each individual holding only 5 of the cards. Information was relayed verbally from one individual to the others but the cards could not be shown. On the basis of this communication the story was reconstructed by the subjects.

The experimenter stopped the group at specified intervals to provide them with information about their progress. One half of each group received the *task-oriented* feedback. The subjects were praised for the effectiveness of their methods, for organizing the information, for outlining the theme of the stories, and for identifying the key features of the story and the characters. The information given the remaining groups was *socially oriented*. These groups were praised for cooperation among members, for giving each person a chance, and for avoiding ridicule if an erroneous judgment was made.

The reader can probably predict the results of this experiment by this point: The achievement-oriented groups performed more effectively under task-feedback, while the affiliation-oriented group's performance was significantly better when the feedback has a more social, or benevolent orientation. On the basis of informal observation, it was found that the groups consisting of achievement-oriented people worked more deliberately toward the goal, argued more violently, and were concerned about finishing the task (speed had been indicated as a factor in judging performance). The affiliation-oriented groups were quieter, paid more attention to the other members of the group, and were smoother in their interpersonal relationship.

There is no one generalization about motivation that is applicable to all situations. Performance is dependent upon a consideration of dominant individual motives, arousal of motive states, the characteristics of the task, and the motive emphasized in the situation in which the task is performed. As psychologists gain greater understanding of these variables, making task requirements congruent with motivational dispositions may ultimately be feasible. In the meantime teachers can profit from what is known and be in a better position, through this knowledge, to improvise in those areas where information is scanty or absent.

Setting Motivational Conditions

An important role of goals is their feedback function. Behaviors which lead to desired goals result in satisfaction; such behaviors are maintained and used again in similar future situations. Behavior patterns which do not lead to goal fulfillment are less likely to be used again in the future and are on the way to being *extinguished.*

Without some form of feedback pupils do not learn. Any consequence, whether extrinsic or intrinsic, provides the pupil with knowledge of results thereby enabling him to modify his behavior accordingly. As noted earlier, all consequences do not necessarily involve material rewards. Merely being able to compare one's answer with a correct answer provides sufficient feedback for the motivating effects of knowledge of results.

The teacher plays an important role in the reinforcement of a pupil's behavior. When the pupil makes responses, the teacher must recognize the incorrect ones and provide the learner with feedback as to why undesirable consequences were attained. When correct responses are made the teacher should also administer praise or other rewards.

The teacher must also be continually alert in his (or her) reinforcing role to see that what he regards as rewards are consistent with

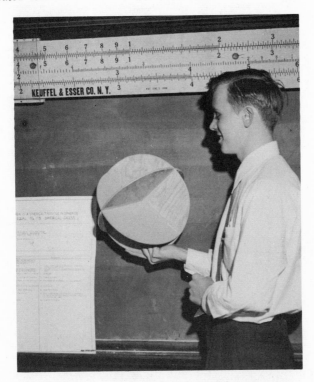

Figure 7-6. This pupil is obviously pleased with his project. What influence will this satisfaction have on his future endeavors in mathematics? (Bloom from Monkmeyer.)

what the pupil perceives as desirable consequences. Failure to do this is well illustrated in one junior high school teacher's experience. He believed that good work should be rewarded by having the pupil sit in front of the room. When one of the boys in the class had earned this "honor" he was given a seat directly in front of the teacher's desk. Almost immediately this pupil's performance slumped. It was not long before the teacher recognized his mistake. Sitting in front of the room made the pupil conspicuous to all of the class and the focus of both friendly and unfriendly jeers from the other pupils. The consequences were anything but rewarding. Such errors in the teacher's perceptions may result because he is using standards appropriate perhaps to himself, or to adults, or maybe to only one of the sexes, or to a particular social class.

Incentive and performance

An important theoretical question in psychology is whether incentive motivation affects learning or performance. Perhaps the ques-

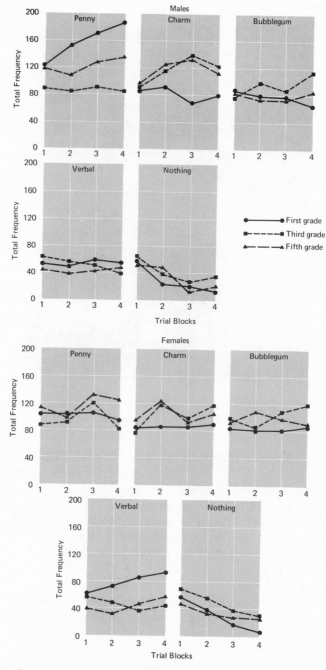

Figure 7-7. Incentive-choice frequencies measured in a discrimination-learning task. In general, material incentives were chosen more frequently followed by verbal incentives, with "nothing" last. (From Witryol, Tyrrell, & Lowden, 1965, p. 216. With permission of authors and publisher.)

tion is of academic interest only. From a practical standpoint any variable that increases the activity of the pupil will also allow the ensuing behavior to be modified through both associative and rewarding processes. While there is still uncertainty concerning the relationship of motivation to learning, as contrasted with performance, evidence from several studies appears important to such an understanding.

The findings strongly suggest that incentives have powerful effects on the utilization of responses. While learning requires some reward, it is possible that only very minimal amounts are necessary. Thus, we often hear the comment that pupils do not demonstrate all they *really know* by their test performance. Perhaps the reason is that they have not been provided sufficient incentive to do so!

As one might expect, the kind of incentive makes a difference in the pupil's motivation as shown in Figure 7-7. Zigler and Kanzer (1962) found differences in the effectiveness of verbal praise ("good" or "fine") compared to verbal indicators of correctness ("correct" or "right") when used with middle and lower class children. As subtle as these distinctions appear to be, they apparently do make a difference in the performance of children in the two groups, as shown in Figure 7-8. Praise reinforcers were more effective for improving performance than "correct" reinforcers for lower class children, while the opposite was the case for the middle class children. Presumably, the use of the "correct" reinforcer is the more abstract of the two. Since lower class children may be at "lower" developmental levels, as far as the school is concerned, they are

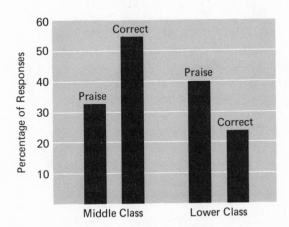

Figure 7-8. "Praise" reinforcers are more effective for lower than for middle class children and, conversely, "correct" reinforcers are more effective for middle than for lower class children. (Based on the findings of Zigler & Kanzer, 1962. With permission of authors and publisher.)

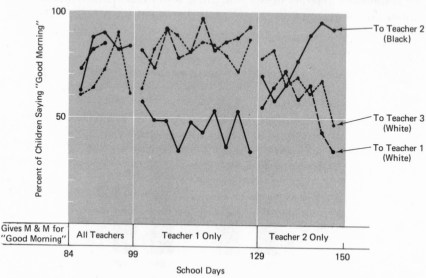

Figure 7-9. Tangible rewards are more powerful than friendly approval. Children greet the teacher who distributes the M & M candies more often than they greet teachers who provided social approval. (Risley, 1968, Vol. 1, No. 8, p. 30. From Psychology Today *magazine. With permission of author and publisher.)*

influenced to a greater degree by the concrete reinforcers. (Nevertheless, the ten-year-old child in the slum leads a much more independent life than do many sheltered middle class children and, accordingly, is much more "advanced" in other ways.)

For the teacher of lower class children such results may imply the periodic use of tangible or concrete rewards for strengthening desirable behavior (see Figure 7-9.) More importantly, however, they imply the wide range of potential reinforcers that must be recognized by the teacher and show that he must be aware of the way different reinforcing stimuli affect the behaviors of different pupils (Baer & Wolf, 1968).

Anxiety and emotion

At the turn of the century Yerkes and Dodson (1908), and, more recently, Broadhurst (1957) demonstrated that the most effective learning situation was not one with maximum motivation. There is some optimal level of motivation, between the maximum and the minimum, most suited to problems of varying difficulty. As the complexity of problems increases, the optimal level is lower (See Figure 7-10). The optimal level of motivation thus is dependent upon the difficulty of the task.

An early experiment by Patrick (1934), using college students as subjects, showed that during intense motivation the range of the subjects' use of rational responses was severely limited. Adaptive behaviors, characteristic of mild motivational states, were replaced by primitive, stereotyped behaviors under intense emotional states. When the individual is optimally motivated, he is more aware of the many cues in his environment. To the extent that some of these are "correct," they can then be used in the solution to problems. The narrower range of cues available to the intensely motivated individual affords less opportunity for the "correct" ones to be identified, thereby seriously impairing adaptive behavior.

In this regard, Tolman (1958) and Biggs (1968) have made the distinction of "broad cognitive maps" to describe the more adaptive behaviors found under optimal motivation and "narrow cognitive maps" to describe the more restrictive behaviors found under intense motivational states. The efficiency of learning very simple tasks is responsive to high levels of motivation. On the other hand, this is the very condition that restricts breadth of learning—that is, how much the individual can learn over and above the immediate demands of the task (Bruner, Matter, & Papanek, 1955).

The counterpart to high motivation induced by stress in the laboratory, is the anxiety provided by extreme competition or other social

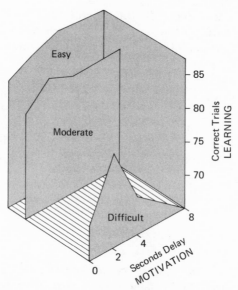

Figure 7-10. A graphic illustration of the Yerkes-Dodson principle. Maximum performance under high motivation is achieved with the easiest task. However, the best performance of difficult tasks is achieved at lower intensities of motivation. (From P. L. Broadhurst, 1957, Figure 2, p. 348. With permission of author and the American Psychological Association.)

conditions in the classroom. The research finding in studies of school learning are not always as clear cut as those from the laboratory, because of the greater number of variables left uncontrolled, but similarities in outcomes can be observed. The efficiency of college students with low test-anxiety was found to be higher in laboratory work than that of students with high test-anxiety (Sarason, Mandler, & Craighill, 1952). The performance of children in the elementary school with low test-anxiety was found to be better than that of children with high test-anxiety on several measures (Sarason *et al.*, 1960). Unfortunately, the anxiety of the high-anxious pupil is compounded further through exhortations that include references to his inadequacy by parents and teachers. These practices undoubtedly increase those interfering responses characteristic of anxiety states. The cold, demanding, deprecating behavior of the instruction-centered teacher provides little encouragement to such pupils. Highly anxious children benefit considerably from the learner-centered and supportive teacher whose criticism is directed toward corrective and constructive measures rather than toward pointing out the personal inadequacy of the pupil (Flanders, 1951).

Measures of anxiety

Some typical items from Taylor's *Manifest Anxiety Scale*—MAS (1953)* are presented below with answers indicative of anxiety:

> I cannot keep my mind on one thing. (Yes)
> I practically never blush. (No)
> I sweat very easily even on cool days. (Yes)
> I do not have as many fears as my friends. (No)
> I certainly feel useless at times. (Yes)
> I am very confident of myself. (No)

This scale was originally developed for studies in which anxiety was conceptualized as a drive state or as emotional arousal. In summation with other drives, anxiety was assumed to multiply the strengths of existing habits. Thus, persons with high anxiety should perform better than those with low anxiety where their dominant responses are correct for the demands of the situation. The reverse would be true where their dominant responses are inappropriate for the situational demands.

Another position is typified by research with the *Test Anxiety Questionnaire for Children* (TASC) and *General Anxiety Scale for Children* (GASC) developed by Sarason and his colleagues (1960). A sample of items from the TASC are as follows:

Do you worry when the teacher says that she is going to ask questions to find how much you know?

Do you sometimes dream at night that you are in school and cannot answer the teacher's questions?

When the teacher is teaching you about arithmetic, do you feel that other children in the class understand her better than you?

Are you afraid of school tests?

While you are taking a test do you usually think you are doing poorly?

When the teacher asks you to write on the blackboard in front of the class, does the hand you write with sometimes shake a little?

Do you think you worry more about school than the other children do?

The format of the GASC is similar as shown in these items:

Do you sometimes worry about whether other children are better looking than you are?

Do some of the stories on radio or television scare you?

Are you afraid of things like snakes?

Do you worry that you might get hurt in some accident?

Do you think you worry more than other boys and girls?

Do you worry when you are home alone at night?

Do you get scared when you have to go into a dark room?

*Items are from J. A. Taylor, 1953. With permission of authors and American Psychological Association.

A "yes" answer to an item in either form of the test contributes to the total score.

The Sarason scales employ the orientation that anxiety acts as a stimulus to elicit responses compatible or incompatible with the task at hand. Which responses are elicited depends upon the person's history with anxiety situations. From this frame of reference it is important to know in what specific situations anxiety is aroused, and the kind of responses elicited in those situations. An example of a compatible (task-centered) response is one in which the person has learned to be extremely careful in problem situations if he is to arrive at a correct answer. An incompatible response tends to be self-centered, is irrelevant to the task, and consists of such behaviors as feelings of inadequacy, hostility, dependency, and self-derogation. The scores from the TASC and the GASC are moderately correlated, being about .65 for boys and .55 for girls. Children with high scores (high-anxious) on either of these tests tend to perform more poorly on typical school tasks than do children with low scores (low-anxious).

The relation between anxiety level (as measured by the MAS) and achievement is illustrated further for different levels of scholastic aptitude in Figure 7-11. There it can be seen that for all but

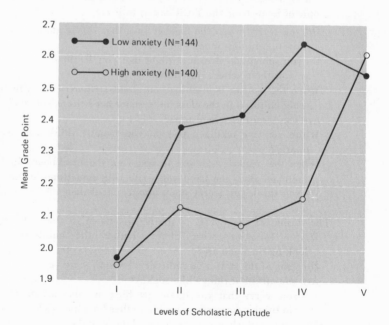

Figure 7-11. Mean grade point averages for high and low anxiety college students at five levels of scholastic aptitude (intelligence). (From C. A. Spielberger, in Mental Hygiene, *1962, Figure 1, p. 423. With permission of author and publisher.)*

the very lowest and very highest levels of aptitude (intelligence)
the low-anxious college student outperforms the high-anxious college student. It can be assumed that persons at the highest level of
intelligence find the work easy; they learn the academically correct
responses and their responses are likely to suffer less from the effects
of misinterpretation than are the responses of persons with lower aptitude. Drive theory would predict that high anxiety would further
enhance the performance of these persons (Spielberger, 1966). This
hypothesis is supported by the crossover of the two curves at Level V
in Figure 7-11.

Success and failure in the classroom

One of the most common ways of providing rewards and punishments in the classroom is through teacher praise, or its opposite, a symbolic "spanking" by reproof. What is the effect of such induced conditions on the performance of pupils in the classroom? Van De Riet
(1964) compared the effects of verbal reinforcers on the performance of
underachieving and normal achieving boys in grades 4, 5, and 6. The
mean Stanford-Binet IQs for all groups ranged from 100.6 to 109.9.
Accordingly, the groups could be assumed to have about the same intelligence. The mean achievement scores of the normal achievers were .69
to 1.01 years *above* the norms for their grade level, while the achievement scores of the underachievers were 1.29 to 1.51 years below their
grade level. After learning a paired-associate task one third of the boys
were told nothing about how they had done, another third were praised
("Boy! You really did well. You learned them faster than any other
kids that took the test.") and the final third received reproof ("Well
that's it. You took a lot longer to learn those names than I expected and
I am kind of disappointed. Do you think if we tried another list you
could do better on it?"). The underachievers took fewer numbers of
trials to learn the second task following reproof and more trials following praise compared to the control group that received neither praise or
reproof. The normal achieving group took about the same number of
trials to learn the second task whether they were praised or received
only the instructions. However, they took more trials to learn after they
received reproof.

Pros and cons of punishment

It is unlikely that the teacher or prospective teacher who reads this
will ever use physical punishment in the control of behavior. Because
of the uncertainty of its outcome, punishment cannot be seriously
advocated for modifying pupil responses. Nevertheless, a further

understanding of the dynamics involved in the use of aversive stimuli can be obtained by examining some of the controversies that have arisen over the effects of punishment.

Solomon (1964), for one, challenges some traditional ideas about punishment. Thus, he suggests that punishment may do more than merely suppress a response. Once a behavior pattern has been established through reinforcement or reward, there is an orderly progression of effects related to the intensity of shock used as punishment: (1) With very mild punishment the noxious stimulus acts to *arouse* the organism to relevant cues. It can also act as a cue, an *emphasizer*, as a reinforcer, or as a response intensifier. (2) Slight increases in intensity act to *temporarily suppress* the response which returns completely intact after punishment is withdrawn. (3) Moderate intensity leads to *partial suppression* of the response, that is, although the response returns, part of it remains changed for relatively long periods. (4) Finally, the greatest intensity of electric shock (4 milliamperes) leads to *complete suppression* of the behavior. As one might expect, the stronger the learned response, the more difficult it is to eliminate it. Furthermore, a noxious stimulus including shock with humans when used too frequently can lead to adaptation so that it is no longer effective (e.g., the pupil can soon "shut out" a continually punitive teacher).

What of the alleged emotional side effects? It is true that in some experiments punishment has led to such effects as ulcers, neurotic behavior, and fixation. But these effects do not occur invariably. Why deviant behavior occurs some of the time and not at other times remains unclear. However, Solomon speculates that abnormal side effects result when the organism is unable to discriminate the circumstances under which punishment is administered. These effects are not obtained (with rats, at least) when a clear signal is given to indicate when a response will or will not be punished. Thus, clear rewarded alternatives, in addition to the punished behavior, seem desirable. When these rewarded behaviors are *incompatible* with the punished behavior very reliable results are obtained (for example, a child may be punished for batting a ball *in* the house but rewarded for batting it *outside*).

Solomon's case provides an interesting *challenge* to the earlier ideas that reward is more effective than punishment, that punishment leads to neurotic (or similar) behavior, and that punishment does not weaken a response. However, much further exploration of the subject is needed before precise conditions can be described under which punishment can be used safely, if at all.

How the teacher is to use praise depends to a large extent on the boy's or girl's needs and prior experience (Lindsley, 1964). A study of individual pupils and the events which are most corrective for each is necessary. The spacing or scheduling of rewarding events must also be considered and controlled. Teachers determine the minimum amount of reinforcement or praise needed before work seems to fall off, as well as to notice where added reinforcements yield diminishing returns. They note the effect that public praise or blame of one pupil has on other pupils. They also observe the differential effects of praise and blame on the performance of pupils with different personalities. It is unlikely that praise and blame can be used most effectively without appreciation of all of these factors.

In a review of 33 studies spanning 50 years of research on praise and blame on the performance of school children, Kennedy and Willcutt (1964) contend:

> It now appears that when one corrects for practice, as with the use of a control group, praise is a reasonable stable incentive, from study to study, contributing an incremental effect upon the performance of school children. An exception is the reaction of severe underachievers whom praise inhibits. Van De Riet (1964), in her explanation of these conflicting results, has suggested what is apparently the largest weakness of studies in this area, that thus far there has been very little control of the reinforcement history of the subjects. ... Blame, on the other hand, has fairly consistently exhibited an inhibiting effect upon the performance of school children. Exceptions to this general debilitating effect of blame are underachievers, Negro subjects performing under Negro examiners, and very bright adolescents* (p. 331).

Social reinforcers and performance

Such comments as "Good!" "That's fine!" and "Keep up the good work!" can act as social reinforcers; that is, they can be employed to strengthen or increase performance of the behavior they follow (Zigler & Kanzer, 1962). Initial investigations in this area (for example, a study by Gewirtz & Baer, 1958) have compared the effects of approval on the performance of pupils who were socially satiated or deprived. Social satiation was induced by a brief period of warm and continual interaction with the pupil while deprivation was induced by minimizing conversation or other interaction. Compared to a control group, socially deprived children were found to be more responsive to approval than were the socially satiated children on a simple performance task. Furthermore, socially deprived children are also more responsive to social reinforcers than to signals such as a buzzer or light to indicate the correctness of a response (Dorwart et al., 1965). Who administers the reinforcer is, of course, also important. The parent or adult of the sex opposite to that of the child was found by Stevenson and Allen (1964) to be a more effective reinforcing agent

*From W. A. Kennedy & H. C. Willcutt, 1964. With permission of authors and publisher.

than the parent of the same sex. Patterson and his colleagues (e.g., see Patterson, 1965) demonstrate that responsiveness to social reinforcement by a peer and by parents correlates positively with teacher ratings, although children most responsive to parental verbal disapproval were rated as inefficient workers by their teachers.

Other investigations have extended these general ideas. Rosenhan (1966), for example, assumed that lower class children were more alienated (meaning a lack of relationship with one's environment) than middle class children from the middle class school culture. Accordingly, the lower class child would be expected to be more responsive to approval and disapproval as a result of his or her uncertainty and insecurity in this setting. Children for the study were drawn from the two socioeconomic classes. Each group was comprised of equal numbers of Caucasian and Negro children. The children played a binary-choice game that required them to press one of two buttons. Approval ("Right!") was given 70 percent of the time for pressing the left button and 30 percent of the time for pressing the

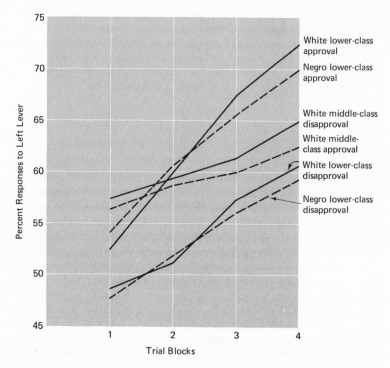

Figure 7-12. Responsiveness of middle and lower class children to approval and disapproval shown by their performance in a simple task. (From D. L. Rosenhan, 1966, 4, Figure 1, p. 255. With permission of author and publisher.)

right button. The ratios were reversed for the disapproval ("Wrong!") condition, i.e., 70 percent of the right and 30 percent of the left button-presses were disapproved. In both conditions, the pressing of the left button can be assumed to be the "correct" response.

The reader can see in Figure 7-12 that the results were as predicted. Social class, regardless of race, was an important variable in determining responsiveness. Approval *elevated* and disapproval *depressed* performance of the lower class children compared to the performance of middle class children on the same task and under the same conditions. This suggests the importance of using approval and of avoiding disapproval in working with lower class children.

Rosenhan suggests several alternative interpretations of his findings, as follows: (1) Alienation leaves the lower class child uncertain of his role in middle class institutions and, accordingly, he is especially sensitive to the reactions of others as an index of how well he is performing. This need not be a detrimental factor if one considers the response approved to be the "correct" response. (2) The middle class child is relatively adapted to verbal persuasions and penalties so is not overly affected by verbal approval or disapproval. The lower class child is subjected more often to physical punishment than to verbal praise and blame by parents and, hence, verbal approval "means more" than it does to the middle class child. The weakness in this interpretation is that if the assumptions about overexposure leading to adaptation or satiation are correct, then the lower class child should be adapted to punishment. As we have seen this is not consistent with the strong effects of disapproval on lower class children. (3) If the alienation assumption is correct, lower class children experience more anxiety in school than do middle class children. Accordingly, anxiety enhances the effects of either approval or disapproval. Middle class children are more secure in this setting and are less affected by verbal or social reinforcers.

Intermittent reinforcement and expectancy

A practical problem arises at this point: Must the teacher provide praise, blame, or some other reinforcing condition after each and every pupil action? The findings of Mech and his associates (1953) are optimistic in this regard. In his study, the cooperating teacher provided approval by walking around the classroom while pupils did problems in arithmetic and pretended to write down the names of the children who were doing good work. Some children were given approval after every set of problems; a second group was given approval spaced on alternate groups of problems (intermittent rewards); and the third group was given no approval. The results indicated that, over a series of problems, pupils improve about equally well whether they are given continued or intermittent rewards. Of added interest is the fact that the group which was not rewarded appeared to benefit by being in the presence of and hearing the approval given the other children. Pupils who hear others being approved work harder than they might if they were alone, because there is the expectation that they too might later be the recipients of the teacher's praise.

Schedules of intermittent reinforcement can be made contingent upon the number of responses, or upon time intervals (Holland & Skinner, 1961). Ratio schedules are based on the number of responses made by the person. They are analogous to piecework where the individual's reward (pay) depends upon output. In the classroom pupils on the *fixed-ratio schedule of reinforcement* might be given a certain number of points for completing a set of 10 problems. Each time they complete a set, they receive some reward (approval, knowledge of results, and so on). The ratio of the number of responses to the opportunities for reward is fixed. On the other hand, the pupil may be given a certain number of points for 10 problems on one occasion, 7 on another, 13 on another, and so on. The number of problems he has to solve in order to qualify for points (reward) varies from one day to the next. The overall average is 10 (or any other number determined by the teacher or experimenter). This is the *variable-ratio schedule of reinforcement.* The fixed-ratio schedule leads to a high rate of performance; the pupil works more since the number of points earned depends on finishing a specified number of problems. Behavior rewarded under the variable-ratio schedule is also emitted at a rapid rate but is also especially resistant to extinction. When reinforcements are withdrawn completely, after experience with these schedules, the behavior persists for long periods.

Interval schedules are controlled according to *time* between reinforcements. The reward for the correct behavior(s) will occur at specified periods of time. If the interval is always the same, it is called a *fixed-interval schedule of reinforcement,* and may be compared with working for a salary. Teachers frequently employ this schedule when they administer examinations periodically (monthly exams, for example). Performance under this schedule is very predictable. In the initial period, work output is low. As one approaches the time for the reward, activity increases at a positively accelerated rate. Once the reward is attained, the performance rate drops significantly. (You may want to compare your friends' study activity immediately *following* the first-quarter examination in a course with their activity the week preceding the second-quarter examination and, again with their activity the week immediately after the second-quarter examination. Parenthetically, your friends' behavior can sometimes be observed more objectively than your own behavior!)

In some interval schedules, the time between reinforcements is varied. Teachers, for example, may give "unannounced" quizzes. The time between quizzes may vary from a day to a few weeks or more. This is called a *variable-interval schedule of reinforcement*. It generates durable and persistent behavior patterns. If the quizzes are important to the pupil, study activity is likely to remain at a consistently higher level than it would if he knew in advance that an examination would be administered once every two weeks on a certain day. Of course this example is used for illustrative purposes only. The use of interval schedules as a technique to automatically control study behavior is not implied. As with the application of all principles, several factors should be considered. In this instance, the teacher would want to consider whether unannounced quizzes might raise anxiety and thereby produce detrimental effects on the performance of some pupils.

Behavior established under either ratio or interval schedules is enduring for extended periods and can be supported by a minimum of additional reinforcements. Only few reinforcements are necessary, under these schedules, to produce a large number of responses and even when extinguished the behavior may be brought back to full strength by only a single reinforcement. By gradually increasing the fixed-ratio schedule to a ratio of 900 responses to 1 reinforcement some laboratory experiments have produced continuous behavior for many hours in infrahuman organisms, notably pigeons.

Most human behavior is reinforced on the variable-ratio or variable-interval schedule. Thus, the teacher, in a good mood, may at one time reinforce mischievous behavior with a smile, but on subsequent occasions attempt to punish the same behavior. After several cycles of such sequences, the pupil's expectancies for eventual reinforcement will be sufficiently established to make the behavior highly resistant to extinction. Some investigators (e.g., Bijou & Baer, 1961) have suggested that the explanation of many enduring personality characteristics may eventually be explained by a knowledge of the individual's past history of variable schedules of reinforcement.

Feedback and correction in teacher-pupil interaction

Aside from the informal hour-to-hour administration of praise or blame, teachers use more formal methods of providing the pupil with knowledge of progress. In this regard, an important study of the effects of teachers' comments when assigning grades was conducted by Page (1958). The participants in the experiment were 74 secondary school teachers and 2,139 pupils. The experiment was conducted in the usual course of teaching. After scoring and grading objective tests in whatever course was being taught, the teachers assigned papers within each grade level to one of three treatment groups at random. The pupils in the *No Comment* group were assigned the earned course grade of A to F with no additional marks or comments. Pupils in the *Free Comment* group were assigned the grade and whatever comment the teacher felt was necessary, or appropriate, on the basis of her knowledge of each pupil and his performance. *The Specified Comment* group received prescribed uniform comments supplied by the experimenter and designed generally to be encouraging. The comments for this group were: A—"Excellent! Keep it up!"; B—"Good work. Keep at it."; C—"Perhaps try to do still better?"; D—"Let's bring this up."; F—"Let's raise this grade." After grading, the papers were returned to the pupils without further attention. Then the teachers recorded performance scores on the next objective test given in the class. The recipients of Free Comments achieved somewhat higher scores on the criterion test than did the pupils receiving the Specified Comments. However, the performance of these two groups did not differ significantly from each other. Both groups performed significantly better than pupils who received No Comments. Comments by teachers thus have a demonstrable effect on the pupil's motivation and work habits. This effect occurred regardless of where the pupil went to school, his year in school, or his ability.

Recitation affords another opportunity for the teacher to administer reinforcements. Typically such interaction involves three steps: a question is raised by the teacher; a response is made by the pupil; and the teacher provides information about the correctness of the response. In an experiment by Van Wagenen and Travers (1963), pupils in a simulated classroom setting learned English equivalents for German words following the three steps in recitation. Over several training sessions those pupils who were reinforced ("That's right") only for correct answers learned more rapidly than if negatively reinforced ("That's wrong") for wrong answers. Telling the pupil only that he is wrong for incorrect answers may be of some help, but it may also act as an emphasizer, thereby increasing the strength of the wrong response for some pupils. Some type of minimum feedback, nevertheless, is essential. Learning is facilitated when the pupil is given information only that he is right and, to a lesser extent, where he is informed only that he is wrong. These experiments also suggest the importance of providing reinforcement with correction (Travers, Van Wagenen, Haygood, & McCormick, 1964). Corrective guidance may consist only of giving the correct answer or it may involve helping the pupil to discover the correct answer himself.

Normally in classroom recitation, not all pupils are active. Some are responding while others are sitting and listening, or perhaps sitting without listening. In the above experiments by Travers *et al.*, only one half of the group actively participated in the interaction with the

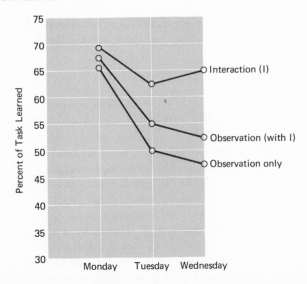

Figure 7-13. Amount of learning is affected by degree of interaction between pupil and teacher. The uppermost curve shows the percentage of items learned with interaction between teacher and pupil; the middle curve shows the percentage of observed items learned by pupils who otherwise interacted with the teacher on other items; the lower curve shows the percentage of items learned by pupils who observed the teacher interacting with other pupils but never with themselves. (From Travers, Van Wagenen, Haygood, & McCormick, 1964, Figure 1, p. 172. With permission of authors and publisher.)

teacher-experimenter; the remaining pupils were merely observers although still a part of the group. The amount of learning was directly related to the degree of participation. Those pupils who only observed performed more poorly than those who more actively participated on one quarter of the items. Pupils who learned three quarters of the items by verbal interaction learned the most. These data suggest the importance of direct interaction and reinforcement. Apparently, pupils do learn when their only participation in the group is that of observer. Nevertheless, they often become bored and easily distracted. Each pupil in the class should be permitted some opportunity to interact. Feedback and correction not only facilitate his learning of the reinforced recitation but also provide sufficient arousal to facilitate his learning of whatever subject matter is being presented when he is merely an observer.

Setting Goal Levels

Capturing the initial interest of the pupil and finding ways to stimulate him to expend more effort in his work are not the only prob-

lems in motivation. Conscientious teachers of course want their pupils
to be challenged, to progress beyond their present levels of achievement.

Level of aspiration

What pupils expect or hope to do in the future is an indication of
their *level of aspiration* and will play a significant role in any activity
where the pupil's subjective evaluations of success are important. A
level of aspiration is fundamentally a working goal. This concept may
be simply illustrated by the pupil who receives a grade of "C" and is satisfied with making a grade of "C" on his next exam, whereas another
pupil with a grade of "C" will be satisfied only with a grade of "B" on
his next exam. He has a higher level of aspiration.

Level of aspiration is closely related to a boy's or girl's self-
esteem (Sears & Sherman, 1964). If there is a discrepancy between his
feelings of what "he is" and what "he would like to be," he may
modify his goals, strive harder, or may simply give up. Ordinarily, level
of aspiration involves some elements of self-competition and is marked
by attempts to "do better" in order to maintain status and to be satisfied
with oneself.

Goals valued by a pupil are those which *he* has successfully
reached in the past. The result is that what is a good performance as
seen by the pupil may be a mediocre performance as perceived by the
teacher. In general, successful performance increases his level of aspiration and unsuccessful performance lowers it. However, this statement
must be qualified to the extent that pupils who are always successful
may develop an expectation of failure more quickly, after single failures, than those whose experiences of successes are mixed with those of
failure. The findings from a number of studies indicate that "changes in
the level of aspiration are (a) adaptively functional—they tend to keep
goals consistent with reality, (b) highly dependent upon recent and/or
similar experiences, and (c) generally dependent upon cultural background, long-run achievement, history and social forces" (Starbuck,
1963, p. 56).

Locus of control and level of aspiration

Related to the pupil's level of aspiration are his expectancies
regarding locus of control with its two aspects of internal and external
control (Rotter, 1966; Lefcourt, 1966). *Internal control* is illustrated
when a pupil perceives that the consequences of an event are due to his
own actions and therefore are under his personal influence. *External
control* is illustrated by the conviction that events are due to more
adventitious circumstances, to powerful forces beyond one's control,

rather than to one's own behavior. Internal control is correlated in positive fashion to higher mental age and to the ability to defer gratification.

Those pupils who believe in strong external control have difficulty in arriving at a stable level of aspiration. They vacillate in estimates of their performance depending on the situation. They tend to raise their expectancies after failure and lower them after success in keeping with the perception that it is the external situation that affects their performance rather than their own abilities. These results are consistent with the findings of Hess and Shipman (1965) that the status-oriented (external) control attitudes are related to lower socioeconomic status where, for example, the mother answers the child's requests with "shut up," "get out," and, in answer to "Why?" arbitrarily replies, "Because I said so." Conversely, the person-oriented (internal control) way of looking at things is related to middle socioeconomic status and to elaborated maternal codes where reasons are clearly differentiated, unique feelings are considered, and a given behavior pattern is justified on the basis of a person's feelings, his relationships with others, the consequences of behavior, and the like.

In our culture a premium is placed on setting goals somewhat ahead of our present achievements. Pupils who believe they can succeed within reasonable limits are in a much better position to learn than those who must protect themselves from failure by setting goals which are too low. Pupils who feel defeated or accept the *status quo* when they are capable of improvement make little progress.

Nor is it desirable for pupils to work toward unattainable goals, for then goal-setting approaches fantasy and unreality. Realistic goals are those one is capable of attaining, at least partially, while unrealistically high goals are certain to result in failure and defeat. Helping pupils to aspire toward reasonable and realistic achievements is an important part of the teacher's task, not only to further the learning process but to help the pupil meet the other basic realities of life.

Achievement motives and the selection of goals

The choice of a task or goal, in formulations by Rotter (1960) and by Atkinson and his associates (Atkinson, 1965; Atkinson & Litwin, 1960), is said to be a multiplicative function of the individual's motives, expectancy of goal attainment, and incentive value of the goal. According to this assertion, if one is to understand a pupil's interest and performance in a given task he must first ask, "Is the pupil's dominant motivational tendency to achieve success or to avoid failure?" The success motive is reflected in high scores on n:Ach measures and "fear of failure" is measured in terms of high Test Anxiety (Mandler & Sarason,

1952) scores. Secondly, one must ask, "Is the task likely to be considered easy or difficult by the pupil?" Expectancy for success-oriented pupils is described in terms of the pupil's belief that he is likely to be successful at the task (high if the task is easy, and low if it is difficult); for failure-oriented pupils, it is the likelihood that he will *fail* at the task (low if the task is easy and high if it is difficult). Thirdly, one asks, "What is the attractiveness of success at this task relative to other tasks?"

Isaacson (1964) made an interesting application of this formulation to the curricular choices of two groups of college seniors who had been identified during their freshman year as success- (achievement) oriented and failure-oriented. He reasoned that the curricular choices of *success-oriented* (high need for achievement) seniors would be made as shown in the upper part of Table 7-1. By multiplying the estimated

Table 7-1. Why students set different levels of aspiration: The probability of taking three kinds of curricula by success-oriented and failure-avoidant students.

Selection of Goals by Success-Oriented Students: Challenging goals, capable of being reached, are selected by those with a high n:Ach; extremes are avoided.

The curriculum is perceived as:	Probability of *Success* (P_s)	Success Incentive (I_p) *	Motive for success high, rated:		Success motivation for taking program:
A. Very difficult	.2	.8	1	=	.16
B. Moderate difficulty	.5	.5	1	=	.25
C. Very easy	.8	.2	1	=	.16

Selection of Goals by Failure-Avoidant Students: Those students with a need to avoid failure tend to select the extreme goals; their behavior is more variable than that of students with high n:Ach.

The curriculum is perceived as:	Probability of Failure (P_f)	Incentive (I_f) **	Motive for failure avoidance high, rated:		Failure-avoidant motivation for taking program:
A. Very difficult	.8	.2	−1	=	−.16
B. Moderate difficulty	.5	.5	−1	=	−.25
C. Very easy	.2	.8	−1	=	−.16

$*I_p = 1.00 - P_s$
$**I_f = -P_s$

probability of success, success incentive, and relative motive for success in each row, the overall probability (shown in the fourth column) for taking the program is obtained. On the basis of these results it is apparent that the pupil with high n:Ach should be motivated to select a program of intermediate difficulty (Program B)—that is, the program yielding the highest resultant success motivation. These students are predicted to select curricula which are neither too easy nor too difficult. The selection of goals by the failure-avoidant persons (with high need to avoid failure) was predicted, by similar reasoning, to occur as shown in the lower part of Table 7-1. Thus, they would be expected to select a program that was very difficult or very easy rather than the one of moderate difficulty. The analysis of the actual curricular choices made by college men in the study provided support for these predictions.

A number of other investigations have supported this formulation regarding the interaction of motives and expectancy on choice of goals (Atkinson, 1965). Experiments with children and adults alike, in tasks varying from dart-throwing contests to choice of academic curricula, continually demonstrate the same selective tendencies of the two groups. The success-oriented pupil desires tasks that provide challenge and that are realistically within his capacities. Accordingly, he selects the moderately difficult task. The failure-avoidant pupil, threatened with the fear of failure, selects the extreme risks. For him, failure in the goal with low-risk is remote. On the other hand, failure in the goal with high-risk assures him of the solicitude of others since "many others may also fail at such difficult tasks." The behavior of the more uncertain and unconfident pupil characterized by fear of failure is more variable than that of the achievement oriented pupil.

Patterning the curriculum to meet pupil needs*

There was a time in the history of education when pupil motivation was given little, if any, attention. Pupils were forced to master what the adults said they should. As a rule, difficult material, whether in English, arithmetic, history, or some other subject-matter area, was prescribed. Whether or not these materials had anything to do with pupil needs was judged to be of little importance. The requirement was that the pupil "get" them one way or another. But learning under these circumstances did not come easily and the teacher found that he had to resort to many harsh disciplinary procedures including the birch rod, dunce cap, and the ruler for a "knuckle rapper."

In reaction against this trend there followed a period in which the educator thought the pupil's happiness and satisfaction was all that mattered. The emphasis was on helping him meet his immediate needs. In its most *exaggerated* form, this program called for a very permissive or even a *laissez-faire* classroom atmosphere. This was the era of the "children-what-would-you-like-to-do-today" method of teaching. (The

*This topic is based on an article by H. F. Wright, "How the psychology of motivation is related to curriculum development." *Journal of Educational Psychology*, 1948, *39*, 149-156. From the AMS reprint, with permission of author and publisher.

reader should not conclude that this was the typical philosophy of all schools at that time, however.) On superficial glance, this seemed like a good idea. It would seem, indeed, that pupils who did what they wanted to do would be motivated. It seemed as though pupils who worked in this fashion would learn what the adults thought they should know in order to get along in a society. Looking more deeply into this philosophy, however, it was soon recognized that pupils, even though propelled to work, were often left rudderless. Pupils who are "free" in only a physical sense are not without restraints especially when they do not know what to do or where they are going when they do begin to work.

There is an important distinction to be made here between long- and short-range goals. Since the former are remote, they are usually much less meaningful to the pupil. The latter are accessible and hence more attractive. However, the reaching of immediate goals often culminates in the achievement of the long-range goals. They are the paths leading to the desired end, to become an educated man or woman. If we find that a particular pupil has needs for status and prestige, and that going to college is a way in which he can satisfy these needs, it is not sufficient to suggest that he should work to go to college and let it go at that. Certainly a goal has been established, but being so remote it alone may result in nothing more than a fantasy for him. He will need help in deciding on an appropriate preparatory curriculum, in evaluating his competence for college work, in making application for entrance at some college, and in making arrangements for financing his college career. If this is done, his activity will have direction. Each course completed, each grade received, and the money earned from his newspaper route will constitute intermediate goals that provide direction to his activity.

The distinction between long-range goals and intermediate goals is useful in even the shorter classroom units. For example, a pupil is left in the mechanical arts class with the project of building a bookcase. Certainly this is an important goal-project and one which can satisfy many needs, like achievement, and peer or adult approval. However, he makes his way to this goal by a path leading through several subgoals which involve the making of plans, determining the amount of lumber needed, computing the cost, saving the pieces, assembling and finishing the whole. The pupil under these circumstances knows what is ahead of him, knows where he is going, and is in a good position to get things done if he knows both the long-range goals and the subgoals.

Classroom planning between pupils and teacher provides an excellent medium for identifying and clarifying these goals. The making of an assignment does not end in merely setting a number of pages to be read before the next class meeting. The boy whose father is in the Air Force, or the pupil who has an interest in airplanes or the design of new cars finds that an important need can be satisfied by learning Newton's laws of motion. The pupil who lives in an overcrowded community, one in which new industries are rapidly growing or one in which a new thruway is being built, has a latent need for studying community planning. Motives can now be tailored to suit the teacher's objectives as well as those of the pupils.

Some mention should also be made of the symbolic rewards. Gold stars, honors, grades, diplomas are all incentives that define goals for pupils. If they are successful directors of performance, as they frequently are, it is probably because they relate back to the satisfaction of some important motive. Used merely as superficial incentives, they may not meet the criteria for optimal motivation. On the other hand, if they are used as signs of accomplishment with guidance as to how work can be improved, such extrinsic rewards can be used to good advantage.

The successful use of motivation in the classroom can be summarized as follows: First, important needs of pupils must be identified by the teacher. They must be aroused by careful classroom planning. Long-range and short-range goals must be clearly defined, and geared to the classroom work so that they are capable of being achieved by pupils. There is no reasonable argument for a rigid classroom structure where pupils are implored or forced to work under inflexible requirements or standards. On the other hand, one cannot defend a curriculum that is without challenge. A reasonable middle-ground approach provides every child with the opportunity to work toward constructive goals commensurate with his abilities and interests.

Summary

Motivation is cyclic. A motive arouses activity and directs it toward a relevant goal. The attainment of an acceptable goal is associated with satisfaction. Then other motives become dominant, or, after a period the same motive arouses activity again, and the cycle continues. Motives energize or arouse behavior; they also provide cues that direct behavior toward goals likely to be appropriate; and through selective reinforcement they further determine which of a number of competing responses will be sustained.

Motives are hierarchically organized. At the most primitive level are the physiological needs, followed by physical security, affection, self-esteem and independence, prestige, and at the most mature level, self-actualization. The more mature motives are dominant forces in the pupil's behavior to the extent that those below them are satisfied. Teachers must be aware of the possibility that the pupil's attempts to satisfy any of the motives may conflict with classroom learning unless their function is recognized.

Goal preferences for the satisfaction of motives can be acquired through association with other preferred goals, through association with rewards, or through imitation. These same processes are responsible for the different valuation of goals among social classes and among different cultures. One characteristic of acquired human goal preferences is that behavior, at first instrumental to the achievement of basic goals, may itself become a long-lasting goal. The concepts of functional autonomy, equivalence beliefs, acquired rewards, or secondary rewards encompass this phenomenon of the transformation of goals.

Much of human behavior is activated by the intrinsic motives, the very motives with which teachers are most concerned, and which provide a substantial portion of motivation to be found in the class-room. Pupils have a need to be active, to explore different opportunities, and to manipulate ideas and events (the manipulation motive). They want to try new activities and their attention is captured by the novel and the surprising situation (the curiosity motive). There is evidence that curiosity about ideas and knowledge can be a very important motive (epistemic curiosity). A postdecisional discrepancy between two cognitions (cognitive dissonance) is a homeostatic-like mechanism which requires that the conflict be removed through the resolution of ideas in order to achieve cognitive balance. White (1959) suggests that much exploration, and engagement in otherwise playful and pleasurable activity, is motivated by the challenge of the task and the attainment of mastery (i.e., satisfaction of an effectance or competence motive.)

Similar to the intrinsic motives are the achievement and affili-ation motives. Both involve relationships with persons, real or imagined. At least one aspect of the achievement motive involves challenge to the person through competition with others. The components of the achievement motive are the hope for success and the fear of failure. The affiliation motive, as the name implies, is reflected in a need to interact with others. Pupils with strong affiliation motives are responsive to socially oriented teaching practices while those with strong achievement motives respond to task-oriented teaching practices.

Some form of informational feedback is essential for efficient learning and continued performance of learned behaviors, whether the consequence is tangible (e.g., a marble or a gold star), symbolic (e.g., a letter grade or phrase), or appraising (e.g., comparison of one's per-formance against an ideal). The magnitude of incentives, whatever their type, is related to performance; increase the value of the incentive and performance level increases, decrease the incentive-value and perform-ance drops off. Incentives such as verbal praise are more effective than abstract indicators of correctness for lower class children while the opposite is true for the middle class children. Children below the fifth-grade level appear to be more responsive to material incentives than to verbal incentives.

A high level of motivation facilitates performance on easy tasks, on tasks where the correct response is well defined, and on well-learned tasks, but hinders performance on difficult tasks, on complex tasks, or on tasks where one or more incorrect responses compete with the correct response.

Stress often results in primitive stereotyped behavior rather than thoughtful, rational behavior. The effects of punishment under typical classroom situations is difficult to predict. Sometimes mild punishment may act as an emphasizer actually increasing resort to the punished response. Stronger punishment may temporarily suppress a response. Traumatic punishment may eliminate responses for extensive periods of time, if not permanently.

In addition to the unpredictability of its effects, punishment also has the disadvantages of its strong emotional concomitants. The consequent noxious stimulation may become associated with other environmental events. Eventually they, too, may become aversive stimuli. Nonadaptive responses are best eliminated by extinction.

The differential maintenance of a learned form of behavior or cognition is accomplished by variations of the ratio or interval schedules of reinforcement. Continuous reinforcement schedules are more effective than intermittent schedules for initial learning, but behaviors maintained under continuous reinforcement are less resistant to extinction processes.

Feedback involving only evaluation is not as effective as when combined with encouraging and corrective comments. There is evidence, too, that feedback provided in teacher-pupil interaction favorably affects not only those directly involved but also those pupils who were, at some time, spectators of the interaction and sharing in the teacher's verbal correction. Pupils who only observe without any direct interaction with the teacher benefit least of all from teacher-pupil interaction involving other pupils.

Level of aspiration refers to either what the pupil expects or hopes to achieve from one attempt at a task to the next. Generally, level of aspiration increases after success and decreases after failure experiences. Pupils who are externally oriented, who believe that events are controlled by circumstances other than their own behavior tend to have a less stable level of aspiration than those whose locus of control is internal.

The selection of goals is influenced by achievement motivation. If the pupil is success-oriented (high need for achievement) he will tend to select goals of moderate difficulty rather than very easy or very difficult ones. If he is failure-avoidant (high need to avoid failure), he will tend to select very difficult or very easy goals rather than those of moderate difficulty.

Teachers can capitalize on motive-goal relationships by helping pupils define the kinds of goals they can and wish to achieve within the society. Classroom experiences can be tailored to meet both short- and long-range objectives. Often neglected in teachers' planning are the many intrinsic pupil motives that can be best satisfied through cognitive activities.

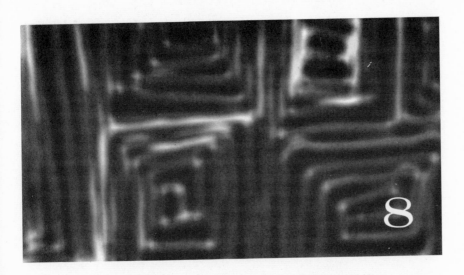

Understanding, identifying, and influencing the motivational antecedents of learning experiences

Man tries to improve his lot by conquest over natural phenomena and by amelioration of inadequate natural and social conditions wherever they may exist. Consider Jane Addams' community projects in slum areas, efforts that initiated the socialwork movement; or Einstein's conquests in unveiling the secrets of the atom; or George Washington Carver's promise of opportunity for the blacks and his contributions to science and education from which all mankind has benefited; or Albert Schweitzer's pioneer efforts to introduce medical care into Central Africa. The annals of history are full of the accounts of great men and women who have been unwilling to accept evil and ignorance in their many forms—bigotry and prejudice, disease and poverty.

It is not to be expected, of course, that many pupils will ever reach such lofty goals. Few have the necessary talents, ambition, and perseverance. To the guidance counselor it may sometimes seem that all pupils want to be eminent doctors, statesmen, or scientists. In some cases these aims are realistic. In many others, they are but ways of testing reality. The individual's goals provide him with objectives toward which he can work and strive, hopefully with spontaneity and enthusiasm. Without definite goals a pupil's behavior is likely to lack the direction required for scholastic success. Furthermore, his goals must be realistic if his potentialities are to be realized, and if the opportunities afforded him are to be effectively exploited.

197

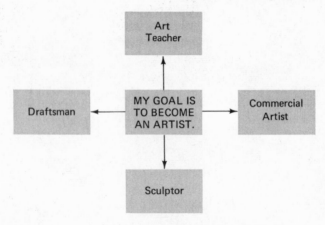

*Figure 8-1. There are many paths to goals. If commensurate with his oppor-
tunity and ability, each may be satisfying to the pupil's aspirations.*

Our aim in this chapter is to point out that the teacher can adopt
a positive approach to the encouragement of striving. When the pupil
is oriented toward achievement as a way of expressing himself, as a way
of contributing to the welfare of others, and as a way of promoting his
own growth, his striving brings with it feelings of self-esteem, a sense of
kinship with others, and an integration with social reality (Maslow,
1956).

Immediate and Long-Range Goals

It is easy to see that pupils' goals are personal, and they must be
recognized as such by the teacher. From a motivational standpoint,
everything that the pupil views as contributing to his major objectives
will be of interest and will be pursued diligently. If a course or activity
has no such meaning then there will be resignation to the extent that he
will do only that which is necessary "to get by" or "to meet requirements." With well-defined goals the pupil can pace his own progress.
When there is commitment to a goal and an opportunity to judge performance against that goal, the pupil's performance will be facilitated
(Kausler, 1959). Threats to achievement-related goals arouse greater
physiological stress reaction in pupils with strong achievement motives
than in persons with strong affiliation motives, while pupils oriented
toward affiliation are more disturbed by threats to affiliation than to
achievement (Vogel, Raymond, & Lazarus, 1959. See Figure 8-2.) Significantly, from a mental-health standpoint, goals provide direction to
the pupil's behavior and provide him with guides for action.

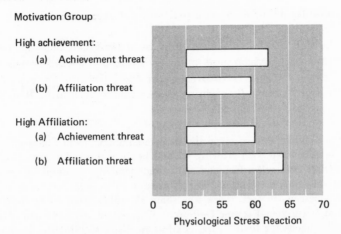

Motivation Group

High achievement:
  (a) Achievement threat
  (b) Affiliation threat

High Affiliation:
  (a) Achievement threat
  (b) Affiliation threat

          0   50   55   60   65   70
              Physiological Stress Reaction

Figure 8-2. Physiological arousal in high school boys as it is related to intrinsic motives and two different threats. Motivation was measured by behavioral and self-report measures. Achievement threat was induced by telling the subjects that the task was a test of capacity for successful academic and occupational achievement. Affiliation threat was induced by instructions that emphasized capacities for warm relations with others. (W. Vogel, S. Raymond, & R. S. Lazarus, 1959, p. 230; and R. S. Lazarus, 1966, Figure 8, p. 122. With permission of authors and publisher.)

In general, a pupil does not have just a single goal toward which he works. Rather there are many which function to influence his behavior. There are the vocational, the social, and the broad ideological goals, all of which can be pursued concomitantly. Each of these invariably has some influence on the others. Favorable evaluations of one's success in performing the tasks instrumental to the achievement of these goals is an important aspect of self-esteem (Sears & Sherman, 1964).

The Nature of Adaptive Striving

Psychological adjustment is a dynamic process. It requires continual striving toward goals and adaptation to a changing physical and social environment (Smith, Bruner, & White, 1956). Most striving is *constructive*. The pupil who tries to reach his goals is constantly learning. New responses are acquired. His activities are directed toward those objectives that will enhance his well-being. But striving can also be defensive. As a compensatory mechanism it can be a protection against events that produce anxiety. Aiming for higher goals helps to make up for some real or imagined deficiency in ability, capacity, or other aspects of one's personality. Striving in these circumstances means that one continually achieves by competition, not only with others, but with oneself (Symonds, 1951).

The delicate balance that must be maintained between personal motives and the environment and the interplay between constructive and defensive striving is illustrated in the following excerpt from a sketch of John Chatwell, a young man studied by Smith, Bruner, and White.

The strivings that received the strongest impetus from Chatwell's parents were those associated with growing up and being mature. The pressure was in the direction of self-sufficiency and independent accomplishment, with emphasis also on investigation and discussion. The values of gregariousness were less stressed; in fact, there was some shielding from early contact with children of lower social status. Definitely discouraged were the dependent tendencies: the needs for loving care, comfort in distress, guidance, help in overcoming anxieties. These remained as residual tensions in a personality organized along lines of independent achievement.

The predominant pattern of strivings received further significant shaping as Chatwell tried out his capacities and skills and learned the channels that would lead him to satisfaction. One of the channels he entered was football, but his light weight and fear of injury prevented this from being a real source of gratification. Another channel was argument, and here the gratification was so high that the love of argument became one of the strongest driving forces in his personality. The assertiveness that could not succeed in athletic channels found in discussion and debate an admirable route toward its goals. In a sophomore story-completion Chatwell symbolized this phase of his own development. Given the plot that a football player was not equalling his famous father on the gridiron, Chatwell had the boy realize that he would never be a good player, but then come to feel that the whole sport was organized wrong; so he suddenly threw himself wholeheartedly into modifying the system, and found that he had just the qualifications for doing this successfully! Politics, persuasion, and human management increasingly appealed to him. In such a role Chatwell won his school success; for the lack of it he was at loose ends in college; resuming it again, he achieved success and rapid advancement in military service.*

Socialization and Striving

A study of the mothers of sons oriented toward high achievement and those of sons with low achievement orientation has been made by Winterbottom (1953). He found that the former group of mothers made more demands *and* placed more restrictions on their sons up to the time

*Reprinted with permission from M. B. Smith, J. S. Bruner, & R. W. White. *Opinions and personality.* New York: John Wiley and Sons, Inc., 1956. Pp. 98–99. Chatwell's autobiography is also described at length and analyzed in terms of vocational choice and adjustment in Tiedeman (1963).

the children were seven years of age than did the mothers of the latter group. After age eight the reverse became true. Thus, the ages between six and ten are critical ones for the development of the achievement motive (Sontag & Kagan, 1963). The distinction between the two groups of mothers rests almost entirely on differences in independence training.

Another pair of investigators (Rosen & D'Andrade, 1959) have found that, in addition to encouragement for independence, some with high need for achievement are likely to come from families where parents set higher standards of excellence. Both parents tend to be warmer and more encouraging and the father tends to be less directive than are the parents of boys with low n:Ach. In summary of their results, they say:

It is unlikely that these variables operate separately, but the way in which they interact in the development of achievement motivations is not clear. Possibly the variables interact in a manner which produces cyclical effects roughly approximating the interaction that characterized the experimental task situations of this study. The cycle begins with the parents imposing standards of excellence upon a task and setting a high goal for the boy to achieve (e.g., Ring Toss, estimates and choices in Block Stacking and Patterns). As the boy engages in the task, they reinforce acceptable behavior by expressions of warmth (both parents) or by evidences of disapproval (primarily mother). The boy's performance improves, in part because of previous experience and in part because of the greater concern shown by his parents and expressed through affective reaction to his performance and greater attention to his training. With improved performance, the parents grant the boy greater autonomy and interfere less with his performance (primarily father). Goals are then reset at a higher level and the cycle continues ... (p. 217).*

Expectations of parents in the different socioeconomic classes undoubtedly have their effect on the ultimate values adopted by the child. As shown in Table 8-1 the reports of middle-class parents indicated that they encourage consideration, self-control, and curiosity. The child is expected to act in a responsible manner as a result of his own values, not as a result of conforming to an authority. The working class parent tends to encourage neatness and cleanliness rather than imagination and exploration in the child's behavior. These differences in child-rearing practices are not without effect on the development of achievement motives.

There are innumerable factors in the socialization process, other than parental behavior, which encourage striving. As the child enters school, he is immediately confronted with a system based on the policies of age-grading and promotion. Here he is rewarded for high levels of

*From B. C. Rosen & R. D. D'Andrade, 1959. With permission of authors and publisher.

Table 8-1. Proportion of mothers and fathers in the middle and working socioeconomic classes selecting each characteristic as one of three "most desirable" in a 10- or 11-year-old child.

Characteristic	Percent of Mothers in:		Percent of Fathers in:	
	Middle SES	Working SES	Middle SES	Working SES
That he is:				
Happy	46%	36%	37%	22%
Honest	44	53	52	58
Considerate of others	39	27	35	14
Dependable	24	21	33	08
Able to exert self-control	22	13	20	06
Obedient to parents	20	33	13	39
Well-mannered	19	24	24	25
Curious about things	18	06	02	17
Popular with peers	15	18	15	25
A good student	15	17	07	19
Neat and clean	11	20	15	17
Able to defend self	10	06	02	17
Ambitious	07	13	17	08

SOURCE: Kohn, 1959, Tables 1 and 2. With permission of author and publisher.

aspiration and is penalized if he accepts the status quo and meets only minimal requirements. The same process is at work in his social relations, particularly if he comes from those with middle status in society. Approval is given for moving up the social ladder. He is also taught to be aggressive in socially approved ways, such as by being ambitious and by showing initiative. The kinds of achievement for which reward is expected may vary—promotion in school, moving up to a better position in an occupation, moving upward in social position. Rewards also vary—social approval, status, economic security are all important. Through these socializing experiences the individual becomes committed to goal strivings. As Baldwin (1955) indicates, the pupil adopts the social concepts that goals fall along some kind of a continuum from low to high, that "high" goals are more difficult than "low" ones, and that the more difficult ones represent greater achievement.

Pupils who are not doing their best can seek an appropriate level for their ability when they are provided challenging tasks which can be completed successfully yet efficiently. Eventually, the success experienced will generate an intrinsic motive for achievement in similar kinds of tasks if not a more general motive for achievement.

Identification and Imitation

Many social roles are learned by imitating the behavior of others (Bandura & Walters, 1963). Individuals believed to be successful in some

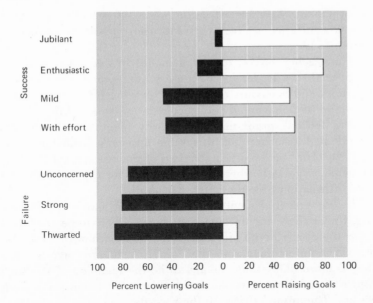

Figure 8-3. The effects of success-failure experiences and associated feelings are reflected in aspirational level. (Adapted from K. Lewin, T. Dembo, L. Festinger, & P. S. Sears. Level of aspiration. In Personality and the behavior disorders, edited by J. McV. Hunt. Vol. I. Copyright 1944 by The Ronald Press Co., New York. P. 338.)

way are selected as models with whom the pupil consciously or unconsciously identifies. They may be athletes, parents, businessmen, teachers, or other highly regarded persons. Through imitation preferred goals and behaviors are selected that the pupil feels promise to help him reach satisfaction. The person imitated often represents an idealized version of the personality he hopes to become like (Bandura, 1965). Some boys or girls decide to become doctors because they identify with their fathers who are doctors. It is not difficult to see why the coach is frequently a popular model for boys in most high schools. When a model is found to have "clay feet" pupils will shift their identification to other models whom they feel are more admirable. Ordinarily, a new model will have unique behaviors in combination with some of the characteristics of previous models.

The teacher as a model

The classroom teacher often becomes a figure with whom the pupil identifies for many different social roles. Every parent of an elementary school child has heard him or her remark, "That's what 'Teach' says!"—and the parent finds himself taking second place to the teacher in the argument. This identification wears off somewhat in the high school years and becomes transferred to peers or some prominent figure in the pupil's life.

The teacher serves, too, as a model in her roles as a subject-matter specialist, a leader in community affairs, or a representative of the attitudes and behaviors expected of an educated person. The pupil may imitate the behavior of the teacher in any one of his or her many roles. The "gifted" pupil may successfully identify with the intellectually talented teacher; but this same teacher's behavior might be entirely out of the realm of the strivings of the average or below-average pupil. Some outgoing teachers provide models for the social strivers but provide little support for the quiet, shy pupil.

In the typical elementary school the staff may be predominantly female. Under these circumstances the boy is likely to be at a disadvantage, for there may be no one other than the coach with whom he can identify. The unfortunate aspects of this situation are magnified because the boy is more likely than the girl to be the recipient of the teacher's disapproval and blame, as shown in Figure 8-4 based on a study by Meyer and Thompson (1956). In their words:

> The teacher who attempts to thwart [aggressive] behavior by means of threats and punishment can only meet with frustration since the boy is confronted with a conflicting social code. A more reasonable plan to follow would seem to be one in which the excess energy and tensions of the male child could be discharged on some constructive activity. . . . Perhaps most important of all, however, is the knowledge that some degree of aggressive behavior is a normal part of the development in both boys and girls and should be treated not as a personal threat to the teacher but as a sign of "normal" social and personality development.*

The teacher's behavior often serves as a standard by which pupils set their goals. His behavior may be imitated if it is perceived as successful for a particular role just as the behavior of *any* other person may be imitated. However, this is not meant to imply, as was once erroneously believed, that the teacher should be an exemplary model of all aspects of personal living. It used to be the case that parents functioning under this assumption frequently tried, to the teacher's great distress, to force him into this uncomfortable and unrealistic pattern. As a consequence of the societal realization that many patterns of living are acceptable, this concept of the teacher's role has all but disappeared.

*W. J. Meyer and G. G. Thompson. Sex differences in the distribution of teacher approval and disapproval among sixth-grade children. *Journal of Educational Psychology*, 1956, 47, 385–396. With permission of authors and Warwick and York, Inc.

Observers' evaluations of recipients of teacher:

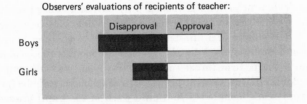

Boys' evaluations of recipients of teacher:

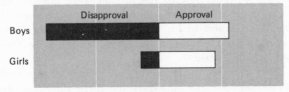

Girls' evaluations of recipients of teacher:

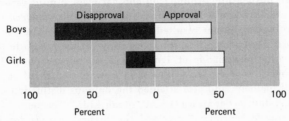

Figure 8-4. Who are the recipients of teacher approval-disapproval evalua-tions? Observers and peers report that boys receive more teacher disapproval than do girls. These negative reinforcements tend to discourage the boys' iden-tification with the school. (Adapted from W. J. Meyer and G. G. Thompson. Sex differences in the distribution of teacher approval and disapproval among sixth-grade children. Journal of Educational Psychology, 1956, 47, 385–396. *With permission of authors and Warwick and York, Inc.)*

Desist techniques and pupil reaction toward the teacher

The teacher who handles the misbehavior of a child by verbal punish-ment, physical restraints, or related ways of indicating disapprobation is often unaware of the influence these procedures have on other pupils who are spectators of the episode. Such control measures are called *desist techniques*. The effects of these procedures on audiences were examined in several contrived, but cleverly realistic classroom experiments by Kounin, Gump, and Ryan (1961) and their students. The typical experiment involved the administration of a questionnaire, the presentation of a lesson, the introduction of deviant behavior by a pretrained pupil who was a confederate of the experimenter, the appli-cation of a desist technique, and, finally, a follow-up questionnaire.

The deviant behavior was managed by having a college student enter a class toward the end of a period or by having a high-school pupil get up in the middle of a filmstrip presentation to sharpen his pencil. The desist technique used by the teacher to handle the problem varied from a sharp, firm threat such as, "Hey you, what do you think you are doing? If you do that again, I'll really make trouble for you! Get in your seat!" coupled with a mild push of the pupil toward his seat; or, a matter-of-fact reprimand such as "Don't do that. Please sit down." Sometimes attitudes toward the teacher were induced by such comments as "Here is a teacher who *likes children* very much;" or, "This teacher is an *expert* in his field. He has worked with codes for the Army intelligence." Some of the questions raised by these investigators are sampled here.

How does relatively intense punishment of a misbehavior affect the audience? One can anticipate the three variations used by these investigators: The teacher in one class severely *threatened* the pupil (even pushed him around), in another class, a mild *verbal reprimand* was employed, and, in the third class the teacher *ignored* the behavior. Punitive techniques resulted in the audience viewing the deviancy as "more" serious and as more interfering with attention to the task than did mild reprimands or ignoring of the misbehavior. The punitive teachers, however, were seen as making too much of an issue over a small incident, and also attained the dubious distinction of being able to maintain order in a class of "tough kids." Teachers who employed the simple reprimand received the highest ratings for fairness and were judged as best able to maintain order in "most" classes. In addition, pupils in these classes reported that they paid more attention to the lesson following the incident than did pupils in the other classes. Ignoring the deviant behavior resulted in the pupils' feeling that the misbehavior would most likely reoccur, but the teachers using this desist technique also received the highest rating for "liking" pupils.

Should desist techniques be approval-oriented or task-oriented? The distinctions here are apparent. An approval-oriented teacher might say, "I see a boy playing with paper clips. I just don't like a person who plays with things when he should be paying attention." On the other hand, a task-oriented teacher might say, "Because the topic we are studying demands concentration, I don't see how anyone can learn much about it when he plays with things instead of paying attention." Compared to one who is oriented toward "liking" or "disliking" pupils, the task-oriented teacher is rated more skillful in handling children, as liking the pupils "more," and as more inclined to reward pupils. In addition, this orientation leads to a higher rating of interest in the subject matter, to a higher rating of the deviant behavior as "serious," and to a decrease in inclinations to misbehave.

Pupil reactions may range from defiance to submissiveness when the teacher employs a desist technique. What effect do these different modes of reaction have on the audience? With a submissive deviant the teacher was rated by the audience as being more capable of handling "kids," more expert in the method of presenting subject matter, and the desist technique (though it was the same for both the "submissive" and the "defiant" deviant) was rated "fairer."

Does like or dislike for a teacher affect the ratings? Whether a teacher is liked or not is apparently a very influential variable in determining how a pupil arrives at an evaluation of the events described. A teacher who is liked tends to be perceived as doing good things and one who is disliked tends to be perceived as doing bad things. Desist techniques of liked teachers tend to be seen as fair, those of disliked as unfair. Those who like the teacher tend to be on his side when he uses punishment, anger, or firmness, while those who dislike the teacher tend to be on the side of the deviant under the same circumstances. The group that liked the teacher tended to judge the handling of the situation, by whatever means, as more fair than did those who disliked the teacher.

In general, and as measured by questionnaires, the observation of another pupil being punished appeared to have little, if any, effect on the motivation of the audience. The primary influence was on their reactions to circumstances surrounding the event, particularly the teacher, the desist technique itself, and the misbehavior.

Models and the media

Through the use of textbooks, story telling, movies, television or any of the other communication media, pupils can be influenced in a significant way by what they see, hear, and read of the great men and women of recorded history, prominent figures of our own day, and of course by the everyday person. A variety of models in the world of ideas is provided the pupil when he learns about men like Newton and Einstein with their systematic, orderly striving and aims; or of men like Ford and Edison with their hard-working, not so systematic, but successfully pragmatic approaches; or of men like Beethoven and Picasso with their creative genius in the fine arts.

In order to produce effects upon the average child the less distinguished person should also be dramatized. Pupils in the ghetto may find it difficult to identify with the various types of personalities described in textbooks. However, they can, and will, identify with the children and adults whom they know in everyday life. The typical occupations and the commonplace roles can be presented as providing opportunities and ways for making a better world for oneself, for one's friends, and for society. For the girls in the classroom there is a need for a departure from the traditional textbook presentation portraying women as sociable, kind, and timid, but lacking the potentiality for great achievement (Child, Potter, & Levine, 1954). A reorientation is required that will help the girl, who in the future may be required to make her own living, to benefit from the same influences as her male peers in the development of motives to work and achieve. The study by Child, Potter, and Levine (1954) leaves little doubt of the influence textbooks have on shaping the motives, strivings and personalities of pupils. But other classroom methods and materials (e.g., curricula) must not be neglected for they too differentiate the roles of the sexes and have the potentiality for shaping the successful citizen. Attention to the implications of these techniques can provide implicit lessons by which pupils can structure their aims and values and by which they can find ways of achieving these ends.

Guiding the Acquisition of Motives

McClelland (1965) has reported the results of a most unique program intended to determine whether groups of business men in India, Mexico, and the United States could profit from a course directed toward the development of the achievement motive (n:Ach). The study is an interesting one for teachers because of several reasons: It was based upon the integration of several theoretical orientations and much experimental evidence from a variety of areas, all of which are related to change in motivations. It was conducted with adults, a group for whom changes in motives were believed to be difficult at best. Finally, it outlined the requirements for methods of developing motives in general, and of the methods used in developing the n:Ach motive in particular. At this writing, it had not been determined whether all of the phases were necessary, or whether only a selected few were important for developing complex motives. The methods used by McClelland are outlined in the following as they would apply to pupils.

Goal setting by the pupil

The pupil should be guided to identify as many reasons as he can why he should develop the motive in question. The more reasons that can be cited, the more likely is the educational attempt to succeed. This step helps to bring the behaviors related to the motive into a dominant position in the habit hierarchy; it presents a concept or image of something the pupil should be, but perhaps is not; and it lessens the defenses against change implicit in such self-verbalizations as, "I've never been good in school, anyway;" "I can't change. Why should I try?" or, "I'm afraid to try this different way of doing what I am supposed to."

Clarify and extend the concept of the motive

The pupil must then perceive some of the realities of the situation and the limitations in developing the motive. Data should be examined from many sources for the purpose of relating the achievement motive specifically to the pupil's academic and vocational endeavors. Any ambiguity in the relationship between the achievement motive and success should be clarified; for example, that n:Ach is related to business success but evidence for its relationship to productivity of researchers is less clear. The course should be presented as a reasonable endeavor within the reality of the pupil's ambitions.

Specific details of the motive must be examined. For example, the business men were taught the coding system used in scoring n:Ach items in stories written to standard sets of pictures by themselves or others. (The scoring procedure was very briefly described in Chapter 7.) To clarify the concept of n:Ach further the business men were taught to write stories loaded with achievement imagery and with references to goals, positive affective components, and to whatever instrumental activity might be indicated as necessary. In addition, stress was laid on how n:Ach was differentiated from other motives such as the need for power or for affiliation.

Translate the verbalizations of the concept into action behaviors

Transfer of a new idea necessitates knowledge of what the motive is, what its consequences are, and what actions are necessary for its implementation. Verbalization alone is insufficient. The pupil at this point can evaluate his activity in n:Ach terms, and whenever he thinks of n:Ach he can think in terms of possible outcomes in action. He can be encouraged to think of the ways in which the development of the motive is consistent with the reality of his own immediate and long-range goals; i.e., to relate it both to reality and to his inclinations. A period of self-confrontation together with honest self-evaluation, through writing of stories about "Who am I?" coupled with counseling would be helpful.

Finally, the new motive must be integrated with the demands and pressures of the larger cultural milieu of which the pupil is a part. Not all cultures are friendly to the development of one or more motives, including the n:Ach. This is true whether one thinks of subcultural groups such as the lower and middle socioeconomic classes or of the distinctions between cultures such as the Mexican, Indian, and English. Conflicts are identified and lessened by role-playing and discussion of values that might be antagonistic to the development of the motive.

Social class segregation and high school boys' aspirations

How are the aspirations of a boy from a working class family affected by attendance at a predominantly middle class school? Conversely, are the aspirations of a boy from a predominantly middle class family more modest as a consequence of attending a school predominantly for working class children? In short, could integration of socioeconomic classes within schools make a difference? These questions were asked by Wilson (1959) about the effects of three different school "atmospheres": (1) Upper white collar—in which 65 percent of the fathers were college graduates, 22 percent were in professional occupations, and 42 percent additional were in white collar jobs; (2) Metropolitan lower white collar—about 35 percent of the fathers had at least some college and a third were in manual occupations; (3) Industrial area schools where only 15 percent of the fathers had any college training, 54 percent had only some high school or less, and 49 percent were in manual occupations.

The effect of the school society on the aspirations of boys who come from families in the different social classes is illustrated in Table 8-2.

Table 8-2. Percentage of boys aspiring to go to college by school groups and fathers' occupations.

Father's Occupation	Kind of School Society		
	Professional	White Collar	Working
Professional	93%	77%	64%
White Collar	79	59	46
Self-Employed	79	66	35
Manual	59	44	33
All occupations	80	57	38

SOURCE: *American Sociological Review*, Wilson, 1959, Table 3. With permission of author and American Sociological Association.

Although there are many factors such as the family that affect occupational decisions, these data show that the school society has a substantial effect. As Wilson (1959, p. 845) indicates, "The Supreme Court has found that, even though the "tangible" provisions of the schools are the same, schools segregated along racial lines are inherently unequal. The 'sense of inferiority affects the motivation of the child to learn.' The *de facto* segregation brought about by concentration of social classes in cities results in schools with unequal . . . climates which likewise affect the motivation of the child, not necessarily by inculating a sense of inferiority, but rather by providing a different ethos in which to perceive values." More than a decade later these ideas are being implemented in many ways, the most unique of which is community control of the schools. What pupils may need to learn most of all is the process of *valuing*.

Set personal goals and keep a record of progress toward reaching them

Once the motive and its consequences are thoroughly understood and integrated with larger units of the personality, the individual is guided to set goals for himself. He is thus committed to an immediate and long-range plan. The plan also provides a basis for the simultaneous provision of feedback. Some record of progress, or basis for judging progress, is particularly important, especially in the development of a motive with the characteristics of n:Ach. Furthermore, progress does not occur instantaneously in this or any other learning. A record helps to maintain the saliency of the motive for longer periods of time.

Provide emotionally supportive teachers as models and a friendly reference group

Learning a motive seems to occur best when the teacher is able to provide a model of that motive in his own behavior. At the same time he should be capable of warm and empathic interaction with his students. Anxiety may serve only to interfere with the learning of a new and perhaps foreign motive. The provision of a supportive learning environment enables concentration on the task and the freedom to accept counsel when necessary.

Coupled with this requirement is the need to provide a new reference group to decrease the influence of other reference groups with antagonistic values during the time in which the new motive is being formed. Isolation from other groups was used by McClelland for a period of a week, ten days, or more depending on the intensity of the training. However, in the typical school setting isolation may be impractical or, in fact, undesirable. Other means of developing group identification can be used such as holding special classes, labeling the group, or just depending upon the informal group identification that occurs when special knowledges or languages are learned by the group.

Evaluate and revise the program

The procedures outlined above are the beginnings of a theory of motive acquisition. The supporting evidence comes from a variety of sources. The effectiveness of this exploration appears to have yielded surprisingly good results as measured by the understanding of n:Ach, by the amount of risk-taking, by the number of job improvements, by the use of time and money, and by the kind of jobs held. The success of the course seems especially important when it is recognized that three quite different cultural groups were represented and the groups of students were already well into their adult careers. As with all such endeavors, whether in laboratory or field studies, there are extreme cases of success or failure. One man in McClelland's group decided that he was not n:Ach-oriented and wanted no part of it. He subsequently dropped out of the course, changed his goals, and became a chicken farmer. The "star" student was a middle-aged businessman who had made plans to retire. After taking the course, he decided to abandon plans for retirement and go into his own business. Within six months he had raised one million dollars and had drawn plans to build the tallest building on the highest hill in the city. The building was to be called Everest Apartments!

While we have described a formal course devoted solely to the development of a single motive, it is unlikely that many readers of this textbook will have an opportunity to take such a course. Some teachers may be involved in the teaching of motives to culturally deprived children. But most teachers will be most concerned about influencing the development of motives by more informal teaching arrangements. For such purposes the principles outlined above, and presented in much more detail in McClelland's (1965) article, should provide hints the teacher will want to test for himself.

An experimental achievement motivation training program for underachieving high school boys

The effect of training in achievement motivation on the academic performance of underachieving high school boys was investigated by Kolb (1965). The program was conducted as part of a summer academic course for underachieving high school boys from high and low SES homes. Another group of boys with similar characteristics took only the academic course and served as the control group.

The program was, in many respects, analogous to the one described by McClelland. The boys lived together in a dormitory. The experimenter was their counselor and behaved in a manner consistent with the behavior of a high achieving person. Thus, he served as a visible need achievement model. Responsibility was gradually turned over to the boys in all matters: external discipline gave way to internal control; structured class meetings gave way to individual responsibility for appointments with instructors. Over several sessions the boys engaged in such activities as writing essays about why the training would work; identifying the characteristics of a person with achievement motivation; playing games to permit a comparison of one's own self-evaluation with the characteristics of an achieving personality; discussing the importance of future orientation, delay of gratification, and ability to control impulses; and applying principles of achievement motivation to life in the pupil's home.

The later academic performance of the boys in the experimental program was compared with that of the control group. For this purpose school achievement was measured 6 and 18 months after the summer program. The main results are shown in Figure 8-5. The boys

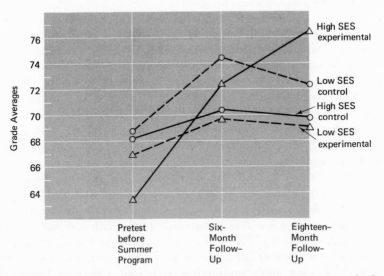

Figure 8-5.   Academic performance of underachieving boys, from high and low socioeconomic status (SES) homes, before, six months after, and eighteen months after a summer training program in achievement motivation. The control group took only an academic course. (From D. A. Kolb, 1965, Figure 1, p. 789. With permission of author and publisher.)

from the higher SES group benefited from the special training relative to their controls while the boys from the lower SES did not.

A tentative explanation by Kolb of these results is based on the different environments to which the boys returned. The underachieving boy in the higher SES group returns to a situation where there is pressure to achieve. The training provided him with the instrumental activities necessary to perform adequately in school and thereby alleviate the tension otherwise produced by a failure to perform up to his capacity. The expectations and aspirations imposed on the boy by the lower SES sub-culture are not so high. Accordingly, he does not feel under the same pressure as does the higher SES boy to improve his performance.

Both Kolb and McClelland provide reasonable cautions in the interpretation of such data as these. Though the study provides encouraging support for the idea that a training program in achievement motivation can enhance academic performance, the study does not permit conclusive statements regarding which factor or factors are directly responsible. Thus, changes might have resulted from identification with a high achievement model; from learning specific instrumental cognitive behaviors for improving performance; from learning to take responsibility; or from mere expectations that participation in the program would be effective.

A final question regarding the development of motives is an ethical one: Should motives be changed? With an adult entrepreneurial group, it is assumed that such persons are interested in improving their performance and that n:Ach is an important factor in effecting this change. The decision to participate in this endeavor is, in the last analysis, theirs. A direct answer to the question with regard to public school education, however, cannot be given from research evidence. We do know that motives are changed by subtle influence from peers, teachers, parents, and other adult groups. The degree to which educational practice is oriented toward the development of such motives as power, achievement, affiliation, or any other must rest with the larger community. The decision itself is based on philosophical considerations such as the values and other factors intrinsic to the cultural milieu where the teaching is to occur. Within this cultural milieu, however, the teacher is a leader not without influence in his or her attempts to move the community toward more productive goals and satisfying human interactions.

Pupil Interests, Career Choices, and the Curriculum

Though interests are sometimes said to be related to motives, many investigators attempt to distinguish between them. *Motives* are the broad, general, and unfocused human needs representing the values, goals, or anxieties that dominate the person's life (Lohnes, 1966). *Interests*, on the other hand, are highly focused, specialized, and unique classes of activities to which the person automatically and effortlessly directs his attention (Roe & Siegelman, 1964). Motives are psychological and physiological forces demanding satisfaction; interests are differentiated means by which valued goals may be attained. Thus, while there is a significant relationship between interests and need hierarchies, present evidence does not support the conclusion that interests and motives are identical, or even more than superficially comparable (Suziedelis & Steimel, 1963; Lohnes, 1966). The manifestations of interests are readily expressed by the pupil and so are more easily identified than are motives. Consequently, such information should be readily available and easily linked to school activities for facilitating motivation and to occupational information for vocational counseling. Nevertheless, the utility of interests is limited as suggested in a caution in interpreting interest by Strong (1955) who said, "In general [the pupil's] *interests* indicate the direction he *should* go; his *abilities* determine how far he *can* go; and his *motivation*, ambition, fight, determination, stick-to-it-iveness indicate how far he *will* go." Thus, the reader is cautioned not to confuse interests with abilities.

Identifying interests

Super and Crites (1962) distinguish four categories of interests according to methods of observation which can be employed by teachers. *Expressed interests* are identified by the verbal expression of a preference for an activity, occupation, or task. A *manifest interest* is assumed from observations of activities in which the pupil participates. *Tested interests* are interests inferred from the pupil's performance on tests of different subject matter areas. *Inventoried interests* are determined by responses of "like," "indifferent," and "dislike" to standardized sets of items about objects, activities, occupations, and so on. Although each of these is a measure of some aspect of interest, the expressed and manifest interests do not necessarily coincide with inventoried interests (Berdie, 1955), and as we will indicate later there may be little correspondence between interests measured by different inventories.

The simplest way to find out about preference is to question the pupil about his likes and dislikes. These yield the *expressed interests*. One may employ, for example, a series of open-ended questions to elicit the pupil's "three wishes;" his most (least) interesting experience; his most (least) preferred school activity; and so on. The replies may be subjectively categorized into attractions and aversions regarding recreational, social, artistic, musical, or any other category of activities. Which specific classifications are used will depend upon the kinds of information the teacher wants. From a practical viewpoint tabulating all responses can be a tedious operation. The teacher may want to get only a general idea of pupil interests by reading all responses and summarizing a general impression.

Although verbally *expressed interests* are rich sources of information for the teacher, the method is unreliable except under most favorable conditions of administration. The interests of young children are characterized by instability, although their stability increases with age. Furthermore, the manner of asking the questions may influence pupil response.

The *manifest interests* are identified by observation of activities in which the pupil participates *when he has a relatively free choice*. Pupils may be asked to keep a list of the books they have read, or to bring their different collections to school to show other children. They may be asked to discuss their hobbies or demonstrate a skill connected with a hobby. The topics pupils discuss during informal play periods and "free discussion" may be noted.

The kinds of part-time jobs held by pupils sometimes reflect their major interests. Although pupils will often work at uninteresting tasks because of the financial return, many a boy has found a business orientation emerging out of experience with a newspaper route or out of his part-time work in a grocery store. Other boys have been led to investigate civil engineering as a vocation after working for a summer with a surveying team.

As a dynamic factor in pupil behavior it is reasonable to expect that interests will find an outlet in preferred activities. However, a few factors tend to detract somewhat from the validity of the inferences that can be made on the basis of informal observations (Super & Crites, 1962). First, a pupil may be participating in an activity for its by-products. Thus, the captain of the football team and the editor of the school newspaper may participate in these activities because they pro-

Figure 8-6. Part-time jobs are sometimes the forerunners of the more enduring interests of the adult. (Ida Wyman from Black Star.)

vide opportunities for increased social interaction. They will be dropped when more preferred opportunities become available or are learned. Second, the number or kind of activities in which a pupil participates is often limited by circumstances beyond his control; i.e., he is not free to engage in any activity he chooses. The pupil may, for example, be genuinely attracted toward photography but may not have the money to purchase the equipment needed to pursue that hobby. Third, environmental circumstances also limit the degree to which an interest may find expression, as in the case of the boy who believes he would enjoy farming but who lives in the center of a metropolitan area and is thus prevented from testing this interest. If these cautions in interpretation of manifest interests are kept in mind, careful observation by the teacher can sometimes spot the beginnings of an enduring interest at an early age.

Development of vocational interests

Psychologists today entertain several alternative explanations of how vocational preferences are developed, although no definitive theory can cover all cases. On the basis of one orientation, for example, some likes and dislikes appear to be gradually acquired because of successes or failures or because of other rewards or threats associated with them. There is much personal satisfaction to be gained when challenging tasks are accomplished easily. Activities that accompany failure, or that lead to thwarting, and threaten one's self-esteem, are eventually disliked. For comparison with such cases, other theories, to be taken up below, are based on the psychology of development, or of personality, or of counseling rather than on the operation of a few principles.

Personality.   Holland (1966) and Bordin (1943) both suggest that interests reflect the more enduring structures of the personality. The patterns that are measured by vocational interest inventories reflect, in large part, the pupil's self-perceptions. Here are to be found the underlying attitudes the pupil has toward his societal role, his sex role, his abilities, and his tendencies to be outgoing and self-confident, or withdrawn. Each of these characteristics is a basic part of his personality. Responses on an interest inventory and preferences for specific tasks are only two, among many, of the means by which the self-concept can be expressed. Feelings toward specific objects will tend to fluctuate. On the other hand, the *patterning* of interests is likely to remain quite stable and resistant to change because it is rooted in the deeper personality structure (Tyler, 1955).

Identification.   Many theories, among which is the one by Super to be discussed below, suggest that interests get their start through identification. In this process, the pupil seeks the approval of

certain favored individuals such as his parents, teacher, some businessman, or other person. As a consequence, he strives to be like them.
Often, on the basis of imitation, he learns the essence of the new role
with little effort (Bandura & Kupers, 1964, 1965b). Success in these imitated roles is often a factor in the development of new interests for the
individual apart from the model from whom they are first learned
(Super, 1949, 1957). Boys appear to have an abundance of models from
which to select vocational roles to be imitated. Girls are not so favored
since their counterparts tend, for the most part, to remain at home.
Thus, as Tyler (1951) has shown, the small boy's interests are more congruent with his measured abilities than are the young girl's.

  Occupational inheritance.   Tiedeman and O'Hara (1963) supply evidence that tracing the origin of interests and vocational goals
is a difficult process. They suggest, however, that studies of *occupational
inheritance* probably provide the most definitive indication of the emergence of interests. Thus, the vocation eventually adopted by the pupil
often coincides with that of his father. Furthermore, the level of education to which the pupil aspires is dependent upon the socioeconomic
level of the family. This dependence, in part at least, appears to be
mediated by parental encouragement (or discouragement) of the child's
scholastic efforts, attainments, and aspirations. Family members are
sources of rewards and punishments, they serve as models to identify
with, and become supportive influences that mold the pupil's expectations of himself.

  Self-concept.   In a more elaborate theory encompassing vocational development, Super *et al.* (1963) emphasize the role of the self-
concept. This theory traces the emergence of interests and vocational
choice through the formation, translation, and implementation of the
self-concept. Important in the development of self-concept are the
processes of (1) *self-differentiation*, in which the pupil gains an identity,
an understanding of what he is like, and a feel for how he differs from
others; (2) *identification* with others perceived to have similar personal
attributes and skills; (3) *role-playing* by acting out a given kind of role
behavior either through imaginative processes or through overt behavior; and of (4) *reality testing*. Translation of the self-concept into vocational choice depends on such processes as testing the validity of a
vocational role suggested by the occupation of a model with whom the
pupil identifies; experience in an occupation into which one was initially cast, perhaps accidentally or involuntarily so because of financial
need; and the canvassing of the possibilities of a vocation that seems to
provide a good fit with one's abilities, interests, and skills. Finally, these
processes culminate in whatever kind of training the pupil undertakes
to implement the self-concept (e.g., training on the job, in a vocational
school, a secretarial school, a college, and so on).

Despite the apparently reasonable conjectures suggested in the theories above, the evidence for factors responsible for, or contributing to, the origins of vocational interests and goals is either nonexistent or, if available, is anything but clear. For example, one theory (Roe, 1956) suggests that occupational interests are dependent on parental control of the person as a child; i.e., the amount of love and attention he gets is relevant to a tendency in the direction of person-oriented occupations, while degree of casualness or demandingness he is accustomed to is irrelevant to a later person-orientation. Roe and Siegelman (1964), on the other hand, found small relationships between some of the measures of family atmosphere and occupational orientation but not for other measures. Moreover, those findings were with male subjects. Fewer significant relationships were found with female subjects. In studies by Holland (1962) and by Hagen (1960), in which retrospective reports were used, only slight evidence was found to support the hypothesis that family atmosphere affected an occupational pursuit. On the other hand, Herriot (as reported in Tiedeman & O'Hara, 1963) did find that educational aspiration was related to the adolescent's self-concept and to his perception of support from others.

Martin: a case study in the development of interest*

Martin is now an eminent theoretical physicist whose history has been studied by Anne Roe. In this account are to be found many of the factors we have already described as contributing to the development of interests. Present in his case are the experiences of success, then dissatisfactions, certain important personality traits, the identifications, and even the chance environmental factors which are frequently so important. You may find it interesting to look for the contributions of these several influences in the sometimes smooth, though sometimes vacillating, molding of his preferences. Here is Martin's story:

I can't remember much about grade school except the fact that I got reasonably decent grades right along and that I was fairly interested in science and mathematics. I had a friend in seventh or eighth grade who was the son of a druggist and we got a chemistry set between us and played around with it and almost blew up the house. We spent our time memorizing the table of elements. I never got along in languages. I couldn't see any sense in memorizing grammar. In history I read so much I had many more facts than the rest whether they were right or not. I think probably the interest in science was partly because of Father. When he was home he liked to do shop work

*The case of Martin is quoted, with only slight abridgement and modification, from *The making of a scientist.* New York: Dodd, Mead, and Co., Inc. Copyright, 1953, by Anne Roe. Pp. 105–111. With permission of author and publisher.

and I used to do some with him. He was rather meticulous and in some ways this was discouraging for a beginner.

I was rather sickly. I imagine that it was more allergic than anything else, although it was not recognized at the time, and I was sick two or three months each year. One term in high school I was only there for a month. . . . This meant that during most of the winter months I didn't get out and I got to reading fairly early. Since I was in the eighth grade I've been in the habit of reading four books or more a week. . . . One spell in high school, when I was sick for three months, I decided I was going into history and I spent the time in drawing up a historical chart beginning with the Egyptians.

I did very little going out in high school. Mother was very worried about it. I felt very shy. I started in my junior year in college and all of a sudden found it interesting and easy and rather overdid it for awhile. Let's see if I can remember how it happened. I just happened to get in with a group of fellows and girls who were interested in artistic things. I started going to the symphony concerts at that time and we got in the habit of going [out . . . sitting around and talking]. Since that time it's [social activity] been a thing I could turn on or off at will. . . . I've always been self-conscious at social functions and never cared very much for them. [When only a few people are present] it's different.

The first few years in high school I don't remember anything special about, except that I managed to get fairly decent grades in mathematics. I took physics and didn't like it. I had taken chemistry before I got there, but there was an extra course that sounded interesting so I took it and it turned out there were only four students in the course and a very interesting teacher. He sort of took personal charge and let us do pretty much what we wanted except that he was extremely insistent that we take care and do a good job. We worked through all of analytical chemistry there and I got a feeling for looking for small traces of elements, etc. This convinced me that I wanted to be a chemist. A little earlier I had gotten a job with the phone company which was with a fellow studying to be a chemist. I read Slosson, *Creative Chemistry*. This was the romantic thing to be. I think that teacher had more individual influence on me than any other.

When I was still in high school I took a job one summer at a Yacht Club. It was a navy camp and one of the instructors had been a radio operator. He got me interested in radio. . . . That winter he and two other radio amateurs decided to open a small radio equipment store in town and they asked me to go in. . . . When the craze hit in 1922 or 1923 the place was about swamped, it was the only store in town. What was made on the store pretty much paid my way through college. While this episode was interesting I was pretty sure I didn't want to go into business. . . . During part of this time in addition to working at the store I had been a part-time radio writer for one of the papers. While that was interesting, too, it didn't appeal as a life work either. By then I was convinced I wanted to go on in academic work.

. . . I just went to college expecting to be a chemist. I had no special idea about it. Two things happened in my freshman year. I took the college chemistry course plus the lab course. The lab course threw me for a complete loss. I think it was taught by a poor teacher who was careless of the reagents and they weren't pure. I got traces of everything and reported it. I didn't like the way the course was taught because I was told everything I was supposed to do and it soured me on chemistry.

I got acquainted with a young man who had just come there as an astronomer and was teaching mathematics. He was perhaps the most inspiring teacher I had. . . . At the end of the year I decided the devil with chemistry, I'm going into physics.

At that time the college had a course in physics which was not popular. . . . There was nothing special about the course except at the end of that year a prize examination was given. . . . The physics course was given with the calculus but didn't use it. So about the middle of the second term I got disgusted and decided I wanted to learn physics the right way and asked the teacher for a text. . . . I studied so that when the exam came along I gave it all in calculus and got the prize. This confirmed me, of course, and the next two years were extremely pleasant. . . .

My teacher felt I should go on to do graduate work. . . . I applied for scholarships at three places and took the second offer. I found it [my first year in graduate school] exciting. I started work on an experimental problem, but then I would get an idea for a theoretical paper and work on that for awhile and then go back to the other.

I think my teacher in high school had given me a few nudges in the direction of research. Both the professors at college with whom I was in close personal contact and saw daily were active in research themselves and I just soaked that stuff up. I find it hard to think back to the time when the idea of research and just spending all the time I had available on trying to understand anything wasn't just there.

Identifying Pupil Interests by Formal Methods

Beginning at about the junior high school level more reliable and valid data than those obtained by direct observation and informal methods are necessary to help the pupil formulate his long-range *curricular and vocational plans*. The inventoried interests, together with other information about the pupil's aptitudes, are important sources of information for *career counseling*. On occasion some professional schools use inventoried interests to *select* students who will have the greatest probability of finding the program appealing and of remaining in the occupation for a number of years after graduation. These purposes are in addition to the more immediate use of inventoried interests that may be made by the teacher for *classroom planning*.

Currently, two interest inventories are popular in the junior and senior high school, and, at present, are the most widely researched instruments. Both were intended as counseling tools only and were never advocated as sole bases for clamping a pupil into a given career or for prematurely hastening a career decision. They are the *Kuder Preference Record* (Kuder, 1956) and the *Strong Vocational Interest Blank* (*SVIB*) (Strong, 1943, 1962, 1964). They represent fundamental differences in the construction and interpretation of interest inventories. Thus, for example, although there are a number of scales (occupational categories) common to the Kuder Preference Record–Occupational Form D (1956) and the *SVIB*, the relationship between the scores on identically named scales for the two tests are rather low, as shown by the average correlation coefficient of .37 found by King, Norrell, and Powers (1963).

The Kuder Preference Record (KPR)

The format of the *Kuder Preference Record* is composed of a series of triads from which the individual taking the inventory is *forced* to choose the one he likes best and the one he likes least. Typical sets of alternatives for the subject to choose between from an early form of the inventory are:

Build bird houses.   Visit an art gallery.
Write articles about birds.   Browse in a library.
Draw sketches of birds.   Visit a museum.*

In the recent forms of the inventory, the items in a triad to be rated in order of preference start with "Be a ..." (For example, "Be a photographer," "Be a physicist," and "Be a salesman.") By a tabulation of items marked "liked" or "disliked" in these sets of alternatives, the ten interest *tendencies* of outdoor, mechanical, computational, scientific, persuasive, artistic, literary, musical, social service, and clerical interests are measured. The total number of responses are scored to determine the relative *strength* of a given interest for the pupil. Fundamentally, the *Kuder Preference Record* provides only a ranking of a pupil's interests from those that are strongest for him to those that are weakest. The interests ranked are, of course, limited to the ten categories.

The scales for each interest tendency relate to the same underlying behavioral tendency. They are based on items that cluster together for each dimension. Occupations can also be described by a set of weights, which is different for each occupation on the several dimen-

*From G. F. Kuder, *Kuder Preference Record: Vocational Form CH*, 1948. Reprinted by permission of author and Science Research Associates, Inc. All rights reserved.

sions. A general impression of the way the inventory is scored can be obtained by comparing some of the "like most" items which contribute to the score for mechanical interest with those that contribute to the score for persuasive interest:

Mechanical Interest	*Persuasive Interest*
Work mechanical puzzles.	Sell tickets for an amateur play.
Build bird houses.	Be an artist for an advertising agency.
Take a course in metal working.	Interview people who are applying for jobs.*

In Figure 8-7 is a profile of interests as measured by the *Kuder Preference Record* for Jim H., a pupil known to one of the authors of this book. In his case the preferences for science, clerical work, and mechanics are strongest and the preference for art and music are weakest. Because Jim is also of average intellectual ability but has better than usual coordination and mechanical ability, it is easy to see why he has selected a vocational curriculum and does well in his industrial arts

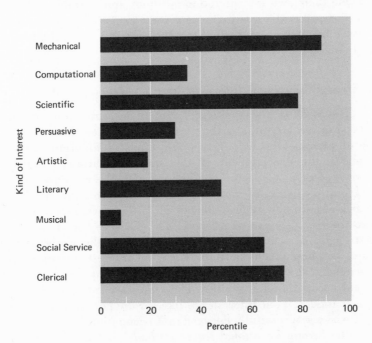

Figure 8-7. Here is Jim's Kuder Preference Record *profile of interest tendencies. In what ways can he be easily motivated? In what ways would it be difficult to interest him in your subject?*

*From the inventory and key of G. F. Kuder, *op. cit.* With permission of author and publisher.

courses. As soon as he is able, perhaps after graduation from high school, he intends to become a television technician.

Pupils with similar interest rankings, but with better than average ability, would probably differ from Jim in their vocational choices. They might hope to attend college to become engineers, physicists, chemists, and the like. The teacher might motivate pupils with preference patterns similar to Jim's by assigning projects that would help them find outlets for their mechanical and scientific preferences. On the other hand, the teacher *might* have more difficulty in motivating such persons in art and music unless it could be accomplished through their other dominant interests.

The reader should be cautioned that the *Kuder Preference Record* scores are relative rankings for a given person. Accordingly, there is no way of knowing whether the lowest ranked preference is an aversive interest or merely a weak but positive interest. Furthermore, the Kuder inventory was intended as a basis for a counseling interview. Thus, it should not be used as a test in which pupils graph their own profiles and make their own interpretations without appropriate guidance. Nor should it become the sole basis for a vocational choice, as we can see if we remember that a pupil who has a high interest in art should not necessarily become a painter by profession.

The Strong Vocational Interest Blank (SVIB)

The *SVIB* is a very different type of measure from any of those discussed so far. It compares the pupil's responses on the inventory with those of persons who belong to many kinds of different occupational groups. In the development of this inventory Strong compared the responses of men in specific occupations with the responses of a reference group consisting of men in general. This procedure was the basis for much of our knowledge on how to apply the mechanics of psychometrics to the measurement of interests. The measure here is not the relative strength of an interest tendency, as it is in the *Kuder Preference Record*, but how much the pupil's general interests resemble those of the scientist, the physician, the teacher, or any one of nearly 50 different occupational groupings. The scores are interpreted in the following manner: "Your interests are like (or are not like) the interests of people who are successfully engaged in X occupation."

The *Strong Vocational Interest Blank** is based on the assumption that successful individuals in various occupations can be differen-

*Although irrelevant to our discussion here, the reader should know that Strong (1962, 1963) and Strong, *et al.* (1964) have reported revisions in the SVIB as a consequence of changes in the meanings of some words and in the nature of some occupations since 1938. The total number of items has also been decreased from 400 to 298.

tiated on the basis of their likes and dislikes of occupations, school subjects, amusements, general activities, and being with people. The scale for an occupation consists of variously weighted items that distinguish the group from the reference group. As you can see, this inventory leans heavily on the *differences* between people in different occupations while playing down the *similarities*. You will see the difference between the preferences of the real-estate salesman and the mathematics-science teacher by examining Table 8-3.

Table 8-3.   Percents answering Like, Indifferent, and Dislike to various SVIB items.

Item	Real Estate			Math-Science			Men in General		
	L	I	D	L	I	D	L	I	D
Being an architect "Not much difference"	39	36	25	46	42	12	46	36	18
Being an artist "Disliked moderately by others compared to men in general"	18	31	51	20	47	33	32	36	32
Being an astronomer "Liked by teachers, disliked by realtors"	18	39	43	53	37	10	33	41	26
Being a scientific research worker "Liked by teachers, disliked by realtors"	21	26	53	75	19	6	48	30	22
Interviewing prospects in selling "Liked by realtors, disliked by both others"	76	16	9	23	36	41	26	34	40
Playing bridge "Liked more by both others than by men in general"	59	23	18	54	31	15	48	29	23
Study algebra "Liked by teachers, disliked by realtors"	44	25	31	86	11	3	60	22	18

SOURCE: E. K. Strong, Jr. *Strong Vocational Interest Blank* (Revised), Form T 399. Stanford, California: Stanford University Press, 1966. With permission. The tabulations were provided through the courtesy of Dr. D. P. Campbell at the University of Minnesota.

Recently Kuder (1963) extended this procedure to his inventory, by comparing responses of one occupational group with another, thereby obtaining a scale that will differentiate between the two groups. Accordingly, specific occupational groups are not compared with a men-in-general base, as in the *SVIB*, but are compared directly, since Kuder believes there is always the problem of defining a reference group when a men-in-general base is used.

A comparison of the KPR and the SVIB

The teacher will probably find the *KPR* more helpful than the *SVIB* for most of the classroom uses suggested in this chapter. For example, it is more useful in the daily management of a class to know that the pupil has strong (or weak) interests in mechanics, science, computational activities, and the like, than it is to know that he has interests similar to those of adults in specific occupations. The scores on the *KPR* also tend to have a closer relationship to self-ratings of interests than do the scores on the *SVIB* (Berdie, 1950). On the other hand, in career counseling, it is necessary to infer whether the pupil will adjust favorably to occupational demands. In this instance scores from the *Strong Vocational Interest Blank*, in conjunction with all other counseling information, would be used since it compares the pupil's interests with individuals who are successfully engaged in specific occupations.

The occupational level (OL) score, based on responses to a number of items throughout the *SVIB*, provides a reasonable basis on which to determine the pupil's general interest level, i.e., whether his interests are dominantly at the skilled, technical, or professional level (Carkhuff & Drasgow, 1963). However, as the reader might have inferred from the introductory comments in this section, the general-level-of-interest score by itself does not have validity for success in a particular occupation (Porter, 1963).

From the standpoint of readability the *Kuder Preference Record* can be used as early as the eighth grade. The *Strong Vocational Interest-Blank* employs vocabulary similar to that of the average pupil halfway through the tenth grade. Thus, the average tenth-grade pupil and the advanced ninth-grade pupil should have little difficulty in responding to either of these inventories (Stefflre, 1947).

When using any interest inventory, it would be well for the teacher to consider that the scores can be, and often are, biased either by deliberate or unintentional "faking." Kirchner (1961) conducted a study on faking in a "real-life" situation and found that applicants for sales positions obtained more extreme scores on several *SVIB* scales than those persons already in the positions. In an experimental study of faking (Bridgman & Hollenbeck, 1961), psychology students were asked to attempt to simulate the responses of applicants for positions as sanitary supply salesmen. They were able to increase their scores on this occupational scale of the *Kuder Preference Record–Occupational, Form D* over that obtained when they were asked only to simulate applicants for "a position in industry."

Some pupils may try to "look good" rather than indicate their real interests. Kuder (1960) has developed a "verification" scale to identify whether responses are biased. If responses have been falsified in an attempt to boost one's score in a particular interest tendency or occupational scale the record becomes worthless for guidance purposes. The reasons for any faking that occurs should be identified and remedied before the pupil is readministered the inventory.

A theory of vocational choice

Holland's (1966) approach to interest measurement and vocational choice is provocative. It differs from either the Kuder or Strong orientation in that the construction of his *Vocational Preference Inventory* is an outgrowth of several assumptions relating personal and occupational information. More importantly, Holland's approach includes a theory of vocational choice broader in scope than just interest measurement. His assumptions derive from empirical evidence from several studies and are briefly summarized below from Holland's (1966, pp. 2–12) work: (1) One's personality is expressed in the choice of a vocation and vocational interests should be thought of as expressions of personality. (2) Accordingly, observations of interests, including those made by use of inventories, are also observations of personality. (3) The sociological and psychological meanings implicit in popular conceptualizations (or stereotypes) of occupations are reliably shared by the population. Though stereotypes of vocations are sometimes inaccurate, there is evidence that they do have some validity. The measurement of interests by most inventories rests heavily on this assumption. (4) People within a given occupation share similar personality qualities and patterns of personal development. (5) As a consequence of similarities in personality, people within a vocational group will respond in similar ways, thereby creating characteristic interpersonal environments. (6) Achievement and satisfaction in an occupation depend on the degree of congruence between one's personality and the vocational environment. (7) Because an organization of conceptual definitions has been lacking in the past, interests have come to mean "interests as measured by an inventory" rather than "interests as related to personality" or "interests as a subject for study by the social psychologist."

Holland's (1958) inventory is composed entirely of occupational titles for which the respondent indicates his degree of preference. In theory this procedure, among the others discussed in this chapter, enables the characterization of the respondent according to his resemblance to one of six personality types prevalent in our culture—i.e., *realistic* (e.g., laborers and skilled tradesmen), *intellectual* (e.g., scientists), *social* (e.g., religious workers), *conventional* (e.g., office workers), *enterprising* (e.g., sales and business personnel), and *artistic* (e.g., writers and musicians). As shown, for each personality type there is a corresponding vocational environment. In making a vocational choice, it is assumed that people will search for compatible environments (vocations) in which their skills and abilities can be exercised, their attitudes and values expressed, and in which satisfaction-giving roles can be assumed and disagreeable ones avoided.

The theory and its implications are not inescapably linked to inventoried interests. Holland says (1966, p. 96) "because the evidence indicates that a person's past choices and tentative future

choices are the most efficient and simple guides to his interests, counselors might make greater use of the client's expressed choices and
reduce or abandon the use of interest inventories." Consequently if a
teacher, counselor, or the pupil himself is aware of the pupil's personality pattern and of the range of possible environments, by whatever
method, this knowledge can in principle be used to predict the outcomes of possible pairings including which occupation will be
chosen by a given pupil, the level of achievement he is likely to attain,
the degree of stability in his situation, and the like.

Holland speculates, too, about the application of the theory.
Incentives and motivational appeals might be made more successfully
with a consideration of pupil personality types than without such considerations, e.g., attempts to interest pupils with "intellectual" inclinations in practical problems might be achieved through the channel of
appeals made in theoretical rather than pragmatic terms. Teaching
efficiency might be improved by assigning pupils to teachers according
to shared personality patterns or by using a knowledge of pupils'
interest profiles in choosing teaching methods.

An important implication of this theory for practical application is the necessity for realistic perceptions of occupations. Thus, the
pupil should be provided with occupational information in order to
develop differentiated understanding, rather than broad and general
impressions, and to emphasize the diversity of opportunities and roles,
rather than the most typical role, within an occupation. Implied in
these statements is the necessity for special work and curriculum
experiences, rather than direct advice, in learning about different
occupations and the compatibility of one's personality with these occupations.

Pupil interests and vocational choice

The first major point at which a vocational choice is formally
influenced is approximately in the grades 8–9 (Katz, 1963, 1966). However, so early in his "career" the pupil is not expected to make a definite
choice. The curriculum offers opportunity for reality testing of alternative possibilities through exploration and development of a pupil's abilities, values, and interests. If choices are made, they should be considered by the teacher as preliminary and highly tentative, since the developmental unfolding of a career choice is a process that continues
through most of the high school years (Super & Overstreet, 1960).

The second choice point, according to Katz (1963), occurs in
grades 11–12. At that time the pupil should be ready to make use of the
model he has constructed of himself. During this period the school will
provide the pupil with a benign climate for inexpensive exploration,
and with an opportunity to make firmer appraisals of himself in relation to anticipated occupational roles. The stakes are now higher than

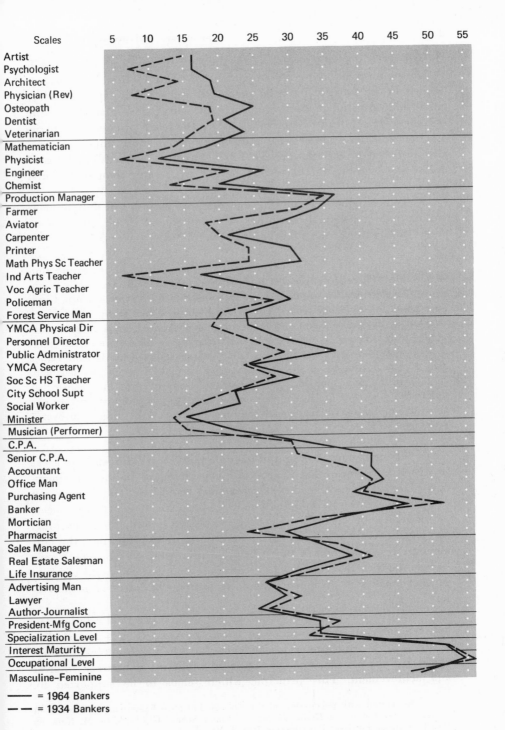

Scales	5	10	15	20	25	30	35	40	45	50	55
Artist											
Psychologist											
Architect											
Physician (Rev)											
Osteopath											
Dentist											
Veterinarian											
Mathematician											
Physicist											
Engineer											
Chemist											
Production Manager											
Farmer											
Aviator											
Carpenter											
Printer											
Math Phys Sc Teacher											
Ind Arts Teacher											
Voc Agric Teacher											
Policeman											
Forest Service Man											
YMCA Physical Dir											
Personnel Director											
Public Administrator											
YMCA Secretary											
Soc Sc HS Teacher											
City School Supt											
Social Worker											
Minister											
Musician (Performer)											
C.P.A.											
Senior C.P.A.											
Accountant											
Office Man											
Purchasing Agent											
Banker											
Mortician											
Pharmacist											
Sales Manager											
Real Estate Salesman											
Life Insurance											
Advertising Man											
Lawyer											
Author-Journalist											
President-Mfg Conc											
Specialization Level											
Interest Maturity											
Occupational Level											
Masculine–Feminine											

——— = 1964 Bankers
— — = 1934 Bankers

Figure 8-8. Comparison of 1934 bankers vs. 1964 bankers holding identical jobs (100 in each group). (From Campbell, 1966. With permission.)

they were in the first period. If he succeeds in reaching a sound self-appraisal in relation to the opportunities open to him, rewards are reaped in the form of eventual successful and efficient career development and adjustment. Ineffectual or capricious career planning at the second stage can lead to such losses as are the result of changing curricula, encountering a need for additional preparation, changing jobs, dropping out of college, and the like. Thus, the "rewards" or "losses" following decisions in the second period are greater than in the first period.

Interest change should be considered as an index of development rather than of personal instability (Dunkelberger & Tyler, 1961). Katz (1963) aptly summarizes this point in the following excerpt:

In short, the exploration of interests involves, first of all, the exploration of activities. There is danger that interest inventories may be treated as a substitute for activities, encouraging mere introspection without experience. Guidance based on inventory scores ignores the likelihood that many interests are developed, discovered, and defined during adolescence. Super (1949) concludes from a survey of the research that "changes do take place in the interests of adolescents and that they are fairly well crystallized by the end, rather than by the *beginning*, of the high school years. They have merely begun to take shape by age 14 or 15." Strong notes that one third of the change that takes place between ages 15 and 25 comes during the first year and another one third during the next 2 years, with the remaining one third spread out over 7 years (pp. 36–37).*

The tendency of the pupil to explore and work diligently in areas in which he is interested is generally considered an important dimension of applied learning. From a practical standpoint, the teacher can capitalize on a pupil's interests to help him investigate many new aspects of his widening world. In the ultraprogressive movement in teaching, the pupil's immediate preferences were permitted to dominate the curriculum as exemplified in the "Children, what shall we do today?" era of teaching practices. This is now considered an extreme point of view, but nevertheless it documents the early doctrine of interests as motivators.

On the surface, there would appear to be a practical relationship between interests, motivation, and learning. Aside from a few studies (Cattell, 1961), educational psychologists have had little success in demonstrating the existence of the supposed relationship between interest and achievement. This principle which seems to be supported by

*Reprinted with permission of the College Entrance Examination Board from *Decisions and Values: A Rationale for Secondary School Guidance* by M. Katz. © 1963 by College Entrance Examination Board, New York.

common sense is a very popular one but unfortunately is not founded on solid factual evidence.

Thus, it seems apparent that the effects of interests on achievement in school subjects are not easily judged by the pupil's grades. There is, perhaps, a more subtle influence prevailing in the way he profits from his experiences that can be hypothesized (though not tested) from Tolman's (1959) concept of wide and narrow cognitive maps. Assume, for example, that two pupils, one with high interest and one with low interest, have equal ability. Both may do equally well in a course if they have similar backgrounds of experience, initiative, and scholastic aptitude. However, there will be important differences in the outcomes of their experiences. The pupil with little interest soon learns about this deficiency and will not take further courses in the area. But the qualities of the pupils' personal experiences in the course itself will also differ. The pupil who dislikes a subject takes it because it is required, does his assignments, and meets whatever other requirements are demanded of him by the teacher. His range of participation and involvement is restricted. The profit he has gained is narrow indeed! On the other hand, many avenues are opened by this experience to the pupil with a great deal of interest in a subject such as algebra. He may see it as a fascinating way of working with unknown quantities, as a way of providing many shortcuts to arithmetic, as a basis for practical applications to problems in many vocational fields and in everyday life. To this pupil his immediate involvement is merely a point of departure for new and fascinating endeavors. He has acquired *breadth* from the experience.

Some indirect evidence for this hypothesis can be found in a study by Lazarus (1955). High school pupils were divided into two groups according to interest and ability. In one group were pupils with average intelligence (Otis IQ of 107) and an enthusiastic interest in writing. The other group was comprised of pupils with superior intelligence (mean Otis IQ of 120) but who lacked particular interest or exceptional talent in writing. Both groups of pupils were guided into a stiff, concentrated course in reading and writing. According to the investigator the high IQ group did not perform as well on the achievement tests at the end of the course and had not produced the quantity or quality of writing as did the high interest group. The latter (high interest) group had read an average of 20.7 books and had written an average of 14.8 papers compared with an average of 5.5 books read and reviewed and an average of 8.2 papers written by the former (high IQ) group. Thus, although interests and achievement do not appear to be related in the usual sense, there may be a relationship between interest and the *quality* of the experience.

Capitalizing on interests in curricular planning

A knowledge of pupil interests may be used by the teacher in course planning at all grade levels. Both informal and formal methods of discovering the preferences of pupils provide useful information. Classwork in any subject-matter area can frequently be structured around the dominant interests represented in a class. General areas of pupils' interests may be used as a stepping-off point from which lesson units are developed. Pupils with similar preferences can be encouraged to work on a common project.

Figure 8-9. Social and technical skills are developed simultaneously while pupils pursue their interests in group activities. Pupils find opportunities for outlets in creative expression and social interaction while exploring their own interests. (Portland, Oregon, Public Schools.)

Adaptation level and creating interest

The degree of interest elicited by an immediately pertinent situation may be dependent upon several factors. A favorable comment from a teacher, for example, will cause some pupils to work harder. Other pupils might not be affected under the same or similar circumstances either because they were not attending and did not hear the comment (focal stimuli are important), or because they have received this same comment too often, perhaps in an outright trivial situation (past experience provides a basis for making judgments), or because the teacher's evaluation is heard only against a background of sarcastic remarks from other pupils (background stimuli change the character of the focal stimuli). In other circumstances, brightly colored stimuli replacing drab, colorless ones in a demonstration or motion pictures replacing filmstrips can be observed to increase the motivation of the pupils. When used too exclusively, such an effect soon wears off. Indeed pupils who at first reacted excitedly to the use of black and white motion pictures soon demand color. If color movies are used too frequently, the pupils may be heard to say, "Movies? Again? Oh, no!"

The above examples serve to illustrate Helson's (1966) Adaptation Level (AL) theory of motivation. His basic premise is that for any motivational influence there is a range of stimulation and incentive for which no adjustment (adaptive behavior) is required. This is the base level. It differs from person to person and from situation to situation, but it is always dependent upon the effective stimuli and the person's past experience. Deviations from this base in the intensity of the affective quality of the situation require adjustment. Thus, pupils may like to perform a certain activity. Upon repetition they adapt, become satiated or indifferent to it, and upon further repetition they may come to dislike (avoid) it. Similarly, a novel activity becomes commonplace through repetition, and "stale" upon further repetition.

Helson (1966, pp. 178–179) shows that cognitive states can act as motivators, and thus the AL theory has substantial implications for teaching:

> In explaining why people behave as they do or what makes them tick—it may be asked: "How do you explain persistence toward future goals and accomplishments? What keeps individuals on a constant course toward certain ends, such as becoming a doctor, a lawyer, or a psychologist?" Predominant ideas serve as inciters to courses of action over extended periods of time. There are emotional and intellectual frames of reference as well as perceptual frames of reference, and they are formed in much the same way. Just as background, anchor, or predominant stimuli exercise influence on sensory ALs, so do predominant ideas and emotions exercise influence on ideational and emotional frames of reference. ... Individuals do better with difficult items of intelligence tests in a difficult context than in an easy one because of the upward adaptation to level of difficulty induced by the preponderance of harder items, thus proving the existence of cognitive ALs.*

Starting with topics the pupils know about and which are close to their personal experiences is one way of making the most of the topic of interests. Take as an illustration the experience of a student teacher known to one of the authors of this book. She was teaching a foreign history course. The unit was to deal with factors contributing to the growth

*From *Nebraska Symposium on Motivation*, © 1966. Used by permission of the University of Nebraska Press.

of selected Grecian ports. The class period was only a few minutes old when she recognized the presentation she had planned was too far removed from the experiences of junior high school pupils in an industrialized small community composed primarily of youngsters in upper lower and lower middle socioeconomic classes. Briefly, the pupils couldn't have cared less about the topic. Adjusting to her momentary dilemma, she discarded completely the elaborate lesson plan she had prepared for the day and brought the subject close to home. She discussed with her pupils the relationship between the development of the Erie Canal (which was but "a stone's throw" away from the school) and of the industrial growth within the town. Eventually, the discussion led to the enumeration of factors responsible for the growth of other nearby cities. After a start along these lines, based on topics of immediate interest, a parallel was drawn with the topic of the day, the study of the development of Grecian port cities.

Interests can be coordinated with curricular planning in other ways as well. A course may be interesting if our culture places a high value on the content. The teaching method which favors an approach involving interests oriented around people, personal experience, and local color is more interesting than one which is more impersonal and distant from the pupil's immediate experiences. Areas of study which result in a clear sense of achievement when the job is seen as finished, where there is a concrete answer, stimulate the greatest interest (Jersild & Tasch, 1949). Thus, with careful planning, pupils can be aided to achieve more while remaining close to what interests them.

Summary

Striving is a pervasive motivational characteristic manifested in directed effort toward the attainment of clearly defined goals. Such objectives can be roughly classified into short-range goals (i.e., those which deal with action, instrumental, or stepping-stone goals) and long-range (e.g., vocational) goals. In the process of achieving either, adjustments and adaptations to the environment will be required.

Striving may also involve behavior typically associated with the achievement, or mastery, motive. This motive emerges from the desire to please parents who encourage excellence in the exploratory achievement efforts of their children and from the identification with parents and other family members who serve as models for intellectual striving and other ways of achieving. A nurturant, accepting parent is a more effective model than is a rejecting, autocratic one.

An effective model is perceived by the pupil as one who is successful, has characteristics similar to his own, is accepting, and is one whose behavior can be successfully or adequately imitated. The teacher serves as a model in the roles of subject-matter specialist, leader, and representative of the educational community.

The influence of textbooks and other media is somewhat less apparent than that of teachers or parents as important models with whom pupils can identify and from whom achieving behavior can be learned. Still, through identification and by descriptions of systems of rewards and punishments these media do influence the growth of motives, social attitudes, and the behavior characteristics of each of the sexes.

Formal methods for developing motives are less well understood than for developing competence in handling subject matter. However, the results of one experimental program suggest that emotionally supportive teachers must be used as models and the pupil must be part of an accepting as well as supporting reference group. The sequence of general activities through which the pupil is to be guided are as follows: First, he must identify and appreciate the reasons why the motive should be developed. This requires clarification of one's personal definition of the realities, with their limitations, and with consideration of possible applications of the motive. The verbalized concept must then be translated into action behaviors. Manageable personal goals must be set that are related to the motive and progress recorded toward achievement of these goals.

Interests are unique classes of activities to which a pupil directs his attention. Several definitions of interests are possible depending on the kinds of observations that are made: *Expressed interests* are judged from the pupil's verbal expressions of preferred activities. *Manifest interests* are identified by observing the kinds of activities in which the pupil chooses to participate. *Tested interests* are inferred from the pupil's knowledge about specific activities and subject matter as judged from his performance on special tests of achievement. *Inventoried interests* are identified from the pupil's responses of like-dislike, or something similar, to a list of occupations, common activities, magazines, and so on.

The two most common measures of interests are the *Kuder Preference Record* and the *Strong Vocational Interest Blank*. The *KPR* is based on several homogeneous scales and yields a ranking of the person's broadly defined interests, such as mechanical, clerical, scientific, and persuasive. The *SVIB* is based upon items which successfully differentiate responses of members within an occupational group from those of a general reference group. It yields several scores indicating how the individuals' responses compare with members of more than 40 different occupations.

Several theories of interest development have been proposed, and none has superseded its rivals. These different theories are represented in the following statements: Activities in which one is successful are preferred over those in which one meets with failure. Interests, particularly vocational interests, reflect one's self-concept. The emergence of interests is, in large part, influenced by what may be called occupational inheritance. Interests get their start through identification.

Similarly, several proposals for the bases of vocational choice were discussed. In one of these vocational choice was traced through the formation, translation, and implementation of the self-concept in relation to vocational goals. In another, it was assumed that vocational interest is an expression of personality. Consequently, successful vocational choice is said to be based on the matching of personality types with vocational environments. A third theory with practical implications for classroom instruction suggests that there are two critical points at which vocational choices are influenced. The first is in the junior high school where the pupil explores his abilities, interests, and competencies, and learns how to plan tentative choices without major disruption of progress. This is done though no definitive choices should be made. The second period occurs toward the end of the high school years when the pupil capitalizes on the lessons gained in the initial period and relates his abilities to specific occupations. Though choices need not be entirely firm during this period, they are much less tentative than in the initial period.

The reliability and long-term validity has led to the popular adoption of the *Strong Vocational Interest Blank* as a vocational counseling tool. However, the presumed relationship between interest, as an important motivational factor, and achievement has received little support from research. There are reasons to believe that school grades are the result of so many different factors that the influence of interest is hidden and cannot be detected.

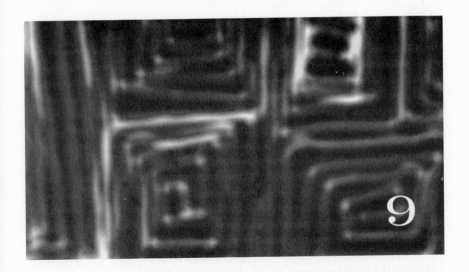

Transfer: a consequence of learning

It is obvious that formal education is a preparation for vocations, avocations, and innumerable other activities to be pursued by the pupil outside of school. Whatever their nature the learning experiences provided in the school are intended to be helpful in other life situations. Sometimes the experiences in and out of school will be related only in subtle ways. This simple premise underlies many curricular decisions. At one extreme, technical education leans toward teaching skills within contexts nearly identical to those encountered in the vocational setting. At the other extreme, a liberal arts curriculum assumes that the student's learning must facilitate the later solution of problems never before encountered by the student; in fact, of problems unanticipated by the society at the time he was educated.

Whenever a current activity is affected, whether beneficially or detrimentally, by previous learning there is said to be transfer. The direction and degree of transfer constitutes the real test of the educational process. After completing a unit, or a term's work, a teacher may advisedly ask, "Can my pupils use what they have learned in another situation, in their next course, or outside of the classroom?" "Is the pupil capable of integrating his learning experiences to solve new problems?" One psychologist has summarized the proper philosophy of the school toward transfer in this way:

That which does not transfer is educationally worthless, if indeed not a positive encumbrance. Except for past learning one could not learn anything in school; the simplest sentence, spoken or written, would be utterly incomprehensible. If a school subject does not transfer in educationally profitable amounts, it is that subject, not transfer, that is invalidated. (From Stroud, 1940, p. 787. With permission of author and publisher.)

The basic set of manipulations employed in the laboratory investigation of transfer defines this process in operational terms, as follows:

Experimental group	Performs Task I. E.g., learns to solve a mathematical puzzle.	Then performs Task II. E.g., learns to solve a mechanical puzzle.
Control group	Does not perform Task I.	Performs the same Task II as does the E group.

The amount of transfer is determined by observing the difference between the performances of the Experimental and Control groups on Task II. Performance may be measured in a number of different ways such as the number of correct responses, the number of errors, the number of trials to learn a task, or the time taken to solve a problem. Of course, the direction of the difference is most important. Here you must keep in mind the fact that only Task I was manipulated. Typically the subjects for such experiments are randomly assigned to different groups. Accordingly, it is assumed that both groups are equivalent before the different treatments. Then if the performance of the Experimental group exceeds that of the Control group there is said to be positive transfer since their performance on Task II benefits from experience with Task I. If the two sets of scores are no more different than one might expect by chance there is zero transfer. Or, if the Control group performs better on Task II than does the Experimental group, the learning of Task I apparently hinders performance on Task II and there is negative transfer. Although the experimental procedures employed are much more sophisticated than the one described above, the same fundamental operations are contained in all discussions of transfer.

Transition to Scientific Explanations of Transfer

Prescientific concern with explanations of transfer ended with the so-called doctrine of formal discipline, a doctrine based on the assumption of faculty psychology. The "mind," it was believed, was composed of several segments; each segment had its unique function or "faculty," such as will power or attention. These formal functions (or *forms* of behavior) could be developed for use in a variety of situations if they were but exercised appropriately, somewhat as the strength of a muscle may be increased for a number of uses by appropriate exercise.

Mental discipline discredited

The doctrine of formal discipline was not without its influence on the school curriculum. The value of a school subject was determined by the degree to which it was thought to contribute to the development of a mental function rather than by its intrinsic worth. Practice in a foreign language was said to develop imagination. The study of German was claimed to be a way of strengthening the scientific intellect. Mathematics was believed to increase or "create" the general powers of concentration and reasoning since attention to detail, memory, problem-solving, and related abilities are demanded of anyone who studies that subject. The common view was that fundamental qualities of the "mind" functioned in the same way on all occasions *regardless* of the kind of material with which pupils had worked providing only that a given "power" or "faculty" was required to perform a task.

As can be seen, this view of transfer held that initial learning had a highly general effect on future learning. The psychologists of that early period erred not in their belief in transfer, but in the notion that transfer was so general it affected all learning with similar requirements. General transfer does occur within certain limits to be described later in this chapter, but seldom as broadly across disciplines as the faculty psychologists believed. This modified view of formal discipline is gaining acceptability as a valid description of transfer (Fleishman, 1967).

The really effective death blow to the doctrine of mental discipline came from the findings of an extensive study by E. L. Thorndike (1924; Broyler, Thorndike, & Woodyard, 1927) of Columbia University. He and his colleagues carefully investigated the transfer of school studies to intelligence test scores of more than 13,500 high school students during an academic year. If some courses had an advantage over others for the "development of the mind," then this fact should be reflected in a test of general mental ability. The amount of general improvement in intelligence due to the kind of courses taken was found to be small. Pupils who took the traditional courses (for example, Latin, geometry, English, and history) performed no better than pupils of initially equal intelligence who took the practical courses (for example, arithmetic, bookkeeping, and homemaking).

Accordingly, the expectation of any general improvement of the mind from one course of study as compared with another was doomed to disappointment. Thorndike said in 1924: "The intellectual values of studies should be determined largely by the special information, habits, interests, attitudes, and ideas which they demonstrably produce" (Thorndike, 1924, p. 98). Which courses were to be selected for the curriculum had to be decided on the grounds of the special training they could provide. Mathematics or languages had no special preeminence. Although it is now an old issue, the weaknesses of the formal discipline account of transfer still are not universally appreciated. Even today, the proposal of a new course or curriculum may instigate the question, "What is its disciplinary value?" or the statement, "We must retain the classic subjects because they teach pupils how to learn, memorize, think, and concentrate."

Transfer theories—then and now

Formal Discipline

1. Based on intuitive-prescientific ideas. The mind was believed to be comprised of several separate and independent faculties, e.g., of reasoning, memory, observation, honesty, attention, volition, and perception. Transfer occurs when these faculties are exercised.

2. Once mental growth had been improved by exercise of these functions, transfer was then automatic.

3. Transfer was assumed to be general: Once a faculty had been "disciplined" it could be used in all settings under all conditions.

4. Once a mental faculty has been developed it was always advantageous for new learning—nothing is wasted or lost. Transfer is always positive—as good as, or better than, in the original learning situation.

Current Theories of Transfer

1. Based on empirical-experimental data. Transfer is based on the individual's ability and previous experience. Interrelationships among tasks are important, as are associations already learned. A background of knowledge is essential.

2. Mental growth is improved by explicit experience with the subject matter. Provision for transfer and application must be made by skillful teaching and effective study habits.

3. Thorndike proposed that transfer occurred only to the extent that components among two situations were identical. This view has been broadened to include more general types of transfer such as transfer of principles and learning to learn.

4. Transfer may be positive, zero, or negative. Even under the most favorable circumstances, transfer is less than that assumed by the disciples of formal discipline.

5. The task of education is to provide the exercises that will strengthen the faculty concerned. For example, to study Latin is to improve one's general ability to use and understand English; the study of literature was said to strengthen imagination; and practice in rote memory would improve memory in general.

6. The general orientation was "do nothing for the student that he cannot do himself."

7. The value of any subject for the curriculum was judged according to its merits for training one or more of the mental faculties. There was no concern for application. Motivation was considered unimportant since it was deemed that eagerness to learn decreased the "disciplinary" value of a course.

8. Since the course content is selected for the purpose of disciplining the mind, the subject matter is irrelevant and need not be of concern to the educator. Although general science, modern languages, and the vocational arts might be practical, their general utility for disciplining the mind was not as great as was that of the more traditional subjects.

5. The task of education is to produce the greatest amount of positive transfer from school to everyday life situations. The most economical approach for one learning French, for example, is to study French. (However, it is recognized that if the teacher emphasizes the derivation of English words in the study of Latin the pupil's vocabulary is likely to be considerably improved.)

6. It must be made clear to the learner that what he is learning can be applied; and how, in what settings, and under what conditions it can be applied.

7. A large part, if not most, of the specific course content of what pupils learn will be useful in many situations outside of school. Thorndike thought that unless the pupil is going to need the specific content there was no need to study it. Today it is recognized that any subject can be taught in a variety of ways. The degree to which the pupil can transfer what he has learned will depend on how skillfully he is taught.

8. As new innovations and discoveries are made they should be incorporated into the curriculum without delay. The pupil will be intellectually handicapped unless he is taught the very latest in the languages, arts, humanities, and sciences. However, teaching the scientific method in one science will have considerable transfer value to other sciences if taught for transfer, i.e., by showing the applications of the scientific method.

Thorndike's theory of identical elements

Upon the collapse of the doctrine of formal discipline there were unduly antagonistic reactions to it. For example, Ward was typical of those who said:

Nothing could be more false than that the study of mathematics strengthens the reasoning faculties. Mathematicians are poor reasoners. I mean those who have studied pure mathematics only. Mathematics, too exclusively pursued, destroys both the reason and the judgment. (Ward, as quoted by Thorndike, 1913, p. 432. With permission of publisher.)

Other positions were more moderate and did not exclude reasonable grounds for the selections of subjects in the curriculum. One such statement read: "No study should have a place in the curriculum for which this general disciplinary characteristic is the chief recommendation." Thorndike's description of his theory of identical elements was simply:

One mental function of activity improves others in so far as and because they are in part identical with it, because it contains elements common to them. Addition improves multiplication because multiplication is largely addition; knowledge of Latin gives increased ability to learn French because many of the facts learned in the one case are needed in the other. The study of geometry may lead a pupil to be more logical in all respects, for one element of being logical in all respects is to realize that facts can be absolutely proven and to admire and desire this certain and unquestionable sort of demonstration. (From Thorndike, 1913, p. 430. With permission of publisher.)

The above quotation provides the essence of the theory of identical elements. It provided more freedom in the selection of courses than the idea that nothing transferred. The introduction of new courses could extend learnings from previous courses. Some transfer of specific content was assumed in the planning of efficient curricula; a view that gave some guidelines for the curriculum-constructor since it would be impossible, and contradictory to common sense, to teach everything the pupil must know in exactly the same form it was to be used in future years.

Through Thorndike's experiments on transfer and his theory of identical elements, course content took its rightful place in curriculum construction. Courses were taught not because they sharpened the pupil's faculties but because the content itself was judged intrinsically useful. The teacher no longer emphasized the formal functions of memorizing, concentrating, and attending. Now the specific skills, facts, and habits that pupils must use in the future became a major concern of the educator. In an indirect way, this theory influenced a renewed emphasis on such subjects as social studies, homemaking, citizenship, and physical education, while other courses such as Latin and Greek were eliminated for most groups of pupils.

Generalization—Learning Bonus and Penalty

Transfer is strongly influenced along two generalization dimensions which now require explaining: The kind of situation the pupil is in (stimulus input) and what he attends to in that situation (stimulus selection); and variability of behavior in a situation. Both sets of relationships affect all learning and are especially important in motor learning.

The selected stimuli affect transfer

Once learning has occurred, a given form of behavior can be evoked by many similar situations (stimulus generalization); for example, feelings of like or dislike for one course may be elicited by other courses. The study of French may come easily to a fluent speaker of Spanish because the same response may be made to words that are either identical or similar in the two languages (stimulus generalization leads to positive transfer).

The extent to which transfer occurs depends on whether similarities between the learning *and* transfer situation are perceived by the pupil. Since situations are highly complex they will differ in many ways. Concomitantly, which stimuli are perceived (or selected) will also differ. If the pupil does not "see" the same elements in the two settings there will be little or no transfer; conversely, if he "sees" both situations as being the same there may be positive or negative transfer depending upon the desired outcome. The personality, motivation, ability, previous experience, and other individual difference variables will also affect what is seen, perceived, and selected by the individual (Maltzman, 1967).

The idea of *stimulus selection* implies that any concept (e.g., of water, democracy, expressionistic painting, or cacophony) should be developed by experiences with it in many contexts so that appropriate stimuli will be attended to on later occasions. The development of the meaning of photosynthesis requires associations with the stimulus terms of leaves, chlorophyll, light, carbon dioxide, oxygen, and the like. In learning a motor skill, appropriate stimuli can be selected only by individual practice. If this provision for practice is not made the pupil can never recognize the *kinesthetic cues* (stimuli that result from movements of the muscles) that guide action of the skill. There is no substi-

tute for these. So important is this fact that special attempts are often
made when skills are being learned to emphasize the kinesthetic cues.
Accordingly, typing teachers remove symbols from the keys of the typewriter when the pupil is learning to type; the shop teacher may blind-
fold the student who is learning to disassemble and assemble a piece of
machinery; and the basketball coach may obstruct the lower part of the
basketball player's visual field with opaque glasses.

The effects of training and of the similarity between the initial
and the new learning situations on stimulus generalization is shown in
an experiment by Spiker (1956) in which kindergarten and first grade
children were subjects. The children were reinforced by receiving a
marble when they responded correctly to a light of a given intensity.
They were not rewarded when they responded to a light of a different
intensity (brightness). After this training, they were given a new task of
responding to lights of different intensities. As the differences in intensities between the lights in the new task and those in the initial learning
task increased, the number of previously learned responses elicited was
decreased as shown in Figure 9-1.

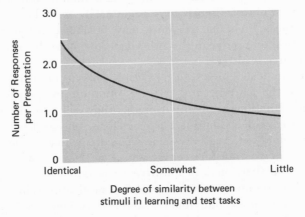

Figure 9-1. *Pupils who learn to press a lever for a marble when they see a
light of one intensity, perform similarly, but to a lesser degree, with lights of
different intensities. This is one illustration of the stimulus generalization gradient. (Adapted from C. C. Spiker, 1956, p. 91. With permission of author and
the Society for Research in Child Development, Inc.)*

Another interesting feature of this experiment was that those
pupils who were rewarded a greater number of times in the original
training generalized (i.e., responded) primarily to the lights most similar to the training stimulus to a greater degree than did those who were
rewarded half as many times (see Figure 9-2). The latter group, on the
other hand, generalized to a wider range of stimuli including those only
slightly similar to those in the original task.

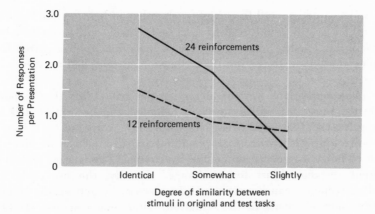

Figure 9-2. The thoroughness of initial learning influences generalization to new tasks. (Adapted from C. C. Spiker, 1956, p. 95. With permission of author and the Society for Research in Child Development, Inc.)

Discriminations are precise and overgeneralization is controlled when the initial task is thoroughly learned, an important result when there is only one correct answer to a problem, or when a single correct response must be made instantaneously and automatically, as in most learning of skills. On the other hand, continued practice of a single response in a limited situation makes the pupil inflexible when it becomes necessary for him to adapt to a slightly different situation.

Variations in responses affect transfer

Just as a given behavior may be elicited by a range of stimuli, so may a given situation elicit a wide range of responses. Although a baseball player has been instructed by a professional on how to drive a golf ball, the baseball player may find himself reverting to a "baseball swing." The swing of a bat has generalized to the drive in golf, probably resulting in negative transfer. When inappropriate new responses are learned to a given situation the result is negative transfer. Nevertheless, as with stimulus generalization, whether positive or negative transfer results from response generalization depends upon the response selected by the learner, upon the relationship between the response and the desired outcome, and upon the similarity or incompatibility of responses in the learning and transfer tasks.

As one might expect, response generalization will occur most frequently among responses that resemble one another. Whatever the situation, a *hierarchy of responses* is always available. This simply means the pupil has many related behaviors that can be ordered in terms of their strength, or probability of being used, in a given situation. Some responses will have high probability of being evoked in a setting; others are there but will have to be "teased" out. Problem-solving for example depends upon variability in behavior, upon a search for a response that is low in the pupil's response hierarchy and must be made salient.

There are many ways of increasing the probability that responses low in the hierarchy will be used. A behavior can be inhibited if it is not reinforced (that is, if it is extinguished). A response that does not help solve a problem will be dropped and another tried in its place. An overused behavior gets tiresome and is dropped. The learner looks for a different response "just for a change." Finally, the use of a long-standing response can be weakened, in a sense, by getting the pupil to perceive new elements in the situation. Thus, one response might be made to the word "club" if placed among the names of instruments or tools, but quite another response would be made if it were placed among the names of different social organizations. By response generalization the former definition of *club* might be "a weapon" while the latter definition of *club* might be "a small organized group." Accordingly, the teacher controls the behavior (definition) by manipulating the situation.

From cognitions to motor skills

Although the concept of response hierarchies has considerable heuristic value the reader should not infer that training in motor skills (or any other type of learning) involves only the raising or lowering of a response in the hierarchy, or only the shaping of a behavior. An interesting alternative approach has been suggested by Miller, Galanter, and Pribram (1960). Though these authors employ a cognitive approach, the principles of response generalization are still assumed to hold. They suggest that the learning of a skill involves two stages (also see Fitts & Posner, 1967, for a similar position): First, there is a verbal plan, an overall strategy for carrying out the skill. The strategy can be communicated from teacher to pupil and can be easily remembered by the pupil. Second, but exceedingly more difficult to implement, is the execution of the plan. Muscular (motor) patterns of behavior identified through search, trial and error, and the like must be coordinated with the verbal pattern. Correction is continually made through perceptual feedback. The *beginner's* implementation of this strategy is, as one might expect, flexible and continually changing. After much practice the *expert* executes the plan, inflexibly and in unitary fashion, through the prescribed sequence of motor activity. The verbal crutch is dropped. Once achieved the behavior plan, whether the "look-remember-hunt-hit-check" plan for typing or the "move-right-rudder-when-extended-finger-touches-panel" plan for the take-off maneuver in an airplane (both examples are borrowed from Miller, Galanter, & Pribram, 1960, p. 88) can then be transferred to new situations. As a consequence of this analysis one would expect that the characteristics of a motor skill change with practice. As the reader can see in Figure 9-3 this is the case.

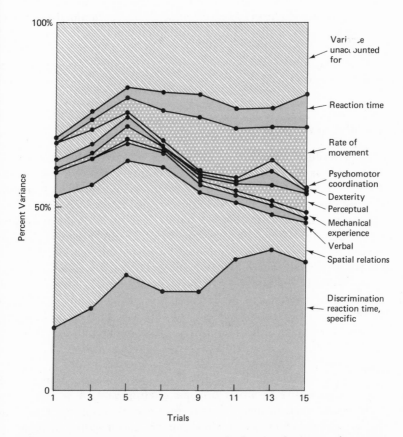

Figure 9-3. The factors associated with the development of a motor skill change in kind and amount with practice stages. (From E. A. Fleishman & W. E. Hempel, Jr., 1954, p. 248. With permission of authors and publisher.)

A very practical way of enhancing a response change is through the principle of *shaping* employed in programmed learning. This principle is based on the notion that the *position* of responses in a habit hierarchy can be deliberately changed by the teacher. Thus, a difficult pattern of behavior in a skill can be taught by starting the pupil with a readily available response (one that is high in the hierarchy) and then gradually changing its topography (shape or form) by rewarding modifications toward a terminal objective (a response low in the hierarchy). An illustration is to be found in teaching the high jump. The pupil is taught to jump a few feet at first. Then, the pole is raised by small degrees, with consequent necessary changes in form as practice progresses, to a height of four or five feet or whatever the aim is. In teaching the concept of *classical conditioning* in a programmed textbook, the programmer also begins with an available response (for example, with the definition of a reflex) and then gradually adds some features, subtracts others, until its topography, too, is modified according to some stated terminal objective.

Verbally mediated transfer

Transfer in humans is most often mediated through words and other symbols whose meanings depend on the kinds of experiences with which they have been associated. Examples are not difficult to find. In learning new skills, such as swimming, speaking a foreign language, or playing an instrument, existing habits can be brought into play by verbal behavior (Fitts, 1964). Demonstration and practice of skills are inevitably preceded or accompanied by verbal instruction. The general process of verbally mediated influence may be described as: Situation ———→Verbal Mediator———→Behavioral Pattern. This can be exemplified in the sequence of activities that might be involved in the learning of French-English equivalents as follows: The pupil first sees the French word terre (the stimulus). Then he verbalizes, "That's very much like the English word *terrestrial* (the mediator), and consequently says, "*Terre* probably means *earth*" (the response).

As a result of their ability to use language, humans have a remarkable ability to adapt to their environment. A wealth of experiences can be transformed (coded) into verbal responses. Coded behaviors are advantageous since they can be stored easily in memory and retrieved readily from memory. The verbal person is more adaptable in many situations than is the less verbal person precisely for the reason that he has more codes for discriminating among situations and for storing new information.

The culturally deprived pupil, the less fluent individual, and the person with the smaller vocabulary are handicapped in their ability to profit from experience by their language deficiency (see Deutsch, 1966). This distinction can be seen in the performance of children with greater language facility (i.e., children from middle socioeconomic status families) compared with the performance of children with less language facility (i.e., children from lower SES families). When children in the two groups worked on a task of sorting cards into several categories both groups performed equally well. However, when questioned after completing the task, the middle SES children could describe the basis for categorizing the cards while the children from lower SES families could not (John, 1963). Such evidence provides at least partial justification for the special attention given to labeling experiences in the compensatory education of disadvantaged children.

Once experiences are stored in verbal form they of course can be retrieved or evoked by numerous other situations and cues, even by orders to oneself, just as can other kinds of responses. Through verbal review, introduction to a topic, pretraining, examples, descriptions, and other verbal devices, the teacher can help the pupil to link his past experience with the demands of the new task.

Labels, attached to a new situation, function to make some stimuli more distinctive and, thereby, more influential than others in affecting a behavioral pattern. This effect of labels is called *acquired distinctiveness* of cues. Other times the use of labels can make the situation more like one already experienced so that a ready response is elicited as in learning the English equivalent of the French word "terre." This effect of labels is called *acquired equivalence of cues*. The notion of transformation of incoming stimuli by labels can be seen in the formation of some attitudes. Imagine that one sees a very average-appearing person who is a complete stranger walk into the room. Most likely, reactions to him will be quite neutral. Now suppose that someone indicates the person is a dogmatic authoritarian. The perception of the person (stimulus) has probably been transformed dramatically, as a result of this verbal label, into a negative stimulus-object. As a consequence, reactions to him will probably be unfavorable.

Characteristic of dependence on mediators, such as labels, in learning a skill is that it takes time to use them. To go from stimulus to verbal mediator to response requires more time to perform than to go from stimulus to response or to go from stimulus to kinesthetic cue-producing responses to overt responses (see Figure 9-4). The mediating verbalization *does* facilitate the initial learning of the movements of a skill, but is much like a "crutch" which might hinder peak performance unless discarded. With sufficient practice these crutches are discarded and the response is made directly to the incoming pattern of stimuli and to the kinesthetic cues. The response is smoother, more coordinated, and more automatic than when a mediator was present. Then, and only then, can one say that the performance takes on its "skilled" characteristics.

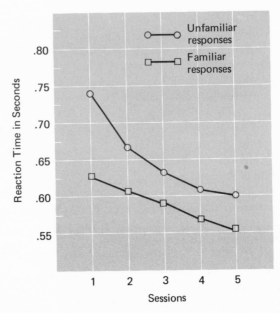

Figure 9-4. With more mediators reaction time is increased. In the familiar response condition, subject associated pictures of objects (such as bird, letter, dress, and chair) with the first letter of the object name (e.g., B, L, D, and C). The mediation chain was assumed to be Stimulus———▸ Familiar object name ———▸ Vocalization of first letter. In the unfamiliar response condition the 12 pictures were associated with the same letters but different pairings. The mediation chain was assumed to be Stimulus———▸ Familiar object name ———▸ Some other name———▸ Vocalization of first letter. The lowering of reaction time over trials suggests the dropping out of mediators. (From Fitts, 1964, p. 263–2( ). With permission of publisher.)

Verbal facilitation of motor patterns of behavior

The effectiveness of *verbal* pretraining in learning a *motor* skill was demonstrated in an interesting experiment by McAllister (1953). The subject worked with an apparatus called a Star Discrimeter. As the name implies it had six channels crossing at the center in the form of a six-pointed star. A vertical rod located at the center could be moved into any one channel by a push or pull motion. The stimuli were six colored light bulbs on a panel viewed by the subject, whose task was to associate a given channel with one of the light-colors. For example, when the blue light was on, he was to move the rod into the 60° channel, i.e., at the 2 o'clock position. When the yellow light was on, he had to move the rod into the 180° channel and so on.

Before performing this task, the subjects were given verbal pretraining. One group learned associations between terms (for example, *inert-valiant*) that were irrelevant to the task. Neither the stimulus nor response in the pairs of words had anything to do with the task of learning color discriminations as cues for lever adjustment. This group was used to provide a control for any effects that might be due to warm-up, i.e., practice. Another group learned to associate the *relevant* color names of the stimulus lights with other words *irrelevant* to the task (for example, *blue-valiant*). Three other groups learned to associate the color names *relevant* to the task with "degrees" (for example, blue-0°), with "clock" (for example, blue–twelve o'clock) or with "directions" (for example, blue–forward right) analogues of the channels on the Star Discrimeter. The latter three groups were called the *relevant stimulus-response* groups. After verbal pretraining the subjects in each group then learned the motor task of moving the vertical rod into the appropriate channel when signaled by the colored lights.

When both stimulus and response verbalizations in the pretraining task were direct analogues of the movements required to perform the task, learning of the motor response was facilitated. The group receiving irrelevant pretraining on both stimuli and responses, and those groups receiving pretraining with relevant color names but irrelevant verbal response, performed less efficiently and made many more errors than did the three relevant stimulus-response pretraining groups.

Teachers of motor skills, including sports, music, driving, and typing, inevitably use pet analogues to help their pupils relate physical movements to the strategy for performing the skill. One tennis instructor, for example, instructs his student in this strategy: Pivot the entire body so that when making the backhand stroke the right shoulder is perpendicular to the net; and when making the forehand stroke the left shoulder is swung toward the net. In executing either stroke unwind toward the original position. To aid the pupil in performing the precise movements he uses the "clock" analogues such as "hold the left foot at 12 o'clock" and "bring the right foot to 5 o'clock."

Verbal pretraining

Words and labels, richly laden with association from prior experience, then, provide pupils with an important means of generalization that can often be used effectively in new situations (Russell & Storms, 1955). They provide the necessary readiness patterns for the successful initiation of an activity. However, without *meaning*, a label, rule, or other mediator, is a functionally useless and empty verbalization. The meaning of a word or a label indicates the kind of situations in which the word applies and the types of response needed.

Verbal pretraining is most effective when the relevant cues for subsequent learning are emphasized as shown in the study of motor learning by McAllister described above. A similar conclusion was reached by Levin, Watson, and Feldman (1964) who investigated writing as pretraining for word recognition. They provided preschool children training on graphemes (i.e., symbols analogous to letters of the alphabet) such as ∏ X 8 I ⋈ and then tested the children on real words such as MAGIC. Greatest positive transfer to the learning of a real word was found when children were pretrained with the first *grapheme* of the artificial word, some transfer when the children were pretrained on the last grapheme, and least transfer when pretrained on the middle grapheme.

The range of pretraining studies is exemplified further by Wittrock, Keislar, and Stern's (1964) experiment. In a concept-identification task, kindergarten children learned the French names of 12 common objects and animals, the article (*la* or *le*) associated with each noun, and to label *la* or *le* as an *article*. In a new discrimination task the children had to match pictures according to the correct article associated with it; thus, *La Maison* (house) would be correctly matched with *La Chemise* (shirt) but incorrectly matched with *Le Bateau* (boat). One group was told only that "something you have learned will help you to find the correct answer." Another group was told, "The article will help you find the right answer." A third group was told, "The top picture is a *La* (*Le*) word. Find a *La* (*Le*) picture on the bottom that goes with it." The fourth group was told, "The top picture is (French noun). Find the picture that goes with it." In this study it was found that a verbal cue leads to more efficient transfer than does a more general or more specific cue; i.e., pupils were able to transfer the instruction that the *article* was important, more effectively than the instruction that "something you have learned is important," or the instruction to find the *la* or *le* word.

Pretraining is effective because it (1) increases the distinctiveness of the important attributes of the task, (2) reduces the generalization among the varied cues present in the total task, (3) increases attention to the important cues, or (4) increases the meaningfulness of the task (Arnoult, 1957). If teachers are to guide pupils toward more effective transfer by the processes described in this chapter and the chapter on language and concept formation, it is necessary that pupils label their experiences and that they see how concepts identify both similar and different characteristics among different events. Pupils can be encouraged to recognize the specific ways one responds when a situation is coded one way as compared with another. Codes and labels *are* learned. Their acquisition is influenced by the same processes as are all learning. The articulate pupil who possesses a rich and wide store of codes (among which is his vocabulary) has a decided advantage in his ability to benefit from new experience.

What Transfers?

The facts, concepts, skills, and general information taught in school subjects transfer extensively to new learning situations. In addition, some behaviors are learned as by-products of experience and may demonstrably transfer to later situations. We can see how many of the factors which transfer in these ways are brought to bear on the activity of the pupil in the following illustration.

In a chemistry laboratory a pupil is making chlorine. He knows what compounds must be combined (facts transfer). In setting up his apparatus he first bends glass tubing (skills transfer). The apparatus is then assembled cautiously with neatness and care (methods transfer). He proceeds with an air of confidence and deliberation (attitudes transfer). If we overview the whole process we find that he works systematically, almost rigidly following the procedures he used in previous experiments. Everything is constantly checked routinely and his findings are recorded as though he were unaware of the actual processes (learning sets transfer).

Attitudes, sets, problem-solving orientations, and other general behavior tendencies may be acquired in subtle ways without "conscious" awareness by the pupil. Because of their pervasive nature they transfer to many kinds of situations and are worthy of special attention in the curriculum by the teacher of special courses (especially remedial ones) and by the teacher of subject-matter areas. With the aid of appropriate experiences, a pupil can be helped to develop positive abilities and attitudes in addition to the specific facts and skills taught in any subject which has a rightful place in the curriculum.

Rules, concepts, and principles facilitate transfer

Rules and principles are among the cognitive tools for facilitating transfer. If one were to memorize the string of numbers 137153163127 it would be a somewhat difficult task if only rote memory were used. However, with little study, the rule by which the string of numbers is organized can be found. First, the sequence 1 - 3 - 7 - 15 - 31 - 63 - 127 is noted (Katona, 1940). Then, the rule or structure becomes apparent. It is simply: multiply by two and add one to get the next number. The rule permits the person to *recall* the string of numbers but it also transfers so that he can *generate new additions* to the series as necessary.

Psychologists who conduct experiments in verbal learning often find difficulty in devising tasks which can be performed entirely by rote association. Their subjects inevitably seek the underlying rule that is the basis for reinforcement or that links the stimulus-response elements in a paired associate task even where no linkage was intended. Principles and formulas in mathematics, physics, chemistry, and other school subjects are rules, too. They help to summarize a wide range of details in a single relationship. Their transfer to other situations makes possible the generation of data that could be obtained only by extensive tables. Examine a simple problem such as finding the area of a triangle. When the height and base are known the principle (formula) can be applied and the area found with little trouble. For college students and most high school students such problems are mere "exercises." However, without the formula the person would have to resort to voluminous tables and each new set of data would constitute another problem. These illustrations exemplify the notion that rules or principles help to organize what is learned. Understanding is thereby enhanced, and in turn transfers to make learning another task easier.

Minor variations from "sameness" may sometimes hinder positive transfer of rules. Many years ago Thorndike conducted a study in which entering college freshmen were given the following problems at widely separated points in the same test:

$$\text{Expand:} \quad (x + y)^2$$
$$\text{Expand:} \quad (b_1 + b_2)^2$$

Since only the symbols are varied it is clear that both problems are algebraically equivalent. The correct solution of each depends upon the same rule or principle. About 30 percent of the students taking this test were able to solve the first problem successfully. Yet only about 6 percent of the same students correctly solved the problem restated with the symbols b_1 and b_2. From this example, it is obvious that one cannot assume automatic transfer of a rule to new situations even where it seems apparent that pupils should do so. If the pupil employs only the symbols X and Y in solving algebraic problems, he may never learn that the notations of b, $\square$, p, or ∞ may also function as symbols without changing the basic nature of the process. Formerly the X and Y notation was used almost exclusively in teaching algebra. Furthermore, algebra was taught primarily at the junior high school level. In modern schools, the meanings of algebraic symbols, as symbols, are learned as early as the second grade. As a consequence we would not expect a replication of Thorndike's little experiment to yield the same results today. Nevertheless, the same implications for education remain. Provision for positive transfer must be made at the time the subject matter is taught.

The best way to assure transfer is to teach for it. The pupil must be able to "see" that some elements in what he is learning are similar to important elements in a variety of potential transfer situations. In a real sense, this is one definition of what is meant by the popular cliché that says ". . . experiences should be meaningful to the pupil." All courses present information, facts, and skills potentially useful in problem-solving and reasoning, however, facts and skills are not always automatically available to facilitate learning or problem-solving in new situations. Many applications must be made of the material at the time it is being taught by teaching it within a realistic context (Overing & Travers, 1966, 1967). Diagrammatic presentation of an idea may help to make it more discriminable in the future, but it is not as effective for transfer as teaching the material within contexts where many irrelevant cues, such as those found in everyday situations, are present.

Buswell (1956) has also emphasized the importance of principles and generalizations in facilitating transfer in the following quotation: "The [cognition] embodied in the arithmetical generalization . . . 'when both the numerator and denominator of a fraction are multiplied by the same number, the value of the fraction is not changed' . . . is more transferable than the specific fact that two-thirds and four-sixths have equivalent value" (pp. 180–181).

One cannot deny the wide applicability of principles, but the operation of the principle and the situation to which it applies should be made explicit. In an early study Wesman (1945) found that training in arithmetic reasoning, good judgment in problem situations, logical reasoning, and interpretation of fables facilitated the solution of other problems but the improvement was mainly on performance of the kinds of problems used in training. In the absence of special applications there was only slight transfer from any one of these learnings to the other three. Thus, principles are transferred most effectively by teaching methods which define the similarities between situations and the relevant applications of the principles (Ulmer, 1939). The broader possibilities for transfer become evident through studies such as those described. However, none of the suggestions from the investigations cited obviates the need for teaching pupils the necessary facts and habits for successful living. Rather, the evidence implies the need for supplementing experience and instruction with general principles.

Transposition

Closely related to transfer of principles is *transposition*. This term refers to the transfer of a *relationship* learned in one setting to a new, appropriate situation. (See Figure 9-5). The meaning of this term is parallel to its meaning in music. When a musical composition is transposed, the specific notes may be changed according to prescribed rules but the relationship of each note to the others remains the same. Consequently, the key is changed but the melody remains the same. Transposition in learning depends upon similar relationships between the relevant attributes of the pairs of stimuli used in the training and the test

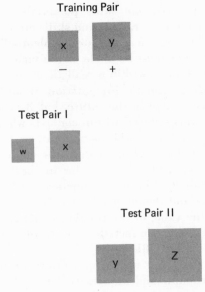

Figure 9-5. In the transposition experiment the subject will be reinforced for selecting stimulus Y during training, regardless of its position. When the choice is correctly made, the subject will be tested on other pairs. When presented with Test Pair I the subject will select X even though it was not previously reinforced. Stimulus Z will be selected in Test Pair II even though Y was reinforced in the training series. It is assumed that the subject in each case is reacting to relationships rather than to absolute stimuli.

task. The subject may respond to "smaller," "darker," "lighter," "farther," or any other perceptible relationship.

    With children 3 to 4 years of age, transposition occurs with *"near"* tests, i.e., tests with stimuli near to the sizes involved in the training stimuli. Transfer does not occur for the *"far"* tests, that is, with tests where the stimulus sizes are several steps removed from the training stimuli.* Older children and adults respond to the relational properties on both near and far tests. While the exact nature of transposition is still not completely understood, some evidence indicates that verbal processes are important (Kuenne, 1946). Young children may not possess the concepts required for transfer of the principle to the far tests. Older children transpose on both near and far tests since they have both the mediational facility and the applicable conceptualizations.

    *Other evidence (Zeiler, 1963), it should be noted, suggests that the *ratios* (as subjectively experienced by the subject) between stimuli in the original learning task are important determiners of transposition. The ratio provides a base against which new judgments are made. Subjects tend to choose the stimulus closest to the ratio experienced in the initial training. As the ratios depart radically in the test task from those in the training task choices become more random.

The implications of the transposition experiment for education is of particular consequence in the teaching of cognitive behaviors. Effective reasoning and problem-solving depends upon the transfer of general principles defining the relationships among objects or events. This requirement underlies a broad range of applications. Older children behave quite differently from young children in their transposition behavior. Presumably, the older child's facility results from his ability to attach relevant verbal labels to the stimuli and to conceptualize the relationships among them. Transposition occurs to the extent that the relationships are perceived against an accurate base as a guideline. If the basis of the relationship is not readily identifiable, the pupil can be helped to discover it for himself and to label it appropriately.

Transfer of attitudes

A very subtle carry-over from one situation to another is seen in the transfer of attitudes. Prejudices and biases about one ethnic group are likely to transfer (or generalize) to other groups with like characteristics, and other groups that are perceived to have similar characteristics. Attitudes transfer and, as with other learnings, may affect further learning or performances.

An experiment by Sherriffs and Boomer (1954) illustrates that the class of attitudes toward oneself, called the self-concept, may influence responses to a testing situation. One group of students (high-anxious) lacked self-assurance, had low self-esteem, were retiring, and were overly concerned with the impression they made on others. The students in the second group (low-anxious) were confident of their ability, had little difficulty in making decisions, and were not easily threatened in ambiguous situations. These groups were then given a true-false examination. They were told that the examination was to be scored with a "rights-minus-wrongs" penalty for guessing. After the tests were completed they were instructed to circle all items that had been omitted. The students were then given the opportunity to indicate what they believed to be the correct answers to the omitted items. Their test papers were scored by the rights-minus-wrongs formula, by the number correct, and by penalty incurred through the omission of answers. The results are shown in Figure 9-6.

The pupils who lacked self-assurance omitted a greater number of items on the true-false test than did their more confident counterparts. Lacking self-assurance and confidence in their own judgment they took the middle-of-the-road course of action. They probably thought something like this: "Taking the chance of putting down an answer might result in a higher score but it might also result in a severe penalty. The safest alternative is to omit an item I am uncertain about."

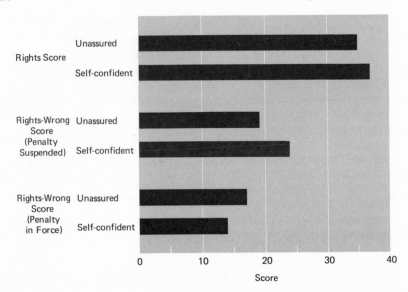

Figure 9-6. Anxiety and lack of self-confidence generalizes to performance on an achievement examination. The anxious pupil is penalized when "rights-minus-wrongs" scoring methods are used. (Adapted from A. C. Sherriffs & D. S. Boomer, 1954, p. 88. With permission of authors and publisher.)

In another study (Updegraff *et al.*, 1937) it was found that pupils who proceed from easy problems to more difficult ones, with success experiences at each level of difficulty, tackle new problems with more confidence and persistence than do those children confronted with continual failures. Teaching activities should be programmed so that the pupil is continually challenged, provided the tasks are always within his capabilities. A reasonable number of success experiences are necessary if favorable attitudes about oneself are to transfer.

Innumerable attitudes about responsibility, patriotism, loyalty, honesty, and other social and cultural attitudes are important in adjustment and may carry over to new situations. In addition, there is the whole realm of attitudes toward oneself, family, and other persons that can transfer to a variety of related situations. Accordingly, the school has a responsibility for developing attitudes that will promote a realistic and mentally healthy adjustment now and in the future.

Transfer of learning processes

"The acquisition of general techniques such as how to use a library card catalogue, is of far more general value than to learn the location on the shelves of a specific reference" (Buswell, 1956, p. 181).

Every activity involves a way of doing things, a procedure, a "how to
. . . ." The pupil may learn these informally, out of his personal experience, or through school experience. If the methods are not formally
taught they may be learned incidentally in connection with course content, and often in a slipshod fashion. Such methods range from learning
to use an outline in taking course notes to social techniques at a party.

Transfer of methods justifies an emphasis on general procedures.
In arithmetic the pupil may be taught how to use multiplication, how to
check results, how to use "crutches" in the first step of learning, how to
estimate quotient figures in division, and the like. Tasks can be set to
provide the pupil with an opportunity to learn these procedures while
at the same time helping him to establish meanings, as is currently being
done in the teaching of modern math. An emphasis only on "correct
answers" in routine drill exercises, an emphasis that gives no attention
to the processes involved in arriving at a solution, may result in little
positive transfer to new situations (Buswell, 1956). In courses other than
arithmetic, the teacher might highlight the processes of interpretation
and discussion of printed matter, the processes involved in laboratory
techniques, and so on. The National Training Laboratory at Bethel,
Maine, for example, has as its primary function the training in methods
of handling group interactions, now known as sensitivity training.

Over the past two decades there has been an increased interest in
the teaching of study methods in the so-called "study skills" courses.
These courses deal, in the main, with improvement of reading, general
study skills, and vocabulary. After a review of 38 of these courses,
Entwistle (1960) concluded that the learning of study skills leads to an
average achievement gain of about one half letter grade. The results are
interesting because a wide variety of content was represented. However,
the gains did not appear to be related either to course content or to the
duration of the course. It may be that methods transfer in a general
way, and indeed, this summary of results is being used to exemplify that
possibility. However, Entwistle's conclusions also raise the question of
whether gains following study methods courses are due to motivational
factors since students who want to take the course seem to be the main
beneficiaries. The answer to this question is clarified by noting that students who wish "to take a study skills course but are prevented from
doing so, and therefore presumably of comparable motivation to those
enrolled, fail to show significant improvement" (Entwistle, 1960, p.
250).

Woodrow's experiment

Specific instruction in procedural methods can produce effective
results. In an important experiment, Woodrow (1927) compared the

gains in ability to memorize of three groups of pupils who were taught different techniques of memorizing over a period of 4 weeks and 5 days. One group was given a test before and after the experiment but no training or practice. A practice group memorized poetry and nonsense syllables with neither explanation nor discussion of methods to be used in memorizing. They were told only to practice memorizing the passage. A total of 177 minutes was spent in this activity during periods, averaging 22 minutes in length, held twice a week. The third group was called the training group. These pupils spent the same amount of total time in the activity except that their time was *budgeted between actual practice in memorizing and listening to an exposition of the techniques of memorizing.* The subjects were taught to employ self-testing, learning by wholes, rhythm, and imagery or otherwise putting individual meaning into the poem when learning it. They were also taught to concentrate and to have self-confidence in their ability to memorize. Seventy-six minutes were devoted to listening to and practice of these rules, 76 minutes to memorizing poetry, and 25 minutes to memorizing nonsense syllables. (The reader should note the similarity between these training methods and those proposed in the section which describes the effects of principles on transfer.) The training group far surpassed either of the other two groups on six different tests of memorization given at the end of the experiment. A summary of the results is presented in Figure 9-7.

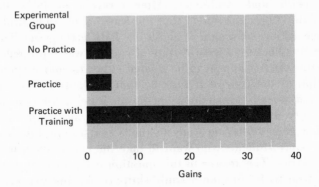

Figure 9-7. Average gains in memorizing by pupils who previously had no practice in memorizing, and practice in memorizing plus training in methods of memorizing. The same amount of total time was spent in the activity by the latter two groups. The time spent on teaching pupils good study methods results in better performance and more time available for other class activities. (Adapted from H. Woodrow, 1927, p. 168. With permission of publisher.)

Transfer of learning strategies, or learning to learn

We have all had the experience of finding the first of a series of poems more difficult to memorize than those later in a series. A similar observation may have been made in learning a series of mechanical or mathematical puzzles. Students often indicate better performance on multiple-choice or essay examinations, although they report having had difficulty, originally, in taking the type of examination that is later preferred. These observations imply that the person's facility in learning situations is somehow enhanced by experience and extends to problems that are quite unlike those in the originally learned tasks.

The phenomenon illustrated above is called *learning set* or *learning how to learn* (Harlow, 1949). Laboratory investigations are conducted by a relatively standard technique in which the subject is given a series of problems, sometimes many hundreds of problems, each with a common solution rule (see Chapter 6).

In articulate organisms learning sets probably reflect the influence of a *win-stay, lose-shift* strategy, i.e., of some such mediating verbalization as "Stay with the object chosen if it is rewarded, shift to the other object if the first object is not rewarded" (Reese, 1965, p. 153).

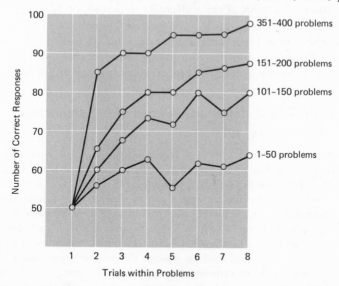

Figure 9-8. With practice on many problems, new problems of a similar nature are solved with the rapidity characteristic of insight, demonstrating that insightful behavior depends, in part, on experience. (From Learning set and error factor theory, H. F. Harlow. Copyright 1959. Used with permission of author and McGraw-Hill Book Co.)

Unlike other kinds of learning, transfer of learning sets is measured by the amount of facilitation from one problem to the next. Since the problems are different on each occasion, the transfer is called *nonspecific* transfer.

The rapidity with which a learning set is developed depends upon how much is transferred from problem to problem (Harlow, 1959; Morrisett & Hovland, 1959). (See Figure 9-8.) On the first few tasks very little new behavior is acquired on each trial (thus, there is little that can be transferred) compared to the amount learned on each trial later in the series of problems (where there is more learning than can be transferred). Accordingly, it is important to allow much practice in an early period of training. Then, since this training will transfer, less practice will be necessary in subsequent stages.

A most important implication of research on learning sets is that insight, thinking, reasoning, and problem-solving can be enhanced by extensive practice on problems. Flexibility in these processes requires practice in many contexts. Extended practice in the early stages of learning seems essential if reliable learning sets are to be developed. These conclusions are most important in planning all educational experiences but especially so for planning preschool curricula, and for compensatory education of the culturally deprived, or for other special education groups. When pupils have well-developed verbal abilities and where teachers wish to make a deliberate attempt to teach learning to learn there is no question that the process may be shortened considerably by didactic instruction in the best strategy for a given problem.

Individual differences and the formation of learning sets

A study by Harter (1965) is important to education because it shows the relationship of IQ and MA to the formation of learning sets. Her study followed the standard procedure: Each trial consisted of selecting the correct stimulus from a pair of objects. The correct object was blind-baited, i.e., a marble was placed in a hole beneath the object. The stimuli were 200 "junk" objects such as spools, ash trays, cups, boxes, and so on presented in pairs. A problem consisted of four trials in which the child had to choose the object representing a given attribute such as roundness, angularity, blueness, or softness. The child received a marble as a token reward for each correct choice and later exchanged the marbles for a colored decal prize. There were ten problems on each of several consecutive days until a learning set had been formed satisfactorily.

The slowest rate of acquisition was found in the group with the lowest MA (five) and IQ (70); the fastest rate of acquisition was

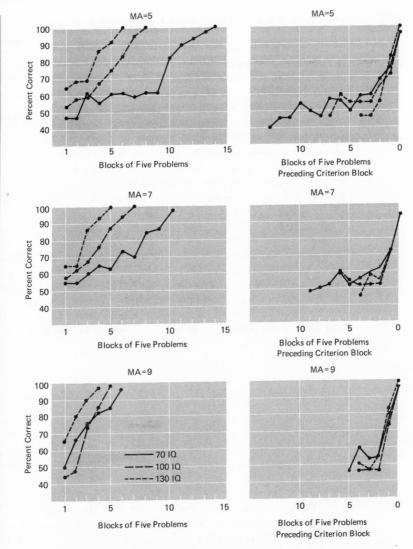

Figure 9-9. Learning set curves for children with different mental and chronological ages. Note especially the lengths of the presolution periods (before the sudden and abrupt rise in the learning curves) as they are related to different levels of maturity. (From S. Harter, 1965, Figure 2, p. 36. With permission of author and publisher.)

found in the group with highest MA (nine) and IQ (130). Both groups had a chronological age of seven. Comparisons of other groups can be made from the graphs shown in Figure 9-9. Note that a child of 3½ years with an IQ of 130 (MA = 5) performed with fewer errors and developed a learning set more rapidly than a seven-year-old child with an IQ of 70.

Figure 9-9, which depicts acquisition of learning sets, does not tell the entire story. It hides the fact that acquisition curves for individual subjects generally revealed chance or slightly above performance on early problems and then the quality of performance increased abruptly as the subject neared the criterion. Note, for example, how slowly the first problems were solved by subjects with a mental age of five and an IQ of 70. Toward the last of the problems there is a sudden rise in performance. To highlight this two-stage process in the acquisition of learning sets Harter (1965) plotted backward learning curves* for the same data. These are shown in the curves to the right of Figure 9-9, which clearly display the insightful characteristic of learning sets. At the point where the subject "catches on," "forms a hypothesis," or "learns the strategy," the rate of acquisition accelerates rapidly, that is, the subsequent problems are solved quickly with few errors. The main difference between the performance of high and low IQ groups appears to be in the length of the period prior to the sudden rise. This observation carries with it the implication that children with lower IQs can learn to form learning sets but must be given considerably more time, more experience, and perhaps more help in verbalizing their experiences than is necessary for children with higher IQs.

Teaching a cognitive skill in mathematics

An arithmetic teacher's objective was to teach pupils an understanding of number base according to learning set principles. The teacher scheduled a short lesson once a day over several weeks and decided to cover all number bases from base 2 to base 12. The parallel between the tasks required in meeting this objective and those in the laboratory study of learning sets is immediately apparent, as follows:

Each number base was considered as a single *problem*. There were, then, 10 problems. (Base 10 was eliminated since the student was familiar with it.) Within each number base there were a series of exercises including conversions to and from base 10, counting, place values, addition, subtraction, and so on. Assuming these were fully designed exercises, as they would be in a programmed learning sequence, each exercise constituted a *trial* within a problem.

A decision was made to start with base 2 for motivational reasons. The teacher was able to demonstrate the utility of number bases because of the advantages of base 2 for computers. The order of the remaining problems were random.

*Backward learning curves are plotted backward from the criterion rather than forward to the criterion.

At this point the teacher decided how much time to spend on each number base. There were several alternatives, the most obvious being the following: spend equal amounts of time on each problem; schedule more time on the first problems than on the later problems; plan less time on the first problems to expose the pupil to a variety of problems with more time given to the later problems; or allot varying amounts of time among problems.

Since the teacher's decision about scheduling of time was made on the basis of learning set principles the second alternative was used. Thus, when the base 2 problem was presented it contained many exercises (trials) to assure sufficient acquisition by the pupil that the processes involved were easily transferred to the next problem. Pupils were given all the time they needed to go over the problem until they thoroughly understood it. Each successive problem was allotted proportionately less time than the previous one. When the teacher arrived at the last problems, the processes were so well understood that the pupils needed to spend only a few minutes to acquire the operations for *any* number base.

Cognition and Transfer

All subject matter can be concisely summarized in the form of general principles that are often referred to as the *structure* of the subject matter. During recent years much attention has been given to helping pupils discover for themselves the underlying generalizations of the subject matter. One investigator (Bruner, 1966) claims that through this "discovery method" pupils learn not only the details of knowledge, but some of the higher order habits essential to problem-solving. Among these are: attitudes toward finding out information for oneself; fitting newly acquired information into one's existing frames of reference; confidence in one's ability to "think"; practice in the skills related to the use of information and problem-solving; and reflection upon the existing knowledge one already has in order to put it into a form for productive use in new situations.

Despite its advantages, learning by discovery need not be considered the ultimate teaching method. If it is important only that the pupil understands principles, directed teaching is an economic procedure. The unsatisfactory performance often encountered after directed teaching may be due to the pupil's failure to study after the initial learning period, rather than to any intrinsic difficulty with the method. The main advantage in the self-discovery of principles lies in its motivational benefits. As a result of involvement in the task and gratification with discovering an idea by himself, the pupil independently pursues the task after the formal learning period. Accordingly, his level of achievement is raised, he remembers for a longer period of time, and he exhibits more transfer (Kersh, 1962). Perhaps the most unique benefit of learning by discovery, however, is the resulting increase in the pupil's confidence that he can solve problems for himself.

The discovery of an hypothesis

Bruner delightfully describes a class of young pupils learning to define hypotheses by the discovery method, as follows:

> What the children needed were opportunities to test the limits of their concepts. It often requires a hurly-burly that fits poorly the decorum of a schoolroom. It is for this reason that I single it out.
>
> Training in the skill of hypothesis making has a comparable problem. Let me give you an example of what I mean. We got into a discussion in one of our classes of what language might have been for the first speaking humans. We had already had a similar session with one other class so I knew what was likely to happen. Sure enough, one child said that we should go out and find some "ape men" who were first learning how to speak and then you would know. It is direct confrontation of a problem, and children of 10 like this directness. I was teaching the class. I told the children that there were various people in the nineteenth century who had travelled all over Africa on just such a quest, and to no avail. Wherever people spoke, the language seemed about the same in sophistication. They were crestfallen. How could one find out if such ape men existed no longer? I thought I should take drastic measures and present them with two alternative hypotheses, both indirect. It is usually a fine way of losing a 10-year-old audience! They had the week before been working on Von Frisch's bee-dance "language" so they knew a little about other than human forms of communication. I proposed, as a first hypothesis, that to study the origin of *human* language they look at some animal language like bees and then at present human language, and perhaps *original* human language would be somewhere in between. That was one hypothesis. I saw some frowns. They were not happy about the idea. The other way, I proposed, was to take what was simplest and most common about human language and guess that those things made up the language man first started speaking.
>
> This discussion, weighing the worth of the two hypotheses, took the whole period. What struck me was that in the course of the discussion the children were learning more how to *frame* hypotheses than how to test them, which is a great step forward. One child asked whether what would be simple in one language would necessarily be simple about another. They were trying to invent a hypothesis about

language universals. Or another pupil suggested that the way babies speak is probably the way in which man first spoke. They enjoyed discussing not only whether the hypotheses were "true" but also whether they were testable. I told them finally that the Cercle Linguistique de Paris in the 1880's had voted that nobody should be permitted to give a paper on the origin of human language, and that they were not doing badly, all things considered. They took a dim view of Paris as a result! I was struck by the avidity of the children for the opportunity to make hypotheses. I believe children need more such practice and rarely get it. (From Bruner, 1966, pp. 110–111. With permission of author and publisher.)

Structure and transfer

Structure helps to guide discovery and understanding. Correct and fully illuminating presentations together with explanations should not be bypassed because they seem too complicated; nor should partially correct explanations be presented because the correct explanation seems too difficult. Correct explanations and examples are as easy to grasp as the partly correct explanations if they are carefully adapted to the pupil's level of achievement.

In *The Process of Education* by Bruner (1960, pp. 23–25), three values are said to accrue from teaching the fundamental structure of a subject, as follows:

1. *Teaching structure makes a subject more comprehensible.* "Once one has grasped the fundamental idea that a nation must trade in order to live, then such a presumably special phenomenon as the Triangular Trade of the American Colonies becomes altogether simpler to understand as something more than commerce in molasses, sugar cane, and rum in an atmosphere of violation of British trade regulations" (p. 23).

2. *Structure facilitates human memory.* "One of the basic things that can be said about human memory ... is that unless detail is placed into a structured pattern, it is rapidly forgotten. ... A scientist does not try to remember the distances traversed by falling bodies in different gravitational fields in different periods of time. What he carries in memory instead is a formula that permits him with varying degrees of accuracy to regenerate the details on which the more easily remembered formula is based. So he commits to memory the formula $s = 1/2 \ gt^2$ and not a handbook of distances, times, and gravitational constants. ... [One remembers a theory] not only for understanding a phenomenon now but also for remembering it tomorrow" (p. 24–25).

3. *Structure facilitates transfer of training.* The idea of structure suggests that a specific event is understood as belonging to a more

general case. If a general principle is understood, then the pupil not only learns about the specific thing or event but also a model for understanding other things like it that he may encounter. "... If a student could grasp in its most human sense the weariness of Europe at the close of the Hundred Years' War and how it created the conditions for a workable but not ideologically absolute Treaty of Westphalia, he might be better able to think about the ideological struggle of East and West—though the parallel is anything but exact" (p. 25).

Summary

The study of transfer antedated the experimental study of most other learning processes. The priority of this emphasis was a natural consequence of a concern for formal education, since without transfer there would be no justification for education as we know it today.

The mental-faculty theory led to one of the earliest transfer theories. It asserted a most general benefit to such presumed functions of the mind as concentration, will power, and memory. It supported the inclusion of courses in the curriculum for their disciplinary value rather than for their content.

Experimental evidence quickly destroyed the view of such general, positive benefits from all learning. Transfer was said to occur only to the extent that two situations contained identical components. A highly practical technical school orientation was suggested by this approach. These extremes were soon tempered by the evidence forthcoming from analytic investigations of transfer processes. It became universally recognized that earlier learning did not always have a beneficial effect on new learning; its effects could be positive, negative, or neutral.

Generalization, either of stimuli or responses, is a well-demonstrated phenomenon in the study of transfer. In stimulus generalization a wide range of situations becomes capable of eliciting a given pattern of behavior, depending upon which stimuli are selected. Stimulus selection might be affected by attention, readiness, motivation, contextual cues, and the like. Response generalization refers to the process whereby a range of behaviors become capable of being evoked by a given situation. Generalization of responses occurs especially within a family of responses that are said to exist in a hierarchy. Variability can be effected through extinction of undesirable responses, shaping processes, spontaneous recovery, fatigue of competing responses, and the like. Stereotype of responses is essential for some kinds of skills whereas creativity depends almost exclusively on variability of responses.

The degree of positive transfer is directly related to the degree of similarity between two tasks, provided the responses are identical. However, negative transfer is greatest when the responses to two functionally identical situations are antagonistic. Facilitation (positive transfer) results when two tasks are functionally identical; the greatest amount of interference (negative transfer) results when two tasks appear to be similar but are functionally dissimilar; and zero transfer occurs when the two tasks are dissimilar.

In all cases two practical points about transfer are certain: The first is that learning from in-school situations does not transfer to real-life situations unless the two settings are functionally equivalent, that is, unless the pupil perceives where, when, and how the learning is to be applied. Secondly, positive transfer is not necessarily automatic. To assure beneficial amounts of transfer to desired situations the teacher must point out or otherwise instigate the necessary applications.

Language may affect transfer in at least two important ways: through verbally mediated generalization as in the attachment of labels, and through the use of verbal plans which can guide the development of motor and cognitive skills. Through associations with experiences, words can acquire both stimulus and response properties. Two similar situations will acquire distinctiveness, i.e., will be discriminated as different, if different labels are attached to each. Conversely, two different situations will be capable of evoking similar responses, i.e., will generalize, if they are given the same label. Language can also be employed in establishing verbal plans or cognitions that form the base for the acquisition of motor skills. A large part of practice in learning skills seems to be devoted to finding and implementing the motor response patterns that correspond to the verbal ones. Accordingly, such factors as coordination and the proper rate of movement are found in the later stages in the acquisition of a skill to a greater extent than they are in the early stages.

There are many sources of general transfer of importance to the teacher. Among these are the transfer of concepts, principles, attitudes, and methods. Perhaps the most pervasive of all is learning to learn or the formation of learning sets. As pupils solve many problems of a given sort they initially sift out ineffective habits and establish useful habit patterns. In later learning stages these simpler patterns may be organized into behaviors useful for solving complex problems. Thus, some form of organization is essential to transfer. Subject matter will be organized by the pupil through such processes as clustering, but the teacher must assist in the process by making the subject matter meaningful (in the sense of relating it to the pupil's background), by providing structure in the form of advance organizers, and by providing meaningful organization in the presentation of the subject.

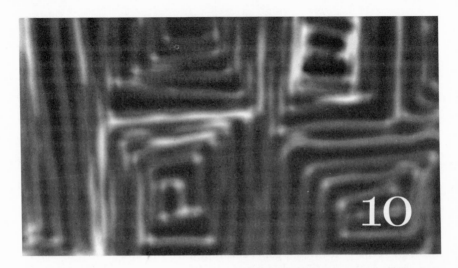

Remembering
what is learned

To student and teacher alike forgetting is a most annoying feature of
behavior. Both would like to strengthen and prolong retention and generally neither is as successful as he would like to be in doing this.
Although forgetting seems to be at all times undesirable, it has its
beneficial side. When useless information is lost it does not stand in the
way of currently usable and functioning information. Forgetting has a
superficial resemblance to extinction, since both are decremental factors
in performance. Forgetting is the unintentional loss of learning where
there is no further practice, apparently through disuse. Extinction is the
elimination of a bit of behavior from an organism's behavior pattern
owing to the failure of an external agent to reinforce its occurrence.
Both extinction and forgetting are important in the educational process
but their roles in changing behavior differ.

Retention is measured by *recall*, by the savings upon *relearning*,
or by *recognition* of the material learned, following a period of time. In
the *recall* method the pupil is required to reconstruct an answer to a
question, as in an essay test. He may be asked to write his answers or to
give them orally with minimal cues. The *recognition* method requires
the pupil to select a correct answer from a series of alternatives in
which the correct answer is imbedded, as in a true-false or multiple-
choice test. The *relearning* or *savings* method was originally used by
Ebbinghaus. As in other methods, the person first learns the task, then
after some specified period of time relearns it. One simple measure of
"savings" is the number of trials, or time required, to relearn the task
compared to the time or number of trials for the original learning. Most

of us have experienced savings in ability to relearn skills that have not been practiced for some time, such as reciting nursery rhymes and poems or riding a bicycle, provided of course, that the skill was originally learned to some minimal criterion level. Forgetting is measured in the same way except that the score is the difference between the amount of original learning and the amount retained upon retesting.

A contemporary model of storage and retrieval processes in memory

In the diagram below, Shiffrin and Anderson (1969) display a representation, or model, of the different stages of memory with particular emphasis on the processes by which information is stored in and retrieved from long-term memory.

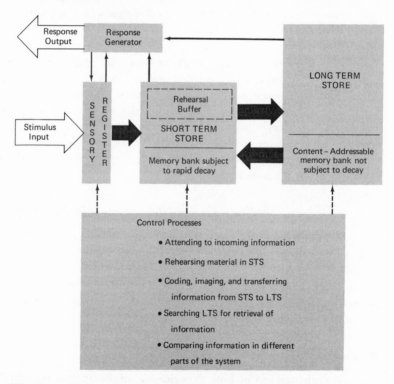

The flow of information in memory. (Solid lines indicate the direction in which information is transferred from one stage to the next. Dashed lines indicate where control processes are relevant and where information in one part of the system, at a given time, can be compared with information in another part.) (Adapted from Shiffrin & Atkinson, 1969, p. 180. With permission of authors and publisher.)

Incoming information is held briefly (less than a second for visual stimuli) in the sensory register where, by the control process of attention, it is transferred to the short-term store (STS). Information can be retained in the short-term store by the process of rehearsal; otherwise it will decay in less than a minute. Via such processes as coding, imagery, and mediating instructions relevant information is transferred to identifiable locations in the long-term store (LTS). Stated in a slightly different way, information is transformed into a form congenial to existing cognitive structures. Information placed in LTS is assumed to remain there permanently. The LTS is also said to be content-addressable. Accordingly, information coded for storage in a given location may be retrieved (recalled) on later occasion by reversing the process. Thus, information placed in a specific location can be relocated by employing the same code, a process analogous to placing a book on a library shelf according to the Library of Congress system and locating it later by use of the same number. The stages and processes described in this overview are presented at greater length in the remainder of this chapter.

The measures described above vary in their sensitivity. The recognition measure, for example, ordinarily yields higher retention scores than does recall, which in turn is more sensitive than relearning. Regardless of how retention is measured, the greatest amount of forgetting characteristically occurs immediately after learning and gradually decreases over longer periods of time. There are many notions about what happens in the process called forgetting, most of which involve some aspect of negative transfer.

Changes in the Structure of Experience

An adult may nostalgically recall an old swimming hole as a tranquil, picturesque spot. Upon revisiting the place of this cherished memory he finds it to be nothing more than a "hole" filled with muddy water. Many memories of past events undergo systematic changes toward an ideal through what seem to be the reconstruction and restructuring of experiences at the time of recall.

Reconstruction of experiences

An illustration of how experiences might be reconstructed is displayed in Figure 10-1. The display was taken from a report of an experiment by Bartlett (1932). He presented the picture of the owl to the first subject, who viewed it for a minute or two, and then drew from *memory* his impression of the picture. The drawing was then passed to the second subject, who in turn drew his impression from memory of the first drawing; and so on, until a number of subjects had made their

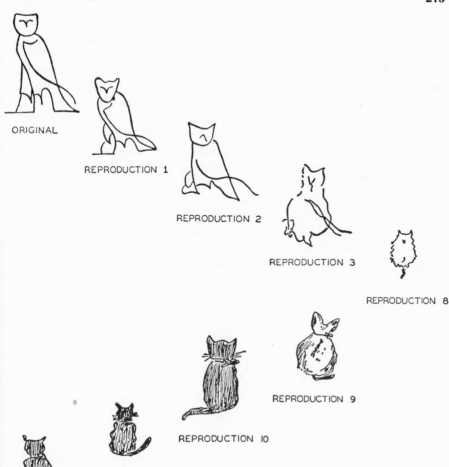

ORIGINAL

REPRODUCTION 1

REPRODUCTION 2

REPRODUCTION 3

REPRODUCTION 8

REPRODUCTION 9

REPRODUCTION 10

REPRODUCTION 15

REPRODUCTION 18

Figure 10-1. The reconstruction of experiences. As pupils passed the drawing from one person to another the drawings became modified. The processes illustrated are those of transformation, elaboration, and simplification. Can you account for the change from the original to the later drawings? (From F. C. Bartlett, 1932, p. 180–181. With permission of author and Cambridge University Press.)

drawings. As you can see, the picture of the owl eventually evolved into the depiction of a cat. Presumably, with the passage of time, the memory trace (an assumed change in the neural system due to activation from experience) of the original stimulus has undergone structural modification.

Were the changes in these figures really due to a change in the memory trace or were they the result of some other factor? Verbal labels appear to be a most important part of the explanation as shown in a study by Carmichael, Hogan, and Walter (1932). Their subjects learned symbols such as those shown in Figure 10-2. During the course of learning one group was told that the symbol was one thing and another group was told that it was another thing. A recall test was administered a short time later. It was found that the figures were reconstructed according to the labels with which they were associated originally. Labels, codes, and images that occur at the time of original learning help the pupil to summarize what is learned in a form that can be easily stored for later recall, but if inaccurate, can also lead to distortions at recall. In Bartlett's experiment, if and when the drawing was labeled a cat, the subject would try to draw a cat and not an owl. The verbalization used to label his original experience biased his later recall. Beginning students of psychology often label the course content as

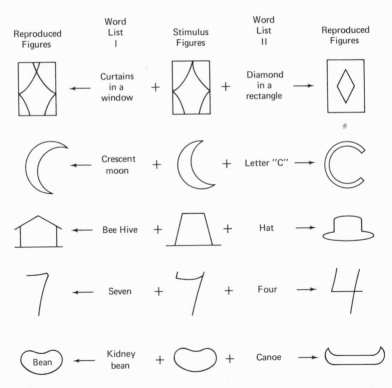

Figure 10-2. Reconstruction of experience. The recall reproductions demonstrate the effects on reorganization of labels (based on previous similar experience) associated with the original task. (Adapted from L. Carmichael, H. P. Hogan, & A. A. Walter, 1932, p. 80. With permission of authors and publisher.)

"commonsense." These interpretations are ordinarily made after they have read an assignment and often have only chance correspondence with the evidence and the conclusions presented in their assignment. On a recall test the student's interpretations are made according to the commonsense label. Under the circumstances, the commonsense interpretations rather than the new learning will be recalled. The student's answer is likely to be incorrect. Such distortions, due to the effect of variations in coding, bear a strong resemblance to forgetting.

Organizational factors in memory

Recently, there has been renewal of interest in reorganization as a factor in the retention of verbal materials. Two currently popular conceptualizations for this process are *clustering* and *organizational factors in memory*. These newer views hold that the person imposes a verbal structure on materials to be learned according to his previous habits. The subject matter is organized implicitly within an existing cognitive framework. Later recall is then made in terms of the cues provided by the basic structure.

A much cited experiment by Bousfield (1953) illustrates the nature of clustering. A list of 60 words was equally divided into commonly acceptable classifications of animals, vegetables, professions, and names. These words were read off to the subjects with instructions to remember as many as possible. A recall test was administered immediately afterward. Subjects in the experimental group recalled many more words than did a control group who were read a random selection of words. The experimental group also recalled the words in clusters based on the categories represented in the list.

In other studies (Seibel, 1966) subjects were permitted to look at long lists of words and categorize them in any subjectively meaningful fashion. As one would expect there were many different subjective organizations of the list. Some subjects arranged the words alphabetically, others arranged the words according to their meanings. But, interestingly, the subjectively organized lists resulted in retention of even greater numbers of words than when the organization was built in by the experimenter. Thus, organization of subject matter can be made on a number of bases. It is not restricted by any means to categories formally prescribed by experimenter or teacher. Any prominent categories may provide bases for clustering (Cofer, 1965).

Mnemonic aids

Occasionally, someone comes along with a training program for improving one's memory. Invariably the claims have popular appeal. Who would not want to be able to perform such feats as recalling the

names of 20 people an hour after having heard each name only once!
If there is any validity to these procedures they should be of interest
to teachers, if for no other reason than the possibility of gaining further insights into retention.

Most of these methods involve first the learning (really overlearning) of one set of concepts as "keys." The keys serve as "hooks"
on which the to-be-recalled items can be "hung," through association,
as responses. A common example is one given by Miller, Galanter, and
Pribram (1960, p. 136) to exemplify the role of mental "plans" in
remembering. They say that one may first learn a simple plan or conceptual peg on which to hang other items to be recalled later, as follows: One is a bun; two is a shoe; three is a tree; four is a door; five
is a hive; six are sticks; seven is heaven; eight is a gate; nine is a line;
and ten is a hen. Then a list of items is read aloud slowly and only
once to the person for later recall as in the following example: (1)
ashtray, (2) firewood, (3) picture, (4) cigarette, (5) table, (6) match-
book, (7) glass, (8) lamp, (9) shoe, and (10) phonograph. When
each is read the subject attempts to make an association with its counterpart in the plan, as for example, the following: the bun is in the
ashtray; the firewood was burned with the shoe; the tree looks like a
picture; and so on. When the subject is to recall the third item in the
list he can recall the tree-picture sentence. Since three-tree was the
conceptual peg he knows that "picture" was the third item. A similar
procedure would be employed for recalling the remaining items. One
of the authors has used this demonstration in educational psychology
classes where one half the class was taught the plan and one half was
not. Those students who employed the aid could, after only one listening, write with 90 percent recall the item occurring in any position
while those students who were not taught the aid could recall with
only 40–50 percent accuracy.

Mnemonic aids have been passed down informally from one
pupil to another or from teacher to pupil to help in recalling serial
order lists which are not made meaningful at the time they are taught.
Thus, the order for the arithmetical operations in solving statistical
formulas is first multiplication, then division, next addition, and
finally subtraction. The aid is *My Dear Aunt Sally*. Others are also
familiar: *Every Good Boy Does Fine* for the notes represented on
each line of the treble clef and *F-A-C-E* for each space. The "Thirty
days hath September . . ." mnemonic aid is so well known as not to
require more than mention. The order of the planets according to
their nearness to the sun is Mercury, Venus, Earth, Mars, Jupiter,
Saturn, Uranus, Neptune, and Pluto. Because this serial order is
difficult to remember, the following aid has been invented: "*My Very
Extravagant Mother Just Sent Us Ninety Parakeets.*"

One study by Smith and Noble (1965) attempted to evaluate
the effects of a mnemonic technique used by Furst (1957), a self-
styled "world's greatest memory expert," and by Roth (1961). The

technique was fundamentally the same as that given above, that is, a primary list was learned as an associative base for the secondary (to-be-recalled) items. The mnemonic technique did not facilitate the acquisition of a list, but it did have some beneficial effect in recalling items of low or medium meaningfulness. This, of course, is just the kind of situation in which students are forced to use such artificial aids to memory. The mnemonic aid appeared to have no efficacy for recall of highly meaningful items.

If mnemonic aids are useful it is because they provide a basis for coding information into a form that can be easily stored. Furthermore, by being placed into an existing context, call it structure or meaning, if you like, the fragment (item) of information is kept from being battered by the effects of interference. The difficulty with such mnemonic aids is that an extrinsic structure is imposed on the study material. The present authors believe that more permanent aids to memory are to be found by relating the course content to any of the many intrinsic (natural) structures of the disciplines. Such procedures are part and parcel of the many suggestions for enhancing organization and reducing interference to facilitate retention that are in this chapter.*

Advance organizers

In learning complex cognitive tasks, structure can be provided by *advance organizers*, a form of overview providing the basic scheme or structural image under which the subject matter may be organized or *subsumed*. Thus, the subject matter is organized in advance of a study period. It provides a signal to the student about what is to be learned and how the new learning will fit into his existing cognitive structure (knowledge). The retention of the learned material is increased since the organizer provides a simple cue to the relevant characteristics of the subject matter and increases its discriminability (Ausubel & Fitzgerald, 1961). Where the student cannot relate prior knowledge to what is being learned then organization by the teacher is a helpful device for introducing unfamiliar material.

These ideas reemphasize the importance of verbalizations for coding information and point out that subject matter is best retained when organized. If learning can be fitted into the individual pupil's previous personal experience, so much the better. Otherwise, a sensible organization of subject matter by the teacher will be necessary.

*The study of mnemonic aids, coding, and organizational factors in memory has become a burgeoning research area in the past few years. Many interesting articles extending the findings described above are to be found by such investigators as Bower & Winzenz (1969), Mandler (1966), Seibel (1965), Tulving (1962), and Wood (1967).

Subject-matter presentations are too often made in an arbitrary unstructured fashion. Pupils may be required to memorize lists of remotely related historical events. Poems are sometimes learned in rote, mechanical fashion. Valences of elements may be learned out of the context in which they will later be used. Any subject matter can be, and should be, meaningfully organized. Art, for example, can be classified (structured, categorized, organized) according to the painter, period, or form; and historical events can be structured according to their political or economic implications. But the most durable and persistent effects on retention will be obtained when pupils are taught to discover for themselves the ways in which the subject matter can be organized.

Subsumption and retention

The transfer value of subsumption was investigated by Ausubel and Fitzgerald (1961). In a three-stage study, they first required their subjects to read introductory passages based on one of three types of organizers: The *comparative-organizer* passage pointed out differences and similarities between Buddhist (the material to be learned) and Christian (familiar material) doctrines. The *expository-organizer* passage presented only material on Buddhism at a high level of abstraction and inclusiveness with no reference to Christian doctrine. The *historical-organizer*, used as a control condition, presented historical and human interest facts about Buddhism and Buddha, without ideational information. Two days later all subjects studied a long and detailed passage on Buddhism. A test of the material was administered three and ten days following the reading of the long passage. Retention after three days was best for the group studying the *comparative-organizer*. After ten days both the "comparative" and "expository" groups remembered more than the "historical" group. However, these differences were observed only for those subjects who were relatively unfamiliar with Christianity to begin with. Subjects in all groups with previous knowledge of Christianity performed better than did those without this knowledge.

This and other studies conducted by Ausubel and his associates (Ausubel & Fitzgerald, 1962; Ausubel & Youssef, 1963) imply that existing cognitive structure based on previous learning provides an important basis for organizing subject matter.

Changes in stimulation

All parts of a learning situation are potential associates of what is being learned. If they do, indeed, become associates, and if some are missing as cues in the recall setting, then recall will be correspondingly decreased. The probability of recall is dependent upon the number of functional cues present in both the learning and test situations. More explicitly, it can be assumed that if a response is equally associated with four cues in the learning setting, the probability of recall will be 100 percent, 75 percent, 50 percent, 25 percent, and 0 percent if four, three, two, one, or none of the cues, respectively, are present in the recall setting.

These ideas help to understand why a change in situations sometimes causes forgetting. Learning takes place with one stimulus pattern that, at best, is only partially represented in the recall setting. A pupil may study, for example, in a room at home with the radio going. He may quiz himself to prepare for an examination. When he has difficulty with a question, he glances surreptitiously at the page, finds a cue, and comes up with the answer. The radio, self-quiz, and page of the book, have become part of the stimulus pattern. At examination time these particular cues are absent, and, in addition, there are many cues foreign to the study setting. He is now in a classroom surrounded by other pupils and confronted by the teacher. The sound of the radio is absent. He cannot glance at his book to see the picture or paragraph heading which provided him with the necessary cues to answer some questions during his study. The wording of the test questions is quite different from that of his own questions. There is a groping for familiar cues until the original situation and its details are sufficiently reinstated to provide the necessary stimuli for the answer. If the major stimuli cannot be brought into focus, recall will be impossible and the individual may say that he is "blocked."

Interference in Recall

The nature of the activity in which he engages both before and after learning will modify the pupil's ability to recall what he has just learned. Almost all new learning (retroactively) has some detrimental effect on previous learning and all past learning will have some effect (proactively) on new learning.

Retroactive interference

The story is told of a professor of ichthyology who gave up learning the names of his students because every time he learned a student's name he forgot the name of a fish! While there may be some doubt about the truth of this incident, it illustrates the notion of retroactive interference. Names have some properties in common, if nothing more than the fact that they are symbols associated with persons, events, and so on. Once names have been learned, any new name encountered later will interfere, retroactively, with the recall of the first name to a greater or lesser degree. The design of an experiment to test this principle in its simplest form provides an operational explanation of forgetting, as follows:

Experimental Group
  Learns Task A: Learns Task B: Takes a retention test of
  e.g., French   e.g., Spanish   Task A

Control Group
  Learns the same Task   Does not learn Task B but   Takes a retention test of
  A as the experimental   may perform some other   Task A
  group   activity such as playing
                          bridge

Typically, the experimental group in the example above will perform more poorly on the recall test than will the control group. Spanish has more similarities to French than does mathematics, playing bridge, or doing nothing and accordingly will cause more interference. Interpolated learning works in a *backward* direction to hinder recall or original learning, hence it is called *retroactive* interference.

The greatest hindrance to remembering under these circumstances occurs if original and interpolated learning are perceived by the pupil as being similar when, in reality, they are functionally different. If learning the names of metallic elements is followed closely with learning the names of the gaseous elements, the pupil will have more difficulty in recalling the first list than if he had followed it by playing cards or by learning to prove theorems in geometry. All intervening activities have some effect, however small, on forgetting.

Teachers can minimize the effects of interference by making certain that materials are taught and learned in a thorough and meaningful way. The beginning student and those who learn only at a superficial level will have difficulty if they first memorize an unstructured list of

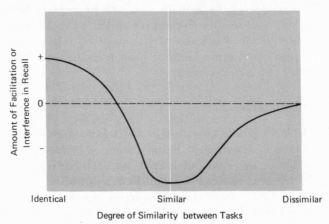

Figure 10-3. Similarity between learning and transfer tasks as a factor in transfer and retroaction. The greatest degree of interference occurs when the interpolated activity is similar to the original learning. (After Robinson, 1927, p. 299.)

the major events in Eisenhower's first administration followed immediately by the major events in his second administration. These ideas will be difficult to recall separately, especially if they are not meaningfully related, because of the similarities—the same person, similar platforms, and the like—all of which will interfere with associations between events and administrations. An advanced political science student will have less difficulty with this task, as will a highly intelligent student, since each has more background with which to provide distinctions between the two administrations. The inverse relationships between CA, or IQ, and the amount of retroactive interference are due not to age and IQ proper, but to the probability that older children and those with higher IQs have learned the first material more thoroughly (Keppel, 1964b).

While the provision of structure and meaning can effectively decrease the harmful effects of retroactive interference, the teacher may also use study hints to advantage. Knowledge of the detrimental effects of interpolated activity on retention and an active effort by the learner to resist these effects were potent in reducing the amount of interference on a recall test (Lester, 1932).

Proactive interference

As one grows older, details of new experiences seem to be forgotten more readily than in the past. College students report that they forget movie titles more quickly than when they were children. Poor performance on a test is often attributed to differences between definition of concepts currently being learned and those learned in another course during the previous semester meaning that interference from previous learning is being experienced. Parents may find difficulty in matching their memory with that of their children on the details of events in which they have both shared. In certain experiments subjects recalled about half of the material learned prior to eight hours of sleep even though there had been no interpolated activity between the time of learning and recall. These simple examples illustrate the effects of previous learning on the recall of new learning. Interference from past experiences occurs in a forward direction. Accordingly, it is called *proactive interference*, for which the defining operations are:

Experimental Group

| Learns Task A: Algebra | Learns Task B: Geometry | Takes a retention test of Task B: Geometry |

Control Group

| Does not learn Task A but may perform some other activity | Learns Task B: Geometry | Takes a retention test of Task B: Geometry |

The relative effects of retroaction and proaction on retention were investigated by Underwood (1957). He analyzed several similar experiments on forgetting that were reported in the literature. One part of the analysis is summarized in Figure 10-4. The conclusion from this analysis was "the greater the number of previous lists learned, the greater the forgetting [thus implying] that the greater the number of previous lists, the greater the proactive interference" (p. 53). Other things being equal, the young child will experience less proactive interference than will the older child. The young child's history of cognitive development is relatively short compared to that of the pupil in high school. Nevertheless, all have some prior experiences to interfere with retention. As with retroactive interference, the more similar the learning and recall situations the greater the proactive interference.

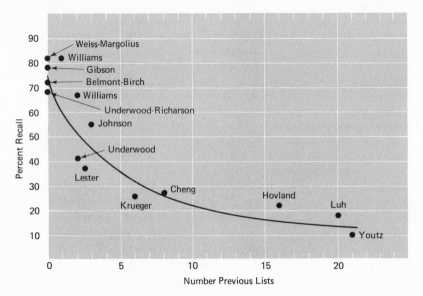

Figure 10-4. The greater the number of previous lists learned the greater the forgetting due to proactive interference. Underwood plotted these data from the results of a number of studies conducted under similar experimental conditions. The investigators' names are shown on the graph. (From Underwood, 1957, p. 53. With permission of author and publisher.)

Short-term retention

Learning, transfer, and long-term retention are necessarily dependent upon short-term retention. Yet, it is a commonplace experience for people to respond to some stimulus, and then seconds later not be able to recall what they have done. Some illustrations follow: A pupil may not recall the first part of a long sentence that he read only seconds earlier. Sometimes the early details of directions for getting to a street are forgotten even before the directions are completed. Other times, one may fail to recall the name of a person to whom he was introduced at a social gathering minutes earlier. A telephone number is forgotten immediately after it has been found in the directory.

Currently, explorations in this area are being made through the memory span technique employing single units, a technique introduced by Peterson and Peterson (1959). In typical experiments the subject is presented a single trigram composed of three consonants (for example, TRX) and then asked to recall it after a period of 3 to 18 seconds. The interval is filled by requiring the subject to count backward by three's in order to prevent rehearsal of the trigram. [The reader should note, however, that retention is not always improved by rehearsal since subjects may practice errors as well as correct responses (Postman & Phillips, 1961)].

The apparent simplicity of this task proves to be deceptive. Subjects (college students) do forget the single item after these short-time intervals. The length of the time interval, of course, is important. Peterson and Peterson (1959) have shown that after a three-second interval about 80 percent of the trigrams are recalled correctly and after 18 seconds less than 10 percent are recalled correctly. The surprising feature of these experiments is that while the recall interval lasts only a few seconds, recall is far from perfect.

Coding and the memory span

An analysis of coding was made more than a decade ago by Miller (1956). He suggested that the memory span is 7 ± 2 units. This simply means that a person can retain about 7 discrete, independent (i.e., unrelated at the time of learning to anything else) items such as numbers, nonsense syllables, words, or other units. One may now inquire whether this is a reasonable finding since even casual observation would indicate that the average person can recall a span containing far greater numbers of items. The explanation is that recall in immediate memory is enhanced by reorganizing cognitions into chunks. An illustration provided by Miller is most appropriate at this point: if you were to observe an individual repeat back a series of 40 discrete binary digits (0 and 1), in the order in which they were presented, and after a single presentation, you would be more than a little surprised. Basic to an understanding of this feat of memory, however, is the fact that the digits were recoded or restructured to increase the amount of information handled in any single response.

An example of recoding 18 digits is shown in Table 10-1. In the first row is a sequence of 18 digits, far too many for the large majority of people to memorize after one presentation. If these are encoded according to the rules or "plans" related to translating base 2 into base 10 by groups of two, so that $00 = 0$, $01 = 1$, $10 = 2$, and $11 = 3$, the sequence to be memorized is now reduced to 9.

Table 10-1. Ways of recoding sequences of binary digits.

Binary Digits (Bits)	1 0 1 0 0 0 1 0 0 1 1 1 0 0 1 1 1 0								
2:1 Chunks	10	10	00	10	01	11	00	11	10
Recoding	2	2	0	2	1	3	0	3	2
3:1 Chunks	101	000		100	111		001		110
Recoding	5	0		4	7		1		6
4:1 Chunks	1010			0010		0111		0011	10
Recoding	10			2		7		3	2
5:1 Chunks	10100			01001			11001		110
Recoding	20			9			25		6

SOURCE: Miller, 1956, p. 94. With permission of author and publisher.

(As the reader may know, the transformation can be achieved by summing the product of the first, or right, digit multiplied by 1 and the product of the second, or left, digit multiplied by 2.) At the time of recall, the base 10 digits are decoded back to the original series and it appears that 18 single digits have been recalled. If the digits are encoded in groups of three the sequence to be memorized is reduced to 6 and the list is still more easily memorized. With this "plan," the rule for working with 2 digits is simply extended by multiplying the third digit by 4 (double the weight of the previous digit) and adding it to the other products. Thus, as the digits are presented, the person encodes 101 as 5, 111 as 7, 100 as 4, and so on. On the recall task each of the digits 5, 0, 4, 7, 1, and 6 are decoded back to base 2 by reversing the rule and the 18 binary digits (or even 40 after training) can be recalled with relative ease. The groupings by "fours" and "fives" are shown in the last two lines of the table.

Reorganization or structuring places less strain on memory since information is condensed in the recoding process. This is equivalent to saying that learning materials must be organized into meaningful units. It is a strong argument for teaching pupils the underlying theory or explanation of the material being learned.

One factor affecting short-term memory is the meaningfulness of the items to be remembered. Words are recalled more accurately than are units of three-letter trigrams. Word triads (three unrelated words) are recalled with about the same degree of difficulty as the trigrams. Note that the trigram is stored in memory as three discrete items (for example, T – R – X), a whole word though consisting of three, four, or more letters is stored as a single meaningful unit, and the word-triad is stored as a series of three discrete items (see Figure 10-5). Accordingly,

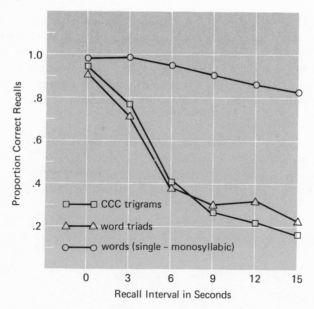

Figure 10-5. Several units, whether letters or words, are more difficult to retain in short-term memory storage than many lettered words that function as units. Retention drops rapidly as a function of time. (From B. B. Murdock, Jr., 1961, p. 619. With permission of author and publisher.)

adding meaning is a way to code the information in a convenient form with a corresponding reduction in the total amount of material to be stored. In the above example three items (bits) tax the memory span to a greater extent than meaningful wholes or chunks (Murdock, 1961).

As with long-term retention, short-term memory is subject to interference by previous learning (Postman, 1964). With an increase in the number of trigrams or words presented, the difficulty of recalling subsequent items is increased (Keppel & Underwood, 1962).

Reducing the effects of interference

From the laboratory research on retention Underwood (1966) has come up with some interesting ideas: Lists of high meaningfulness words are learned more rapidly than lists of low meaningfulness words. Lists of words that have low similarity among the items are learned faster than lists with high similarity. Bright pupils learn faster than those less bright. *Yet in all cases the rate of forgetting remains the same.* Furthermore, the amount forgotten (or retained) by a naive learner is almost constant and is affected mainly by the length of time between learning and recall. But it should be said with emphasis that these results are obtained *only if the amount of learning is held constant.*

In all investigations of retention analyzed within the framework of interference theory no variable emerges with greater influence on retention than does the degree of original learning. This conclusion was reached many years ago by Krueger (1929) who investigated the effects on retention of 100 percent, 150 percent, and 200 percent original learning. The smallest percentage represents the number of trials to one per-

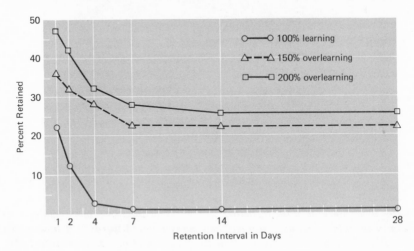

Figure 10-6. Rapid forgetting occurs when minimal levels of learning are achieved. Overlearning effectively enhances retention over long periods of time although increases beyond 150 percent overlearning are not as dramatic as increases over the threshold. (Adapted from W. C. F. Krueger, 1929, p. 73. With permission of publisher.)

fect recitation of monosyllabic nouns, while the other two figures indicate the percentage amount of additional practice. Both levels of increased practice led to increased retention. It would appear to be advantageous for both teacher and pupils to capitalize on this finding that has stood the test of time and of replicated experimentation. Effective teaching methods can and should employ whatever techniques are necessary to clarify course content and to structure it meaningfully for the pupil. Such methods include the use of discovery techniques, advance organizers, projects, and the many other devices described elsewhere in this text, and in texts on teaching methods. But there is no substitute for overlearning, to the extent that lessons are studied beyond the point where the student can barely pass an examination, if a high degree of retention is to be attained.

Practice, if it is to be effective, should not be meaningless repetition. Motivated rehearsal can be accomplished by laboratory demonstrations of information learned in other contexts, field trips to large markets to observe the operation of principles of economics, and conversational French to practice one's French grammar. Good study habits should be developed by the student (including the college student) that will include self-examination, rereading, outlining, and consistent review. One never learns a poem or a part for a play without using some of these practices to increase frequency of repetition. Once they are learned there is a great deal of savings. Similar procedures should be employed for academic work, provided meaning is not sacrificed.

Massed and distributed practice

Learning schedules, too, can contribute to permanence of learning. Keppel (1964a) examined such effects in a task that involved a great deal of proactive inhibition. The subjects were required to learn four sets of words to the same stimulus items. Then they were tested at a later date on the fourth set. One group of subjects learned all of the lists at one time (massed practice). The other group studied the last list for two trials a day over several days until it was learned (distributed practice). Proactive inhibition from the first three lists caused the group studying under massed practice to forget the fourth list after a week. The group studying under distributed practice, on the other hand, still retained a third of the list after a month. The obtained differences are dramatic for the relatively simple tasks employed in the learning laboratory. They are obtained whether the distributed practice is on the original learning (Task B) or on the prior learning (Task A). Such findings clearly imply the importance of frequent practice periods or reviews over several days or even months. (See Figure 10-7.)

It would be poor teaching practice, from the standpoint of improving retention, to teach a unit all at one time and then drop it without returning to it, or to employ massed practice. A practical prob-

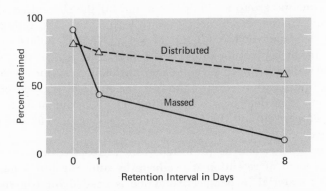

Figure 10-7. Distributed practice favors retention. Massive amounts of proactive interference occur under massed practice even after a day or two. (From G. Keppel, 1964a, p. 97. With permission of author and publisher.)

lem arises, however, with regard to how one determines when practice is massed in school subjects. This question is not answered easily because the definition varies with the subject matter and task characteristics. However, if the period is so long that the pupil loses interest, loses motivation, becomes fatigued, or is exposed to so many different topics that interference will result, one can say the period was too long. On the other hand, the period must be sufficiently long for a passage in a musical composition to be played with reasonable competence, for the meaning of a poem to be acquired, for the underlying structure of a debate to be grasped, and the like.

The implications with regard to distribution of practice are clear. Study or review periods should be spaced close enough together so that most learning from the previous period will be retained. When a topic is first being taught or learned it is necessary to have frequent and closely spaced reviews. As learning proceeds, the reviews can be further apart. Again, it must be emphasized that reviews are not only drill-like repetitions, or formal brief abstracts of previously taught material. They should be continually incorporated as applications of important content in new contexts throughout a course.

Finally, the research on short-term retention suggests that an association cannot always be retained until some *consolidation* occurs. In accordance with notions about distributed practice, rapid presentation of materials, or topics presented too rapidly in succession will be difficult to retain. The learner requires time to put the material in its proper place. This effect has also been demonstrated with long-term retention in a study by McGaugh and Hostetter (1961). As described by Hilgard (1962) these investigators arranged the following conditions: One experimental group of subjects learned a task, followed by sleep, and then they relearned the task. The control group learned the task, followed by waking activity before relearning the task. The savings for the experimental group was 82 percent and for the control group it was 64 percent. Another experimental group learned the task, followed by 8 hours of sleep and then by 8 hours of waking activity before relearning the task. In the control for this experimental arrangement the two activities intervening between original learning and relearning were interchanged, that is, after learning the task the subjects engaged in waking activity and then slept before relearning. The experimental group's savings was 86 percent and the control group's savings was 59 percent (see Figure 10-8).

The learner can be protected from retroactive interference and the impairment of retention it produces by allowing him enough time to put the material in perspective. Time is needed for contemplation, for the learning to "sink in." In view of the findings summarized in this section, one may well question the validity of such practices as three-

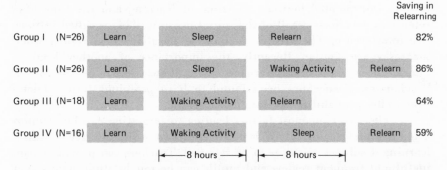

*Figure 10-8. Evidence for a consolidation period in learning. When sleep
follows immediately after learning, retention is high (82–86 percent), regardless of whether the sleep is followed by waking activity before relearning. When
learning is followed by waking activity, retention is less (64–59 percent), regardless of whether sleep intervenes before the test of retention. The results
show Group I to have higher savings (i.e., retention) than Group III, and
Group II to have higher savings than Group IV, with equal elapsed time in
each comparison. These results are statistically significant. (After McGaugh &
Hostetter, 1961. From E. R. Hilgard, 1962, p. 313. With permission of author
and publisher.)*

hour lecture periods where the student may be bombarded in rapid-fire
succession with dozens of new (often unrelated) ideas; or of one-week
workshops where a semester course is taught in one week.

Summary

   Closely related to transfer is retention and its opposite, forgetting.
Retention is commonly measured by recall, anticipation, or relearning
(savings) methods. These techniques differ in their sensitivity, a statement not to be misinterpreted to mean that they measure different
amounts of retention or forgetting.

   Forgetting is the loss of modification of a behavior pattern when
it goes unused for a period of time. Some changes seem to occur as a
result of reconstruction or restructuring, that is, as a consequence of cognitions associated with the original learning. Unintended idiosyncratic
clustering may have occurred in the original learning, there may have
been contextual changes of relevant stimuli in the situations, some
details are elaborated toward an ideal, some details because of motivational or emotional factors may not be perceived, and so on.

   Interference has gained the most widespread acceptance of all
explanations of forgetting. One kind of interference occurs when any

activity interpolated between the time of learning and the time of a retention test affects recall of the initial learning. This is called retroactive interference. The greatest amount of negative effect results when the tasks are similar. Recently, the importance of another kind of interference, proactive interference, on recall has come to be recognized. Previous experience has been found to have profound (often deleterious) effects on ability to retain new learning.

The effects of most factors leading to forgetting can be counteracted by overlearning. There is no substitute for a high degree of initial learning if subject matter is to be retained. Teachers can provide meaningful and frequent review and pupils can be taught study habits that emphasize overlearning. Distribution of practice is more effective, in the form of continual use of the course content, than is massed practice. Classes and study periods can be scheduled to avoid similar subjects succeeding one another. Mnemonic aids may be used within narrow limits to enhance retention even though they are recognized as artificial strategies to impose structure on learning. Often times such aids are forgotten and the student is left to search helplessly for the behavior required of him in a given situation. Teaching methods that capitalize on the intrinsic organization and structure of the material to be learned are more effective than mnemonic devices. Coding allows larger amounts of material to be retained as units, while good organization of course content relates it to the pupil's existing cognitive structure rather than leaving isolated bits of information to be lost through interference.

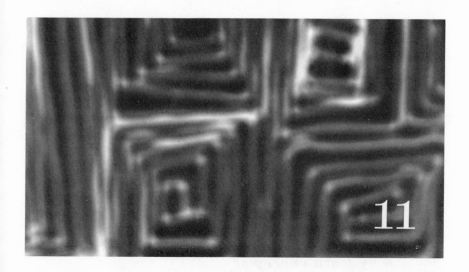

The role of concepts
in cognitive processes

At any stage of their formation, concepts, as classifications of experience, are destined to have a major influence on new learning and on
communication with others. In effect, they modify and temper all
aspects of behavior. They code experiences into small classes with the
result that people come to deal more with categories of experiences than
with independent events.

An example of their profound effects on behavior can be clearly
seen in superstitions, stereotypes, and prescientific explanations. The
coincidental occurrence of a misfortune with the breaking of a mirror or
the presence of a black cat results in an association of the two events in
a way that leads to the erroneous categorical conclusion that a black cat
or a broken mirror brings bad luck. An individual under the influence of
such a concept will go through a complex routine to avoid "bad luck."
In the social realm, false stereotypes based on biased abstractions of
experience (direct or vicarious) with racial, religious, or other ethnic
groups, are manifested in various forms of prejudices and bigotry. In
science it was once believed that an object would remain in motion only
as long as it was propelled by some external force. Until Newton formulated the first law of motion (that a body in motion will remain in
motion unless acted upon by some external force), it was unlikely that
any man could have recognized that some day he would have the technological capabilities required for sending a man to the moon. The
amount of fuel that would be required for a trip to the moon would be
impossibly large if the rocket required a continual supply of propellant.
Early concepts of illness considered that some illnesses were caused by

evil spirits possessing the body of the sick person. Elaborate rituals for curing the person thus consisted of chasing the spirit out of the body. Many attractive and highly competent individuals, as a result of prior experiences and social interaction, have been led to make verbalizations about themselves equivalent to "I am unattractive," "I am unacceptable to others," or "I never seem to perform adequately." Such verbalizations (not necessarily conscious or overt) often lead to (mediate) behavioral patterns characterized by withdrawal, lack of confidence, hesitancy, and anxiety. Casual experience in any area inevitably leads to concept-formation. Nevertheless, such informally acquired concepts are rarely precise enough for a person to function effectively when it comes to any highly technological matter.

Why learn concepts?

Bruner, Goodnow, and Austin (1956) ask the question, "What does the act of rendering things equivalent [through concepts] achieve the organism?" (p. 11). They answer it by saying the following functions are achieved:

... the organism reduces the complexity of its environment.

... categorizing is the means by which the objects of the world about us are identified.

... a category based on a set of defining attributes reduces the necessity of constant learning.

... the concept provides direction for instrumental activity.

... categorizing permits ordering and relating classes of events.

(From J. S. Bruner, J. J. Goodnow, & G. A. Austin, 1956. With permission of author and publisher.)

Choosing Concepts to Be Taught

The meanings of concepts conveyed by symbols are important to the communication system of any culture. History has been transmitted down through the ages, by the first drawings of cavemen, by later abridged drawings and hieroglyphics, and still later by uncounted systems of written language. In this way the records of philosophy, mathematics, and history have contributed to the growth of civilization. Modern cultures have thereby profited by the discoveries and the mistakes of earlier generations.

In even the simplest of cultures there are many hundreds if not thousands of concepts to be acquired. The pupil's task is proportional to the complexity of the society around him; in most present day societies his preparation must necessarily be prolonged as a consequence of the knowledge "explosion." Through problems and assignments set for him in each course of study, the pupil is provided opportunity to organize

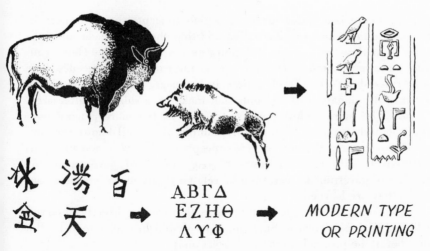

Figure 11-1. The cruder forms of symbolic representation illustrated in the early caveman drawings and Egyptian hieroglyphics were the forerunners of today's efficient language systems.

this knowledge in special unique ways and is provided with a set of words (i.e., labels) to correspond with his experience. Thus, in chemistry courses the concepts of atom, ion, compound, catalyst, and isotope are taught. In physics courses the pupil learns the concepts of momentum, acceleration, and energy. In language courses he learns the distinction between singular and plural verbs, and between nouns and pronouns. In nutrition, the student learns to differentiate vitamins, carbohydrates, and proteins. In music, he learns to classify experiences related to harmony, pitch, rhythm, cacophony, atonality, and so on. By looking at a listing of concepts taught in a course, one could identify with some degree of certainty not only the subject matter area but its level and complexity.

Since concepts influence one's perceptions, explanations, and applications of knowledge, the prospective teacher should choose carefully those concepts in his subject-matter area that are essential for students to know. Though it would be impossible to state here what these should be for each and every course, some rules-of-thumb may be helpful in making this selection:

1. Teach the simplest concepts first. Concepts with clearly identifiable features, with few features, or with simpler combinations of features are easier to learn than those with the opposite characteristics. For these reasons, "touchdown" (i.e., crossing a goal line) is easier to learn than "strike" (i.e., swinging at and missing the ball or referee's decision). The more complex concepts generally incorporate some characteristics, or features, of the simpler concepts and so should be taught later.

2. There is a logical order in which concepts should appear in the curriculum. Thus, understanding addition should precede multiplication in arithmetic, knowing the notes on a scale precedes chord construction in music, and identifying vowels and consonants precedes their use in rules about letter combinations in language. This order should be determined by analysis of concepts that make up a subject-matter area.

3. The more inclusive concepts (that is, the more general concepts) should be taught first. If, for example, the pupil knows the concept of government then other new concepts can be *subsumed* under it. Progressively differentiated concepts (e.g., forms of government, or branches of government) can then be related to the more inclusive concept as they are learned.

4. Concrete concepts have features that can be directly observed or linked with experiences. Such concepts should be understood by the pupil before he proceeds to more abstract ones.

5. The concepts to be taught should be matched to the preparation of the pupil and to his maturational level, a topic to be discussed at length in the next section.

The Development of Conceptual Ability

Not all cognitive skills involved in thinking are available at every stage of growth. The abilities to form concepts and principles develop gradually. The following description of intellectual development as observed and reported by Jean Piaget, Director of the *Institut Jean Jacques Rousseau* at the University of Geneva, is helpful in viewing the stream of cognitive development.* The concern of the Geneva group has been with the *progressive stages* of the child's *cognitive growth*, especially in mathematics, formal logic, and the principles of science. Within these contexts the development of perceptual constancy, reversibility, conservation, and formal operations have been foremost considerations. Two unique contributions of the Geneva Institute's research are the finding that all normal children's misunderstandings at a given age are very similar and also that the emergence of stages of cognitive development occurs in an orderly and uniform pattern in all children. An understanding of these stages provides a basis for matching teaching strategies to the pupil's conceptual ability.

The sensory-motor period (birth–18 to 24 months)

As the name of this period of growth implies, this stage is essentially a preverbal one. The sensory abilities present at birth are used and

*This presentation is largely based on a summary by J. McV. Hunt (1961).

exercised. For example, the infant's cries are interrupted when an agreeable voice or sound is heard. Later it may try to mark the sound, then smile at the voice. Still later it locates the voice and turns its head toward the source of the sound. Then it can locate the sound accurately with a glance. In the course of its activity, the infant learns to recognize objects, to perceive, to begin to see the separation of means and ends, to play, and to recognize the permanence of objects. Some notions of space and of causality appear to be learned.

During this first period the infant's behavior suggests it has begun to know how to learn, how to control external events. Sensory motor behavior patterns become differentiated and coordinated. The constancies in the environment are beginning to be learned, thereby providing the bases for more mature intellectual operations which occur later. Finally, its use of imitative behavior suggests that the child has learned the rudiments of representing absent objects to himself through imagery.

The concrete operations period

The concrete operations period is divided into *three phases* over a span of 10 to 12 years. Though ages are provided for all periods and phases, the reader is cautioned that it is the progression of cognitive development that Piaget emphasizes rather than a close link between age and stage of development.

The Preconceptual Phase (*18* to *24* months–about *4* years). In this phase of the second period of development, the child engages in make-believe (symbolic) play. Language is important from the very beginnings of this period although symbolic actions precede the use of language symbols. Speech is largely unsocialized and egocentric. The child appears to assume that the listener is aware of his intentions and understands his explanations. The child engages in mental games for the first time during this period. For example, he is willing to guess where an object is, pretends to drink out of a box, and laughs at his dolls. Such games have a definite pattern of imitative responses and are repetitively practiced. Later, symbolic games are played in which he may lay his head on a shawl and imitate sleep. Thus, he learns that some actions represent other actions. At the end of this phase, games are played with simple rules. Together with the emerging development of language ability, these activities teach the child to associate experiences with words. The use of language enhances his ability to make mental manipulations, sharpens his perceptual ability, and initiates his ability to think in terms of the past and the future.

Child's World—Young children, Piaget found, believe the sun follows them when they go out for a walk. They also think that anything that moves is alive, that clouds have motives, and that dreams come in through the window while they're asleep.

Figure 11-2. (From David Elkind. Giant in the nursery—Jean Piaget. The New York Times Magazine, May 26, 1968, Section 6, 52.)

Out of Sight— . . . "The infant behaves as if a ball that has rolled out of sight has gone entirely out of existence."

Figure 11-3. (From David Elkind. Giant in the nursery—Jean Piaget. The New York Times Magazine, May 26, 1968, Section 6, 77.)

The Intuitive Phase (Four years–seven or eight years). This is a transition period of growing intuitions about the environment through commonsense classifications of events. The child vastly extends the operations used in thinking, but he makes characteristic mistakes. Although he differentiates among cues, integrates new information, and corrects his intuitions, his attention appears to be centered only on what he can see directly. For example, water in a tall, thin beaker, poured from a short, wide beaker is said by the child at this stage to be of larger volume because it stands higher in the taller of the two beakers. He focuses his attention on a single dimension of the problem, but can not shift his attention from height to width. No permanence is seen to a given quantity of liquid poured from one container into several other containers or into a container of a different shape. Thus, logical structures of the cognitive operations in this phase are said to lack the properties of conservation and reversibility.

Monologists—"Piaget noted that when two nursery school children were at play they often spoke *at* rather than *to* one another, and often about unrelated topics."

Figure 11-4. (From David Elkind. Giant in the nursery—Jean Piaget. The New York Times Magazine, *May 26, 1968, Section 6, 79.)*

The Concrete Operations Phase (Seven or eight years–eleven or twelve years of age). The elements of abstract conceptualization make their initial appearance in this last phase of the concrete operations period. Reversibility as a property of concepts is apparent. Quantity is seen to be conserved when, for example, the child is shown a ball

moulded from a sausage-shaped piece of clay and he explains they are
the same because nothing has been added or taken away. During this
phase the child makes classifications based on concrete attributes and is
learning how to learn. He is able to form classes, to order objects in a
series, and to number, all of which are fundamental processes in concept
formation. He can perform these operations with concrete objects or
events that are actually before him, but he cannot use them in more
abstract situations, as he must, for example, in multiplication.

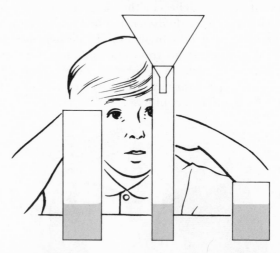

*Figure 11-5. Michael wonders about whether a given quantity of liquid be-
comes "more" if it is poured into a taller glass. Piaget argues that intelligence
—adaptive thinking and action—develops in a sequence of stages that is related
to age. (From David Elkind.* Giant in the nursery—Jean Piaget. The New York
Times Magazine, *May 26, 1968, Section 6, 27.)*

The trainability of the concept of conservation

In the typical conservation experiment (Piaget, 1952a, 1952b) four-
year-old children, when confronted with a problem showing two rows
of four pellets, equally spaced, correctly say that the two arrays are the
"same." Then the experimenter changes the pattern by adding two pellets to the bottom row and shortens it by moving the pellets closer
together, while leaving the top row unchanged. Four-year-olds fail to
conserve the relationships. They incorrectly say there are "more" in
the top array. Five-year-old children correctly say there are "more" in
the bottom array. Four-year-old children are unable to reverse (irreversibility) the pattern of pellets seen initially. Consequently, they are
unable to recall where the two pellets were added.

On the basis of many such observations of children in different
countries the general conclusion suggests that the emergence of intel-

lectual stages is more dependent on maturational factors than on cultural factors. In other words, the sequence of emergence of the fundamental schemata appears to be a universal achievement of children regardless of the culture in which they have been raised (see for example, Wallach, 1963).

Nevertheless, the research findings are not uniformly in agreement regarding the way the stages develop. Nor is there complete consensus regarding the effect of training on the development of a given stage. Mehler and Bever (1967), for example, challenged the results of the conservation experiment described above. They indicate that no one had investigated conservation in children younger than four years of age, since it was assumed that if four-year-olds did not conserve quantity it could hardly be expected that younger children would be able to do so. But these investigators felt that further evidence was required before the assumption could be accepted. Accordingly, they repeated the study with these modifications: (1) Their 200 subjects were children ranging in age from 2 years and 4 months (2.4) to 4 years and 7 months (4.7). (2) Each child performed the task in one sequence with clay pellets in the arrays and in another with M & M candies. When clay pellets were used, the child was asked whether the rows were the same or which row had more. When M & Ms were used the child was told to "take the row you want to eat, and eat all the M & Ms in that row." (3) They used a third set of problems in which the row with more objects was also the longer row to make certain that conservation responses were not due to a tendency for children merely to pick short rows.

The interesting results of this study are depicted in Figure 11-6. Children from age 2.4 to age 3.7 exhibit a form of quantity conservation. Between ages 3.8 and 4.3 they indicate the longer row with fewer objects to have "more." After the age of 4.6 they again discriminate correctly.

The investigators explain these results by suggesting that very young children apparently do have the capacity for logical operations required to perform these problems. The temporary inability at about 4.0 years is the result of overdependence on perceptual expectancies based on experience with correlations of shapes and quantity. Thus, "longer arrays (shapes) have more (quantity) than shorter arrays." The experimental task, in a sense, misleads the child into using this rule. However, given sufficient motivation, as in the task employing M & Ms, the four-year-old, too, can be trained to make the correct choice. Around the ages of 4.6 to 5.0 the child gains an explicit understanding of the rule. As a consequence, he ignores the perceptual expectancy when not confirmed by the logical operation of counting. Presumably the four-year-old is unable to divorce the two operations. On the basis of these observations Mehler and Bever (1967, p. 142) conclude, "nonconservation behavior is a temporary exception to human cognition, not a basic characteristic of man's native endowment."

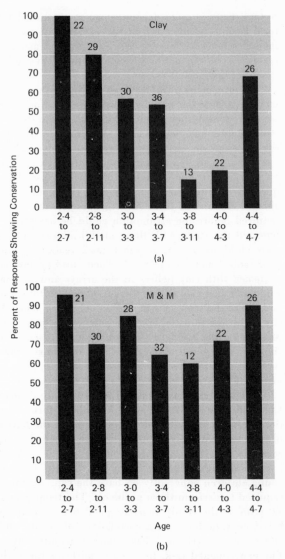

Figure 11-6. The proportion by age of responses choosing the row with more members in the conservation task. Numbers at top of bars indicate total number of subjects of that age. (From Mehler & Bever, 1967, p. 142. With permission of authors and publisher.)

Formal operations period

This period starts at about 11 or 12 years of age and comes to maturity at 15 or 16 years of age. The problems used in the Geneva laboratory remind one of the laboratory exercises that might be found in a general science class. In a typical task, the subject attempts to hit a target, placed at different locations on a table, with a marble shot from a spring-loaded plunger. But the task is not as simple as it might at first seem since the rules require that the target must be hit only after the marble rebounds off a wall inside the apparatus. Thus, the child must discover, at least implicitly, that "the angle of incidence equals the angle of refraction." Such tasks require the child to use concepts involving relations among objects or events. The symbolic behaviors required in reasoning and the formal operations of logic are essential. He can now handle such problems as "A is larger than B; A is smaller than C; which is the largest of the three?" He can consider hypotheses which may or may not be true and deduce what may follow if they were true. These behaviors imply that he can follow the *form* of an argument while disregarding its concrete content. Hence, the term *formal operations*.

Some applications of Piaget's theory to teaching

The implications of Piaget's theory for teaching method, curriculum, and testing have been considered separately by Flavell (1963) and Stendler (1965). One of the important applications, on which both agree, is based on Piaget's dictum that the pupil must be actively engaged with the content to be learned; or, in a much-cited phrase, *Penser, c'est operer*. Thus, the pupil is said to build stable and enduring cognitive or mental structures only if *he* is mentally active. He *can be told* what the relations are in the material to be learned, he *can be told* of his errors but they will not be *incorporated* into his mental structure unless he is actively engaged with the data of his experience. On this basis overt activity becomes transformed into the kind of mental operations represented in reversibility, associativity, additivity, identity, and so on. At adolescence these thought processes emerge in the form of propositional thinking.

Some illustrations from Stendler's (1965) discussion are as follows:

The preoperational child can learn the rudiments of classification by being given the task of classifying objects differing in size, shape, and color (or other attributes). Children can make a grouping based on one attribute (for example, size) and then shift the criterion for grouping. Such activities aid the pupil in learning the requirements for the formation of classes and the rudiments of hierarchy of classes. He can also learn to arrange things in a series (for example, nested cups, days in a week, and numbers) and perform tasks involving simple relations among elements in the series (e.g., two comes after one; three comes after two; does three also come after one?) although he still is unable to learn the logic of seriation.

In the concrete operations period the child can be expected to give concrete rather than abstract explanations of activities involving such operations as reversibility and additivity. Thus, the pupil might be given a billiard-game type of problem to illustrate the principle of refraction. However, he is likely to say, "The more I put it like that (the cushion inclined to the right) the more the ball will go like that." It does not occur to him that two equal angles are formed from the total angle.

Flavell (1963) provides additional examples of how teaching might proceed according to the tenets of Piaget's theory. Recognizing the ingenuity demanded of the teacher in extending these recommendations, he suggests that the teacher (1) analyze the content of the lesson in terms of the mental operations required, (2) arrange the materials so that these operations will become apparent in the pupil's activity, and (3) see to it that the pupil performs the task. For example, to teach the concept of fractions, the teacher might require the young pupil to divide pictures of objects into equal parts instead of demonstrating with a concrete object before the entire class; and to teach the concept of contours on a map, the student would be allowed to cut a model mountain into horizontal layers. If one were to teach the property of reversibility in arithmetic he would alternate addition and subtraction, or multiplication and division in such problems as, $(8 \times 14 = ?\ 132 \div 8 = ?$ and $5 + 7 = ?\ 12 - 5 = ?)$. When teaching the serial order of cause and effect (A will cause B), the effect-cause (the effect B is caused by A) order would be alternated with it.

Implicit in these recommendations is the need to: (1) identify the activity required in the operation and then have the pupil use it, and (2) assist the pupil to gradually transform these activities into mental operations. The latter is accomplished, according to Flavell's interpretation, by gradually withdrawing external support when the pupil performs the task. In this way the operations become internalized by reproducing the developmental process in the classroom in much the same manner as it occurs in life. A mental operation is first performed with physical (concrete) objects, then with pictorial representations, and finally only with ideas, anticipations, or expectations. The pupil ultimately performs the operation independent of environmental support.

Implications of the stage notion for the teaching of concepts

There are a number of implications suggested by Piaget's observations for the practice of teaching (Hunt, 1961). It is to be noted that some aspect of most concepts can be taught to any school-age child, however, the total richness of meaning associated with any concept cannot be achieved until the final stage is reached. It is apparent that the practice of teaching must carefully match the concepts one is teaching with the behavioral patterns and concepts the pupil has acquired as represented by his stage of development. The teaching method one uses requires adaptation to the pupil's conceptual level. For example, the first-grader can be introduced to some of the principles of geometry but this does not mean that he has to be taught Euclidian definitions, axioms, and postulates. He can be taught such notions as a "straight line is the shortest distance between two points" by asking which of two paths to a grocery store, one winding and one straight, would be the quickest way to the store. Evaluations of the discrepancy between the level of the pupil's acquired concepts and the concepts to be taught need to be continually appraised, not only at the outset of teaching, but during the course of teaching when it may be necessary to "step back" if the teaching units are too large or presented too rapidly. Small but challenging steps are motivating to the child; as he acquires new concepts he will work to rehearse these new tools. On the other hand, large steps may be frustrating and are likely to be detrimental to motivation. The questions involved in matching the presentation of materials with the pupil's knowledge are: What skills of coordination, learning how to learn, perception, and the like does the pupil have? What is his knowledge, that is, his concepts and level of development of concepts? What logical processes does he use?

The observations regarding the details of intellectual development at each stage suggest the necessity for providing direct, concrete experience in the early school years. The teaching of thought processes should correspond to the pupil's stage of development. The most sensible general rule is to gradually incorporate increasing complexity by small steps into the child's conceptual scheme (Hunt, 1961). In the intellectually more mature pupil, i.e., at about the time he is able to use formal operations, verbal experience becomes the important mode of learning. Once the pupil has a sufficient foundation of primary experience, the use of verbal principles and statements is more efficient and important to the development of concepts than concrete experiences. There is some evidence to indicate that subsumption (the incorporation of new learnings into already existing meaningful categories) improves both the retention and the assimilation of new material and of details by making them more meaningful (Ausubel, 1963). Verbal experience during the formal operations period may compensate to some extent for deprivation during the earlier stages, however, the degree to which this can be accomplished requires further investigation.

Influencing Concept Learning

The acquisition of concepts can be facilitated by the following teaching practices as described by Carroll (1964) : (1) Teach those classifications that have been found useful in the trades, business, science, and the arts. Recognize that knowledges presented in different courses differ because of the ways in which pupil experiences are organized. (2) For a given classification provide several experiences which are similar in one or more respects. (3) Both positive *and* negative instances of a concept must be provided in the sequencing of activities. If the concept is taught vicariously then the verbal explanation must contain the positive and negative instances. As there are more discriminations necessary in complex concepts, more negative instances are necessary. (4) Guidance must be provided, usually in the form of feedback and correction, to inform the learner of the correctness of his response. The remainder of the section will be devoted to further discussion of these and related topics.

Perceiving concept dimensions

Concept formation involves the perception of relevant cues (Haber, 1964; Bourne, 1966). Perceptibility and salience of the concept dimensions affect the ease of learning. The pupil must be able to identify cues he is to look for. If after being presented many examples of the concept the pupil still does not "catch on," the teacher may choose to provide definite direction through questioning, comparison and contrast with other concepts, and the like. When a characteristic is viewed in many situations it stands out clearly and undeniably. For example, a piece of coal in strong sunlight may reflect more light than snow on a dark night; yet the coal is always perceived as darker than the snow.

Figure 11-7. An apparently bent stick. No matter how much experience one has had with straight sticks in water, and no matter how much knowledge one has about the laws of refraction, the edges still seem to be bent at an angle. This illusion must be one of the oldest experienced by man. A sophisticated modern observer, however, can see more than just bent edges—he can perceive edges bent by refraction. (From Gibson, 1966, Figure 14.1, p. 289. With permission of author and publisher.)

Similarly, the distant telephone pole is seen as being nearly the same as the one closeby, although the retinal image of the far object is much smaller than that of the near one. (These examples illustrate the notion of *perceptual constancy*.) The ability to identify an attribute is a prerequisite to concept-learning even with older pupils. All must be taught "to observe" as well as "to see." The cognitive skill of observing and perceiving can be learned if all teachers require the pupil to identify for himself, through guidance and direction, the differences in experiences, in objects, in ideas, and in events.

Establishing patterns and categories

The world is full of differences that can be perceived by informed human beings. Few events contain the same combinations of attributes on successive occasions (Bruner, Goodnow, & Austin, 1956). If a wholly different response were made to all of these minor changes and fluctuations, our world would be complex indeed. However, underlying these differences there is to be found the stability provided by patterning the environment. This tendency is continuously present. Whenever the unfamiliar is experienced, the person identifies those features which are most familiar to him on the basis of his existing concepts.

By establishing categories we reduce the number of discriminations that have to be made (Bruner, Goodnow, & Austin, 1956). When new objects with similar characteristics are encountered, they can be conveniently placed in an existing category. If a new shade of yellow is encountered, we can call it yellow without renaming it or without learning a new name for it. In this way the environment is almost always meaningful. If some perceptual experience cannot be explained, i.e., cannot be placed into àn existing classification system, we say it is puzzling and feel insecure about it.

The tendency tò simplify may be carried to extremes and consequently to errors (Hildreth, 1941). Young pupils frequently exhibit this tendency in their behavior. When they do not understand problems, or when they find words and perceptions unfamiliar or too difficult, they try to make them meaningful in terms of·what they know. In the salute to the flag, they have been reported to say, "I pledge allegiance to the flag of the United States of America and to the *Republicans* for which it stands, one nation, *invisible* . . ." or, "I led the pigeons to the flag." In an informal report, the following answers were said to have been found on high school test papers, "A *caucus* is a dead animal." "The seats of the Senators shall be *vaccinated* every six years." "An *octopus* is a person who hopes for the best." "*Penelope* was the last hardship Ulysses endured in his journey." Such errors as well as others that frequently

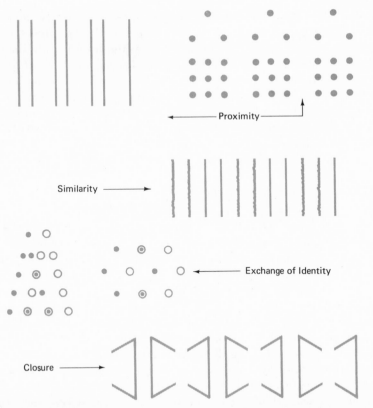

Figure 11-8. Examples of some principles governing the patterning of experiences as described by the Gestalt school of psychology. (From K. Koffka. Principles of Gestalt psychology. Harcourt, Brace & Co., Inc., 1935; and W. Ellis. A source book of Gestalt psychology. Routledge, Kegan Paul, Ltd., 1939. With permission.)

occur in reading or thinking are seldom random. At one time or another, most of us react to apparent similarities among events rather than to their uniqueness in attempts to bring clarity to otherwise unfamiliar situations.

From the teacher's standpoint, errors similar to those above become apparent through test results or by other observations of behavior used to determine the child's comprehension of a concept. When an erroneous concept is identified it is important to diagnose just where the cognitive deficit lies (Kagan, 1966). In the above examples the pupil's difficulty might have been in spelling, in labeling, in attribute identification, or in syntax. Then the alternatives available for correction of any of the above mistakes include comparisons of differences between correct and incorrect words, in their spelling, referents, or attributes. If no attempt is made to dissociate the misunderstanding from the originally learned concept, it becomes unavailable for later use by the pupil. When this happens the experience has suffered obliterative subsumption, which means that it has been absorbed as a part of a more general and, in the case of each illustration above, incorrect, concept (Ausubel, 1967).

Abstracting relevant attributes

The attributes of a concept never occur in exactly the same setting on all occasions. Accordingly, they must not only be perceived, they must be selected from within any of a number of contexts. To facilitate abstraction, learning experiences should be organized to focus on relevant features of the concept as they appear in different settings. Without such direction, the resulting concept may be fuzzy, i.e., the pupil may ignore the essential dimensions of the concept on one occasion, or he may claim that there are more attributes associated with the concept than are really important or necessary on another occasion.

In a now classic study of concept formation Hull (1920) found that familiarity with a variety of instances facilitated abstraction of the precise characteristics required to identify a concept. However, Morrisett and Hovland's (1959) study also indicates that practice in many

Figure 11-9. Concepts permit pupils to make discriminations. However, communication is difficult, if not impossible, when the meanings are not precise. (United Feature Syndicate.)

different settings and with many different problems is as important for transfer as it is for initial learning. Hull's study also demonstrated that a simple-to-complex presentation was important for identifying the relevant attribute. Furthermore, the alternate presentation of the attribute in isolation (e.g., in a graphic presentation) and in context (e.g., as it appears in a "real life" situation) is an important technique for facilitating the learning of a complex concept. Thus, some simplification of the relevant pattern seems necessary for presenting concepts.

As often as not, concepts in real life involve not only those attributes that are associated with a given classification (positive instances), but also those that are not (negative instances). To illustrate, an insect is distinguished from an arachnid (e.g., spider) by the fact that it has a complete metamorphosis and not an incomplete metamorphosis. In the adult stage the insect has three body segments, six legs, and breathes through spiracles, to name but a few of its identifying features. On the other hand, insects do not have only two body segments or eight legs, as does the arachnid. If the pupil is to distinguish between the two he must distinguish between what an insect *is* and what it *is not*. The use of negative instances appears to be more important as the complexity of the concept increases.

When teaching a new concept, gross, easily perceived distinctions should first be made to facilitate later abstraction. In the later stages of development complex and refined discriminations will be required. This point emphasizes the importance of continuous experience through all grades with as many socially important concepts as possible. For example, in the early grades the child can be taught to distinguish trees as a class from other plants such as shrubs or flowers. Later he can be taught to discriminate deciduous from evergreen trees. Then comparisons of oaks with maples can be made. These experiences prepare him for comparisons of species of trees when he learns, for example, the bark, leaf-bud, and leaf cues that differentiate the Sugar from the Norway Maple, or the needle cues that differentiate the White from the Red Pine.

Whether the pupil learns by either concrete or vicarious experiences, inquiry is always helpful. For example, he should be asked, or he, himself, should be encouraged to ask, such questions as, *"When is a* (combination of compounds a solution)?" *"When is it* (a mixture)?" *"How do* (compounds) *differ from* (solutions and mixtures)?" *"When are* (clouds) *called* (cirrus)?" *"When are they called* (cumulus)?" Questioning and illustrating raise the pupil's curiosity, call his attention to the attributes that are to be perceived, and teach him to discriminate the relevant from the irrelevant attributes. Routine events are likely to be sterile experiences unless the pupil's curiosity about them is stimulated (Berlyne, 1965).

Generalization and discriminability

Both discrimination and generalization are important in bringing breadth and precision to a pupil's concepts (Bulgarella & Archer, 1962). Through generalization selected groups of things, events, or ideas can be seen to have something in common and to be related to previous experiences; that is, there is *integrative reconciliation* (Ausubel, 1967). However, if concepts are to be made precise, generalized objects or events must often be shown to differ; that is, they must have *discriminability* (Ausubel, 1967). For example, the pupil may have learned first that ants live in "ant-hills" which may lead him to believe that they are *always* located in the ground, the only place he has ever seen the ants' nests. Then he is shown that though some nest in the ground, some, like termites, form tunnels and feed on wood close to the ground, while still others, like carpenter ants, drill holes in wood located anywhere above the ground. His generalization is revised accordingly. Depending upon his previous experiences, if the pupil has first learned to observe small differences in nature and to give them distinctive names, then in going to a generalization he must overlook some of these differences and assign new names to indicate that they share the same attributes with other objects or events. Names, verbal labels, symbols, and the like serve to code such information in a form that can be readily stored in memory (Chan & Travers, 1966).

The reader can observe for himself the formation of increasingly inclusive categories by working with the collection of stimuli shown in Figure 11-10. First, try giving each one of the stimuli a name to distinguish it from all others. This is the highest level of discriminability. To retain these the person must store nine different items. However, by categorizing these items a great amount of information can be condensed into a few words. Generalization *within* classes of objects is mediated by a concept, for example, "all angular figures," or "all curved figures." *Discriminations* among classes are to be found in the distinctions between angular or curved figures, between closed or open figures, between black or white figures, and so on. This exercise can be carried further to indicate the hierarchy of inclusiveness of concepts by answering these questions: What are all of the possible categories that can be formed for these nine items? Order these categories from least to most inclusive. What is the most inclusive category? Which features are included and which are overlooked at each level in the hierarchy?

Generalization, always present to some degree in concept formation, enables the pupil to see relationships among his experiences (Gibson, 1940; Bourne & Restle, 1959). Thus, the extent to which he can identify an object as a member of another class (for example, rock is a mineral, or democracy is a form of government), provides an indication

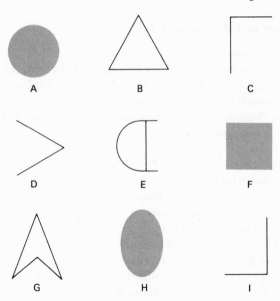

Figure 11-10. A collection of figures which might be used in a study of concept formation. How many classifications can you make? (From W. E. Vinacke. The investigation of concept formation. Psychological Bulletin, *1951, 48, 4. With permission.)*

of the breadth of meaning he has acquired (Noble, 1963). The extent to which he can indicate, by different verbal labels, the variations between classes reflects the precision of his meanings. Such labels become most useful and especially precise when the concept is experienced in many contexts. For example, sophisticated concepts about classical music would be developed through encounters with the music in many different settings. Ideally, the student would become an active participant as a listener, musician, and composer; he would study the lives of the composers, musical composition, historical periods in which music assumed different characteristics, and comparisons with other forms of music.

Attributes of the concept of "tort"

Examples of concepts are often taken from the physical sciences and, therefore, sometimes convey the impression that the majority of concepts are to be found in physics, chemistry, or biology. To illustrate that concepts in the social sciences can be analyzed in much the same way as concepts in other areas, an example by Carroll (1964) showing how the concept of "tort" might be developed is presented below:

Tort

The concept of *tort* is very likely to be unfamiliar or at least vague to the average reader. Even a dictionary definition may not help much in deciding whether arson, breach of contract, malicious prosecution, or libel are positive instances of torts. The case method used in many law schools, whereby students examine many positive and negative instances of torts in order to learn what they are, is somewhat analogous to a concept formation experiment of the purely inductive variety.

A study of the various laws and decisions relating to torts yields the following approximate and tentative characterization of the concept as having both conjunctive and disjunctive aspects:

$$\text{TORT} = (A+B+C+D+E+F+G+H)\ (I+J)\ (K)\ (-L)\ (-M)\ (-N)\ (-O)$$

where A = battery
    B = false imprisonment
    C = malicious prosecution
    D = trespass to land
    E = interference to chattels
    F = interference with advantageous relations
    G = misrepresentation
    H = defamation
    I = malicious intent
    J = negligence
    K = causal nexus
    L = consent
    M = privilege
    N = reasonable risk by plaintiff
    O = breach of contract

Within a parenthesis, terms joined by the plus sign are mutually disjunctive attributes; a minus sign within a parenthesis signifies "absence of"; the full content of each parenthesis is conjunctive with the content of every other parenthesis. Thus, we can read the formula as follows: "A tort is a battery, a false imprisonment, a malicious prosecution, a trespass to land, . . . or a defamatory act which is done either with malicious intent or negligence, which exhibits a causal nexus with the injury claimed by the plaintiff, *and* which is done without the plaintiff's consent, *or* without privilege on the part of the defendant, *or* without a reasonable risk by the plaintiff, *or* which is not a breach of contract."

Thus, *tort* turns out to be a concept very much on the same order as *tourist*—a collocation of criterial attributes with both conjunctive and disjunctive features. Deciding whether an act is a tort requires that one check each feature of a situation against what can be put in the form of a formula (as done above). Presumably, a person presented with a properly organized series of positive and negative instances of torts could induce the concept, provided he also understood such prerequisite concepts as *battery, misrepresentation*, etc. (From Carroll, 1964, pp. 198–199. With permission of author and publisher.)

Capitalizing on corrective feedback

Reward and nonreward with corrective feedback help to make the precise discriminations that are necessary for the formation of concepts. Learning experiences should provide pupils with opportunities to make fine distinctions. When mistakes are made they can be corrected and later appropriate distinctions can be rewarded. The following is an illustration of the way a demonstration was used for this purpose:

Mr. Sills teaches pupils in his general science class the difference between chemical and physical change. He thinks the pupils understand these concepts but wants to make certain. He has placed on the laboratory bench these groups of objects: a regular nail, a rusty nail, and a bent nail; some granulated sugar, a caramelized piece of sugar, and a sugar solution in water; and a beaker of water, a piece of ice, and electrolysis apparatus in operation. Pupils then make discriminations as to which of the objects in each group is an illustration of chemical and which of physical change of the first object in that series. If they are correct, they are rewarded by good grades or praise. If they are wrong or inaccurate, he corrects them or allows the pupil an opportunity to discover for himself why he was in error.

More precise identifications of attributes must still be made after this initial exercise, so Mr. Sills provides further opportunity for feedback and correction. He has his pupils discriminate between chemical actions in which precipitates are formed, in which solutions become saturated, in which solutions become clear, in which heat is absorbed, in which heat is produced, in which solids are formed out of combinations of liquids, and in which gases are produced out of liquids. All of these demonstrations provide opportunities for misunderstandings, i.e., incorrect concepts, to come to light.

Mr. Sills initially provided his pupils with an opportunity to see the relatively gross differences between physical and chemical change and the ways in which the instances of each were similar. The pupils had an opportunity to abstract the critical attributes of each, just as a child abstracts the concept of "redness" from red wagon, red dog, red leaves, and Red Riding Hood, to form a concept of red. But if concepts are to be precise, the teacher must allow for still further discriminations. Hence, the second set of exercises was provided for broader experience, requiring more precise discriminations. In this way, from one period to the next, from one course to the next, with increasing experience the pupil's concepts become more complex and loaded with new elements.

Although immediate feedback is important, it is interesting to note that there may be some advantage in a slight postfeedback delay before going on to another part of an assignment. Bourne and Bunderson (1963) found that a longer delay period after reinforcement led to more efficient learning of a concept than a very short delay or no delay. This effect was more important for learning complex concepts than for learning simple concepts. Apparently, the delay period following correction allows the pupil time to determine why he was wrong or right and thus permits a degree of self-correction. In a classroom, postfeedback delay is less likely to be a problem than in the laboratory, except perhaps when drill cards or other paced learning situations are arranged. Nevertheless, these results emphasize that mere reinforcement without some opportunity for correction is insufficient (Postman, 1961). The reasons for the "correctness" or "incorrectness" of a pupil's response should be explained; he should understand (find out for himself) why his response was correct or incorrect (Wallace, 1964); and, then he should be provided with an opportunity to rehearse or practice what he has learned (Kendler, 1964).

Decreasing the complexity and difficulty of concepts

Concept attainment requires the formation of rules about the relationships among attributes. As a consequence, learning difficulty is related to the number of attributes required to identify the concept. With increases in the number of attributes or dimensions that characterize a concept there is a corresponding increase in the amount of information that the pupil must compress or code to arrive at the concept name. Interference among the attributes also increases with complexity (Fallon & Battig, 1964). Similarly, if the attributes are not easily identified, that is, are not easily perceived or discriminated from the other attributes of the stimulus, as in abstract concepts, concept attainment increases in difficulty.

The application of these understandings requires that the teacher in his teaching methods emphasize the essential features of the concept by such procedures as pointing, magnification, coloring, slow motion, simplified drawings or diagrams, introductory reviews, outlines, or other procedures that strip the concept of irrelevant attributes. The teacher can also point out the relevant *redundant* attributes, that is, attributes which overlap and to some extent are predictable from one another. For example, a parallelogram has four sides, opposite sides are parallel, and opposite angles are equal; a white pine is evergreen, has needlelike leaves, and the needles occur in clusters of five; and fire engines are big, red, and have sirens. The effects of redundancy of relevant and irrelevant characteristics are shown in Figure 11-11, which demonstrates that even a single irrelevant dimension increases the difficulty of learning the concept.

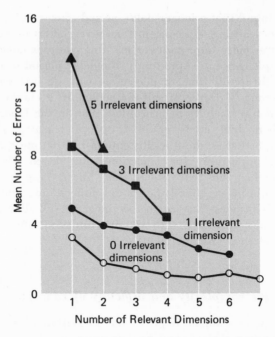

Figure 11-11. Complex concepts are learned more easily when there are many correlated attributes and when stripped of irrelevant dimensions. The bottom line represents a diagram or other means of focusing only on significant conceptual features. (From Bourne, 1966, Figure 1, p. 59. With permission of author and publisher.)

Irrelevant attributes are not defining ones and contribute only to "noise." The ways in which the attributes can be combined contribute further to the complexity of a concept. Thus, a young elementary school pupil can easily see that a set of five green marbles and a set of three red apples are the same as a set of three red apples and five green marbles. From putting things together in this way in concrete situations he can see how the principle works. Later, the child can make discriminations among classes of features or "sets." However, he is unable to see what happens when one "set" is subtracted from another. Since little use is made of negative instances by young pupils, initial presentation of a concept might employ use of only positive instances. At about eight years of age the child can use negative instances more effectively than at the earlier years. Early in the formal operations period, when verbally presented materials are important bases for learning, he can acquire disjunctive concepts (those involving either one attribute *or* another, for example, to be a resident of a community the individual must either reside there, own property in the community, or operate a business there). At this time he is ready to learn the formal versions of such algebraic concepts as associativity and identity. At each stage in his learning of these concepts, the teacher has employed a different version of the algebraic rule for combining elements. Concomitantly, the pupil has acquired some information that will contribute to his total understanding of the complex concept.

Concept Attainment Strategies

Concept attainment is not a hit-or-miss process. Rather, pupils use different ways of selecting attributes from positive instances of the concept and testing whether the attribute is relevant or not. This process is especially prevalent in teaching procedures where the pupil is guided to discover for himself the attributes that define a concept.

An experiment by Bruner and his associates (Bruner, Goodnow, & Austin, 1956) was specifically designed to identify the methods (strategies) people use to learn a concept. Interestingly, all of the methods employed by their subjects could be classified within the four basic categories described below. However, because only conjunctive concepts (that is, concepts in which attributes are connected with "and" such as *black and square*) were learned, the reader should realize that these strategies may not be descriptive of those used for attaining more complex concepts. Nor is it to be assumed that these processes are used with awareness. Indeed, if one were to ask subjects how they went about learning they would probably be unable to provide an answer. Accordingly, strategies such as these are *inferred* from the subject's responses. These strategies differ in terms of how the person validates his hypotheses about the concept, how much he learns from each experience, how much he has to remember, how many instances he must encounter before identifying the concept, and the speed with which the concept can be identified.

Simultaneous scanning

The person who uses this strategy considers all ways that a concept might be represented in the exemplar (representative instance of the concept). Then he tests one of his hypotheses by selecting an instance (example) that represents that hypothesis. If he is wrong, the information gained is used to eliminate other related, thus invalid, hypotheses. If he is correct, he can restrict himself to a greatly reduced number of hypotheses. The remaining potentially valid hypotheses are then tested until the correct concept is attained. This would be an ideal strategy since it employs all information about all hypotheses (i.e., whether the hypothesis was selected and tested yet; if so, whether it was supported or rejected, and so on). The knowledge gained on each experience must be remembered. Thus, this apparently efficient strategy has the great disadvantage of placing large demands on the person's memory capacity. Even when only three attributes are involved there are nine possible outcomes, all of which must be retained. Then a record must be kept, as each instance is reviewed, of the unlikely concepts and of those that remain as possibilities. Concepts learned in school are much more complex and most pupils would be unable or unwilling to employ the elaborate analysis required by this strategy.

Successive scanning

When the person uses this strategy he tests only *one* hypothesis at a time. If this hypothesis fails, he turns to alternative hypotheses until one of them receives support by a number of correct solutions. Unlike the simultaneous scanning strategy, hypotheses are not systematically eliminated. The person may test the same hypothesis a number of ways or may examine instances which contain features that have already been examined (e.g., he may have found out that a pine tree is not a deciduous tree, but then asks whether a hemlock is a positive instance). Consequently, the testing of hypotheses by this strategy can be redundant and inefficient; the learner rarely makes full use of his knowledge of positive and negative instances. On the other hand, it is a relatively easy strategy to use since the pupil does not have to remember which hypotheses were tested or what decisions were made.

Conservative focusing

In the use of this strategy, the person notes the attributes of a positive instance and focuses on the values of one of these attributes. The values are then varied systematically and conservatively. The importance (relevance) of the values of the attribute is tested in a manner that decreases the complexity of the task since irrelevant attributes are eliminated one by one. This strategy, as used in an experimental situation, is described in more detail in Figure 11-12.

Focus gambling

This is a variation of the previously described strategy; that is, the person uses the positive instance as a base from which to work. However, instead of changing one value at a time, he may decide to change two or more. He may jump from one attribute to another without an apparent system. The gambling strategy *is* "gambling!" Accordingly, it involves greater risk than conservative focusing. If the person makes the right "guesses," identification of the concept will require few choices. If the guesses are wrong, the solution will inevitably require many choices, especially if many attributes are manipulated at one time.

Figure 11-12.   A description of the use of the conservative focusing strategy.

The following is given as an example of the conservative focusing strategy
by Bruner, Goodnow, and Austin (1956, p. 87): The subject has for his use 81
cards, each with different combinations of borders (one, two, or three), shapes
(crosses, circles, or squares), color of figures (green, red, or black), and number
of figures (one, two, or three). His task is to identify the concept (in this case,
it is any card with red circles) by selecting cards which illustrate the concept. After selecting a card he is told whether it is or is not a positive instance.
As he selects cards the first positive card encountered contains three red circles
with two borders. This and the remaining choices are described below.

Choice	*Instance*	*Response*
1. Sees the first correct instance—a card with three red circles and two borders.	Positive	This is first correct instance. Note the respective values of the attributes (3 red circles and 2 borders). First, let us determine whether the concept of "three figures" (of any kind whether squares, circles, or crosses) is a relevant feature. Go to 2.

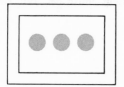

2. Selects the instance with two red circles and two borders.	Positive	Two, instead of three red circles, and still the choice is correct! The requirement of "3 figures" is unimportant; it is not a relevant value of the concept. Now let's test the relevance of color as an attribute of the concept. Go to 3.

3. Selects the instance with three green circles and two borders.	Negative	With the exception of the color green, this card was the same as the focus card. But it is incorrect! "Green" is wrong and "red" is right! Redness, then, is an important attribute value of the concept. Now determine the importance of kind of figures; i.e., is the "circle" a relevant attribute value? Go to 4.

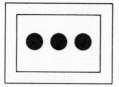

Figure 11-12 (continued)

Choice	Instance	Response
4. Selects the instance with three red squares and two borders.	Negative	Another negative instance! The only variable changed from that of the focus card was that of the circle. We had better retain circles as a relevant feature. Now let's test the relevance of the values of the last attribute, i.e., of the number of borders. Go to 5.

| 5. Selects the instance with three red circles and one border. | Positive | Only one border and the selection is a positive instance. Apparently the number of borders makes no difference. *Voilà!* the concept must be "red circles!" |

SOURCE: Bruner, Goodnow, and Austin, 1956.

These four strategies were isolated through observations in the learning laboratory, with college students, and with conjunctive concepts. The implications are, thus, limited in their applicability to all situations. However, it should be noted that these experimental tasks are not unlike those engaged in by pupils in a chemistry class who must identify the dimensions of elements belonging to the halogen family; or the pupil in a biology class who must form a concept of cocci forms from a display of bacteria; or the pupil in a language class whose task it is to determine the characteristics of verbs. School learning tasks are undeniably more complex than tasks in the psychological laboratory. Pupils are often younger than the subjects used in experiments. Nevertheless, it would appear that some strategies, similar to those described, would be used by children in the later grades of the elementary school and, certainly by junior and senior high school pupils.

Teaching concept-learning strategies

Suchman (1960), Hunt (1961), and Bourne (1967) all suggest that the cognitive skills embodied in these strategies can be taught through some form of inquiry training. The teacher might begin with a presentation of positive and negative instances of a concept through demonstration, motion pictures, reading, or discussion. Then the responsibility for discussion can be shifted from the teacher to the pupils. At first, they can ask questions that can be answered with a "yes" or "no" much after the fashion of the game of "20 questions." This procedure is analogous to that used in laboratory investigations. At the later stages of development, the simpler strategies can be extended to include the systematic strategies described by Bruner, et al. Pupils can develop hypotheses about the concept in question and then indicate "how they would find out whether they are right." They can indicate the kind of grouping into which each could be made. They can indicate the systematic tests that could be made on the basis of a single positive instance. They can practice verbalizing a hypothesis and testing it before going to another. A strategy might be tried with and without the use of aids (such aids would include a visible list of attributes, lists of hypotheses to be tested, or lists of hypotheses tried but found to be inadequate, notes, outlines, diagrammatic sketches, and so on). At whatever level the pupils are being taught, they should learn how to determine whether the absence or presence of some attribute makes a difference in identifying the concept. Verbalizing their observations about how they used the strategies provides pupils with the foundation for formulating the sophisticated relational hypotheses required in advanced, independent study. In this regard, a period in which the class has had to cope with a strategy can be concluded by pointing out the weaknesses and the strengths of each

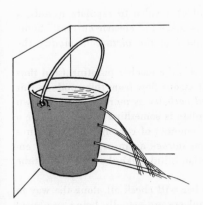

Why does the water spurt out farther from the lower holes?

Why does Jack have to hold on to the spinning merry-go-round?

What force is pulling him off?

Figure 11-13. Some ideas for inquiry training. (From J. Richard Suchman. Inquiry development program: Idea book. Chicago: Science Research Associates, Inc., 1966. Pp. 53, 80.)

of the techniques employed. Even lecture-like summaries describing the basic elements of the strategies in concept formation and problem-solving have been found to be helpful (Suchman, 1960).

A model for teaching concepts

Concepts can be taught either by didactic or by inquiry methods. An advantage of didactic teaching is its efficiency. It helps the child learn that he is able to discover ideas for himself, and shows him how to test the validity of assumptions regarding everyday matters of the world about him. The elements in the process of concept formation, common to the two procedures, are illustrated below from an example provided by Suchman (1966) as they would appear in didactic teaching. In inquiry training the initial presentation would be in the form of a problem and the essential features would be developed through questions and answers.

Suppose a teacher wants to provide his pupil with a new *set of organizers* that will enable him to comprehend the essential structure and functions vital to electronic tubes. He might begin by showing his pupil an actual tube or a cut-away model. This would be *an encounter* in the form of *direct sensory intake*. He might then say, "A tube is something like a valve." In doing this he is instructing the pupil to *retrieve from storage a particular organizer* (in this case a system or concept) and bring it down into the arena of thought for further consideration. By bringing in the "valve" concept the teacher is also suggesting the model of a "flow being regulated," since that is what valves are for.

He continues, "But instead of a valve to regulate liquids, a tube regulates the flow of electrons, a kind of electric current." Some *new organizers have been brought into the picture to modify* the earlier one.

"Notice this object here," says the teacher pointing (and thus *generating a new encounter*). "Electrons flow from this anode to this plate." The *encounter is extended verbally* as more data are thrown in. "Between the anode and the plate is something which acts like a venetian blind to admit varying amounts of current." Once again a *model or system is retrieved from storage* as an organizer. Past encounters plus a concept of a venetian blind make the grid of the tube immediately more meaningful.

Of course, the skillful teacher will check all along the way to be sure that he knows what organizers are actually being employed by the learner and what meanings for the learner they are generating when applied to the encounters.

The main distinction between this process and inquiry is in the role of the mediating function. It is, in this case, being carefully manipulated by the teacher. Each retrieval from storage, each new encounter taken in, is the result of the teacher's decision, not the

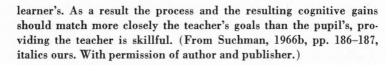

learner's. As a result the process and the resulting cognitive gains should match more closely the teacher's goals than the pupil's, providing the teacher is skillful. (From Suchman, 1966b, pp. 186–187, italics ours. With permission of author and publisher.)

Concepts should be servants, not masters of men

The effective use of concepts permits man to understand the world he lives in. By the labels and associated meanings, he can sift out similarities and distinctions. As an aid in thinking and problem-solving, concepts provide him with a means of manipulating several objects or classes of experience in verbal experimentation. He can summarize and transmit, through symbols, his past experiences to the younger generation, thereby contributing to human progress.

In the formation of concepts there sometimes occurs a failure to make adequate discriminations. The individual, consequently, overgeneralizes. The child who is bitten by *a* dog may be frightened of *all* dogs, irrespective of color, breed, or size. In other words, he predicts the outcome of a new dog's behavior on the basis of experience with one dog and fails to see the differences among them. Sometimes this process provides a protective device against hazards and dangers. In threatening situations, similarities may be more important in safeguarding one's person than the "irrelevant" differences. Later differentiation may occur through wider and more cautious experience.

Yet it is in this very process of overgeneralization that the tyranny of concepts may develop, making them the "masters" of men, for not only are the good and helpful aspects carried over to new situations but the bad and obstructive as well. There are many such incorrectly or incompletely labeled objects or events in the experience of most individuals. There is always the danger that inadequate generalizations may bring on emotional upsets, as is often the case with superstitions. Other labels such as those involved in prejudice, may be considered as final, or as "truths," and serve to inhibit further exploration by the individual. The label provides him with an excuse for *not* examining further. A concept which is only partially or incorrectly developed can be a serious deterrent to effective problem-solving and further learning. Here the teacher can guide the pupil against ready-made concepts borrowed all too readily from a model or authority, e.g., the statement, "It's right because I read it in a book" or "I heard it on the radio." Rather, the pupil through methods of inquiry can be taught to ask and to find out for himself the answer to such questions as "What is the evidence?" "How do you know it is so?" "Is the evidence reliable?" (See, for example, Suchman, 1966b, for detailed discussion of techniques for developing inquiry.)

The damaging features of incorrect labeling are dramatically

illustrated in their effects on speech. All preschool children* repeat on
the average 1 out of 4 syllables, words, phrases, or sentences. Ordinarily,
these are of little concern to adults. On the other hand, anxious parents,
teachers, or other adults who appear to have high standards for speech
behavior attempt to correct these supposed speech deficiencies. When
these corrections fail the child may be labeled a "stutterer," and treated
accordingly.

It is interesting to note that such well-meaning "diagnoses" are
usually accompanied by a failure to understand definitions of normal
and stuttering speech or the behavior of children at different stages of
development. In any event, the label "stutterer" appears to be more
than just another term to which the child is exposed but is a significant
factor in the beginning of real stuttering. Wendell Johnson (1955) discusses this influence as follows:

In general, the studies so far made of the onset of stuttering have
yielded substantial indications that the children who develop stuttering are
essentially normal . . . there is always the mother or father, occasionally a
teacher, or some other responsible adult listener, or even several such listeners
in the picture along with the child. At first, indeed, in most cases there appears
to be serious question whether the child is doing anything at all that can be
properly judged as of clinical significance. What the parent, or other adult listener, is doing, however, appears to be of very considerable importance. The
parent or other listener in such a case is found to be making and acting upon a
judgment—a judgment to the effect that the child's speech is not as it should
be, a judgment that becomes overt in postures, frowns, or even actual statements that the child interprets as disapproval. And so it is the listener's judgment rather than the youngster's speech that appears to have the kinds of
consequences that need to be counteracted.

This illustration should make any adult who is responsible for
the development of a child extremely wary of making diagnoses and
labeling what he thinks he observes without sufficient understanding
of the definitions of the terms used and of the expected behavior patterns at various ages. The haphazard use of such terms as "fatty," "neurotic," "stupid," "introvert," and the like, implying final judgment,
should be viewed with considerable apprehension in the light of available research evidence.

The tyranny of overgeneralization can be avoided by the use of
the many principles leading to the development of accurate concepts.

Children do learn to understand their environment and to see distinctions. The culture demands the use of appropriate terms to identify
these specific experiences. Through constant appraisal, logical explanation of the phenomena about us helps to avoid obvious contradictions.

*From the Editor's Introduction to D. Davis, Speech patterns of young chil-
dren. In R. G. Kuhlen & G. G. Thompson (Eds.) *Psychological studies of human
development.* New York: Appleton-Century-Crofts, 1952. Pp. 231–232.

No pupil's concepts will have the entire wealth of all possible associations. The breadth of the pupil's specific understandings will depend upon his maturity and background of experiences. It is the teacher's responsibility to establish teaching objectives and to provide experiences at whatever the pupil's level of development that will lead to precise concepts.

Words . . . weapons or tools?

Examples of color-bias emphasize the force of language in our lives and the very significant part it plays in shaping our relations with others. God, truth, beauty, virtue, chastity, and honesty are associated in our culture with whiteness, whereas the Devil, falsehood, ugliness, evil, promiscuity, and dishonesty are expressed by various shades of black. Polite people tell "white" lies, hold "white-collar jobs," visit the "White House" in Washington, and proudly announce they are "free, white, and 21." On the other hand, disliked individuals are "blacklisted," "blackballed" from clubs and associations. Every family has its "black sheep" who may, on occasion, be hauled off in a "Black Maria" to the accompaniment of "black looks" from relatives and friends. When we appreciate that a Dutch treat is not a treat at all, Dutch door is only half a door, a Dutch oven is a pot, and a Dutch widow is not an attractive warm individual but a bamboo and cotton contraption to keep one cool while sleeping, we become aware of words as weapons which sometimes can be beaten into useful and colorful tools of the language. Inasmuch as teachers are keepers of the language, we can make a significant contribution to improving relationships between people by remaining alert to language's power and force and by resisting its influence when used to the detriment of our fellow citizens. (From Keach, Fulton, & Gardner, 1967, p. 3.)

Summary

Concepts are classifications of environmental objects, events, or ideas. Categories thus formed reduce the complexity of the environment and enable the organism to identify different objects in the world about him. A learned category reduces the necessity for constant learning, provides direction to the attainment of goals, and permits the ordering and relating of classes of events.

Laboratory investigations typically employ either the *reception* or *selection methods*. In the reception method, the stimuli are presented one at a time; the subject responds to indicate that it is or is not an instance of the concept, and receives feedback. Attainment of the concept depends on remembering the effects from one trial to the next. In the selection method, the subject is shown the entire sample of instances at the outset and also an instance of the concept to be attained. He then selects from the sample of stimuli an instance with which to test his hypotheses. Feedback is provided for each selection.

The development of conceptual ability was described by Piaget as proceeding through three major stages: the sensori-motor period (up to about 18 or 24 months); the intuitive or preoperational period (about 24 months to 7 years); the concrete operations period (about 7 years to 10 or 11 years); and the formal operations period (about 11 years to maturity). The stage notion implies a hierarchy of learning in which the development of early behaviors is essential if the pupil is to make the most of his capabilities in the succeeding stages. The most general implication of this theory for teaching is that teaching methods, content, and material should match the pupil's level of development.

The acquisition of a pupil's concepts can be facilitated by providing many experiences, within a given conceptual classification, which are similar in one or more ways. In the presentation of materials both positive and negative instances are necessary to enable the pupil to determine and learn the conceptual rule, that is, what is included and what is not included in the classification. The pupil must be provided with feedback and correction if he is to develop precise concepts. Information about the correctness of the pupil's concepts follows the principles of all reinforcement. However, there is evidence that a delay period after correction (postfeedback delay) allows the pupil to determine for himself why he was correct or incorrect and thus leads to efficient concept attainment.

The learning of concepts is not a chance process. Pupils tend to follow strategies in selecting and testing the rule that defines a concept. These strategies appear to be ways for reducing the memory load. In simultaneous scanning the pupil systematically tests the alternative rules for defining the concept while utilizing all information gained from positive and negative instances. The successive scanning strategy employs the procedure of testing a single hypothesis at a time. Because the pupil does not attempt to remember what happened on every trial, he may attempt hypotheses already tested and found to be incorrect. Though it is somewhat inefficient, this method has the advantage of making slight demands on memory. In conservative focusing the pupil will attempt to vary the attributes of a positive instance systematically, though conservatively. It too, makes only small demands on retention as does focus gambling in which the pupil jumps from one attribute to another in the hope that he will hit upon the correct hypothesis by chance or, at the least, that he can quickly eliminate the incorrect alternatives. Efficient strategies for attaining concepts, for problem-solving, and reasoning can be taught by inquiry methods, followed by a critique of the techniques employed and by lecture-like summaries about the elements of strategies.

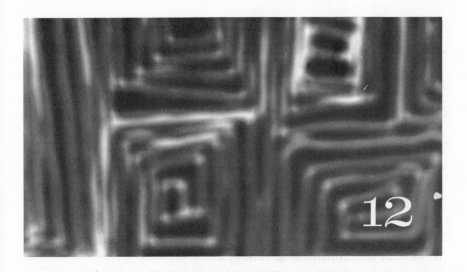

The unique functions
of language in
learning and thinking

So much of our experience involves symbols that we are likely to over-look them and become unaware of their very existence and vast impor-tance. Words, numbers, gestures, and formulas are among the many signs often taken for granted as realities without recognition that they repre-sent, or stand for, meanings, ideas, and experiences.

The eastern European psychologists have conceptualized the role of symbolic behavior, especially language, by adopting Pavlov's theory of a "second signalling system" (Simon, 1957). The *first signalling system refers to primary or direct contact man makes with his environment through his senses.* Both higher and lower organisms have this capacity. Many organisms also have the capacity to sort selected features of quite dissimilar experiences into classes and so to associate them with a common response, an essential characteristic of *concept formation.* Man, however, is unique in his ability to use language and other symbolic stimuli for thinking and reasoning. These comprise the *second signalling system that dominates man's ability to comprehend, communicate, and generalize his experiences.* The nature of the processes in the second sig-nalling system can be seen in the following passage from Liubinskaya (Simon, 1957).

Initially, the word is connected with one concrete object, having a number of particular characteristic features which belong to it alone (e.g., white spots on a pink cup). The same word later signalizes features common to a multitude of objects which, though different in many ways, constitute a single

325

group. At first the word "cup" signalizes a combination of features belonging to the object, fortuitously as well as essentially. Later, the word signalizes the *essential* feature of the object, *irrespective* of change in secondary features. This essential feature, found in the concrete and single instance, remains unchangeable and common for all objects of the same kind and is the means of distinguishing them from other similar classes of objects. Only at this stage has the word acquired for the child that "comprehensive" character distinctive of signals of the second system which cannot be compared either quantitatively or qualitatively with the conditioned stimuli of animals (Pavlov), i.e., with signals of the first system.

Concepts and Word Functions

As a result of the processes we have been discussing, words may be used by the individual to classify environmental events, on the one hand, and to control the environment on the other (Skinner, 1957). Words of the latter kind serve a *mand* function. They control the behavior of the listener, and function primarily for the benefit of the speaker. Typical mands (demands) require some action from the listener; for example, "come here," "catch the ball," "write on the blackboard," "stop," and the like. Other words serve a *tact* or naming function, for example, "this object is a ball." This function serves to benefit the listener, and since it is used for naming abstracted qualities of objects and events it is especially important in the development of concepts. Through continual association of experience with such terms as water, dog, molecule, compound, and with appropriate reinforcement, a word comes to "stand for" the respective experiences. (See Figures 12-1, 12-2.)

At first concepts are defined in terms of function and action (Feifel & Lorge, 1950; Carson & Rabin, 1960). When asked for the definition of a ball, the child is likely to respond, "You throw it," or when asked for the definition of a telephone, the response may be, "You dial it." These are not arbitrary definitions but are directly related to functions that can be performed with the objects, and once again, suggest that direct experience is important in the early stages of concept learning. Later, after the child runs out of actions, language constructions are used for building new concepts. Once the child begins to encode meanings grammatically, there does not seem to be a fixed order, for example, concrete to abstract, in which concepts related to the tact function are learned.

Brown (1958) indicates that whether the child learns from the concrete (Prince) to abstract (dog) or from abstract (money) to concrete (dime) depends on whether the category is maximally useful to the child. In the final analysis it is less the preference of the child and more the imitation by the child of the naming practices of the adult that determines "how a thing shall be called."

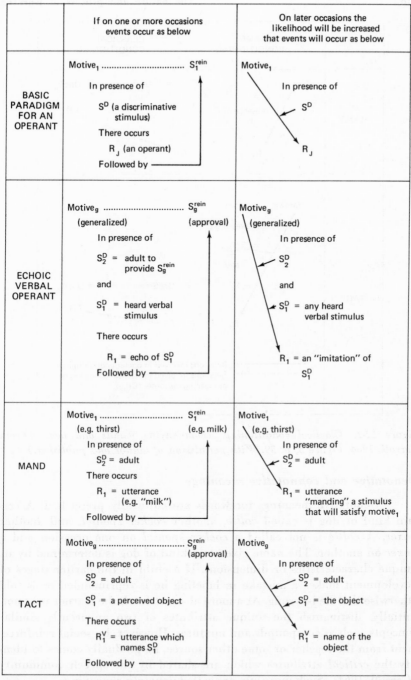

Figure 12-1. Operant paradigms for the learning and maintenance of verbal learning. (From Carroll, 1964, Figure 4, p. 37. With permission of author and publisher.)

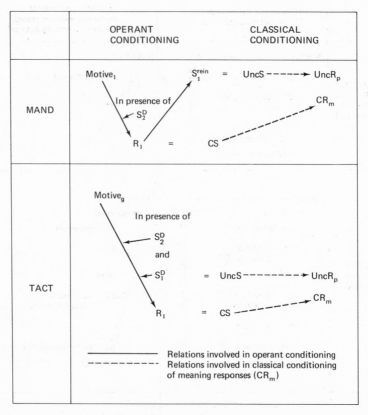

Figure 12-2. Classical conditioning accompanying mands and tacts. (From Carroll, 1964, Figure 5, p. 39. With permission of author and publisher.)

Denotative and connotative meanings

Denotative meanings for words are culturally prescribed. A certain kind of dog is called *collie,* another *cocker spaniel,* and another *boxer.* A *collie* is not called a *cocker spaniel* on one occasion and a *boxer* on another. The name given to a kind of dog is determined by its unique characteristics or dimensions. If a child in the earlier stages of development makes a mistake in labeling he is reprimanded or is told otherwise that he is wrong. At a more abstract level, the learner may not, initially, distinguish the unique attributes of two apparently similar concepts such as compounds and mixtures. However, by social reinforcement from the teacher or some other source, he gradually comes to identify the *critical* attributes which are shared by the speech community (Carroll, 1964). Such meanings are called *denotative* meanings.

During the acquisition of concepts, the stimulus patterns are also associated with other dimensions which, though not critical in the sense of being shared by the speech community, do occur regularly in repeated experiences (Carroll, 1964). These are the *affective* attributes of concepts. They are idiosyncratic to individual experience and are not regularly reinforced by social approval. Thus, while the word *horse* has definite critical attributes commonly accepted by the speech community, it also has associated with it meanings of an affective quality such as good or bad, large or small, weak or strong, and so on, depending largely on one's experiences with horses. These affective qualities of experience are called *connotative* meanings. As in the development of denotative meanings, the patterns of stimulation resulting in such associations may be from external sources (direct experience with horses) or from linguistic contexts (for example: Compare the feeling tone toward *horses* in the sentence "Horses are smelly," with that toward *horses* in the sentence "Horses are beautiful"). Within a given speech community personal experiences with concepts are usually similar, so that connotative meanings are also similar.

The dimensions of connotative meaning that appear to be most salient, even across a variety of cultures, are evaluation, potency, and activity (Osgood & Miron, 1966). The *Evaluation* dimension corresponds to the individual's tendency to make approach-avoidance responses to an object or event. It reflects the extent to which a concept has been positively or negatively reinforced, that is, its satisfyingness, for the individual. The *Potency* dimension corresponds to the amount of effort needed to adjust to the event or the amount of resistance it offers. *Activity* meanings connote the necessity for making rapid adjustments to stimuli.

The connotative meaning of objects calls attention to the emotionality conveyed by linguistic symbols. Communication (including the teaching process) involving highly affective words (either strongly positive or negative *Evaluative* words) may affect learning and retention. Through the simple associative processes involved in classical conditioning such words may be used to form new attitudes or change prevailing attitudes (Staats & Staats, 1963). The meanings for several concepts as rated by children are shown in Figure 12-3.

Concepts, then, can be organized according to their cognitive, affective, and phenomenological bases in experience. Connotative meanings are restricted to underlying affective properties of concepts. But the fact that the speech community, including children, shares these kinds of meanings provides an important initial (though primitive) basis for teaching new concepts. Thus, the meaning of a word, such as "poison," which might be unfamiliar to a young child can be easily conveyed by verbally associating it with other verbal connotative equivalents, with similar imagery responses, such as "Don't touch *poison*, it is dangerous," or "If you go near the *poison* you will be punished," or most simply "*Poison* is bad." Indeed, this is the procedure followed by parents and

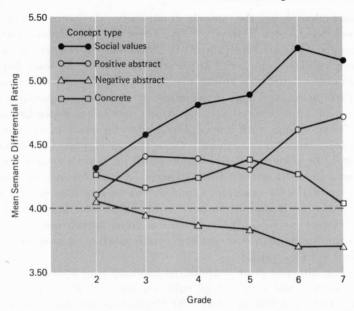

Figure 12-3. Changes with age in the ratings of four classes of concepts on the evaluation dimension of connotative meanings. (From Di Vesta, 1966, p. 159. With permission.)

teachers for developing approach-avoidance responses to new objects or events.

There is another implication of research on connotative meaning for teaching situations. In any learning environment the affective responses become readily linked, not only between words associated together but also to the situation itself or to parts of it such as the teacher, other pupils, or events in the classroom. Interesting in this regard is the finding that when the objective meanings have been long forgotten, the connotative meanings remain (Yavuz & Bousfield, 1959; Yavuz, 1963). Thus, it would not be uncommon to hear a person say, "I can't remember any of the details but I certainly disliked that class" or "I can't recall his name but he was a teacher who certainly put the pressure on us to work hard." Affective meanings associated with the classroom climate, the subject matter, or the teacher may persist to influence the pupils' behavior to as great an extent as the subject matter he has learned.

Coding and Verbal Mediation

A process similar to Pavlov's second signalling system, called verbal mediation (e.g., Goss, 1961), has been of much interest to American psychologists and is potentially important for the teacher to understand. Although the elements of the principles of verbal mediation are to be found in Hull (1952) and Spence (1956), the currently accepted theories are probably based primarily on the work of Osgood (1952). The acquisition of word meanings (Osgood, Suci, & Tannenbaum, 1957) by classical conditioning is explained immediately below.

Sentences in learning and comprehension

In an experiment with human subjects, a neutral word might become associated with shock. Shock elicits avoidance reactions. After repeated pairings with shock the word alone would elicit the avoidance response. Words developed in this way are called *signs*. Other words, paired with these signs acquire meanings through higher-order conditioning and are called *assigns*. Thus, a neutral reaction may be first elicited to the word "Tom." However, if one says "Tom is a thief," some frac-

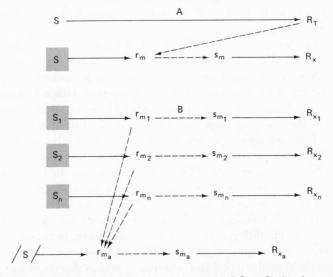

Figure 12-4. A. Development of a sign. A minimal but distinctive portion of the total behavior (R_T) originally elicited by an object (S) comes to be elicited by another pattern of stimulation (S) as a representational mediation process (rm), the self-stimulation (sm) from which mediates various instrumental sequences (R_x). This representational mediation process is the meaning of the sign. B. Development of an assign. Portions of the representational behaviors (r_{m_1} - r_{m_n}) associated with a set of signs (S_1 - S_n) transfer to a new pattern of stimulation, the assign (/S/), as a 'distilled' representation process (r_{m_a}), which becomes the meaning of this assign. (From Osgood, 1953, p. 697. With permission of author and publisher.)

tion of the avoidance reaction made to "thief" will also be made to Tom. Moreover, if the reaction to Tom is to change, the listener must already know that Tom (the stimulus) is a person and "thief" must previously have been conditioned as "a person who is bad" or "one who takes things, or steals." Once these conditions are present, word meanings can be shifted (assigned) from one word (sign) to another (assign) through predication.

Mowrer (1960, pp. 147–152) indicates that similar conditioning may be accomplished by the following four kinds of sentences:

1. *Thing-thing* sentences: E.g., the parent may use direct punishment such as spanking (*thing*) or slapping the child when the child is caught hitting (*thing*) his brothers. In the laboratory a shock is paired with cheese through classical conditioning, and after several trials the rat avoids the cheese. Note that, in both examples, directly observable and primary events are being associated.

2. *Thing-sign* sentences: E.g., the child about to throw (*thing*) an eraser at one of his peers sees the teacher's glare (*sign*), and the child's action is inhibited. In the laboratory the sound of a buzzer (*sign*), previously paired with shock, will inhibit the eating response when paired with eating (*thing*).

3. *Sign-thing* sentences: This form of learning is exemplified when the parent verbally reminds the child that he was to have come home directly after school (*sign*) and then administers punishment (*thing*). In the laboratory, a rat may eat cheese in association with a blinking light. When the blinking light (*sign*) is presented alone it will be accompanied by some of the chewing responses present in the initial conditioning. If the sign (*blinking light*) is then paired with shock, the inhibition produced will generalize to other occasions in which the rat eats cheese.

4. *Sign-sign* sentences: This sentence contains the "sign" elements of the two previous sentences and is clearly evident in the example employing the sentence "Tom is a thief." Here, we call attention to the fact that through training the learner's responses are so modified that he behaves much differently than he would have behaved otherwise. The parent, for example, might verbally reinstate (*sign*) the situation in which the child misbehaved and administer verbal threats of punishment (*sign*) for subsequent occurrence of that behavior.

Much of what goes on in the classroom parallels the sign-sign sentence. Teachers provide instructions that give directions or rules by relating representations of ideas. They control behavior by relating verbal representations of the behavior with verbal representations of favorable or unfavorable consequences, depending on the nature of the outcome desired. Accordingly, the teacher, if he is to provide precise guidance to the pupil's behavioral growth, must be certain that his meanings for signs and assigns are also shared by the pupil.

The sentence and reading readiness: what does the pupil see when he reads?

In contrast to Mowrer's "sentence paradigms" for conditioning, the sentence, as spoken or written, is considered by the psycholinguist to be a basic unit of comprehension. As such it is fundamental to the transmission and acquisition of knowledge as well as being fundamental to most activities conducted in the school. Its comprehension depends upon how much competence has been acquired in the rules that govern the grammar of the language.

The spoken or written sentence may be analyzed, according to Chomsky (1968), at two levels: the surface structure or what is actually heard, read, spoken, or written; and the deep structure, which is understandable by the member of the speech community, though unexplained, and which corresponds to the underlying fundamental meaning of the sentence. For example, the following sentences seem, on the surface, to be syntactically similar:

i I expected the doctor to examine John.
ii I persuaded the doctor to examine John.

But replace the phrase "the doctor to examine John" with its passive counterpart "John to be examined by the doctor" and the differences in meaning or deep structure immediately become apparent, as follows:

ia I expected John to be examined by the doctor.
iia I persuaded John to be examined by the doctor.

The meaning of the first sentence is readily accepted by the native speaker as unchanged, while the second sentence is perceived as conveying an entirely different meaning. The "correctness" of these meanings in everyday speech is interpreted instantaneously, without conscious effort, and requires no demonstration such as the one above. The rules that govern the identification of the meaning of the sentence's deep structure are highly abstract and, interestingly, seem to be acquired at a very early age, probably long before the child reaches kindergarten (Lenneberg, 1967). However, as McNeill (1966) says:

> Early speech of children, so much as we have seen of it, reflects a severely limited grammatical competence. They have a few grammatical classes, which are used in simple hierarchical rules, and the rules reflect the basic grammatical relations; there is little else. However, it is important to note that these aspects of children's competence—classes, rules, relations—are all properties of the base structure of sentences. On the other hand, children's earliest speech does not reflect the transformational rules; those seem to come into

children's grammar only later. Full adult competence includes semantic interpretation of base structures to obtain meaning, transformations of base structures, and phonological interpretation of surface structures to obtain a representation of speech (p. 51).

As in most psychological characteristics there are individual differences in the mastery of the deep structure. Consequently, some psycholinguists suggest that control of the deeper levels of language is a most important characteristic of reading readiness.

Coding, verbal mediation, and transfer

In single unit learning the response is assumed to be associated directly with the stimulus, thus S→R. However, in coding, imagery, and verbal mediation other processes are assumed to intervene between the stimulus and response, thus:

Stimulus → Verbalization → Response;
Word → Meaning → Response;
Situation → Image → Behavior.

In effect, these descriptions indicate that people react to their personal interpretation of the situation. Thus, the situation is transformed and the resulting behavior is not the one that might have been made without the presence of mediators.

Verbal mediation can be illustrated by showing how it has been used in the laboratory to facilitate the learning of a motor skill (Eckstrand & Morgan, 1953). When the same verbal response (the word "green") is used to label both a color (green) and a colorless shape (e.g., a square) the two stimuli become functionally equivalent by association with a common response (i.e., the label). The shape-stimulus comes to elicit the word "green" as a response. Now, there is another interesting property of any response; when it is made the response produces proprioceptive or kinesthetic cues (stimuli) of its own that can be associated with other responses. So it follows that actually saying the word "green" provides stimuli that can be associated with other responses in chaining fashion. A motor response such as closing a predetermined pattern of switches, learned initially only to the color green, can also be made to a square *without the response ever having been learned directly to the square*. The one provision, of course, must be that the square had been associated previously with the color name, "green." The process may be diagrammed as follows:

Stage 1

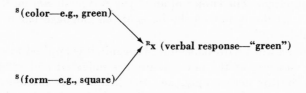

Stage 2

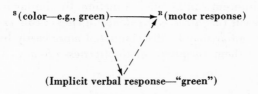

Stage 3

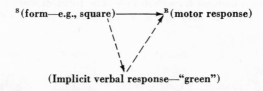

Verbal mediation can also affect attitude formation. As a consequence of pairing a neutral figure with positive-evaluative words such as good, pretty, clean, and smooth, the figure will be ranked as being "more attractive" and if paired with negative-evaluative words the figure will be ranked as "more unattractive" (Di Vesta, 1962; Di Vesta & Stover, 1962).

Verbal labels and behavior

Eisman (1955) taught children to call both a white triangular and a green rectangular block by the name "egg," to call a white square block and a black rectangular block by the name "shoe," and a white circular block and a yellow rectangular block by the name "car." In a second phase of the experiment the children were rewarded for picking up one particular geometrical white block (e.g., the block labeled "shoe"). Attitude in this study was defined as the choice of a valued object rather than of an object without value. Accordingly, after the training task, the children were given the remaining unrewarded blocks and were asked to find the one that would be followed by a reward. They immediately picked up the block with the same *label* as that reinforced earlier. The importance of the language as the second signalling system is apparent. The choice of an object was made *not* on the basis of its primary attributes but on the basis of the language labels associated with the objects.

When a word with its acquired meanings is applied to a new situation, the meaning of the new situation is modified and influences the person's behavior accordingly, i.e., the behavior is influenced by the word and its concomitant meanings. This fact can be used to influence generalization and discriminability of ideas. Two situations that are superficially different can be made functionally similar by applying the same label to each (*acquired equivalence of cues*); conversely, two situations that are similar may be discriminated more easily by applying different labels to them (*acquired distinctiveness of cues*) (Spiker, 1956).

Labels in concept formation

Heidbreder (1946) used the several series of pictures shown in Figure 12-5 for a concept formation task. The pictures were presented one at a time on a memory drum. A few seconds later the "name" (a non-

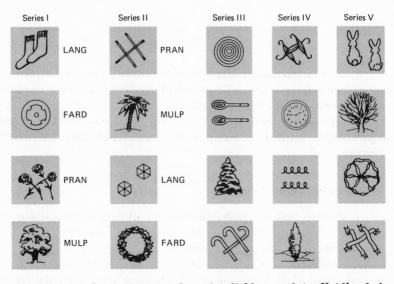

Figure 12-5. Lists of materials and syllables used in Heidbreder's (1946) concept-formation task. The concepts are based on concrete objects, numerical quantities, and forms. After relating the syllables with the objects in Series I and II, the reader should find it increasingly easier to name those in Series III, IV, and V even though no object is repeated in any series. (Adapted from Heidbreder, 1946, Figure 1, p. 182. With permission.)

sense syllable) of the picture was spoken by the experimenter. The subject's task was to anticipate the name before it was given by the experimenter. The subject was not told that it was a concept formation task, only that he was to learn the name of each object. No series was ever repeated so no picture was ever shown twice; that is, after each picture in the first series was presented the experimenter went right on to the second, third, fourth, and fifth sets of figures without a pause or other interruption between series. (Because instances are given to the subject one at a time and he must place each in a given category, this procedure is an illustration of the *reception* paradigm used in many concept formation tasks.)

The subjects in this experiment learned the last list quite easily. By the fifth set of figures most of them had learned the linguistic labels that were codes for similar cues. Each of the morphemes (new words) functioned as signals that some of the figures over the five series, though different and never identical were, nevertheless, similar in some way. Thus, the subject might have learned that "pictures of a building are always called *leth*," and, "an array of six objects is called *dilt*." Conversely, a morpheme such as *dilt* signals the subject that objects so labeled are different in some way from objects called *leth*.

In this study, then, the subject (1) responded to each pronunciation of a single label as equivalent due to his history of experience with the language in which he has learned that the same order of phonemes are equivalent even though their pronunciation varies slightly; (2) abstracted the attribute common to all instances to which the label was attached, or, in other words, learned the semantic rule that defined the concept; and (3) generalized the rule to new instances in the succeeding series.

Such learning is an important part of, if not essential to, the early stages in the teaching of concepts. At first, some of the meaning of one word is acquired by association with another and is parallel to something like learning French equivalents for English words, or to learning the meanings of symbols in chemistry. When learning statistics, for example, difficulty is often encountered when the student tries to make sense out of statistical notation. This may be because the teacher has ignored the simple first step of meaningful learning. The first experiences with entirely new material should be provided by pretraining in which the pupil can link the new ideas with something he already knows—one procedure is simply to pair the "nonsense term" with meaningful material.

If new course material is not related to previous experience the student may view the substance of statistics or other course content as nothing more than a matter of rote learning; that is, of arbitrarily associating one nonsense syllable with another. Carroll (1964) clarifies this point with the notion of correlation. He says that for the beginning student of statistics the word "correlation" may be a "nonsense term" and should at first be paired with other already meaningful experiences. Thus, the term *correlation* might be associated with "signs" the pupil has experienced. For example, that a positive correlation means the X'ier . . . the Y'ier, or within a more realistic context, the individual who has a high score on test X, also has a high score' on test Y. Another paired association is required to relate the term "correlation" with its symbol r (i.e., r stands for correlation). This process may be used in most subject-matter areas although its use often is not apparent to the teacher or pupil.

Growth of the Pupil's Facility in the Use of Language

Verbalizations must have similarity of meaning from person to person if adequate communication and shared thinking are to become possible. The beginnings of this achievement appear in infancy and continue throughout the pupil's development.

The emergence of meanings

The emergence of meanings is marked by qualitative changes in behavior, particularly the bases used for classification. In an experiment by Sigel (1953), children 7, 9, and 11 years of age were asked to classify 20 toy objects such as a blue and red plastic lounge chair, a brown metal soldier, a green plastic truck, and a plastic man in a black suit and white shirt. They could make as many groups as they chose. The 7-year-old group classified the objects principally on the basis of *perceptual characteristics* such as the use of the objects, their structural similarities, and their common geographical location. The 11-year-old children grouped the objects as *members of an abstract class*, such as living and nonliving, furniture, human, or vehicle, rather than on their overall appearance. The findings are summarized in Figure 12-6.

As verbal concepts grow there are changes in the meanings of words, the richness of their associations, and precision in their use. These developments also reflect increasing accuracy in the use of vocabulary. Welch and Long (1940) found that preschool children have a number of concepts which they are unable to name, i.e., these children categorize objects with common properties but are unable to provide a label. With further language development, more and more verbal discriminations occur. Some of the simpler categories are given names. Later, the pupil combines these simpler categories to form broader and more inclusive classifications or to form complex differentiated patterns. To illustrate, preschool pupils say that men and women are people, and

Basis of
Grouping

Percentage
Using Classification

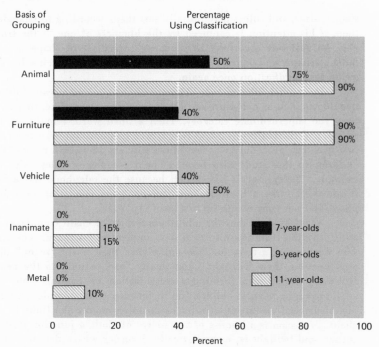

Figure 12-6. The percentage of children in three age groups identifying classi-fications of toys. Note the growth from perceptual classification based on struc-ture to conceptual classification based on abstract classes. (Adapted from I. E. Sigel. Developmental trends in the abstraction ability of children. Child Devel-opment, 1953, 24, 138. With permission.)

that apples and potatoes are food. Later they combine these concepts into more complex categories. Potatoes are labeled as food–vegetables and apples as food–fruit; soldiers are people–men and nurses are people–women. After their fifth or sixth birthday children combine many classes into a single category, or they may combine a given set of categories in different ways.

Chain complexes: the child's basis for understanding words

Children do sometimes grasp the meaning of abstract concepts but it is often only a very small part of the potential meaning and is arrived at in quite a different manner than the one adopted by adults.

The chain complex is considered by Vigotsky (1962) to be a basis for the child's understanding of words in which the meaning of one object among several being classified is carried over to the next. For example, the child upon being asked to classify blocks of varied shapes, sizes, and colors may initially sort them according to triangles; then, if his attention is captured by the blueness of one of the triangles, he will sort according to blueness, regardless of shape or size until, perhaps, he is attracted to the large blocks and switches his criterion for classification once again.

In another kind of task Bruner and Olver (1963) read children two names such as *bell-horn* and asked how they were alike, that is, to form the superordinate category. Then a third word, *telephone*, was added, and the child was asked how it was like and different from the first two. The procedure was continued with six additional names. The children in this study also formed chain complexes. They said, for example, "Telephone is like a bell because the telephone has a bell inside it; it's like a horn because you put your mouth up to a telephone and put your mouth up to a horn" (p. 131).

Vigotsky describes the adult counterpart of chain complexes by an illustration from the historical development of language: The Russian word *sutki*, a term for "day-and-night," first meant "seam," then any junction, then "twilight," and finally "one twilight to the next." However, rather than forming a classification by leaping from one attribute to the next, as children do in forming chain complexes, there is a clear relationship or transfer of meaning among the links in the chain . . . a seam is a joining of two pieces of cloth, a junction forms a corner, and twilight is, metaphorically, a corner where day and night come together.

In other studies, Di Vesta (1966) found that children have only partial meanings in another sense; they have connotative meanings for abstract concepts but cannot give definitions of the concept or tell in anything but vague terms what the concept is about. For example, they may say, "Communists are bad," but have no other response to the concept.

Thus, with increasing intellectual maturity, conceptual skill changes dramatically; many rather than only a few attributes can be employed to form a classification. Attributes such as ideas, only indirectly related to immediate sensory experience, become important in the development of new concepts. Combinations of attributes are organized into hierarchical structures according to increasingly complex logical rules (Bower, *et al.*, 1969). Cognitive skills, related to forming and using principles and rules, and the syntactical features of language play more important roles than previously for expressing innovative relationships among ideas or attributes (Chomsky, 1968; Carroll, 1968). As a consequence of all these processes, the names given to the resulting classifications or categories refer to discrete, highly abstract experiences. The acquisition of precise meanings for these names requires an accumulating body of knowledge by the child, that is, a growing cognitive structure.

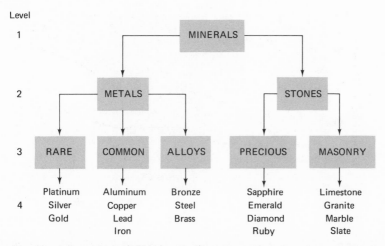

Figure 12-7. Conceptual organization facilitates recall. The above diagram is one of many conceptual hierarchies that could be made for "minerals." Level-four words, in nested category lists of words, were recalled 2–3 times better when the lists were presented in a hierarchically organized manner than when the words were presented in random order. (From Bower, Clark, Lesgold, & Winzenz, 1969, Figure 1, p. 324. With permission of authors and publisher.)

Implications of vocabulary growth for teaching

The changes in verbal ability become represented in the size of the pupil's vocabulary. It provides a rough index of the concepts available to him as indicated by the substantial correlation between the number of words the person uses and his concept scores (Vinacke, 1951). Thus, although the child ordinarily understands more words than he is able to speak (Russell, 1956), the estimates of vocabulary used by children (Figure 12-8) provide an indication of the pupil's basic conceptual abilities at different grade levels. Such indices can only be approximate because words are only useful to the extent they can be employed "inventively and metaphorically." As Glaser (1968) has suggested, the pupil does not have a complete concept of *tree* until he can speak of the "tree of life," or of *river* until he can talk of the "river of fear," or of *ocean* until he can relate it to "oceanic feeling," or to "ideas that are oceans apart," or of *spiderweb* until he can speak of a "spiderweb of decisions."

With the development of the conceptual characteristics of vocabulary, there is a corresponding growth in cognitive skill. Teachers can capitalize on these trends by using verbal organizers in advance of the material to be learned. These organizers not only explain and integrate the material but also indicate what is to be done with it—whether to compare, trace historical trends, or identify salient points. Most impor-

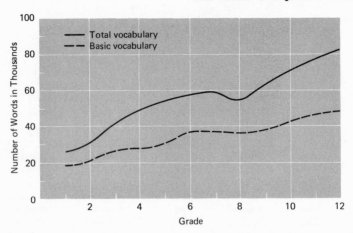

Figure 12-8. Basic and total vocabulary increases immensely over the elementary and high school years. Growth in the use of language is essential to adequate concept development. (Adapted from M. K. Smith. Measurement of the size of general English vocabulary through the elementary grades and high school. Genetic Psychological Monographs, 1941, 24, 327–328. With permission.)

tantly, these organizers tie what is being learned into previously learned concepts already coded and stored as part of the vocabulary, and at the same time provide the basis for discriminating new ideas from the old.

The pupil's ability to employ an ever-increasing vocabulary permits the teacher more flexibility in sequencing of materials. He can, of course, use the inductive approach by presenting examples and having the pupil arrive at the conceptual rule. Beyond six or seven years, children will summarize their experiences verbally whether you want them to or not. On the other hand, the teacher can use the deductive approach in which rules are used as instructions. By providing the rule and then asking pupils to find only illustrative instances, to find instances that are exceptions of the rule, or to find instances that refine it further, the teacher can direct the pupil's behavior remarkably well.

Finally, in the sequencing of materials teachers can use a verbal label to identify an abstracted version of a complex stimulus pattern. Thus, a response is learned to the total pattern first. Then the pupil can begin to abstract intermediate patterns, rules, or details (Binder, 1966). This use of verbal labels parallels that of organizers described above.

Development of mediational facility

"Speech, for the child, acts initially as a means of communication with others, and later as a way of organizing his behavior and in thinking." In this statement Luria (Simon, 1957) emphasizes the importance of mediation of activity through language.

Investigations of mediation in children and in college students by Kendler and Kendler (1962) strikingly illustrate this point. The application of this technique to the study of concept formation, though simple, was clever and ingenious.

In the first learning task, the Kendlers presented children with two cups at a time. The cups varied on two attributes, size and brightness. Thus, on one trial a *large black* cup might be paired with a *small white* cup; on another trial a *large white* cup might be paired with a *small black* cup; on the third trial the *large white* cup might be paired with the *small white* cup, and so on. The task was to select either large cup, regardless of color. The correct choice was rewarded.

In the second task, the children were required to learn to shift the criterion for their discriminations without being informed that the rules were changed. One-half of the original group was required to make a reversal shift. They were now reinforced for selecting objects based on "smallness"; i.e., the same attribute (size) was relevant but its *value* was reversed. The other half of the group made a *nonreversal* shift. They were now reinforced for selecting objects based on brightness; i.e., a value of the other attribute (brightness) was now relevant. (See Figure 12-9.)

Young children who have not developed well-established meanings for words tend to make a nonreversal shift more easily than a reversal shift. Lower organisms also make the nonreversal shift more easily. On the other hand, older children and adults make the reversal shift more easily than the nonreversal shift, thereby suggesting that language facility causes the difference.

The theoretical explanation of these differences in performance is based on the mediational role of language. Recall that in the first learning task, the children were reinforced for selecting the large cups and, as a consequence, were not reinforced for selecting the small cups. But it is assumed that very young children respond to concrete attributes and simple associations rather than to relationships among attributes. Presumably they do not depend upon language in mediational processes to the same extent as adults. Accordingly, in the reversal shift they first "unlearn" and then "reverse" their original learning by single independent steps. On the other hand, when the nonreversal shift is learned, the attribute that was relevant on the first task is ignored. They need respond only to the other attribute (brightness), the one that was irrelevant in the first task. Since brightness was neither reinforced nor extinguished more often than by chance in the first task, only a small amount of "unlearning" was required. Thus, very young children, without mediational facility, learn nonreversal shifts more easily than reversal shifts.

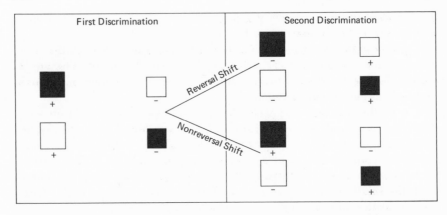

Figure 12-9a. Examples of reversal and nonreversal shifts in discrimination learning. In a reversal shift, after learning to select the large stimuli in the first discrimination, the subject is reinforced for selecting the small stimuli in the second discrimination. In a nonreversal shift, he is required to respond to another dimension (brightness) in the second discrimination. (After Kendler & Kendler, 1962. With permission of authors and publisher.)

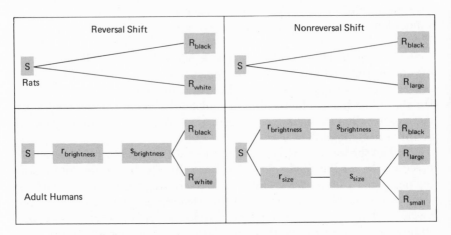

Figure 12-9b. A schematic representation of the differences between behavior of rats and of adult humans in executing reversal and nonreversal shifts. (From Kendler, Basic psychology, 1963, pp. 360, 361. With permission.)

Older children and adults, as we have said above, find reversal shifts easier to make than nonreversal shifts. A reasonable interpretation is that, unlike the very young child, the older person's discriminations are linked to a verbal response. The discrimination task becomes one of classifying the attributes (large, medium, or small) according to the concept of size. Since the same verbal response is required in the reversal shift, nothing new has to be learned. The transition from the value of *largeness,* important in the initial learning, to the value of *smallness,* important in the second task, is facilitated by the use of the same relevant mediator for both tasks (i.e., the word "size" or its equivalent). However, when the individual with language facility makes the nonreversal shift, he must extinguish his original learning that size was important; he must learn that reinforcement is contingent upon an entirely different attribute, represented by the symbolic response *brightness,* and then must identify which value (white or black) of the dimension is relevant.

Kuhlmann (1960) also discovered developmental differences between the cognitive processes of very young and older children. The young children depend on imagery for organizing material in memory. Accordingly, they are highly successful when the material to be coded is highly concrete and "pictureable." With increasing age and facility in the use of language children and adults become less dependent on the habit of imaging and more adept in the use of symbolic processes. It seems, however, that maturity in cognitive skills is reflected in an increase in the use of the much more flexible codes provided by language symbols, although there are some adults who depend upon imagery as a coding mechanism to a greater extent than do others. Those adults who depend on verbalizing mechanisms seem to use symbolic methods of organizing material. As a consequence, while both "imagers" and "nonimagers" perform equally as well on concrete materials the performance of the "nonimagers" (i.e., those who are dependent on verbal or other symbolic processes rather than imagery) significantly exceeds that of the "imagers" on learning abstract materials (Stewart, 1965). The nonimagers clearly have more flexibility in coding.

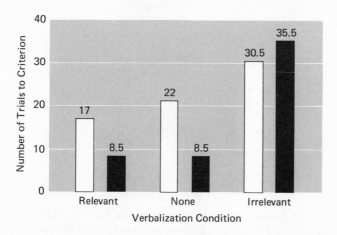

Figure 12-10. The effect of verbalizations on a reversal shift for 4- and 7-year-old children (Kendler & Kendler, 1962, Figure 7, p. 10. With permission of authors and publisher.)

Adapting teaching method to differences in coding ability

These findings nicely illustrate how the verbal and symbolic processes essential to mediation affect concept formation and simple problem-solving. Verbal mediation enables the individual to relate what he has learned regarding the attributes of one concept to other instances of the concept class. The findings also demonstrate how the role of words and their meanings lead to quite different behaviors in the preverbal and verbal stages of development. Quite different modes of thinking by the child in the elementary grades compared to the child in the later grades are suggested. Once again the necessity for employing different teaching methods at different grade levels is emphasized.

In terms of Gagné's hierarchy of learning (see Figure 12-11) a demarcation in the pupil's learning facility and in the teacher's teaching requirements occurs after the chaining of associations has been accomplished. Most of the objectives in the preschool and early elementary grades should be taught by procedures that emphasize simple learning processes such as associating concrete experiences with words; single-

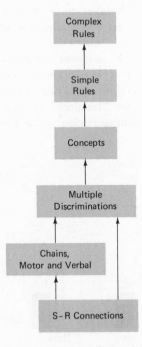

Figure 12-11. A general sequence for cumulative learning. This plan assumes that most of what is learned by children and adults takes the form of meaningful (as opposed to arbitrarily learned) rules. Each of the learnings is believed to depend upon the availability of those below it. (From Gagné, 1968, Figure 1, p. 182. With permission of author and publisher.)

unit learning in which simple associations between words are formed; and chaining deliberately and consciously by linking single ideas, words, or experiences with one another. While pupils in these early grades might be given practice in discovery methods and in verbally describing their experiences, it is not likely, in terms of any of the stage theories, that very young pupils will gain much facility in these inductive methods until they have a backlog of experiences upon which verbal processes depend. Such experiences provide the bases required for the range of mediational processes found in the remaining parts of the hierarchy—from the use of simple verbal mediators as in the Kendlers' experiments, to the labeling of attributes identified in concept formation and attainment, and finally to the formation of relational principles characteristic of Piaget's formal operations period. In fact, the initial activities in the hierarchy of learning or stages of development are essential if "the child is to learn by being told." Where the groundwork for mediational processes is firm, teaching method can depend heavily on verbal presentation and can compensate in large part for deficiencies that might have been experienced in the earlier education of the child.

The Teacher's Role

Schools were originally instituted to give instruction in the proper use of symbols. The pupil's first educational experiences are today heavily weighted with the learning of concepts and related symbols. The major foci of curricular content require that the pupil be immediately concerned with the acquisition of skills in reading, writing, and arithmetic.

In the elementary school of the past, the pupil was literally "plunged" into oral reading and the alphabet. There were periods for penmanship and oral spelling. There was drill in arithmetic. Through the influence of European educational leaders such as Rousseau and Pestalozzi, and those in our own country such as Horace Mann, Henry Barnard, John Dewey, and many others, teaching procedures have changed and school objectives have been broadened. Today, educational goals include physical security, ability to get along with others, consideration of others, and acceptance of the values of society. But the pupil's use of concepts is still a major part of the curriculum, whether the objectives are understanding our physical world, appreciating beautiful objects, being able to communicate with others, or understanding quantitative relationships. In each of these curricular objectives. there remains, as a central core, the mastery of those symbols which contribute to the socialization process. Pupils must know facts, words, numbers, and a multitude of other simple and complex concepts. All of these help him to describe the world about him and to function effectively in his culture.

Cultural influences on word meanings

The use of symbols with their associated meanings is universal among all cultures. However, each society has its own set of concepts peculiar to its requirements. For example, in our society, yams are relatively unimportant and to most of us a single name is sufficient to identify this food. To the Trobriander, however, the yam is an important source of livelihood and ten names, each with highly refined distinctions in meaning, are required. Dorothy Lee's vivid account of the many meanings given this tuber in the Trobriander tribe follows:

If I were to go with a Trobriander to a garden where the *taytu*, a species of yam, has just been harvested, I would come back and tell you: "There are good taytu there; just the right degree of ripeness, large and perfectly shaped; not a blight to be seen, not one rotten spot; nicely rounded at the tips, with no spiky points; all first-run harvestings, no second gleanings." The Trobriander would come back and say "taytu;" and he would have said all that I did and more. . . .

In fact, if one of these were absent, the object would not have been a taytu. Such a tuber, if it is not at the proper harvesting ripeness, is not a taytu. If it is unripe, it is a *bwanawa*; if it is overripe, spent, it is not a spent taytu but something else, a *yowana*. If it is blighted it is a *nukuonokuna*. If it has a rotten patch, it is a *taboula*; if misshapen, it is a *usasu*; if perfect in shape but small, it is a *yagogu*. If the tuber, whatever its shape or condition, is a post-harvest gleaning, it is a *ulumadala*. When the spent tuber, the yowana, sends its shoots underground, as we would put it, it is not a yowana with shoots, but a *silisata*. When new tubers have formed on these shoots, it is not a silisata, but a *gadena*. An object cannot change an attribute and retain its identity. Some range of growth or modification within being is probably allowed, otherwise speech would be impossible. . . . As soon as such change . . . is officially recognized, the object ceases to be itself.*

Variations in meanings among subcultural groups

The fact that words convey shades of meaning is not limited to the Trobrianders' language habits, of course. Most of the readers of this book can provide the several contrasting definitions for such terms as "tough," "cool," or "fuzz" when used by different societal groups. Meanings of common words also take on a different color when compared across socioeconomic groups. Miller (1958), for example, found the following focal concerns associated with value-oriented words by persons in the lower socioeconomic class:

1. *Trouble* is an unwelcome or complicating involvement with official authorities of the middle class. A person's status is evaluated in

*From D. Lee, Being and value in a primitive culture. In C. E. Moustakas (Ed.) *The self: Explorations in personal growth.* New York: Harper & Bros., 1956. Pp. 121–122. With permission of author and publisher.

terms of his ability to "keep out of trouble." In the middle class his status is evaluated in terms of his "achievement" and associated symbols.

2. *Smartness* refers to a person's ability to outsmart, outwit, dupe, "take," or "con" others. It also involves the ability to avoid being "taken" or "outsmarted." These skills are practiced by children and adolescents in the street-corner society, who earn prestige as their competence in these skills improves. In the middle class the parallel to "smartness" is associated with intellectualism, defined in terms of formally acquired knowledge.

3. *Fate* is the direction provided to one's life pattern by a set of forces over which the person has little control. This conception undoubtedly reflects the feeling of being "locked-in" since it is often associated with a view that effort is futile. Concerns here are with "being lucky," changing one's luck from being "unlucky" to "lucky" and so on. By comparison, the middle class norm emphasizes that the control of one's progress rests on his own efforts.

But differences in meanings can also affect the acquisition of specific subject matter. One of our graduate students has called our attention to a neat illustration of such a possibility. Boyle's law, that the volume of a gas is inversely related to the pressure exerted on it, was being taught to children in a uniquely homogenous cultural group. The concepts of gas, volume, and mass appeared to interfere with the pupils' grasp of the principle. Their understanding of these concepts were taken for granted by the teacher. However, upon careful analysis of recordings made of the class discussion it was later found that the pupils were associating *gas* with gasoline, *volume* with loudness of a TV set, and *mass* with a church service. It was apparent that these concepts had been so absorbed into the students' existing cognitive structures that their new meanings became obliterated for use in understanding Boyle's law.

The teacher's role is to guide the acquisition of meanings in ways that will make them functionally useful to the pupil. Other alternatives than "being lucky" can be shown to play a part in determining one's "fate." The classifications of experiences that have been found useful in daily life, in business, in politics, in the trades, in science, or in the arts are the bases of the concepts that are taught the pupil. If they do not contribute to the socialization process in some way, their place in the curriculum is questionable. The efficient selection of concepts to be taught requires a thorough understanding of the culture in which the teacher plays a part, of the meanings words have for pupils in that culture, of the concepts in his or her subject-matter area, of the methods by which pupils acquire concepts, and of characteristics which affect the acquisition of meanings. The task of all who are associated with education is to provide systematic opportunities for the development of formal concepts used to interpret subject matter in specific fields. It is imperative that these concepts are related to the needs of the culture and have communicable meanings shared by the speech community.

Social dialects and their meanings

The speech form also carries implicit meaning that cannot be disregarded. It will come as no surprise to the reader that there are several dialects (speech patterns that differ among groups but are similar within a group) in American society. They differ across regions (e.g., Boston, Southern, or Midwestern dialects); among ethnic groups (e.g., almost any foreign group); and across socioeconomic classes (e.g., working and middle class or among prestige classes as defined by society). Differences in dialect can occur at the phonetic level where, for example, the "g" or "r" might be omitted from words; at the syntactic or grammatical level, as for example, when the small words (prepositions, conjunctions, etc.) are used with greater or lesser frequency depending on the social group; and, at the semantic level where word meanings differ among groups.

The teacher as a model for the learning of a dialect

The learning of speech patterns may be compared to the learning of concepts. Sounds of words are heard, common attributes are abstracted, a rule is formed for saying the sound, and the rule is generalized to subsequent speech. What effect then does the teacher's speech have on the pupil's speech patterns? Why is it that young people who are exposed to the Standard English of their teachers for 10 or 12 years still retain a variant (dialect) indigenous to their region? Labov's (1964) study of the acquisition of Standard English identified some interesting differences among the speech patterns of different socioeconomic classes in several speaking contexts. His findings have implications not only for a better understanding of the pupils' speech development, but also of the effect of the speech of a teacher who has been raised in a geographical area where some variant of Standard English was ordinarily used.

The study was conducted in the New York City area where two common contrasts were found: When saying words such as "thing," "three," and "thought," some people use the stigmatized version in which [th] is pronounced [t] and the words are pronounced t'ing, t'ree, and t'ought. The prestige form, as elsewhere in the U.S., is of course the former or [th] pronunciation. The other contrast is identified when New Yorkers speak such words as guard, car, board, and beer. The stigmatized form of these words is virtually [r]-less while in

the prestige form the [r] is pronounced. Labov collected speech samples, containing representatives of the two variant forms, from persons
in the lower, working, lower-middle, and upper-middle socioeconomic
classes when using casual speech, when using careful speech, when
reading a text, and when reading pairs of words in which the contrasts
were dominant.

The results of his study, related to the differentiation of [th]
and [t] by people in different socioeconomic strata are displayed in
Figure 12-12. (Since the class stratification of [r] is essentially the

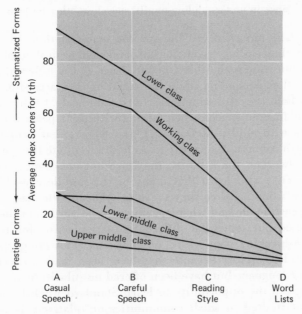

*Figure 12-12. The social stratification of the [th] phoneme (the
initial consonant of thing, through, three, etc.) in New York City. All
groups tend to omit the "h" more frequently in casual speech than
when reading aloud. The middle class speaker uses the prestige forms
to a much greater extent than does the speaker in the working and
lower class. (From Labov, 1964, Figure 1, p. 83.)*

same, those results are not shown.) The reader should note in Figure
12-12 that the stigmatized [t] form occurs to some extent at each
socioeconomic level and that its use decreases with increasingly formal
situations. Thus, intrapersonal styles depend on personal perceptions
of social situations. People have different speaking styles for formal
and informal levels of speech.

According to Labov the middle class users of the stigmatized
[t] or [r] forms are unaware of this fact and the belief of persons in
the middle class is that the form only occurs in the speech of lower
socioeconomic people. Thus, teachers, in the mistaken belief that their

own speech is stable, and being unaware of the shifts in style, understandably condemn their pupils for variants in form that they themselves use in casual speech. The pupils, on the other hand, are reluctant to abolish a behavioral pattern with which they feel at ease and which is essential to their status in their peer groups.

The contrasts will differ with the geographical area (for example, Labov estimates half the people in the U.S. do not differentiate between "hock" and "hawk" or between "cot" and "caught"), but Labov's study provides a basic model that can provide helpful guidance in understanding pupils' speech in other parts of the country.

Less apparent are the specific manifestations of the differences and of their social, psychological, and pedagogical implications. When communicating with others, people learn to use different modes of communication depending upon the situation and according to the people with whom they are attempting to communicate. Children, for example, use one form of speech when talking with their peers and another when talking with adults. McDavid (1964) reports that people in one small Southern community quickly learn to differentiate the speech patterns of the millworker, the hillbilly, the "nice but unassuming" white, and the black. They also learn that many of the middle class blacks are bidialectical; that is, when they speak to other middle class people they use one speech mode and when speaking to the yard man they use another. A related but somewhat different situation exists for the Cajuns, the French-speaking poor whites of Louisiana. This group has been placed in double jeopardy because they have been made to feel French is an inferior language but have been offered no substitute, i.e., they have not been given the opportunity to learn Standard English. Such conditions are not limited to small communities or relatively isolated groups of families. Differences among class dialects also exist in all large cities including Detroit, Cleveland, Chicago, San Francisco, Oakland, Memphis, and New York. Thus, the teacher of English, whether in college remedial English classes or in the public school, whether in the inner city or in the small rural community, is faced with teaching Standard English as a second foreign language (McDavid, 1964). Other teachers, too, will influence the development of dialects, or will be influenced by them, when making evaluations of the pupils' performance.

Social dialects: some implications for teachers

Dialects emerge according to definite speech patterns on a continuum ranging from the highest prestige form (the acrolect) at one extreme to the early developmental form (the basilect) on the other (Stewart, 1964). The young child is believed not to incorporate the prestigious dialect until approximately seven or eight years of age, at which time definite shifting takes place as in the acquisition of new morphemes (for example, kliynt becomes "cleaned," rentit becomes "rented," and wetit becomes "wetted"). More evidence is needed to determine whether this will prove to be a valid generalization. However, a number of sources suggest that major changes do occur in the behavior of the child around seven to nine years.

One implication is that the school might rechannel the energies required in making this transition by non-Standard-English-speaking pupils into a formal, intensified course in Standard English around the time they are eight or nine years of age. Secondly, the teacher should be aware that even where the speaker himself shifts to Standard English, the consequences of early experience with the basilect might be uncertainty about structural agreement between the two (for example, he may not realize the difference in acceptability of "I don't like it" compared to "I ain't like it"); and grammatical interference (for example, the child who reads "he brother" for "his brother" may not be making a reading error but is transforming the meaning of the printed phrase into the basilect equivalent).

When working with children from different cultures or subcultures it is also helpful to know that social dialects are highly resistant to change. One reason may be that dialects are deeply rooted in value systems (Labov, 1964). The vernacular is supported by identification with one's own people since many people in the working class have no desire to be identified with the middle class. They identify with people who are their friends and family, and whose style of casual speech is considered to be identified with masculinity. These attitudes obviously will interfere with the acquisition of Standard English.

The notion that social dialects symbolize relationships with others within some social group is shared by other linguists. Haugen (1964) indicates that changing a dialect is, in many ways, similar to learning a new language, requiring a dual identity for optimal motivation. The speaker of English who learns French most successfully is the one who likes and admires the French. The Northerner who moves to the South and likes the people there will acquire a southern dialect and will not relinquish it when he moves North again. However, if he likes both groups equally well, he will become bidialectical.

Baratz and Shuy (1969) stress the point that black children "speak a well-ordered, highly structured, highly developed language system which in many ways is different from standard English" (p. 94). Accordingly, if it is desirable that all children reach a similar degree of proficiency in reading, writing, or speaking Standard English, it will be necessary for the schools to identify major differences in the structure of language as used by blacks and whites. Then it will be necessary to develop new teaching techniques and materials, based on these differences, for use by the teacher whose methods, which may have been developed for other goals, are virtually worthless for these new goals. However, teaching any of the English-oriented subjects (reading, writing, or speaking) requires more than an understanding of contrastive descriptions about the phonological, grammatical, syntactical, or lexical components of the language. It is becoming increasingly apparent, from what is now known in the emerging field of sociolinguistics, that a complexity of social-psychological variables including group norms, attitudes, values, loyalties, and even status or power positions are entwined with the language patterns adopted by the pupil.

These observations of differences in speech patterns imply that the black citizen will not be ready to change to the Standard English speech patterns, necessary for success in the present educational system, unless there can be some identity with a white community which is actively willing to accept and integrate him (Haugen, 1964). There is also the implication that to change a dialect is to tear asunder some fairly strong emotional ties with one's social group. Thus, the better alternative may be to teach children in such a way that they remain bidialectical rather than to eradicate the dialect entirely.

Golden (1964) has pointed out that a visit to the U.S. Senate would provide convincing evidence of the many acceptable varieties of American English. There are also the amusing variations provided by the lovable Hyman Kaplan or the Boston dialect, to name but two others. All add a richness to the flavor of the language. As long as the speaker is effective, slight variations are acceptable to the listener. Where major variations lead to communication difficulties, however, they should be remedied.

As with all learning, the teacher can provide guidance but in the end it is the pupil who must change. In the course of this process the child is permitted to retain pride in the language he already has, whether it be a dialect, or German, Italian, Spanish, or other foreign language. In fact, in the case of a foreign language, he might be encouraged to increase his proficiency in it. At the same time, the pupil can be made aware of leaders and models from his ethnic group who have changed their speech habits. Unacceptable structural deviations require remedial attention. The teacher then focuses on language as a tool and skill. The pupil's focus is toward facility in the use of language. In a sense the teacher is saying to these pupils, "This brand of English you are using is a language in itself which has its uses. It is like a comfortable suit of clothes that we keep because we may still want to wear it on some occasion. But perhaps we would decide not to wear it to a job interview if we had another one to wear. Here in class you can acquire the language used by most Americans. This language will then be yours to use when you need it" (Golden, 1964, p. 104).

Summary

Words are said by some psychologists to serve two major functions: mand and tact. The mand function is a demand requiring some action by the listener. It is reinforced when the demand has been fulfilled. The tact function is used to name objects and serves to benefit the listener. Since it is used for naming abstracted qualities of events it is important in concept attainment.

Other properties of words include their denotative and connotative meanings. Denotative meanings are the criterial attributes commonly agreed upon by the speech community for distinguishing a concept class. Connotative meanings refer to the affective attributes of concepts as idiosyncratically defined. The results of some studies suggest that connotative meanings are retained for a longer period of time than are denotative meanings.

The development of word meanings has been explained in terms of classical conditioning, operant conditioning and verbal mediation. More recently, there has been an emphasis on the effects of such features as syntax in the development of meanings. In addition, verbal mediation is an important theoretical explanation of many effects language has on behavior. Various experiments have demonstrated that the skills of learning and attitude formation can be made materially more efficient by verbal mediation. In terms of a hierarchy of learning processes it appears to be the immediate antecedent of concept formation, principle learning, and problem-solving.

From an educational viewpoint symbols and concepts have always had a salient place in the curriculum of the American schools, although it should be recognized that the use of symbols is universal among all cultures. However, concepts are more differentiated for events closer to the central concerns of a given culture than for those events that are of little concern. Thus, the teacher would be well-advised to teach those concepts from business, science, and the arts that will contribute most to the socialization of the pupil.

Frequently overlooked in teaching is the importance of the social dialect as a kind of concept, although most teachers generally consider lower prestige forms undesirable. However, there is some evidence to suggest that dialects, whatever their form, are retained because the person identifies with other persons sharing the dialect. Accordingly, the dialect appears to be a part of his concept of the group. In a sense, to relinquish the dialect is also to relinquish emotional ties with the group. Thus, there is the suggestion that the better alternative is to teach the child in such a way that he remains bidialectical.

Teaching of concepts can be facilitated by recognizing that some aspect of most, if not all, culturally important concepts can be taught at any age. This requires that the teacher match the level of the concept with the level of the child's development. At the younger ages the teaching of concepts will require considerable amounts of concrete experience and learning will have to be in small steps. At the later ages (junior and senior high school) the teacher can depend more on verbal presentations. However, it will still be necessary to provide both positive and negative instances, to employ the principles of feedback and correction, and to monitor the formation of rules and generalization to new instances of the concept.

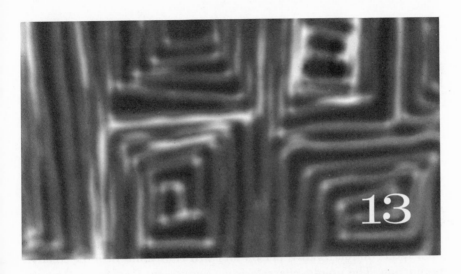

13

The cognitive skills of reasoning, problem-solving, and creativity

Solving old problems and learning to solve new ones are highly representative processes in human cognitive abilities. These skills are built upon an integrated set of prior learnings which include simple associations, verbal mediators, concepts, principles, and rules. They can transfer to facilitate and sometimes, as we note later in this chapter, to hinder the achievement of a solution to a problem. Often, in a dynamic society, adaptation (accommodation) requires that pupils learn to achieve successful solutions to problems that have no prescribed answer in the cultural heritage. Or, as Piaget has suggested, "The goal of education is not to increase the amount of knowledge, but to create opportunities for a pupil to invent and discover, to create mature persons who have the capacity for doing new things" (Ripple & Rockcastle, 1964, p. 3).

For many years Dewey's (1910) description of thinking was popular among educators because of its implications for curriculum development. Briefly, five steps in problem-solving were proposed: (1) A degree of motivation exists in the person due to a felt need aroused by a question. (2) The problem is restated in understandable terms, interpreted, and analyzed. (3) Possible solutions to satisfy the problem requirements are proposed. (4) These solutions are examined for their effectiveness against the problem criteria. (5) A "good" solution is selected as meeting these criteria and then applied. If the person becomes blocked at any one of the steps, then the problem will not be solved.

Since the time Dewey made his analysis, psychologists have proposed many other theories and models of reasoning behavior. All suggest that problem-solving is much more complicated than indicated in a description of five steps (Davis, 1966).

Convergent and Divergent Processes in Cognitive Skills

In recent studies of the intellect, Guilford (1959, 1966) has distinguished between convergent and divergent factors in thinking and reasoning. *Convergent* thinking singlemindedly leads to traditional conclusions drawn from given information. The pupil seeks solutions that appear to be correct and that comply with acceptable cultural norms. An individual who depends entirely on convergent thinking is likely to be a rather unimaginative person and will contribute little to creative production. The unique characteristic in *divergent* thinking is the production of a variety of answers from available information, answers that are likely to be considered novel, unique, or creative. The *convergent* thinker seeks only the obviously correct answer. The *divergent* thinker, on the other hand, is characterized by *fluency* (number of solutions he produces in response to a problem); *adaptive flexibility* (restructuring of interpretations and approaches); *spontaneous flexibility* (freedom from inertia in thinking); *originality* (novel or new ideas); and, *elaboration* (development and extension of ideas and solutions).

Convergent and divergent thinking abilities

The distinctions of divergent and convergent thinking are based upon differences in abilities. Divergent thinking requires the ability to produce a diversity of answers, using many kinds of information as a springboard to many alternatives. Convergent thinking is the kind most often measured on traditional intelligence tests and is often sought in classrooms when a teacher has a correct answer to be identified by the pupil. The information given to the pupil is used to produce the one correct answer. The two kinds of thinking can be distinguished by their products and the kinds of test items used in their measurement, as illustrated in the examples below.

Production of Units

Divergent thinking is measured by word fluency (for example, when the requirement is to produce as many words as possible beginning with a given letter) and by ideational fluency (for example, when required to respond with many ideas to an unrestricted situation, as in the Uses of Things test).

Convergent thinking is measured by facility in naming familiar forms (such as circles, triangles, and hexagons) presented in random order and in such tasks as naming concepts represented in groups of words (e.g., movie, bowling, circus, and game).

Production of Relations

Divergent thinking described by this factor is measured by the ability to think of words that can substitute for one another in different ways, that is, by associational fluency (e.g., name two synonyms for "exaggerate" and two antonyms for "approve," rapidly). This facility is probably one important requirement for writers who must seek means of inventively expressing ideas.

Convergent thinking requires that a response is produced to a given relationship, as in this example from the "inventive opposites" measure: Give two antonyms to Strong beginning with f ——— and w ———.

Production of Systems

Divergent thinking requires the facile production of organized discourse and is measured by such items as this one for expressional fluency: Write a four-word sentence beginning each word with these letters, Y ——— c ——— t ——— d ——— .

Convergent thinking involves the ability to arrange things in their most appropriate or reasonable order, as in the example: In what order would the following events occur? (1) Many roads were blocked and homes flooded. (2) The river overflowed because of heavy rains. (3) Traffic was held up all over the area.

Production of Transformations

Divergent thinking requires originality. Tests include the writing of clever titles for simple story plots or listing of consequences for sudden and striking hypothetical events (e.g., what would happen if electricity was suddenly turned off all over the world for one hour?).

Convergent thinking is measured by the ability to reorganize objects or events in a way to come up with a single new or different use, as in the question: Which object could be used to start a fire?
A. Fountain pen   B. Onion   C. Pocket watch   D. Peanut   E. Bowling ball
Answer: The pocket watch by using the crystal as a lens with which to focus the rays of the sun. (Adapted from Wilson, 1968, pp. 25–28.)

Both characteristics are necessary for reasoning and thinking. Convergent thinking is essential to critical thinking, and, furthermore, enables the pupil to benefit from history and tradition, i.e., from man's past experience as embodied in his culture. There *are* correct answers to known problems. These should be accepted for the sake of economy in thinking, provided they are responsibly derived and subjected to critical, public evaluation. Divergent thinking becomes important when better, unique, or novel solutions are sought. Complete insistence on a single correct answer is often stressed in school settings encouraging the development of convergent rather than divergent thinking. A balance between the two modes can be achieved by encouraging the pupil to seek new answers to problems, to identify a variety of potential solutions, and to evaluate the adequacy of alternative solutions to whatever problems are presented. If the teacher insists on a single correct answer, as he often does to save teaching time, the pupil may eventually develop a learning set to seek only the one acceptable answer. When the teacher encourages productivity of alternative solutions, the pupil is more likely to learn divergent thought patterns that contribute to creative problem-solving.

As a result of highly directed experience in authoritarian settings many pupils become predominantly convergent thinkers. They learn by the time they are in high school that there is one unique answer or conclusion to a problem. Other pupils as a result of their experience in democratic and accepting atmospheres become predominantly divergent thinkers. They tend to try many alternatives, uninhibited by the necessity to conform to a goal or to accepted standards; they reject the common, old solution in favor of the novel solution (Guilford, 1959).

The creative pupil

Getzels and Jackson (1962) made an intensive comparison of pupils classified into these two groups: high IQ and high creativity. Intelligence test scores were taken as a measure of convergent thinking since a high score typically depends on knowing the "correct" answers. Creativity was measured by tests of the number of different definitions given for words, the number of different uses given for common objects, the identification of geometric figures in complex designs, the number of different endings composed for fables, and the number of problems made from given information. The pupil's score was based upon the number, variety, appropriateness and complexity of his answers. The following example, from Getzels and Jackson (1962, p. 18), illustrates how the "uses for common objects" test was scored:

The subject was required to give as many uses as he could for objects that commonly have a stereotyped function attached to them, for example, "brick," "paper-clip," "toothpick." His score depended on the number and originality of the uses he mentioned. A student obtaining a low score on this test might reply to the object brick, by saying, "A brick can be used for building purposes. You can build a wall with brick, or you can build a sidewalk or fireplace with brick." A student obtaining a high score might say to the same item, "Bricks can be used for building. You can also use a brick as a paperweight. Use it as a doorstop. You can heat a brick and use it as a bedwarmer. You can throw a brick as a weapon. You can hollow out the center of a brick and make an ashtray."

The pupils in the two groups were selected according to their scores on the IQ and Creativity tests. The High Intelligence group was comprised of pupils in the top 20 percent on the IQ test but below the top 20 percent on the Creativity tests. The High Creativity group was comprised of pupils in the top 20 percent on the Creativity tests but below the top 20 percent on the IQ tests. The mean IQ of the High Creative group was 127 points, 5 points less than that of the school as a whole and 23 points less than that of the High IQ group. Despite differences in IQ the school achievement of the two experimental groups was similar and was significantly superior to that of the total school population. Thus, at least among pupils above average in IQ, creativity seemed to be as important to school achievement as a sheer increase in IQ points. (The reader should note that the average IQ of the Low IQ group was, relative to the general population, very high.)

Written products from two High Creative and High IQ subjects

Of the many comparisons between the High Creative and High IQ pupils provided by Getzels and Jackson (1962) the following are interesting because of the highly contrasting responses:

... in response to the picture stimulus perceived most often as a man sitting in an airplane reclining seat on his return from a business trip or professional conference, are case-type stories given by a High IQ subject and a High Creative subject.

The High IQ subject:

Mr. Smith is on his way home from a successful business trip. He is very happy and he is thinking about his wonderful family and how glad he will be to see them again. He can picture it, about an hour from now, his plane landing at the airport and Mrs. Smith and their three children all there welcoming him home again.

The High Creative subject:

This man is flying back from Reno where he has just won a divorce from his wife. He couldn't stand to live with her anymore, he told the judge, because she wore so much cold cream on her face at night that her head would skid across the pillow and hit him in the head. He is now contemplating a new skid-proof face cream. (From Getzels & Jackson, 1962, pp. 38–39)

In another phase of the Getzels and Jackson study, the teachers in the school were asked to rate each child on a five-point scale according to whether his presence in a class was enjoyed by the teacher. The High Creative group did not fare well in this comparison. Teachers rated the pupils in the High Intelligence group significantly more desirable than either the rest of the school population or the High Creative group. The High IQ pupils may have been favored because of their conventional cognitive and social orientations as reflected in the differences described by Getzels and Jackson (1962, pp. 60–61) :

> ... The high IQs tend to converge on stereotyped meanings, to perceive personal success by stereotyped standards, to move toward the model provided by the teachers, to seek out careers that conform to what is expected of them. The high creatives tend to diverge from stereotyped meanings, to move away from the model provided by teachers, to seek out careers that do not conform to what is expected of them.

"Creativity," like "discovery," is an appealing concept; nevertheless, the results of studies in this area of research need to be scrutinized carefully. Creativity is still a poorly defined concept and much of the theorizing has not progressed beyond the point of educated guesses. Before accepting the findings in the area of creativity, appealing as they may be, as the final word, the cautious reader will want to consider the following criticisms made by McNemar (1964) : The relation between IQ, creativity, and school achievement needs more clarification than is presently available in the literature. All of these measures are substantially correlated, a most important fact in the interpretation of data since both groups came from a restricted (upper) range of IQs but from an uncurtailed range of creativity. Where IQs, or any other scores for that matter, are highly homogeneous their correlation with another variable tends to be attenuated. Under the circumstances, then, the correlation of .40 between creativity and intelligence found by Getzels and Jackson (1962) represents more than a moderate relationship. The differences in the ranges of the IQ and creativity scores probably account, too, for the finding that creativity tests correlated higher than IQ tests with achievement in courses high in verbal content.

Conceptual distinctions between the creative person and the so-called convergent thinker may not yet be clearly made. Furthermore, in the aforementioned studies, subjects high in both intelligence and creativity were not compared with the High Creative and High IQ groups. But perhaps a more important criticism, because it relates to the logic involved in the interpretation of the data, is that although the high creative group is said to have achieved high grades despite a lower IQ, the reversed argument is also true, i.e., that the high IQ group also achieved satisfactory grades despite lower creativity scores. Thus, since intelligence and creativity scores were highly correlated and since the groups subdivided into clearly distinct levels of IQ and creativity, the relative contributions of creativity and intelligence to achievement scores was indeterminable.

Cognitive Skills in Problem-Solving

The principal attributes of a problem-solving situation are the statement of the problem and the procedures for arriving at its solution. Either attribute may range, in varying degrees, from known to unknown (Getzels, 1964). At one extreme, both the problem and the procedures are known. A solution can be readily achieved by systematically following the required steps. At the other extreme a problem exists but remains to be identified, or discovered, and a standard method of solving it is unknown to the persons involved. These extremes are illustrated by Alice Toklas' report, in her autobiography, that Gertrude Stein on her death bed said over and over, "What is the answer?" Her very last statement before death was, "Then, what is the question?" In between these extremes is the circumstance where a problem exists, but remains to be identified by the problem-solver; the method for solving it is known to others but not to the problem-solver himself.

A pragmatic approach to problem-solving

Understanding the Problem

What is the unknown? What are the data? What is the condition? Is it possible to satisfy the condition? Is the condition sufficient to determine the unknown? Or is it insufficient? Or redundant? Or contradictory?

Draw a figure. Introduce suitable notation.

Separate the various parts of the condition. Can you write them down?

Devising a Plan

Have you seen it before? Or have you seen the same problem in a slightly different form?

Do you know a related problem? Do you know a theorem that could be useful?

Look at the unknown! And try to think of a familiar problem having the same or a similar unknown.

Here is a problem related to yours and solved before. Could you use it? Could you use its result? Could you use its method? Should you introduce some auxiliary element in order to make its use possible?

Could you restate the problem? Could you restate it still differently? Go back to definitions.

If you cannot solve the proposed problem try first to solve some related problem. Could you imagine a more accessible related problem? A more general problem? A more special problem? An analogous problem? Could you solve a part of the problem? Keep only a part of the condition, drop the other part; how far is the unknown

then determined, how can it vary? Could you derive something useful
from the data? Could you think of other data appropriate to determine the unknown? Could you change the unknown or the data, or
both if necessary, so that the new unknown and the new data are
nearer to each other?

Did you use all the data? Did you use the whole condition?
Have you taken into account all essential notions involved in the problem?

Carrying Out the Plan

Carrying out your plan of the solution, *check each step.* Can
you see clearly that the step is correct? Can you prove that it is correct?

Looking Back

Can you check the result? Can you check the argument?
Can you derive the result differently? Can you see it at a glance?
Can you use the result, or the method, for some other problem?
(From G. Polya, *How to solve it.* Princeton, N.J.: Princeton
University Press, 1945. Inside front cover. With permission of author
and publisher.)

The pupil's preparedness for problem-solving

The typical experiment in problem-solving employs a statement
of the problem to be solved and the subject discovers the method for its
solution. In one situation, nine equally spaced dots, forming a square,
are presented. The subject's task is to connect them by drawing four
continuous lines without lifting his pencil from the paper. In another
situation, the subject is given six wooden matches with the requirement
that he assemble these to form four congruent equilateral triangles, the
sides of which are equal to the length of the matches. Duncker (1945)
asked his subjects to solve this problem: given a human being with an
inoperable stomach tumor, and rays which destroy organic tissue at
sufficient intensity, by what procedure can one free him of the tumor by
these rays and at the same time avoid destroying the healthy tissue surrounding it? Luchins (1942) gave his subjects problems involving water
jars of varying capacity, e.g., 21 quarts, 127 quarts, and 3 quarts, with
the requirement that they successfully obtain a given quantity, for
example, 100 quarts. In all of these problems, the problem is given
(known) and the standard method of solution is unknown to the subject
but known to others.

These, and problems in practical settings, must have been
preceded by learning if they are to be solved. In order to solve the
matchstick problem, the pupil must be able to relate possible solutions
to principles in geometry, at least on an intuitive basis; in order to solve

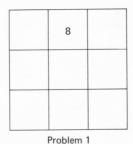

Problem 1

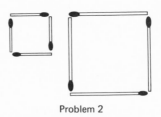

Problem 2

Number the remaining squares (without repeating numbers) so that each row, column, and diagonal add up to 15.

Arrange the eight matches to make three squares of equal size. No part of any match may extend beyond the edge of any square.

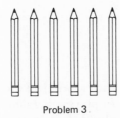

Problem 3

Arrange the pencils to form four congruent triangles each side of which is equal to the length of the matches.

Hints:

Problem 1. The instructions do not say to limit yourself to whole numbers.

Problem 3. Most people assume the pencils must lie flat. Try to form a pyramid.

Figure 13-1. The solution of puzzles is often used to examine problem-solving processes. Try to solve some of the above puzzles. Describe your activities and compare them with the processes described in this chapter.

the ray problem, he must deal with principles from physics; and to solve the water-jar problem, he must be able to perform elementary arithmetic operations. The pupil approaches any problem with certain basic aptitudes, learned abilities, a way of organizing the elements in the situation, and some statement of the problem. In seeking the solution, he must reorganize elements of the problem situation into new patterns (transformation), redefine the solution in his own words (coding), relate previous learning to the question (transfer), and match his activities to the solution (evaluation).

Reasoning and thinking, to be successful, require a preparatory phase during which relevant experiences and knowledge have been acquired. The person who is more intelligent, who has more information, has a distinct advantage in solving problems over his less favorably

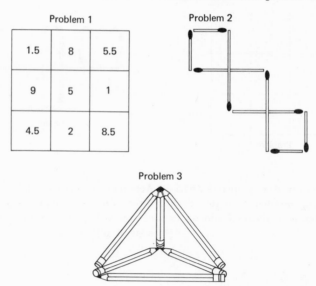

Problem 1		
1.5	8	5.5
9	5	1
4.5	2	8.5

Problem 2

Problem 3

Figure 13-2.   Solutions for problems in Figure 13-1.

endowed counterpart. In the course of dealing with a problem the pupil must call on this information in various ways. In playing Scrabble or in solving anagrams, a large vocabulary is most helpful. Just as important, if not more so, is the pupil's storehouse of intellectual skills for processing information, for reorganizing elements (e.g., letters) into meaningful patterns (e.g., words), for predicting outcomes from "knowns" and for evaluating the importance of an outcome. Gagné (1968) indicates that these skills probably emerge in a given order: "Specific responses transfer to discriminations, which transfer to classifications, which transfer to rules, which in turn may transfer to more complex forms of rule-governed behavior . . ." (p. 9). The teacher assists in this process by instructions, verbal directions, clear specifications of the nature and characteristics of the situation, and by questioning to guide discovery of alternative hypotheses (Gagné, 1966).

Factors in problem-solving

Functions of Instruction	*Internal Processes*	*Individual Differences*
Presentation of problem; instructions on kind of goal to be attained.	Abstracts and defines problems. Sets goals.	Individuals differ on bases for goal setting —some have higher standards than others.

Functions of Instruction	*Internal Processes*	*Individual Differences*

Stimulate recall of facts, concepts, and rules that are essential to the understanding of the problem and its solution. The teacher may say something like, "You may recall the formula for Boyle's law."

Recall of subordinate rules.

The number of previously learned rules available and the number that can be recalled differ from person to person. If one doesn't know the word, for instance, he cannot solve the crossword puzzle. The more information the better.

Make the relevant cues distinctive. When solving the nine-dot problem the number of dots is unimportant, the fact that the boundary of the solution is not the square formed by the dots is important.

Search and select the rules relevant to the stimulus situation. Reject those that are not.

Different pupils will perceive different relationships or patterns, not just stimulus elements. Some will be unable to see any but a few patterns. There are individual differences in distinguishing relevant and irrelevant cues, and relevant from irrelevant concepts.

Guide thinking. Give direction to making hypotheses. Guided discovery, or instructions that narrow the combinations, will speed up the process of hypothesis formation.

Combining subordinate rules to form hypotheses.

A source of differences will be in the strategies habitually used by the pupil. Fluency in making new hypotheses is dependent, too, on ingenuity and flexibility.

PROVISIONAL RULE

A provisional hypothesis is formed. It will be matched against an internal idea which is a "form" or "model" of the solution.

Functions of Instruction	*Internal Processes*	*Individual Differences*

Check against solution model. Provisional hypothesis is tested against an interpretation of the goal. If they are not matched, the process is initiated once again from any of the previous stages.

Verification.

Retention of features of solution model differs among pupils. Accuracy of checking of provisional hypothesis against solution differs and depends upon accuracy of retention.

SOLUTION RULE

(After Gagné, 1966, pp. 138–146 and Figure 1, p. 139. With permission of author and publisher.)

Understanding the problem

The statement of a problem and the questions that are asked about it contain direction and clues to possible answers. Thus, most investigators recognize this feature as a critical part of problem-solving (Duncker, 1945; Maier, 1930; Simon & Newell, 1964). If the statement is vague there can be little opportunity for the pupil to find the necessary meanings and directions that will lead to adequate solutions. Without clarity there can be no objective basis for evaluating solutions. Successful problem-solvers manipulate the directions by shortening them or by emphasizing the essential details *without losing the intended meaning.*[*] Poor reasoners are likely to give the problem statement a haphazard or superficial examination as though it had no relevance to the solution. Some may even fail to read the instructions, or fail to understand the meanings of some of the phrases or terms.

Sometimes the successful pupil will substitute an illustration or example for a vague term and think in terms of this illustration. The unsuccessful pupils may consider the term as it is given without doing anything to reduce its vagueness. Understanding and meaningfulness not only help in an immediate solution but make transfer to similar problems more likely (Hilgard, Irvine, & Whipple, 1953).

[*]This discussion is based on a detailed comparison of successful and unsuccessful problem-solvers in B. S. Bloom & L. J. Broder, *Problem-solving processes of college students: An exploratory investigation.* Chicago: University of Chicago Press, 1950. (Copyright, 1950, by the University of Chicago.) With permission of author and publisher.

Helping, guiding, and directing the pupil's efforts toward learning ways to restructure the problem will enable him to gain a better comprehension of its meaning. Such direction cannot be overemphasized as an important part of the teacher's role in helping the pupil to learn the intellectual skills required in reasoning. Successful problem-solving depends on these first processes (Schroder & Rotter, 1952).

Information search and cognitive conflict

As we have seen in the preceding sections, thinking and problem-solving are initiated by the statement of a problem. The pupil has some notion of the final goal, but lacks information about how to get from the problem status to the solution status. The resulting discrepancy between where he "is" and where he would "like to be" is an important motivation for engaging and remaining engaged in problem-solving activity (Berlyne, 1960). Without some degree of uncertainty, pupils would feel no need to solve a problem (Salomon & Sieber, 1969). Bartlett's (1958) notion of motivational influence is also very similar, as can be seen from his description of thinking as ". . . the extension of evidence, in line with the evidence, and in such a manner as to fill up gaps in the evidence probably accomplished by a series of interconnected and articulated steps . . ." (p. 20).

Within this framework cognitive conflict is the energizer of the pupil's search for information. Berlyne (1960) suggests that one skill for reducing conflict consists of searching for ways the competing responses can be made less incompatible. Thus, a person may be at a loss to identify a parasitic plant because he had always associated parasites with animal forms. However, by finding out that parasitic plants (e.g., mistletoe) do exist makes the question more compatible (sensible) in terms of what he knows. A second skill for reducing conflict is to make a new response more dominant than conflicting tendencies. The following is a detailed illustration from Berlyne (1960, p. 293) :

If a person with no special knowledge of marine biology is asked, or asks himself, "How does the starfish eat?" he will have no associations available that are peculiar to the thought of a starfish eating. The most likely responses are thus going to be those associated with eating, and those associated with the starfish. "Eating" will predominantly evoke thoughts about vertebrates inserting edible objects into holes in their faces, and this will be recognized as inapplicable to a starfish, which does not appear to have a face. "Starfish" will evoke thoughts derived from memories of pictures of a starfish, which are usually of the dorsal surface and so include no feature that seems pertinent to eating. The subject may even find himself completely at a loss and allow his fancy to wander farther and farther from any line of thought that could lead to a solution. When, however, he has ascertained that the starfish has an aperture on its ventral surface and that its stomach emerges through this

aperture to envelop prey, he has some strong associations that will in the future
be called up by the unified concept of an eating starfish and will exclude the
less apposite thoughts that would have occurred earlier in the same context.

The new line of thought, since it permits a solution to the problem, is reinforced through reduction in conflict. The old sequence of
behavior is concomitantly extinguished.

The effect of cognitive *conflict* in the child's learning of the concept of conservation of substance was studied by Smedslund (1961, 1963)
in this way: If a piece of material is added to or subtracted from a plasticine ball there is no conflict. The child easily notes that the object becomes heavier or lighter. However, if the ball is elongated, the child, at
first, also believes it has become lighter. When the object from which a
piece has been taken is compared to the elongated material, conflict is
aroused, since both objects had been viewed as becoming lighter in
weight. Now the child must make a decision regarding which is the
greater change. After several such comparisons, the child learns the idea
of conservation. (See Figure 13-3.) These findings and others (Smedslund, 1963) *suggest* that the problems are solved through a reduction in
conflict, apparently without other external reinforcement. Each new decision is a choice point where fractional changes in thought occur. After
a number of such experiences, the solution (rule), "change in shape does
not affect the weight of the objects," is reached.

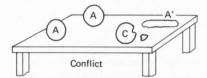 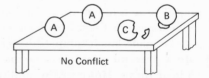

Child perceives A' as lighter than A,   Child readily perceives B as heavier
and C as lighter than A. The conflict   than A, and C as lighter than A.
is produced by asking which produces
the greater change: subtracting a piece
of plasticine or elongating the ball.

*Figure 13-3.   The reduction of conflict facilitates the child's learning of con-
servation.*

Cognitive conflict can be employed usefully in the classroom
through the use of so-called discovery methods. While it is premature to
judge the relevance of such methods to learning (Ausubel, 1961), there
is some evidence that discovery can be, at the least, a useful motivational technique in problem-solving (Kersh, 1962), and thus can help
even the very young pupil attain otherwise difficult solutions to problems. Berlyne (1965, p. 265) provides an interesting example:

I once witnessed a demonstration by Professor D. A. Page, Director of the University of Illinois Arithmetic Project. He was acquainting third-grade children with the position that the difference between the square of an integer and the square of the preceding integer, that is, $[(n + 1)^2 - n^2]$, must be an odd number. He showed this to be the case with 2^2 and 3^2, and then with 3^2 and 4^2, etc. Would it work with 4^2 and 5^2, 5^2 and 6^2, etc? The tension with which the moment of revelation was awaited and the excitement on finding the principle vindicated once more grew visibly with each succeeding instance. Questions asked by Professor Page elicited all the standard signs of schoolroom zeal—climbing on desks, hissing, stretching of hands toward the ceiling. After enough specific instances had been examined and it was becoming clear that the proposition was true throughout the number system, the question of why it was true was raised, and the equivalent of a proof was presented with the help of colored blocks of wood. . . .

This example serves to illustrate the point that the discovery technique arouses the pupil's curiosity; a condition essential to problem-solving. This motivational condition is established essentially through the problem itself which is presented in a manner to create doubt, to be perplexing to the pupil, to indicate a possible contradiction, to require a clarification of the implications of given information, or even to present a resolvable incongruity or confusion. As a result the pupil's behavior is oriented toward the reduction of conflict by inquiry; he notes the properties of the question asked, formulates alternative hypotheses, and asks fruitful questions in the exploration and search of alternate routes to the solution (Kersh, 1965). A "reinforcement-like" effect occurs, as a consequence of this activity, through the reduction of conflict. If the discovery method has a beneficial effect on learning, beyond that of its motivational properties, it is through the fostering of inquiry which leads to intelligent learning or understanding. Since such learning is integrated into the pupil's own experiences and is justified by him during the course of learning, the knowledge he acquires is particularly resistant to forgetting or extinction (Ausubel, 1966).

Learning by discovery

Very often the teacher has as his objective techniques of discovery, per se. The actual subject matter involved may be of secondary importance. The purpose of the learning experience is to exercise and to reinforce the learner in what may be called "searching behavior"—strategies of problem-solving, divergent as opposed to convergent thinking, flexibility in thinking—in essence, the characteristics of what is often labeled "the creative person." With such objectives, discovery or guided discovery techniques are most appropriate. However, if the task is so difficult that the learner does not succeed in discovering the relationships which he is supposed to discover, there will be little opportunity for reinforcement of that very process which is being taught. It is most important that the learner have success experiences when learning by discovery.

It has become increasingly apparent that the learners' attitudes towards a subject-matter area may be as important as what he learns in the cognitive sense. If a student is highly interested in a subject, he is likely to continue to learn. Under appropriate conditions of practice and reinforcement, the discovery technique will foster favorable attitudes and interests. It is interesting and challenging for students to discover, particularly if their efforts are successful, or at least occasionally so. The opposite effect may result when their efforts never or almost never meet with success. (From Kersh & Wittrock, 1962, p. 467.)

The integration of experiences to arrive at successful solutions

No clear-cut set of steps always characterizes the problem-solving process. The pupil seems to go through a cycle involving (1) clarification of meaning, (2) establishing proposals about possible solutions, (3) attempting to incorporate relevant information, (4) evaluating the extent to which the information bears on the problem, and (5) rejecting the information as being of no use or accepting it as necessary to the solution. These processes may be repeated many times before the acceptable solution is found.

In their study of problem-solving, Bloom and Broder (1950) found that the successful problem-solver, in his search for information, constructed hypotheses (intelligent guesses) as to the direction in which the correct solution might appear, or he might have established some standards (criteria) against which the correct solution could be evaluated. Successful problem-solving behavior requires feedback. Without some criteria there can be no knowledge of progress. The successful problem-solver also analyzed a complex problem into simpler subproblems. Alternative answers were considered systematically. If correct, they were accepted. If incorrect, they were dropped once and for all.

The unsuccessful pupil may have no plan for attacking the problem, he may arrive at an answer with only superficial consideration of the elements involved, or he may not use all of the available clues and try to give an answer on the basis of an "impression." Also, an answer is sometimes selected on the basis of elimination, i.e., "None of the others appears reasonable so this is probably the right one." Unfortunately, the person who does this frequently has the information he needs but fails to use it or to realize that it can be used. Sometimes he is on the right track but gives up on the very plan which would yield results. The successful reasoner ties together several isolated experiences and reorganizes them for his solution. His products reflect continual appraisal of the appropriateness of his answers.

Pupils can be helped to analyze their own problem-solving processes by comparing them with successful models. Training and practice in abstracting, analyzing, generalizing from the general to the concrete, and other skills that can be brought to bear on the task show considerable transfer to new problems as reflected in some of the new curricula, e.g., in science (see AAAS Commission on Science Education, 1967).

Detrimental Factors in Reasoning

Attitudes may transfer to facilitate or hinder problem-solving processes, just as they influence other pupil activities. Pupils who feel that reasoning is of little value, who feel that either they know the answer to a problem at once or not at all, who are easily discouraged and lack confidence in their reasoning ability, are handicapped before they begin.

The personal convictions and values of the pupil may operate in still more subtle ways to hinder logical reasoning. An objective attitude toward the considerations involved in thinking is desired if one is to be successful. For example, Bloom and Broder show in their study that pupils often become distracted by ideas that are unrelated to the problem. The pupil's concern is with the *ideas* and the *inferences* contained in possible answers rather than their relation to the question asked. Their convictions and biases about these may be so strong that the basic meaning itself is neglected.

The effects of bias

The influence of bias can be seen in the results of an experiment by Thistlethwaite (1950). Students were asked to examine the following problem and determine whether the conclusions, *in view of the assumptions made*, were valid or invalid (Thistlethwaite, 1950, p. 443):

Given: If this is a desirable neighborhood, then it is close to transportation services. This is not a desirable neighborhood.
Therefore: It is not close to transportation services.

Like the subjects in the experiment, the reader will quickly recognize that the conclusion is invalid. As can be seen, there is no statement with respect to the proximity of transportation in an undesirable neighborhood. Now examine the following, which was also given to the individuals in the experiment (Thistlethwaite, 1950, p. 444):

Given: If production is important, then peaceful industrial relations are desirable. If production is important then it is a mistake to have Negroes for foremen over Whites.

Therefore: If peaceful industrial relations are desirable, then it is a mistake to have Negroes for foremen and leaders over Whites.

The reader will notice that the logic involved is the same as that in the earlier problem. The conclusion here is also an invalid one, in view of the assumptions given. Although most subjects in the experiments were able to recognize that the conclusion in the syllogism having to do with transportation services and neighborhoods was invalid, they made errors on the industrial situation in direct relationship to the amount of prejudice.

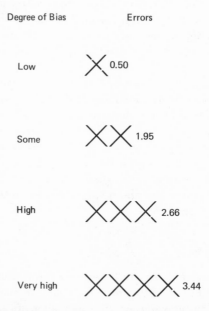

Figure 13-4. *Errors in reasoning about racial problems are related to degree of prejudice. The pupil with strong beliefs is hindered in solving problems on topics involving his biases. (Adapted from D. L. Thistlethwaite. Attitude and structure as factors in the distortion of reasoning.* Journal of Abnormal and Social Psychology, *1950, 45, 442–458. With permission.)*

Material with high emotional content tends to be perceived less accurately by pupils than neutral material. The greatest amount of distortion of meaning occurs with subject matter which involves the pupil's most strongly held attitudes and beliefs. The pupil's thinking can also be distracted by many other external considerations, such as opinions about a course, about the instructor, and about examinations.

When pupils are first exposed to problem-solving it appears best for them to work on fairly neutral material. The fewer the distractions at this point, the better. However, it would be virtually impossible, and certainly undesirable, to continue presenting problems void of emotional content throughout the pupil's school career. Everyday problems *do* contain emotional elements which must be recognized. The teacher's task is to help pupils to see the basic questions involved in a problem, to answer these questions objectively and logically, and to avoid being sidetracked or pushed to a false solution by bias and emotional connotations.

Rigidity and stereotyped behavior

Continuing difficulties in problem-solving are often the results of stereotyped behavior. Finding correct answers to problems requires a considerable amount of variability in pupils' responses. Usually they must try several alternatives. Flexibility and adaptability are among the prerequisites for suddenly becoming aware of the structure of the problem and its solution (a process sometimes referred to as *insight*). Anything related to rigidity, perseveration, stereotypy, or inflexibility is its foe.

Good reasoners do not rigidly pursue unsuccessful or inefficient approaches to problems. They are flexible in their attempts to find a solution. Poor reasoners, on the other hand, often continue in an inappropriate direction, trying for hours on end to achieve the impossible (Maier, 1933). Children exhibit this characteristic to a considerable extent up to the age of five or six, but it is present in pupils of all ages to some degree (Maier, 1936).

Luchins (1942) has demonstrated the effect of rigidity on both public school pupils' and college students' attempts to solve problems. The subjects were given tasks in which they were to use three water jars with different capacities. By filling jars and pouring water from one to the other they were asked to arrive at a given quantity. One such problem and its solution are shown in Figure 13-5. The formula is $B - A - 2C$. Following this problem the pupils solved several other exercises by the *same formula*. Then the following two problems were given:

	Given		Obtain
Jar A	Jar B	Jar C	
23 qts.	49 qts.	3 qts.	20 qts.
15	39	3	18

Although these could also be solved by the original formula, the *first one* could also be solved by the simpler solution of $A - C$, and the

PROBLEM:	Jar A	Jar B	Jar C	Obtain
	21 quarts	127 quarts	3 quarts	100 quarts

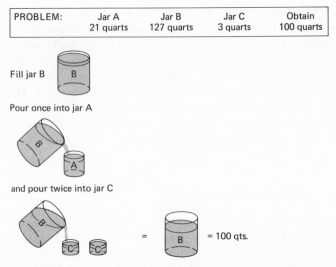

Fill jar B

Pour once into jar A

and pour twice into jar C

= 100 qts.

Figure 13-5. How the water jar problem is solved. (Adapted from A. S. Luchins. Mechanization in problem solving: The effect of Einstellung. Psychological Monographs, 1942, 54, No. 6. With permission.)

second by A + C. Having become habituated to the original solution, however, some pupils failed to see the new possibilities and continued to use the more cumbersome formula B—A—2C.

The rigidity or *set* demonstrated in this experiment is a persistent expectation in reasoning and is clearly a case of negative transfer, assuming that the application of the simpler formula is desired (Schulz, 1960). Pupils whose problem-solving behavior is dominated by this set try to arrive at a solution quickly. They feel they are wasting time if they deal with each problem in a unique fashion. Accordingly, they stereotypically employ the solution that has appeared to work best on previous attempts.

Sets are often induced by the teacher through instructions or may exist as a result of pupils' experiences in similar situations during the past. The pupil will often have difficulty in adapting new approaches unless hints about directions and parts of the solution are given (Chown, 1959). Similarly, massed practice on one type of approach tends to produce a less flexible set than distributed practice (Kendler, Greenberg, & Richman, 1952).

These findings suggest the kinds of preparation needed for different sorts of problems. Teaching methods that require pupils to feel certain of the correctness of their responses, acccording to a single culturally acceptable standard, emphasize convergent thinking and thereby reduce the adaptive flexibility required for many types of problem-solving. On the other hand, sets do not always hinder performance. If the dominant habit is a correct one for the question at hand, problem-solving will be facilitated by these expectations which are detrimental only when incorrect habits are made dominant.

What may be called atmosphere effects are in the same class of behavioral phenomena as sets. They occur in problems or other situations in which there is a closed series of responses to a single task. The result is that the person makes a response which is consistent with the tone of the whole situation. In some early studies, Sells (1936) was responsible for a number of interesting findings regarding this effect in syllogistic reasoning. He demonstrated that a syllogism such as "All X's are Y's," and "All Z's are Y's," often led to the wrong conclusion that "All X's are Z's" because of the "all yes" atmosphere established by the first two sentences.

As with the water-jar problems, the expectancy can be changed somewhat by the caution, "Don't be blind" or "Think carefully." However, Sells also suggests that an atmosphere leading to the correct cognition can be created by substituting concepts for the letter-symbols. For example, when students see the syllogism "All cats are animals," and "All whales are animals," they immediately see the fallacy of their earlier incorrect conclusion since "No cats are whales."

Personality factors

The above discussion describes the difficulties a pupil may encounter in overcoming established habits because of situational elements. Another form of resistance to change is due to a pervasive and enduring rigidity represented by the cognitive styles of closed- (dogmatic) and open-minded persons (Rokeach, 1960).*

A distinction between set and dogmatism can be made clear by their respective influences on different phases of the problem-solving process. Rigidity is assumed to affect the early stages of the analysis of a problem where previous habits have their greatest effect. Dogmatism is assumed to have its greatest effects in the synthesis stage when the solution becomes apparent and may not be accepted if it is contrary to existing beliefs. The dogmatic (closed-minded) person may be unable to relinquish or alter his beliefs. The open-minded person is more flexible. He is more able to accept or reject a novel solution on its merits. Closed-minded persons tend to be more source-oriented than content-oriented. They consider information or evaluations from authoritative

*There have been numerous criticisms of conceptual characterizations and resulting studies of the authoritarian personality, the stepping-stone to studies of dogmatism. Although these criticisms are only indirectly related to the orientation presented here, the interested reader may wish to read the detailed analyses to be found in a volume by Christie & Jahoda (1954) entitled *Studies in the Scope and Method of "The Authoritarian Personality."*

figures as extremely important. Information from socially unimportant persons is more likely to be rejected. The open-minded person is more content-oriented than source-oriented. His concern is with the validity of the information. Doubtful information is checked against other existing bodies of knowledge.

Rigidity affects performance on oddity problems

In a test of the validity of the assumptions about closed- and open-minded persons, Restle, Andrews, and Rokeach (1964) investigated the performance of both types of subjects when learning to solve two different kinds of problems. One task required the subjects to learn a sequence of unrelated learning-set problems where the attributes necessary for reinforced discriminations were reversed from time to time. Successful performance demanded that the experimenters' rein-

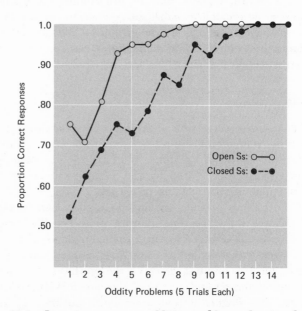

Figure 13-6. Learning curves on oddities problems, showing the effects of differences in personality. Open-minded subjects look for a durable principle underlying solution of the problem. In this task the principle is "the odd item will be reinforced," so looking for the principle aids their performance. The closed-minded (dogmatic) subjects rely mainly on extrinsic factors (e.g., reinforcement by the experimenter) rather than on such intrinsic factors as a durable principle. Thus, their performance is hindered. (Adapted from Restle, Andrews, & Rokeach, 1964, Figure 1, p. 651. With permission of authors and publisher.)

forcements (verbal "yesses" and "noes") be followed closely. Another task, called the oddity problem, required the subjects to solve many different problems with a single common underlying principle (the odd one of a triplet was correct). Although feedback was provided, a new problem could be solved best only if the correct principle had been identified. Closed-minded subjects performed more efficiently on the learning-set problems, implying that they depend more on the rule to "follow the authority." Feedback from the experimenter, however capricious, is the important consideration. Less attention is given to the requirements of the task or to the information conveyed through experience with the task. Open-minded subjects, on the other hand, performed more successfully on the oddity problem which involved a principle. They seek the abstraction that will help in the solution of new problems. Concomitantly, since they depend less upon authority, they do not perform as well on the learning-set problems where the principle capriciously varies from time to time. Furthermore, they seek a principle which has more durability than being applicable to a few problems for the shorter range effects.

Like sets and rigidity, dogmatism may be detrimental to problem-solving (Vacchiano, Strauss, & Hochman, 1969). Open-mindedness is a characteristic sought where novel solutions are necessary. But the extent to which closed-mindedness interferes with or contributes to the pupils' adequacy differs according to the stage (analysis or synthesis) of problem-solving being considered, and the kind of task being performed.

Anxiety and stress

When pupils are afraid of failing or are strongly motivated by some other anxiety, they are likely to be poor problem-solvers (Spielberger & Lushene, 1969). Their productive thinking is disrupted by a compelling preoccupation with inadequacy and failure (Lazarus, Deese, & Osler, 1952). Stereotyped behavior is the result.

An analysis of the changes in rational behavior under stress compared with normal conditions is shown in Figure 13-7. The striking finding of the study by J. R. Patrick (1934) illustrated in this figure was the marked reduction of rational, deliberate, and adaptive effort under stress. On the other hand, the stereotyped, primitive tendency to repeat a trial over and over again, and the tendency to remain inflexible even when effort was wasted was characteristic of individuals under conditions that aroused strong fear. Indeed, the emotional reactions were so severe that college students in this study required almost as many attempts to solve the problem as a 26-month-old infant!

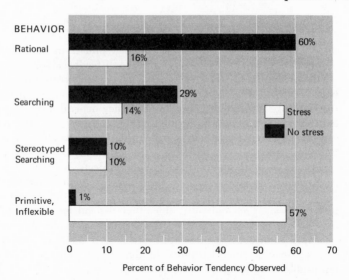

Figure 13-7. Stress blocks rational behavior. Under such conditions stereo-typed, primitive, and inflexible behaviors may be substituted for rational be-havior. (Adapted from J. R. Patrick. Studies in rational behavior. Journal of Comparative Psychology, 1934, 14, 167. With permission of author and Williams and Wilkins Co.)

Emotional reactions and the production of irrational behavior

The effect of an emotional situation on the rational problem-solving behavior of organized and unorganized groups was cleverly demonstrated by French (1941). Different groups of subjects were left in a room to fill out a questionnaire after a period in which frustration was produced by working on insoluble problems. After they were in the room, the door was locked without their knowledge. Then wood smoke was made to seep under the door. A few moments later a fire siren was sounded in a distant room but could be heard by the subjects. Thus, the event had the appearance of a dangerous fire. During this time the subjects were observed through a one-way screen and their verbal responses were recorded.

The results were similar to those caused in panic. Individuals within a given group all behaved very much the same way. However, the organized group's behavior was more irrational and emotional than that of the unorganized group, probably because of their greater interdependence which led to better communication of the fear response, social facilitation of emotional expression, and circular social stimulation. In addition, groups with less education seemed to be more suggestible, less critical, and more submissive to the prestige of the experimenter than groups with more education, as evidenced by the recordings of subjects' verbal responses and by their descriptions written after the event.

Experiments stimulated and guided by Taylor's (1956) orientation have led to explanations of the circumstances under which anxiety may be a help or a hindrance in problem-solving (see Chapter 7). In problem-solving or other complex tasks, a number of interpretations are possible at each choice-point; two or more response tendencies often compete for dominance. If the correct response is the strongest one available, the high-anxious subjects will learn the task more readily than the low-anxious subjects. Anxiety, conceptualized as a drive, increases the probability that a well-learned interpretation will be used to a greater extent than a weaker one. By the same rationale, if the *dominant* interpretation is *incorrect*, high-anxious pupils will have more trouble in thinking. For example, high-anxious subjects tend less than do nonanxious subjects to shift from one approach to another in solving the water-jar problems (Maltzman, Fox, & Morrisett, 1953). Highly motivated children have more difficulty solving the Umweg or Detour problem than do those children less motivated (Lewin, 1935). However, for a problem to be solved, a correct hypothesis must eventually occur somewhere in the course of events. Heightened drive at that point should facilitate performance (Hill, 1957).

While the relationship between anxiety and performance has been supported in a number of experiments, it has not been fully clarified (Levitt, 1967). Anxiety, in some cases but not all, seems to increase set in problem-solving, thereby leading to a decrement in performance. When pupils are overly excited or strongly threatened by failure, impaired performance can be expected. Pupils who find competition exceedingly motivating, those who must work rapidly to keep up with the rest of the class, or those who work under the threat of failing grades meted out by a punitive teacher can usually be expected to display unvarying and stereotyped responses.

Creative Thinking

Modern science, industrial technology, communication, and the arts are replete with the products of creative thinking. Inventors find new ways of doing things. They plan and build new and improved devices. Scientists discover new relationships and find new solutions to problems. Poets, musicians, and artists find new forms in which to express familiar experiences. The contributions these innovators make to our personal security, daily convenience, and enjoyment are recognized by all. On the other hand, there never seems to be an oversupply of creativeness. High premiums are often paid in the form of increased financial remuneration, promotions, and prestige to those who are exceptionally creative. Whatever the teacher can do to contribute to the development of creativity is valuable to society as well as to the individual himself.

Some creative persons' intuitions about creativity

Albert Einstein's self-searching suggests "The psychical entities which serve elements in thoughts are certain signs and more or less clear images of what can be combined. . . . This combinatory play seems to be the essential feature in productive thought."

Samuel Taylor Coleridge is described as having developed his ideas in the following manner: "Facts which sank at intervals out of conscious recollection drew together toward the surface through the most chemical affinities of common elements."

In the field of art, we find André Breton referring to a collage by Ernst as being distinguished by a "marvelous capacity to grasp two mutually distant realities without going beyond the field of our experience and to draw a spark from the juxtaposition."

Most explicit, however, is the oft-quoted statement by the mathematician, Poincaré, who talks about an evening when "ideas rose in crowds; I felt them collide until pairs interlocked so to speak, making a stable combination. By next morning I had established the existence of a class of Fuchsian functions." From these experiences Poincaré felt that he could state that "to create consists of making new combinations of associative elements which are useful. The mathematical facts worthy of being studied . . . are those which reveal to us unsuspected kinships between other facts well known but wrongly believed to be strangers to one another. Among chosen combinations the most fertile will often be those formed of elements drawn from domains which are far apart." (Quoted from Mednick, 1962, pp. 220–221, based on selections from Ghiselin, 1952. With permission of author and publisher.)

A description of creative thinking

Creative thinking involves many of the factors and processes that are involved in reasoning, problem-solving, and transfer. The different factor is the requirement that the pupil should depart from his old ways of organizing information and reject hypotheses which are ordinarily transferred, without change, from previous learnings. He must learn to solve important problems by using familiar materials and methods in *new*, original ways. He must erupt into unique lines of activity that might not have occurred to him before. This is illustrated in the following example of young Gauss (who, in later life, became a famous mathematician) solving a mathematics problem in elementary school:

The teacher gave a test in arithmetic and said to the class: "Which of you will be the first to get the sum of $1 + 2 + 3 + 4 + 5 + 6 + 7 + 8 + 9 + 10$?" Very soon, while the others were still busy figuring, young Gauss raised his hand (and said,) "Here it is." "How . . . did you get it so quickly?" exclaimed the surprised teacher. Young Gauss answered—of course we do not know exactly what he did answer, but on the basis of experience in experiments I think it may have been about like this: "Had I done it by adding 1 and 2, and then 3 to the sum, then 4 to the new result, and so on, it would have taken very long; and, trying to do it quickly, I would very likely have made mistakes. But you see, 1 and 10 make eleven, 2 and 9 are again—must be—11! And so on! There are 5 such pairs; 5 times 11 makes 55." The boy had discovered the gist of an important theorem. (Wertheimer, 1959, p. 109.)

Here Gauss was able to break away from tradition, a necessary condition in creative thinking. The procedural differences are illustrated in Figure 13-8. A new and important discovery was the result.

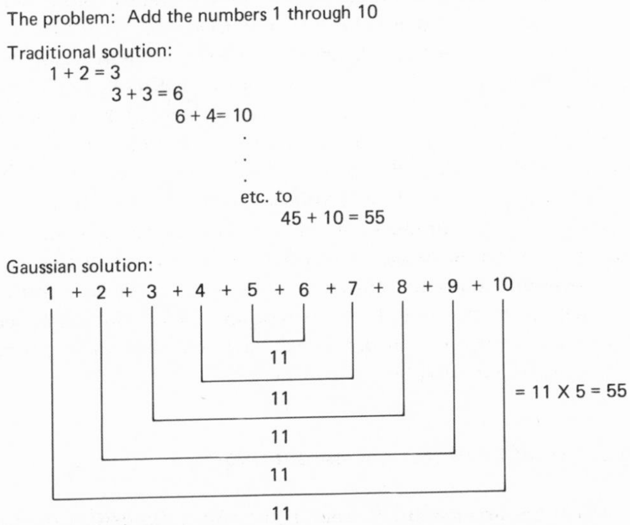

The problem: Add the numbers 1 through 10

Traditional solution:
$1 + 2 = 3$
$3 + 3 = 6$
$6 + 4 = 10$
.
.
.
etc. to
$45 + 10 = 55$

Gaussian solution:
$1 + 2 + 3 + 4 + 5 + 6 + 7 + 8 + 9 + 10$
11
11
11   = 11 X 5 = 55
11
11

Figure 13-8. A diagram comparing the traditional and Gaussian solution to the problem of adding the numbers 1 through 10. (From M. Wertheimer. Productive thinking. New York: Harper & Bros., 1959. P. 109. With permission.)

Creativity—cognitive ability or cognitive style?

Gallagher (1966) raises the question of whether creativity is a cognitive style or a cognitive ability. Drawing on evidence from the research of Wallach and Kogan (1965) he characterizes four groups of children classified on the bases of intelligence and creativity measures in much the same way that Getzels and Jackson (1962) did. The comparisons were as follows (Gallagher, 1966, p. 52):

High creativity—high intelligence: These children can exercise within themselves both control and freedom; they evince both adultlike and childlike kinds of behavior.

High creativity—low intelligence: These children are in angry conflict with themselves and their school environment and are beset by feelings of unworthiness and inadequacy. In a stress-free context, however, they can blossom forth cognitively.

Low creativity—high intelligence: These children can be described as "addicted" to school achievement. Academic failure would be perceived by them as catastrophic, so that they must continually strive to make excellent grades in order to avoid the possibility of distress.

Low creativity—low intelligence: Basically bewildered, these children engage in various defensive maneuvers, ranging from useful adaptations such as intensive social activity, to regression such as passivity or the development of psychosomatic symptoms.

Gallagher further points out that the *high intelligence—low creativity* pupils performed rather poorly on thematizing tasks where such articles as comb, lipstick, watch, pocketbook, and a door had to be linked as belonging together because they all have something to do with "going out." The poor performance of this group was attributed not so much to inability as to a dislike for such tasks. When specifically asked to do so these pupils performed adequately. There is also evidence that preferences of this sort may have far-reaching effects on other cognitive processes, e.g., what is filtered out in the perception of a problem, thereby further affecting thinking and creativity. According to these and other similar ideas, Gallagher argues that creativity represents a preferred way of performing, or, in other words, a cognitive style.

Verbal aspects of training for originality

At all stages successful thinking, whether divergent or convergent, by humans is especially dependent on language behavior. Initially, the verbalizations that are necessary to reach the solution are probably quite low in the hierarchy of responses, especially in creative thinking. If the responses were high in the hierarchy, of course, the problem would be solved immediately. As experience is gained with the conditions stated in the problem and with the criteria for the solution, the salient attributes are abstracted in the form of concepts. These concepts can then be related to one another in a variety of ways, but especially in the form of principles related to the stated goals. These principles guide the selection of alternative solutions to be tested.

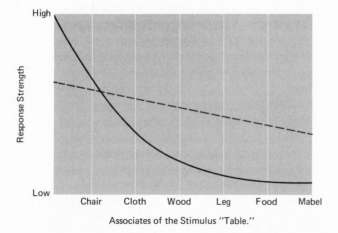

Associates of the Stimulus "Table."

Figure 13-9. Associative hierarchies around the word "table." The solid lines show the relative strengths of some popular or common responses in the form of a steep hierarchy. The creative person is assumed to have a flatter hierarchy as shown in the dotted line. The less creative could provide chair and cloth as associates of table rather rapidly, but would have considerable difficulty in eliciting the other associates. The creative person would take more time in making the associations but would also elicit many more associations. (From Mednick, 1962, Figure 1, p. 223. With permission of author and publisher.)

One of the classic studies used to demonstrate the directive role of verbalizations, in the form of instructions, is Maier's (1930) pendulum problem. The subject is given two poles, a clamp, a piece of board, some string, and pieces of chalk. The problem is to construct two pendulums that will make marks at designated places on the floor as they swing back and forth (see Figure 13-10). One group was given only the problem statement. Another group was also shown how to perform each of the necessary operations. That is, the subjects were shown how to clamp poles together, how to make a pendulum, and how to wedge a board against a surface by use of a pole. A third group of subjects was shown each of the operations but, in addition, they were shown how the operations might be combined. A fourth group was told only the problem statement and that it would be convenient if the pendulum hung from the ceiling; that is, they were given the "direction" that the solution should take. The final group was given the problem, operations, and direction. The fourth and fifth groups were more successful than any of the other groups. These findings suggest how verbalization increases the saliency of new combinations of words that direct the solution of problems (Maltzman, 1955). The effect of verbal directions and

Problem: Construct two pendulums suspended from the ceiling so that when they are swinging, chalk marks will be made on the floor.

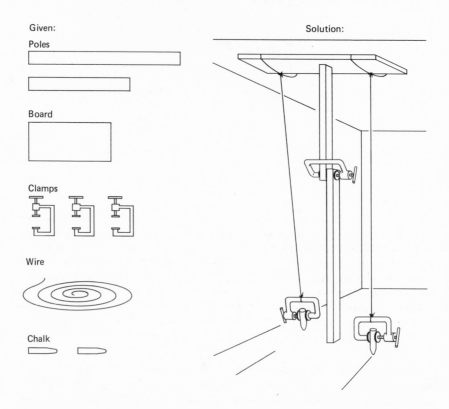

Figure 13-10. The problem, materials, and solution for Maier's (1930) pendulum problem.

hints in guided discovery on the solution of problems was shown more recently by Gagné and Brown (1961). (See Table 13-1.)

Verbalizations, to be useful, must be available to the pupil and he must have sufficient intellectual capability to integrate the concepts into compound relationships. However, the context in which the words are used can make a profound difference in their relevance to the problem situation. Cofer (1957) illustrates this point in the following four-word problem: Given the words,

Add   Subtract   Multiply   Increase

the problem is to identify the word that "does not belong." There are at least two principles that might be functional here. The subject who verbalizes these as arithmetic operations uses the answer "increase." The subject who verbalizes the problem in terms of processes that indi-

Table 13-1.   Average time and the numbers of hints required to solve new problems after pupils were taught by the rule and example, discovery, and guided discovery methods.

| | Measure | |
Condition	Time in Minutes	Number of Hints
Rule and Example	27.4	6.5
Discovery	19.8	2.2
Guided Discovery	16.7	1.5

SOURCE: Gagné & Brown, 1961, p. 318. With permission of author and publisher.

cate increases in magnitude uses "subtract" as the answer. (One of our students pointed out that "Add" doesn't belong because it is the only word that doesn't have eight letters.) Thus, the context of words, and the way the problem is transformed, directs the nature of the solution. The reader will note the similarity between this phenomenon and the "atmosphere effect."

Sometimes verbal symbols can be made relevant to the problem by sensitizing the pupil to *problem-related words* through pretraining as shown in the "two-string" problem. This problem requires the subject to tie the ends of two strings suspended from the ceiling. The strings, however, are too short to permit the subject to take the end of one, walk to the other and then tie them together. There are several solutions to this problem, but Cofer and his associates decided to increase the number of pendulum solutions by planned preproblem experiences, sometimes called "priming." The subjects in the experimental groups first learned a list of 11 words immediately before attempting the problem but independently of the problem situation. The words *rope, swing, pendulum, time,* and *clock* were embedded in this list. The control group also learned a list of 11 words but the embedded words were not included. As a result of priming with pendulum-related words, the men in the experimental group produced a higher number of pendulum solutions than did those in the control group. The subjects in the experimental group tied an object such as a blackboard eraser to one of the strings, made it into a pendulum, started the pendulum swinging, grasped the other string, walked to the pendulum and when it was in the right position caught it. The ends were then in a position to be tied. The appropriate stimuli in the problem situation were, thus, activated to a dominant position in the habit hierarchy by the verbal preproblem training. As a consequence, it is assumed that verbal associations (see Figure 13-11) generalized to facilitate the solution of the manipulative problem.

Since verbal responses appear to be important in directing problem solutions there remains the question of how to increase the produc-

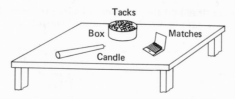

Figure 13-11. Duncker's Candle Problem. This problem requires that the candle be firmly affixed to the wall, burn properly, and not drip wax on the table or floor. The solution is attained more quickly by subjects who saw the objects labeled as above than by those who saw only the tacks labeled or the objects without labels. The box is a functionally-fixed object, especially when it is filled with tacks. It is not noticed unless labeled. Thus labeling facilitates problem solving where certain cues are important. (Glucksberg & Weisberg, 1966, Figure 1, p. 660.)

tion of original verbal responses. Both instructions to produce many different responses and the reinforcement of unique responses have been found to produce significant increases in originality (Maltzman, 1960). When the person is asked to give (or reinforced for giving) the same response upon repeated presentation of a given stimulus, the production of original responses on subsequent tasks is decreased or restricted. Changes in the production of original responses by these means undoubtedly results from nonspecific transfer (learning to learn) of a principle learned through reinforcement of uncommon responses.

Although these procedures contain positive implications for classroom practice, reasoning must still be viewed as a complex process subject to the influence of many variables. To provide but one illustration, the pupil who has only limited conceptual ability or who is a "convergent thinker" can probably be started on the path to produce the variability so desirable in reasoning. It is unlikely, however, that such simple procedures will help him develop into a highly "original thinker" in the absence of some "ideal" combination of early training, adequate intellectual ability, personality traits such as independence and self-confidence, and so on.

An associational interpretation of creativity and the RAT test

Mednick (1962, p. 221) defines the creative thinking process as "the forming of associative elements into new combinations which either meet specified requirements or are in some way useful. The more remote the elements in the new situation, the more creative the process or solution." The creative solution can be achieved, within the framework of this definition, by three processes: (1) *serendipity* or the accidental associations leading to such discoveries as the x-ray and penicillin; (2) *similarity of associations* so often found in creative writing which exploits homonymity, rhyme, similarities in word structure, and the like, or in expressionistic approaches to music, painting, and sculpture; and (3) *mediation* of remotely associated events through some common property or element.

If these associations are to be linked to form a creative combination, they must be in the person's associative hierarchy: "an architect who does not know of a new product can hardly be expected to use it creatively." In addition, a creative person will be able to produce many ideas, though at a somewhat slow rate since it is assumed that he has many associations of about equal strength for given ideas. Thus, the hierarchy of associations is relatively flat (see Figure 13-9). An uncreative person will have a few very strong stereotyped associations with the remaining ones few in number and weak. The hierarchy is steep. A creative person may also have a steep hierarchy but, if so, the strong associations are likely to be unusual or unique (deviant) associations. Consequently, he may be a one-shot producer, whereas the person with a flat hierarchy is more likely to be a multiproducer.

As a result of these assumptions Mednick developed the *Remote Associations Test* (RAT) to measure individual differences in creativity. The measure is based on linking sets of three words with a fourth uncommon or remote association, as illustrated in the following examples:

RAT   BLUE   COTTAGE   _____

RAILROAD   GIRL   CLASS   _____

OUT   DOG   CAT   _____

(The answers are: cheese, working, and house.)

The student's scores on this test correlate .70 with professors' ratings of their creativity. Low RAT scorers received higher grades from teachers rated dogmatic than from teachers rated flexible. High RAT scorers gave more word associates in a limited time than did low RAT scorers. There is a negative correlation ($r = -.38$) between the RAT scores and conformity scores. Finally, improbable associations can be used as a reinforcer to increase the learning of high RAT scorers. (Abstracted from Mednick, 1962.)

Reducing inhibition in the search for original solutions

Pupils need to know the formal rules of logic if they are to reason properly. They need to become conversant with the accepted facts in any field. However, dependence of pupils on *memorized* formulas, methods, concepts, and skills, without broader understanding, is an enemy to effective learning for the years ahead not only in mathematics but in all education. The more intelligent pupils should certainly be encouraged to search for new procedures (as exemplified in the highly creative achievements by Gauss).

Pupils become limited in their ability to see new uses for familiar objects when the use-meaning (functional fixedness) has become deeply entrenched in their thinking. When objects have been used for one purpose, pupils may fail to use these objects for other purposes even when a new use would help them to solve a problem (Di Vesta & Walls, 1967). The use-meaning of a paper-clip as an object for holding paper may be so much a part of the pupil's understanding that he fails to see that it can be unbent to form a hook. Or a box may be so often viewed as a container that he may fail to see it as a possible platform (Glucksberg, 1964). Even in experiments where the use of an object may be restricted to a single purpose for a very limited time, a use-meaning interferes with the solution of new problems for a day and continues to some extent for as long as a week, as shown in Figure 13-12 (Adamson & Taylor, 1954). Functional-fixedness strength is increased under high drive (Glucksberg, 1964) as are other dominant responses. Functional fixedness shares with set in the water-jar, Umweg, "atmosphere effect," and other similar problems, the competition between a dominant incorrect pattern of behavior and the behavior necessary to the solution of the problem. The difference among them is only in the kind of task used.

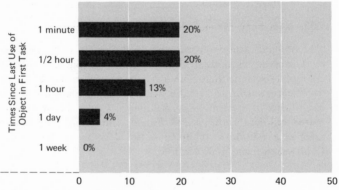

Figure 13-12. The immediate use of an object hinders the individual from seeing its use for other purposes. This is one reason why problems sometimes are solved more easily when they are left for awhile and returned to later. (Adapted from R. E. Adamson & D. W. Taylor. Functional fixedness as related to elapsed time and set. Journal of Experimental Psychology, 1954, 47, 122–126. With permission.)

Facilitating the production of novel ideas

The "brainstorming" technique of posing such questions as "What new uses can be made of these products?" has been found in industrial circles to be one way of overcoming the hindering effects of rigid use-meanings in creativity. To illustrate, though there are at least 50,000 known uses for the gases which are the by-products of coke ovens, industrialists believe there may be as many as 50,000 more uses as yet undiscovered. One worker saw pieces of surgical tubing being thrown away into a waste barrel. He asked, "Why not cut them into rubber bands of the size and width used by the millions to hold small items together?" A new use for what was wasted previously was discovered. Such incidents are everyday occurrences in industry.*

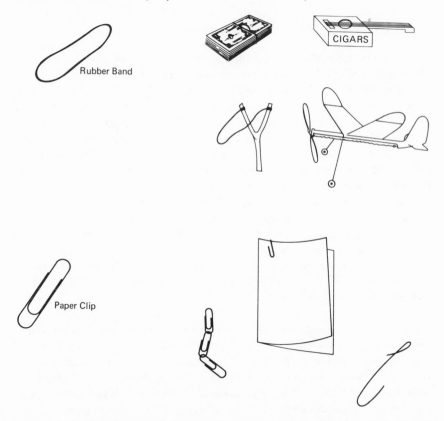

Figure 13-13. What new uses can you name for these common objects? The "brainstorming" technique requires the overcoming of traditional use-meanings.

*The illustrations presented here, and many others, appear in A. F. Osborn. *Applied imagination: Principles and procedures of creative thinking.* New York: Charles Scribner's Sons, 1962. With permission of publisher.

The effectiveness of the "brainstorming" procedure was demonstrated in a study by Parnes and Meadow (1959). Subjects who were instructed to give all the solutions to problems that occurred to them, regardless of quality, gave more good quality ideas than those who were instructed to give only good quality solutions. In addition, those subjects trained in problem-solving provided more good quality solutions than did untrained subjects, *implying* that problem-solving procedures can be taught. The best quality answers appeared among the later ideas produced (Parnes, 1961). One of the advantages of "brainstorming" is that the technique encourages a greater number of ideas. Restrictive instructions tend to inhibit the production of ideas, whether good or bad, perhaps as a result of self-criticism or fear of criticism from others.

Guiding creative thinking in the classroom

Any activity that restricts the pupil's freedom of expression, independence, curiosity, exploration, or self-confidence is likely to be a deterrent to the nurture of creativity. Specifically, a few examples can be used to illustrate the potential deleterious side effects some teaching practices have on creativity: A teacher may give assignments that are too long for the pupil to handle as anything more than a mere exercise. The hope and sincere interest of the teacher, of course, is that the pupil will "really" achieve. The outcome, however, is ordinarily a pupil whose main aspiration is to get the assignment done at whatever minimal level of accomplishment will please the teacher. The pupil tries to outguess the teacher. An even less desirable outcome is that the pupil has no time for contemplation or for divergent thinking. Sometimes, perhaps too often, school marks are overemphasized. Again, an artificial goal is established and becomes the criterion toward which the pupil works; a goal that has nothing to do with the encouragement of creative behavior. The main problem for the pupil becomes one of "how to get good grades."

Similar effects are to be noted from too many objective tests and "cut and dried" assignments. Pupils do set their goals by the kinds of examinations they are administered, although the teacher might prefer other and more intrinsic bases for the setting of standards. Objective tests, when used too exclusively, establish a restrictive study pattern that can become habitual. Not the least of the adverse effects on creativity, however, may be created by the teacher himself. One who is too rigid or too much of an authority figure may not be able to tolerate more than an occasional incident of divergent thinking. Too often such teachers tend to encourage the correct answer, the authoritative opinion, the convergent style, rather than the occasional departure from the popular response, the variability of behavior, the fluent production of different ideas, and the flexibility required for the nurturance of creativity.

Creative thinking requires that the pupil be continually inquisitive about such questions as "What about . . . ?" and "What if . . . ?" Then they should be continually probed with the question "What else?" (Osborn, 1953). Pupils should be encouraged to try different routes to goals. Once the pupil knows the logic of reasoning and has the necessary facts, his creativity is limited only by the bounds of ability, fixations, and interference from previous learning. The teacher can promote creative processes by *guiding* the pupil's thinking instead of telling him the right answer (Reid, 1951). The intellectually able pupil should be encouraged to develop personal and unique approaches to life's problems. Moreover, when creativity is required, sufficient time must be allowed. It is senseless to direct the pupil to "write an original poem" in the last fifteen minutes of a class period. Creativity, which results in a product characterized by originality, is an extended process. The complex requirements of sensitivity to problems, flexibility, fluency, originality, elaboration, and redefinition come to fruition by gradual increments, not suddenly.

Although the teaching methods that hinder or benefit creativity have been suggested, the routine application of such methods as a "bag of tricks" is likely to be less than optimally effective. A systematic approach integrating a style of teaching to encourage divergent thinking as a central part of the curriculum seems necessary (Aschner & Bish, 1965). If decisions about teaching methods are based on scientific knowledge of psychological processes and principles, they can lead to an improvement in the art of teaching.

Summary

Human problem-solving has been of interest to educators and psychologists for more than a half-century. Early approaches described thinking simply as a procedure involving the five step-like requirements of being motivated, perceiving the problem, interpreting the problem, generating hypotheses, and verifying one of the solutions. The ability-factors model distinguishes between the production of a variety of answers required for problems that have a number of possible solutions (divergent thinking) and the production of correct answers to problems for each of which there is only one correct answer (convergent thinking). Creativity and originality appear to be related to divergent thinking processes whereas critical thinking seems to be related to convergent processes. This approach rejects learning processes and emphasizes cognitive structures involved in thinking.

There is general agreement that success at problem-solving requires a preparatory phase during which relevant information is brought to bear on the problem and is made available for the formulation of hypotheses. Additionally, the pupil abstracts and defines goals, recalls rules, selects and integrates rules to form provisional hypotheses, verifies the hypotheses against the criteria required for a "good" solution, and finally selects the solution that meets this set of criteria. Cognitive conflict, an important motivational element in human thinking, represents a more mature level of functioning since it depends on cognitions related to the gaps between the problem and its ultimate solution and because of its dependence on verbal processes.

Thinking efficiency is sometimes hindered by a number of detrimental factors. Biases may influence the pupil's answer or solution by predisposing him to react to the emotional components of the problem statement rather than to the cues necessary for the solution of the problem. Several similar problems in succession will tend to establish a response tendency, or set, that will limit the availability of novel or alternative ideas. These tendencies are present in the phenomena of functional fixedness, set, and atmosphere effect. Dogmatism, a more pervasive form of rigidity, is an enduring and general personality tendency, manifested in reliance on a prestigious source for information rather than on the validity of the content provided in communications and problems.

An increase in anxiety, according to some theories, is comparable to an increase in drive. Accordingly, where only one response is required, as in simple learning situations or where the correct response is dominant, an increase in anxiety can facilitate learning. However, in typical thinking situations there are many alternatives, from which a correct one must be selected. Typically, the correct response is low on the habit hierarchy of responses. Under these circumstances thinking will be hampered by high anxiety. Most emotional states tend to interfere with problem-solving behavior because they may modify the interpretation of the problem (even distort it) or because they lead to interfering (competing) responses.

Creativity calls for divergent thinking. It has the characteristic of offering the opportunity for a variety of solutions to a problem. Especially sought are the original, unique, and productive solutions. The stages, as defined on intuitive bases by famous artists and poets, are much like those in convergent thinking: preparation, incubation of ideas, formulation of hypotheses, verification of alternative hypotheses, and revision of solutions. Most descriptions of creativity suggest the importance of verbal behavior. Verbal instruction provides "direction" to the whole process and strongly influences the solution obtained since the criteria for solutions must be stored in memory in verbal form.

Which verbalizations are available to the pupil, and their relative strengths, affect their ultimate availability and consequently affect the efficiency of problem-solving. It is quite likely that encouraging pupils to have confidence in themselves, to be inquisitive, to "brainstorm," or to make uninhibited best guesses has some beneficial aspects for the facilitation of creativity. In the teaching process, the deterrents to the nurturance of creativity include assignments that are too long for the pupil to handle as anything more than an exercise, overemphasis on school grades, an excess of objective tests, cut and dried assignments, and the teacher being too much of an authority figure.

Part IV

Personality
development
and socialization

A majority of social scientists will agree that the home is still the most important socializing and character-building institution in contemporary culture, notwithstanding some experimental programs to supplant it in the U.S.S.R. and in Israel. Such experimental programs have always involved only a small proportion of the available infants and of preschool children. Furthermore, these programs have generally been short-lived in the communal societies of the past, and the continuance of related current social experiments seems uncertain. The home thus remains clearly primary as the nurturant, socializing agency during the early years of childhood.

But what of the middle years and especially the adolescent ascent to early maturity? Probably the home again is still primary, but state, private, and parochially supported schools must run a very close second within the Western cultures. In Part IV we attempt to describe the principal dimensions of personality and character development in terms that will have meaning to the classroom teacher. We further try to show that the informed classroom teacher can have a real and beneficial influence on the adaptation and adjustment of his pupils. We offer and defend the thesis that modern teachers cannot avoid the responsibilities involved in guiding and counseling pupils—neglect and rejection of the guidance role are in a sense a type of counseling, albeit one with generally negative consequences. We further propose and illustrate in some detail that the classroom teacher is often in a uniquely favorable position to help some pupils take important steps toward positive mental health. Although the teacher is not a psychotherapist, nor should he pretend to be one, he is often the deciding social force in the lives of young people who find themselves at crossroads where important social and personal decisions must be made.

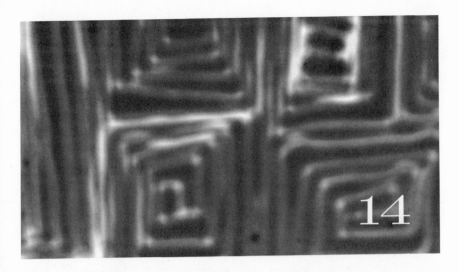

The structure and dynamics
of personality integration

Since personality structure and dynamics define the totality of man's psychological processes, they will undoubtedly be the last to be encompassed in satisfactory explanatory and predictive theories. Even the most rationally oriented and best prepared teachers can be expected to have difficulty in functioning within this arena because psychological theorists are not in agreement among themselves on what is the most fruitful approach to this ambitious undertaking. Measurement in this domain is admittedly crude, and the obtained data are usually subject to several interpretations.

One can reasonably ask whether or not teachers should even concern themselves with this complex problem. It is one that is inadequately formulated in psychology at the present time. Furthermore, isn't the old saw "a little knowledge is a dangerous thing" especially applicable here? Even though we might like to spare today's teacher the pain of another commitment, and one so especially difficult, such an alternative is not defensible. Whether he likes it or not, the teacher *will* have a theory of personality structure and dynamics, however crude and antiquated it may be. This follows simply because a teacher can't function in a modern classroom without one. The teacher's theory may be the naive one that everyone perceives the world as he does or that others feel and are moved to action in the same ways as himself, or some other casual and offhand way of conceptualizing the personalities of his pupils. But there seems no doubt that his understanding will be at least somewhat enhanced if he is familiar with a sampling of the theoretical constructions—conjectures, if you will—now current, which seek to clarify the forces at play in personality structure and dynamics. It is not necessarily true that "a little knowledge is a dangerous thing," if the knower fully appreciates the fact that his knowledge is indeed meager and that he should appeal to specialists in difficult cases.

First impressions of personality differences among pupils

When the teacher first steps into a new classroom he is usually most impressed by the many physical and psychological differences among the pupils. There are wide variations in size, posture, neatness, and other similar characteristics. Some of the pupils appear poised and eager, some anxious and apprehensive, some bored and lethargic. After the class begins and the days pass and the school year draws to a close, the teacher gradually feels that he has somehow come to know many of the personality characteristics of his pupils.

The observant teacher soon finds that each of the pupils is an individual in his own right. For example, John appears to be an attractive boy with an easygoing disposition, able and willing to accept the challenges of daily living, and rarely at odds with his classmates. When he fails to measure up in some activity, he shrugs his shoulders, smiles at his errors, and either tries again or starts some new activity. In contrast, Robert never seems to be happy, whatever the situation. He is an attractive boy with superior intellectual ability and above average motor and social skills. Although he usually manages to reach the very difficult goals he sets for himself, his accomplishments leave him tense and anxious. He always seems to be anticipating failure and punishment even though he seldom experiences them. Or consider Mary, who comes from a poor but community-oriented family. Mary is an intelligent and physically attractive adolescent girl who won't accept friendship from any of her classmates. She goes out of her way to offend anybody who makes friendly overtures. She wears an air of "I'm just as good as you are" but it is apparent that she isn't convinced that this is true.

These thumbnail sketches are fragmentary but they illustrate some of the average teacher's early impressions of his pupils. They go somewhat beyond the superficial aspects of personality in their emphasis on needs, goal setting, and unconscious motivation. It is the purpose of this chapter to augment the teacher's knowledge so that a better understanding of what lies behind these personality differences may be realized.

The meaning of personality integration

Personality integration is an ideal state which may be approached ever so closely but never consistently reached. A near approximation to the ideal would be represented by an individual whose needs, satisfactions, and achievements were *always* harmonized and never in a state of *internal* conflict. He would be optimally happy and productive, with nearly complete knowledge and use of his abilities and acceptance of his limitations. His anxieties would be relieved through smoothly productive channels of recreation and work. He is the picture of an extremely well-integrated personality. The individual thus ideally integrated could be of any level of intelligence and of other psychological assets, because the criteria for personality integration pertain to *internal* balance and harmony. The integrated person is "at peace" with himself, and thereby optimally effective (within the limits of his talents) in relating himself satisfactorily to the external environment.*

In contrast to such persons, there are nonintegrated personalities of every degree. An imbalance of needs, self-deception, unrealistic goals, and crippling anxieties may combine in many patterns to produce various degrees of personality disharmony. The nonintegrated personality may be unusually successful by external social standards (a straight "A" pupil, a popular beauty queen, a star athlete, a musical prodigy, and so on), and still be a miserably "unhappy" and poorly integrated person. The modern adage "be glad you're neurotic" is a half-truth and a dangerous one. Although it is easy to cite cases of poorly integrated persons who have accomplished great things because of unhealthy compulsive drives and compelling anxiety states, they are the infrequent exceptions rather than the rule. Far more of the nonintegrated persons spend their lives in chronic frustration. They are usually unhappy, maladjusted, and typically rejected by others because of their "peculiarities."

Personality integration is, as can be seen, a relative condition for the majority of individuals. Each person has his own peculiar problems. Self-consistency is not always possible, successful coping procedures are not always available, and ego defenses are not always recognized or understood. Because of this relativity, we are inclined to speak of "well-integrated" and "poorly-integrated" personalities.

A "well-integrated" personality: The case of John Desmond

The following brief description of a twelve-year-old boy who has achieved an above average level of personality integration may help to clarify the concept.

*Various other interpretations of personality integration may be found in: Cameron (1963), Fromm (1955), Erikson (1963), Horney (1950), and Maslow (1954).

John Desmond is one of three children of striving, upper-lower class parents. He is of average intelligence and has consistently earned "C's" and "B's" in his school work along with a few "D's" and "A's". He has superior motor skills and is regarded by his classmates as a "good athlete." He is about average in physique and physical attractiveness for boys his age. He works part time after school at a neighborhood grocery to earn spending money, out of which he must purchase some of his clothing. The majority of his classmates come from middle-class homes and dress somewhat better than John. They enjoy a number of privileges which John's employment doesn't permit.

We consider John's personality integration to be somewhat above average: He is acceptant of his modest home conditions. "We're not rich, but we get along all right." He is sometimes resentful that his after-school work keeps him from going out for Junior High basketball, but this is a temporary response. "I admit that I'd like to try out for the team, but all of us have to work around our place to make ends meet." He is presently making plans to get a weekend job in a neighborhood radio and TV shop so that he can participate in sports.

John is aware that his scholastic talents are only average. "I have to work hard in school to make the grade, but I don't mind too much. I want to get a high school diploma and a year or two of training at some tech school for radio and TV. Dad and Mom want me to get an education so I won't have it as hard as they've had it."

John and a close friend, Fred, have built a transistor radio with odds and ends picked up from repair shops. They are presently working two nights a week on a shortwave transmitter. They are winding their own coils and saving money to buy more elaborate equipment. John and Fred have been good friends for several years. They are members of the local Boy Scout troop and informal members of a neighborhood group of boys who go swimming together and play basketball and football in their backyards. John "sticks up for his rights" and sometimes takes his aggression out on other members of the group. However, he usually recognizes social situations in which he is in the wrong and makes amends or admits that he "blew his top." He is well accepted by his peers as a "right guy."

John's relationships with girls are casual. He participates in the social dancing instruction at school but laughingly admits that it isn't too much fun. "I guess I'm not old enough yet."

He is affectionately tolerant of his older sister and younger brother and fond of his parents. He has the usual difficulties in trying to establish his independence, but is able to accept parental authority most of the time.

Although this is far from a complete picture of the personality integration of John Desmond, it highlights a number of important behavior tendencies. He has his problems but is not overwhelmed by them. He is generally self-acceptant and realistic. His needs, goals, and abilities are in fair balance, and he usually relieves his anxieties by positive actions.

Some Important Dimensions of
Personality Integration

Since the personality integration of a particular person is a complex pattern of response tendencies, a detailed analysis of the component functions is difficult, if not impossible, to make. Each pupil strives
to strike a balance between inner needs and perceived opportunities for
need satisfactions. Some pupils are obviously more successful in maintaining a stable balance than are others. The more subtle intricacies of a
given pupil's pattern of personality integration can be evaluated only
through an intensive study by an experienced and insightful psychologist or psychiatrist. However, the conscientious teacher can approximate
such an understanding by making intelligent observations guided by
the formal constructs of personality theory. In this section we review
some of the dimensions of personality integration which are frequently
overlooked or underestimated by the inexperienced observer.

Unconscious motivation

One of man's most powerful tools in his eternal quest to understand and control the forces of nature is his mastery of signs and symbols. Language in the form of words, logic, and mathematics permits
him to invent systematic ways of viewing the workings of the universe.
These theoretical inventions when appropriately implemented by engineering talents produce electrical power, atomic energy, and the many
other advances of modern civilization. Man's ability to manipulate
verbal symbols is indeed his most valuable skill for channeling the
resources of nature to his own advantage. However, modern psychology
has demonstrated that words and their associated symbols can also en-
snare man in the labyrinth of their abstractions and blind him to his less
noble needs and behavior tendencies. He develops verbal skills of ration-
alizing to himself (using wishful thinking or arguing from biased premises to support the propriety of some course of action he desires to take).
In the process of justifying his behavior to others he deludes both himself and them. These processes in combination with behavior tendencies
acquired during the preverbal period of early childhood keep man from
understanding, or even recognizing, many of the forces that drive and
direct him in his daily living. He tends to rationalize many of his
actions after they occur because at this stage he has no other choice. He
does not know, nor can he ever know, many of the primitive forces that
lie behind much of his behavior.

To ask a boy why he slashed his neighbor's automobile tires is
like asking the west wind why it blows toward the east. He simply does
not know. If pressed socially he may say that he saw it done on televi-

sion or in a comic magazine, or he may trump up a charge discrediting his neighbor, but these statements are merely after-the-fact rationalizations of an action he does not understand. Although this state of affairs does not condone his aggressive response, it does illuminate one of the facets of unconscious motivation and does emphasize the complexity of the youth's problem.

Each individual adopts a unique pattern of behavior for satisfying his needs in socially acceptable ways. This process of adjustment involves compromises, self-denials, and self-deceptions along with attaining of some of the desired satisfactions. The following adjustment mechanisms, drawn here and there from psychoanalytic theory, define some of the more important dimensions of human adjustment.

> Our right to assume the existence of something mental that is unconscious and to employ that assumption for the purposes of scientific work is disputed in many quarters. To this we can reply that our assumption of the unconscious is *necessary* and *legitimate*, and that we possess numerous proofs of its existence.
>
> It is *necessary* because the data of consciousness have a very large number of gaps in them; both in healthy and in sick people psychical acts often occur which can be explained only by presupposing other acts, of which, nevertheless, consciousness affords no evidence. These not only include . . . dreams in healthy people, and everything described as a psychical symptom or an obsession in the sick; our most personal daily experience acquaints us with ideas that come into our head we do not know from where, and with intellectual conclusions arrived at we do not know how. All these conscious acts remain disconnected and unintelligible if we insist upon claiming that every mental act that occurs in us must also necessarily be experienced by us through consciousness; on the other hand, they fall into a demonstrable connection if we interpolate between them the unconscious acts which we have inferred. A gain in meaning is a perfectly justifiable ground for going beyond the limits of direct experience. When, in addition, it turns out that the assumption of there being an unconscious enables us to construct a successful procedure by which we can exert an effective influence upon the course of conscious processes, this success will have given us an incontrovertible proof of the existence of what we have assumed. This being so, we must adopt the position that to require that whatever goes on in the mind must also be known to consciousness is to make an untenable claim. (From Freud, 1915, pp. 166–167. With permission.)

Sublimation and repression

According to the psychoanalytic theory of human motivation proposed by Freud, the infant and young child are invested with primitive drives which are pleasure seeking, asocial, amoral, and illogical. They demand satisfaction. In the socialization process the infant finds that certain responses evoke punishment from his parents and other individuals in his social environment. The discomfort of punishment forces the infant to modify or suppress his primitive pleasure-seeking activities. The most personally satisfying adjustment to this conflict situation is a deflection of the drive toward a socially acceptable goal object. The deflected drive is satisfied without provoking punishment and displeasure. This mode of adjustment is called *sublimation*. Drives toward destruction and personal aggression may be sublimated in ways that are

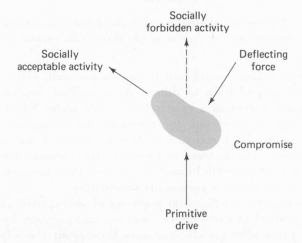

Socially
forbidden activity

Socially
acceptable activity

Deflecting
force

Compromise

Primitive
drive

Figure 14-1. A schematic illustration of a deflected drive, which defines sublimation.

personally satisfying and at the same time praised by others as worthy activities. The construction engineer, the surgeon, and the teacher have sublimated their aggressive impulses which they shared in early life with the less fortunate individuals who have become delinquents and criminals. As may be seen, sublimation permits need gratification as well as social approval, and favors a high level of personality integration.

If the demands for social conformity are too severe or are made too early in the infant's development, he may be unable to sublimate his primitive impulses. Repeated punishments of "reality testing" may force the infant to deny himself all forms of need gratification for a particular drive. He may be forced to *repress* a given drive tendency. Repressions are doubly frustrating. They prevent need gratification and they also limit the individual's capacity for further psychological growth. The pupil with many repressions is unable to engage in the academic and

Figure 14-2. A schematic illustration of a drive and a counterpsychological force which prevents the satisfaction of the drive. The counter force defines repression.

social activities that would satisfy his needs and bring him the approval and approbation of others. As a further disadvantage, his repressions are always in a relatively unstable state. When he is off guard in sleep or distracted, the repressed drives may overcome or evade their restraining forces in ways that are highly disturbing. Nightmares, impulsive actions, fears, and phobias are common. It is as if the individual were at war with himself. Repression thus produces an unstable and inefficient basis for personality functioning.

Although the fundamental processes of sublimation and repression are developed in early infancy and are unrecognized by the individual, his personality growth continues throughout the school years. Many instances are on record where insightful and resourceful teachers have helped pupils find socially acceptable outlets for their aggressive impulses. Withdrawn and repressed pupils have also "come to life" under wise supervision and guidance. Such improvements in personality integration are often associated with a host of secondary gains in academic achievement. The pupil who "finds himself" in some creative activity also usually forges ahead in his school achievements.

Identification and introjection

The origins of identification are complex in psychological theory, but it may suffice to state that the young child usually identifies with the parent (or parent substitute) of the same sex. The little girl tries to pattern her behavior after her mother's, and the little boy attempts to emulate his father. Identification is a most important process in personality growth because it serves as a generalized guide to socialization and an acceptance of the cultural standards of personal conduct. Identification paves the way to and is a prerequisite for the introjection of society's values. The self-restraints and the aspirations by which man guides his daily living are the products of *introjection*. The child comes to demand of himself the ways of behaving which are initially demanded by the adults with whom he identifies. His aspirations and hopes become similar to those of the persons with whom he identifies. He punishes himself whenever he fails to live up to his own standards of conduct which are the mirrored demands of the adults with whom he has identified.

Thus it can be seen that identification and introjection perform two important functions in personality growth and integration: (1) They mold the ego ideal, which defines what activities are important in life, and (2) they impose the self-restraints of personal conscience, or superego, which dictate forbidden activities. The child who fails for any reason to experience relatively normal identification and introjection processes is often a miserable person, one who is not infrequently found in a penal institution or a mental hospital. Individuals with extremely weak superegos are typically diagnosed as having a psychopathic personality and are recognized as being without stable purpose or conscience, which makes them potential menaces to the welfare and safety of others.

Strong identifications and the accompanying introjections are necessary for healthy personality growth. However, these processes are not without hazard. The child sometimes interprets the demands of others as far harsher than they really are. He may consequently make such heavy demands upon himself that he is doomed to frustration, guilt, and despair. His long-term goals forever elude him and even his daily conduct never appears to himself to be consistent with acceptable standards of excellence. He is paralyzed by feelings of guilt and inadequacy.

It can be seen that the socialization processes of identification and introjection can err in two directions, too little or too much. Neither extreme favors a healthy personality integration.

The subtle human relationship which promotes identification and favors introjection is not well understood in contemporary psychology. However, research findings on imitation and modeling suggest that children and adolescents do respond in these ways to adults outside, as well as inside, the family unit (Bandura & Walters, 1963). Common observation shows that some master teachers are able to establish such close personal relations with their pupils that the latter imitate their faults and idiosyncrasies as well as their socially desirable habits and personality tendencies.

The Coping Functions in Personality Integration

In classical psychoanalytic theory, with which the nonprofessional person is most familiar, the defensive aspects of personality integration are emphasized. The ego is conceived as being a somewhat helpless buffering agent between or among the demands of the id, the superego, and reality. The modern interpretations of psychoanalytic theory regard human personality as less passive, and reveal man to have a more striving, coping, and mastering orientation (White, 1966). Both the older and the newer views offer useful perspectives to the teacher. The human personality *does* defend and deceive (including self-deception), and the teacher must be continuously alert to those situations in which pupils use these defenses—for through such observations of correlated personal-social variables, the teacher may discover some of the latent factors in an individual pupil's personality structure and dynamics. Such knowledge does not always permit the teacher to help the pupil relinquish his defenses, but it may prevent the teacher's misinterpreting some of the pupil's troublesome behavior and adopting a punitive attitude toward him or in other ways making his problems of adjustment and adaptation even more difficult than it is.

> In recent years we observe certain marked improvements in theory, shifts in the direction of functional autonomy. What is known as neo-Freudianism shows two striking advances: a fuller recognition of the contributions of culture, and a postulation of a far more active, purposive, forward-reaching "ego." Originally Freud conceived the ego as a relatively helpless, though intelligent, rationalizer, beset by three "tyrants"—the id, the superego and external reality. More often than not, it could do nothing but repress its bitter conflicts, which would finally erupt in neurotic anxiety. Even the most orthodox psychoanalysts now say that Freud died without completing his ego theory. Nor is it customary today to regard this enlarged and improved ego as an agent only of defense; it contains mature motives approximately of the order demanded by the doctrine of functional autonomy. (From Allport, 1960, p. 29. With permission of Beacon Press.)

In a society that recognizes many alternative forms of adjustment the person, of necessity, must learn to cope with his environment. Coping has been described as a problem-solving process (Jahoda, 1958), one that reflects the positive, adaptive aspects of behavior. The person not only appreciates his problem but actively engages in doing something about it; there is improvement in feeling tone (whether by partial solution, or passive acceptance); and the person attempts to regard the problem in its own right rather than as a recurrent nuisance (Scott, 1958). Here we see a person engaged in active adjustment, seeking to master his environment, while retaining correct and realistic perceptions of himself in relationship to his surroundings, and while maintaining a stable integration (unity) of his personality. He accurately perceives himself and his environment to be independent entities, a process similar to self-realization or self-consistency. The coping mechanism is mentally healthy behavior even if it does not result in success. Sometimes the environment does not permit success. Nevertheless, striving maximizes the possibility of arriving at a solution (Jahoda, 1953). By comparison, the pupil who faces a threatening situation may use defensive reappraisal, i.e., he finds new ways of appraising the situation so that it no longer appears threatening (Lazarus, 1966). Scott (1958) points out that there may not be a one-to-one relationship between striving (or coping) and happiness. Unhappiness may be a result of the pupil's attempts to compensate for deficiencies by excessive coping. Such behavior, in turn, may lead to negative reactions from others.

Coping behavior is influenced by cultural values: An achievement orientation as a means of coping is characteristic of the Protestant ethic; a regimented society precludes the possibility of active adjustment; where conformity pressures exist, active adjustment is hardly necessary; and in the lower socioeconomic groups, defeatism is a more prevalent attitude than it is in the middle socioeconomic groups (Miller & Swanson, 1958, 1960). Among different ethnic groups, the Jewish family tends to encourage the achievement ethic and striving while the Italian family tends to encourage the affiliation ethic (Strodtbeck, 1958). There may be pressures from the adolescent peer group in the present educational system that facilitate the affiliation rather than the achievement orientation (Jacob, 1960; Coleman, 1961).

Although our attention in this chapter is directed toward encouragement of striving, coping, and achievement motivation, this is not to be interpreted as an endorsement of the mastery ethic in its most radical form. Striving behavior should be handicapped neither by its submission to other motives nor by the subordination of other motives to it. The individual should be able both to advocate and support his progressive ideas without fear of retaliation from others and to achieve an approximation of them without damaging his social relationships (the affiliation motive). If the pupil's behavior is directed only toward that of gain (achievement), whether for himself or society, he may sacrifice the satisfactions to be derived from outcomes associated with other motives (Miller & Swanson, 1958). Furthermore, he may even find that achievement is difficult where friendly relationships are necessary to the fulfillment of his goals.

A comparison of defense and coping mechanisms

Haan (1963) notes that the processes in handling stress, threat, and frustration by defense (dealing with one's feelings about a situation) and coping (dealing with the situation) mechanisms may appear to be identical or at least similar; however, they differ in their properties. Her analysis of the different properties of these two kinds of mechanisms are presented below (1 through 6) together with a comparison of the ego mechanisms as they appear in each (7 through 9). (From Haan, 1963, pp. 2-3. With permission of author and publisher.)

Properties of a defense mechanism	*Properties of a coping mechanism*
1. Behavior is rigid, automatized, and stimulus-bound.	1. Behavior involves choice and is thus flexible and purposive.
2. Behavior is pushed from the past, and the past compels the needs of the present.	2. Behavior is pulled toward the future and takes account of the present.
3. Behavior is essentially distorting of the present situation.	3. Behavior is oriented to the reality requirements of the present situation.
4. Behavior involves a greater quantity of primary process thinking, partakes of unconscious elements, and is thus undifferentiated in response.	4. Behavior involves secondary process thinking, conscious and preconscious elements, and is highly differentiated in response.
5. Behavior operates with the assumption that it is possible to remove disturbing effects magically.	5. Behavior operates within the organism's necessity of "metering" the experiencing of disturbing effects.
6. Behavior allows impulse gratification by subterfuge.	6. Behavior allows forms of impulse satisfaction in an open, ordered, and tempered way.
7. Impulse control is through displacement, reaction formation and repression.	7. Impulse control is through sublimation, substitution and suppression.
8. Defensive cognitive activity includes isolation, intellectualizing, and rationalization.	8. Coping cognitive activity includes objectivity, intellectuality, and logical thinking.
9. Those defenses which contain both impulse control and cognitive activity are doubt, denial, projection, and repression.	9. The coping variations of these defenses are tolerance of ambiguity, concentration, empathy, and regression in the service of the ego.

This analysis has been described by Lazarus (1966, p. 276) as a useful way of differentiating between pathological and normal processes but does not distinguish between other defenses and cognitive styles. The distinctions drawn have the difficulty of depending largely on the quality of reality testing and tend to treat defenses "as necessarily bad." Regardless of such criticisms there is relative consensus that the "adjusted" person copes rather than defends. Haan (1963) also showed that, in a comparison of IQ's at adolescence and at later maturity, those persons who typically employed coping mechanisms accelerated in intellectual performance. Defensive behavior also was correlated with a reduction in effective intellectual performance.

Mechanic's (1962) study of students under stress: A field study of adaptation

Most readers of this book will probably agree that taking general course examinations can be a source of discomfort. Perhaps for some this is an understatement! The serious student is intensely involved. The spirit of competition that prevails at examination periods may add to whatever threats are perceived (correctly or incorrectly) and to whatever ensuing anxiety or torment is experienced. Thus, it will be easy for the reader to empathize with the difficulties experienced by students as a consequence of the perceived challenge posed by an important examination (stress) and the manner in which the student actively attempts to master the situation (coping or adaptation) as described in a study by Mechanic (1962).

Although the following abstracts are necessarily brief and do not always relate the actual sequence of events as they unfolded, the presentation remains loyal to the original.

The Stress Situation

A written examination for the Ph.D. and M.A. provided the situation for the investigation of stress and adaptation to stress. The test covered 9 different content areas and took 18 hours, distributed over a week, to complete. Most of the 22 students in the study spent a period of about 2 months prior to the exam preparing for it. Each student learned about his performance approximately 2 weeks after the exam.

An idea of the importance of the examination can be had by realizing it represented the achievement of the transition (*rite de passage*) from precandidate to candidate for the advanced degrees. After investing 2 years in the program a student could be "flunked" out of it if he performed poorly. At best, poor examination results would mean repeating the entire process a year later. Of course, the students also had feelings of personal involvement related to self-esteem. Married students felt greater stress because of responsibilities to their families. Mechanic investigated many aspects of the situation for a period of 3 months prior to the exam extending to about 3 weeks afterward. He examined, for example, faculty perception and adaptations to students at various

stages in the total period. He describes the relationships of students
with faculty, with other students taking the examination, with students
not taking the examination, with families, and the like. He describes the
students' feelings toward the examination, toward other students, toward
faculty, toward family, and toward passing or failing. He observed the
support the student received from a variety of sources ranging from the
impersonal institution to the student's own adaptive mechanisms.
Finally, the data were collected, summarized, and examined, within a
social psychological theory of stress and adaptation. The presentation
here is necessarily a brief abstract, but it should provide illustrative
examples of coping mechanisms.

The Period of Preparation

Not until the examinations actually approached did they become a prime
concern, although from time to time the student did think about them and
experience some anxiety. Once the examination neared, the student began to
seek information actively and plan his approach (pp. 50–51). In short, the student taking examinations for the Ph.D. attempts to ascertain what the examinations mean, why they are given, how they are evaluated, and what the strategies
are for approaching them, and then plans an approach for the anticipated
examinations (p. 45).

The most consistently observed defense device used by the students
under study was that of seeking comforting information from the environment
that was consistent with the attitudes and hopes the student held about the
examinations. Often these comforting cognitions were made on the basis of
comparing oneself favorably with others ... (pp. 119–120). [For example,]
"I'm as bright and knowledgeable as other students who have passed these
examinations" (p. 121). [Such social comparisons provided one basis on which
the student could pace himself.] Others *drew on past experience* and, by reassuring themselves of their competence in the past, they felt more competent in
the present: "I wouldn't have gotten this far unless I knew something," "I've
handled test situations in the past," and other similar statements (p. 121).

Well before examinations, joking consisted mainly of poking fun at the
material—a form of tension release. As examinations approached, however, ten-
sion-release humor still was present, but avoidance banter seemed to increase
in significant quantity. A possible explanation for the change in the kind of
joking forms was that as the examinations approached, time pressures
increased and students became aware that time for future coping effort was limited. Therefore, a useful defense would allow for avoidance of serious discussion about examinations and avoidance of anxiety stimuli. For example, a few
days prior to the examinations, it would be of little use for a student to discover that five important textbooks had been read by others while he had spent
his time on less significant details. Joking as an avoidance technique allowed
for keeping further information that might have been disruptive out of one's
frame of reference (pp. 126–127).

As examinations approached and there was little more the student could do, reassurances were accepted more readily; it was during this period that cues were most often perceived. Early in the preparation period, when student motivation was still important, faculty reassurances had been more likely to be rejected, for fear that they might interfere with the motivation to prepare adequately (p. 133). As the examinations approached, the students began to get evidence of having attained mastery over the materials they had been studying. Mastery is objectively indicated by the student's realization that he can now handle questions on old examinations that he was not able to handle earlier (p. 135).

The weekend prior to examinations severe psychosomatic symptoms seemed to appear. . . . On the morning of the first examination most students reported stomach pains; a number reported diarrhea; and a few reported that they had been unable to hold their breakfast (p. 162).

The Confrontation: Examination Week

[After the series of examinations began] there was an apparent decrease in the hostile jabbing that had taken place just before the examinations. Once examinations started, however, students became more genuinely friendly to one another and supported one another more than they had at any prior period. It would appear that once the examinations had begun and some of the tension was reduced, the competitive jockeying was no longer necessary. The clearly defined threat now was not other students but the examinations themselves. And the group seemed to unite against this threat (p. 132).

It appeared that the student who was most effective at studying was the one whose motivation was high, but who at the same time was able to control his anxiety. . . . Thus, the most effective student was able to explore alternatives openly (cope) and then to defend when his anxiety level became too great. Defense helped him to contain his anxiety and insulate himself against perceived threat, thus allowing him to continue to cope with some effectiveness (p. 102).

During the examination week the student's feeling states were highly dependent on how he perceived he had done on the examinations he had already taken. If he believed that he was doing satisfactorily, he began to feel more comfortable and confident. . . . After each examination students congregated and discussed the questions to some extent, as well as the answers they had given. . . . The student who already had perceived that he had done a poor job attempted to avoid the discussion; those who felt that they had done well hashed over the answers and gave each other encouragement and support (p. 163).

Decision Time

During examinations many students perceived that faculty members become aloof and distant, that they became impersonal toward those taking examinations. . . . [However,] when examinations ended and faculty began grading, students became extremely sensitive to the expressions and behavior of the faculty. They interpreted faculty behavior as meaningful in regard to their examination performance (p. 166). . . . All of the students reported . . . heightening of anxieties as decision time came (p. 172).

The anxiety over the results increased to its most intensive point during the day of the final faculty meeting, [approximately *two weeks* after the exams were written] especially during the hours of the meeting in the late afternoon. As tension and anxiety mounted, students found themselves incapacitated for work (p. 172).

At the faculty meeting the chairman requested that each student be informed of his outcome by his advisor (p. 180). The feelings described by [a student who passed] are similar to those sometimes described by a person awaiting a very important decision, who has been holding tight reins on anxiety and aspiration level. When he heard the favorable result, he still seemed to have a feeling of "residual anxiety" which took some time to disappear (p. 181). A number of students, soon after hearing the result, experienced an empty, depressed feeling and found it difficult to return to work. Although students in their longing to be through with the examination saw a euphoric future, the postexamination period was not so experienced. The student's anticipation of the period after examinations was so favorable that a letdown was inevitable (pp. 181–182).

The Aftermath

A feeling of social distance very quickly developed between those who had passed and those who had failed . . . a desire for mutual avoidance developed (p. 183). In most cases the students did express sympathy for their friends who had not been successful. . . . The intense sympathy the student develops for those who fail is in part a defense against his own fleeting thought in which he obtains gratification from others' failures. One student, for example, expressed considerable resentment that others who had not studied equally as hard as he had passed; this was followed, however, by an indication of extreme regret for those who had failed. Thus, this feeling of intense sympathy in part may represent a way of hiding one's own feeling of being victorious in departmental competition (p. 185).

Failure on the examinations seemed to lead to either of two reactions, both having as their basis a considerable loss in self-esteem and esteem in the eyes of others. Some students experienced a feeling of utter humiliation; others felt a surge of great hostility toward the examination processes and toward the examiners. . . . The second reaction—anger-out—seems to have been a defense against the discomfort of the first reaction—humiliation (or anger-in) (p. 187).

After examinations ended and the results were known, students found that there was still much to do . . . (p. 189). Most students experienced great difficulty in returning to work. Thus, the period after examinations was experienced as an anticlimax, and many students reported mental fatigue, loss of motivation and restlessness (p. 190).

Character: The Social Dimension of Personality Integration

Psychological adjustment necessarily involves increasingly active and independent adaptation to one's society. This point cannot be emphasized more strongly than it is in the pupil's development. In his growth toward maturity, the pupil varies his mode of adapting to challenges with different styles of living. Some pupils have characteristic strivings aimed solely at self-satisfaction; some may be interested only in complying with the demands of others. Some immature pupils live by a set of abstract principles, applied rigidly to each and every situation, while the mature pupil is guided by a rationality of purpose, including a feeling of responsibility for the progress of himself and others.

A number of psychologists have analyzed the dimensions of growth toward maturity and the typical adjustment problems of the school years. Peck* has an interesting approach, one on which the following discussion is based, and summarized in Table 14-1. The reader should, of course, recognize that this is only one of a number of schemes that might be used for a classification of the modes of adjustment made by the maturing pupil.

Table 14-1. The developmental stages of psychosocial development.

Character Type	Developmental Period
Amoral	Infancy
Expedient	Early Childhood
Conforming	Later Childhood
Irrational-conscientious	
Rational-altruistic	Adolescence and adulthood

Source: Peck & Havighurst, 1960, p. 3. With permission of John Wiley & Sons, Inc.

During the period of growth from infancy to early childhood, the pupil exhibits behavior which is typically *self-centered* (amoral and *expedient*). His mode of adjustment is characteristically toward the attainment of satisfaction of his own needs. As he strives to accomplish this, he may be aware of the demands of others, but he ignores them. He will act in "honest" ways, for example, to retain a favorable reputation or he will conform to the immediate situation because this behavior will help him to achieve long-range goals. If more can be gained by other means, particularly if he can avoid censure or detection, he will adopt them. Carried into the later years this style of living or personality organization is obviously not constructive. A basically hostile person may find an outlet in delinquent behavior. A tendency to have a pleas-

*Adapted from R. F. Peck. *The psychology of moral character*. Ph.D. dissertation, University of Chicago, 1951. With permission of the author. Also see Peck & Havighurst (1960).

ant outlook on life may be perceived as "charming but irresponsible."
This mode of adjustment has the major disadvantage of ignoring the
harmful effects that may accrue to others when one acts in disregard of
them.

Later development in the growth toward adolescence brings on
the emergence of a tendency toward *conformity*. The pupil appears to be
guided by one general principle—"to do what others do and what they
say one 'should do.'" He develops an awareness of the demands of

*Figure 14-3. Extreme conformity does not necessarily lead to universal popu-
larity. (© 1956 United Feature Syndicate.)*

others. The violation of some code such as truth-telling may produce a
feeling of shame or guilt, not because "lying" is "wrong" and might be
harmful to himself or others, but because "others say it is wrong." The
approval of others is the major reward at this stage of development.
The conformist accepts the dictates of his family and other social groups
in a placid, uncritical way. The rules he lives by may call for kindness to
some people and cruelty to others. Since these are the social rules, he
feels no responsibility or guilt in obeying them. Such individuals seldom
depart from prescribed rules of conduct. The *rigid* conformist may
follow a prescribed set of ritualistic behaviors, learned in childhood and
now habitual. The *pliant* conformist adapts to any group he is with. His
behavior depends upon the social structure of which he is a part at any
one time. The individual who is arrested at this stage of development

has difficulty in setting goals of his own, because he continually bows to the requirements of others. He fails to gain a place for himself as an individual.

The next stages of personal development are entered in the later adolescent years and extend into maturity. These are the socialized stages in which the individual is guided by codes and principles. The typical *irrational* conscientious person abides by a set of abstract principles. No longer is the group standard in and of itself important. At this stage, feelings of anxiety come from having violated "what one believes in." We recognize that standards of truthfulness, loyalty, neatness, honesty, and the like are important guides for living in a social world. Difficulties of adjustment spring from the fact that such rules are not recognized by the irrational-abstract person as man-made expedients contrived to serve mankind in a functional way and that some give and take in their use is necessary on exceptional occasions. As a result this person is sometimes caught between two conflicting principles. Honesty and kindness, for example, may conflict if pushed too far.

Although the irrational conscientious style of living may be a favorable one for most situations, it is the *rational-altruistic* stage in which the behaviors most characteristic of mature development are found. Here too, principles guide and direct behavior—honesty, integrity, and so on—and dependably so. However, behavior of this kind is *not* the result of a blind application of abstract principles, but rather the result of rational assessment of one's actions and their possible effect on others. There is strong interest in the welfare of others as well as of oneself. Such a person permits circumstances to alter cases. This individual's style of life allows him to develop continually, and to adapt to a variety of situations without a serious conflict of values.

Piaget's observations of character development

Piaget's (1948) conceptualization of the development of morality in the child, as described by Kohlberg (1963), emphasizes changes in the child's attitudes toward rules (a sense of duty) and toward justice (a sense of rights). Maturity in the use of rules is represented by mutual respect growing out of the ability to differentiate one's own beliefs from that of others. Basic to development in this area is peer group interaction. In addition, maturity in attitudes toward justice involves internalized standards rather than passive conformity to norms.

Flavell (1963) has interpreted some of the interesting observations made by Piaget (1948) to illustrate the stages in the development of the child's character. It should be noted that the individual differences in this area are large and the "stages" are not always as clearly defined as they appear to be in the examples that follow.

On playing marbles: The child in the first stage (before 3 years) treats the marbles as playthings only. Rules are not a part of his life-space. At Stage 2 (about 3–5 years) the child imitates the rule-regulated behavior of older children whom he has seen playing the game. Rules are seen as emanating from a higher authority. The child's play is egocentric and socially isolated. He unintentionally changes the rules according to his own desires. At Stage 3 (7–8 years on) the game is played with social awareness. It is a truly social endeavor but the rules still have a vague and ambiguous quality about them. It is not until Stage 4 (around 11 or 12 years of age and on) that the child appears really to understand the rules and to follow them according to a sense of duty. In fact, he now takes special pride and enjoyment in making up new rules for unforeseen circumstances as long as there is mutual agreement.

On lying: Young children see a lie as a string of bad words, akin to swearing. It is blameworthy to the extent that it deviates from the facts. The offense is perceived as worse when the lie fails to deceive than when it succeeds and an unintentional lie with serious consequences is perceived as worse than a deliberate lie that leads to no consequences of importance. Falsehoods are wrong especially if one gets punished for them or especially if they are told to an adult.

The attitudes of older children toward lies or other deviant actions are determined, in large part, from the motives of the person and from the effects of his action on others. Thus, a lie is defined as any statement that deviates from the truth and is especially reprehensible if it is deliberate. Whether others are successfully or unsuccessfully deceived by a lie, or whether one is punished for the deceit or not; or whether the lie is told to an adult or a peer are not the fundamental distinctions for the older child. All are equally "bad" if there is an intent or motive to deceive others.

On punishment: Young children tend to favor expiatory punishment, that is, the wrongdoer should be made to suffer for his deeds according to the *magnitude* of his offense. Other children tend to favor reciprocity in punishment; that is, the punishment should be in direct relation to the logical consequences of the offense upon others. In other words, their attitude is one of "letting the punishment fit the crime."

On justice: Younger children more than older children tend to believe in immanent justice—that deviance will lead Nature to take care of the culprit. With regard to distributive justice, i.e., how punishments and rewards should be meted out to a group, Piaget's evidence seems to point to three distinct stages. Prior to 7 or 8 anything done by the adult or other authority is considered "fair" even if individuals are treated unequally. About 7 to 11 or 12 the child believes that everyone should be treated equally regardless of the circumstances. Then from 12 or so on, the child sees a necessity for the members of the group to be treated very much, but not altogether, equally.

Naturally, a number of environmental influences will shape the individual's growth toward maturity of character. The culture sets the content and organization of moral values through its symbols, communicative processes, and institutions (Warner, 1959). The peer group acts as a reinforcer of moral values and behavior patterns originating in the adult group. It is also used as a testing ground for consequences of independent thought and of moral behavior. Piaget (1932), in *Moral Judgment of the Child*, asserts that the peer group is basic to autonomous moral development. The community through its communication media, ethical principles, social stratification, and opportunities for religious affiliation has an effect primarily when the parents have defaulted and failed to play their proper role.

An important factor in character formation appears to be the family climate as can be seen in Table 14-2 (Peck & Havighurst, 1960). To illustrate this point we can compare the familial patterns for the two extreme character types. The amoral–self-centered adolescents in the Peck and Havighurst study:

. . . had familial relationships that were chaotically inconsistent and so lacking in mutual trust or affection as to deserve to be called actively rejecting. Several of these families were autocratic and severe in their punishment of the child. The rest were lenient and rather laissez-faire in their discipline (p. 176).

The common pattern of family experience for those adolescents described as rational-altruistic was one in which:

their rearing was consistent, strongly trustful and loving ("approval" does not do justice to the evidence in the case materials), highly democratic, and lenient in its punishments. . . . Further, in order to be intelligently and effectively ethical it appears necessary to add to this pattern the element of democracy; the opportunity to experiment in making decisions, and to develop and trade ideas, unafraid, with parents and other family members.

Table 14-2. Correlations of family characteristics with the character maturity scale.

Family Characteristic	Child's Maturity of Character
Consistency	.58
Democracy-Autocracy	.26
Mutual Trust and Approval	.64
Leniency-Severity	—.16

SOURCE: Peck & Havighurst, 1960, p. 106.

The importance of the family and of the specific patterns of family interactions in character formation are supported in a number of the findings of other investigations (Whiting & Child, 1953; Sears, Maccoby, & Levin, 1957).

The teacher, as a parent surrogate, can be a key figure in this growth toward an integrated personality and a mature style of living. In the curricular materials he uses, in his methods, and in his example he can guide the pupil toward seeing and understanding the rationality in the many rules and behavior guides established by society. The pupil can be encouraged at the same time to find his own identity as a worthwhile and important person, who trusts himself and others. Classroom experiences can foster initiative and industry (Child, Potter, & Levine, 1954). The pupil can learn, in this setting, to live intimately with others without yielding to their every demand, retaining his independence.

> It has been my pleasure recently to work up a speculative description of a psychological Utopia in which all men are psychologically healthy: Eupsychia, I call it. From what we know of healthy people, could we predict the kind of culture that they would evolve if 1000 healthy families migrated to some deserted land where they could work out their destiny as they pleased? What kind of education would they choose? Economic system? Sexuality? Religion?
>
> I am very uncertain of some things—economics in particular. But of other things I am *very* sure. And one of them is that this would almost surely be a highly anarchistic group, a laissez-faire but loving culture, in which people (young people too) would have much more free choice than we are used to, and in which wishes would be respected much more than they are in our society. People would not bother each other so much as we do, would be much less prone to press opinions or religions or philosophies or tastes in clothes or food or art or women on their neighbors. In a word, the inhabitants of Eupsychia would tend to be permissive, wish-respecting and gratifying (whenever possible), would frustrate only under certain conditions, that I have not attempted to describe, and would permit people to make free choices wherever possible. Under such conditions, the deepest layers of human nature could show themselves with great ease. (From Maslow, 1954, p. 350. With permission of Harper & Brothers.)

The Self-Defense Functions of Personality

According to psychoanalytic theory the individual ego (or self) is in the middle of oftentimes conflicting psychological forces. His unconscious needs must be met either directly or in sublimated form, otherwise life seems empty and without purpose. He must satisfy the demands imposed upon him by parents and other authority figures in his environment in order to satisfy his complex array of dependency needs. And he must comply with the dictates of his own ego ideal and conscience in order to avoid feelings of guilt and consequent self-punishment. Personality integration is thus a delicately balanced series of compromises and decisions—the majority of which occur at the unconscious level.* This is the reason that we so often experience feelings of guilt, social rejection, and personal frustration without being able to identify reasonable causes.

In view of the many conflicting demands made upon the ego (or self) one can readily understand why an individual so frequently feels frustrated and discontent, anxious and apprehensive. The denials, delays, and compromises which are the warp and woof of psychological adjustment are never completely satisfactory. Hence the individual is in a more-or-less continuous state of anxiety about his adequacy to maintain the ongoing processes of personality integration. Confronted with this difficult assignment the individual adopts a series of self-defenses or self-deceptions that help to maintain a semblance of self-consistency and logical order even when the adjustment conditions are actually chaotic. For the average person the self-defenses function largely at an unconcious level so that he is never aware that he is defending or deceiving himself. When employed with moderation the ego defenses *do* contribute to personality integration and feelings of self-esteem. However, when used to excess they may blind the individual to his real needs and problems, and thereby hamper healthy personality growth. It is often the teacher's role to help pupils recognize and adjust to personal problems which their ego defenses have obscured or hidden completely. For example, the pupil who consistently blames others for his own inadequacies and failures (defense by projection) must somehow be helped to face his problems in a more direct way. Otherwise he will fail to develop the necessary skills for a happy and productive life.

Rationalization

This is the most commonly recognized mechanism of self-defense. The individual unconsciously attempts to make his behavior appear adequate and consistent at all times. Defense by rationalization is well illustrated in Aesop's fable in which the fox who is unable to reach a particularly luscious looking bunch of grapes says, "They are probably sour anyway." Because of the popularity of this fable, rationalization is sometimes called the "sour-grapes" defense.

Pupils' rationalizations are often serious deterrents to academic progress. For example a pupil may say, "I'm not very good in mathematics because I don't like it. It's a dumb subject." This rationalization excuses his inadequacy and also prevents him from expending very much energy trying to discover the meaning and importance of this intellectual experience.

*An interesting and highly readable discussion of psychoanalytic theory and its variations can be found in Mullahy (1949).

Consider the difference in attitude of John and Bill who are both deficient in spelling achievement. John recognizes his relatively poor talent for spelling and has started a program of home study with the aid of his parents. He says, "I'm not too good in spelling, but I'm improving." In contrast, Bill studies less and less on spelling as time goes by and excuses his poor performance by saying, "Spelling isn't important anyway. When you grow up you can always get a secretary to do your spelling for you." There is some truth in Bill's rationalization, although it glosses over glaring instances in which poor spelling may be a handicap in everyday life. However, Bill's rationalization does illustrate the perniciousness of this form of defense. Most rationalizations are based on half-truths and are therefore especially resistant to change by argument or persuasion. The more effective approach by the teacher is to help the pupil solve his underlying problem. Then the rationalization will fade out because it is no longer needed or useful.

Projection

By projecting, the individual attributes the causes of his frustration or failure to some other person, to events beyond his control, or to inanimate objects. He may also project his own needs to other persons and state that they want to do things that he himself unconsciously wishes that he could do. When Mary says, "Sandra wants to cheat but is afraid she will be caught," she may be revealing her own unconscious wish and accompanying anxiety.

Projection is a favored way of self-defense because it so frequently satisfies two purposes. When Billy stumbles in the marching band and says, "Carl pushed me," he may be satisfying two needs: (1) he excuses his own awkwardness, and (2) he hurts Carl, toward whom he feels hostile and aggressive over some real or imagined injury in the past. Projection in this instance permits Billy to maintain his self-esteem and also to vent his aggression under conditions that usually preclude immediate retaliation.

Since projection is an ego defense it is aimed at maintaining an integrated personality. More strikingly, it is also a means of self-deception and therefore a potential danger when used to excess. The pupil who projects the blame for most of his failures on to other people is in double jeopardy. He deceives himself and thereby overlooks opportunities for self-improvement. He also reaps a harvest of hostility and ill favor from individuals falsely accused for his frustrations. The teacher may be able to help his pupils understand this aspect of adjustment by class discussion. Thus his pupils may become more sensitive to their more obvious and flagrant instances of blame and need projection. However, most projections occur at the unconscious level and constitute behaviors to be understood and taken into consideration by the teacher, but not to be dealt with directly.

Psychosomatic defenses

This is a drastic form of self-defense. Its occurrence usually implies extreme frustration, so intense that other methods of defense have proved inadequate. The individual unconsciously adopts the symptoms of some physiological malfunction such as an upset stomach, asthma, headache, visual difficulty, paralysis, or other disorder which automatically removes him from a recurrent problem. Although the cause of his illness or physical infirmity is psychological, his physical suffering is clearly real and disturbing.

The pupil who has an upset stomach or a sick headache on school mornings and is completely all right over the weekend is expressing his chronic frustration through the conversion mechanism of self-defense. The teacher may be able to adjust the school program to lighten the psychological pressures, but more importantly he should be provided the therapeutic services of an expert. Fortunately, such pupils are often taken to their family physicians through whom they may be referred to competent clinical psychologists or psychiatrists for treatment.

Other mechanisms of personality integration

The following mechanisms of human adjustment are presented in less detail because they are judged to be less relevant to the teacher's understanding of the typical pupil. An understanding of their meaning and functioning is more important to the therapist or counselor who works with severely disturbed pupils.

When the individual is particularly unsuccessful in solving a personal problem, he may *regress* to a more infantile or childish response pattern. The temper tantrum is a good example. It is by no means restricted to early childhood. It sometimes occurs in the lives of fairly well-adjusted adults who are temporarily overcome by the vexations of unusually frustrating circumstances. An individual's rational faculties are temporarily routed and primitive patterns of shouting, kicking, and so on appear. The tensions of frustration are reduced but the individual is now confronted with new problems: guilt feelings, loss of self-esteem, and imperiled social relations. The temper tantrum acts as a safety valve in personality integration. When it occurs frequently in children of school age it is an indicator of severe personality disturbance and should be regarded as such.

There are several other defense mechanisms which are employed in an effort to maintain an integrated personality. They are complex in their origins and functioning. However, they may be of some academic interest to the teacher-in-training. The *reaction formation* describes a condition where the child unconsciously does the opposite of what he views social reality as demanding of him. The child from a home characterized by an extreme emphasis on cleanliness and orderliness may delight in grime and disorder. The negativism of the two- and three-year-olds is a good example of reaction formation at an early developmental level. It is an attempt to deal with demands that are viewed as unreasonably stringent or harsh. A reduction in social pressures for conformity, so that the child can make a more positive adjustment, is desirable. A sullen and resistant pupil is often able to adopt a more cooperative attitude when he realizes that he has a real voice in managing his own affairs.

In *displacement* the individual unconsciously displaces an idea or action that he cannot easily face by one that is more acceptable. He may start worrying excessively about his school work when his real concern is being accepted and appreciated by his classmates. He may resent and reject his teacher when the real antagonism is toward an overprotective mother who smothers him with affection and restraints.

The *isolation* mechanism permits the individual to deprive an unpleasant experience of its distasteful emotional content. It produces a stoical attitude. Such a child may be confronted by a difficult adjustment situation without betraying any sign of emotional disturbance. This mechanism of self-defense is related to repression and may produce some of the same serious consequences when used excessively.

By the foregoing mechanisms and a few others too technical for description here the individual defends himself and attempts to maintain an integrated and self-consistent personality. The self-defenses are symptoms of psychological distress just as an abnormally high body temperature is a symptom of physical illness. An observant teacher can learn a great deal about a pupil by noting the kinds and frequency of occurrence of situations in which he is forced to adopt one or more of these self-defenses.

Summary

An understanding of some of the more obvious dimensions of personality integration is an extremely important part of the teacher's intellectual equipment. In this chapter the psychoanalytic viewpoint has been employed because it is the most complete and has permeated so much of the ordinary layman's psychological thinking. Personality integration is conceived as being an "ideal state" that may be approximated but never fully realized. Sublimation and identification are recognized as the most important dynamisms for positive movement toward the integrated personality. The coping functions of an integrated personality are discussed in some detail, as are the functions of self-defense. The reader should be mindful that there are other, quite different, theories purporting to explain the structure and dynamics of personality integraion. The psychoanalytic model was selected for inclusion in this book because of its comprehensiveness and its record of stimulating so much research, as well as its general familiarity to the average reader. We have urged that teachers be forced to look for subtle antecedents of behavior in their attempts to understand and influence their pupils. Some knowledge of an internally consistent model of personality functioning is essential for teachers. The psychoanalytic model meets this test extremely well.

Self-esteem and psychological health

In the course of development, the pupil develops a gradual awareness of himself as a person. There is the emergence of fairly stable evaluations about his physical abilities, his appearance, his intellectual capacities, and his social skills. A number of his attitudes relate to his general self-confidence, self-respect, and adequacy. They will benefit or hinder his ability to make choices for himself, to express himself, to rely on his own judgment, and to make his influence felt, depending on whether the attitudes are favorable or unfavorable (Rogers, 1956; Skinner, 1956). The verbal responses associated with each experience are important consequences of these experiences (Staats & Staats, 1963). Some will be in the form of self-criticism or self-blame after infractions of rules. Other verbal reactions may direct hostility inward toward oneself and thereby function to reduce anxiety (Aronfreed, 1968).

These verbalized abstractions of one's attributes comprise the concept about oneself (self-concept). Important in this regard are all evaluations, whether reflected in scores on examinations, in subjective estimates of one's ability by other people, or in one's own introspective evaluation. Whatever these appraisals are, they get translated into personal form. At first the child may be told, "*You* shouldn't do that!" or "*You* were mean!" Then he may be made to repeat the phrases modified to, "*I* shouldn't do that!" and "*I* was mean!" In this manner the individual learns a repertory of verbal responses to himself as a stimulus based on responses of others and which are descriptive (though not always an accurate description) of his behavior (Staats & Staats, 1963; Staats, 1968). As one learns about his capabilities and limitations (whether accurately or not) they become the (inferred) bases for predicting future success or failure in similar situations (Hall & Lindzey, 1957).

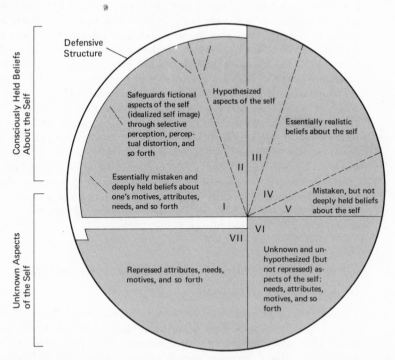

Figure 15-1. Some inferred aspects of the self-system. This is a symbolic representation of some attributes that might be included in the self-image. The ratios into which the quadrants are divided are also only representative. Obviously, wide ranges of individual differences may occur. Exploratory experiences related to hypothesis-testing are considered to be especially important in providing new information about social reality and about oneself. (Jordaan, 1963, Figure 1, p. 62. With permission.)

The teacher and the pupil's adjustment

Whether wittingly or not, each teacher engenders in her classroom attitudes toward learning, tests, failure, and success. We realize that there are many sources of such attitudes but there can be little doubt that the teacher is one of them. From our observations we have concluded that one of the most important dimensions on which teachers vary is the degree to which they establish an atmosphere in which the child's sense of security and level of self-esteem are very much determined by the adequacy of his performance. In some classrooms failure or lack of progress by a child is responded to by the teacher in a way that increases the child's feeling of inadequacy. In other class-rooms such a child is responded to in a way that, while it recognizes the child's failure or rate of progress, does not make him feel that the teacher is rejecting or derogating him, i.e., the teacher likes and accepts him despite his inadequacy or failure. It is too frequently for-gotten by parents (and also by teachers) how important a figure the teacher is in the life of a child. From the standpoint of the child, what he thinks is the teacher's attitude toward him is of great moment to him, *particularly if he likes the teacher and wants to be liked by her.* We emphasize this last point because we have observed classrooms in which it was quite clear that the children had little respect for the teacher, and what she thought of and said to them carried little weight in the sense of affecting their self-attitudes. It is when the child is dis-posed to like and respect the teacher that the ways in which the teacher responds to an inadequate performance of the child are of great significance. This would be especially true of the anxious child, who, as described previously by us, is dependent on the positive atti-tudes of others toward him for a sense of security. (From Sarason, *et al.*, 1960, p. 272. With permission.)

Three self-concepts—three different reactions to the same situation

Through trial and error teachers found that varying their techniques assured greater success than adhering to any single teaching proce-dure. They also discovered that classroom behavior could not be understood without knowing something about each child and how he perceived himself and the world about him. An illustration may serve to clarify this point:

The setting is a fifth-grade classroom. Three boys have been "cutting up" and in the process have managed to spill a can of paint on the nearly completed mural the class has been making for the school's Christmas festival. Livid with rage, the teacher reprimands them severely in front of the entire class. Among other things she calls them stupid, disloyal, and irresponsible. She threatens to make them do the mural over after school.

Because she does not single out any one boy for chastisement, one can assume the external stimulus is the same for the three boys. Yet their responses are different because different self-concepts are involved. One boy responds with only a shrug of his shoulders. Through many similar experiences in his five years of schooling he has learned to see himself as a person who does not do what is required, who gets into trouble, who is stupid and a failure by school standards. This latest experience fits perfectly the picture he already has of himself and consequently produces little response. A second boy similarly shows no overt reaction; yet within him hot resentment flames up at being called stupid and irresponsible.

Unlike the first boy his previous school experiences have been successful, happy ones. Being interested in biographies and identifying himself with George Washington, his hero at the moment, he sees himself as he perceives Washington—strong and silent in the face of adversity, one who "can take a beating and face it like a man." If in the heat of his anger he forgets his idea for a moment and blurts out some excuse for his action, he rationalizes to himself that even Washington stood against injustice and fought for what he thought was right. Only by such rationalization can he protect his image of himself as a Washington. The third boy responds still differently. A leader in physical activities on the playground, he has often played the role of bully among his classmates. He sees himself as a tough character whom "nobody pushes around and gets away with it," even a teacher. Therefore he argues with her over her remarks and claims that the paint can should not have been left near the mural. When her back is turned but when all the children can see, he sticks his tongue out at her. One stimulus but three self-concepts and three different responses—this is the relation of self to behavior. (From Brandt, 1957, pp. 26–27. With permission of author and publisher.)

The Measurement of the Self-concept

A number of personality inventories contain items that, in conjunction with other information, can be used for informal interpretations of a pupil's self-perceptions. More frequently, however, specialized inventories, ranging from relatively simple paper-and-pencil questionnaires to very highly specialized projective devices are used to measure this aspect of behavior.

The simplest measure to administer requires the pupil to rate whether or not an attribute is characteristic of his response patterns. In obtaining such self-evaluations, the pupil is presented with a number of statements illustrated by the following (see e.g., Coopersmith, 1959) :

I am happy most of the time.	Yes ? No
I make friends easily.	Yes ? No
Most people regard me as odd.	Yes ? No
I often feel self-conscious because of my personal appearance.	Yes ? No
I feel that nobody quite understands me.	Yes ? No

Another kind of inventory simply lists 50 to 100 adjectives such as nonchalant, humourless, self-assertive, self-confident, attractive, good natured, aggressive, slow, strong, and sociable (Rogers & Dymond, 1954, pp. 78, 275–276). The pupil checks only the adjectives which he feels are most like him, rates the degree to which an attribute characterizes him, describes his feelings by simple "yes" or "no" responses, or indicates the desirability of each trait.

Self-ratings are not always consistent with the objective estimate of the pupil's ability gained by achievement measures or by other outside criteria. In describing themselves, pupils sometimes resort to defensive maneuvers (Rogers & Dymond, 1954; Jones, 1964): A pupil with low self-esteem may "overrate" himself in an attempt to gain some measure of self-enhancement. An overly modest person may tend to underevaluate himself. This, among other factors, tends to lower the reliability of self-rating measures, so careful investigators (e.g., Coopersmith, 1968) often obtain supplementary indexes based on teacher's reports and on psychological tests. When inventories are administered in an impunitive atmosphere that guards the privacy of the pupil's response, bias in either direction will be reduced. As with all personality measures, self-concept ratings are obtained only when the results will, in some way, be of benefit to the pupil. Furthermore, the rights and privileges of even the youngest pupils who do not wish to respond to such inventories are respected.

Figure 15-2. The pupil's self-concept is reflected in his behavior while interacting with others. Describe the different self-concepts represented in this picture. (From E. S. Joy. A book about me. Chicago: Science Research Associates, 1952. With permission.)

Ratings by "others" in the pupil's environment can yield significant insight into his behavior since these persons tend to have strong influences on how the pupil will respond to himself (Coopersmith, 1967; Rosenberg, 1965; Sears & Sherman, 1964). Evaluations of the pupil are continually being conveyed by subtle verbal or expressive symbolic behavior and will eventually be incorporated into his cognitive structure as are all other experiences that result in learning (Staats & Staats, 1963). Conversely, established self-evaluations will inevitably be conveyed in the pupil's behavior and reflected in the ratings by others.

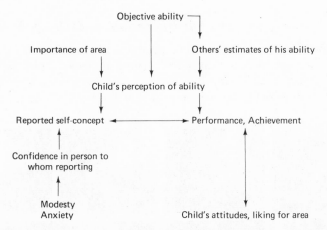

Figure 15-3. A suggestive model incorporating potentially influential factors in the relationship between the pupil's reported self-concept and in his achievements in school related tasks. (From Sears & Sherman, 1964, p. 12. With permission of author and publisher.)

Some measures of the self-concept are indirect as illustrated in an inventory employed by Sears and Sherman (1964, p. 37–38).* The questions on their scale were stated in both direct or projective methods as illustrated below for purposes of comparison (the italicized words illustrate some possible, but fictitious responses):

Direct	*Projective*
When the teacher criticizes my work, I—*feel bad.*	When the teacher criticized his work, Greg—*was very unhappy.*
Giving oral reports makes me—*sick.*	Giving oral reports made Beatrice —*scared.*
Not having others notice me makes me feel—*pretty good.*	Not having others notice her made Ruth feel—*unhappy.*
Having to do things in school that don't seem interesting to me—*makes me bored with schoolwork.*	Having to do things in school that didn't seem interesting made Stu —*mad at the teacher.*

An assumption behind the indirect (projective) measure is that whatever response is made will be among the highest in the pupil's hierarchy of expectations and evaluations of himself. Thus, his ratings of Greg, Beatrice, Ruth, Stu, or other persons' behaviors are likely to reflect his own true feelings. But because they are reactions assigned to other people, the pupil's feelings may not be hidden by defenses.

*Adapted from a scale described in Getzels & Walsh, 1958.

Identification and the Self-concept

The self-concept, like other products of the learning process, is acquired in part, at least, through learning processes involving principles of association and reward (Staats & Staats, 1963, Staats, 1968). However, everyday observation will reveal that the behavior of a boy push-

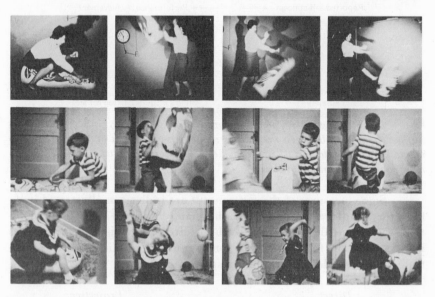

Figure 15-4. Photographs of children spontaneously reproducing the behavior exhibited by an aggressive adult model. (From Bandura & Walters, 1963, p. 62–63. With permission.)

ing a toy lawnmower will contain many of his father's mannerisms in performing that task. His stance and warm-up before pitching a baseball will probably be a replica of the warm-up by his current favorite in the major leagues. Even his haircut will correspond to the fad most popular among his peers. While reinforcement processes are undoubtedly influential factors in the development of these behaviors, there is evidence that many are learned through imitation. Girls, too, imitate grooming, dress, mannerisms, and postural behaviors of their popular peers, teachers, and movie actresses.

Recently, the role of social imitation (or identification) has been receiving renewed attention as a basis for understanding how such behaviors, emerging as a result of the socialization of the individual, are learned. Consequently, related research has contributed to our understanding of how the pupil's self-concept is learned. However, it should be recognized that a few decades ago Freud (1948, pp. 62–63) also called attention to a similar process when he described identification as follows: "One's parent is what one would like to be. . . . Identification endeavors to mould a person's own ego after the fashion of one that has been taken as a model."

Children in modern cultures acquire many patterns of behavior by observing and imitating others. Though they may imitate real-life models pupils are not provided, as directly as are the children in more primitive societies, with miniature replicas of the actual behavior patterns adults use in social interaction. (Children in simpler cultures may, for example, perform adult chores with small versions of the tools used by adults.) Nor are they provided with the opportunity to participate in the extremely complex social interactions that occur among adults.

In complex societies, the child's contact with models is mainly in symbolic form. They are presented as abstractions of exemplary behavior wherein a given person may be identified as one to be imitated by directing attention to the desirable behaviors. Similarly, unfavorable models may also be identified and their deviant behavior abstracted from their other behaviors to illustrate unsuccessful or forbidden behaviors. However as Bandura and Walters (1963) suggest, the use of deviant models for this purpose may be unfortunate since the child's attention is directed to patterns of behavior that might otherwise have been ignored.

In practical situations the pupil does not imitate only a single model. Bandura and Walters (1963) indicate that most of the pupil's behavior will be modeled after the abstracted configuration of behaviors represented in a composite of real-life, exemplary, and symbolic models. The result is not a simple miniature replica of one person's behavior. It is more a synthesis of attributes from all models. As a result, children who have been raised in the same family constellation of parents and siblings may exhibit quite different behaviors.

The diversity of the child's models increases as he grows older. Accordingly, the total pattern of behavior undergoes gross changes. Nevertheless, the selection of models by any given individual, even where many are available, will probably be more homogeneous than might at first be assumed. Each model tends to be selected in terms of the previously acquired values and attitudes, thereby resulting in relatively stable patterns of behavior with increasing age.

The ideal self-image of pupils: Who are their ego-ideals?

In a study of the development of the ideal-self, or ego-ideal, Havighurst, Robinson, and Dorr (1946) used the following questions to identify the kinds of people that influenced the pupil's ideal-self:

Describe in a page or less the person you would most like to

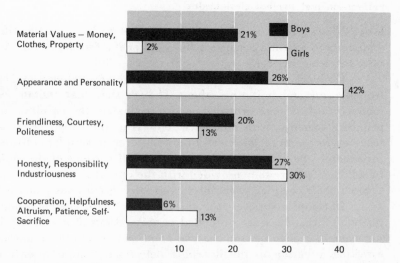

Figure 15-5. Boys and girls differ in the kinds of character and personality traits they mention as important in their descriptions of the ideal-self. (Adapted from Havighurst, et al., 1946, Table 4, p. 253. With permission.)

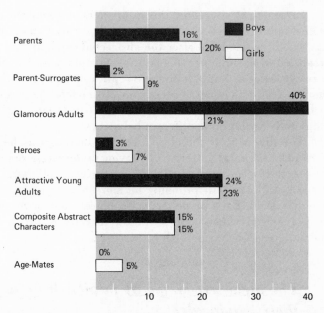

Figure 15-6. Boys and girls choose different kinds of people as representative of their ideal-self, i.e., "the person they would most like to be like when they grow up." (Adapted from Havighurst, et al., 1946, Table 3, p. 252. With permission.)

be like when you grow up. This may be a real person, or an imaginary person. He or she may be a combination of several people. Tell something about this person's age, character, appearance, occupation, and recreations. If he is a real person, say so. You need not give his real name if you do not want to. (Havighurst, *et al.*, 1946, p. 242).

The pupils ranged in age from 10 to 17 years of age and represented small and large communities as well as several minority groups. The results in Figures 15-5 and 15-6 should only be taken as suggestive. In times of rapid changes in social influences the nature of children's identifications change with equal rapidity. As important, are the cautions by Havighurst, *et al.* (1946) who indicate that the children's specific choices in any era are likely to be influenced by short-term and superficial factors (currently popular heroes, popularity among peer groups, and so on). In addition, there may be a question about the ability of children in this age-group to "fully report on their ego-ideals" (Havighurst, *et al.*, 1946, p. 257).

Nevertheless, with this caution in mind, these investigators suggest that in principle, parents are increasingly less important as models after the child is 8 years of age than are glamorous adults. People with "romantic or ephemeral fame" play an increasingly important role in the life of the 10- to 15-year-old pupil. A teacher or other person in the child's immediate life-space may take the place of this "glamor figure" and, thus, also symbolize the ego-ideal. While changes in models often appear to be frivolous, the core of values on which choice of models is based is probably quite stable and less capricious then it may seem from the child's apparently changing loyalties. Finally, from this study it appears that pupils are deeply influenced by such qualities of prestigious persons as their power, age, and possessions.

Educational processes and self-concept of the black pupil

"It is clear that the life experiences of the black child are not such as to aid him in developing a positive sense of himself or of his place in the world. What does this suggest to us? It would seem that a very compelling hypothesis is that *the black child, from earliest school entry through graduation from high school, needs continued opportunities to see himself and his racial group in a realistically positive light. He needs to understand what color and race mean, he needs to learn about those of his race (and other disadvantaged groups) who have succeeded, and he needs to clarify his understanding of his own group history and current group situation.*

"At the moment, these are missing ingredients in the American public school classroom. Numerous studies of textbooks have shown them to be lily white. Pictures do not show black and white children together; when blacks appear they are usually either Booker T. Washington, George Washington Carver, or foreign. Neither whites nor blacks have an accurate picture of the American Negro and his history. One observer noted that a commonly used contemporary civics book had no index entry for *urban renewal, transportation, transit, or Negro*. The lily white nature of text materials is true also of other visual aids used in the schools. If blacks appear in school films, they are in stereotyped roles. One film, for instance, showing "community helpers" illustrated the work of repairing the street with a black crew and a white foreman. . . .

"That these materials can and do have a strong impact on the child's perception of himself and others was well documented in the study by Trager and Yarrow (1952). When a story describing a black child as a funny savage (*Little Black Sambo*) was read aloud to young children, white and black children's feelings were affected, particularly when the white children referred to the story in the schoolyard. The only thing that is surprising about these findings is that educators and others have consistently ignored them. It is interesting that the Trager-Yarrow research report is probably the only study made of the differences in education (textbook) content that is reported in the literature. . . .

"If teaching materials present a slanted view of him and his place in the world to the black child, what does the teacher tell him? It is no very startling piece of news that teachers, too, bear the majority version of the black. Studies of their attitudes toward children show that the black child is rated lowest in all rankings of groups on a Bogardus-type social-distance scale. The original study was completed in 1940; teachers-in-training in 1963 give the same responses. Attempts to change teachers' attitudes through human relations, workshops, and special courses have reached very few. In formulating some guidelines for the education of the culturally disadvantaged, Niemeyer (1963, p. 81) stated:

"Our hypothesis is that the chief cause of the low achievement of the children of alienated groups is the fact that too many teachers and principals honestly believe that these children are educable only to an extremely limited extent. And when teachers have a low expectation level for their children's learning, the children seldom exceed that expectation, which is a self-fulfilling prophecy. . . .

"It is not our purpose here to provide a blueprint for educational innovations which might be the object of experimentation. What is significant, however, is that the school has not as yet been used deliberately to change the self-concept of students. . . .

"We are suggesting that education *can* make a difference. One difference, so far cited, as far as Negro youth are concerned, is the deliberate provision in guidance procedures to demonstrate to Negro youth that other Negroes have succeeded in moving up and out of the ghetto, becoming skilled and white-collar workers." (From Grambs, 1965, p. 21–25. With permission.)

At the time the above quote was published the need for Afro-American studies, for diversity of educational opportunity as well as equality of educational opportunity, for textbooks oriented toward different ethnic groups, for improvement in educational and vocational opportunities, and for community control of schools was most apparent. While much still remains to be done, some progress in each of these areas has been made. At the same time there are greater demands being placed on the teacher for keeping up to date as a resource person and representative of the community in a period of rapid social change. He must recognize the multiplicity of definitions associated with the terms *disadvantaged, social class,* and *ethnicity* since such definitions convey different implications for educational practice. The term *disadvantaged,* for example, is used most often to refer to people who are limited in housing, job, and educational opportunities by their socioeconomic status. By providing people in lower socioeconomic status groups with the same opportunities as those in the middle socioeconomic groups the differences between the two groups in achievement levels and social patterns are decreased considerably if not entirely eliminated. However, ethnic groups differ in *patterns* of ability, and these differences remain even with increases in social advantages. (See Chapter 19 for an example of differences in patterns of mental abilities.) The problem here is one of providing educational advantages to maximize the capabilities of all groups regardless of ethnic or racial origin. In so doing, the consequence may be one of increasing differences among differently identified groups. Stodolsky and Lesser (1967) indicate that, on the basis of these observations, a new definition of "disadvantaged" would eventually be based on child characteristics and instructional environments in which the child must function, rather than on gross classifications provided by "social-class" distinctions.

Some behaviors acquired by imitation

Self-criticism, aggression, and aspiration are among the behaviors learned by imitation. Children's patterns of self-reinforcement, for example, closely match those of the model they imitate. In experimental situations described by Bandura and Kupers (1964), children who imitated models with low standards were highly indulgent. They rewarded themselves generously, even for poor performance. The children imitating models with high standards, on the other hand, displayed considerable self-denial and took rewards sparingly.

The pupil's self-evaluation, thus, may be dependent in part upon matching his behavior with that of an esteemed person (such as an adult), whatever such behaviors may be. Several illustrations are given

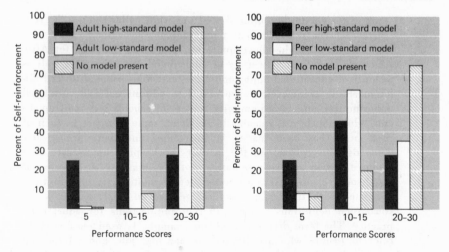

Figure 15-7. Children tend to model their behavior after the prevailing patterns established by their peers or by adults. Self-reinforcement was contingent upon the performance criterion which matched that of their respective models in the experimental conditions whereas the children in the control conditions reinforced themselves independently of their task performance. (From Bandura & Kupers, 1964, Figure 1 and Figure 2, p. 5. With permission.)

by Bandura and Walters (1964, p. 64) to illustrate this point: parents of dependent children tend themselves to be dependent; parents of children with inhibited dependency behaviors tend to show generalized inhibition dependency responses; girls tend to be passive-dependent whereas males tend to be much less so—that is, males tend to be independent and adventurous presumably because of the influence of symbolized models in children's books and because of same-sex modeling. A child who observes a model being punished acquires emotional reactions that are evoked in other similar situations even though he himself has not been personally punished (Berger, 1962). Fear and withdrawal reactions to specific situations may be learned through vicarious participation in an activity (Walters, Leat, & Mezei, 1963).

Self-esteem

A generalized outcome of the self-concept is the pupil's evaluation of his overall ability and worth—his self-esteem. The term designates the extent to which a person holds a generally favorable opinion (high self-esteem) or unfavorable opinion (low self-esteem) of himself. For any single trait one can appraise the *amount* of self-esteem by such statements as "I am a worrier but wish I weren't;" the *clarity* by statements such as "I am somewhat aggressive;" and the generalized *abstraction* of the self-concept by such verbalizations as "I like working by myself" (Super, *et al.*, 1963).

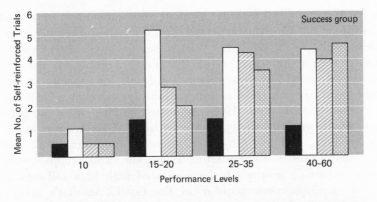

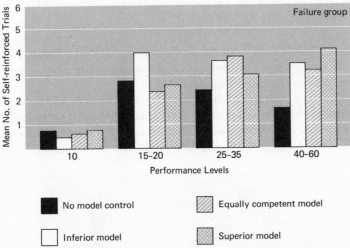

Figure 15-8. In each of the modeling conditions children who had previously experienced failure rewarded themselves less frequently than did their successful counterparts. Children in the control group (no model) who experienced failure rewarded themselves more frequently for poor and moderate performance than did their successful counterparts. Bandura & Whalen (1966) suggest that such self-gratification after failure is more therapeutic than self-congratulatory, much like the consoling experience of treating oneself to a dinner or to a show after a disappointing failure. (From Bandura & Whalen, 1966, Figures 1 and 2, p. 377–378. With permission.)

Antecedents of self-esteem

An antecedent of self-esteem is the degree of identification with one's parents. Pupils with high self-esteem identify with emotionally supportive parents; those with lower self-esteem identify with emotionally nonsupportive parents, or fail to identify with their parents (Carlson, 1963). The pupil lacking adequate internal sources of self-esteem relies upon meeting the expectations of others for evidence of his achievements (or failures). His behavior emphasizes current social relationships (what the *other person* thinks) in defining his self-concept. The extreme need for social orientation limits his capacity for spontaneous, warm, and successful social relationships (Carlson, 1963).

Coopersmith (1967, 1968) conducted an interesting and extensive study, which we will briefly summarize here, of factors associated with high, medium, and low self-esteem in boys who were 10–12 years of age. Unimportant in differentiating among the three groups were many factors commonly assumed to be associated with high self-regard. For example, socioeconomic position of the family, mother's occupation, family size, physical attractiveness, early trauma, or athletic prowess were not consistently related to self-esteem. Many of these same factors, incidentally, were found also to be unrelated to the self-esteem of adolescents and adults in a study by Rosenberg (1965). These events are probably unimportant since they do not consistently play a direct role in the pupil's evaluation of himself.

On the other hand, the day-to-day experiences of the pupil and, particularly, his experiences in the interpersonal environment with family and peers were significant. Important were the reactions of others that lead to feelings of being accepted and of being an "important

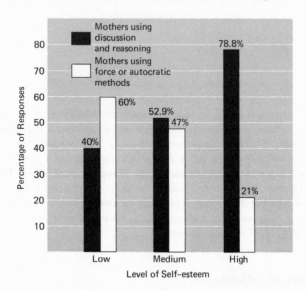

Figure 15-9. Mothers of high self-esteem children reported that the child's cooperation and compliance was obtained by discussion and reasoning (solid) rather than stress on force or autocratic methods (white) to a greater extent than did mothers of low self-esteem children. (Based on Coopersmith, 1967, Table 11.8, p. 214. With permission.)

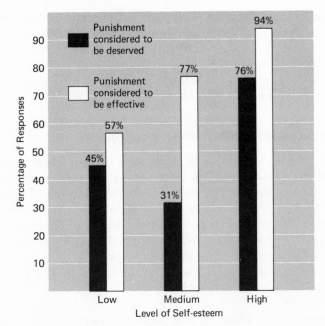

Figure 15-10. Boys with high self-ratings also tend to be of the opinion that punishment administered by parents was generally deserved (solid) and that it was effective (white) to a greater extent than boys with low self-esteem. (Based on Coopersmith, 1967, Table 10.7, p. 194. With permission.)

person." Coopersmith points out three child-rearing practices especially correlated with the boys' ratings of high self-esteem:

First, the parents demonstrated a sincere interest in the boy's activities by direct active participation rather than by overprotective indulgence or by insincere, extravagant gestures of affection. The parents showed an interest, too, in the boy's companions, knew his friends' names, and were genuinely concerned about his welfare.

Second, high standards for the boy's behavior were set and enforced by rewarding appropriate conduct rather than by harsh punishment for infractions of rules. The boys, themselves, indicated that the punishments, when given, were fair and necessary. On the other hand, parents of the boys with low self-esteem tended to be permissive, did not bother to establish or enforce rules of conduct, and administered harsh punishment when the boys became "troublesome." The boys with low self-esteem considered these practices to be unfair.

Third, the general home climate of boys with high self-esteem was democratic, although the power structures and privileges of the family members were well established. The children's rights were recognized, their dissent was acknowledged, and they participated in plans that affected the family.

The factors associated with high self-esteem are those that contribute to one's sense of worth and significance as a person. On the other
hand, extreme permissiveness and inconsistent punishment lead to feelings that parents have little interest in the boy, even to feelings of rejection, and consequently to low self-esteem. Both of these general conclusions were also reached by Rosenberg (1965).

Behaviors associated with feelings of adequacy

Self-esteem is associated with many far-reaching behavioral
manifestations which depend in large part on whether or not the pupil
perceives his accomplishments to be successful. Coopersmith (1967) has
suggested that pupils take as the criteria of success their *competence*, or
the extent to which they can perform proficiently, in the tasks expected
of them; their *power*, that is, their ability to adequately persuade, influence, and otherwise engage in social interaction so as to result in the
control of others; their *significance*, or the extent to which they have
gained acceptance by others; and *character*, or adherence to ethical and
moral standards.

These classifications appear to be attractively simple but on
closer inspection the reader can easily see their complexity. Thus, for
example, one who is successfully powerful may also have difficulty in
gaining acceptance of his confederates. Accordingly, it should be recognized that the way in which the four qualities are combined may vary to
some extent from person to person. With this caution, the remainder of
this section will be devoted to general descriptions of pupils with high
and low self-esteem synthesized from the investigations of Coopersmith
(1967, 1968), Diggory (1966), Rosenberg (1965), and Sheerer (1949).
The differences between the groups will be found to be primarily in the
criteria of *competence* and *significance*.

Pupils with high self-esteem are energetic, active, and expressive.
At least one important advantage on their behalf is their relative freedom from anxiety and psychosomatic symptoms. Too, they have realistic
assessments of their abilities and, accordingly, are confident that their
efforts will meet with success. They feel that they have contact with
others around them, and that they can share feelings, ideas, and enthusiasm with others. Their confidence in themselves, their standards, and
their convictions are based on rational grounds rather than on arbitrary
acceptance of the conventions and traditions of others. They are fully
aware of their limitations and do not try to evade or deny the existence
of these weaknesses. The pupil with high self-esteem expects to be
accepted for what he is—both for his assets and despite his liabilities.

In his interpersonal relationships the pupil with high self-esteem
displays similar levels of confidence. He is outgoing and socially success-

ful. He accepts others with full expectations that he in turn will be well-received, and they do tend to accept him. In discussions, he is eager to express opinions, is not afraid to argue or enter into a disagreement, and is not "hurt" by criticism. He is a dominant member of a group, taking leadership roles rather than the follower role. He is assertive when it comes to making decisions. In the high school community he participates in extracurricular activities, especially clubs, and is likely to be found in a leadership position.

Community and its potential for contributing to the search for an identity

There are many ways in which social and educational factors affect the self-esteem of the black, the Puerto Rican, the Mexican-American, as well as the children of other ethnic origins who live in the complex of our larger cities. The school can fulfill its role as an instrument of education only by cooperation of the community, through citizen and parent participation in community action, social agencies within the community, and legislative support.

The feeling of inadequacy experienced by many of the ethnic groups, but especially of the black, are in part tied to the inescapable reality of color as an inherent part of self. With increasing awareness of this distinction the evidence suggests that the child may reject his status. He may become the subject of unwarranted derision, blocked opportunities, and social rejection. Without compelling reason for accepting another image, he sometimes develops a deep-seated negative self-concept.

Fortunately, things are changing. There are new vocational and educational opportunities available, about which teachers must learn. There are many ways in which the individual can learn about his heritage. So rapid are the changes that the teacher will want to keep apprised of them through newspapers, journals, and professional literature.

The newer opportunities are all intended to contribute to the child's search for an identity; to open the doors to self-fulfillment. This means equal opportunities in education and jobs, pride in one's culture, and civil rights that contribute to self-esteem. In addition to all of these factors the black movement itself is making a very vital contribution to promotion of these changes. At the same time there must be provided appropriate means by which the person can take advantage of these opportunities when they are made available to him. These are not easy objectives to implement. There are no panaceas, and sound arguments can be made for or against any recommendation. (This caution must be kept in mind during the reading of the possibilities for change suggested below.) Some changes might be made in the family and in the community, as well as in the school, if deep-seated

adjustments either in individual character or societal malfunctioning
are to be achieved. Desegregation of schools, while requiring new
adjustments for all concerned, can help to change the disadvantaged
child's level of aspiration by providing other opportunities, other challenges, and additional yardsticks for measuring his progress. It has
already been pointed out in an earlier section of this book that the general characteristics of the social milieu of the school affects aspirational level. Programs such as Headstart can help to bring out the
potential of preschool youngsters, as can Upward Bound for the high
school graduate. But the gains resulting from these programs can easily
be subverted by adverse influences outside of the school. Consequently,
there must be concerted community action to see that advantages
gained by the school are supported both in the home and the community.

In all of these activities the search for identity remains a major
objective. No single instrumentality for achieving this goal, on a mass
basis, clearly stands out exclusively over all others. Yet, in addition to
those mentioned immediately above, there are many which are clearly
constructive toward these ends. Involvements which are only beginning at the time this is written include the drive for Afro-
American studies, the "black is beautiful" theme, and the impetus to
change textbooks (beyond the inclusion of a few pictures of black
children) and curricula. These activities emphasize the connectedness
of racial and ethnic cultures in the history of American society, and of
ethnic communities-at-large. Community participation is being encouraged in these endeavors through the drive for the community-centered
school in which parent-student-teacher linkages in the conduct of
school business are being organized.

All of these activities decry ethnic or racial exclusiveness. At
the same time they provide for cultural diversity. Equalization and
diversification are not necessarily incompatible educational goals. As
Stodolsky and Lesser (1967) indicate in thoughtful conclusions to
their research, "If accelerating the feasible gains in jobs, education,
and housing of lower-class families accelerates the gains in intellectual
development of their children and reduces the difference in intellectual performance between social-class groups, we can all agree on the
desirability of this outcome. On the other hand, if recognizing the particular patterns of intellectual strengths and weaknesses of various
ethnic groups and maximizing the potential power of these patterns by
matching instructional conditions to them makes the intellectual
accomplishments of different ethnic groups more diverse, we can all
accept this gain in pluralism within our society" (p. 586).

The pupil with feelings of inadequacy

The pupil with low self-esteem inversely reflects the attributes of
his high self-esteem counterpart. These pupils are easily discouraged

and sometimes depressed. They feel isolated, unloved and unlovable, and incapable of expressing themselves, of defending their inadequacies. They are so preoccupied with their self-consciousness and anxiety that it all but destroys their capacity for self-fulfillment. Their anxiety may be due to an uncertain evaluation of themselves; to the possibility that, in trying to overcome their feelings of worthlessness, they present a false front to others which must then be defended; to their vulnerability (sensitivity) to criticism; and to their feelings of isolation. Each of these factors according to Rosenberg (1965) is further related to the psychosomatic symptoms (insomnia, headaches, and intestinal disorders) of anxiety.

The pupil with low self-esteem is also vulnerable in his interpersonal relationships. Others are not responsive to him and at the same time he is submissive and unassertive. He tends not to initiate conversations and waits until others approach him first. He is fearful of raising the ire of others and shrinks from attracting their notice probably as a protection from further hurt. He avoids participation in extracurricular activities and is less frequently elected to office than his high self-esteem counterpart. He engages in social interaction with the expectation that he will not be well-received. Accordingly, he listens rather than participates in discussion, sidesteps disagreement, and divorces himself from concern for public affairs.

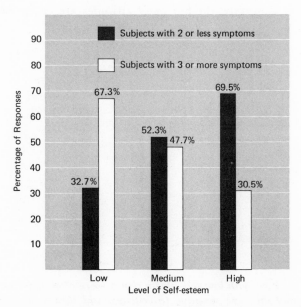

Figure 15-11. Psychosomatic symptoms of anxiety are experienced in greater numbers by adolescents with low self-esteem than by adolescents with high self-esteem. (Based on Rosenberg, 1965, Table 14, Ch. 8, p. 166. With permission.)

An unfortunate consequence of low self-esteem is in the nature of ensuing identifications. Pupils with low self-esteem tend to give lower evaluations of their performances when they learn the model performed poorly on a task, but fail to adjust their self-evaluation when the model's performance was adequate (Stotland & Hilmer, 1962). The person with low self-esteem assimilates information that is consistent with his general self-concept. On the other hand, persons with high self-esteem are more readily influenced by optimistic, gratifying, and potentially self-enhancing communications than by pessimistic, threatening ones (Leventhal & Perloe, 1962, pp. 387–388). This factor may also account for the greater ability of high self-esteem persons to sympathize with others (Stotland & Dunn, 1963).

Self-esteem and social skills

Self-esteem is also related to persuasibility. The pupil with low self-esteem is more conforming, field dependent, and persuasible in his self-evaluations than the pupil with high self-esteem (Hovland & Janis, 1959). Such persons seem to be concerned with others' views and opinions because of implications for themselves. Favorable attitudes toward oneself tend to increase resistance to outside influence and conversely, unfavorable attitudes toward oneself are related to decreased resistance to influence. However, whether one's attitudes are easily changed also

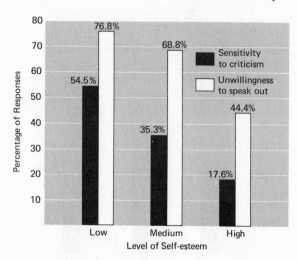

Figure 15-12. Boys with low self-esteem report more often than boys with high self-esteem that they are sensitive to criticism and that in a discussion they would prefer to say nothing than to say something that would arouse the anger of others. (Based on Coopersmith, 1967, Table 3.7, p. 66, and Table 3.8, p. 67. With permission.)

depends on the similarity of the model or communicator to the recipient of the information (Dabbs, 1964). High self-esteem persons tend to accept information from one who, like themselves, is portrayed as active, optimistic, and ambitious. Low self-esteem subjects accept information from a source portrayed as passive, pessimistic, lacking in self-confidence, depressed, and displaying little information, even though he was viewed as a relatively *unattractive* person because of these qualities.

The tendency for individuals to limit the information they accept to that which is consistent with their self-image, was also shown by Silverman (1964). Upon completion of a quiz on current events, the subjects in the experiment were given the correct answers against which to score their tests. The scores were then compared with the "average" of the current college student populations. In actuality these "norms" were contrived to induce conditions of failure and success. The norms given to the "failure group" were set sufficiently high so that most scores could be interpreted as being "below average." Those given to the "success group" were sufficiently low so that all but a few scores in the group would appear to be well "above average." After this treatment the subjects were again administered the same test. (Note that they had an opportunity to learn more about the subject matter when they were given the correct answers for scoring their papers.) The subjects with high self-esteem improved more after the success than after the failure treatment. Conversely, the low self-esteem subjects improved more after failure than after success.

Rosenberg says of the adolescent with low self-esteem, he "manifests that peculiar combination of qualities which is least likely to make him a leader among his peers. ... The individual's self-conception is not only associated with his attitudes toward other people, it is also associated with his actions in social life and with the position he comes to occupy in his high school peer groups" (Rosenberg, 1965, p. 205). He goes on to say, "Hence those social conditions and family experiences . . . which operate to destroy the child's sense of his own worth are at the same time undermining the personality prerequisites of a democratic society" (Rosenberg, 1965, p. 223).

Contributing to the pupil's confidence

Enhancement of self-esteem is clearly related to those aspects of one's experience which contribute to singling the person out as a unique individual of some importance. Approbation, reinforcement, approval, acceptance, consistency, attentiveness, and all of the other signs of success, all administered sincerely, or which occur as a natural consequence of the pupil's behavior, and which occur without unctious over-indulgence, can contribute to one's confidence in his ability and hence to his feeling of worth. On the other hand, when *significant* others (teachers, parents, or peers) continually reject, ignore, isolate, or disapprove of the pupil, either directly or psychologically, these actions, because they are signs of failure, can accomplish little else but lower the pupil's regard for himself.

Such effects can even be demonstrated in experiences of relatively short duration as is the case with many psychological experiments. In a report of his investigations on ingratiation Jones (1964) concludes:

> . . . subjects who present themselves amidst recurrent approval from an attractive peer show at least a temporary increase in generalized self-esteem. [The findings from two experiments] may be interpreted as reflecting the normal human desire to treat approval from others as a signal of basic personal worth, even though the behavior eliciting approval has been colored by such tactical considerations as concealing or minimizing negative self-attributes. The relative ambiguity of one's self-concept, and one's pervasive uncertainty concerning where one stands on most evaluative dimensions, make this kind of retrospective distortion possible. Vanity, the wish to believe the best of oneself, provides direction to the distortion. When one is approved of, one's basic self has been glimpsed and admired. When one receives disapproving feedback, one is reluctant to accept this as evidence about one's true character and one readily entertains other hypotheses. (From Jones, 1964, p. 78. With permission of author and publisher.)

Contributing to the pupil's self-esteem

In a setting where understanding prevails, evaluations are not detrimental to psychological health. Used judiciously and effectively they can promote mental health. Indeed they are necessary to help the pupil meet the realities of life. By these means the pupil becomes aware of his potentialities and learns how they can be applied to greatest advantage. He also becomes aware of his weaknesses and limitations. He learns to accept failure without demoralization and without "giving up." However, if the pupil has low self-esteem he is especially sensitive in situations where possibilities for self-evaluation exist, and to feedback he might obtain about himself in such situations (deCharms & Rosenbaum, 1960; Rosenbaum & deCharms, 1960). Even the person who has momentarily lost self-esteem will have his need for positive feedback aroused but, even so, the person who momentarily fails at an important task responds less favorably to praise than does a person who has succeeded) Deutsch & Solomon, 1959).

Some of the specific areas in which schools may foster unhealthy (unwarranted and unjustifiable) self-evaluations are highlighted by Jersild (1952). He points out that in school the emphasis on some kinds of achievement is greater than merited by the outcomes. In this category are placed such activities as sports, some social organizations like fraternities and sororities, and even an overemphasis on academic accomplishment. The adolescent who fails to be a "star" in these areas may be subjected to a contrived or false evaluation (Coleman, 1961a; 1961b). He may feel that because he does not meet the so-called standards in one area that he is inferior in all respects. These self-deprecating circumstances may be humiliating and provocative of the unwarranted debilitating effects of anxiety (Schumacher, *et al.*, 1968).

Other areas in which pupils may be affected adversely are also suggested by Jersild. The "poor" monthly or quarterly report of the pupil's progress is sometimes used by parents as a tool for further rejection of an already rejected child. Social status differences frequently exert a subtle influence on evaluations made by both teachers and peers. Pupils who are in the upper social classes are graded higher by their teachers than those in the lower social classes even though intellectual ability and performance are the same (Heintz, 1954; Rosenthal & Jacob-

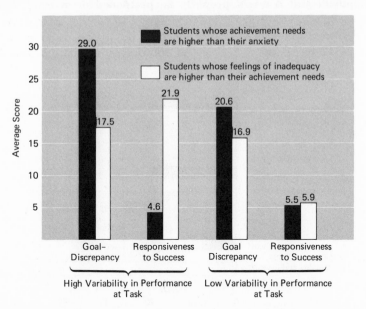

Figure 15-13. When the success of the pupil's performance at a task varies from one occasion to the next, as it often does in typical classroom situations, pupils with debilitating anxiety (feelings of inadequacy and uncertainty) are more responsive to success than pupils with low levels of anxiety. The anxious subject increases his level of aspiration after success experiences (responsiveness to success). However, his goal-discrepancy (average increase in level of aspiration after each trial) is lower than that of the pupil with feelings of self-adequacy. (Based on Feather, 1967, Table 3, p. 44. With permission.)

son, 1968). Test results may be used out of all proportion to their value (especially when tests are poorly constructed) as the final answer to the pupil's adequacy. There are also less tangible contributing factors. Sears (1963), for example, found the somewhat surprising result that teachers prefer the bright pupil with medium or low self-esteem, and the less bright pupil with high self-esteem. Evaluations made on these bases often invite invidious comparisons, resulting in judgments that fall short of helping the child gain a realistic understanding of himself.

In addition to paying some attention to the *areas* in which self evaluations occur, the teacher should also consider the best *time* for contributing to specific phases of the pupil's emotional development. Thompson and Witryol (1952) have shown that pupils who are 6–12 years of age find feelings of guilt and being teased or ridiculed as being among their most unpleasant experiences. During these years the pupil is pressured to conform to adult standards. Feelings of inadequacy are experienced when he does not, or is unable to, meet these demands. Perhaps this phase of socialization is imposed on the child too early in his development and it might properly be postponed or at least initiated more gradually. Other problems were found to emerge as important in the adolescent years. Adults recalled that when they were in the age range of 12 to 18 years, feelings of inferiority, insecurity, and social

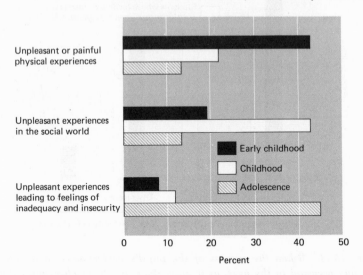

Figure 15-14. Adult recall of unpleasant experiences during three stages of childhood. The specific problems of adjustment are peculiar to each stage of "growing up." (Adapted from G. G. Thompson & S. L. Witryol. Adult recall of unpleasant experiences during three periods of childhood. Journal of Genetic Psychology, *1948, 72, 111–123, Figure 1, p. 118, Figure 2, p. 119, and Figure 3, p. 120. With permission.)*

inadequacy were foremost among their unpleasant experiences. These feelings of inadequacy may be engendered by the unrealistic values and standards conveyed through equally unrealistic models in advertisements and popular media. The prime target of such influences is the adolescent who, as a consequence, feels he must meet these standards or be doomed to social failure. Thompson and Witryol (1948) suggest: "Perhaps parents and teachers ... need to instigate counteractive measures (to advertising, unrealistic generalizations about successful living and the like) to build up the individual's sense of personal worth and to help him set up levels of aspiration in work and social affairs that are commensurate with his abilities and needs."

Creating classroom climates conducive to the development of self-esteem

Within the classroom itself, the pupil's confidence can be enhanced by providing him with increasingly greater demands; demands that are not overwhelming, but which are challenging, and within his capacity to perform successfully. This is particularly important during first experiences with new tasks. If the pupil receives nothing but jeers from his classmates and admonitions for poor grades from his parents and teachers, he will quickly develop a feeling of helplessness, vulnerability, and inadequacy in academic and school tasks. Competence can be increased by self-initiated activities. Early experiences with control of problem situations can lay the foundation for dealing with later troublesome experiences (Held & White, 1965). Helplessness in those with low self-esteem is probably learned in the same way as are control, power, and adequacy by those with high self-esteem.

Through opportunities for expression the pupil is encouraged to test his capacities and abilities without fear of humiliation when failure occurs. Through mastery and success in the exploration of fundamental academic and social skills a tolerance for occasional frustrations and disappointments, which one is bound to encounter, is acquired (Overmier & Seligman, 1967). Some schools dote on harsh methods of control including severe criticism, sarcasm, reprimands, restraint, and failure. Pupils who bear the brunt of these attacks tend to evaluate themselves as inadequate. This is not to imply that the pupil should do as he pleases under all circumstances or that he should never be reprimanded. If we can extrapolate from findings related to child-rearing antecedents of self-esteem, favorable self-judgments are facilitated by structured, demanding (challenging) situations in which rules and limits are clearly and firmly established. Accordingly, what we are saying is that the pupil should not be criticized or subjected to humiliation and failure because he is a convenient target for the projection of the teacher's own inadequacies. The inevitable occurrence of occasional task-oriented difficulties (or failures) make excellent opportunities for helping the pupil to learn how to profit from his errors.

The classroom atmosphere recommended in this chapter is not one of extreme permissiveness. Nor is it one in which the pupil must bow to every dictate of the teacher. It is intended to be one in which the pupil is treated with fairness and justice.

Helping pupils learn the strategies of adjustment

The pupil with low self-esteem can be helped even more directly in self-understanding by identifying the criteria he uses for judging his worth (Schuldt & Truax, 1968). He may be making judgments on his deficient traits while ignoring his superior ones. Or, he may be using two or more incompatible bases for self-evaluation. As Coopersmith (1967) suggests, the recognition and adjustment of incompatibilities between the bases for evaluations or between the bases for judgments of his worth and of his capabilities may afford the pupil with low self-esteem a way of changing the content of conceptualizations about himself.

Finally, Coopersmith (1967) suggests that greater cognizance of the modeling process may be advantageous to teachers willing to help pupils with low self-esteem. Many theories of imitation call attention to the specific responses (e.g., aggression or self-reinforcement) of the model. However, the *strategies* (*styles* or *skills*) employed by the effective model for dealing with anxiety, resolving ambiguities, and for making decisions may be equally important but often ignored. By observation of methods with which the effective person handles insults, meets failure, makes friends, and otherwise gains control and power, the pupil can incorporate effective strategies into his own self-concept. Accordingly, the pupil with low self-esteem who already has difficulty in defining and dealing with his environment is provided with a behavioral alternative that is vastly more efficient (and probably more effective) than learning solely by his own mistakes or by first learning a verbal rule and then waiting an indefinite period of time for an opportunity to see how it is employed.

Summary

An outgrowth of the developmental processes is the self-concept which includes the person's abstractions and evaluations about his phys-

ical abilities, appearance, intellectual capacities, social skills, physiological self-image, self-confidence, self-respect, and self-adequacy. Thus, the
self-concept deals with the self-perceptions of the person. However, it
also can be considered as an inferred process that will affect the pupil's
other behaviors. Accordingly, it can be expected that one's self-
perceptions will, in turn, affect his social interaction, level of aspiration,
psychological health, school achievement, and, indirectly, his popularity
and approval by other people in his environment.

The pupil's self-concept can be measured in an informal way by
observing the pupil's behavior and by inspecting his responses to those
items in personality inventories which are typically employed to obtain
a measure of the person's characteristic traits. There are also inventories
specifically designed to obtain indices of the person's self-evaluation,
self-esteem, self-image, and self-ideal. When administering a direct measure of the self-concept one must be especially aware of the defensive
maneuvers that respondents sometimes employ to gain a measure of
self-enhancement. The pupil with low self-esteem might be tempted to
overrate himself or, conversely, an overly modest pupil might tend to
underevaluate himself in his responses to certain items. These difficulties can be avoided to some extent by administering the inventories in
an impunitive atmosphere that guards the confidential nature of the
pupil's responses and that guarantees the responses will be used to his
advantage.

In addition to the principles of association and reward, the processes of identification and imitation contribute to the acquisition of
one's self-concept. By comparing themselves with various models, the
pupils acquire not only self-attitudes and self-ideals, but they learn
other behaviors related to level of aspiration, prejudices and biases, and
self-criticism. At present a missing ingredient in the American public
school classroom is the absence of appropriate models for children in
the disadvantaged and minority groups; particularly absent are
appropriate models for the black child.

Children select models that possess the qualities of being pres-
tigeful, competent, high in status, and capable of controlling rewarding
resources. Imitation is encouraged if the model is seen as having power.
In the complete developmental process it is unlikely that the pupil imitates only a single model. More probably, his behavior will be modeled
after the configuration of behaviors represented in a composite of real-
life, exemplary, and symbolic models.

A generalized outcome of the self-concept is the pupil's evaluation of his overall ability and worth, that is, his self-esteem. Socioeconomic position of the family, mother's occupation, family size, physical
attractiveness, and athletic prowess were *not* found to be consistently
related to self-esteem. The factors associated with high self-esteem are

those which contribute to one's sense of worth and significance as a person, such as the pupil might derive from emotionally supportive parents. The factors that contribute to low self-esteem are extreme permissiveness and inconsistent punishment which lead to feelings that parents have little interest in the pupil, even perhaps to his feeling rejected.

Pupils with high self-esteem tend to perceive themselves as successful. They are relatively free of anxiety and psychosomatic symptoms. They realistically assess their abilities and are confident that their efforts will meet with success. On the other hand, they are also fully aware of their limitations.

Persons with high self-esteem are outgoing and socially successful with full expectations that they, in turn, will be well received. They accept others and others tend to accept them. Conversely, persons with low self-esteem tend to assimilate information that is consistent with their general self-concept. They tend to be more highly persuasable than are persons with high self-esteem.

Most authorities agree that the school can make major contributions to the pupil's feelings of adequacy and, accordingly, to his psychological health. Schools may foster unhealthy self-evaluations by greater emphasis on some kinds of achievement than is merited by the outcomes; an overemphasis on sports, some social organizations like fraternities and sororities, and even an overemphasis on academic accomplishment can penalize the person who is unable to compete effectively. The poor monthly or quarterly report card showing the pupil's progress is too often used by parents as tools for further rejection of an already rejected child. Sometimes pupils who are in the middle social strata are graded higher by their teachers than those in the lower social strata even though the performance of pupils from the two groups is similar.

Success for the pupil means that demands are not overwhelming, but are challenging and within his capacity to perform successfully. Through mastery of fundamental academic and social skills the pupil will acquire a tolerance for occasional frustrations and disappointments which one is bound to encounter, without seriously deflating his self-esteem. In fact the inevitable occurrence of occasional task-oriented difficulties or failures may provide excellent opportunities for helping the pupil to learn how to profit from his errors.

Social reality and the self-actualizing pupil

Different theories of motivation place correspondingly different valuations on human nature. Contemporary motivational theories based on extrinsic and intrinsic drives typically take the relatively neutral view that the character or potential of the person as an individual is irrelevant to understanding motivational dynamics. On the other hand, Freud (for example, 1938) emphasized conflict and defense mechanisms. His observations of the maladjusted persons with whom he dealt led him to believe that the bases of their problems were in the unconscious, presumably a continual source of difficulty for the person, against which frequent defenses were necessary, using mechanisms that distorted reality. More recently, several psychologists, psychiatrists, and sociologists, among whom are Allport (1960), Horney (1950), Fromm (1955), and Riesman (1950), have espoused theories of self-actualization in which are emphasized the person's potentialities for continued growth and emergence as an integrated being. While these theories recognize that the person does react to pressures, drives, and conflicts they also consider that, above all, man has the potential for growth and self-realization beyond that of sheer reactivity presumed in most traditional theories of drives and conflict.

The Self-actualizing Person: Beyond Self-esteem

According to Maslow (1962, 1967), one of the leading proponents of actualization theory, motives guiding the self-actualized person begin

where self-esteem leaves off. In the growth toward independence, the
D-motives (deficient- or deficiency-need–motivation) of physiological
needs, safety, belongingness, affection, self-esteem, and respect from
others are important motivational forces. But the satisfaction of D-motives requires dependence on others for gratification, as Jones (1964, p.
86) also suggests. With full growth toward maturity, and to the extent
the D-motives are satiated, the person is then motivated by self-actualization, which is at the top of Maslow's hierarchy of needs. The person
then can become self-sufficient with the full capacity for becoming what
he is, of "advancing toward the fulfillment of hopes and plans. . . ."
(Allport, 1961). His dependence on D-motives is replaced by the *B-motives* (being-motives or growth-motives) of trust, loyalty, justice, and the
like, which are characteristic of the self-actualized person. The B-motives
guide him toward the full realization (actualization) of his potentiality,
capacity, and talents (Maslow, 1962, 1967). Growth, whether in one's
hobby, vocation, or other pursuit becomes a rewarding, exciting process
and a sufficient reason for working and performing.

Maslow (1954, 1962, 1967) analyzed the attributes of several
people whom he considered to be self-actualizing. Though the procedures he used were not completely objective, they allowed for the identification of characteristics that, to a degree, are measurable. (See the
following for a summary.)

Attributes of self-actualized persons

Maslow (1954, 1962) has described the self-actualized persons in his
study as having certain attributes (that separate them from persons
motivated by the lesser needs) as follows:

Realistic.   Self-actualized people have a clearer and more
efficient perception of reality than other people. The accuracy of their
perceptions extends to art, music, science, politics, public affairs, and
all intellectual matters resulting in superior cognitive capacity and
problem-solving ability.

Acceptant.   They accept the inevitable strengths and weaknesses of themselves, others, and nature without complaint and as natural events. They may have guilt feelings but these are related to their
own improvable shortcomings such as laziness or a stubborn, lingering
prejudice.

Spontaneous.   Their behavior is spontaneous, expressive,
fully functioning, and alive. Their guide for conduct is based on fundamentally accepted principles rather than on convention. Unconven-
tionality is principally a matter of a way of thinking rather than of
rebellion against authority. Thus, they are relatively independent of
their physical and social environment.

Problem-centered.   Self-actualization is a way of life open to experience and oriented around tasks to be accomplished, a mission to be achieved. The means are secondary to the ends. Their problems are the problems of the larger society rather than the ego-centered concerns of the less mature person. They identify strongly and compassionately with the human race even though they may be disturbed by some of its members.

Objective.   They are objective. The strength of their convictions enables them to retain a detached, objective composure in trying or difficult circumstances. They are not bothered by solitude and may even seek privacy unlike the person who is not self-actualized and who depends on the presence of others for the satisfaction of his needs.

Autonomous.   They experience more frequently than others "the greatest attainment of an identity, autonomy, or selfhood. . . ." (Maslow, 1962, p. 99) in which they feel the peak of their powers through intensified experiences of problem-centering or concentration.

Affectionate.   They have especially strong and deep emotional ties with relatively few people. Others demand much of the self-actualized person. Though they are sometimes hostile to others they seldom show it. Moreover, their hostility is situational rather than characteristic of their personality and is directed primarily at the hypercritical, pretentious, pompous, or self-inflated person.

Democratic.   In a sense the self-actualized person exhibits a humility, in relating to others, by his recognition that much is to be learned from everyone regardless of occupation, birth, family, power, and the like. However, they do not equalize all persons indiscriminately, since the selection of their own friends is based on the attributes of character, capacity, and talent.

Creative.   Initially Maslow (1954) limited creativity to the source of discovery and of novelty which is fundamental to artistic and scientific endeavors. More recently (1962), however, he separated productive creativity, conventionally defined, by the work of any painter, scientist, inventor, poet, or composer, from self-actualizing creativity, which is prerequisite to the former and, if absent, inhibits the full development of the potential of the "special talent creativity." Self-actualizing creativity is a tendency to do *anything* creatively and need not require special talents. It includes everything whether it is setting a table, constructing a business organization, or teaching, as long as it is first an outgrowth or expression of the personality and only secondarily stresses the achievement. It is characterized by "qualities like boldness, courage, freedom, spontaneity, perspicuity, integration, self-acceptance . . ." (Maslow, 1962, p. 136) and the other characteristics of the self-actualizing person.

As Allport notes (1960, p. 282) these characteristics are not the ones typically given by psychiatrists. The psychiatrist, when asked for a definition of the psychologically healthy person, is likely to emphasize the opposite attributes of the not-so-sound personality he treats. Thus, he is apt to describe the healthy person as optimistic, cheerful, able to enjoy work and play, able to control his emotions, and as socially responsible. However, everyone encounters conflict and guilt as a part of life. Adequate psychological health means to accept and handle these and other adjustments with "self-control, personal responsibility, social responsibility, democratic social interest, and ideals" (Allport, 1961, p. 282). In addition to these attributes the self-actualization theorists also emphasize "the serious side of maturity, and include the achievement of meaning and responsibility, as well as acceptance and the 'courage to be...'" (Allport, 1961, p. 282).

The reader should not leave this section with the impression that the self-actualized persons studied by Maslow are without imperfections. He observed that, as with all human beings, self-actualized persons are subject to the lesser weaknesses of mankind. They have habits which are wasteful, silly, or unproductive. They have their moments of unjustified temper and stubbornness. On occasion they can be downright boring. Sometimes their strength of character enables them to make and implement difficult decisions in an objective manner giving them the appearance of being ruthless and "surgically cold." Often their detachment immerses them in periods of intense concentration that causes them to appear absent-minded and humorless. And, as we have indicated in our summary, they, too, are not without guilt, self-castigation, anxiety,

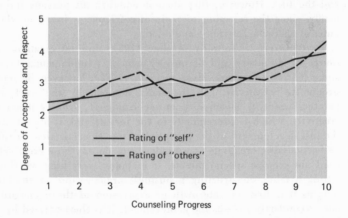

Figure 16-1. As the individual proceeds through counseling his self-acceptance increases. Note the corresponding increase in his acceptance of others. (Adapted from E. T. Sheerer. An analysis of the relationship between acceptance of and respect for self and acceptance of and respect for others in ten counseling cases. Journal of Consulting and Clinical Psychology, 1949, 13, *Figure 1, p. 174. With permission.)*

strife, or conflict though such maladjustment "arises out of nonneurotic sources ..." (Maslow, 1954, p. 229).

We would be remiss in our responsibility if we failed to caution the reader that while theories in the self-actualization, phenomenological, and existential modes are provocative and intriguing in many of their conceptualizations, nonetheless they have led to voluminous writings but to few empirical demonstrations of their claims. A major difficulty is their failure to provide much more than descriptive accounts of their viewpoints in relatively vague terms. A precise explication of basic premises and of relationships to other aspects of behavior appears to be necessary.

The Self-concept and Social Reality

In all societies the individual's environment includes psychologically important cultural factors, norms, and standards. These are the social conditions that function as general guides for each person's behavior. Although there are major differences among societies the regulations, the idiosyncratic standards, the values, the morals, and the laws of each exist as cultural demands.

The differences in social reality for boys and girls in various cultures are well documented in social anthropology. By way of illustration, we briefly describe a simple demand in each of three primitive cultures (Erikson, 1963). In Kwoma, the child learns a respect for food "poisoned" by sorcerers. The Sioux learns what to us would be a distorted concept of "generosity." (Their ideal of generosity means an unlimited sharing of one's goods with others—even to the extent of what in our society is stealing.) The Yurok, on the other hand, learns to be angry, "stingy," and suspicious.

Facing reality in these tribes means knowing the values of the culture to which one belongs and living in accordance with them. In Kwoma, reality consists of following the rules about eating—that is, you would not eat food which came from another tribe, for it might carry the curse of the sorcerer hired by your enemy. The Sioux, because he believes in an unusual concept of generosity, might be accused of stealing by the standards of our society. The Yurok is a most restrained person! He eats in complete silence so that he can think of fishing and of ways "to make money." His restraint gives him the appearance of being unsocial, if not antisocial.

By our standards none of these behaviors would be considered acceptable or desirable. The Kwoma, Sioux, or Yurok might be described by some as odd, defiant, or deviant. For that matter, it is conceivable that some behavior of the typical Black, Puerto Rican, barrio Mexican-American, reservation-bound American Indian, or person in any other minority group might also be taken to be as unacceptable or as undesirable as the behavior of people in the more distant, exotic cultures. What is needed here more than anywhere else is anthropological information of equal quality and objectivity on many of the subcultures in our own communities. The persons in all of these groups are facing the social realities of their particular cultures. One behaves in accordance with cultural demands in order to satisfy his social needs. When he strays outside the defined social restrictions, he may be ostracized in such informal ways as exclusion from his peer groups.

The pupil in the United States lives in a dynamic society. His social interactions are in a continuous state of change around a more or less stable fulcrum of cultural values. To maintain satisfying social relations he finds that he must share the beliefs of the majority of the group (as is the case in every society). His social contacts permit him to judge when his attitudes are "different" or "incorrect" (Festinger, Schachter, & Back, 1950). Sometimes pupils introject the myriads of cultural value patterns (e.g., disobedience is bad; making money is good; cooperation is better than working alone, and so on) as their own without ever considering their source or, indeed, their validity (Rogers, 1964). Fortunately, *individual* appraisals of various kinds do occur and are permitted for it is recognized, in most democratic societies at least, that society is made by its members and, accordingly, can be changed by them. The pupil's task is one of learning to stay close enough to social realities so as to remain effective while at the same time he retains his individuality.

Social reality

There are two major dimensions in the pupil's learning to face social reality. The first is a highly personal one involving the pupil's own experiences and perceptions. No two people identically share an experience since each extracts different elements or meanings from the experience. Accordingly, each individual's expectations about the outcomes of his behavior will be somewhat different.

The second dimension of social reality relates to the broad values of the culture. These affect the pupil's behavior in all social settings whether in interaction with his peers or with representatives of societal institutions. Each situation has its own demands for specific kinds of behavior since socially commendable behavior in one is not necessarily appropriate for all social situations.

Mannheim (1966), for example, obtained a number of different descriptions persons had of themselves. Among these descriptions were scores of the subject's *self-image* (how do you ordinarily think of yourself?); of his *reference-group self* (how do people in the main group with which you affiliate see you?); and of his *membership-group self* (how do people in your dormitory see you?). These indices yielded the finding that reference groups were important factors in the development of the self-image. Thus, an unstable reference-group self was related to an unstable self-image and over time the self-image corresponded to an increasingly greater degree with the reference-group self.

The self-fulfilling prophecy

In a recent series of investigations Rosenthal and Jacobson (1968, p. 174) applied the idea that "one person's expectation of another could become a self-fulfilling prophecy" to teaching of disadvantaged children in the elementary school. Thus, they speculated that how a child was treated might affect his performance on measures of intelligence. Briefly, the procedure in their investigation was as follows: All children in the school were tested at the beginning of the school year on a standard intelligence test represented to the teachers as a special measure for predicting spurts in intellectual growth. Following the testing session, each of eighteen teachers in Grades 1 through 6 was given the names of "special" children who were expected to show dramatic increases in academic ability during the year. However, the children were actually selected by reference to a table of random digits and not by test scores so the difference between the "special" children and the remainder of the class existed ". . . only in the mind of the teacher." The children were retested at the end of the semester and once again when they were in the next grade.

The reported results of the study were as follows: The "special" children in the experimental groups had a distinct expectancy advantage which was reflected in their gains in IQ points. The gains were especially great among the first- and second-grade children. Nevertheless, the follow-up testing a year later revealed that the younger children who were the most easily influenced lost their advantage after they were separated from their original teacher while the other children "showed an increasing expectancy advantage." Only in reading was a report-card advantage reflected. Finally, the children in the medium track benefited more in both IQ and reading score gains from the teacher's favorable expectations than did children in the "fast" or "slow" tracks. (The "track" was an administrative device which grouped children according to their reading ability.)

The exact nature of the mechanism accounting for these changes is a matter of speculation for the present. As Rosenthal and Jacobson (1968) indicate nothing was done directly to or for the disadvantaged child. Only the teacher was influenced to believe that there was something in the performance of the child that bore watching. As a consequence she may have done a number of things: she may have been more friendly or more encouraging thereby increasing the motivation of the "special" children; she may have watched them more closely thereby permitting her to administer feedback and correction more immediately and more frequently after a child's responses; or she may have been more reflective in her evaluation of the pupil's performance thereby providing cues upon which the pupil could model a change in strategy for performing on the intelligence test. That teacher expectation can result in improved performance of the disadvantaged (and advantaged) pupil has been demonstrated. The explanation of this effect must await further research. Rosenthal and Jacobson conclude:

As teacher training institutions begin to teach the possibility that teacher's expectations of their pupil's performance may serve as self-fulfilling prophecies there may be a new expectancy created. The new expectancy may be that children can learn more than had been believed possible, an expectation held by many educational theorists though for different reasons. The new expectancy, at the very least, will make it more difficult when they encounter the disadvantaged for teachers to think, "Well, after all, what can you expect?" The man on the street may be permitted his opinions and prophecies of the unkempt children loitering in a dreary schoolyard. The teacher in the schoolroom may need to learn that those same prophecies within her may be fulfilled; she is no casual passer-by. Perhaps Pygmalion in the classroom is more her role. (From Rosenthal & Jacobson, 1968, pp. 181–182. With permission of author and publisher.)

Some cautions regarding the importance of the effect must now be observed. We wish to note that the study is clever in its conception, rationale, and design. Furthermore, the kind of results reported appear to have both theoretical and pragmatic usefulness. But, unfortunately, the study appears to have some serious methodological flaws, one of which is the inappropriateness of the level of the pretest for the first- and second-grade children. One critic (Thorndike, 1968) said, "The general reasonableness of the 'self-fulfilling prophecy effect' is not at issue, nor is the reported background of previous anecdote, observation, and research (p. 708) . . . [it is] the basic data upon which this structure has been raised [that] are so [lacking] that any conclusions based upon them must be suspect" (p. 711). The reader may find other criticism in Snow (1969) and in Barber and Silver (1968) with replies by Rosenthal (1968, 1969) and Thorndike (1969).

The conclusions and criticisms are briefly presented here to indicate how necessary it is to examine data carefully. Where studies are as appealing and where the conclusions are as well-intentioned and as attractively drawn as they are in research on the "self-fulfilling prophecy effect" objective examination is difficult. Nevertheless, it must be done before such data are used for making major innovations in educational practice.

Pupils who perceive social realities accurately are also those characterized by feelings of adequacy. They act accordingly and are commonly described as "socially sensitive" or "tactful." They sense the moods and unwritten codes of the groups to which they belong, and adapt effectively to them with a delicate sensitivity. They pick up subtle social clues which enable them to understand and appreciate the behavior tendencies of others (Mussen & Porter, 1959). At the other extreme is the socially "blind" pupil. He constantly provokes others by his actions and by his apparent insensitivity to their feelings or neglect of the group code. They are unskilled in inferring how others may feel toward them and are bewildered when it comes to predicting the reactions of others. They cannot seem to size up what makes one popular or unpopular in a group, or to recognize the limits of acceptable behavior. The following report by Redl and Wineman (1957, p. 125) describes an incident in the life of a young socially inept child who was undergoing psychological treatment:

On the afternoon that he was scheduled to go with me to have his haircut, Larry was in a transport of joy. He was going around gaily chanting and bragging, "My haircut, my haircut, Emmy's goin' to take me for a haircut." This incensed the group against him and caused a flurry of attacks on him by the others. Joe punished him viciously, calling him "baby" [and other names] and had to be pulled off him by the counselor. As usual, the sibling hatred of the group was stirred up into open rage by his injudicious bragging. He has been in the same situation innumerable times. So far we have been unable to make him aware of what he was letting himself in for. (From Redl & Wineman, 1957, p. 125. With permission of author and publisher.)

Here was a child who had not learned the habits and customs of his playmates. Severe cases of social maladjustment usually require long periods of training and therapy for overcoming their inadequacies and should be referred to qualified personnel. The pupil with minor difficulties in facing social reality can be helped by the classroom teacher. He can be taught to see the consequences of what he is doing by observing his peers and drawing inferences as a "bystander." He can learn to take success in stride without making himself intolerable by excessive bragging. He can learn to regard failure as a stepping-off point instead of a demonstration of his inadequacy.

Distortions of social reality can be corrected

Reality distortions in the form of the defense mechanisms are directed at the reduction of anxiety and its betrayal rather than at the removal of the original causes of the problem. Prejudice and displacement also represent departures from social reality.

Evidence that such defense mechanisms are learned was provided in a classic experiment by Miller (1948). Pairs of rats were trained to attack one another as soon as electric shock was applied to the grid on which they were standing. When the animals were striking vigorously, the shock was turned off. This served as a reinforcement of the striking activity. When one of the two animals was replaced by a celluloid doll, the remaining animal then struck at the doll. (See Figure 16-2).

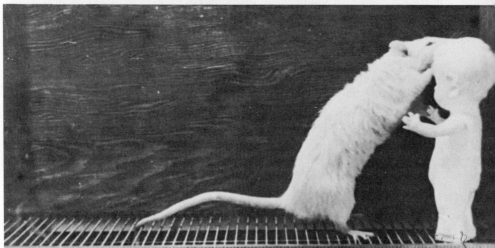

Figure 16-2. Striking displaced from other rat to doll. When two rats were placed in an apparatus with an electric grid along with the doll, they struck at each other as soon as the electric shock was turned on. When they were placed on the apparatus one at a time, they struck at the doll. (From N. E. Miller. Theory and experiment relating to psychoanalytic displacement to stimulus-response generalization. Journal of Abnormal and Social Psychology, 1948, 43, Figure 2, p. 157. With permission.)

The "hostility" of the animal toward the doll is an example of the defense mechanism of displacement, and contains elements of the process of stimulus generalization. The doll, similar in size, shape, and color to that of the target animal, was the most convenient object for attack in its absence. In everyday situations, too, displacement replaces rational attempts to solve a problem. If one dislikes a neighbor, the neighbor's dog might be mistreated. If a child is angry at his friend's mother for not permitting the friend to play with him, he may aggressively tease his young sister.

Fortunately, most of the training that pupils receive in our culture is against the use of displacement or other defense mechanisms. Youths are trained to consider details. Rewards are obtained for making accurate judgments. Reports must correspond to those of others. Even the very young child is told that there is a difference between his fantasies and reality and that he cannot solve problems by "sitting and dreaming." These experiences protect the pupil in the long run from fantasy, delusion, and hallucinations. Training in being fair, in not blaming others for something which is one's own fault, tends to protect the individual from the dead-ends of rationalization, projection, and displacement.*

When left to informal controls such training is often imperfect. If consistent reality distortions are observed, the skillful teacher guides the pupil to a point where he can refocus one or more of his key perceptions of social reality. Dollard and Miller (1950) illustrate the details of this process with the story of an adolescent boy who teased his sister because his friend was denied permission to go on a camping trip. The boy could first be shown the reason for his behavior. He could be shown that when his goals were blocked, he was aroused to anger; that the more he thought about it, the more angry he became; that he gave in to a primitive impulse to take his anger out on a convenient nearby object, in this instance his sister. The boy could then be shown that restraint was required and that it was not fair to punish his sister who, in reality, had nothing to do with his problem.

Leaving the boy at this point may help to teach him restraint but still fail to solve his original problem. Thus, he might then be brought to see that there are alternative solutions. First, there may be other boys with whom he could go camping. Secondly, there might be equally attractive alternative or substitute activities. Perhaps he could get his stamp collection in order, or complete his chores today so that he could play softball tomorrow. Thus, the pupil is not just restrained from

*The illustrations and discussion in this section are drawn from J. Dollard & N. E. Miller. *Personality and psychotherapy.* New York: McGraw-Hill Book Co., 1950. With permission of author and publisher.

giving vent to his feelings because he fears the reactions of others, but is helped to understand his feelings and how to handle them.

When pupils understand their motives and goals, they are in a better position to cope with anxiety. They can and must learn to postpone immediate satisfactions, to tolerate frustration and to alter their goals, but the process of promoting these behaviors is a slow one. The teacher must proceed patiently and cautiously with unobtrusive guidance rather than direct instruction.

Distortion of social reality in delinquency

Relationships (not necessarily causal) have been found between delinquency and adverse conditions existing in slum areas; unfortunate family conditions including rejection by parents, sibling rivalry, and the like; and inherited characteristics including physical anomalies, extreme body types, or poor health. In view of these many factors it is never possible to isolate a single cause for a given "type" of delinquency. However, it is helpful to recognize that the "kinds" of delinquents do parallel to some extent different ways of relating to society (Sanford, 1966).

The psychopathic delinquent appears to have stopped growing at an immature stage of personality and character development (Kvaraceus, 1954). Such individuals fail to foresee the consequences of their behavior, which may include violence toward others. Though they know that their actions will injure others they appear to strive toward the unhealthy goal of self-satisfaction at the expense of others, in defiance of societal values. They appear unable, even unwilling, to comprehend social reality and lack the capacity to maintain satisfactory and mutually profitable relationships with others.

A more common kind of delinquent behavior, reflecting distorted social realities, manifests itself in the pupil's relationships with authority figures (Glueck, 1966; Glueck & Glueck, 1959). Normally a pupil recognizes that he must be protected by the family, school, and church during the period when he is unable to take care of himself. He realizes that as he matures he can become increasingly less dependent upon those older and stronger than he, that is, he develops an identity. Yet in the process of growing up some boys (and girls) suffer severe frustrations from oppressive authoritarianism, the deprivations of poverty-stricken homes, the inability to achieve satisfactions in the face of demands by peers and adults, and the failure to win love and approval from parents. Some may submit to bad treatment with a sense of crushing wretchedness. Others react by regarding society (authority) as their natural enemy. Delinquency provides the means by which a kind of status can be achieved and a retaliatory outlet against a society which makes him feel inferior, miserable, and resentful (Cohen, 1955). Jean, as described by Young (1954) was just this kind of a person:

> She was 15 years old and the court designated her a delinquent. Young as she was she had defied adults and their rules. She had gone her own way, angry and violent, running away from home, spending her nights at dubious clubs and dance halls, stealing now and then, recklessly inviting trouble from strange men who saw in her youth and defiance an invitation and an opportunity for exploitation.
>
> Attitudes toward the authority of parents, teachers, men, and so on are important for the development and establishment of the individual's place in society. To pupils like Jean, authority is not recognized as something which will be replaced later as one's own capacities and abilities mature and after supervision is no longer required for their protection. Rather it is viewed as an interference with their enjoyment, as a frustrating impediment to life as they want to live it. (From Young, 1954, p. 62. With permission.)

Following aggressive episodes that bring partial relief from tension there may be an opportunity for wise teachers to help the pupil reappraise his position, to guide him toward more appropriate goals (Sontag, 1955). Such exhibitions of hostile behavior in boys and girls can be prevented or treated by a considerate, kind, and trusted person with whom they can identify. Adolescent boys are especially vulnerable to engaging in deviant behavior because of the frustrations encountered in developing an identity associated with their sex role. The adolescent girl is in a more advantageous position since her role as wife and mother is relatively well structured, is labeled as important by the society, and requires limited technical training (Mussen, Conger, & Kagan, 1963, p. 582).

Prejudices feed on distortions of social reality

Prejudices, too, are sometimes anchored in the social reality of the principal group of which the pupil is a member (Festinger, *et al.*, 1950).

[The attitudes of a significant number of people in one's primary social group can be important motivators for attaining a dominant prejudice as illustrated by] the white youngster who, in rural Mississippi, may begin life on very favorable terms with his Negro playmates. Still, as he matures, his adjustment to and acceptance by the white community depend in some measure upon the extent to which he has come to share the prevalent anti-Negro biases. If he rejected these biases, he might be vulnerable to social ostracism and even more severe manifestations of disapproval. (From Sarnoff & Katz, 1954, p. 117. With permission).

More familiar as prejudices are the attitudes of intolerance associated with feelings of hostility and aggression, sometimes bearing the marks of maliciousness (Frenkel-Brunswik, 1954). These are the attitudes possessed by pupils who may be living under conditions similar to those described under the etiology of delinquency—i.e., economic or social frustration. The feelings of insecurity arising under these circumstances may be experienced, for example, by some families who are seeking success (social prominence, rapid promotions, material possessions) but who may not find the road upward as smooth as they would like it to be. Such families may seek out other groups as targets for the aggression generated by their frustrations. They may describe other groups as inferior—"*they* are dirty, stupid, and crude," and as threatening—"*they* are trying to run this town" or "*they* are to blame for my not being promoted." Such attitudes will be immediately recognized as gross distortions of social reality. The group on which the blame is placed is frequently weaker than the individuals who feel threatened!

Prejudices of this nature involve an either-or, all-or-none type of perception. When reinforced sufficiently, they produce more and more distortion. A single characteristic stands out and is attributed to each and every member of the group as well as to other groups with similar characteristics. These distortions are difficult to change because of the individual's many defenses. If the prejudiced pupil visits the community where the out-group lives, he may tend to notice only its unfavorable or "different" characteristics. He may notice an unpainted house, a neglected lawn, or a person with distinctively different features. Typical comments may follow, "Just as I thought, they can't take care of their things!" and "See, they all look alike—strange and foreign!" When he hears bits of favorable evidence about the group he may develop a negative attitude and appear not to hear the favorable arguments or he may label the evidence as indications of deception. He might say, "They never do anything worthwhile intentionally. If they did something for others it was purely by accident and they are getting all the credit for it." or "They must have done it for some (suspicious) reason. They must be trying to get something or they must be trying to hide something." All of these are forms of distortions, which maintain a prevailing unfavorable attitude. They are the distortions on which prejudices feed (Adorno, 1950).

Helping pupils learn tolerance

Pupils can learn to be tolerant (Allport, 1955). They can be helped to understand the nature of group differences, that all individuals within a group are not alike. They can be helped to see the rich values and the broader meanings of race by experience with customs of people with varying ethnic backgrounds. Children within the classroom provide an excellent source of information and understanding. These experiences may be coupled with participation in the activities of these cultures—exhibits, festivities, and religion—to provide deeper understanding. On the basis of these experiences, children can be given the opportunities to talk about their experiences. They can be guided toward precise meanings rather than fallacious stereotypes, labels, and overgeneralizations by objective summaries of their experiences. (See, for example, Silberman, 1969.)

Pupils may also be helped to understand the causes of prejudices. Even the young pupil can be helped to understand the scapegoating mechanism as a form of displacement or projection of one's own inadequacies. Most pupils can understand that a trait attributed to an ethnic group may frequently be the expression of prejudice seeking a victim. They may be brought to understand that the uncertainty, the insecurity under which some minority groups live may give rise to tensions and defensiveness which lead to undesirable behavior.

Gordon W. Allport points out:

[This] is a delicate lesson to teach. The danger lies in creating a stereotype to the effect that *all* Jews are ambitious and aggressive in order to compensate for their handicaps; or that *all* Negroes are inclined to sullen hate or petty thievery. The lesson can, however, be taught without primary reference to minority groups. It is essentially a lesson in mental hygiene. Through fiction, to start with, a youngster may learn of the compensations a handicapped (perhaps crippled) child develops. He may go from that point to a discussion of hypothetical cases in class. Through role-playing he may gain insight into the operation of ego defenses. By the age of fourteen the adolescent may be led to see that his own insecurity is due to his lack of firm ground: he is sometimes expected to act like a child, sometimes like an adult. He wants to be an adult, but the conduct of others makes him unsure of whether he belongs to the world of childhood or of adulthood. The teacher may point out that the predicament of the adolescent resembles the permanent uncertainty under which many minority groups have to live. Like adolescents, they sometimes show restlessness, tension, ego defensiveness, which occasionally lead to objectionable behavior. It is far better for the young person to learn the grounds for ego-defensive behavior than for him to be left with the idea that objectionable traits are inherent in certain groups of mankind. (From Allport, 1954, pp. 512–513. With permission.)

The "Causal" Approach to Self-understanding

Insight into the dynamics of one's own behavior and into the causes of one's behaving in an undesirable way are essential conditions for attaining mental health (Calvin & Holtzman, 1953; Rogers, 1967). Even though the pupil is encouraged to give up whatever he is doing that shows he is maladjusted, he will change his behavior only if he recognizes that the behavior is not in his best interest. He cannot arrive at this realization until he is able to perceive himself and others in a more objective light. When this reorientation has been accomplished, the psychotherapist would say the pupil has attained insight. Once low esteem has been established the difficulties to be surmounted in effecting a change are enormous because there is strong resistance to this change (Rosenberg, 1965). Accordingly, one of the aims of the school should be to prevent poor psychological health by fostering insight *before* maladjustive behavior patterns have developed. This viewpoint places the responsibility for mental health on both parents and teachers from the kindergarten through the high school years (Levitt & Ojemann, 1953).

Levitt and Ojemann (1953, pp. 394–399) propose that self-understanding may be promoted through a "causal" orientation in

Figure 16-3.   Helping pupils overcome their fears. The other pupils accept Don's fear of turtles with understanding. When he does approach the turtle, they provide him with support rather than jeers. (By permission from The teacher and the child, by C. E. Moustakas. Copyright 1956. Used with permission of McGraw-Hill Book Co., Inc.)

which several steps are suggested: The pupil first learns that behavior is complex and caused by the existence of a number of factors interacting in complex ways. Secondly, the pupil must be able to recognize that there may be several alternative explanations for his behavior and that of others. For example, the same desire for prestige may result in quite different behaviors in different pupils. One may go out for the presidency of his class, while another may turn to delinquency for attaining prestige in his peer group. Conversely, different motivations may lie behind the same behavior. Four children arriving late for school, for example, may have been motivated in quite different ways, one by family problems, another by his need for companionship, a third for fear of school, and a fourth because he overslept as a result of fatigue. The pupil must also be encouraged to perceive this behavior from the viewpoint of the other person. In his interaction with other people he must realize that *his* behavior will have an effect on what others do. This view has been a major crosscurrent throughout this chapter. Recognize, for example, the effect that the teacher's actions or the parents' attitudes have on the pupil's feelings of adequacy. The pupil must also learn to suspend judgment of another person until he has sufficient information for this judgment.

First steps must be mastered before later ones can be taken. The individual must be able to adapt readily to changing situations and changes in his self-understanding as they occur. He must be able to avoid making black-and-white decisions about others and to accept them with their good and bad points. He must be able to maintain affectionate and permissive interpersonal relationships. And during this process there must continually be self-acceptance.

Pupils taught by teachers with a pupil-centered orientation have been found to be less authoritarian, more responsible, and less self-blaming than pupils taught by the class-centered approach (Levitt, 1955; Ojemann, *et al.*, 1955). The teachers who understand the causes of behavior (their own as well as that of their students) will contribute most to the mental health of their pupils since they convey what they know by their manner of talking with the pupil and by the information about human relations that they provide.

The school and pupil achievement

Pettigrew (1967, p. 282–283; 1968) has summarized many conclusions from the Coleman Report (Coleman, *et al.*, 1966). The report, though subject to criticism on several counts from some quarters (e.g., Levin, 1968), is still a landmark contribution as Pettigrew (1968, p. 76) indicates. Thus, this summary is worth bringing to the attention of the teacher who would understand some of the factors that must be considered for effective teaching in today's schools.

1. *Socioeconomic status of the pupil's family* is a correlate of the pupil's achievement. The correlation is higher in the primary grades and for white children than it is in the later grades or for Negro children.

2. Academic achievement test scores are correlated with an index based on the socioeconomic status of all the families of pupils in the school (social class climate). This correlation is higher for Negro pupils than it is for white pupils and higher for pupils in the upper grades than it is for pupils in the lower grades.

3. In the upper grades and for Negro pupils *teacher quality* is a third important correlate of achievement scores. Beyond this, such school facilities as teacher-pupil ratio, laboratories, curriculum, school size and the like are unimportant when the effect of other factors is removed. This finding is probably due to the fact that the diversity among schools in these factors is insufficient to make a real difference in view of other compensatory factors such as remedial programs, willingness of teachers to help the pupil, quality of teachers, and so on.

4. Negro children in classrooms where the majority of children are white perform better on achievement tests than do other Negro children. The effects of early *interracial schooling* is particularly pronounced.

5. *Variation* (standard deviation) *in performance* on academic tests is greater for Negro children in white schools than it is for those in schools where there is less than a majority of white children. A similar finding, in quite a different context, was reported by Jensen (1968) and Rapier (1968) who conclude that the poor performance of culturally disadvantaged children is attributable to a greater variety of correlates (e.g., lack of opportunity, ineffective teaching, inadequate stimulation, and so on) beyond that of mere differences in intellectual ability. The performance of children in the lower socioeconomic groups does not differ from that of children in the middle socioeconomic groups on serial learning tasks where chaining is the important process. However, where verbal processes are important (in paired-associate learning) the performance of disadvantaged children is poorer and more variable than the performance of pupils from the middle socioeconomic groups.

6. White pupils in school with Negro children are least likely to reply that they prefer to be in all-white classrooms or prefer only white children as close friends.

7. *Self-attitudes* are strong correlates of academic test performance for all pupils, though different items are correlates for white than for Negro children. Thus, the self-concept item—"How bright do you think you are in comparison with the other students in your grade," is a significant correlate of the white pupil's achievement. On the other hand, an item related to control of one's fate by the environment or by fate was a more important correlate of the Negro pupil's achievement.

Negro pupils who *disagreed* with items such as "good luck is more important than hard work for success" made higher scores than did those who agreed with the items. Internal control, that is the locus of control of environment and of one's own fate residing in oneself, was higher for Negroes in desegregated schools. Pettigrew (1967), with Coleman *et al.* (1966) speculates that the Negro pupil first must learn that he can do something about his surroundings, and secondly he must "evaluate relative capabilities for mastering the environment ..." (Pettigrew, 1967, p. 283).

As Coleman speculates:

Having experienced an unresponsive environment, the virtues of hard work, or diligent and extended effort toward achievement appear to such a [minority] child unlikely to be rewarding. As a consequence, he is likely to merely "adjust" to his environment, finding satisfaction in passive pursuits. It may well be, then, that one of the keys toward success for minorities which have experienced disadvantage and a particularly unresponsive environment —either in the home or the larger society—is a change in this conception (Coleman *et al.*, 1966, p. 321. In Pettigrew, 1967, p. 284).

Coleman's report seemed to argue that schools in a democratic society should bring white and black (as well as other ethnic and minority group) pupils to equal levels of achievement; however, pupils in various subgroups are not equally able in academic achievement when they finish high schools; therefore the schools are unequal and ways should be sought to reduce such inequality. Stodolsky and Lesser (1967), on the other hand, believe that Coleman's argument may not have been carried far enough, especially in view of the evidence from their research (see Chapters 15 and 19). They indicate, "... If lower class children now perform intellectually more poorly than middle class children—and it is clear that they do—and lower class status can be diluted or removed by a society clearly dedicated to doing so, this gain seems to be one legitimate aim of education. If the maximum educational promotion of particular patterns of ability accentuates the diverse contributions of different ethnic groups, this gain in pluralism seems another legitimate aim of education" (p. 586). "We raise the issue because we are committed to our program of school-based research; whether ethnic-group differences are in fact minimized, held constant, or inflated by the programs which match individual differences to instructional strategies, we believe it is important to pursue these programs nonetheless" (p. 587).

The Teacher Understands His Own Behavior

The antecedents of the emotional and disciplinary problems are often related to the self-concept. We have already described those pupils with a lack of self-esteem. There are also those with a ready temper who burst into fits of anger at a moment's notice. Some seek to deny their own weaknesses by blaming others. Others are frightened, unwilling to take a reasonable chance, and worry about what "others" may think. Still others betray their anxieties by inability to learn, impertinence, inattentiveness, and restlessness.

One aspect of understanding the social reality facing these pupils is that of understanding one's own behavior in relation to others (Jersild, 1955). The teacher must be able to face his own anger, fears, anxieties, strengths, and weaknesses if he is to understand similar reactions in his pupils. He can comprehend the boy or girl's hostility when he recognizes the forces of his own anger. He can better understand the devices for self-deception when he recognizes how he uses them himself. Self-understanding is not always an easy process and even with the help of others, it may be a painful if not nearly impossible task. It is always a gradual process which is never complete because the self-concept is always in a state of change.

If the person genuinely wishes to determine what others think of him toward the management of an attractive impression in the eyes of others, wish—he would have a difficult time finding out. The same motives that push him toward the management of an attractive impression in the eyes of others, push the others toward seeking attraction in his eyes. Since one of the first rules of being attractive is to be supportive and agreeable, the person is not likely to see himself and his worth, clearly reflected in the communications presented to him by others (Jones, 1964, pp. 18–19).

With insight into his own behavior the teacher is in a relatively favorable position to accept the maladjusted pupil. He will recognize without effort that the admonitions of "Snap out of it!", "You ought to know better!", "Aren't you ashamed!" are just as ineffective as any lecturing that is supposed to have a remedial purpose (Staines, 1958).

As shown by deGroat and Thompson (1952) different amounts of approval and disapproval by the teacher have a marked influence on the pupil's adjustment. Boys and girls who received the combination of a high amount of approval with only small or moderate degrees of disapproval exhibited better self-adjustment than groups who received large amounts of disapproval and only little or moderate approval. The child's evaluation of himself and his self-confidence are influenced by the degree of teacher approval or disapproval that he receives. Teachers must attempt to distribute their approval evenly and fairly. It is important that they be on guard against favoring selected pupils because they happen to have some specific advantage such as high achievement or upper social status. You will want to compare the characteristics of such pupils by referring to Table 16-1.

Table 16-1.   Characteristics of pupils approved and disapproved by teachers.

Pupil Characteristic	Pattern of teacher approval-disapproval	
	High approval— Low to moderate disapproval	Low to moderate approval— High disapproval
	Average Score	Average Score
Mental maturity	101	83
Academic achievement	277	241
Total personality	120	98
Self adjustment	57	47
Social adjustment	66	51

SOURCE: Adapted from A. F. deGroat and G. G. Thompson. A study of the distribution of teacher approval and disapproval among sixth-grade pupils. *J. exp. Educ.*, 1949, *18*, 57-75. P. 70 With permission of authors and publisher.

The following experience of one teacher in promoting self-understanding is typical:

... Previously, the pupils who seemed to struggle with the [class] material were a source of annoyance, but I have changed on this point.

One girl is a good case in point. At the start of the year she seemed to be a compulsive talker. Other teachers found her unpleasantly aggressive; I made up my mind that I'd listen to her. When she found she was accepted and felt more free to speak her thoughts, she began to argue at any opportunity. Gradually this has disappeared. Just the other day, she stopped after class to tell me that at the beginning of the term she talked a great deal because she was unhappy since she simply couldn't memorize lessons and wanted to make an impression. When she realized I was listening to her, she felt she ought to stop talking and think things out for herself before she spoke. Now, she went on to say, she thinks about what she studies, something she never did before, because I consider what she says important. (From Cantor, 1953, pp. 273–274. With permission of author and publisher.)

The pupil needs to be accepted as he is, to feel that someone knows how he feels. Under these circumstances he can verbalize his feelings. The teacher may help by putting into words those feelings which the child has difficulty in expressing. In this way the pupil will also recognize that he is understood.

Rogers (1967) recently summarized his view as follows:

... It is most unfortunate that educators and the public think about, and focus on *teaching* ... [rather than] on the facilitation of *learning*—how, why, and when the student learns, and how learning seems and feels from the inside. ... We have some knowledge, and could gain more, about the conditions which facilitate learning, and that one of the most important conditions is the attitudinal quality of the interpersonal relationship between facilitator and learner. ...

Those attitudes which appear effective in promoting learning can be described. First of all is a transparent realness in the facilitator, a willingness to be a person, to be and to live the feelings and thoughts of the moment. When this realness includes a prizing, a caring, a trust and respect for the learner, the climate for learning is enhanced. When it includes a sensitive and accurate empathic listening, then indeed a freeing climate, stimulative of self-initiated learning and growth, exists.

. . . Individuals who hold such attitudes, and are bold enough to act on them, do not simply modify classroom methods—they revolutionize them. They perform almost none of the functions of teachers. It is no longer accurate to call them teachers. They are catalyzers, facilitators, giving freedom and life and the opportunity to learn, to students.

. . . [There is] cumulating research evidence which suggests that individuals who hold such attitudes are regarded as effective in the classroom; that the problems which concern them have to do with the release of potential, not the deficiencies of their students; that they seem to create classroom situations in which there are not admired children and disliked children, but in which affection and liking are a part of the life of every child; that in classrooms approaching such a psychological climate, children learn more of the conventional subjects (Rogers, 1967, pp. 16–17).

Achieving self-understanding

Menninger (1953) suggests that teachers can begin to understand their own reactions to stresses that inevitably occur in any classroom and to their life-styles in general by asking themselves such questions as these:

Am I always unhappy and dissatisfied?

Do I frequently have vague physical complaints for which the physician can find no physical cause?

Do I feel more or less lonesome and discouraged all the time?

Do I have a continuing feeling that people don't like me?

Am I always in friction with children or other adults—always arguing about one thing or another?

Do I complain a lot? Are most things—my work, my social life, my friends—unsatisfactory to me? (Menninger, 1953, p. 333. With permission.)

One should not be disturbed if he answers "yes" to one or two of these questions. Nor should he be concerned about occasional feelings described in the above question. Everyone experiences such reactions now and then. That is why Menninger uses the terms "always" and "frequently" in each. However, when these traits are persistent and characteristic of the teacher's behavior then it is time to recognize that steps can and should be taken for its improvement. This involves (1) changing oneself, (2) changing one's environment, or (3) changing both. One can, for example, be more sympathetic, patient, and friendly. Sometimes a teacher takes out [his or her] hostility on pupils because impossible demands are made of [him or her] in which case it may only be necessary to tackle the problem systematically in small, manageable steps. Occasionally, one's deep-seated and over-learned habits prevent his seeing the seat of his difficulties. If all attempts to realistically see [his or her] problems and to improve [his or her] behavior fail, then the teacher should seek outside help.

Menninger (1953) suggests that the amount of satisfaction one gets from life can be facilitated by the following:

Stand aside and look at how you may be contributing to your own unhappiness. (You may be too dependent or too aggressive.)

Do something out of the ordinary now and then. Use your imagination—explore new ideas and activities.

Make a serious effort to find ways of doing your job better.

Recreate and refresh yourself. The more fun you have in leisure, the better it is for you. Everyone needs time to do what he wants, with full freedom of conscience to be happy in his own way.

Develop the art of friendliness. Most of the joys of life, and sorrows, too, depend on how you get along with other people. Friends can be your greatest source of satisfaction—your strong support in times of crisis.

Finally, take a look at your life goals. If you have a goal that is high enough and worthy enough, your achievement will come with your growth toward emotional maturity. (Menninger, 1953, p. 333.)

Summary

During the course of development the individual is initially dependent upon deficiency-motivations. At this stage the person is dependent for his motivation on the satisfaction of physiological needs, safety, self-esteem, and respect from others; all of which depend upon other people for their gratification. However, the fully developed individual becomes self-sufficient with the full capacity for fulfilling his hopes and plans independent of other individuals. He is guided by the Being-motives or the Growth-motives of trust, loyalty, justice, and independence. These enable the person to reach his full realization and potentiality of his capacities and talents.

In the growth toward maturity, and even at maturity, the individual must face social reality. These are the restraints and demands made by the culture in which one's social needs are satisfied. In the American culture the restraints are there but one is permitted a great deal of freedom in considering the source of the cultural values as well as the validity of the value itself. In a democratic society it is recognized that

society is made by its members and, accordingly, can be changed by
them. The pupil's task is one of learning to stay close enough to social
realities so that he can remain effective but at the same time, to retain
his individuality.

In learning to face social reality the pupil's experiences depend
in part upon his perceptions of his relationships with others and in
addition to the broad values of the culture itself. It is quite apparent
that the individual's reference groups are important in this regard. An
unstable reference group is related to an unstable self-image. However,
the person with accurate perceptions of social realities adjusts well in
many diverse groups as reflected by such adjectives as socially sensitive
and tactful that are often used to describe him.

The testing of social reality is based in part on the reactions of
other significant persons to one's activities although the pupil will also
anticipate the outcomes of his behavior by tests in play or fantasy, a
process that parallels the mature adult's experimentation and planning.
Social reality becomes sidetracked when distortions produced by excessive conformity, overdependence on society, and associated defense
mechanisms take over.

Delinquency, too, may be seen as a distortion of social reality. In
one type of delinquency the psychopathic delinquent fails to foresee the
consequences of his behavior which may include violence toward others.
He appears unable, even unwilling, to comprehend social reality and
lacks the capacity to maintain satisfactory and mutually profitable relationships with others. Another kind of delinquent behavior is characterized by reaction against authority figures. The child learns at a very
early age that authority represented in the family, school, and church
protect him during a period when he cannot take care of himself. It is
expected that as he matures he can become increasingly less dependent
upon such people. That is, he develops an identity. However, oppressive
authoritarianism sometimes stifles the development of such individuals
who react by regarding everything about society as their natural enemy.
Delinquency provides them with a means for achieving a kind of status
and retaliatory outlet against a society that makes them feel inferior,
miserable, and resentful.

Prejudices, too, are anchored in the social reality of the principle
group of which the pupil is a member. However, sometimes prejudices
emerge out of economic or social frustration. Other groups are sought as
targets (scapegoats) for the aggression generated by their frustrations.
These distortions, once formed, are difficult to change because they are
fundamentally defense mechanisms.

Several authorities have advocated that contributions to adequate
self-concepts and realistic perceptions of social reality can be acquired
through self-understanding both from the pupil's standpoint and from

that of the teacher. A procedure that is suggested quite often is the pupil-centered orientation. Such teaching procedures tend to be less authoritarian, develop more responsibility on the part of the child, and place more emphasis on problem-centered approaches than on ego-centered activities. Teachers who themselves are emotionally healthy tend to have a beneficial effect on the pupil's psychological health.

The academic self-concept, that is, the internal locus of control, is more highly correlated with performance for white children than it is for the black child. On the other hand, a measure of fate control, or external locus of control, predicts a black child's performance or achievement more strongly than for the white child. The internal locus of control exists more strongly among black children in the desegregated school than it does in the segregated school. Thus, the favorable consequences of interracial classrooms may be considered a result of the opportunities these classrooms afford for self-evaluation and a wider range of friendships for pupils of both races.

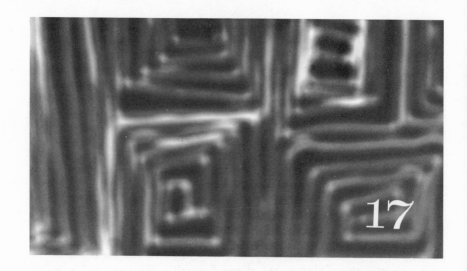

Cultural demands
and individual values

The American public schools have long been an important socializing agency in this country's homogenization of individuals with different backgrounds of culture. During the "melting pot" era of mass migrations of other nationalities into the United States, it was the schools that carried the burden of teaching a common language and of initiating the young (and often the old, as well) into the cultural practices of their new national home. The schools have also been a most important force in equipping the children of economic and social "have-nots" with knowledge and skills that have permitted upward movement in socioeconomic status and the acquisition of property and positions of respect in their communities.

At the present time our culture is again looking to the schools (and downward extensions of customary school programs) for help in meeting the emerging but as yet not clearly defined educational needs of economically and socially underprivileged groups. We are embarked on a program of social-racial integration and an equalization of educational opportunities across state and other geographical boundaries. Whether or not this approach will be satisfying in the long run to those Blacks who are calling for cultural pluralism remains open to serious question (Friedman, 1969). The gains (and probably some inevitable losses) to come from the neighborhood's school being replaced by a socially and socioeconomically integrated one will not be known for some time, although early findings by Coleman (1966), and others indicate that we may enjoy what some will consider gains that are not educational in the

480

narrow sense of the word—changes in need for achievement, self-esteem, etc.

The teacher of tomorrow's schools will have to strain his resources to be adequate in the new socializing role. It would be easy just to persist in expecting, and demanding, middle class performances and the mere proliferation of middle class attitudes and values. This could be disastrous—a missionary effort that would deny that our culture had gained strength and new perspectives from a pooling and sharing during the earlier "melting pot" days.

Cultural Demands

During the growth period, civilized man is exposed to a series of environmental demands which define a central core of the socialization process. As boys and girls grow toward maturity they are expected to develop certain competencies and to assume socially conventional responsibilities. For example, the infant of eighteen months is expected to get around pretty well on his own two legs, the child of seven years is expected to display the rudiments of reading skill, and the youth of sixteen is expected to have fairly definite plans for his vocational future. Similar cultural demands are made throughout the life span.

These developmental tasks differ somewhat from community to community or across racial and socioeconomic lines within the same community. They are, however, remarkably consistent within a given subculture. Grandparents pass their developmental expectations on to parents, neighbors exchange child-rearing attitudes over the back fence, schools have a prescribed curriculum formalized by state departments of education, and so on.

Ideal child for each age and sex group
(As perceived by the New Englanders of Orchardtown, USA)

Although children with different potentials might be expected to behave differently, there are a certain number of characteristics which might be considered as ideal in a child of a particular age and sex. Some of the traits which were felt to be ideal are presented in summary form below.

Ideal infant (both sexes): The ideal infant cries very little, and then only to indicate the pain of sticking pins. He has no physical defects, eats well, needs no entertainment. He goes happily to all adults. He has a nice odor about him (no odor of vomiting, feces, etc.) and is not ugly.

Ideal preschooler (male): This child is ideally aggressive in defending himself, but is not aggressive otherwise. He trains easily (bedtime, toilet, eating, etc.) and gets along with other children. He is not spoiled, or shy, or a show-off.

Ideal preschooler (female): She is not aggressive. She stands up for her rights only verbally. She, also, is not spoiled, shy, or a show-off. She trains easily and shows feminine tendencies like an interest in dolls, babies, etc. She likes to appear very helpful to her mother. However the female role is not quite as sharply defined as the male role at this age and during grade school. The female "tomboy" is censured less than the male "sissy."

Ideal school-age boy: A poem from the second-grade blackboard at school gives an idealistic prescription for the school-age child, both male and female:

Whole Duty of Children

A child should always say what's true,
And speak when he is spoken to,
And behave mannerly at table;
At least as far as he is able.

This poem probably represents current adult standards of "company behavior" for their children and should not be taken too seriously as reflecting the actual expectations of the adults as to their children's daily behavior, although there is certainly some increase in parental standards when the children go to school.

A child of this age to be ideal must not be "sneaky"; he must appear alert. (This no doubt gives the impression that he has a high potential.) Although quiet is needed in the schoolroom, a too-quiet child is not admired either by parents or teachers. One statement relating to this was, "He was so quiet I didn't know who he was." Other similar remarks indicate that although teachers are constantly emphasizing orderliness and quiet, this is not entirely congruent with their picture of the ideal child. (A too-submissive child gives evidence of a damaged potential, perhaps.)

An ideal school-age boy should be open, liked by both adults and peers. If he gets into troubles these must be of such a nature that they can be excused by the phrase "he is a typical boy." He should be willing to fight for his rights and be able to do so. He should also be willing to defend weaker children, not be a bully, and yet not be self-righteous, a tattle tale, etc.

Ideal school-age girl: This child, ideally, should never engage in physical aggression. She should be alert, popular with boys and girls, not a scapegoat, and not rebellious. She should be neat, pretty or cute, get good marks in school, but not appear to be a "brain." Ideally she is shorter than most girls her age. She runs errands and helps mother willingly. She likes feminine games (dolls, etc.) and feminine frills. (Abridged from Whiting, 1963, pp. 928–929. With permission.)

Taking the American middle class society as an example, one can easily see that children are expected to master certain learning assignments according to a pretty standardized timetable. For example, children are expected to learn to read somewhere between the sixth and the seventh years of life. Examples from the Vineland Social Maturity Scale illustrate some of the common cultural expectations in our middle class society.

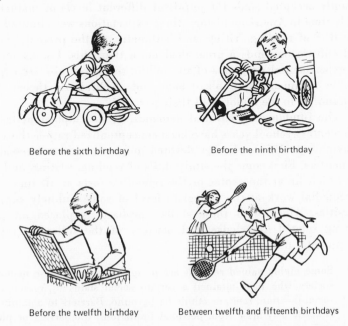

Before the sixth birthday   Before the ninth birthday

Before the twelfth birthday   Between twelfth and fifteenth birthdays

Figure 17-1. Pupils are expected to display certain behaviors at different age levels. Some of the developmental demands are shown in these illustrations. (Based on Edgar A. Doll. Vineland scale of social maturity. Educational Test Bureau. Redrawn from Your child grows up. John Hancock Mutual Life Insurance Co. With permission.)

It is easy for the teacher to forget that there are huge social class and cultural differences in the timing of the demands that are made on the growing child. For example, the middle class home may make demands at an earlier age for some learnings (such as responsibility for personal belongings), whereas the lower class home may expect the child to get his own lunch at a much earlier age.

And of course when one moves across cultures, or even subcultures in the United States, one can observe vast differences in what learnings are expected of children at different developmental levels.

Cultural demands of middle class American society

Members of the American middle class dictate the cultural demands of our public schools. They constitute the teachers, the principals, the superintendents of instruction, the writers of textbooks, members of governing boards, and so on. They set the pace and apply the social pressures for meeting the expectations that they believe to be the commonly accepted goals for pupils of different levels of maturity. At an early time in American history, these expectations were limited to the "three R's" of reading, 'riting, and 'rithmetic. At the present time, the school culture demands a great deal more than this. For example, in some experimental programs of the public schools pupils are expected to master rudiments of Boolean logic and algebraic set theory, which are unfamiliar to the majority of their parents!

The fundamental cultural demands, or developmental tasks, of the elementary school years have been conceptualized rather thoroughly by Havighurst (1953) who has devoted much thought and research to these matters. First come the study skills of reading, writing, and arithmetic which lie at the center of the school's efforts at all times—even into remedial work at the collegiate level of some publicly supported universities. Along with these skills, emphasis is placed on pupils' acquiring related knowledge and mastery of the following types of developmental tasks.*

Some highly valued rewards are permitted only to those members of society who have attained a certain social status by reason of age, social position, rank, or ethnic background. Barriers to obtaining such rewards may arise from personal limitations, intellectual or physical, and other fortuitous factors, over which the individual has little or no control. They may arise also from a lack of sociovocational skills, possession of which gives access to the financial resources that are, for the majority of people, the primary means of obtaining highly rewarding goal-objects. Since proficiency in such skills is often dependent on an early commencement of training, which must then continue over a lengthy period of time, persons not infrequently find that lack of opportunities or guidance during their childhood and adolescent years has, in effect, imposed a life-time barrier to their legitimately acquiring possessions and status, or participating in activities that for other persons are evident sources of enjoyment and means for obtaining additional social and material rewards. Thus, both genetic and early-experience factors may create conditions under which persons are tempted to acquire socially acceptable rewards by socially unacceptable means.

In the generally competitive atmosphere of North American society, achievement demands are made on the majority of children.

*Adapted from Havighurst (1953).

Cultural achievement norms include the attainment of a level of academic or vocational proficiency that is likely to lead to economic self-sufficiency, and the establishing and maintaining of a home in which a family may be raised. Achievement demands are highly variable among social class, ethnic, and other subcultural groups; nevertheless, in a society in which upward-mobility is a cultural ideal, parents and other adults in the family usually exert pressures on young people to surpass, or at least equal, the attainments of the previous generation. (Abridged from Bandura & Walters, 1963, pp. 165–167. With permission.)

Boys and girls are expected to acquire the necessary motor-intellectual skills for playing various popular games, such as basketball, football, baseball, hockey, tennis, or whatever is stressed in a given community. The pupil's social acceptability and personal happiness often depends on his ability to master this developmental task, although this is obviously not so true for girls as for boys (Kuhlen & Lee, 1943). Being good in the games is an ideal that has descended to us from the culture of ancient Greece. Most of the public schools employ special teachers of health and physical education to give instruction in the coordinated body movements related to these games.

Closely associated with the foregoing developmental task is the cultural expectation that boys and girls will be instructed about the best ways to care for the health and safety of their bodies. Teachers and other school personnel stress physical hygiene, cleanliness, and rules for safety. This developmental task is stressed in both curricular and extracurricular contacts.

Learning how to relate meaningfully and satisfactorily with classmates is another developmental task, and an important one in American middle class society. This is a cultural demand where teachers frequently fail to understand the lower class pupil's difficulties in accepting middle class standards and social skills.

Achieving a masculine or feminine social role

Nature of the Task.   To accept and to learn a socially approved adult masculine or feminine social role.

Biological Basis.   The pubertal growth cycle broadens the physical differences between the sexes. Women become definitely the weaker sex, in terms of physical strength. They also become physically attractive to men, and thus gain one kind of power while losing another.

Psychological Basis.   Since the masculine and the feminine roles are different in our society, a boy has to accept the idea of becoming a man and a girl has to accept the idea of becoming a woman. For boys, this seems easy in our society, which offers its principal places to men. Most girls also find it easy to accept the role of wife and mother, with dependence on a man for support. But a number of girls find this to be difficult. They want a career. They admire their fathers and their older brothers and want the freedom and power and independence of the male. For them it is not an easy task to accept the feminine role. Fortunately, our society's definition of the feminine role is broadening to give more satisfaction to girls of this type.

Cultural Basis.   The approved feminine sex role is changing. Especially in the urban part of our society women are given much more latitude than they were a generation or two ago. This means that adolescent girls are under less pressure to adopt the traditional feminine role. Some of them can choose to be independent, to go into business or a profession, to be married without becoming mothers, to do a number of things that would have been impossible or at least unpopular in an earlier day.

Educational Implications.   For most boys this task is so easy to achieve that it hardly appears to be a task at all. Only a few boys, who may have been brought up without much masculine attention or influence, or who have learned certain feminine or sexually neutral interests and habits, need help with this task. For them, the school may provide help through guidance and counseling.

With girls, on the other hand, there is often much more hesitation among normally well-adjusted girls to assume the usual feminine expectations of becoming a wife and mother. This is especially true of girls in the upper middle class, where it is expected that the girls will go to college and prepare for a career outside the home.

The school can *help girls to think through the problem of accepting the feminine sex role.* In senior high school and college there should be opportunity for girls, individually or in groups, to discuss the problem of accepting a feminine role. Courses in psychology and in literature are probably best for this purpose. A woman's college could deal with this problem through the study of literature. Free class discussion with a skillful teacher would meet the problem for most girls. Women who have been outstandingly successful in the usual feminine role of wife and mother should be available to lead such discussions, as well as women who have been successful in other accepted feminine roles. (From Havighurst, 1953, pp. 115–116. With permission of Longman's, Green and Co.)

Another extremely important cultural demand is that boys and girls will learn to assume appropriate sex roles. This is a difficult developmental task because sex roles are in transition and it is not always possible to discriminate between what is distinctly male and female with respect to activities or attitudes. Here again, there are often serious discrepancies between lower class and middle class expectations.

Boys and girls are also expected to "grow up" during the school years, to achieve a considerable degree of personal independence. This is accomplished by their being given an increasing degree of freedom and opportunity to experiment, to be on their own, to make mistakes and to correct them. Related to this cultural demand is another with which it goes hand-in-hand: developing a personally satisfactory set of prescriptive values—conscience and ideas.

Consequences of failing to meet important cultural demands

What happens to the individual pupil who is consistently unable to master the more important developmental tasks of his school and community? An answer to this question can be attempted on several levels. For example, one might speak of truancy, school phobia, dropping out of school, vandalism of school buildings, delinquency, and so on. Or one can respond on a theoretical level via some conceptual schema such as the one proposed by Thelen (1950). Such theoretical attempts are typically more useful in the long run. Thelin has proposed that, in general, individuals go with, against, or away from the group.

"Going with the group" implies that the pupil who has failed to meet a given societal expectation develops other competencies that successfully offset his failure to master this particular learning assignment. It may also mean that the group is so important to the pupil that he is willing to accept extremely low status in it as long as this permits maintenance of membership. And, of course, there is always the case where school failure enhances the pupil's social status with certain individuals in a group—however, this appears not to be common at the older age levels.

"Going against the group" is the behavior mode adopted by many boys and girls who end up in our penal and behavior correctional institutions. The lack of success associated with being assigned to one of the latter institutions is well known. The need for such institutions serves as an indication that our society has failed, as yet, to cope with this type of problem.

"Going away from the group" is a most dismal solution. It is often the beginning of anomie, despair, and a decline toward serious mental illness (types of personality disorders discussed at some length in Chapter 14 of this book).

The pupil who fails to master developmental tasks that are regarded as important by the schools and their supporting middle class values may be variously treated in the American culture. His failure may be temporarily ignored; then if mastery of the task is a necessary precursor of subsequent learning assignments, he may find it increasingly difficult to make normal progress in mastering later learning assignments. He may be denied the privilege of attempting more advanced learning assignments until the task at hand is handled in some satisfactory way (retention in grade or assignment to special classes are commonly employed procedures). He may be given special tutorial care. This may have positive effects in advancing his learning, but may have deleterious effects on his self-esteem and his social stimulus value to others. And, of course, he may drop out of school at the legally permitted age.

What can be done to aid those pupils who experience great difficulties in meeting the middle class cultural demands made manifest through the goals of the American public schools? There is no simple answer to this question. Special tutorial sessions with the help of automated teaching devices are sometimes helpful in those cases where the pupils' needs for achievement are sufficiently high to sustain a learning orientation. Permitting pupils to work against their own previous records of achievement is often a successful approach. The placing of pupils who are falling behind in an ungraded group where their deficiencies in mastering some of the developmental tasks will not completely mask their adequacy in meeting other cultural demands is practiced successfully by some school systems. There are many more teaching procedures that are commonly used to advantage by teachers who support their art by a comprehensive knowledge of how pupils learn and solve their problems.

The reader is reminded again that curricular and extracurricular activities of the public schools have been selected by teachers and parents who accept and attempt to perpetuate the currently espoused middle class values; that is, from the traditional middle class point of view, the success of our American culture has been based on such honored values as strong striving, persistence, dependability, quality workmanship, and reliability, to mention only a few salient qualities. This being so, it is easy for teachers to forget that some pupils come from homes and neighborhoods in which these middle class values are not given high priority as guides to conduct. What can the teacher do when confronted with these pupils who do not respect the basic values and cultural expectations of the school and community? Possible answers to this question are discussed in the following section; however, let the reader be forewarned that there is no simple solution to such social problems.

Individual Values

It is well known that boys and girls learn many things from their school experiences besides those encountered in the curricular and extracurricular offerings. For example, in a minor vein, they may learn, when in the depths of scholastic despair, to hate the image of a particular American President whose portrait hung in the classroom. They may learn to love the light strains of the music played during the festivities of May Day, marking the nearness of summer vacation. They may learn to fear numbers in any form because of their invariant association with bewilderment and failure in arithmetic. They may learn to like all women with long, hooked noses because an especially kindly and sympathetic teacher had this feature.

Most of these learnings go on unconscious to either teacher or pupils. These kinds of experiences frequently have an emotional overlay of pleasantness or unpleasantness. They provide the basis for many of our appreciations and attitudes which are often very strong, even though their sources in experience are usually uncommunicable.

There is also an emotional tone in the learning of many of our more rationalized or quasi-logical attitudes. When the flag and the big brass band come marching by we rise, bare our heads, and in these ways show our respect and love for country. At least this is what we say in an attempt to explain our behavior to somebody from another culture. All the time there is a thrill and excitement about our behavior that cannot be easily verbalized, a feeling of joyous pride that can be understood and shared only by others who have developed similar patriotic attitudes.

Following related principles, many of our negative or rejecting attitudes toward persons of other racial or religious groups have strong emotional overtones of apprehension and fear. We respond to these people and everything associated with them by active avoidance or aggressive attack. In some long-forgotten ways they symbolize threat and danger. We typically rationalize and defend our negative regard by prejudiced statements that come readily to mind. Some person in our very early childhood may have said that these people are different from us and cannot be trusted. It must be true, for they are indeed different and we feel uneasy in their presence. We may put our prejudiced attitude into words in talking to others or we may transmit it just as effectively by our nonverbalized actions.

Some attitudes influence our behavior only when we are in the presence of the evoking stimuli. That is, they are aroused by conditions in our surroundings. For example, we may live for months without experiencing some of our favorable attitudes toward certain infrequent social occasions, like a picnic or party. Some acquaintance mentions one of them casually and we immediately start to expend energy to bring about a recurrence. "Yes, let's do have a get-together. They're lots of fun."

Other attitudes are more persistent and enduring. By some means they have become part and parcel of persisting needs and thereby function as long-term goals, shaping our daily routines in very direct and significant ways. These self-arousing and more or less sustained attitudes are often placed under the rubric of personal *values*. They do much to influence behavior and perpetuate cultural norms and styles of living. A pupil may have come to appreciate the value of scholarship, not from his own achievements but from others' aspirations and hopes for his scholarly future. He studies hard, is attentive, anxious to please his teacher, and becomes severely distressed when any situation threatens his hopes of achievement. Another pupil may have developed a strong value for athletic proficiency. He will neglect everything else in his school life in order to promote his status and skills in athletic events. Still another pupil may value participation in musical events. To him musical production is the most worthwhile activity and he may go to great lengths to convince others that musicians are the bulwark of our civilized culture.

The acquisition of wholesome attitudes and of more generalized values are integral parts of a pupil's education. They can be influenced in culturally approved directions by the informed teacher. The dedicated teacher derives many of his richest satisfactions from the knowledge that his influence has extended beyond the sheer transmission of facts and skills. Parents often evaluate such a teacher by saying, "He is more than a good teacher. He is a good *influence* on his pupils."

At times the term "value" is employed to refer to the tendencies or dispositions of living beings to prefer one kind of object rather than another. ("Object" in this connection signifies whatever can be preferred to something else; physical things, persons, colors, emotions, images, thoughts, symbols, forms of physical activity, can all be objects in this sense.) Such values may be called *operative* values.

In contrast to this employment, the term "value" is often restricted to those cases of preferential behavior directed by "an anticipation or foresight of the outcome" of such behavior. In contrast to operative values, such values may be called *conceived values*.

A conceived value thus involves preference for a symbolically indicated object. The problem of the relation of conceived values to operative values is a phase of the problem of the relation of behavior controlled by symbols to behavior not so controlled. As abstract possibilities, one can imagine an extreme case where every conceived value issued into an operative value and another extreme case where no conceived value influenced the system of operative values. But human beings seldom, if ever, find themselves at either extreme; some interaction and some incompatibility between conceived and operative values is the common state.

A third employment of the term "value" is concerned with what is preferable (or "desirable") regardless of whether it is in fact preferred or conceived as preferable. Since the stress is upon the properties of the object, such values may be called *object values.*

What is preferred (operative values) can be found through a study of preferential behavior. What is conceived to be preferable (conceived values) can be studied through the symbols employed in preferential behavior and the preferential behavior directed toward symbols. If, then, it could be shown that while the preferable is not identical with the preferred (the "ought" not identical with the "is") it still cannot be defined without relation to preference, then all three usages of the term "value" would have in common a reference to preferential behavior. Preferential behavior would then define the value field, and the various employments of the term "value" would be explicated not as referring to different entities (different "values") but as delineating different aspects of the value field. To the extent that this could be done, axiology (the theory of value) would, as the science of preferential behavior, become part of the general science of behavior. (Abridged from Morris, 1956, pp. 10–12. With permission.)

How are appreciations, attitudes, and values acquired?

Appreciations, attitudes, and values are acquired and modified in the same ways and according to the same learning principles as other human behaviors. However, these attitudinal and "emotionalized" learnings (as contrasted with learning skills in arithmetic or some of the other more formally presented tasks) are often based on low-level conditioning processes and unconscious imitations of others' behaviors. Studies of animal behavior demonstrate that they too can be taught to appreciate a generalized attribute of objects—such as working for one type of token and not for another (Wolfe, 1932). Most of us would agree that a gold star is more attractive and symbolizes a greater value than a red star. The origins of this attitude can be traced back to early school days. However, the conditioning of some of man's attitudes lies forever buried in the experiences of early childhood or the repressed memories of later life. For example, in the experiences of one individual: Why is he repelled by bright colors in men's clothing? Why does the smell of cigar smoke dredge up feelings of well-being and affluence? Why does awakening in the middle of the night evoke feelings of quiet loneliness?

It is sometimes impossible to determine what needs an individual pupil may be satisfying through clinging to a personally troublesome or socially unacceptable attitude or value. Even "deep" therapy like psychoanalysis may fail to unearth information that would support a reasonable inference. One pupil we know feels grief-stricken and comes to tears when she hears a certain strain of classical music. Another pupil cannot tolerate any act of kindness from others.

It seems probable that many of our less emotionalized appreciations, attitudes, and values build up slowly according to a generally accepted reinforcement theory of learning (Bijou & Baer, 1961). That is, stimulus events are associated with other stimulus-response associations which result in need reduction, thus producing a satisfying state of affairs. After many pairings the coincidental stimuli come to have need-satisfying properties and are sought after in their own right as desirable stimulus conditions. For example, the child who hears certain soothing music at bedtime when his mother is fondling him and preparing him for bed may come to enjoy the music (in the absence of the mother) for its relaxing effects. Or the pupil who is continually praised and approved by her teachers for her neat handwriting will prefer and strive toward this goal even when writing notes to herself that no one will ever see. And, of course, there is the same set of principles for negative attitudes and aversions. For example, the small son of a southern farmer hears his father damning the bankers of Wall Street for his financial difficulties. The little boy is disturbed by his father's emotional behavior, which is very similar to that displayed when he punishes his son. The immature boy perceives the verbal stimulus as "bankers in general" and is fearful of his father's strong emotion. This occurs on many occasions. The son grown to manhood cannot understand his distrust and aggressive feelings toward bank personnel, stock brokers, and the like. His negative attitudes appear somehow justified and yet unreasonable. They handicap him in his financial transactions and in his investment planning.

Boys and girls also appear to have a strong tendency to adopt the attitudes and values of a preferred adult. The boy tries to be like his father in every respect, and the girl like her mother. Later the father's and mother's influences are extended to imitation and copying of the attitudes and values of other adults, the "parent surrogates." Psychoanalysts speak of "identification" with others and the "introjection" or "internalization" of the other's attitudes and value systems—sometimes without conscious awareness or any discrimination of the others' desirable as contrasted with their undesirable characteristics. Thus we may find pupils imitating some of our most embarrassing mannerisms as well as our more estimable behavior patterns.

Each of these explanatory approaches (conditioning by sheer association, conditioning with need reinforcement, and identification-introjection mechanisms) seems plausible. They have many components in common. In this book we are not interested in their relative theoretical merits, but have called attention to them as illustrations of current thinking in psychology. On one point there seems to be general agreement. Many of our attitudes and values develop in strength from socially obscure origins.

Attitudes and values motivate other patterns of behavior

It is the motivating and guiding effects of attitudes and values that make them so important in human affairs. They instigate and then sustain complex behaviors over long periods of time. They guide and cast an emotional coloring over many of our everyday routines.

Negative attitudes have an adverse effect on motivation in that they keep the individual away from certain goal-striving situations. The pupil who has acquired negative attitudes toward reading because of his early failures usually does everything possible to avoid the reading situation. Clinicians and teachers of remedial reading report that the first task is one of eliminating the retarded reader's negative attitudes toward printed materials. He cannot learn to read until he can be helped to "release the brakes" of his negative evaluations of reading as a personally unsuccessful activity.

The *absence* of a favorable attitude or value leaves the pupil in a state of behavioral inertia. We say that he is not interested or that he is not motivated to learn. The teaching of handwriting to boys offers an excellent illustration of this condition. It is frequently difficult to encourage them to improve the aesthetic quality of their writing. They typically place a low value on neatness and are satisfied merely with writing legibly. Or consider the mother's plight who tries vainly to get her preadolescent boy to comb his hair every morning. With his entrance into adolescence he seems transformed. Now he may comb his hair *ad nauseam* or let it grow to shoulder length.

The motivating effects of a positive value are well known. History is replete with instances of persons undergoing extreme hardships and even death in pursuing positively valued goals. It should be noted that the behavioral consequences of pupils' positive values are not always pleasing to the teacher, because he may possess different values. Nevertheless, the teacher will do well to take cognizance of the potent effects of his pupils' positive values. They are expressions of enduring and powerful trends toward behavior.

Attitudes and values influence perceptions

Pupils' perceptions of the external world are highly influenced by their attitudes and values. They may consistently perceive objects as being considerably different from what they really are. For example, in one experiment it was found that economically less privileged children remembered coins as larger than did a more privileged group of children (Bruner & Postman, 1947).

Pupils also perceive the presence of objects and events which do not exist in fact. This has been interestingly demonstrated in the psy-

Figure 17-2. When the story of this picture is told "round robin" from one person to the next, it frequently changes in content so that the razor is in the hand of the Negro who is interpreted as an aggressor. This illustrates the influence of attitudes on perceptual and memory processes. (From Gordon W. Allport. Psychology of rumor. New York: Henry Holt & Co., Inc., 1947. With permission.)

chology of rumor (Allport & Postman, 1947). The sometimes negative attitudes toward the American Negro may influence perceptions, as shown in Figure 17-2. The pupil who has apprehensive attitudes toward the school and his teacher may perceive many of the teacher's routine behaviors as personally threatening and damaging to his self-esteem (see Sears & Sherman, 1964). Almost everything that the teacher says is twisted into further evidence that "The teacher doesn't like me."

Attitudes and values also make the pupil sensitive to what may superficially seem to be very weak stimuli. Anything that is related favorably to his value system is perceived, even though the triggering situation is fleeting or otherwise obscure. The pupil may be completely oblivious to contrary or threatening circumstances. That is, his values have made him unusually sensitive to barely perceivable conditions in the external world, provided they are in accord with his own organization (Bruner & Postman, 1947). Examples of this human tendency abound in our everyday experiences. The pupil with a highly developed value system related to academic achievement sees the tiniest evidences of progress and is perceptually sensitive to the minor ways in which he can make greater gains. Stimulating conditions that threaten his value system are handled in two ways: he is unusually alert to threats that he feels he can handle, and very insensitive to those for which he has no ready defense.

Conditions That Favor Changes in Attitudes and Value Tendencies

The teacher can do many things to influence the attitudes and values of his pupils. Probably his best approach is the indirect one of exhibiting sympathy and understanding toward his pupils. If he is successful in projecting a genuine concern for each pupil's happiness and welfare, he will exert a strong influence on their attitudes and values.

Most pupils will have adopted their strongest identifications outside the classroom with parents or other adults. The teacher will not be able to establish a close relationship with every pupil. Boys sometimes find it difficult to identify with women teachers. There are values and attitudes to be encouraged for which outlets are impossible to find through everyday behavior within the classroom. These difficulties make it desirable to consider more formal methods of influencing the attitudes and values of pupils.

Conditioning by frequent association

When we reflect about the sources of our own positive attitudes and values it is easy to see that many of them were acquired through casual association with pleasant experiences. The poems and stories that were read to us and the carols that were sung at Christmas time still arouse pleasant feelings of warmth and well-being. They represent positive values inasmuch as we like to repeat them each year and feel deprived if conditions interfere with a full measure of enjoyment. If, perchance, circumstances threaten to prevent such pleasurable activities, we are willing to expend a lot of energy to preserve what we feel are our inalienable privileges. It takes something like this to make us recognize how strong are our positive values. They are felt to be the most desirable way of living. We explain them as the products of conditioning by frequent association with pleasurable early experiences, family love with its special intimacies, feasting, reverence, and so on.

The school offers many opportunities for transmitting similar positive values. For many boys and girls the school is the only setting in which they are exposed to the culture's best literature, art, and music. If these experiences can be made a pleasurable part of the school's curricular and extracurricular offerings, there is a good chance that pupils will adopt them as positive values. If on the other hand they are associated with apprehension and threats of failure, we can be almost certain they will represent negative values—activities to be avoided.

"Ugly part of town, ain't it?"

Figure 17-3. Negative values are acquired on the basis of pain, threats of failure, and the negative evaluations of one's associates. They represent activities to be avoided. (Courtesy of Stan Fine. Reprinted from The American Magazine.)

The influences of music, art, and literature are often sadly curtailed by the way in which they are presented. The pupil who knows that he will be tested and graded solely on the names of great artists and their productions is not in a favorable state for acquiring positive attitudes and values. The warmth and humanity of Lincoln's address at Gettysburg is forever lost to the unfortunate pupil whose first exposure to it was to be forced to memorize it "word for word" in an English assignment. The emotional appeal of our best poetry can be destroyed by an emphasis on intellectual analysis and memorization. Under these conditions the pupil may be able to "recite" and interpret the meaning of "Paul Revere's Ride" yet feel none of the excitement or patriotic fervor inherent in this stirring chronicle of our early history. How unlike the days of poetry's beginning when the minstrel sat at the fireside and told his stories in song after the evening meal. One can almost see the excitement and enjoyment of the boys and girls in this setting.

It is not our purpose to attempt a comprehensive listing of the values that should be transmitted through our schools or the best teaching methods for reaching desired goals. However, it seems probable that some teachers with the best of intentions may be defeating their own purposes, because they are not aware of the psychological principles by which positive attitudes and values are acquired.

The influence of prestige figures

Perhaps the best illustrations of influencing attitudes and values through prestige labeling and association can be drawn from modern advertising. It is a widely used and effective method for selling everything from dental creams to Cadillacs. The usual technique is to have some well-known public figure endorse the product or merely be photographed in its presence. The inference is made that the potential consumer will want to identify herself in every way with such an admirable figure—even down to the superficial detail that she uses Beauty soap. This inference has a solid foundation in fact, as is shown by the following research study.

Children of preschool age were told an interesting story about an appealing hero who (among other things) was very fond of one type of food but violently disliked another kind (Duncker, 1938). For several days the children had opportunities to try the two foods and tell which one they liked best. The story had been so written that the hero's favorite food was initially least liked by the children. After hearing the story the children changed their preference to the hero's best-liked food. Although they tended with time to slide back toward their initial ranking of the foods, they still showed a positive influence on the twelfth day after listening to the story.

Everyday observation also attests to the sales appeal of a hero's endorsement of some product. When this prestige association is combined with an invitation to send in a box top and become a member of the hero's inner circle, the influence is even more enhanced. Nor is such prestige influence restricted to small children. Older boys and girls adopt the attitudes and values of movie stars and other celebrities. Even adults are by no means immune from prestige suggestion. In the present era of great technological progress the unsupported statements "Science has shown . . ." or "Four out of five doctors recommend . . ." will send the majority of adults scurrying to the supermarket.

As a matter of fact, we are so heavily influenced in our attitudes and values by prestige factors that we consider it necessary to exercise some degree of social control. Review and censure boards monitor our books, movies, and radio and television programs to protect us from unscrupulous promoters. The government appoints special committees

Figure 17-4. It is not always possible to predict the effects of experience upon attitudes and values. The best laid plans often go awry. (Drawing by R. Mac-Donald, copyright 1944, The New Yorker Magazine, Inc.)

to examine the products that "Science has proved" will enrich our way of life.

How fares education in this struggle to influence our youth toward the acceptance of civilization's most cherished attitudes and values? There appears to be room for considerable improvement. In the first place, teachers appear reluctant to accept a fair share of the responsibility for pupils' developing values (Thompson, 1968). They decry the influence of commercial interests but too frequently offer no alternative attractions. In the second place, they too often passively adopt antiquated methods and materials handed down from a previous generation of teachers, or vaguely remembered approaches drawn from their own childhood.

That this is the case is well illustrated in one analysis of third-grade textbooks in reading (Child, *et al.*, 1946). Over 900 stories selected from thirty readers were analyzed according to type of story, central character, behavior shown, consequences of the behavior, and so on. The analysis showed an extreme emphasis on work and skills as means of reaching one's goals. Success is the keynote, for of course the hero almost always succeeds. Girls and women are characterized as kind, timid, inactive, and lacking in ambition. We consider the optimism of always succeeding through hard work as an unrealistic picture of life for the average third-grade pupil who sometimes works very hard without success. The picture of womanhood is neither realistic nor attractive. It is small wonder that boys and girls are little influenced by such a selec-

tion of stories. Few pupils can identify with a character who is fictionalized to success through *hard work*. They like their *fiction* in pure form where the hero always succeeds through the extraordinary gifts of Superman. Heroes and heroines with whom they can identify must be susceptible to the same winds of misfortune as themselves. And they must seem as real as the celebrities of today in order for their qualities to compete successfully with the innocuous attitudes and values of the popular movie star or singing idol (as fabricated by their press agents). The pedagogical task is a difficult one, but the psychological facts are clear. New teaching materials and methods of instruction are demanded if the school is to become a leader in the transmission of values via prestige figures. It is unrealistic to believe that the virtues of Washington will be preferred to the glamorous charactertistics of a contemporary idol.

Influencing values by group discussion and decision

Attitudes and values that have become well established are difficult to change. In the modern era of rapid communication through radio, television, daily newspapers, magazines, and elaborate billboards the individual is bombarded from all sides with information designed to influence his attitudes and style of living. In response to these pervasive tools of persuasion the child acquires an attitude of skepticism and disbelief. He may have sent in a few box tops and found that the attractively described gifts were really pretty shoddy merchandise. He comes to distrust the motives of others who try to influence his behavior. This callous regard generalizes to all spheres of life. It makes the teacher's task much more difficult, but on the positive side it permits the pupil some degree of freedom in establishing his own attitudes and values.

The teacher can no longer feel confident that his words of advice will be accepted at face value. The pupils may wonder "What's he after?" "What's he trying to sell?" New techniques are required which permit the individual pupil the freedom of personal decision which he demands. The group-discussion approach seems especially tailored for classroom use. Its effectiveness is illustrated in the following experiment with adults.

This study was conducted under the supervision of Lewin (1952) who initiated the "group dynamics" movement in social psychology. The objective of this study was to encourage housewives to increase their use of sweetbreads, beef hearts, and kidneys during World War II when the usually consumed meats were in short supply. Two approaches to the task were employed with several groups of women ranging in size from 13 to 17 members. Only 45 minutes of time were available with any one group. In three of the groups the women were given an attractive lecture which appealed to their desire to help the war effort, emphasized the superior nutritional value of such meats, and gave detailed directions for preparing them in attractive ways. Mimeographed recipes were distributed. For the other three groups a leader skilled in group work presented the problem in terms of nutrition and the war effort. After a few minutes he initiated a group discussion. The advantages and disadvantages were discussed freely. Then the nutrition expert offered the same recipes as given to the lecture groups. At the end of the discussion session the women were asked to raise their hands if they were willing to try one of the meats during the next week. A follow-up inquiry revealed that 32 percent of the women in the discussion groups served one of the meats the following week as contrasted with only 3 percent of the lecture groups.

The effectiveness of the group discussion and decision approach has been demonstrated within many other settings like factories, cooperative dining halls, and mothers' groups. It has been used successfully in one of its variant forms within the classroom to promote interpersonal understanding and tolerance. It is a powerful approach which is especially amenable to classroom use. When handled with reasonable finesse it also provides valuable opportunities for pupils to explore their own attitude and value systems against the backdrop of the group. This experience is a good mental hygiene measure in itself.

Mass media influences on attitudes and values

Mass media are available to all and are demonstrably effective. They include radio, television, movies, books, newspapers, magazines, pamphlets, billboards, lectures, and any conceivable means through which communication with groups of people becomes possible. There can be little doubt that they have a substantial influence on our attitudes, values, and daily behavior.

Teachers have many of these approaches available for their use. The library, which is the heart of the academic side of our educational programs, is an invaluable aid. The teacher can through personal suggestion and group discussion have a significant influence on the types of books and magazines that his pupils read. Many of our schools have banded together to support radio and television programs that are educational in purpose. And almost every school has film projectors and contractual arrangements with a film library for renting films on almost any topic.

Although the mass media are valuable resources for presenting information and teaching skills, they may be less influential in molding attitudes and encouraging the development of values. Generally they are less dramatic and exciting than the media sponsored by advertising interests. This is the reason that we have emphasized the approaches that are uniquely available to the teacher. He can interact with his pupils under social conditions shared by very few other individuals. This is the teacher's principal advantage. If he is resourceful and understanding, he can do much to encourage pupils toward an integrated and personally satisfying philosophy of living that will insure a maximum of freedom for the individual without encroaching on the rights and privileges of others. It is just as important for the teacher to help pupils acquire a stable hierarchy of socially acceptable values as to give instruction in the three Rs. This can often be best accomplished through group discussions in which pupils are unobtrusively guided by the teacher toward individual decisions consistent with their backgrounds and general styles of living.

Summary

There are certain cultural demands for personal-social development and behavior which growing boys and girls must recognize and satisfy in order to enjoy social approval and opportunities for personal advancement. The school is one of the most important agencies for helping young people acquire the skills and values necessary for meeting these cultural demands. The teacher's functions as a special representative of the culture are discussed in some detail, with some comments about helping those pupils who find it difficult to meet societal expectations.

The pupil is also viewed as acquiring attitudes and values that define his unique orientation toward the "good life." An attempt is made to show that as long as these appreciations and values are not in direct conflict with societal restrictions, the pupil has a wide range of available behaviors, interests, and attitudes for expressing his individual approach to getting the most satisfaction from daily living. Teachers are reminded that there is more than one way of simultaneously meeting society's demands and satisfying one's own idiosyncratic needs. The manner in which attitudes and values are acquired through learning processes and how they may be altered (when deemed necessary for all concerned) are discussed; however, this dimension of learning is considered in much greater detail in the chapters on learning in Part III of this book. In this chapter we take the stand that the teacher's role in modifying and building pupils' attitudes and values is an important, although often overlooked or underestimated, part of the teacher's proper functions.

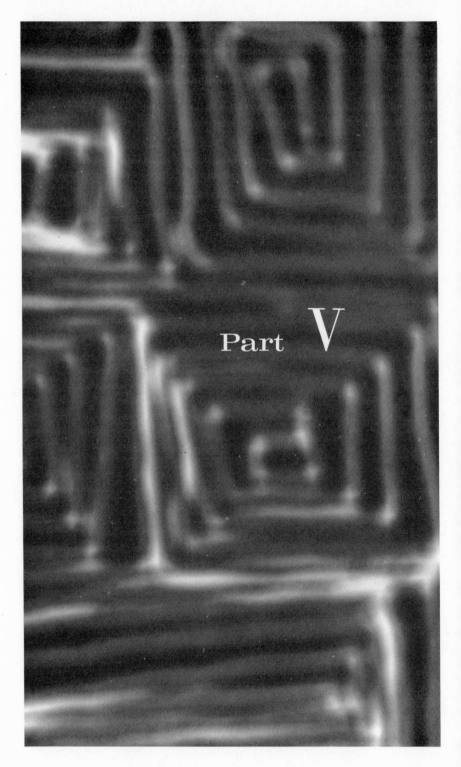

Part V

Measuring and
evaluating
behavioral change

When Socrates said, "Man is the measure of all things," he was undoubtedly referring to a necessarily valid generalization that some person must be present to discriminate the operations involved and to keep a record of the prescribed events for any particular measurement. Without this human observer there can be no measurement whether the operations be relatively simple and direct or complex and remote. The discriminations, operational procedures, and recording into some communicable logical system are just as important for the valid measurement of something like verbal intelligence as they are for measuring nuclear weights.

The classroom teacher is an observer, a discriminator, a recorder of human events, and a measuring instrument, whether by intention or not. Almost any statement that a teacher can make about a particular pupil is based on some comparison with other pupils and is, in this sense, a type of measurement. The more information that the classroom teacher has at his command about the conditions that favor or disfavor reliable and valid measurement, the more probable it seems that his descriptive and evaluative statements about pupils will serve as useful guides for educational planning and teaching procedures. At least this is the philosophy that lies behind this Part of our text.

We have emphasized functional measuring techniques that translate most easily into teaching and remedial actions. Realizing that the contents of this Part of the book constitute only a meager introduction to the theories and technical operations of psychological and educational measurement, we nevertheless believe that a teacher who becomes thoroughly familiar with these contents will be in a better position to evaluate pupil progress and to initiate more promising programs of curricular enrichment and remedial action. In the last analysis, the classroom teacher is the most important evaluator of the totality of educational experiences, the only person who can shift courses of action in light of the day-to-day happenings as they are observed, discriminated, recorded, measured, and evaluated. The teacher can be helped on the measurement side by some reliance on commercially available tests (provided he knows how to select and use them to advantage), but he cannot escape the responsibility of making the value judgments that define the very heart of evaluation and that can most intelligently lead to differential teaching behaviors. We have emphasized the informal case study as the culminating act in the process of observing, discriminating, recording, measuring, and evaluating behavioral change. The statistical and measurement concepts presented in Appendix A and the clinical skills illustrated in the case study in Appendix B are presented as a useful supplement to the present discussion.

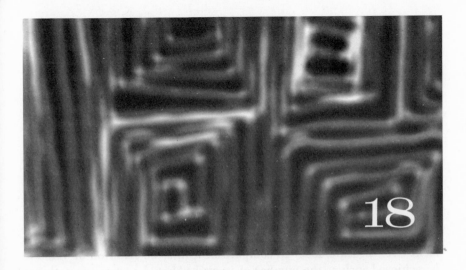

The measurement of learning achievements: Assessing readiness, interim objectives, and terminal objectives

Measurement in its many forms touches the lives of even the most care-free of persons. Plans are made for different parts of the day with the aid of a clock; food is purchased by the pound; and the speed of an automobile is measured by a speedometer. However, there are several levels of measurement that can be described (Stevens, 1951). Some of the measures that we use permit only classifications into gross, mutually exclusive descriptive categories, such as boy-girl, Democrat-Republican, or plant-mineral-animal. They are called *nominal* scales of measurement. Other kinds of measures allow us to go a step further toward precision by permitting us to rank or to order individuals or events from high to low, as do scores on personality tests, attitude-scales and ratings of social interaction. They are *ordinal* scales of measurement. Still other kinds of measures, such as the thermometer and possibly some standardized tests, yield scores having the characteristic of *interval* scales. In addition to ranking individual events, these scales permit us to say that the distances between all adjacent ranks are equal, but the zero point is arbitrary. Thus, we can compare gains qualitatively. When the temperature goes from 70° to 80° it can be said that the gain is the same as when it goes from 35° to 45°. However, we cannot say that 70 is twice as hot as 35°. The most precise measures, such as length and weight, are *ratio scales* of measurement. They have a zero point and they allow us to express any relationship (e.g., zero means absence of the characteristic, 16 pounds are twice as heavy as 8 pounds, or 3 yards are half as long as 6 yards) that can be expressed by numbers. However, measures with the characteristics of ratio-scales have not been developed for use in practical educational situations.

Categories, test scores, clocks, balances—these are all measurement devices that yield descriptions of objects, events, or persons. When the qualitative or quantitative descriptions obtained from them are judged in relation to some objective, purpose, or goal the process is called *evaluation*. Thus, the judgment that a pupil is proceeding slow or fast (evaluation) must be based on a description of his scholastic achievement (or other behavior) as it is obtained from a "pointer reading" such as the number of items he answers correctly on an achievement test (measurement) in comparison with some criterion or value to be achieved such as the number of items he should answer correctly for mastery of the subject (objective).

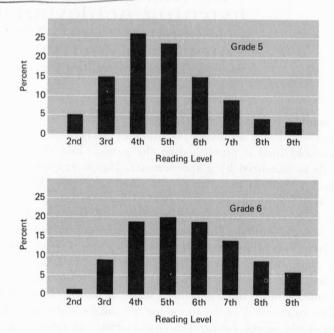

Figure 18-1. The percentages of children at various reading levels within grades 5 and 6 at the beginning of the school year. The large variability in reading ability within the same grade is readily apparent in this figure. It is important that the teacher recognize the variability that exists among pupils as well as the vast differences in abilities, skills, and competencies within an individual pupil. (Adapted from data in the Stanford Achievement Test Manual. *World Book Co., 1953, 1966. With permission.)*

Education and evaluation are closely related as shown by Gronlund (1965) and Gagné (1965) in these four steps in the teaching-learning process:

1. The teacher identifies the behavioral changes to be accomplished by the end of the instructional period. He specifically states what the pupil is able to do when the instructional period is initiated (readiness); what the pupil must be able to do enroute to the satisfactory achievement expected of him at the end of the instructional period (auxiliary, interim, short-term, or means objectives); and what the pupil can reasonably be expected to accomplish, together with the characteristics of the expected performance, at the end of the instructional period (terminal objective). Clear specifications of objectives provide the teacher with a basis for knowing what to evaluate and the pupils with a basis for knowing what to study.

2. The pupil's learning experiences are planned and directed in accordance with the projected objectives. This step, of course, requires construction of teaching plans and the use of teaching methods. Evaluation is only indirectly involved.

3. Periodic observations are made of pupil progress toward the terminal objectives. This clearly involves evaluative decisions, particularly the question of "how to evaluate?"

4. The results of evaluation should be used to help arrive at decisions about the pupil's readiness for further work; the pupil's need for remedial help; and placement of the pupil in special groups if necessary. Evaluation helps the pupil to clarify the teacher's objectives, to identify his degree of progress, and to recognize his special weaknesses or strengths.

Evaluation, at the initiation of a new unit, helps to determine what the pupil has already acquired. This information aids immensely in arriving at decisions regarding the initial experiences the pupil must have if he is to profit from later work. As the unit of work progresses, evaluation is again important to see whether ideas, concepts, attitudes, or skills essential to achieving the terminal objective have been grasped by the pupil. If so, the teacher can go ahead with the work as planned; if not, some remediation may be necessary. Finally, evaluation is used once again at the end of a period of instruction to determine the level of the pupil's performance; that is, to determine how well the terminal objective has been achieved. While we typically consider these three kinds of objectives as important to the elementary and secondary school, the measurement of achievement at the preschool level is becoming a major concern (Goslin, Epstein, & Hallock, 1965) as preschool education becomes a reality (Hechinger, 1966).

The Need for Instructional Objectives

In Chapter 6 behavioral objectives were said to have these characteristics (Mager, 1962): (1) They precisely specify the nature of the behavior expected of the pupil at the end of the instructional period. (2) They describe the conditions under which the behavior is expected to occur. (3) They designate the level of performance (e.g., efficiency, rapidity, complexity) considered acceptable by the teacher. Above all, the objectives should be realistic and inclusive of all the goals of the course that pupils will be expected to achieve and that the teacher expects to evaluate.

The Taxonomy of Educational Objectives: I. Cognitive Domain, (Bloom, 1956) and II. Affective Domain (Krathwohl, et al., 1964) are aids that can be employed in determining objectives, in specifying what is to be evaluated, and in assuring that all major objectives are included. Bloom defines a hierarchy of six levels in the cognitive domain, as follows:

... knowledge involves the recall of specific facts ranging from terminology to the structure of theories.

... comprehension is the basic level of understanding in which the pupil grasps the meaning or intent of the meaning including the ability to use non-literal meanings (e.g., metaphors, symbolism, and the like), translation of mathematical into verbal symbols, the grasping of a generalization, and the ability to extrapolate trends.

... application requires the person to use abstract generalizations or principles in concrete situations such as the application of any of the principles of physics to practical problems, the application of principles of civil rights to current events, or the application of trigonometry to navigation.

... analysis is the achievement of skill in breaking content down into its parts in a manner that reveals the elements of a communication (e.g., to see distinctions between facts and assumptions in a research report), relationships among them (e.g., seeing the main ideas in a paragraph), and their organization within the material as a unit (e.g., seeing the pattern of elements in a work of art).

... synthesis is the identification of the parts of the material and organizing, arranging, or combining them into structures not previously apparent.

... evaluation is the ability to make judgments about the material against established criteria of worth or utility such as identifying "logical fallacies in arguments" or weighing values in making a decision.

When this or any other classification is employed in stating course objectives it must be imposed on the specific changes the teacher is attempting to make in the pupil's behavior. Sometimes measures intended to evaluate the higher levels of knowledge (e.g., meaning) may be measuring only lower levels as in those circumstances where the test employs content in precisely the form it was presented to the pupil. In this instance, correct answers are based on recall through sheer memorization of the material rather than through any productive cognitive processes such as reasoning or problem-solving.

Levels of objectives in the affective domain

Some of the objectives of the school are aimed at the development and change in attitudes. This area is less developed than that of measuring achievement. Nevertheless, one group of investigators (Krathwohl, Bloom, & Masia, 1964) has attempted to identify the attitudinal levels to serve as practical bases for statements of classroom objectives. An outline of their analysis of levels of objectives in the affective realm with an illustration for each is presented below:

Receiving and attending—the student's attention must be directed to the preferred stimuli.

He becomes *aware* of something . . .
"Develops awareness of aesthetic factors in dress, furnishings, or good art" (p. 177).

He is willing to *receive* . . .
"Attends carefully when others speak—in direct conversation, as with the telephone, or in audiences" (p. 177).

His attention is *selective* . . .
"Listens to music with some discrimination as to its mood and meaning . . ." (p. 178).

Responding—the student becomes actively engaged in the activity.

He is *acquiescent* . . .
"He complies with health regulations" (p. 179).

He is voluntarily *willing* to engage in an activity . . .
"Acquaints himself with significant current issues in international . . . affairs through voluntary reading and discussion" (p. 179).

He achieves *satisfaction* from the activity . . .
"Finds pleasure in reading for recreation" (p. 180).

Valuing—the student becomes committed to the underlying values of the affective behavior.

He *accepts* the value and is willing to be identified with it . . .
"Grows in his sense of kinship with human beings of all nations" (p. 181).

He is sufficiently *committed* to the value that he seeks out opportunities to pursue it . . .
"Deliberately examines a variety of viewpoints on controversial issues with a view to forming opinions about them" (p. 181).

Organization—as the student encounters many situations more than one value is involved. These are then differentiated, correlated, and synthesized into an organized system.

He *conceptualizes* the value by abstracting the quality that relates it to values already in the value structure and to values yet to be incorporated . . .

"Attempts to identify the characteristics of an art object which he admires" (p. 183).

He organizes his values into proper relationships with one another . . .

"Weighs alternative social policies and practices against the standards of public welfare rather than the advantage of specialized and narrow interest groups" (p. 183).

Characterization by a value or value complex—the pupil acts so consistently in accordance with certain values that he becomes characterized by the behavior they control and by their integration into a philosophy or world view.

He is able to act consistently and effectively to events around him . . .

"Judges problems and issues in terms of situations, issues, purposes, and consequences involved rather than in terms of fixed, dogmatic precepts or wishful thinking" (p. 184).

He is so internally consistent that these objectives characterize him almost completely . . .

"Develops for regulation of one's personal and civic life a code of behavior based on ethical principles consistent with democratic ideals" (p. 185). (From Krathwohl, Bloom, Masia, 1964, pp. 176–185.)

The two following examples from Gronlund (1965, pp. 52–54) suggest how Bloom's taxonomy can be used in conjunction with statements of behavioral objectives for the construction of items and for selecting tests with appropriate kinds of items.

Specific objective. The pupil should be able to differentiate between relative values expressed in fractions. This is a Level II objective: Comprehension.

Item: Which one of the following fractions is smaller than one-half?
  (A) 2/4   (B) 4/6   (C) 3/8   (D) 9/16

Specific Objective. The pupil should be able to apply biological principles and concepts to everyday problems. The next two items illustrate the measurement of this objective at Level III: Application.

Item: Which one of the following best explains why green algae give off bubbles of oxygen on a bright, sunny day?

(A) Transpiration (B) Plasmolysis (C) Photosynthesis

(D) Osmosis

Item: Which one of the following best explains why bread mold can be grown in a dark room?

(A) Some plants do not produce their own food.

(B) Photosynthesis can take place in the dark.

(C) Chlorophyll aids the growth of plants in darkness.

(D) Bread mold takes in carbon dioxide and gives off oxygen
in both darkness and light.

Upon examining the above objectives in relationship to those
stated according to Mager's (1962) specifications the reader will readily
see that there is considerable leeway acceptable in the way objectives
are stated. Compare the objectives above with the following illustrations:

Specific Objective: When the pupil is provided a list of fifty compounds
containing carbon he will be able to classify at least thirty of them as to
whether they are gas, liquid, or solids at normal temperature and pressure
(Ahmann & Glock, 1967; Mager, 1962).

Specific Objective: The pupil should be able to describe the relevant events
leading up to the Boston Tea Party (Gorow, 1966).

In practice the important characteristic is that you state as precisely as possible just what the pupil is expected to accomplish. The
more precise statements serve as efficient and accurate guides for identifying which skills and knowledges a pupil must have as he enters and
emerges from each period of instruction.

Characteristics of Evaluative Procedures

The extent to which subject-matter objectives have been achieved
can be measured by a number of different procedures. Which procedure
is used depends in large part on what is to be evaluated. For appraising
readiness in reading, for example, teachers often use commercially prepared examinations or standardized tests; for measuring knowledge of
terms the student needs to know for later comprehension of the subject
matter of a given course, the teacher might prepare an objective test; for
evaluating whether the pupil can relate a current event to earlier historical events, an essay question might be used; to see whether the pupil
can use references, a written report might be the basis for evaluation;
and to determine whether the pupil has made progress in social skills,
the rating scale, anecdotal record, or observation with the aid of a
checklist are useful devices.

Sometimes teachers fail to recognize that the kinds of data suitable
for evaluating one kind of objective (e.g., knowledge and comprehension) are not necessarily suitable for evaluating other kinds of objectives (e.g., analysis and synthesis). Thus, items or tests which require
only that the pupil define terms can be used for measuring interim
achievements but will tell very little about his ability to balance equa-

tions. Similarly, a written test in which the pupil explains the process of streaking an agar plate to prepare a bacterial culture in biology is not a substitute for the actual performance if the objective clearly indicates that he is to "*perform* the process in (a specified amount of time) and (with results that have certain specified characteristics)." Thus, regardless of the method of assessing pupil performance the teacher is concerned with the relevance of the measurement and its dependability.

Validity: Observations of behavior must be relevant

The first and foremost question to be asked with respect to any evaluation procedure is: How valid is it? This question is concerned with whether the test measures or predicts, (1) what we want it to measure or predict, (2) all of what we want it to measure, or (3) nothing but what we want it to measure. Does the test really measure what it purports to measure? For example, whether a so-called arithmetic reasoning test is valid or not depends upon the extent to which it measures reasoning ability in arithmetic rather than other things, such as general intelligence or reading ability.

Validity, then, refers to the soundness of the results of the instrument or of the soundness of the interpretation of the results for the purpose at hand. It is always the instrument's most important characteristic. All other merits of the test are preempted if it lacks validity. The types of validity to be described below are similar to those defined by a national committee established for examining technical characteristics of tests.*

Content Validity. One approach to identifying the validity of a test involves a logical analysis of the content of the instrument. Using one's best professional judgment, the topics and areas included in the test are compared with subject-matter content and behaviors that might have been included. Validity obtained in this way is referred to as *content validity.* This procedure can be simply illustrated by showing how a test of social studies might be judged as valid. The content of the test is examined to determine how well it matches what the teacher has been trying to teach, i.e., how well it relates to his objectives. If the test contains a representative sample of the important aspects of the course, it is said to have high content validity. Similarly, the activities and processes that correspond to a specific concept, such as "good citizenship," might be analyzed. The first problem is to define what the concept means. The term "good citizenship" is broad, abstract, and indefinite. Test items

*Committee on Test Standards of the American Educational Research Association, National Education Association and National Council on Measurements Used in Education, *Technical Recommendations for Achievement Tests* (Washington: NEA, 1955).

must be specific, concrete, and precise. They must consist of definite limited tasks. Accordingly, the concept is analyzed to determine the kind of behaviors implied by the objectives. Then the test is examined to determine whether it will permit a representative sampling of behaviors and of related situations in which the behavior is expected to occur. The problem in preparing a test that has concept validity is one of translating the concept into specific tangible tasks or test items.

Concurrent and Predictive Validity. The second type of validity is determined empirically or statistically. In this case, the test user determines the extent to which performance on the test predicts some future performance (*predictive validity*) on an important criterion task, or the extent to which it is related to some current performance (*concurrent validity*). The measure of performance on the criterion might be very similar to the test for which validity is being determined, or it might be quite different. Empirical validity, thus, is studied by comparing test results with those of a criterion known to measure some characteristic of importance. For example, if one wished to know whether a test successfully predicts college grades, i.e., whether it has *predictive* validity, it would be given to high school seniors prior to admission to college. At the end of their freshman year in college their scores on the test would be correlated with their average freshman grades. Or, if one wished to know whether the test yields results similar to those obtained from an intelligence test already known to predict academic achievement, then the scores from the first test would be correlated with scores from the second (intelligence) test administered at about the same time. The criterion in this example of *concurrent validity* is the score from the intelligence test.

The magnitude of the relationship, in either situation, is expressed by an index called the *validity coefficient* which indicates how well the test predicts performance on the criterion measure. The validity coefficient is a coefficient of correlation. As such, it can vary from —1.0 to 1.0. A correlation of .00 indicates no validity. A correlation of 1.0 indicates perfect validity, or ability to predict without error, the rank of any person on the criterion measure by knowing his test score. A correlation of —1.0 indicates a perfect inverse relationship between the predictor and the criterion. It indicates that the highest value of the predictor is associated with the lowest values of the criterion; the next highest with the next lowest and so on to the lowest value of the predictor which is associated with the highest value of the criterion. For the purpose of prediction a negative validity coefficient is as useful as a positive one of the same numerical value. Validity coefficients between .00 and —1.00 or +1.00 indicate that the relationship is either negative or positive, respectively, but in either case the relationship would be less than perfect. Of course, the closer the validity coefficient approaches

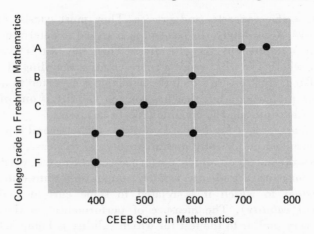

Figure 18-2. The CEEB (College Entrance Examination Board) examination is a good predictor of college grades. The students obtaining high scores on the CEEB examination obtain in general the best grades in college.

1.0 (whether positive or negative) the more accurate will be the predictions of the criterion scores from knowledge of the predictor score.

In the illustration of concurrent validity it was suggested that the score on the predictor test might be correlated with the score on an intelligence test. Since validity may be determined by any kind of performance, test designers frequently validate their instruments by correlating them with well-established tests. For example, group tests of intelligence have been frequently correlated with the Stanford-Binet test of intellectual ability which has been thoroughly studied both empirically and logically. If a test correlates highly with the Stanford-Binet test, it is assumed to measure whatever the Binet measures and therefore it should be valid for similar purposes.

Using Information about Validity. Validity coefficients are seldom as high as one would like them to be. Rarely does a validity coefficient exceed .70. However, any degree of correlation, provided it is reliable, indicates that predictions from the test are better than decisions made without such data. Practical considerations such as methods already in use, time and money available for testing, and gains to be achieved are among the factors which enter into deciding whether a particular validity coefficient is sufficiently high to justify using that particular test.

Reliability: How dependable are the observations?

Any test score is, to some extent, an inaccurate measure of performance, because errors occur whenever a *sample* of behavior is obtained. For example, most readers of this book have taken tests where they knew a considerable amount of the subject matter being tested, but received "poor grades" because the teacher just happened to ask the "wrong" questions. The reader probably felt that the test was not a fair test, i.e., it was not a very reliable index of his performance. Had he been administered another test with other items he might have made a much higher score. This is the same as saying that the first test score would not be consistent (not reliable) with performance based on a different sample of questions.

When measuring achievement in an area such as multiplication the pupil is presented with many items drawn from all over the appropriate range of multiplication combinations. A *sample* of his performance is obtained by administering a test containing these items. The assumption is that this sample provides an *estimate* of what his work will be like on other occasions. A given sample of items will yield erroneous estimates of the pupil's ability if the combinations happen to be those especially easy or difficult for him. The sample of behavior will also not be representative of his talents if we test him on a day when he is ill, lacks motivation, or works under adverse physical conditions of lighting, ventilation, and noise. Such factors contribute to errors of measurement which, when added to the pupil's "true" score, may lead to incorrect inferences about the pupil's ability. An index called the *reliability coefficient* expresses the extent to which errors of measurement are present in the scores. The reliability coefficient varies from .00 to 1.00. A zero correlation indicates absence of reliability and 1.0 indicates perfect reliability.

In a word, reliability means consistency. Whatever technique is used for gathering information about the pupil and whatever the source, the information should be evaluated for its dependability. Unlike validity, little can be told about the reliability of a test from examining the test itself. Reliability is a statistical concept and requires that the test be administered on one or more occasions to a group of people. The consistency of the relative standing of the individuals from one occasion to the next is then expressed in terms of their shift in ranks (*reliability coefficient*) or in terms of the amount by which any individual's score can be expected to vary (*standard error of measurement*) on successive occasions. Usually, for a standardized test, the author performs these analyses and reports the results in the test manual.

The Equivalent Forms Method. Sometimes the user of a test is interested in the consistency of performance of pupils on two equivalent forms of a test, that is, how much a pupil's score would change from one sample of questions to a different sample testing the same ability. This method is commonly used by makers of standardized tests. It involves the preparation of two or more equivalent forms of the test which are then administered to a large number of pupils with little or no time lapse between administrations. The test is said to be reliable if the scores based on the two forms are highly correlated. A reliability coefficient obtained in this way is called a *coefficient of equivalence* and indicates how precisely the test measures the person's performance at the time of administration.

Closely related to the coefficient of equivalence is the coefficient of *internal consistency*. Its determination involves: (1) administering a test once to a group of pupils, (2) obtaining two sets of equivalent scores (e.g., a score based on odd-numbered items and another based on even-numbered items) from the test; and (3) correlating the two sets of scores.

The Test-Retest Method. The user of tests is also concerned with the stability of test scores over a period of time. Accordingly, the same test is administered to the same pupils on two different occasions without intervening opportunity for the pupils to increase their knowledge of the material. The reliability coefficient obtained by correlating the two sets of scores is called a *coefficient of stability*.

The length of time between tests is an important consideration when making decisions based on indexes of stability. Thus, for quizzes given at different points in a course, short-term stability would be important while long-term stability would be relatively unimportant. On the other hand, an intelligence or achievement test given in high school for predicting success in the first year of college should be stable over long intervals of time. These considerations are especially important when teachers use information from school files, or when counselors use information to predict later adjustment in vocations or college. The stability of test scores may vary considerably for the same interval at different stages of maturity. The intelligence test score, for example, is more stable over a three-year period at maturity than it is over the three-year period between 6 and 9 years of age. However, in both cases the score is reasonably reliable over a one-year period. Thus, the score obtained at maturity is more dependable for making decisions over a long time range than is the score for the six-year-old child. On the other hand, the score from the younger pupil can be used for making decisions about readiness requirements and the like that do not extend over periods beyond a year. Doubt about the reliability of a test score always calls for retesting.

The coefficient of correlation

In Figure 18-3 are diagrams showing different degrees of reliability based on coefficients of equivalence. Each dot represents an in-

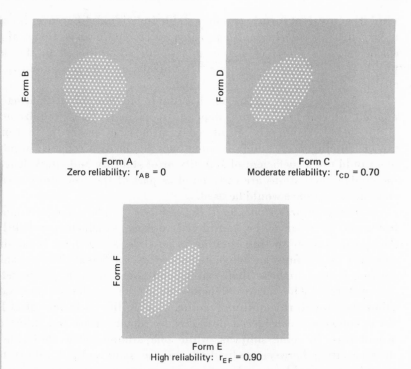

Form A
Zero reliability: $r_{AB} = 0$

Form C
Moderate reliability: $r_{CD} = 0.70$

Form E
High reliability: $r_{EF} = 0.90$

Figure 18-3. Diagrams showing varying degrees of reliability.

dividual pupil's score on two forms of a test. The correlation coefficient (r) indicates the *degree* of relationship represented by the array of scores, but it is *not* a percentage. Note that it would be a difficult matter to predict scores on Form A knowing the person's score on Form B. Pupils with Form-B scores in the middle range fall in the high, middle, and bottom range of Form-A scores. However, by knowing Form-F scores, one can efficiently predict Form-E scores; pupils with low Form-F scores also earn low scores on Form E and those with high scores on one earn high scores on the other.

These diagrams could be used equally well for representing validity coefficients simply by substituting criterion scores on the ordinate and predictor scores on the abscissa. Or, they can be used to represent the general case of the coefficient of correlation by substituting Variable X on either axis and Variable Y on the other. What would the axes be labeled if any of the above figures were used to represent split-half reliability coefficients? coefficients of stability?

The Combined Approach.   A third method of estimating reliability considers, simultaneously, the fluctuations due to day-to-day changes in the person and fluctuations due to the particular choice of items in the test. An index which shows the extent to which the test (and its equivalent form) measures stable individual differences is called a *coefficient of stability and equivalence*. To obtain an estimate of this coefficient, *two forms* of the same test are administered to the same pupils on *two different occasions*. The correlation between these two sets of scores is taken as the desired estimate.

As noted above, the most suitable method of estimating the amount of error in test scores depends upon the teacher's requirements. If day-to-day variation is considered as a source of errors (as in a measure of "intelligence," which is sometimes assumed to remain constant), one would use a coefficient of stability or of stability and equivalence. If day-to-day fluctuations are considered as part of the true score, a coefficient of equivalence would be used.

Using Information about Reliability. What standard must a test meet in order to be considered to have satisfactory reliability? No simple answer to this question is possible, since there is no single standard that defines an adequate reliability coefficient. The reliability desired is the highest that can be obtained with a given set of circumstances. The answer depends upon the particular purpose in mind. As a rough rule-of-thumb guide, a reliability coefficient of at least .50 is commonly considered desirable for determining the status of a school class in some subjects, while one around .90 is desirable for differentiating between individuals in the same subject. Short tests, though less reliable than longer ones, are often convenient for initial screening purposes or for making tentative judgments in the absence of more reliable tests or where time is at a premium. Of most importance, the teacher should not treat a score with low reliability in the same manner that he does a score with high reliability. If it is essential to have a great deal of confidence in the results, then a high reliability is demanded. Although reliability and validity are related they are not one and the same concept. A test may yield consistent results time and again without having concurrent or predictive validity. On the other hand, for a test to be valid, that is, for it to predict a criterion score successfully the score must be dependable. Thus, the validity of a score cannot be higher than its reliability.

Reliability coefficients are influenced by such factors as the length of the test, its difficulty, its objectivity of scoring, and the homogeneity of the pupils tested, as follows:

(*a*) *Test Length.* The longer test is more reliable than the shorter one, provided the items in both are of equal quality. The reason behind this rule of thumb is that the greater number of items in the long test is more likely to be a representative sample of the pupil's behavior than is the fewer number of items in the short test.

(*b*) *Test Difficulty.* The most effective test for reliably differentiating among pupils is one of moderate difficulty. If the test items

Effect of length of test on reliability

Short test of 10 items	Long test of 100 similar items
Reliability coefficient, r_{11}=0.50	Reliability coefficient, r_{11}=0.90

Effect of difficulty of test on reliability

Class	8B	Class	8B	Class	8B
Teacher	Miss Jones	Teacher	Miss Jones	Teacher	Miss Jones
No. of items	50	No. of items	50	No. of items	50
Class average	45	Class average	25	Class average	10

Very easy test of 50 Items	Moderately difficult test of 50 Items	Very difficult test of 50 items
Reliability coefficient, r_{11} =0.60	Reliability coefficient, r_{11}=0.85	Reliability coefficient, r_{11} =0.65

Effect of homogeneity of group on test reliability

Test	MAT	Test	MAT
Class	6A	Class	5A, 6A, and 7A
Teacher	Miss Jones	Teacher	Miss D, Miss J, and Miss K
No.of items	50	No.of items	50
Class average	30	Class average	30

Test administered to 6th-graders only	Same test administered to group of 5th-, 6-, and 7th-graders
Reliability coefficient, r_{11}=0.80	Reliability coefficient, r_{11}=0.96

Figure 18-4. Effect of length of test, of difficulty of test, and homogeneity of the group on test reliability.

were too easy (or too difficult) for most pupils in a class the scores would tend to be lumped together in one group, i.e., most pupils would have either high scores or low scores. Whatever differences were found among them would be due, to a large extent, to such temporary factors as guessing, fatigue, motivation, or other characteristics of the situation which can be expected to fluctuate from one occasion to the next, rather than to permanent changes in behavior.

On occasion, some teachers construct examinations with difficulty levels of 70 percent on the assumption that 70 percent is a passing score (Wood, 1960). This is an incorrect premise and leads to an examination that is too "easy" for grading purposes. However, even this conclusion may need to be qualified somewhat according to the results found in an experiment by Sax and Reade (1964). They caution that the results of their study must be considered tentative, but the data suggest that where a very low cut-off point is used for determining the "passing" point, "easy" examinations are more accurate than are "hard" examinations. On the other hand, difficult examinations lead to higher motivation for further study than do easy examinations. These results suggest that fairly difficult examinations might be used during the year to motivate students and easier examinations might be used at the end of a unit or course for grading purposes.

(c) *Test Objectivity.*   The scoring procedure is not objective when two scorers obtain widely different scores for the same paper. The reliability of the test is decreased accordingly. Tests composed of true-false or multiple-choice items are less subject to this difficulty than essay test items.

(d) *Homogeneity of the Pupils Tested.*   If pupils are very much alike the differences in their scores are likely to be small and their rank in class or their shifts in scores will be due to chance or other temporary factors, thereby decreasing the size of the reliability coefficient. On the other hand, where differences among pupils are large the scores will be widely separated and, concomitantly, there will be less opportunity for such factors as fatigue and minor changes in motivation to cause a change in the pupil's rank in class. Consequently, reliability coefficients for heterogenous classes will be larger than those based on homogeneous classes.

Appraising Scholastic Achievements

The art of examining and obtaining information about student achievement is an ancient one. Oral quizzing has been part of the daily classroom routine from time immemorial. Although written examinations are more recent than oral testing, they also have a long history. They were firmly established in the educational system of China thirteen hundred years ago, and were familiar to Grecian and Roman teachers.

The emphasis on the kind of information needed about pupils and the most appropriate methods of obtaining it have both varied over time. Oral, essay, and objective examinations have been stressed and attacked in turn. Modern emphasis on the psychology of individual differences and the attendant problems of measurement make it probable that the high esteem in which examinations are held will continue to be maintained for some time. The present trend is to make use of many types of examinations to evaluate the several dimensions of pupil achievement. The use of teacher-made examinations and certain stand-

ardized tests gives the teacher information about his pupils which was
unavailable to even the most skillful and experienced teacher a century
ago.

Constructing tests

Teacher-made tests can contribute significantly to an accumulation of diagnostic and achievement information. They have the great
advantage of being especially tailored to the aims and objectives of the
course as defined by the teacher. In fact, the materials emphasized in
tests implicitly tend to define objectives and to be accepted by pupils as
important. With care, teacher-made tests can be exact and important
communicators of the teacher's intent in a way not possible with other
kinds of measures. On the other hand, if his tests ask only for names,
dates, and sentences, from the textbook, these will become the *functional* objectives and pupils will study accordingly. Tests tell much of
what the teacher really values in his pupils' achievements regardless of
what he may verbally profess to value. When constructing their own
examinations, teachers customarily employ the essay and the short-
answer exam for measuring pupil achievement. The construction of
either type necessitates an explicit set of objectives from which to work.

Distinctions between essay and objective tests

Whether the teacher decides to use an essay or objective test depends
on his objectives and the functions to be served by the test. Most
measurement specialists differentiate between the two kinds of tests on
the bases of the requirements for constructing them, the objectivity of
the obtained scores, and the thought processes that are involved in
answering the questions. Among representative descriptions of these
matters is the one provided by Ebel (1965). It is briefly summarized
below by showing how each characteristic appears in both types of
tests. This summary should prove useful to the reader when making
decisions about the kind of teacher-made tests to use in conjunction
with specific objectives.

Test Characteristic	Essay Test	Objective Test
Preparation by Teacher	Easy to prepare. Composed of a few general questions that call for lengthy and detailed answers.	Tedious and difficult to prepare. Requires the construction of many questions requiring brief but carefully chosen and carefully worded alternatives.

Test Characteristic	Essay Test	Objective Test
Student Activity	The student composes his answer by relating facts, organizing them in logical order and expressing his ideas in written form. Most of the student's time is spent in thinking and writing.	The student chooses a correct answer from several alternatives. If carefully constructed, the student's choice will require knowledge and understanding rather than recognition or rote memory. Most of the student's time is spent in reading and thinking.
Expression by Student	The student can answer the question according to *his* own unique style, in terms of the knowledge *he* has acquired, and on the basis of the information *he* chooses to bring to bear on the question. Essay tests, however, may encourage bluffing.	The student is limited by the kinds of objectives reflected in the questions. He can only express his knowledge by his choice of alternatives. Objective tests may encourage guessing.
Expression by Teacher	The teacher can explicitly express his objectives by stating the basis for scoring and by making demands for specific qualities in the answers. He implicitly states objectives by his scoring requirements. Typically, larger units of material are emphasized.	The teacher expresses his values and objectives clearly and definitely, by the kinds of questions asked. Often, small units are emphasized in a single item, but because there are more items, the test can permit a more representative sampling of the material than do essay tests in a given time limit.
Objectivity	Though the task *can* be made definite, it often is not. The course objectives are not always apparent from inspection.	Task requirements, bases on which answers will be judged, and objectives to be tapped are openly reflected. Because these points are unambiguously apparent, the objective test is subject to more criticism than is the essay test.

Test Characteristic	Essay Test	Objective Test
Scoring	The quality of the scoring procedure rests entirely on the care employed by the scorer. Essay tests are time-consuming to score accurately. The scorer must take special precautions to prevent his biases, and other extraneous factors, from influencing the score. The distribution of scores is controlled by the weights, minimum scores, and maximum scores assigned by the scorer.	The quality of scoring is determined by the care with which the questions are constructed. These are easy tests to score objectively. Because of this, the teacher with large classes or who intends to use the test with many classes, might reasonably consider spending the extra time required to construct objective test items. The distribution of scores is determined exclusively by the statistical characteristics (determined by quality of items) of the test.
Similarities	There are some misconceptions about the two kinds of tests that can be dispelled by summarizing their similarities.	

(1) Either test can be employed to measure adequately any important educational achievement objective that can be clearly defined.

(2) Both kinds of tests can be used to encourage students to use such desirable practices as studying for understanding, organizing of material, relating material to previously learned knowledges, and applying information to problems.

(3) Some subjective judgment is required by both the teacher who constructs the items and the pupil who responds to the items.

(4) The score from either test is valuable only to the extent that it is objective and reliable.

SOURCE: Ebel, 1965, pp. 84-109. With permission of author and publisher.

Essay tests

The essay examination has long been popular with teachers although it came under attack in the early 1920s. Studies by such pioneers in the measurement field as Starch and Elliott (1912) showed that when the same set of English essay examinations was submitted to presumably competent teachers, the grades assigned to the same paper ranged all the way from 50 to 98 percent. Grading in geometry (Starch & Elliott, 1913) proved to be as inaccurate.

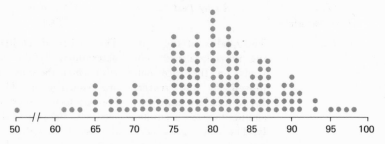

Grades assigned to the same English paper by 142 teachers of English

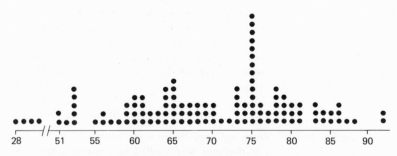

Grades assigned to the same mathematics paper by 115 teachers of mathematics

Figure 18-5. The top diagram shows the marks in percentage assigned to the same English paper by 142 teachers of English. The bottom figure indicates that 115 teachers of high school mathematics do not agree in their grading any better than did the English teachers. (Adapted from D. Starch & E. C. Elliott. Reliability of grading high school work in English. School Review, *1912, 20, 442–457 and D. Starch & E. C. Elliott. Reliability of grading work in mathematics.* School Review, *1913, 21, 254–257. With permission of authors and publisher.)*

The importance of these findings, along with those of many other research workers, is that they led to a critical analysis of the essay test as an effective evaluation procedure. Research showed that the essay test could be improved, leading the way to recommendations for helping teachers construct better essay tests that could be evaluated more objectively and reliably (Dressel, 1954). Such tests are neither easy to make nor easy to score as is sometimes believed. Both processes require considerable care and time. Carelessness may result in scores not better than descriptions obtained from casual everyday observations. Properly conceived and scored, they have no equal for measuring the higher level objectives of production, analysis, synthesis, and evaluation of ideas within and among subject-matter areas.

The following suggestions are guides that have been found helpful in improving essay test questions (based on Gronlund, 1965, 1968; Gorow, 1966; and Solomon, 1965) :

1. Relate essay questions to higher level objectives that do not lend themselves readily to measurement by true-false or multiple-choice tests. If a multiple-choice or other form of objective test will serve the teacher's purpose it should by all means be used instead of an essay test.

2. Focus the question on eliciting the kind of behavior called for in the learning outcomes and understood as such by the pupil, especially of behaviors related to abstractions and principles.

3. Explicitly request an interpretation, an application, or other requirement. Unless this is accomplished the question will yield an unscorable set of answers. An example of a poor item is: "Compare the Greeks and the Romans." An example of a better item is: "Show how each of the following has been a factor in the development of democracy in the United States:

(a)   The characteristics of life on the western frontier.

(b)   The public schools.

(c)   Newspapers and periodicals."

4. A sufficient amount of time should be allowed for pupils to complete the question and to demonstrate their abilities.

5. The efficiency of the items will be increased if the instructions to the test include its purpose, the desired objectives, the sorts of answers that will be rated highest, and the amount of time to be allocated to each question.

After the essay test items have been constructed and *before* administering them to pupils the teacher would be well advised to set up the scoring system. Not only does this provide a basis for judging the papers but it can also serve to indicate ambiguities in the question. Some guides to scoring suggested by Solomon (1965) and Gorow (1966) are summarized below:

1. *Block out a framework of the model answer and possible answers to the questions before the test is administered.* If some of the "possible" answers are irrelevant then the question should be reworked to eliminate the chance that the uninterpretable or ambiguous answer will be elicited. An illustration of an essay test with criteria and model answer is highlighted immediately below.

Grading standards for an essay test

The following is an example of grading standards, in this case from the College Entrance Examination Board's *Advanced Placement Examination in American History*, a test for students in senior high schools.

Question: "The reform movements of 1820-1850 embodied certain old and persistent American qualities."
Assess the validity of this generalization.

Guidelines for Grading

Extremely Well Qualified

Specific discussion clearly relating several reform movements with American qualities. Wider range of examples, more elaborate or precise descriptions.

Evaluates generalization by showing where it holds and where it does not, in each case providing specific illustrations.

May note paradoxical nature of reform—some reforms at cross-purposes with others, yet both drawing on traditional elements for sanction.

Well Qualified

Specific discussion of several reform movements and specific indication of American qualities.

Clear relation between qualities and reform movements.

Evaluates generalization both by supporting it with specific examples *and* by some indication of reform aspects where generalization does not hold.

Qualified

Fairly specific discussion of several reform movements.

Fairly clear relation between qualities and specific reform movements.

Reasonably accurate.

Evaluates generalization with clear and appropriate examples.

Possibly Qualified

Some indication of reform movements—should mention more than one unless one is very well done.

Some brief indication of old and persistent American qualities.

Attempts to relate qualities with reform movements.

No glaring errors or inconsistencies.

Attempts to evaluate generalization.

Not Qualified

No recognition or specific indication of reform movements; just superficial treatment of reform in general.

No clear indication of old and persistent American qualities.

Major factual errors, inconsistencies, irrelevancies.

Checklist of Facts

Reform movements, 1820–1850:

Abolitionism
Penal reform
Temperance
Naval reforms

Mental illness
Other handicapped
Women's rights
Peace movement
Working conditions
Utopianism
Public education
Political: spoils and rotation, franchise, etc.
Economic reforms: monopoly, labor organization, etc.
Transcendentalism and religious groups

Old and persistent American qualities:

Optimism
Progress
Individualism
Moralism
Sense of mission
Natural rights
Moderation in making changes
Concern for social ills
Opportunity for all

New and temporary qualities:

Romanticism
Democratic mood in contrast to earlier deferential mood
Millennialism
Perfectibility of man and society

2. *Score a single question on all papers before going to the next question.* Each item can be scored by assigning points depending on the degree of correspondence between the pupil's answer and the teacher's "ideal" answer.

3. *Provide for objectivity in scoring.*   Different scorers often vary in the grades they assign a given paper because they are distracted from the content of the answer by extraneous factors. This means that individual teachers inadvertently introduce bias into their scoring procedure by basing their scores on such irrelevant factors as grammatical structure, neatness, spelling, or punctuation, even when they are clearly instructed to base their score only on content (Marshall, 1967; Scannell & Marshall, 1966). Where these factors are related to the objectives they should, of course, enter into the scoring system.

Objective tests

As a countermeasure against the weaknesses of the essay form of examination, professional test-makers in the early 1920s developed and offered to the schools short-answer or objective type tests. Numerous tests using true-false, multiple-choice, and matching items were published. These were not only used widely but in a short time many teachers began to construct and use similar tests.

In principle, objective tests can be used for evaluating a wide range of behaviors from facts to complex learning outcomes. Thus, it is possible to measure content detail which depends primarily upon the pupil's ability to memorize minute detail as in the following item given by Berg (1965, p. 49):

The clause "the powers not delegated to the United States by the Constitution, nor prohibited to it by the states, are reserved to the states, or to the people" is to be found in the
1. Fifth Amendment
2. Eighth Amendment
3. Tenth Amendment (Keyed correct)
4. Fourteenth Amendment

Berg properly notes that the exclusive employment of such items results in a distorted functional description of the course objectives and is, literally, an abuse of the objective test item. On the other hand, it is possible to use the objective test to measure a variety of the higher level outcomes presented in the *Taxonomy of Educational Objectives* (Bloom, 1956), as illustrated in the three items by Gronlund (1968, pp. 60–61). (See adjoining highlights.)

Examples of objective items for three levels of outcomes

Directions: Read the following comments which a teacher made about testing. Then answer the questions that follow the comments by encircling the letter of the best answer.

"Students go to school to learn, not to take tests. In addition, tests cannot be used to indicate a student's absolute level of learning. All tests can do is rank students in order of achievement, and this relative ranking is influenced by guessing, bluffing, and the subjective opinions of the teacher doing the scoring. The teaching-learning process would benefit if we did away with tests and depended on student self-evaluation."

Objective: Recognize Unstated Assumptions

1. Which one of the following unstated assumptions is this teacher making?
   A. Students go to school to learn.
   B. Teachers use essay tests primarily.
   *C. Tests make no contribution to learning.
   D. Tests do not indicate a student's absolute level of learning.

Objective: *Ability To Interpret*

2. Which one of the following types of tests is this teacher primarily talking about?

A. Diagnostic test.
*B. Mastery test.
C. Pre-test.
D. Survey test.

Objective: *Ability To Identify Relationships*

3. Which one of the following propositions is most essential to the final conclusion?

*A. Effective self-evaluation does not require use of tests.
B. Tests place students in rank order only.
C. Test scores are influenced by factors other than achievement.
D. Students do not go to school to take tests.

(From Norman E. Gronlund. *Constructing achievement tests.* Englewood Cliffs: Prentice-Hall, 1968, pp. 60–61.)

The construction of good objective test items is time consuming and requires considerable skill and knowledge. However, the following are worthwhile introductory guides.*

1. *The item should be related to a teaching objective.* The main concern of the teacher should be with the extent to which his pupils have achieved the defined objectives.

2. *The main question should be clearly phrased in the stem of the item.* For example, the following item would be considerably less confusing to pupils if the stem were rewritten along the lines indicated:

(Poor) The great circle, one-half of which is the Greenwich Meridian, is on the other side of the

(1) International Date Line
(2) Equator
(3) Tropic of Cancer
(4) Tropic of Capricorn

(Improved) The Greenwich Meridian is one-half of a great circle. What do we call the other half?

(1) International Date Line
(2) Equator
(3) Tropic of Cancer
(4) Tropic of Capricorn†

*For a more detailed description the reader may want to refer to Gronlund, 1968; Ebel, 1965; or Gorow, 1966; all of whom, among other outstanding measurement specialists, have granted permission to use some of their materials, and whose views are introduced to the reader in one or another sections of the chapter.

†From a manual prepared by S. N. Tinkelman, *Improving the classroom test: A manual of test construction procedure for the classroom teacher.* Albany: University of the State of New York, 1957. With permission of author and publisher.

Although the stem should be positive for most items occasional negative wording is permissible in which case the negation should be emphasized.

3. *Alternatives should have the same relationship to one another.* The sentence formed by the combination of stem and each alternative should be grammatically correct.

4. *The keyed alternative should be viewed as correct to the knowledgeable student.* The other alternatives should appear as correct to the pupil who does not know the material; but avoid "trick" alternatives. In the illustration below "writer" is a possible correct answer not intended by the author of the question. The item is improved by "spoiling" this response so that it is definitely incorrect.

(Poor)   H. L. Mencken has achieved his greatest fame as a
    (1) writer   (2) biographer of Abraham Lincoln   (3) poet
    (4) psychologist   (5) student of the American language

(Improved)   H. L. Mencken has achieved his greatest fame as a
    (1) writer of popular novels

In the following illustration, the alternatives contain material that may well be incorporated into the stem.

(Poor)   Milk can be pasteurized at home by
    (1) heating it to a temperature of 130°
    (2) heating it to a temperature of 145°
    (3) _____

(Improved)   Milk can be pasteurized at home by heating it to a temperature of
    (1) 130°   (2) 145°   (3) _____

5. *Avoid irrelevant cues that might be used by the student who is "guessing."* Frequently, grammatical clues such as "a" or "an" at the end of a stem or differences in grammatical construction of stems and alternatives reduce the number of choices that have to be made. Other times the correct answer might be a "dead giveaway" if it is always shorter or longer than the distracters. The use of such phrases as "all of the above" and "none of the above" is not recommended. In the following question the article "an" provides a clue to the correct answer:

(Poor)   The least objective measure is an _____ item.
    (a) matching   (b) multiple-choice
    (c) true-false   (d) essay

(Improved)   Objectivity is most difficult to achieve in scoring _____ items.
  (a) matching   (b) multiple-choice
  (c) true-false   (d) essay

6. *Do not limit items to memorized content but include items that measure transfer of knowledge*; include items of the type that Bloom (1956) calls comprehension, analysis, synthesis, and evaluation. Examples are provided in the highlight below.

Objective items to measure critical thinking

The ... items [below] can be answered after a critical analysis of the reference material alone, i.e., the student need not recall social science content not included in the test exercise to answer the given item. Test items of this kind are useful in measuring critical thinking objectives such as the ability to make generalizations, to distinguish fact from opinion, to recognize assumptions, to detect biases, and others of a similar nature. Some examples are given in the exercise which follows:

Read the following statement about education in the United States.

Financial support for public education in the United States comes almost entirely from local and state tax revenues. States of low financial ability, with few exceptions, rank at the top in the percentage of their income devoted to schools. Nevertheless, these states rank at the bottom with respect to the quality of schooling provided. It has now become evident that no plan of local or state taxation can be devised and put into operation that will support in every local community a school which meets minimum acceptable standards.

The central thought of the statement above is that
  1. the poorer states devote a greater part of their income to education than do the richer states.
  2. the richer states have better schools than the poorer states.
  *3. education will be inadequate in many areas as long as it depends on local or state revenues.
  4. no fair system of state or local taxation can be developed.

The author of the statement apparently assumes that
  *1. minimum educational standards should be higher than the levels now maintained by some schools.
  2. there is no way to achieve greater educational equality in the United States.
  3. people in the United States are taxed too heavily.
  4. there is a direct ratio between the percentage of state income devoted to education and the quality of the schools.

Which of the sentences in the statement deals most nearly with a matter of belief or opinion rather than of facts? The sentence beginning with

1. Financial support ....
2. States of low ....
3. Nevertheless, they rank ....
*4. It has now become evident ....

(From Harry D. Berg. *Evaluation in social studies.* Washington, D.C.: National Education Association, 1965. Pp. 56–57. With permission.)

Improving tests

Once the teacher has made his first objective test items and administered them to the class, he has made a start toward a pool of items for future use. Each item can be typed on an individual card for filing purposes and classified according to a category meaningfully related to the class objectives.

In addition, there are many simple things that can be done to improve the item before its next use as illustrated in "Recording Item Information After Use." After the test has been administered the responses of the pupils provide a basis for revising or eliminating items. (For extensive treatments of this topic see Ahmann & Glock, 1963, and Ebel, 1965, in addition to other measurement books referenced in his chapter.) Item analysis data, for each of the questions below, can be recorded on the back of the item card for reference when making revisions.

1. *What learning outcome was assessed by the item?* This is a statement of the *objective* tapped by the item, the *purpose* (e.g., diagnosis) for which the item was used, and the *level* (e.g., knowledge, comprehension, or evaluation) of behavior represented.

2. *How difficult is the item?* Difficulty is measured by the percentage of all pupils taking the test who answered the question correctly. The percentage is recorded. Maximum differentiation among pupils is obtained with a difficulty of 50 percent (Gulliksen, 1945; Ebel, 1955). Most items that are constructed for the first time will not meet this standard and so will require some revision. If the item is too easy (difficulty of 80 percent or higher) it may be measuring an outcome at a low level or there may be unusual clues to the correct answer. An item with a difficulty index of 20 percent or lower may require revision because the item was unclear, the alternatives were ambiguous, or because some event during instruction misled the pupils to select an incorrect alternative. Of course there is also the possibility that the item was really too difficult for the level of the class, in which case the item should be adapted to the pupils' readiness.

3. *Does the item discriminate among pupils in the upper and lower achievement groups?* The first step in answering this question requires that the test papers be arranged in order from high to low scores. Then the highest and

lowest 27 percent of the papers are separated from the rest. This percentage appears to be best suited for separating the extremes while still retaining a sufficiently large sample on which to make judgments. However, in practical situations teachers may want to use the upper and lower thirds or even larger fractions in order to obtain enough papers within a group, especially if the class is a small one. The discrimination index is then obtained, for a given item, as follows: subtract the number of pupils in the lower 27 percent who answered the item correctly from the number of pupils in the upper 27 percent who answered it correctly; divide this difference by one-half the total number of pupils included in the analysis. Indexes near .00 indicate minimal discriminating power; larger indexes reflect greater discriminating power, though they rarely reach 1.00. A negative discrimination index indicates that more of the low achievers than of the high achievers responded correctly to the item.

4. *How useful are the alternatives?* Information about the number of pupils in the upper and lower 27 percent of the class (based on the total score of the test) who selected each alternative, including the correct answer and the distracters, can be recorded in a simple table on the back of the card, as shown in the illustration from Chauncey and Dobbin. A distracter needs to be revised (or eliminated and replaced) if (1) more pupils in the high-scoring group use it than do pupils in the low-scoring group, (2) no one in the whole class uses it, or (3) no one in the lower group selects it.

The teacher-made "objective" or short-answer tests reduce the possibility of unreliable grading. When skillfully constructed and standardized on representative groups of pupils in the local school, they are effective instruments for obtaining information about the growth and development of individual pupils. In fact, if the requirements of scientific construction and adequate standardization are met, the teacher-made test may be more easily adapted to the teacher's purpose than the commercially published achievement tests.

Recording item information after the item has been used in a test

Below is an item that was part of a set of questions administered to high school students who were completing a year of high school physics. The question illustrates the kind of response that can be expected of well-trained students of high school age when they are presented with a relatively novel situation which is based on fundamental concepts from the field of mechanics.

This question requires that the student consider the nature of a possible mechanism for providing a "down" direction in a space station to simulate the gravitational "down" so important in our normal activities on Earth. Choice (C) is the direction normally considered "down" in diagrams. Although this direction is not significant in the space station, a sizeable number of the poorer physics students chose it. Other students assumed that the "down" direction would be that one toward the center of rotation of the station, choice (D). However, objects free to move in the space station behave as do particles in a centrifuge and "fall" to the outer edge. This direction, (B), then is the "down" direction in the rotating station. The other choices, (A), "up" as it is usually represented in diagrams, and (E), a direction which depends on the speed of rotation, were not selected by many students.

One method of obtaining "artificial gravity" in a space station is to have the station rotating about axis AA as it revolves around Earth.

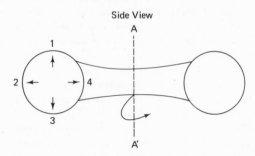

The inhabitants of the space station would call which direction "down?"

(A) Direction 1
(B) Direction 2
(C) Direction 3
(D) Direction 4
(E) Any one of the four, depending on speed of rotation

Some of the statistical characteristics of this item as determined after its use with 170 students are shown below.

Statistical Analysis

Responses	Students Classified by Total Test Score				
	Lowest Fifth	Next Lowest Fifth	Middle Fifth	Next Highest Fifth	Highest Fifth
Omit	3		1		
A		1		1	
*B	12	17	19	29	28
C	8	4	6	1	
D	7	9	6	3	6
E	4	3	2		
Total	34	34	34	34	34

Percent of total group of 170 students answering correctly   62%
Correlation between success on this question and total score on test .44

* Correct answer

SOURCE: Chauncey & Dobbin, 1963, Question 10. With permission.

How should items be arranged?

Sax and Cromach (1966) review several speculations concerning the effects of item arrangement. They point out that some authors say the arrangement of items makes little difference on test performance; others insist that a logical order is most beneficial: others suggest an easy-to-difficult organization, and still others maintain the difficult items should be interspersed with easy items to maintain motivation.

They conducted a study to examine the effects of different orders of the same items on test performance. The results are shown in Table 18-1 for groups given a short period of time (30 minutes) and a longer period of time (48 minutes).

Table 18-1.   The Effects of Item-Order and Time-Limits On Test Scores

Order of Items	Time Limits 30 Minutes	48 Minutes
Easy to Hard	37.83	47.54
Hard to Easy	21.39	45.58
Easy and Hard Mixed	27.00	42.65
Random	29.12	42.02

SOURCE: After Sax & Cromach, 1966, Table 1, page 310.

As the authors conclude there is little advantage to arranging items in any specific way when time limits are ample for students to finish. However, when the test is long or when time limitations are imposed, then test constructors should be certain to order the items from easy to difficult in ascending order.

Interpreting Test Scores

Suppose a teacher reported to you that one of his pupils obtained a score of 40 on a standardized arithmetic test. What does this score mean? What information does it convey? The score might express the percentage of correct answers. However, unless one knew something about the difficulty of the test and of the scores obtained by other people with certain amounts of training, the percentage itself would be relatively meaningless. As an exaggerated illustration, consider the following spelling tests:

Test A		Test B	
dog	the	ricochet	naphtha
sit	fat	simultaneous	supplementary
boy		insignia	

It would be nonsense to infer that 40 percent on Test A was the equivalent of 40 percent on Test B.

The score of 40 might be the actual number of items answered correctly by the pupil, i.e., it might be a *raw* score, in which case it would convey even less meaning. You wouldn't know whether this represented 40 items correct out of 80, or 40 out of 40. Nor would you know whether these were very difficult or very easy items. In order to interpret any test score or observation some frame of reference is necessary.

The authors of most tests provide information for interpreting a raw score relative to "normal" performance. These conversion tables are based on scores of groups of people selected by the test constructor to represent some special characteristic such as all eighth-grade pupils, all rural pupils in the Midwest, or inner-city children on the East coast. The reference group is called a *norm* group. A raw score can be given meaning only by referring it to the performance of some norm or standardization group or groups. A score is not high or low, good or bad. It is higher or lower, better or worse than scores made by some individual or group with which it is compared. In selecting standardized tests it is essential that the teacher refer to the manual and carefully study the sample on which the test characteristics are based. Before a test is selected, before any score is interpreted, or before any decision is made on the basis of test scores the teacher should be certain that the norm group permits a relevant comparison with pupils in his class.

There are two widely used methods for relating a person's score to a more general framework. One method is to compare his score with a graduated series of groups and see which one he matches. Such normative groups are often based on school grades which provide *grade norms*, or chronological age groups which provide *age norms*. Grade norms represent the average performance of children in each of a series of grades. Age norms represent the average performance of children in each of a series of age levels. The second major method of describing test performance identifies the pupil's relative position within a norm group (or within each of a number of groups), in terms of the percent of the group he surpasses. The resulting types of norms are called *percentile norms*.

Age norms

Age norms can be prepared for any trait which shows a progressive change with age. A person making a score equivalent to the average performance of a typical age group is assigned a score corresponding to the age of the group. For example, the average score made on a specific test by a typical group of seven-year-olds at the beginning of the year is simply assigned a score of 7.0. Individual pupils are given an age score of 7.0 if they obtain a raw score on the test equal to the *average* raw score of all seven-year-olds in the norm group. The average raw score made by a typical group of eight-year-olds is assigned a value of 8.0. Similar values are assigned for other such age groups. Intermediate scores are usually determined by interpolation.

The age framework is relatively simple and familiar. "He is as big as a twelve-year-old" is a relatively common way of describing a child. However, age norms do have some serious limitations, the main one being that it is not reasonable to believe that age units are comparable throughout the measurement scale. For example, growth in height is not the same between ages five and six, as it is between eleven and twelve. Also, man eventually reaches an age where further increases in height no longer occur. Used with caution, age norms are useful aids for the teacher in the elementary school and for appraising abilities that grow as part of the general development of the pupil.

Grade norms

Grade norms have many of the same characteristics as age norms. The difference is that the scores are obtained from pupils in representative groups of several school grades. The norm is defined as the *average* performance of the pupils within a grade. For example, the average score made on a specific test by a typical sixth-grade group at the beginning of the school year is assigned a value of 6.0. Pupils are given a grade score of 6.0 if they obtain the average raw score of sixth-grade children in the norm group. The average raw score made by a typical

Table 18-2.   Some raw scores and corresponding grade equivalents in paragraph meaning.

Number Right	Grade Equivalent	Number Right	Grade Equivalent
1	1.8	18	5.2
2	1.9	19	5.4
3	2.1	20	5.7
4	2.2	21	5.9
5	2.4	22	6.2
6	2.6	23	6.5
7	2.8	24	6.7
8	2.9	25	7.0
9	3.1	26	7.3
10	3.3	27	7.7
11	3.5	28	8.0
12	3.8	29	8.3
13	4.0	30	8.7
14	4.2	31	9.1
15	4.5	32	9.5
16	4.7	33	10.0
17	5.0		

SOURCE: *Stanford Achievement Test, Advanced Battery, Form N.* World Book Co., 1953. With permission of the publisher.

seventh-grade group at the beginning of the school year is assigned a
value of 7.0. Similar values are assigned for other grades in the same
manner. Again, intermediate values are usually determined by interpolation. Thus, a grade norm of 6.5 represents the average performance of
a typical group of sixth-grade pupils who are halfway through grade six.

Percentile norms

Although age and grade norms provide useful bases for interpreting a pupil's test score, it is quite common to use percentile norms. An
individual's position in his group can be estimated by a statement of the
percentage of the group he exceeds in a given trait. For example, if
exactly 30 percent of his classmates are lighter in weight than a given
pupil, that pupil's weight would be at the thirtieth percentile, and he
would have a percentile rank of 30.

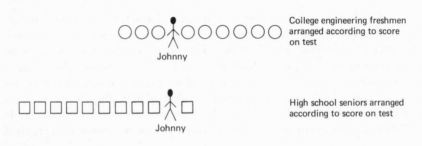

*Figure 18-6. The importance of knowing the normative group. John's raw score
of 68 on a mathematics test gives him a percentile rank of 90 when high school
seniors constitute the normative group and a percentile rank of 40 when the
normative group consists of college engineering freshmen.*

Percentile norms are applicable to any situation where there is a
relevant normative group to serve as a yardstick. The appropriate norm
group is in every case the group to which the pupil being evaluated
belongs according to such factors as experience, aptitude, and cultural
characteristics. The closer the normative group approaches the pupils in
a class on these factors, the more meaningful will the comparison be.
Most tests have percentile norms for many distinct groups depending
upon the use anticipated for the test by the test constructor. Thus, the
teacher should choose the normative group judiciously. It would make
little sense, for example, to compare the academic potential of college
juniors with norms based on unselected adults. Very often schools col-
late the results of tests administered year after year to compile their
own local norms and thereby provide an additional frame of reference
for interpreting individual scores.

Some cautions to be observed
in interpreting scores

None of the scores under discussion are to be interpreted literally or without supplementary evidence. An eight-year-old pupil who achieves an *age* score in arithmetic of ten years is not necessarily the same as a ten-year-old pupil who achieves the same age score. The pupil has clearly exhibited superior performance but it is not necessarily the performance of the higher age levels. He may have attained that score by superior performance on quite different patterns of correct responses than would be the case for the older pupil or the one in the higher grade. For example, his higher score might have resulted from better than average performance on items representing his own age or grade level rather than on items representing the typical performance of older pupils or of pupils in the upper grade levels. Thus, it would be quite inappropriate to make decisions related to the pupil's readiness for advanced work on the basis of these scores without such supplementary data as the level of maturity of the pupil and the kind of achievement represented in his score.

Percentile ranks are more easily interpreted than age or grade norms provided the appropriate norm groups are available. It is meaningful to say that a person whose performance is better than 80 percent of a specified reference group has demonstrated a degree of excellence, whether the concern is with reading Greek or running the 50-yard dash. The principal difficulties in interpreting percentile norms are: (1) Many sets of norms are required and the one most appropriate for the teacher's purposes might be unavailable. The only possible interpretation of a percentile score is in terms of some norm group. If the reference group is irrelevant then the score will be meaningless. (2) Another limitation of percentile rank is that the scale units are unequal. Thus, a difference of 5 between percentile scores at the middle of the range is not the same as a difference of 5 between percentiles at the extremes. A pupil requires only a few more correct items to go from a percentile of 50 to 55; a relatively greater number is required to go from a percentile of 90 to 95 or from a percentile of 5 to 10. The teacher can compensate somewhat for this difficulty by taking it into consideration when interpreting any score or sets of scores.

Under no circumstance does the score, from any test, by itself provide a standard of performance that all children in a school or class should reach. A score is merely a description in standard units which provides one of the essentials necessary for making comparisons. Nothing in it tells who shall go to college, who to the trades, or who to business. Nor does it say who should be educated, when they should be educated, or where they should be educated. These are philosophical and evaluative judgments that can only be made after careful consideration of all data available against the relevant values that must be attained either by the individual or the society.

Selecting and Using Standardized Achievement Tests

Although commercially available tests are made up of the same types of items and cover many of the same areas of knowledge as many teacher-made tests, there are five main differences between them.

1. Standardized tests are based upon content and objectives common to many schools throughout the country, whereas the teacher's test is usually adapted to her course content and objectives.

2. They usually deal with large segments of knowledge or skills, whereas the teacher-made test is prepared for more limited topics.

3. The commercially available test is developed with the aid of professional writers, reviewers, editors of test items, and statisticians, whereas the teacher-made test usually rests upon the skills of one or two teachers.

4. Norms for various groups that are broadly representative of performance throughout the country (e.g., national norms) characterize the standardized test, whereas the teacher-made test lacks this external frame of reference.

5. The commercially standardized test usually appears in two or more comparable forms, whereas the teacher-made test is rarely constructed with more than a single form.

The use of standardized achievement tests results in a considerable saving of teacher time and provides information beyond that which is possible with locally produced measures. For example, in teacher-made tests there is no way to compare pupils in the local school with boys and girls at corresponding academic levels in other schools.

Consider an example that illustrates the latter advantage of the commercial achievement test: Sam came from a nearby community and John from the local eighth grade. When they both entered the same ninth grade algebra class the teacher, in examining their records, discovered that John had an eighth-grade class average of 90 in arithmetic while Sam had an average of only 77. After a week in which a series of arithmetic tests were given it became clear that Sam knew much more about arithmetic than John. They had apparently been given different kinds of teacher-made examinations or had been graded on very different standards. If they had been given a common standardized achievement test in arithmetic in their respective schools, this confusion could have been avoided. If the algebra teacher had attempted to section the group on the basis of their marks she would have misplaced both John and Sam.

Alternate forms of a test are desirable for many purposes. They are especially needed for accurately measuring growth over a period of time where familiarity with specific items, gained from taking the initial test, reflected in higher scores on the later administration of the test, would be undesirable. Standardized tests, with their carefully constructed comparable forms and a broad frame of reference for interpretation (such as national norms), enable the teacher to interpret a pupil's score more precisely than do teacher-made tests. Thus, extraneous factors, such as practice on specific items, that might decrease the validity of the test can be eliminated by using alternate forms or an interpretation more closely tailored because, ordinarily, more than a single set of norms is available.

There are standardized achievement tests for almost every subject-matter area including arithmetic, mathematics, physics, chemistry, history, and social studies. There are some that attempt to measure such skills as studying, reading, listening, critical thinking, and creativity. Many cover the entire range of grade levels from kindergarten, through grade 12.

The *Iowa Test of Basic Skills* (Lindquist & Hieronymus, 1964) is available for measuring several levels of achievement from grades 3 through 9. It has tests and norms for vocabulary, reading comprehension, language skills (spelling, capitalization, punctuation, and usage) work-study skills (map-reading, reading graphs and tables, and knowledge and use of reference materials) and arithmetic skills (arithmetic concepts and arithmetic problem-solving). Some typical items from the popular Stanford Achievement Tests (1964–1965), illustrated in Figures 18-7 and 18-8, represent those found in most achievement tests.

Figure 18-7. Some items from the reading, science, and social studies areas of the Stanford Achievement Test Form X_R, High School Battery.

Test 1: Reading

DIRECTIONS: Read each passage. Decide which one of the words or phrases below is *best* for each blank, or *best* answers the question asked about the passage. Then, on your separate answer sheet, fill in the space which has the same number as the word(s) you have chosen.

SAMPLES: Fine embroideries are a specialty of the Swiss women. Most people have seen dotted Swiss __A__ . Formerly these were made entirely by hand, but they are now made largely by __B__ .

A 1. silks   2. embroideries   3. cheese   4. woolens

B 5. farms   6. machinery   7. children   8. retired women

Figure 18-7. (continued)

Test 2: Science

DIRECTIONS: Read each question. Decide which one of the answers given
below is *best.* Then, on your separate answer sheet, fill in the
space which has the same number as the answer you have
chosen.

SAMPLE: A The earth is in orbit around —

1. Venus   2. the moon   3. the sun   4. Mars

Test 3: Social Studies

DIRECTIONS: Read each question. Decide which one of the answers given
below is *best.* Then, on your separate answer sheet, fill in the
space which has the same number as the answer you have
chosen.

SAMPLE: A The resource which has helped most to make southwestern
Asia more prosperous is —

1. water   2. cattle   3. electricity   4. oil

SOURCE: Stanford Achievement Test, Form X_R, High School Battery. New York: Harcourt,
Brace & World, Inc. 1965. With permission.

Figure 18-8.   An item taken from the Study Skills Test of the Stanford Achievement Test.

Study Skills

DIRECTIONS: Look at each graph or map and read the questions that go
with it. Decide which of the answers given is *best.* Then fill in
the answer space which has the same number as the answer
you have chosen.

Use the graph below in answering questions 51-55

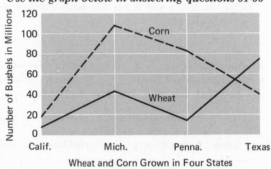

Wheat and Corn Grown in Four States
during One Year

Figure 18-8. (continued)

---

51. Which state grew more wheat than corn?
    5. California   7. Pennsylvania
    6. Michigan   8. Texas

                  5 6 7 8
          51 ○○○○

52. The state which grew the most corn was —
    1. California   3. Pennsylvania
    2. Michigan   4. Texas

                  1 2 3 4
          52 ○○○○

53. About how many more million bushels of corn than wheat were grown in Michigan?

   5. 42   6. 50   7. 65   8. 106

                  5 6 7 8
          53 ○○○○

54. The state which grew the least wheat was —
    1. California   3. Pennsylvania
    2. Michigan   4. Texas

                  1 2 3 4
          54 ○○○○

55. How many million bushels of corn were grown in Pennsylvania?

   5. 18   6. 66   7. 80   8. 82

                  5 6 7 8
          55 ○○○○

SOURCE: Study Skills Test, p. 26, Stanford Achievement Test, Form W_R, Intermediate II, Complete Battery. New York: Harcourt, Brace & World, Inc., 1964. Experimental Edition. With permission.

Among the tests available for the upper grades, the Cooperative English Test (1960) is representative of tests sometimes employed to measure objectives related to reading comprehension. It is available in three forms and at two levels of difficulty. The lower level of difficulty is for high school pupils and the more difficult level is for college freshmen and sophomores. The performance of the student on this test yields four scores: *Vocabulary, Speed of Comprehension, Level of Comprehension,* and a *Total Reading Comprehension* score which is based on the average of the first two scores. There are a number of other tests available for measuring "reading skill" at both the elementary and secondary school levels as well as at the college level. However, it is important to recognize that in this area as well as in other skill and subject-matter areas there may not be complete agreement on the kinds of pupil behavior to be sampled when measuring reading comprehension, level of comprehension and the like. Thus, because one test purports to measure reading comprehension, the kinds of performance required by the pupil may not be at all like "reading comprehension" as measured by another test. In the final analysis it is necessary for the teacher to inspect the test itself, as noted below, to determine whether it appropriately measures behaviors related to his objective.

The three best sources of information about standardized tests for the average classroom teacher are Buros' *Mental Measurement Yearbooks* (1953, 1959, 1965), catalogues of commercial publishers, and "Specimen Sets" (each of which contains a copy of a given test and its manual). The *Yearbooks* list and critically review each new standardized test which is published. A complete index and detailed directory section make it easy to locate information about a particular test or to determine what standardized tests are available in different subject-matter areas. The *Yearbooks* also include much factual material about the tests which a potential user is likely to need—such things as author, publisher, publication date, cost, time required to administer, grades for which the test is suitable, number of forms available, evidence about such characteristics as norms, validity, reliability, and so on.

The most up-to-date information on standardized achievement tests can be obtained from the publishers themselves, either through correspondence or through their catalogues. It is not reasonable to suppose that test publishers are completely unbiased sources on the value and limitations of their own tests. However, they are helpful as sources of information provided one interprets them according to the criteria of purpose, objectivity, reliability, validity, and adequacy of normative groups as described in this chapter.

When a teacher becomes interested in a particular test, the contents and the accompanying manual should be carefully studied. He should not depend on a superficial description for determining whether it is adequate for his purposes. In fact, it is recommended that the teacher administer the test to himself, following the directions as carefully as though he were administering it to a class, yet scrutinizing it carefully as he proceeds from item to item. "Specimen Sets" containing a copy of the test, instructions for administering and scoring, and supplementary materials on norms and interpretation are sold at a nominal price by the publisher. Many publishers refuse to distribute tests if the prospective purchaser does not give evidence that he or she has the necessary professional skills and background to use the materials properly. A letter on the official stationery of the school or a note from a professor at the university where the teacher is studying will often suffice.

The *manual* provides detailed information about the use and interpretation of the test. Manuals differ greatly in the amount of information they provide, and unfortunately, a few of them are little more than promotional devices designed to increase the sales of the test. The teacher should concentrate on the *evidence* presented in the manual and examine claims made in the light of this evidence. Since there is often an inverse relationship between the magnitude of the claims and the evidence, a teacher may well be suspicious of the test whose manual makes dramatic claims but presents very few supporting data.

Achievement tests are often organized into batteries covering many skills and areas of academic knowledge as illustrated in Figure 18-9. Since the normative data for each subtest in the battery are obtained from the same sample of subjects, it is possible to make comparisons of a pupil's performance on the different parts. The content areas included, the emphasis on work-study skills, and the relative emphasis on the various basic skill areas vary somewhat from test to test. Certain of them are also published as individual tests or in smaller battery groupings.

Use of achievement tests in diagnosis

A diagnostic test is one that provides a picture of the pupil's strengths and weaknesses through subscores or analyses of specific items. In a real sense any test that yields more than a single-score can serve for diagnostic purposes provided, of course, that the scores are reliable and are sensibly related to the teacher's diagnostic objectives. Even with only two-part scores (for example, arithmetic computation and arithmetic reasoning), the test permits one to say that a pupil performed better in one area than in another. Such information provides a relatively general diagnostic cue. Other tests are designed to provide a more detailed type of diagnosis. There are two important cautions here: Since there are many subscores from diagnostic tests, each score tends to be based on a fewer number of items. Accordingly, the score will be less reliable than that from a general survey test of equal quality. Secondly, as with survey tests, each diagnostic test, even in the same subject-matter area, reflects the author's definition of a specific weakness. This definition may or may not be like that of another author.

Figure 18-9.   Examples of items from the Test of Academic Progress.

Test 1: Social Studies

This test examines knowledge, understanding, and skills in the area of social studies.

SAMPLE: Who was the first President of the United States?

      1. George Washington   2. Andrew Jackson
      3. Theodore Roosevelt   4. Woodrow Wilson

ANSWER:

Figure 18-9. (continued)

Test 2: Composition

This test examines ability to write and organize various types of compositions.

SAMPLE: 1   Alaska, which was admitted   Which of the following is
          2   as the forty-ninth state   the correct way to write
          3   increased the total area of   line 2?
          4   the United States by nearly
          5   twenty per cent.   1. as the forty-ninth state

                                                   2. as the forty-ninth state,

                                                   3. as the forty-ninth state;

                                                   4. as the forty-ninth state.

ANSWER: ① ● ③ ④

Test 3: Science

The purpose of this test is to measure knowledge, understanding, and skills in the area of science.

SAMPLE: Which of the following animals has feathers?

               1. Kangaroo   2. Turtle   3. Porpoise   4. Duck

ANSWER: ① ② ③ ●

Test 4: Reading

The purpose of this test is to find out how well the pupil understands the materials he reads.

SAMPLE: Pure oxygen can be a   What gas makes up the main
          dangerous gas because of the   part of our atmosphere?
          ease with which it combines
          with other substances. If   1. Oxygen
          nitrogen gas did not make   2. Nitrogen
          up the largest portion of our   3. Carbon dioxide
          atmosphere, even ordinary   4. Water vapor
          fires would be extremely   5. The selection gives no
          dangerous.   clue.

ANSWER: ① ● ③ ④ ⑤

Figure 18-9. (continued)

Test 5: Mathematics

The purpose of this test is to find out how well the pupil is developing his knowledge, understanding, and skills in the area of mathematics.

SAMPLE: What number is two-
            thirds of 24?

            1. 8
            2. 12
            3. 16
            4. 18
            5. None of the above

Which of the following fractions, if any, is (are) equal to
1/2?

(a) 2/4   (b) 3/5   (c) 5/10

1. (a) only
2. (a) and (b) only
3. (b) and (c) only
4. (a), (b), and (c)
5. None of the above
    answers is correct

ANSWERS: ① ② ● ④ ⑤   ① ② ③ ④ ●

Test 6: Literature

The purpose of this test is to find out how well the pupil can interpret selections taken from many different kinds of literature.

SAMPLE: 1   Listen, my children,
              and you shall hear
          2   Of the midnight ride
              of Paul Revere,
          3   On the eighteenth of
              April, in Seventy-five;
          4   Hardly a man is now alive
          5   Who remembers that
              famous day and year.

Who accompanied Paul Re-
vere on his famous ride?

1. Washington
2. Adams
3. Jefferson
4. The selection does not
    tell.

ANSWER: ① ② ③ ●

SOURCE: Scannell, 1964, pp. 5, 17, 31, 45, 67, 81. With permission.

The Diagnostic Tests and Self-Helps in Arithmetic (Brueckner, 1955) is a typical diagnostic test. Initially, a screening test for achievement in whole numbers, fractions, and decimals is administered to the pupil. Then, on the basis of an analysis of his errors, he is given one more of twenty-three diagnostic tests which measure such processes as arithmetic facts, arithmetic operations with fractions, arithmetic operations with decimals, percent, and operations with measures. Coordinated with this test is a series of self-help exercises related to the diagnostic tests. To illustrate the use of tests in diagnosis consider the case of Jane, a seventh-grader.

Late in the spring she reported her dislike for school and especially for arithmetic. This announcement came as a surprise to her parents, since she had always attained a high score on tests of general scholastic aptitude and had always been a good student. Arithmetic also seemed to have been one of her favorite subjects. An examination of her recent scores on the *Metropolitan Achievement Test* showed that she was well above the norm in reading, vocabulary, and, in fact, all subjects except arithmetic. She was slightly above the norm in arithmetic reasoning and slightly below in arithmetic computation. The previous year she had been two grades above the norm on both tests. The information supplied by this achievement test battery is diagnostic at a very general level. Her arithmetic performance, although about average, had dropped relative to her previous year's performance and relative to work in other subjects.

A diagnostic arithmetic test containing separate tests of several different computational procedures was then administered to her in order to obtain more information in an attempt to localize her difficulty. On this test she did reasonably well but showed an inconsistent performance on items involving fractions and decimals.

This information provided the basis for a still more detailed diagnosis by the teacher. She asked Jane to "think out loud" while doing some additional problems on fractions and decimals. Jane's errors and reports of the arithmetic processes she was using were recorded systematically. The teacher dicovered that Jane apparently did not understand the role of the denominator in working with fractions. She also showed little understanding of the processes involving the use and manipulation of the decimal point. Remedial work in fractions and decimals was undertaken. The success Jane experienced in arithmetic subsequent to overcoming her deficiencies had a beneficial effect on her general attitude toward school.

In general, diagnostic test results must be interpreted with caution. Each step in diagnosing academic difficulties provides information from which the teacher may obtain some tentative suggestions as to the individual's strengths and weaknesses. Possible solutions such as tutorial help, placement in special remediation groups and the like should be clearly recognized as *tentative* hypotheses. If the remedial activities are successful, well and good. If not, the teacher must be ready to review what she has done and explore other leads. Often, many tests, interviews, performance tasks, or exercises will have to be employed to detect the deficiency in the student's learning. The teacher's patience may even be taxed to its limits. Even if the weakness is found, he will recognize that the diagnosis only tells what the weakness is and not its causes. Accordingly, one should think of test results as suggestions, rather than commands.

At the present time there are few standardized diagnostic tests outside the fields of reading and arithmetic. Hence, diagnosis must usually be made with tests developed by the teacher or through personal interviews with the pupil. Although diagnosis is an important teaching function, each diagnosis should be made with care and much tentativeness. Faulty diagnosis may lead to an aggravation of problems. There should be no hesitation about engaging the assistance of such school personnel as the school psychologist, reading specialist, or speech therapist when there is a question related to diagnosis.

Effective use of achievement information

Achievement information is of little value unless reliably obtained with valid tests and then effectively utilized. The desirable operations that enter into decisions about obtaining and using such information can be conceptualized in four steps.

A reliable and valid test should be selected. If a standardized test cannot be found for the purpose in mind or if material supplemental to the standardized test is needed, the teacher should construct the necessary tests. Whatever test is used it should call for those behaviors related to one's objectives. Every attempt should be made to use tests that are reliable. (Reliability coefficients should be at least in the high .80s or low .90s.) Other things being equal, the higher the reliability the better.

The test should be administered under favorable conditions. The test room should be a quiet one with good lighting facilities. Follow the directions for standardized tests explicitly, especially with respect to such things as timing and parts to be read verbatim. It is reasonable to say that if a test has not been previously used by the teacher, he should practice administering it to be certain he thoroughly understands the procedure.

Use the results to diagnose the difficulties of individual pupils. Take remedial steps and then reappraise the pupil's achievement status. If the desired results have not been achieved, continue to obtain information, make additional diagnoses and try new remedial steps. Obtain the help of specialists if necessary.

Keep intelligible and systematic records of pupil performance to transmit to future teachers. The most extensive testing program is worthless unless the results are in a readily available form that can be used to the pupil's advantage.

Collating information and evaluating potentials for growth

Information obtained by the methods just described must be brought together and interrelated in some fashion. One procedure is to make a case study of a pupil. This is a broad investigation of the pupil's family history, home environment, medical history, school record, test scores, social environment, and personal reactions. Such a study is usually made in an attempt to discover which factors are relevant to the pupil's maladjustment. Typically, only pupils with serious problems warrant a thorough case study by one or more of the following experts: psychologist, psychiatrist, or social case worker. However, the cumulative records of a school often approximate the completeness of case studies. Many factors related to a pupil's adjustment are brought together in them. Consistent patterns of behavior can be recognized from a careful study of all information, if sufficient information has been gathered. These procedures are described in greater detail in Chapter 20 and Appendix B.

Summary

Measurement may occur at several different levels depending upon the degree of precision desired. Nominal scales permit one to classify objects or events on the basis of counting and nothing more. Ordinal scales assign numbers to indicate rank or order of objects. Accordingly, one can tell whether one object is higher or lower than another by the use of such scales. Interval scales, in addition to having the characteristics of the former two kinds of scales, permit one to compare differences among scores. The intervals or distances among points on the scale are equal. However, there is no absolute zero point in these scales. Ratio scales are the most precise methods of measurement and do have a true zero point. The use of all arithmetic operations is permitted with the scores they yield.

When the descriptions of objects, events, or persons are obtained from a given measurement and judged against some criterion, the process is called evaluation. Evaluations are used for identifying the pupil's readiness, for identifying the pupil's progress or achievement essential to achieving the terminal objective, and for evaluating the extent to which the terminal objective has been achieved.

Objectives are essential for instruction and for evaluation. Objectives should be behaviorally stated to provide the most explicit guidance for the teacher. Objectives in either the cognitive or in the affective domain may be stated at several levels. For example, objectives in the cognitive domain may consist of knowledges, comprehension, application, analysis, synthesis, and evaluation. Objectives in the affective domain can be stated at the receiving and attending, responding, valuing, organizing, and integrating levels.

The worth of teacher-made tests and standardized tests are judged against similar criteria. The observations of behavior made from the test must be relevant to the teacher's objectives; that is, the test must be valid. Among the types of validity are content validity, concurrent validity, and predictive validity. A test must also yield dependable observations or scores; that is, the test must be reliable. Reliability may be determined by the test-retest method to determine the stability of results, by the equivalent forms method to determine the representativeness of sampling of items in two different forms of the test, and by internal reliability to determine the consistency of scores yielded by the items within the test itself. Reliability is affected by the length of a test, the difficulty of a test, the objectivity of a test, and the homogeneity of pupils tested. The correlation coefficient, a statistic which indicates the degree of relationship between two sets of scores, is typically used to express the degree of a test's validity or reliability.

Teacher-made tests may be typical of the essay and objective types. Essay test questions are often used to evaluate higher level objectives. If they are to be effective, the focus of the question should be on eliciting the kind of behavior called for in the learning outcomes; they should be explicitly stated in their requests for interpretations, applications and the like; and their purposes should be clear to the pupil. Model answers identified prior to administration of the test are worthwhile helps to provide objectivity in scoring. It is especially important that essay questions be scored only in terms of relevant course objectives.

Objective tests of the multiple-choice, matching, and true-false varieties can often be used in evaluating most objectives for any course, including those that would be typically measured by the essay test. When constructing objective tests each item should be related to a teaching objective, the main question should be clearly phrased in the stem of the item, alternatives should parallel one another, the keyed alternative should be correct to the knowledgeable student, irrelevant cues to the correct answer should be avoided, and the items should not be limited to memorized content but should include comprehension, analysis, and synthesis. Once administered, objective test items can be improved for later use by capitalizing on information provided through the responses of pupils who have taken the test. Such information includes the difficulty of the item, the extent to which the item discriminates among pupils in the upper and lower achievement groups, the extent to which distractor alternatives are functioning properly, and the degree to which each item appears to be related to the stated objectives of the course.

Test scores may be absolute or relative. The absolute score consists of a raw score or a percentage score. However, such scores may be meaningless without knowledge of the difficulty of the test, of the group taking the test, or of some other frame of reference. Accordingly, relative scores are typically used for interpreting test scores, that is, a raw score is interpreted relative to normal performance of specified groups of people who have already taken the test. The reference group is called a norm group. Grade scores are obtained by comparing the individual's raw score with average raw scores of pupils in different grades. Similarly, age scores are based on comparisons of the pupil's raw score with the average performance of children on the same test who are of different ages. A common method of relating a person's score to a more general reference group is by percentile norms. The percentile indicates the percentage of a specified reference group that the individual surpasses.

Under no circumstances does a score from any test by itself provide a standard of performance that all children in a school or class should reach. Such decisions must be based upon a number of other factors including the kind of reference group that is used, the emphases in the school itself, and the purposes of instruction.

Standardized achievement tests are based upon content and objectives common to many schools throughout the country. They are typically developed with the aid of professional writers, reviewers, and statisticians. One of their distinct advantages is that norms for various groups, broadly representative of performance throughout the country, are available. Another advantage is that such tests may appear in several forms, for within and across grade levels. The standardized achievement test is available for almost every subject matter area including arithmetic, mathematics, physics, chemistry, history, and social studies. They are also available for measuring various academic skills, such as studying, reading, listening, critical thinking, and creativity. Many of the standardized tests for achievement can be used as aids in diagnosing pupil difficulties in various subject matter or skill areas.

Information obtained by all methods of evaluation should be brought together and interrelated in some fashion. Typically this takes the form of a case study of a pupil in which the pupil's family history, home environment, medical history, school record, test scores, social environment, and personal reactions are summarized. In exceptional cases the case study may be interpreted, not only by the teacher, but by several of the specialized school personnel such as the school psychologist and the social case worker.

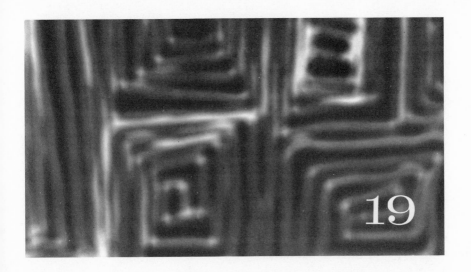

The measurement of individual differences in learning aptitudes

Aptitude tests can be separated from achievement tests simply by defining the *purpose* to be served by the test in question (Tyler, 1963). Thus, if the test is to be used for predicting whether the pupil will profit from training, whether in a general college curriculum, in arithmetic, in social relations, in foreign language, in music, or in vocational school, then the test is called an *aptitude* test. The intelligence test is said to measure scholastic aptitude because it is used to predict general success in school situations. Aptitude tests, by this definition, are typically used to select people for certain jobs or training programs. On the other hand, if the purpose of the test is to evaluate what the pupil has accomplished, what he knows, or what he has gained from a training experience, then the test is called an *achievement* test. "Abilities" is a more general term that includes both aptitude and achievement.

One of the best ways of predicting what a person will do in the future is on the basis of his past performance. Thus, it is easy to see why both aptitude and achievement tests often contain very similar items. For example, if one wished to predict success in arithmetic the "aptitude" test should contain arithmetic items. Similarly the reader can see that a test can sometimes serve both functions; for example, an achievement test in foreign language can be used to evaluate past accomplishments in the subject-matter area, but it is also likely to be a good predictor of what the person will accomplish with further training in foreign language.

Intelligence (scholastic aptitude) and other aptitudes are not directly observable entities. They cannot be measured directly. They are not specific things that people have or do not have in varying amounts. An aptitude is simply an inference based on observations of (1) how the pupil performs certain kinds of tasks represented on a test, and (2) the relationships between this performance and performance in a training or work situation. Our knowledge and inferences about an individual are dependent upon the behaviors we observe.

The logic underlying the construction of intelligence tests assumes that given *equal* opportunity the person who earns the higher score will have learned more from his general experience than one who earns the lower score. Presumably, he will be able to use past experiences more effectively in solving problems, sensing relationships, and in performing other types of intellectual tasks.

Aptitudes: Implications of a "model for school learning"

Carroll's (1963) model of school learning suggests some implications of the study of aptitudes for understanding pupil achievement. The model is "a description of the economics of the learning process in a situation that takes learning for granted" (p. 725), and is briefly summarized below:

Aptitudes for a given task can be estimated by relevant and reliable measures, all of which are based on the pupil's past performance. The *time* required for learning the task will be inversely related to the aptitudes relevant to the task minus any savings from previous achievement in the area. Those pupils with high scores on aptitude measures will learn the task rapidly, those with low scores will take longer to master the task.

In these terms, achievement, defined as degree of learning, is a function of *time actually taken* in relation to (divided by) *time needed to learn* the task. "Underachievement" results whenever some learning condition adversely affects, to a greater degree than is normal, the time spent on a task. The perseverance of some pupils may be lower than that of other pupils with similar aptitudes; instructional quality may be poor; or there may have been insufficient opportunity for learning. "Overachievement" occurs when these conditions are especially favorable; that is, when pupil perseverance is high; when instruction is of better than average quality; and when there is ample opportunity for mastering the task.

As Bloom (1968) points out, the high correlations between aptitude test scores and achievement scores have traditionally led us to believe that only the more capable pupils are able to reach high levels of mastery of a task. Carroll's model, on the other hand, suggests that attaining given levels of performance is within the reach of the majority of pupils. It goes beyond the view that only some pupils can acquire complex ideas and skills while others must be content with simpler ones.

According to this model, whether a pupil masters a given task depends upon factors that determine the amount of time needed for learning and the amount of time spent in learning. The amount of time needed for learning depends on, in addition to *aptitude*, the pupil's *ability to understand instructions*, as determined in part by his general intelligence or verbal ability. The latter can be directly affected by the third determinant of amount of time needed, that is, by the *quality of instruction*. To be effective, instruction must provide carefully prescribed learning goals including specifications of performance levels to be attained for each task; and must communicate, in terms that the pupil can understand, goal descriptions and procedures to be followed for mastery of the task.

Time spent in learning is affected by time allowed for learning, i.e., by the opportunity afforded the individual. It should be apparent that schools geared to the "average" pupil may be allowing too much time for some pupils but too little time for many other pupils to master a task. Some schools use such procedures as nongraded plans, programmed instruction, and tutorial methods that permit students to proceed at their "own rate" (and, incidentally, also do much toward improvement of instructional quality). Finally, the amount of time spent is affected by the pupil's perseverance, that is, the amount of time he is willing to spend at a task. Persistence comprises a number of the pupil's existing attitudes toward learning and work, but it can also be affected by the things teachers do, such as rewarding pupils when they are successful and encouraging them to go on when they encounter failure. In fact, it is one of the exciting features of Carroll's model that it implies there is much the teacher can do in helping pupils achieve mastery at all levels of "aptitude."

The test items for measuring intelligence are selected in a number of ways. Binet and Terman used many vocabulary and reasoning items in the *Stanford-Binet Intelligence Test* (Terman, 1916; Terman & Merrill, 1937). Since much of what a child is required to do in school involves vocabulary and reasoning, it is not surprising that, in general, a pupil who shows a high level of verbal and reasoning facility on such tests will have a higher probability of succeeding in academic situations than will one who shows low facility. From a purely pragmatic view it would be unnecessary to speculate further than the fact that scores from such tests correlate with performance in a number of academic and academic-like situations (e.g., see Churchill & Smith, 1966; Conry & Plant, 1965). But the theorist has also been interested in integrating knowledge about the many correlates of intelligence test scores to attempt descriptions of the structure of intelligence.

Figure 19-1. Subtests from the Wechsler Intelligence Scale for Children (top picture) and from the Stanford-Binet Intelligence Test (bottom picture). (Courtesy of The Psychological Corporation and Houghton Mifflin Co.)

The Structure of Intelligence

What functions comprise the intellect? What are the components of intelligence? These definitions might be derived by understanding the relation of intelligence measures to all other performance measures (Deese, 1967). However, if we were to calculate all such correlations resulting matrix would be so detailed that any interpretation would be impossible. Accordingly, psychologists have attempted to simplify this problem by a number of procedures. Some, such as Binet, intuitively identified the content to be included in an intelligence test, and thereby provided a kind of operational definition of intellectual structure. Others, such as Piaget, choose to define the structure of the intellect by imposing a theoretical model from another orientation (e.g., mathematics or philosophy) on empirical observations of behavior. Some, such as Guilford (1959), employ the statistical operations of factor analysis, a popular procedure for defining intellectual components.

The emergence of intellectual structures

Piaget's theory has been described previously. However, since his work is oriented toward understanding of the development of intellectual structures, it should also be considered in any discussion of intelligence. Piaget's concern in this regard is with schemas, that is, with the organization and adaptive sequence of cognitive and motor patterns of behavior, as they emerge in the course of maturation (Baldwin, 1967).

The reader will recall from our earlier discussions that in the elementary school years the pupil's thinking is marked by concrete operations. At about adolescence formal operations emerge in his thinking and reasoning processes. In the concrete operations period the child understands such relations as groupings of equalities, multiplication of classes, and adding asymmetrical relations. But an operation can be performed only if it is exercised independently rather than as a part of a complex set of possibilities and only if the operation is based on concrete events.

In the formal operations period, the cognitive structure is comprised of abilities related to hypothetical thinking. At this stage the youth is able to deal with logical relations and the operations necessary for their verification or refutation. He can consider the possibilities that might occur as well as those that actually do occur. He has also gained the use of processes to allow for the combination of classes of events and of strategies for the systematic arrangement of classes of events to enable the making of choices and decisions. He has an intuitive grasp of formal logic that is used to obtain an understanding of new (to him) relationships among events so necessary to the testing of alternative hypotheses.

Piaget's description of the cognitive structure contains a number of other behavioral groupings. However, this brief description illustrates one method of describing cognitive structure by imposing mathematical constructs on empirical observations and intuitive knowledge of children's behavior (Baldwin, 1967).

One of the principal implications of Piaget's approach is that educational processes should match the cognitive structure of the pupil at a given grade level. Perhaps, at some date in the not too distant future, curricula will be oriented around structures (schemas) suggested in Piaget's description of developmental stages. Some of the recent preschool innovations appear to be heavily weighted with tasks that undoubtedly owe their invention to Piaget's formulations, (for example, see Gray & Klaus, 1968; or Kohlberg, 1968). It seems likely, too, that this theory has implications for the testing of intelligence. The level of intellectual maturation attained by the pupil might be expressed in terms of the structure represented in the Piagetian stages. Successful tests of this sort would provide useful bases for decisions about adapting teaching processes to the pupil's readiness patterns, though they have not as yet been devised. While the thought of educational innovations based on Piaget's theory is provocative and seems to hold promise, there has been little research conducted to apply it directly to educational programs.

Intelligence as a two-factor structure

One of the early theories of the structure of intelligence proposed that intellectual ability was comprised of many independent abilities among which were social intelligence, or the ability to deal effectively in social interaction; concrete intelligence, or the ability to work with things; and abstract intelligence, or the ability to deal effectively with symbols, abstractions, and ideas (Thorndike, 1921). However, it soon became apparent that scores of a representative group of people based on separate tests of these abilities are not independent but are correlated in a positive direction. Similarly, many other positive characteristics tend to go together and to go with higher intelligence. Contrary to popular belief, children who are bright tend to be taller, heavier, healthier, and to have fewer physical defects than their less fortunate counterparts. The relationship between intelligence and positive physical characteristics, although slight, is definitely positive (Terman, et al., 1925).

Although there are many exceptions, pupils who obtain high scores on the intelligence test are likely to be superior in all subjects, but not equally so in all. Thus, there is apparently a kind of *general* aptitude in combination with varying degrees of unique aptitudes that affect the pupil's performance. Figure 19-2 illustrates schematically this Two-factor Theory of Intelligence. If test results on the two abilities of arithmetic and reading are represented by two overlapping ovals, then the amount of overlap represents the degree to which the two tests are related. This is the "general" ability (vocabulary and word meaning) common to answering written questions about arithmetic problems and questions about the meaning of a paragraph. It is represented by the shaded region in the left-hand diagram. The shaded portion of the second diagram represents the "g" (general) factor or common ability represented in performance scores on three tests. Each of the letters S_1 (e.g., number facts), S_2 (e.g., computation), and S_3 (e.g., speed of reading) identifies the part of each test which is not common to all but unique to the specific test. Thus, the two-factor theory describes the structure of the intellect as being comprised mainly of a "g" factor common to performance on all tests and a group of "s" (specific) factors unique to the tests used.

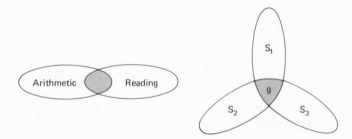

Figure 19-2. Schematic illustration of Spearman's Two-factor Theory. The shaded areas represent the element common to a group of tests. The remainder of the ellipses represent the unique portion of each test.

The multiple-factor structure of intelligence

The rather simple theory of a pervasive general "g" intelligence factor was short-lived. Soon it was suggested that there were additional equally important factors or aptitudes. Much of the impetus for this view came from the use of factor analysis, a statistical procedure that attempts to describe as simply as possible the main factors that account for the relationships among several different tests.

Thurstone (1947, 1948; Thurstone & Thurstone, 1938) was among the first to use this procedure by correlating the results from approximately 60 separate tests. The factor analysis of the resulting correlations yielded the following abilities providing the basis for the construction of the Primary Mental Abilities (PMA) test (Thurstone & Thurstone, 1941, 1946–1958) :

Number factor. The ability to perform numerical operations with facility—rapidly and accurately.

Verbal factor. The ability to comprehend verbal materials and to work with the similarities and differences they contain.

Space relations. The ability to perform operations with pictorial representations as they are imaginally moved in different spatial positions.

Memory. The ability to memorize materials quickly for later recall.

Reasoning. The ability to discover rules, principles, or abstractions as in concept-formation, inductive cognitive processes, and deductive processes.

Word fluency. The ability to name the same object with many different words, quickly and accurately.

Perceptual speed. The ability to identify similarities, differences, errors, and the like in pictorial forms.

Today there is rather general agreement among psychologists that there are many intellectual dimensions. However, there remains a factor that might be called general scholastic aptitude, a conclusion supported by the fact that factors on such tests as the PMA are not completely independent but are correlated to some extent with one another. Underlying success in school is the ability to comprehend, to reason, to see relationships, to be verbally fluent, and so on.

Despite the analytic nature of the multiple-factor approach, it is still based on a limited conception of intelligence since little weight is given to social intelligence, mechanical intelligence, and to abilities in special fields such as athletics, music, drama, and oratory. An attempt in this direction has been made in Guilford's (1959, 1966) model described in the adjoining summary.

The structure of intellect model

The total number of abilities in all of what we infer as "intelligence" is unknown. The PMA and the DAT postulate about eight or nine mental abilities. Guilford (1959, 1966) has made a more ambitious attempt to identify the many different factors that would describe the cognitive structure. He and his colleagues initially segregated several distinct abilities that were then summarized into a heuristic model. The basic components of the model, shown in Figure 19-3, are *operations*, or the processes the person uses as he reasons; *contents*, or the way in which objects, events, or other materials are handled in the thinking process; and *products*, or the results that emerge from thinking.

While there are only a few subcategories for each component, the reader will note that there are 120 different possible combinations. Guilford (1966) and his colleagues have inferred, by testing procedures, the existence of 80 of these different abilities and have made some initial entries into the area of social intelligence. Although

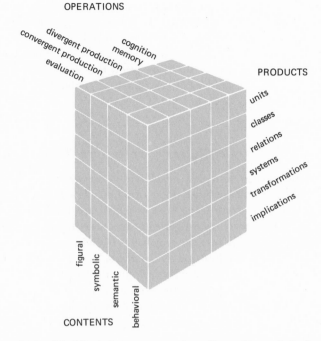

OPERATIONS

divergent production
convergent production
cognition
memory
evaluation

PRODUCTS

units
classes
relations
systems
transformations
implications

figural
symbolic
semantic
behavioral

CONTENTS

Figure 19-3. Model of the structure of intellect. (From J. P. Guilford. Intelligence: 1965 Model. American Psychologist, *1966, 21, 21.)*

the significance of these factors and some of the tests developed from them must still be determined, a few interesting observations have been made by Guilford. First, the factors of intelligence do not emerge by differentiation of a comprehensive "g" factor. Presumably they emerge independently, becoming differentiated at an early age. One reason is that the child's encounters with the four kinds of information occur at different stages in his life. Second, despite the fact that all factors still are not known, attempts at predicting algebra scores from appropriate factor test scores "added significantly to prediction obtainable from standard aptitude tests" (Guilford, 1966, p. 23). Other of the tests developed have permitted clearer distinctions between convergent and divergent thinking than previously had been the case thereby providing a basis for understanding the development of creativity.

From this discussion it should be apparent that the term intelligence can be used in many ways. A pupil may have high general intelligence and social intelligence, he may be high on one and low on the other, or he may excel in other unmeasured intellectual factors. Some pupils may have high ability in science but low ability in mathematics. The distinctions that do exist are important for making such educational decisions as those related to remediation practices. Nevertheless, different intelligence test scores *are* more or less interrelated, a relationship that is reflected in the *general* intelligence tests described in the next section of this chapter. The items in these tests sample a wide range of abilities on the assumption that scholastic success depends on many kinds of performances, most of which must be sampled if grades in school are to be predicted successfully.

Intelligence Tests and Their Interpretation

Intelligence tests can be classified according to their manner of administration and purpose. One common classification compares *individual tests* with *group tests*. Most teachers are familiar with the results of group-administered intelligence tests since they often assist in administering them in fall testing programs. Individual intelligence tests, on the other hand, are administered by the school psychologist or guidance counselor when initial screening of pupils by group tests suggests the need for verification or for future data. The results and interpretations of individual tests will often be made available to teachers for aid in making decisions about instructional procedures to be used with individual pupils.

Individual intelligence tests

The most widely used individually administered intelligence tests in today's schools are the 1960 revision of the *Stanford-Binet Intelligence Scale* (Terman & Merrill, 1937, 1960) the *Wechsler Preschool and Primary Scale of Intelligence*, or WPPSI (Wechsler, 1967), the *Wechsler Intelligence Scale for Children*, or WISC (Wechsler, 1949), and the *Wechsler Adult Intelligence Scale*, or WAIS (Wechsler, 1955).

The Stanford-Binet is the oldest of the four scales. It is also typical of individual tests in general. The test requires about an hour to administer and consists of a ladder-like series of tasks ranging from those that are appropriate for the average two-year-old child to others which tax the ability of adults, i.e., the items are grouped according to age level (difficulty) and within each age level there may be several mental abilities represented (see example below).

The examiner begins administration of the test at a level of tasks which is judged easy for the person being tested. An average nine-year-old child, for example, might be started with tasks at the eight-year-old level. The examiner then proceeds through questions at each of the age levels until the problems become too difficult (all are failed) for the pupil being examined. The purpose is to see how far up the ladder of

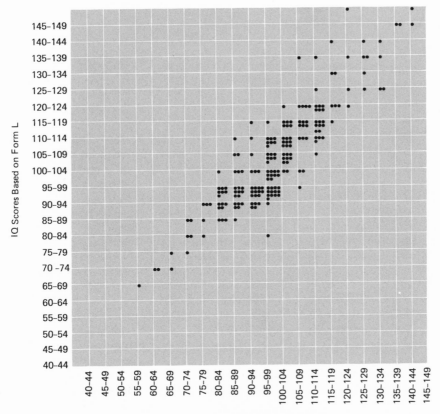

Figure 19-4. Parallel form reliability of Stanford-Binet. Scatter diagram of IQs obtained by 7-year-old children on Forms L and M (1937). Note the high degree of consistency of performance on the two forms, but that there is more agreement between the two forms at the lower than at the higher IQ levels. The Stanford-Binet test is more reliable, in general, at the lower than at the higher IQ levels. (After Terman & Merrill, 1960. With permission.)

tests the pupil can go, without regard for speed or fluency, in order to measure his mental growth or mental age (MA).

Some typical items from the Stanford-Binet (1960) are presented in Figure 19-5 to illustrate the kinds of tasks the average child at different ages can perform. The majority of children at a given age level will correctly answer items for that level, only a small proportion of children at the age level immediately below will answer them correctly, and most children at the next age level will answer them correctly.

The 1960 (Form L-M) revision contains the most discriminative items from the two forms (Form L and Form M) of the earlier 1937 version of the test. In addition, the intelligence quotient (IQ) tables have

Figure 19-5. General descriptions of some typical items from Year IV, Year X, and Year XIV levels of the Stanford-Binet Intelligence Scale.

Year IV (Preschool)	*Year X* (Elementary School)	*Year XIV* (High School)
1. Names common objects from pictures.	1. Defines 11 common words.	1. Defines 17 words.
2. Names objects from memory.	2. Counts blocks in different arrangements and perspectives.	2. Draws inferences based on facts given in a problem to arrive at a solution.
3. Indicates opposite analogies.	3. Knows meanings of abstract words such as "grief."	3. Performs water jar problems without paper and pencil.
4. Identifies object by knowing its function.	4. Gives reasons for common situations such as "Why children should not be too noisy in school."	4. Orients himself according to different verbal directions.
5. Discriminates "X" from other forms.	5. Names 28 words in a minute.	5. Knows similarities and differences in opposites such as winter and summer.
6. Comprehends "Why we have houses."	6. Can repeat six digits such as 4-7-3-8-5-9	6. Can draw what a folded paper with a notch cut out of it will look like when it is unfolded.

SOURCE: Terman & Merrill, 1960. With permission.

been extended from 16 to 18 years and the use of the *deviation* IQ has been introduced to replace the older *ratio* IQ. The latter is discussed in more detail later on in this section. It is one of the weaknesses of this test that the item content and, consequently, what is measured, changes from at least the very young age levels to the older ones. The items for the initial (Year II) MA level are largely nonverbal, while mainly verbal reasoning is encountered at later MA levels. To some extent the Wechsler tests compensate for this difficulty, although the assumption of a general mental ability is the same as that underlying the Stanford-Binet and many of the tasks resemble those of the Binet test. The principle difference is that the Wechsler scales are comprised of several separate verbal subtests (such as vocabulary, information, arithmetic, and comprehension) and several separate *performance* subtests (such as picture-completion tasks, building-block designs, and coding tasks in which different lines in varied positions are matched with geometric designs). Accordingly, while the Stanford-Binet yields a single global intelligence score, each of the Wechsler scales (WPPSI, WISC, and WAIS) yields a verbal IQ, a performance IQ, and a full-scale IQ.

Interpretation of intelligence test results

Scores on intelligence tests are generally reported in terms of mental age, deviation IQs, and percentiles. The mental age (MA) is a derived score based on performance of tasks in age scales such as the Stanford-Binet. It indicates the pupil's level of mental development. Thus, the individual who performs as well on the test as the average 12-year-old child is said to have a MA of 12 regardless of his chronological age. The traditional IQ was introduced to permit a comparison of mental age with chronological age and was expressed as

$$\text{IQ (Intelligence Quotient)} = \frac{\text{MA (Mental Age)}}{\text{CA (Chronological Age)}} \times 100.$$

According to this formula, an 8-year-old child with an MA of 12 would have an IQ of 150, and a 14-year-old child with an MA of 7 would have an IQ of 50. The IQ, derived in this way, said something about the child's *rate of mental development*. It indicated how well he was progressing for his age.

This notion of IQ as it was used with the Binet tests is sometimes referred to as the *ratio* IQ. It is all too familiar to the lay person and professional alike. What may be less known to the lay person is that the psychologist has all but abandoned the use of the ratio IQ with the 1960 revision of the Stanford-Binet. There are several reasons for its retirement as indicated by Terman & Merrill (1960):

First, intelligence reaches maturity at some age level originally thought to be 15 or 16 years of age so, at one time or another, both of these ages were used in the denominator for all persons at age 15 or 16 and over. Then it was recognized that the upper limits of mental maturity probably extended beyond that time, thereby suggesting other increases in the denominator as illustrated in Figure 19-6 (Bayley, 1955). For comparison purposes, changes in verbal and performance scores from 16 to 36 years of age on the WAIS are displayed in Figure 19-6. Regardless of what common denominator is used beyond a critical age, interpretation difficulties are created by the fact that prior to that age the value of the denominator shifts. After that age the denominator remains constant. In essence, the latter yields a standard score for a given group. Accordingly, measurement specialists abandoned the ratio IQ in favor of the deviation IQ (standard score) at all levels.

Secondly, the use of ratio IQ formula requires tests that yield MA scores. Many if not most tests employ point scores (number of items

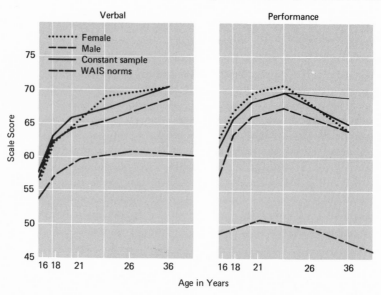

Figure 19-6. Age curves of mean scores on the Wechsler Scales of Intelligence, for the Berkeley Growth Study. The Wechsler-Bellevue Test of Adult Intelligence (1939) was given at years 16, 18, 21, and 26; the Wechsler Adult Intelligence Scale (1955) at 36 years. The constant sample is composed of 25 cases of both sexes who were tested at all five ages. The 36-year point on the curve for the constant sample on the performance scale is shown both for the 36-year WAIS scores (heavy line) and for an estimated corrected score (light line). The number of cases at a given age varies for the female sample from 17 to 24, for the male sample from 16 to 22. (From Bayley, 1966, Figure 2, P. 120. With permission.)

correct); therefore, ratio IQs from different tests cannot be compared without some transformation.

Thirdly, the distribution of scores shifts from one age level to another as can be clearly seen in Figure 19-7. That is, the variability of scores differs at various ages. Thus, the ratio IQ for a given person might shift wildly from one age level to the next as a function of atypical changes in the variability of the scores, rather than as a function of a change in the pupil's performance. Upon examination of such deviations it would be found that the person actually retained his same position or rank within a group of people his age.

Because of these difficulties with the traditional IQ, the recent revision of the manual for the Stanford-Binet Intelligence scales extends the IQs to include ages 17 and 18 and, as with most modern tests, provides tables for *deviation IQs* (standard scores). The latter are scores that indicate the distance the person's score is from the mean of all

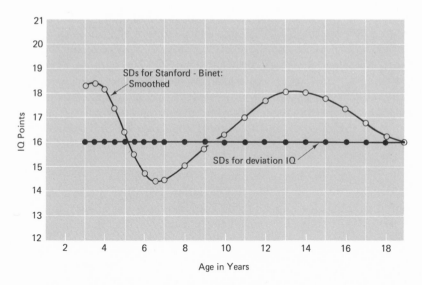

Figure 19-7. Fluctuations in the size of standard deviations of conventional IQs at different age levels. (Adapted from Samuel R. Pinneau. Changes in the intelligence quotient with age. In Testing Today, Boston: Houghton Mifflin Co., *Winter 1962, p. 5.)*

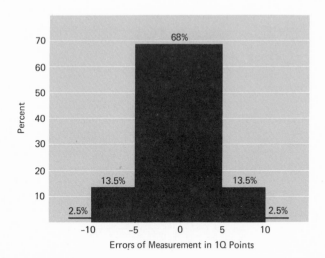

Figure 19-8. There is some error in any measurement we obtain. Note that we would expect errors of less than 5 points in the scores of the majority (68 percent) of children taking the Stanford-Binet. Also note that we would expect errors of more than 10 points in 5 percent of the cases.

scores within some designated standardization group, usually an age group. These norms also take into consideration the variability (standard deviation) of the standardization group, thereby reducing the weaknesses, described above, of the traditional IQ. The authors (Terman & Merrill, 1960) indicate "... a) a given IQ now indicates the same relative ability at different ages, b) a subject's IQ score, ignoring errors of measurement, remains the same from one age to another unless there is a change in ability level, and c) a given change in IQ indicates the same amount of change in relative standing regardless of the ability level of the subject" (pp. 27–28).

The ratio IQ has served its purpose. The older meaning of IQ has been revised to indicate, via the deviation IQ, what the test specialist wanted to know all along, and which incidentally, was always implicit in the ratio IQ—that is, how much the person deviates, in standard score

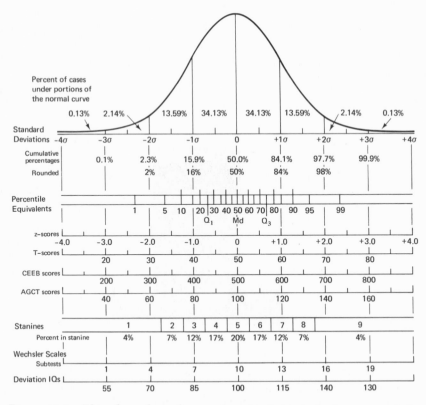

Figure 19-9. This chart shows how various kinds of derived scores and the percentile scale are related to a normal distribution of scores (Seashore, 1955, p. 8).

units, from the average of a representative group of people of his own age. Comparisons of deviation IQs (for the Wechsler scales) with other derived scores and with percentile equivalents in relationship to the normal distribution are shown in Figure 19-9.

Group intelligence tests

In addition to individual tests, the typical school relies heavily on group tests of intelligence for easy administration and for initial screening purposes. Such tests employ items which are fundamentally similar to those in the Stanford-Binet. Instructions are highly standardized for administration by teachers and scoring is often accomplished by machine.

Two widely used group intelligence tests are the Otis–Quick Scoring Mental Ability Test (1939), which has been recently revised (Otis & Lennon, 1966), and the Lorge-Thorndike Intelligence Test (1954, 1957), which has also been recently revised (Lorge, Thorndike, & Hagen, 1964). Both recent editions have two or more forms for measuring intelligence from grades K–12. The Otis provides a single global score and the Lorge-Thorndike provides, in addition, a verbal and nonverbal score. Tables are provided for converting raw scores to percentiles and other derived scores based on large standardization groups. Some illustrations of items from both tests are presented in Figures 19-10, 19-11, and 19-12. The reader will easily see similarities between these items and those in the Stanford-Binet. While there are numerous other tests just as satisfactory, these two are highly representative of the content, organization, scoring procedures, and statistical characteristics of group tests in general.

Group tests have several disadvantages. An uninterested, anxious, or confused pupil may make a poorer score than is typical of his performance. Since group tests rely heavily on pencil-and-paper items, they also tend to emphasize speed (adjusted to the "average" pupil), verbal factors, and reading comprehension to a greater extent than do individual tests. There may be as much as 15 to 20 points variation in the intelligence quotient of individual children over a span of one year when measured on group tests. Consequently, if evidence from group testing does not coincide with evidence based on other observations of the pupil, he is often given an individual test. The reader should keep in mind that the performance on any measure is not only a reflection of what the pupil is *able* to do but also of his *motivation* to perform at a given time and of other temporary factors such as fatigue or anxiety that may be present during the testing period.

Figure 19-10. Illustrations of some types of items that appear in the Otis-Lennon Mental Ability Test *(1967) at levels 7–9.*

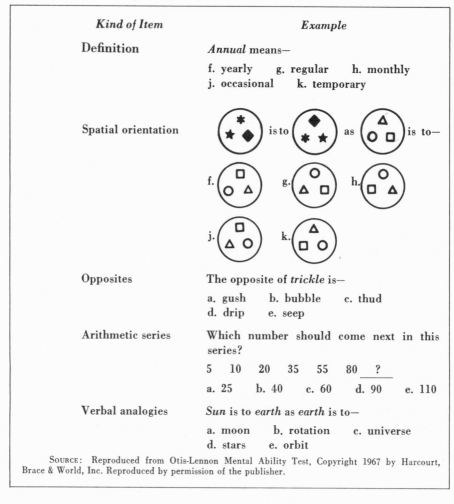

Kind of Item	Example
Definition	*Annual* means—
	f. yearly g. regular h. monthly
	j. occasional k. temporary
Spatial orientation	
Opposites	The opposite of *trickle* is—
	a. gush b. bubble c. thud
	d. drip e. seep
Arithmetic series	Which number should come next in this series?
	5 10 20 35 55 80 ?
	a. 25 b. 40 c. 60 d. 90 e. 110
Verbal analogies	*Sun* is to *earth* as *earth* is to—
	a. moon b. rotation c. universe
	d. stars e. orbit

Figure 19-11. Some representative items from the verbal subtests of the Lorge-Thorndike Intelligence Test *(1964).*

Verbal

1V A - H

For each exercise in this test you are to read the word in dark type at the beginning of each exercise. Then, from the five words that follow you are to choose the word that has the same meaning or most nearly the same meaning as the word in dark type. Look at sample exercise 0.

Figure 19-11. (continued)

0. **loud**   A quick   B noisy   C hard   D heavy
    E weak

The word which has most nearly the same meaning as loud is noisy. The letter in front of noisy is B, so on your answer sheet make a heavy black pencil mark in the B answer space for exercise 0.

1V A-H

In this test you are to work some arithmetic problems. After each problem are four possible answers and a fifth choice, "none of these," meaning that the correct answer is not given.

Work each problem and compare your answer with the four possible answers. If the correct answer is given, fill in the space on the answer sheet that has the same letter as the right answer. If the correct answer is not given, fill in the space on the answer sheet that has the same letter as "none of these." Look at sample 0.

0. If candy costs a cent a piece, how much will nine pieces cost?
    A 1¢   B 7¢   C 8¢   D 9¢   E none of these

The correct answer is 9¢. The letter in front of 9¢ is D so on your answer sheet make a heavy black pencil mark in the D answer space for exercise 0.

1V A-H

For each exercise in this test, a pair of words is given that are related to each other in some way. Look at the first two words and figure out how they are related to each other. Then, from the five words on the line below, choose the word that is related to the third word in the same way. Look at sample exercise 0.

0. laugh   happy : cry
    A wonder   B sad   C hide   D lost   E rough

The right answer is sad because you laugh when you are happy and cry when you are sad. The letter before sad is B so on your answer sheet make a heavy black pencil mark in the B answer space for exercise 0.

Figure 19-12. Some representative nonverbal items from the Lorge-Thorndike
Intelligence Test *(1964).*

Nonverbal

1NV - AH

For each exercise in this test, a series of drawings is
given which are alike in a certain way. You are to figure
out in what way the drawings are alike. Then you are to
find the drawing at the right that goes with the first group.
Look at sample exercise 0. The first three drawings in the
row are alike in a certain way. Find the drawing at the
right that goes with the first three.

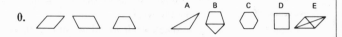

0.

The first three drawings are alike in that each has four
sides and no lines inside it. The drawing at the right that
goes with them is at D. It has four sides and no lines inside
it. Make a heavy black pencil mark in the D answer space
for exercise 0.

1NV   A - H

For each exercise in this test a series of numbers or
letters is given in a certain order. You are to figure out the
order (or way) in which the series of numbers or letters
is arranged, then find the number or letter at the right that
should come next. Look at sample exercise 0.

0.   1   3   5   7   9

A 10   B 11   C 12   D 13   E 14

In the series of numbers, 1 3 5 7 9, each number is 2 more
than the number before it, therefore, the next number in
the series should be 11. The letter in front of 11 is B so
make a heavy black pencil mark in the B answer space for
exercise 0.

1NV - AH

In each exercise in this test, the first two drawings go
together in a certain way. You are to figure out how the
first two go together, then find the drawing at the right
that goes with the third drawing in the same way that the
second goes with the first. Look at sample exercise 0.

Figure 19-12. (continued)

0. The first two drawings go together because you wear a glove on your hand; therefore the right answer is the shoe because you wear a shoe on your foot. The letter above the drawing of the shoe is C so make a heavy black pencil mark in the C answer space for exercise 0.

Nonverbal tests

Intelligence tests can also be classified as verbal and nonverbal. These too exist in both individual and group forms. Special groups of children such as the deaf, blind, and those with foreign language background are often handicapped on the usual intelligence tests. Performance tests and nonverbal tests are thus particularly useful with children who have limited verbal facility of the sort required on the usual verbal test of intelligence. Some intelligence tests have separate verbal and nonverbal (or performance) sections. For example, the individual Wechsler scales have several performance subtests within each on which a total performance score is based, and the Lorge-Thorndike provides for both verbal and nonverbal subscores.

The first nonlanguage group test was the *Army Examination Beta* (1959), originally developed for testing foreign-speaking and illiterate soldiers in World War I. The test was similar to *Army Alpha,* a group intelligence test, but the directions were administered by means of gesture, pantomime, and demonstrations on specially prepared charts. Another well-known nonlanguage scale is the *Pintner Non-Language Test* (1945), which was originally designed for use with deaf children. It has subsequently been employed with many other types of subjects. Ordinarily simple oral directions are used in its administration but pantomime directions are also available for illiterate examinees and for examinees with physical limitations.

Although one of the original purposes for designing nonlanguage tests was to take into account the effect of different subcultures (foreign, urban, rural, race, socioeconomic, etc.), it is clear that some persons would still be handicapped because they lack specific information the test presupposes. Attempts have been made to construct tests that supposedly use only elements common to experience in many cultures and thereby to remove certain kinds of cultural bias. One development in intelligence testing designed to be relatively free from "social-class bias"

TEST 5

In each picture draw what is left out. Work fast

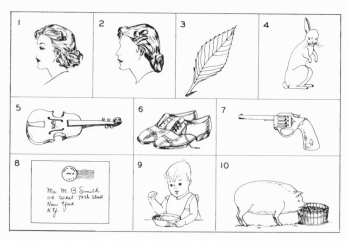

Figure 19-13. Typical items from Pictorial Completion Test *of* Army Beta. *This is a nonverbal test and was devised for the Army to test illiterates. (From C. E. Kellogg & N. W. Morton.* Revised Beta Examination. *New York: The Psychological Corp., 1957. With permission.)*

is the *Davis-Eells Games* (1953). It is applicable from the first to the sixth grades and is entirely pictorial. There is no reading requirement since the directions are given orally by the examiner.

The attempt to develop nonlanguage tests, performance tests, and other culture-free forms of the verbal intelligence tests leads to difficulties of which the reader should be aware. Performance on some nonverbal tests may depend mainly on items that measure spatial, perceptual or manipulative abilities. However, some tests do successfully employ pictorial and other nonverbal material to measure symbolic or ideational functions. Consequently all performance tests cannot be lumped together as measures of reasoning ability.

The social objectives involved in developing culture-free tests are attractive and appealing. It is sometimes the case that the typical intelligence test does underestimate the intellectual abilities of the lower class child. Furthermore, IQ tests do predict learning ability on serial learning and paired-associate learning tasks more successfully in the middle socioeconomic class than for children in the lower socioeconomic class (Rapier, 1968). Nevertheless, the attempts to remove "cultural bias" have *not* been successful. The performance of children in the lower socioeconomic class on culture-free tests remains lower than the performance of children in the middle socioeconomic class, just as it does

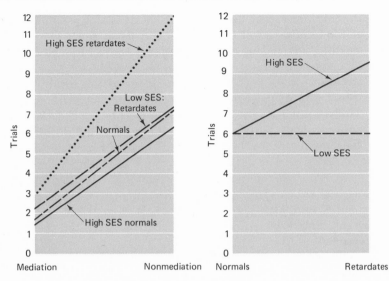

Figure 19-14. The number of trials taken to learn a paired associate learning task by normals and retardates from high and low socioeconomic status (SES) families. Due to fewer learning opportunities there is more variability in the factors causing "retardation" in the lower SES group. Given the opportunity, some children in the lower SES do learn to learn. Accordingly, IQ tends to be correlated with paired-associate learning for high but not for low SES pupils. (Rapier, 1968, Figure 2, p. 106 and Figure 3, p. 107. With permission.)

on the typical intelligence test. Moreover, the tests do not predict scholastic performance as well as do other tests.

This line of attack, though not abandoned entirely, has been largely replaced by attempts to identify successful methods of motivating and teaching the pupil from the lower socioeconomic class. The burden of responsibility for efficiency in learning has been shifted from the pupil to the society, which is as it should be. Teaching procedures, curricula, and other educational experiences are carefully considered with the aim of matching them to the pupil's characteristics. These seem more promising than the disappointing results of previous endeavors to locate the source of social class differences through the development of tests based upon the nature versus nurture controversy (Jensen, 1968).

Use of intelligence test results

Despite their faults, intelligence tests may be used for two very important purposes. The results permit the teacher to estimate the relative intellectual status of a pupil at a given time, so that other aspects of the pupil's behavior can be better understood. It is also possible to *predict* what his relative intellectual status will be at some *future* time, thereby enabling better long-range educational and vocational decisions than could be made if this information was not available.

Intelligence tests have been useful in predicting reading readiness, in predicting school progress in such subjects as arithmetic and reading, and in predicting probable success in college. They have also been used extensively by educational, military, and industrial institutions to help predict probable occupational success. Figure 19-15, which is based on extensive data obtained in World War II, shows the median AGCT score (one type of intellectual aptitude) for enlisted men who were in each of the designated occupations. Although there is considerable variability in intelligence among members of any vocational group, there are substantial differences in intelligence between the *averages* of certain occupations.

Intelligence tests are of great value to the teacher in providing for special learning situations. In combination with scores on reading and arithmetic tests, they can be helpful aids when setting up groups needing remedial instruction. This kind of evidence documents

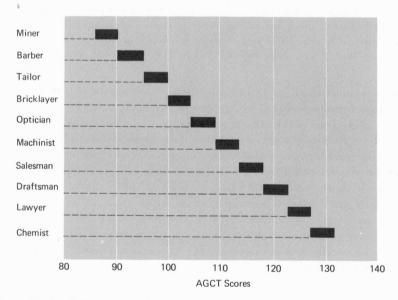

Figure 19-15. Selected occupational groups ordered according to their median *AGCT scores. Note that these are average intelligence test scores and that some miners actually obtain scores higher than, for example, salesmen. (Adapted from D. E. Super.* Appraising vocational fitness. *New York: Harper & Bros., 1949. Pp. 96–97. With permission.)*

the value of intelligence tests at the lower IQ levels. Nevertheless, before the results are used the teacher should become thoroughly familiar, through relevant reading and resource personnel, with the capabilities, strengths, and weaknesses of a given test.

Intellectually Exceptional Pupils

One of the purposes of measuring intelligence is to identify persons who require special educational opportunities or care. They include children who are at one or the other extreme of intellectual ability—those who are retarded and those who are gifted.

Educational retardation

Both educators and psychologists have been concerned, at least sporadically, with prevention of intellectual retardation and with the educability of persons with subnormal intelligence. Recently, there has been a resurgence of interest in this area as documented in a most thorough presentation by Robinson and Robinson (1965) in their book entitled *The Mentally Retarded Child.*

Mental retardation can occur as a consequence of any of a number of different factors, often in interaction with each other, rather than from a single cause. Genetic influences can effect certain little-understood characteristics of the central nervous system; or they may affect the balance of other bodily systems which impair an otherwise normally functioning nervous system (see Figure 19-16).

Physical factors, external to the organism, also may cause aberrations that result in mental subnormality. The mother's condition during pregnancy, for example, may have important effects on the fetus. Control of mental retardation due to such factors is largely a matter of preventive medicine during pregnancy; for example, prevention of mishap to the infant at the time of birth as when premature detachment of the umbilical cord may cause brain damage due to anoxia (lack of oxygen); or prevention of illness or injury of the neonate after birth. Prevention, however, is not as easily achieved as it would seem to be at first thought.

Genetic and physical influences do play their respective roles in affecting intellectual capabilities. But educators and teachers are directly concerned with the effect of the *psychological environment.* Whatever his capabilities at birth, the child's intellectual growth will suffer if the environment does not provide for its nurture. Robinson and Robinson (1965, p. 187) illustrate the effects of extreme deprivation on

Category		Correlation	Groups Included
		000 010 020 030 040 050 060 070 080 090	
Unrelated Persons	Reared apart		4
	Reared together		5
Fosterparent - child			3
Parent - child			12
Siblings	Reared apart		2
	Reared together		35
T W I N S	Two-egg	Opposite sex	9
		Like sex	11
	One-egg	Reared apart	4
		Reared together	14

Figure 19-16. Correlation coefficients for intelligence test scores from 52 studies. This summary shows the consistency in data relating intellectual functioning to hereditary factors. Intragroup resemblance in mental abilities is directly related to the degree of genetic relationship. Some studies reported data for more than one relationship category; some included more than one sample per category, giving a total of 99 groups. Over two-thirds of the correlation coefficients were derived from IQs, the remainder from special tests (for example, Primary Mental Abilities). Midparent-child correlation was used when available, otherwise mother-child correlation. Correlation coefficients obtained in each study are indicated by dark circles; medians are shown by vertical lines intersecting the horizontal lines which represent the ranges. (From L. Erlenmeyer-Kimling & Lissy F. Jarvik. Genetics and intelligence: A review. Science, 1963, 142, 1478.)

"attic children." These children have been prevented from interaction with others of their own age by rejecting parents.

Such children continue to be discovered sporadically even today. K. Davis (1940, 1947), for example, has reported two such isolated girls. Anna was a neglected, illegitimate child who was confined in an attic and was discovered immobile and in an emaciated condition at the age of five. She lived for five years and recovered to some extent, but she gave the picture of a congenitally defective child, as perhaps she was. Isabella, another illegitimate child, was locked up for her first six years by an irate grandfather who could not bear to be confronted with his daughter's baby. She seemed feebleminded when she was first discovered, although she was superior to Anna, but she recovered rapidly and within sixteen months had a vocabulary of 2,000 words. A significant difference between these cases is that Isabella's mother, a deaf-mute, was isolated with her much of the time, perhaps furnishing a much-needed human relationship and the stimulation which established the foundations for future growth (Stone, 1954).

Even though children do interact with others, the level of interaction may be such that it fails to permit full intellectual development. Mentally subnormal or emotionally disturbed parents can produce effects nearly as severe as the rejecting parents of the "attic children." The parents' education and socioeconomic status are directly correlated with the pupil's intelligence test scores. Cultural differences can affect development of verbal or other abilities of children within any ethnic group, as shown in Figure 19-17. With reference to the data displayed in that figure, Stodolsky and Lesser (1967) say, ". . . the study of mental abilities suggests that there may be patterns of attributes (cognitive, personality, motivational, and so forth) which are related in some regular way to ethnic-group membership. [However,] school-based research has not as yet identified the particular patterns of attributes which are educationally important and which (when matched with the appropri-

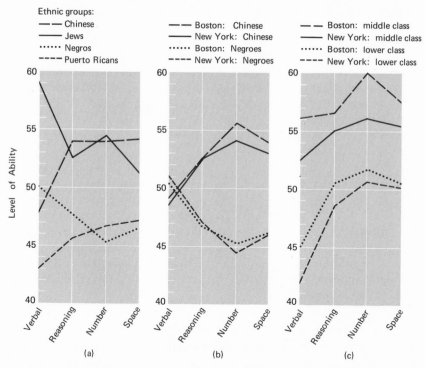

Figure 19-17. Ethnic groups differ in both level of each ability and in the patterns among abilities (A). Social class variations do not alter the patterns though scores tend to be higher for middle class children than for lower class children in each of the groups as illustrated in B and C for two groups. Note, too, how closely the patterns correspond for children from both New York and Boston. (From Stodolsky & Lesser, 1967, A Figure 1, p. 567, B Figure 8, p. 575, C Figure 9, p. 575. With permission.)

ate instructional strategies) will maximize school achievement. Thus, we do not yet know if attribute patterns associated with ethnic group membership will, in fact, be identified as educationally important" (p. 587). Whatever the result of such investigations turns out to be, it is clear that "... a new definition of 'disadvantaged' should include psychologically meaningful statements about the environment and the child. The complexity of such statements ... will be a realistic reflection of the diversity and individuality of children and the lives they lead" (p. 589).

The need for *early* stimulation and experience appears to be essential to compensate for environmental deficit. Special programs such as Operation Headstart for preschool children have met with partial success, but probably are now due for revision (Hess & Bear, 1968). On the basis of existing evidence (Hunt, 1961), the effects of stimulation (or deprivation) appear to begin at birth. Thus, the disadvantaged child at four may have been deprived of opportunity during some of his most formative years. Accordingly, follow-up programs and training programs of longer than one-year duration may be necessary to compensate for deficiencies in school readiness (as reflected in traditional middle class schools) accumulated during the child's initial four years in an environment with minimal educational opportunity. Skeels (1966), for example, showed that prolonged stimulating care in institutions followed by care in attentive adoptive homes of children who initially evidenced marked mental retardation enabled them to enter adulthood as self-supporting and reasonably well-adjusted persons, both personally and occupationally. A contrast group had spent their childhood in a relatively nonstimulating orphanage where the principal provision was custodial care. Of the 12 persons in this group, 4 on reaching adult status were still wards of state institutions. Their occupations, socioeconomic class, and adjustment were, on the average, lower than those persons provided stimulating environments through planned intervention. Remediation of mental retardation due to deficits which are psychological and cultural in origin appears to necessitate, in part at least, prolonged, and rich educational experience.

A mask of mental retardation: lowered achievement needs

Some personality variables may be among the psychological variables that give the pupil the appearance of being mentally retarded. Robinson and Robinson (1965, pp. 201–202) present a case in which a decrease in motivation was correlated with a decrease in intellectual functioning.

Matt was the only boy of three children. The father was a cheerful, happy-go-lucky steward for a steamship line. His work took him to foreign lands but usually gave him a week or two between trips with little to occupy his time. During these periods, he was waited on effusively by his wife and daughters and was the center of attention, full of stories about his exciting travels but playing a clearly passive and dependent role. It was this "vacation" side of his father with which Matt apparently identified. He spent much of his spare time watching television and was never persuaded to put forth much effort in his schoolwork, although intelligence tests during the school years placed him in the average range. His sisters, on the other hand, adopting the rather active and dominant pattern of their mother, did fairly well in school and took turns at household tasks. His father was killed in an accident when Matt was fifteen. Matt's grades fell lower and lower, and finally he dropped out of high school to enlist in the military service. He was soon discharged for ineptitude, however, part of the reason being that even when he was on probation he failed to make his bed or straighten his belongings properly. After his discharge, he made a false start at schoolwork but soon became discouraged. For more than a year he remained unemployed, and he finally became a janitor in a cafe, working from midnight to 3 A.M. On a Wechsler Adult Intelligence Scale administered at age 20, Matt obtained an IQ of 81; he put forth little effort despite much encouragement by the examiner. Lacking the father's good humor and intriguing stories, Matt could not command the center of attention, and he withdrew into a more and more passive state. His prognosis was far from bright; by early adulthood he had seemingly already retired from life and was functioning on no more than a marginal level in terms of his intellectual, economic, or emotional adjustment.

These short descriptions of the bases for mental retardation have been provided to indicate the many definitions for the term "mentally retarded," and the various forms of remediation implied by each. Our discussion indicates why the former classification of subnormals into the categories of idiot, imbecile, moron, and feeble-minded according to IQ scores has all but disappeared. In addition to the opprobrious connotations attached to them, the terms were not functional. In their place is a classification devised by the American Association On Mental Deficiency (AAMD). Other classifications are also being proposed. The three classifications with corresponding IQ levels for each category within them are depicted in Figure 19-18.

Despite the fact that one of these may be more functionally adequate than another, any classification implies a constant social setting within which broad value judgments can be made. Of course, this is not always possible. Normally, pupils interact socially with many subgroups. In some of them, the pupil might be considered dull because the others with whom he is being compared exceed him in IQ level. In a different setting he might be considered bright because he had the highest IQ among a number of pupils with relatively low IQs.

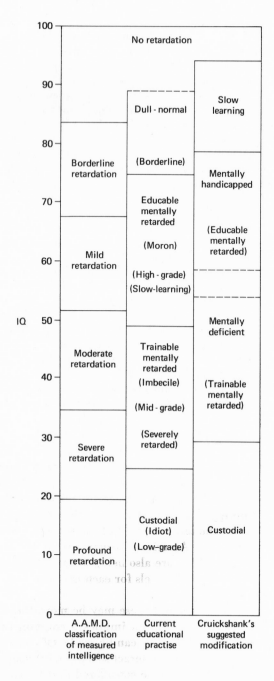

Figure 19-18. Current and suggested classificatory systems (according to Stanford-Binet IQ). (From H. B. Robinson & N. M. Robinson, The mentally retarded child: a psychological approach. *New York: McGraw-Hill, 1965. P. 463. With permission.)*

Genius and the gifted pupil

On occasion one may be informed that another is a genius, often by self-proclamation, because he exceeded the intelligence quotient of 140—a figure originally used by Terman (1925) for selecting gifted children. Such comments reflect an unfortunate outcome of providing an individual with a test score without sufficient explanation of what the results mean. The comment also reflects the examinee's misunderstanding of the nature of giftedness. Most "geniuses" do have an IQ of 140 or higher as shown in Table 19-1 which lists the IQs of a sample of eminent men studied by Terman and his associates (Cox, 1926). However, as the reader can also see from that chart, it is not an absolute necessity to have an IQ of 140 to be classified as "eminent." Conversely, an IQ of 140 without recognizable accomplishment does not automatically make one an initiate of the society of gifted and eminent men or women. There are many, many persons in professions, colleges, and businesses with IQs of 140 or over who are not considered geniuses or eminent by their colleagues.

The eminent men selected for study by Cox (1926) were taken from a report by Cattell (1903) who based his judgments on the length of the description given that person's work in biographical dictionaries. Cox and her colleagues then estimated the IQ of these men from accumulated anecdotal material and reports of their behaviors for the period up to the age of 17 years, and for the period from 17 years to 26 years of age. Judgments were made according to characteristics that compared with behaviors measured on the Binet-type tests. Note, for example, the following much-cited, delightful anecdote concerning Sir Francis Galton's (estimated IQ of over 200) performance in early childhood (Cox, 1926, pp. 41–42):

From early childhood Galton was under the instruction of his sister, Adele, herself a mere child. She taught him his letters in play, and he could point to them before he could speak. . . .

Francis knew his capital letters by twelve months . . . he could read a little book *Cobwebs to Catch Flies*, when 2½ years old, and could sign his name before 3 years. . . .

The letter written to his sister the day before his fifth birthday, runs as follows:

My Dear Adele,

I am 4 years old and I can read any English book. I can say all the Latin Substantives and Adjectives and active verbs besides 52 lines of Latin poetry. I can cast up any sum in addition and can multiply by 2, 3, 4, 5, 6, 7, 8, [9], 10, [11].

I can also say the pence table. I read French a little and I know the clock.

Francis Galton
February 15, 1827

Table 19-1. Estimated IQ's of eminent persons based on records to 17 years and from 17-26 years of age.

Eminent Persons	Principal Occupation	Father's Occupation	IQ 17 Years	IQ 17–26 Years
Francis Bacon	Philosopher	Statesman	(165)	180
Ludwig van Beethoven	Musician	Musician	(150)	165
Robert Burns	Writer	Farmer (renter)	(140)	150
John Calvin	Religious leader	Lawyer	(155)	175
Thomas Carlyle	Writer	Mason	(155)	165
S. T. Coleridge	Writer	Clergyman	(180)	175
Oliver Cromwell	Soldier	Gentleman	(120)	135
Charles Darwin	Scientist	Physician	(155)	165
René Descartes	Philosopher	Councillor	(170)	180
Sir Francis Drake	Soldier	Sailor, Clergyman	(120)	130
Michael Faraday	Scientist	Blacksmith	(135)	170
Benjamin Franklin	Statesman	Tradesman	(160)	160
J. W. Goethe	Writer	Councillor	(190)	210
Thomas Hobbes	Philosopher	Clergyman	(165)	165
Thomas Jefferson	Statesman	Colonel	(160)	160
Michelangelo Buonarrotti	Artist	Gentleman	(160)	180
Thomas More	Statesman	Judge	(150)	155
Napoleon Bonaparte	Soldier	Lawyer	(140)	145
Isaac Newton	Scientist	Farmer	(150)	190
M. M. I. de Robespierre	Revolutionary Statesman	Lawyer	(160)	170
Gouvion St. Cyr	Soldier	Butcher	(120)	135
P. H. Sheridan	Soldier	Farmer	(120)	135
Jonathan Swift	Writer	Member of King's Inn	(145)	155
Leonardo da Vinci	Artist	Farmer	(155)	180
George Washington	Soldier	Farmer	(130)	140
James Watt	Scientist	Merchant	(155)	165
Karl Maria von Weber	Musician	Army officer	(145)	165
Daniel Webster	Statesman	Farmer	(160)	165

SOURCE: Cox, 1926.

Galton's adult achievements included mathematics and meteorology but the accomplishments for which he is best known are his studies of the inheritance of mental abilities and of the measurement of these abilities (Galton, 1869). As such, he has had a major impact on the study of individual differences.

Thus, using Galton as an example, genius is defined by whatever traits are essential, such as a reasonably high level of intellectual functioning but, in addition, by productivity in a form recognizable by society. Tyler (1965) suggests that to achieve such accomplishments requires a combination of special talent, powerful motivation, physical stamina, and good work habits.

These points can be exemplified no more clearly than in Terman's (1925) later study of 1,000 gifted children who were identified by the measured IQ of 140. This figure was selected because it was the average found in the earlier study for most groups of eminent men. Periodic follow-ups have been made since the initial testing. As children, the gifted groups were found to differ from a control group on such characteristics as leadership qualities, high motivation, high perseverance, inquisitiveness, curiosity, and originality, as well as intelligence (Miles, 1954).

Of even more interest were the later follow-ups. In their book *The Gifted Group at Mid-Life*, Terman and Oden (1959) reveal the prodigious accomplishments of the people identified earlier (at about preadolescence) as gifted, and aptly summarized by Tyler (1965, p. 404) as follows:

. . . members of the gifted group, some three and a half decades after their initial selection, were still maintaining their superiority in health, adjustment, intelligence, career success, and contributions to society. Among the men, 86 per cent were working at the professional or semi-professional level, and only 1 per cent were engaged in semiskilled work (none in unskilled labor). Many of them were listed in *Who's Who* and *American Men of Science*; some had acquired international reputations. Altogether they had published more than 2,000 scientific and technical papers, 60 books and monographs, 33 novels, 375 short stories, novelettes, and plays, 60 essays, critiques and sketches, and 265 miscellaneous articles, as well as hundreds of news stories, editorials, and radio, television, and motion picture scripts. They had taken out at least 230 patents.

Individual differences occur in the characteristics of giftedness as they do in every other trait. The range of IQ scores for eminent persons is large. Not all children with IQs of 140 and over were successful in later careers. Tyler (1965) has cautioned that some highly productive people have had poor physical health or stamina, some were poorly motivated, others were indolent and had poor work habits. Despite these "shortcomings" their work has come to earn them the reputation accorded only to men of eminence.

The reader should be warned that from the teacher's standpoint, highly gifted children sometimes encounter difficulty in adjusting to school (Hollingworth, 1942). They may prefer to make their own decisions rather than to depend on others. They sometimes have difficulties in social interaction. If not identified early such children may become bored and uninterested in school work. Further they may develop lazy habits and a bitter attitude toward school. There are personnel such as school psychologists in most of today's schools who provide special service in identifying these pupils and in planning the kind of program that will prevent unnecessary difficulties. Perhaps, then, the best advice to the new teacher is to make the best use of whatever resources are available, including his own knowledge, to identify gifted pupils and once they are found, to nurture the growth of their capabilities through enrichment opportunities.

Tests of Special Abilities

Long before the advent of the multiple-factor theory of intellectual structure it was generally recognized that the usual intelligence tests with their single global scores, though useful, were quite limited in their coverage of the pupil's abilities. Such aptitudes and achievements differ drastically in kind and amount from person to person. They can be combined in an almost infinite variety of ways to differentially affect success in school and in life. The person who is best able to identify his strengths and limitations and to realistically weigh these against the requirements for occupational success is likely to make his maximum contributions to society and simultaneously achieve the greatest satisfactions for himself. A strong impetus to the construction of all special aptitude tests was provided by the urgent problem of matching educational and vocational requirements with the individual's characteristic pattern of abilities. Attempts to fill in the gaps and broaden our understanding of how the matching process was to be accomplished resulted in the construction of special aptitude tests.

Some tests of special aptitude

Among the earliest of the tests were scales designed to measure mechanical aptitude. The demands of vocational selection and counseling also stimulated the development of tests to measure clerical, musical, and artistic aptitudes. Tests of vision, hearing, and motor dexterity were devised to assist in the overall guidance process.

An example of a special aptitude test is the *Horn Art Aptitude Inventory* (1945), designed for estimating probable success of applicants to art school. This test requires the subject to sketch a picture around a pattern of lines as illustrated in Figure 19-19. The pictures are judged by art instructors as to imagination and technical drawing quality.

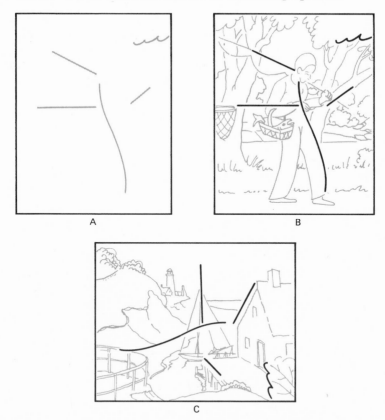

Figure 19-19. Specimen item from Horn Test of Art Aptitude. *Rectangle A shows the stimulus lines. The other two show drawings based on them. In rectangle B, the artist viewed A as shown and in rectangle C he turned it sideways. (From C. A. Horn & L. F. Smith. The Horn Art Aptitude Inventory.* Journal of Applied Psychology, *1945, 29, Figure 1, p. 351. With permission.)*

Obviously, previous experience in drawing is an important factor in the picture produced. Artistic aptitudes are among the more difficult areas of measurement and progress here has been correspondingly slow. There are, however, several tests of artistic appreciation and tests of creative artistic ability. Musical aptitude was one of the early artistic areas to receive the attention of test-makers. Tests to measure discrimination of pitch, loudness, rhythm, time, timbre, and tonal memory are available. There are also tests to rate interest in different types of music.

Motor dexterity tests are designed to measure speed and coordination of movement. The principal use of such tests is vocational placement. Although the classroom teacher is not likely to administer such tests, his knowing that they are available is desirable, since he may send students to the guidance counselor for additional testing. Some

Crawford Small Parts Dexterity Test. *(Courtesy The Psychological Corporation.)* *Bennett Hand-Tool Dexterity Test. (Courtesy The Psychological Corporation.)*

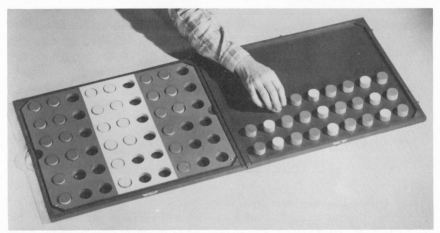

Stromberg Dexterity Test. (Courtesy The Psychological Corporation.)

Figure 19-20.   Some tests of mechanical dexterity.

tests measure dexterity by the speed with which the subject can insert pins into a small hole either by hand or with a tweezer. Another involves the use of common hand tools to remove and replace nuts and bolts. Others utilize no tools but require assemblage of pins, collars, washers, etc. These activities have demonstrated their value for predicting success in certain types of jobs available to pupils leaving school.

Many tests of mechanical ability are also available. They too are tools in the kit of the vocational guidance counselor. Their usefulness is in predicting performance in shop courses, technical and medical courses, art, and dentistry.

For the teacher of business subjects there are various tests of clerical aptitude. Some require the subject to match names and numbers. Others test such things as spelling, vocabulary, typing, and filing skills. Tests of this kind have been used advantageously by students taking a high school commercial course.

It is desirable at this point to comment on the concept of "special aptitudes." The term was introduced at a time when the major emphasis in testing was placed upon "general intelligence." Mechanical, musical, and other special aptitudes were regarded as supplementary to the IQ in the description of a person. With increased study, it was gradually recognized that "intelligence" itself is composed of a number of "special aptitudes" such as verbal comprehension, numerical reasoning, spatial visualization, and associative memory. Special aptitude tests include a miscellaneous collection of instruments, each measuring a narrowly defined area. The multiplicity of such tests is due largely to attempts to find the best predictors of future achievement in both educational and vocational settings. This activity has culminated in the development of batteries of tests to measure several abilities.

Differential aptitude batteries

The multiple-factor tests attempt to provide a set of scores for more accurate prediction of scholastic or vocational success. They attempt to measure the person's relative standing on many different abilities presumably enabling a more accurate matching of individual profiles with academic or job profiles.

The Differential Aptitude Tests (DAT). A characteristic example of the differential or multiple-aptitude test is the DAT (1947–1961). This test samples a range of abilities from clerical to mathematical as shown in Figure 19-21. The reader will observe the resemblance between the DAT and that of the PMA test described earlier. The important features of this test are: it was standardized on nearly 50,000 students in grades 8 through 12; it measures a number of abilities important for educational and vocational guidance purposes; it yields a profile of scores, rather than a single score, thereby making it useful for diagnostic purposes. The person taking this test can usually find some ability which he can use advantageously. If only a test yielding a global score were used, this advantage would be denied him since the information would be an inseparable part of the single score. Extensive norms are available for this test. The difficulty in using aptitude batteries in differential fashion is illustrated by some conclusions based on a study by Milholland and Womer (1965). They indicate that a student scoring high on verbal reasoning, number ability, abstract reasoning, and spatial relations has a better chance of graduating from college, regardless of specialization, than if his scores are low. Mechanical reasoning, clerical speed and accuracy, spelling and sentence scores are not useful predictors. However, DAT profiles do differentiate between groups who have earned a college degree versus those without post-high school education and among high school students and other groups who enter different fields of occupation as shown in Figure 19-22.

Figure 19-21. The Subtests in the Differential Aptitude Test *(DAT) With Illustrative Items.*

Abstract reasoning

This is a nonverbal subtest. Performance depends upon the identification of the principle underlying a pattern series.

Each row consists of four figures called Problem Figures and five called Answer Figures. The four Problem Figures make a series. You are to find out which one of the Answer Figures would be the next, or the fifth one in the series.

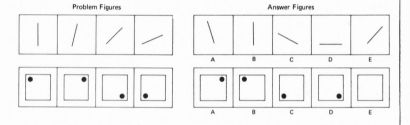

Numerical ability

The items in this test are numerical problems that measure the ability to handle arithmetical concepts efficiently and with understanding.

Next to each problem there are five answers. You are to pick out the correct answer.

Add	13	A	14	Subtract	30	A	15
	12	B	25		20	B	26
	—	C	16		—	C	16
		D	59			D	8
		E	none of these			E	none of these

Clerical speed and accuracy

This test consists of simple perceptual tasks emphasizing speed and retention. It involves the comparison of number and letter combinations.

Notice that in each Test Item one of the five is underlined. You

Figure 19-21. (continued)

are to look at the one combination which is underlined, find the same one after that item number on the separate Answer Sheet, and fill in the space under it.

Test Item				
V.	<u>AB</u>	AC	AD	AE	AF
W.	aA	aB	BA	Ba	<u>Bb</u>
X.	A7	7A	B7	<u>7B</u>	AB
Y.	Aa	Ba	<u>bA</u>	BA	bB
Z.	3A	3B	<u>33</u>	B3	BB

Answer Sheet

	AC	AE	AF	AB	AD
V.	⁝	⁝	⁝	▮	⁝
	BA	Ba	Bb	aA	aB
W.	⁝	⁝	▮	⁝	⁝
	7B	B7	AB	7A	A7
X.	▮	⁝	⁝	⁝	⁝
	Aa	bA	bB	Ba	BA
Y.	⁝	▮	⁝	⁝	⁝
	BB	3B	B3	3A	33
Z.	⁝	⁝	⁝	⁝	▮

Language usage: spelling

This test measures spelling ability by requiring the person to identify words that are misspelled or spelled correctly.

Indicate whether each word is spelled right or wrong.

W. man   X. gurl   Y. catt   Z. dog

Language usage: grammar

A test of familiarity with grammatical principles. It emphasizes recognition of errors in punctuation, grammar or spelling.

Ain't we / going to / the office / next week?
  A   B   C   D

I went / to a ball / game with / Jimmy.
  A   B   C   D

Samples of Answer Sheets

Figure 19-21. (continued)

Mechanical reasoning

This subtest consists of questions that are solved by identifying and applying mechanical principles. It is a measure of mechanical comprehension.

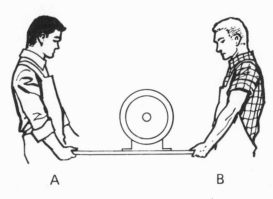

X

Which man has the heavier load?
(If equal, mark C.)

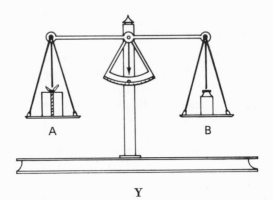

Y

Which weighs more?
(If equal, mark C.)

Space relations

Each problem in this subtest requires the person to visualize how a pattern would look when folded along dotted lines and when rotated in different positions.

Figure 19-21. (continued)

Which one of these figures can be made from the pattern shown? The pattern always shows the outside of the figure.

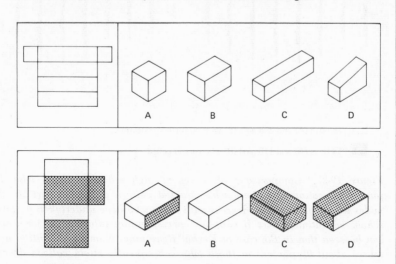

Verbal reasoning

This test measures the ability of the person to comprehend, abstract, and generalize from verbally presented materials.

For each sentence you are to choose from among five pairs of words to fill the blanks. The first word of the pair you choose goes in the blank space at the beginning of the sentence; the second word of the pair goes in the blank at the end of the sentence.

Example X. _____ is to water as eat is to _____

A. continue _____ drive
B. foot _____ enemy
C. drink _____ food
D. girl _____ industry
E. drink _____ enemy

Drink is to water as eat is to *food.* *Drink* is the first word of pair C and *food* is the second word of pair C.

Example Y. _____ is to night as breakfast is to _____

A. supper _____ corner
B. gentle _____ morning
C. door _____ corner
D. flow _____ enjoy
E. supper _____ morning

Supper is to night as breakfast is to *morning.* Pair E has both *supper* and *morning*; *supper* fits in the blank at the beginning of the sentence and *morning* fits in the blank at the end.

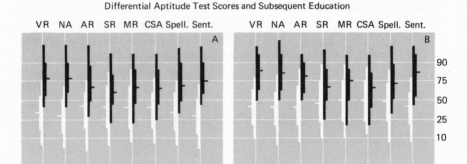

Differential Aptitude Test Scores and Subsequent Education

☐ 178 boys (A) and 398 girls (B) with no further education

■ 214 boys (A) and 118 girls (B) who earned college degrees

Figure 19-22. Comparisons of scores of high school students who did not pursue education and those who attained college degrees. Chart A contrasts males who report college degrees with those who have undertaken no post-high-school education. Chart B supplies corresponding information for women. It can be seen that in the case of Verbal Reasoning, Numerical Ability, and Sentences about 90 percent of those who subsequently attain college degrees are drawn from the top half of the high school population. At the same time, an appreciable proportion of boys (about 30 percent) and an even greater percentage of girls (about 45 percent) who did not continue in school displayed aptitudes in the same range.

The vertical bars in the above figures are used to show the spread of scores in the contrasted groups. The wider portion of the bar includes the middle 50 percent (25th to 75th percentiles) of the group; the upper thin bar represents those between the 75th and 90th percentiles; and the lower thin bar shows those between the 25th and 10th percentiles. The short horizontal line intersecting the wider portion of the bar marks the median or 50th percentile. (From Harold G. Seashore (Ed.). The DAT—A seven-year follow-up. New York: The Psychological Corporation, Test Service Bulletin, No. 49, November, 1955, Figure 1, p. 14. With permission.)

The data in Figure 19-23 showing average profiles of abilities of machinists and accountants are based on scores from the *General Aptitude Test Battery* developed by the U.S. Employment Service. Although such differentiations can be made, success in occupations does not seem to be *predictable* from test scores (Thorndike & Hagen, 1959). If differential test batteries are to make contributions to prediction of success,

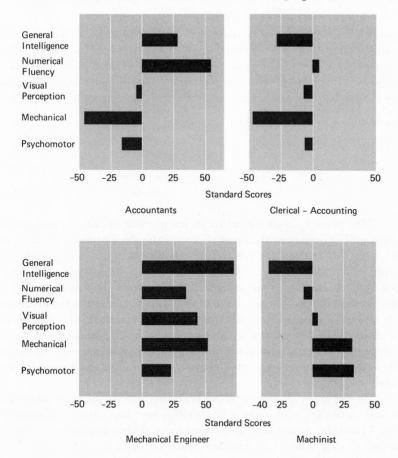

Figure 19-23. A comparison of test profiles for people in two levels of occupations requiring numerical and mechanical abilities. (Robert L. Thorndike & Elizabeth Hagen, 1959, pp. 27–28. With permission.)

over and above that made by survey tests, they must have differential validity. It is not surprising that, since most tests are validated in training situations, measures of verbal and numerical ability tend to have the best predictive validity almost to the exclusion of all other tests (for example, see Ingersoll & Peters, 1966).

Much research remains to be accomplished before the differential tests can be said to have fully met the objectives established by the measurement specialist. A current and most ambitious undertaking in this regard is Project Talent (Flanagan, *et al.*, 1964). Nearly a half-million high school students were administered a two-day battery of tests consisting of 18 tests and several self-descriptive and background inventories. These students will be followed up at periodic intervals (1,

5, 10, and 20 years after graduation) at least up to 1980 and perhaps beyond. Their achievements, career choices, activities, community participation, education, job satisfaction, occupational success, and the like will become a part of the record to be compared with early test scores. Perhaps the results of this project will provide more definitive data regarding what can and what cannot be predicted over long periods of time.

Summary

The term aptitude refers to an inseparable combination of innate talents and experiences that contribute to the development of these talents. If a test is used for predicting whether a pupil will profit from training then the test is an aptitude test. On the other hand, an achievement test is used to determine what the pupil has gained from a training experience. These purposes illustrate the relation between aptitude and achievement. Because what a person will do in the future (his potential) is best predicted on the basis of what he has already gained from past experience (his achievement), it is easy to see why both aptitude and achievement tests often contain very similar, and some identical, items.

In the study of general mental ability, one of the most commonly studied aptitudes, the *nature* of intelligence has always commanded much attention. Some, such as Piaget, have chosen to emphasize the sequence of emergence of the intellectual structures.

Thorndike proposed that intellectual ability comprised many independent abilities among which were social intelligence, concrete intelligence, and abstract intelligence. However, on the basis of correlations among scores from many tests, Spearman proposed a two-factor theory. He felt that performance on any test was determined in large part by a general ability. This ability existed to varying degrees across all tests, but was common to all tests. The other factor comprised those unique abilities required to perform satisfactorily on any specific test.

With the aid of the newly discovered statistical procedure known as factor analysis, Thurstone, in the 1940s, identified the multifactor structure of intellectual functioning. Factor analyses of several tests yielded the several abilities of number operations, verbal usage, space relations, memory, reasoning, word fluency, and perceptual speed. Despite rather consistent agreement among psychologists that intelligence consists of several dimensions, the existence of a "g" or general aptitude is supported by the fact that the several scores from multiple-factor tests are not completely independent but are correlated to some extent with one another.

Intelligence tests are often classified as individual or group tests, or as verbal or nonverbal tests. The most widely used individual intelligence tests in today's schools are the Stanford-Binet Intelligence Scale and the several Wechsler intelligence scales for children and adults. The Stanford-Binet Intelligence Scale is an age scale in which the items are grouped according to age level. The items within a given age level represent several mental abilities. The test yields a global score of intelligence called the intelligence quotient or IQ. The 1960 revision of the Stanford-Binet intelligence test replaced the ratio IQ with the deviation IQ, or standard score. The Wechsler scales are comprised of a series of verbal and performance subtests. They are point scales rather than age scales, each of which yields a verbal IQ, a performance IQ, and a full scale IQ rather than a single intelligence quotient. The content of the individual and group intelligence tests are, in many ways, very similar. Though the group tests are easily and quickly administered the pupil's score may be less reliable than that from individual tests. Performance on any measure is not only a reflection of what the pupil is *able* to do but also of his motivation to perform at a given time along with other temporary influences such as fatigue or anxiety that may be present during the testing period. Thus, a pupil who is not interested and who is anxious or confused may make a poorer score on a group test than is typical of his performance on an individual test. Group tests also tend to emphasize speed, verbal factors, and reading comprehension to a greater extent than do individual tests. Accordingly, group tests are often used only for screening purposes.

The nonverbal tests are used with special groups of children. Among the nonverbal tests are the culture-free ones, designed to control the effect of experience in different subcultures. Unfortunately, attempts to remove cultural bias have not been entirely successful. Nor do they predict scholastic performance as well as do other tests. It no longer seems feasible to locate the source of social class differences through the development of tests based upon the nature versus nurture controversy. Instead, the educator seeks to maximize the efficiency of teaching procedures and curricula by carefully matching educational experience with pupil characteristics.

In addition to predicting academic success, intelligence is measured to identify persons who require special educational opportunities. Among these persons are mentally retarded children on the one hand and very gifted children on the other. The many factors that affect the etiology of subnormal intelligence include genetic influences, physical factors external to the organism, and psychological factors due to environmental forces. Whatever his capabilities at birth, the child's intellectual growth will suffer if the environment fails to provide opportunities for its nurture. Evidence from research in this area implies the need for early stimulation in order to compensate for anticipated environmental deficiencies.

At the other extreme is the gifted child. Terman studied the characteristics of children with IQs of 140 and over and found them to be superior to a control group on such characteristics as high leadership qualities, high motivation, high perseverance, inquisitiveness, curiosity, and originality, as well as intelligence. They were also physically superior to their control counterparts. In their later years, some three and a half decades after their initial selection, these "gifted" people were still maintaining their superiority in health, adjustment, intelligence, career success, and contributions to society. As with any other trait, there are wide individual differences in giftedness and its associated characteristics.

Among the attempts at aptitude measurement has been the development of measures of special aptitudes. Activity in this area of test development has culminated in the development of such test batteries as the Differential Aptitude Test and the General Aptitude Test Battery which measure several different characteristics. Profiles of the separate aptitudes are then compared with average profiles of people in different academic or occupational pursuits. Because of the large number of aptitudes measured by such tests, they have the advantage of providing the individual with greater flexibility in identifying a trait which he can use effectively. In addition he can also find out at least that he has (or has not) the minimum level of aptitude required for a given education. The multifactor test batteries do not appear to have the differential validity necessary for predicting occupational success, perhaps because they attempt to predict performance in training situations where verbal abilities are important. A major undertaking with multifactor tests, at present, is Project Talent. A battery of several tests has been administered to nearly a half million high school students over a two-day period. These students will be followed up at periodic intervals for twenty years. Their achievements, career choices, activities, community participation, education, job satisfaction, occupational success, and the like will become part of their record to be compared with early test scores. Eventually, it is hoped, the results of this project will provide definitive data regarding what can and what cannot be predicted over long periods of time from aptitude tests.

Diagnosis of learning and adjustment difficulties

Many of our larger school systems employ several groups of school personnel whose concern is pupils who fail to make reasonable academic progress or who can't adjust to a stable pattern of social relations with their classmates. School psychologists, visiting teachers, school psychiatrists, remedial reading specialists, speech specialists, and guidance counselors give skilled diagnostic and remedial-therapeutic attention to pupils with chronic learning and adjustment difficulties.

These persons, who never seem sufficiently numerous to meet the schools' demands, cannot function effectively without the classroom teacher's assistance. The classroom teacher must identify those pupils who need this type of attention. Also, implementation of the recommendations for remediation or therapy made by the specialists is frequently the teacher's responsibility. Perhaps of greatest importance, it is the teacher who must be ever alert for minor difficulties that can be successfully handled by his resources before they become full blown, chronic maladjustments that are often difficult to correct even with the most skillful of professional adjuncts. Furthermore, in many of the smaller school systems the teacher is "on his own" with no such professionals available for referring pupils with unusual learning or adjustment difficulties. Under such conditions, the classroom teacher is forced to function as a diagnostician and remedial worker. How can this best be done? The case study appears to be one of the best approaches to making the classroom teacher maximally effective in this demanding role.

Making a Case Study

A case study is the report of an intensive analysis of an individual pupil. The specific purposes of case studies will vary widely as will their completeness. However, their fundamental purpose is to discover the *causes* of the behavior of a pupil who seems to be displaying symptoms requiring special attention. They are the kinds of aid to understanding the individual pupil which help prevent haphazard labeling based on cursory observation of symptoms. Ordinarily the teacher does not prepare a formal case study of a pupil but makes a partial study judged sufficient for understanding the pupil and guiding him toward healthy growth. The case study assures the teacher that all relevant, available information about the pupil's adjustment difficulties has been brought together in organized form. A serious hazard in analyzing a pupil's behavior problems is the almost irresistible tendency to label and to treat mere symptoms instead of searching for underlying causes. Little is gained by labeling a pupil "aggressive" when he bullies others or behaves disrespectfully in the classroom. These activities may be efforts to gain attention or to compensate for lack of affection, understanding, and recognition. If the teacher attempts to curb the aggressive symptoms without altering the predisposing causes, the pupil is likely to shift to other symptoms of hostility.

Stereotyped labels, such as "nice, quiet kids," are often used by teachers to describe pupils who exhibit social withdrawal tendencies. The withdrawing symptom is often overlooked once the pupil is identified as one who causes the *teacher* no trouble. Clinical psychologists are usually more concerned about the mental health of the withdrawing pupil than about the pupil who is mischievous or who flouts strict moral codes.

In assembling a case study on an individual child, the teacher does not collect information in the formal fashion that would be favored by a clinical psychologist or a psychiatrist.* Rather the teacher tries to survey and integrate readily available information and then seeks additional information as it seems needed. Because of limited training in the behavioral sciences, the typical teacher must be frankly experimental. His approach is somewhat similar to that of a general practitioner of medicine. After collating and interrelating the immediately accessible information (observations, informal testing and questioning, plus all the information in the pupil's personal folder), the teacher hypothesizes about the pupil's difficulties, tries some relevant program of remedial action, and then evaluates the outcomes. If the pupil does not make favorable progress, he seeks more information, tries a new approach,

*See Appendix B for an excellent case study prepared by professional personnel.

and reevaluates the outcomes. This process is repeated until satisfactory results are obtained or until he judges it desirable to refer the pupil to another person with more specialized remedial or therapeutic skills.

Who should be studied?

Most pupils are fortunately within the "normal" range and present no unusual problems. Other pupils may have difficulties whose causes are so readily apparent that they require no extended study. However, some pupils with special or exceptional abilities or with serious behavioral problems require detailed study by the teacher. Examples of such pupils are John, a quiet and retiring boy who begins to stutter; Sally, a junior in high school who develops such an intense "crush" on Miss James, her gym teacher, that she completely ignores her classmates; or Sam, who, with the highest IQ in the class and an earlier outstanding academic record, now is failing in all his subjects. The case study provides a more nearly "whole" view of each of these pupils by integrating his history, experiences, and present condition. It provides a good basis for understanding each pupil and for indicating the kinds of help and guidance he needs.

The kinds of information that go into the case study

The case study usually contains information about the pupil's family history, physical development, health, intellectual abilities and progress, social adjustments, emotional patterns, needs, and interests. The pupil's personal folder is a rich source of such information. This folder, which is usually filed in the principal's or counselor's office, contains much of the following kinds of information: age, family, ability indices, results of physical examinations, achievement scores, anecdotal records from previous teachers, school history, and personal and social adjustment records. In many instances there is much duplication of information. These multiple measures of the same characteristic are valuable aids. Multiple indices permit greater confidence in the picture portrayed. For example, several IQs obtained at different times provide a more reliable estimate of the pupil's intelligence than a single estimate. Several scores on the same ability over a period of time also permit an inference about growth or lack of growth. The scores obtained by a child on an achievement test battery administered at different times over a span of several grades indicate the pupil's growth in each of the subjects measured.

In making a case study the teacher tries to obtain as much information as possible about the past history of the pupil. He usually has to rely on the reports of other people. Often their records do not contain objective behavioral data. Untrained observers are inclined to confuse matters of opinion and fact. Consider the following report on Julius:

Julius talked loud and much during poetry. He wanted to do and say just what he wanted and didn't consider the right way of doing things. He was rude to me and talked back when I told him he was naughty and shouldn't be allowed to be with the rest of the children. Had to make him sit next to me. Showed a bad attitude about it.*

This is a confused combination of factual reporting and inferential evaluations. In fact, this anecdotal recording gives more information about the teacher who wrote it than about the pupil!

Sometimes teachers fail to select important incidents or they emphasize irrelevant material in their reports. It is natural and inevitable that teachers will notice and remember most readily the classroom incidents of special interest and concern to them. It is also understandable that they will write anecdotes about happenings related to their own preoccupations. However, the most useful anecdotes are those which are directed toward happenings of importance *to the pupil.*

The following is an illustration of an anecdote which emphasizes the teacher's emotional reaction to a pupil:

King's vocabulary is amazing. His current interest and information are wonderful. He is the most unusual and interesting child I've ever taught. . . . King has been feeling fine since Christmas, the same unusual child. He is the only child in my room who really feels like saying anything he wants to me.†

Contrast this anecdote with the following where happenings significant to the pupil are well described:

Sam (age 12) showed a decided preference for Dora today. Asked to help her committee put up curtains. Said that "girls hardly know how to put up curtain fixtures straight like they should be." Painted a picture with Dora. Told me that he would probably learn to paint a little better if he could paint with an artist like Dora. I wasn't so sure. He especially enjoyed our poetry appreciation period. Asked for "Sea Fever," "Moon Folly," and "Overhead on a Salt Marsh." When James asked for "Hiding," he said, "Oh, boy, stop asking for those baby poems."‡

Much is reported in the pupil's own words. It tells both what was done and what was said. It, along with others, permits important inferences about the pupil's development.

*Adapted from D. Prescott (Ed.), *Helping teachers understand children.* Washington, D.C.: American Council on Education, 1945. P. 33. With permission of publisher.

†Ibid. P. 37.

‡Ibid. P. 39.

Besides a record of the past history of the pupil, a case study includes information about his present situation and behavior. The instruments and techniques described in preceding chapters can be used to obtain whatever information is desirable and well substantiated. Often a picture which seems confusing or unclear is dramatically improved by the addition of more information.

The teacher may wish to have conferences with the pupil, or arrange for interviews with his parents or other teachers. The most important feature of any interview or conference is the achievement of satisfactory rapport. It is vital to establish friendly relations with those one is talking to and to make them feel that you and they share a common interest in the pupil. Once the confidence of the interviewee has been gained, the teacher is more likely to obtain important information about the pupil.

The informed teacher can obtain much help from skillful consultants: the school physician, nurse, school psychologist, guidance counselor, visiting teacher, speech therapist, reading consultant, and various supervisors. Their training and skills can be of great service in providing insights into the pupil's behavior.

Interpreting the case study

An adequate case study should promote a better understanding of the pupil. Interpretation of the case study materials, with identification of consistencies and inconsistencies in behavior, is a prerequisite to understanding. For this purpose more than one frame of reference is desirable. Three very useful ones are: growth, or changes in a particular characteristic over time; idiosyncrasy, or differences between the individual's performances in various areas at a particular time; and relative status, or comparisons with normative groups of various kinds. The first two use the individual pupil as his own frame of reference while the third uses the performances of others, especially groups of fellow pupils.

An individual pupil's *growth* in reading comprehension can be determined by comparing his performance on a reading test in October with his performance on a comparable form of the test in May. By comparing his scores on these two occasions the teacher can tell how much the pupil has gained or lost in his reading ability. For this comparison to be meaningful it is important that the two tests be highly reliable and comparable. One must use either the same test both times or two forms of the test constructed to give comparable scores.

What are the given pupil's relative strengths and weaknesses? The teacher can compare the pupil's performance in reading, arithme-

tic, science, and social studies provided he has adequately reliable scores
which are comparable from test to test. For example, if the pupil has a
percentile score of 70 in reading and 50 in arithmetic on the tests of a
standardized achievement battery, one would be inclined to say that he
is better in reading than in arithmetic. However, the difference in the
two scores must be large enough to represent a "true" difference and not
just errors of measurement.

Numerous types of scores based on *normative* groups are useful.
One can discover a pupil's relative spelling ability by converting his
score on a spelling test to grade norms. If he obtains a grade score of 6.5
we can say that he obtained a score comparable to that of the average
child who has been in the sixth grade five months. If the pupil is in the
fifth grade and was tested in late October he shows superiority since the
score representative of his grade placement would be 5.2. Let us say that
when this score is converted to fifth-grade percentile norms the pupil in
question is at the 85th percentile. One now knows that although the
pupil did as well on the spelling test as the average sixth-grader, so did
many other children in the fifth grade. In fact 15 percent of the fifth-
graders exceeded him.

Thus it can be seen that an examination of a pupil's performance
in many fields over many grades and using many different frames of
reference can give us needed information about the consistency of his
behavior. If a review of his records were to show that he had been
above the norm in most subjects in the third grade, below in the fourth,
and way above in arithmetic in the fifth one would wish to know why.

After identifying unusual *consistencies* and *inconsistencies* in
behavior, a search must be made for the fundamental causes so that reasonable recommendations can be made. All this can take place within
the perspective of the information contained in the case study. Again an
analogy can be drawn with the case studies of the physician. The doctor
considers a "syndrome of symptoms" and by a process of elimination,
adding information, and applying treatments finally diagnoses the
difficulty. For example, he may be called by a mother who observes a
rash on her child. He first observes the kind of rash and where on the
body it occurs. If it consists of flat, pink spots that first began around the
ears and worked down he suspects that the child may have measles. If he
now is informed that the child has had fever and cold symptoms for
three or four days before the rash began he is more certain. On the
other hand, if the rash were a red blush which started in the warm
moist parts of the body such as the armpits, groin, and back he might
suspect scarlet fever. Confirmatory symptoms would be sickness with a
headache, fever, vomiting, and sore throat prior to the occurrence of the
rash. The physician makes the best diagnosis possible in view of known
symptoms and then begins treatment. Knowledge of additional symp-

toms either confirms or refutes the original diagnosis and suggests continued or modified treatment.

The teacher's task in evaluating case study data closely parallels the physician's procedures. The teacher is continuously alert for things which go together. There are a number of syndromes related to pupil adjustment. The "nervous syndrome" is usually composed of restlessness, withdrawal or aggression, nail biting, facial grimaces, daydreaming, or reversal in achievement. These kinds of behaviors are suggestive but not conclusive evidence of the presence of frustration and maladjustment. As a second example, the behavior of the indulged overprotected child is frequently marked by disobedience, impudence, tantrums, unreasonable demands, and varying degrees of tyrannical behavior. Various syndromes of symptoms are associated with social adjustment and academic difficulties. One must always keep in mind that nearly any symptom may have many different causes. Since adequate treatment depends upon the identification of the cause rather than the symptom, an adequate analysis and interpretation of symptoms is a vital part of diagnosis.

Use of case studies

A case study is usually initiated by a problem that comes to the attention of the teacher. The teacher then collects information, integrates and evaluates the significance of the data by setting up hypotheses, and attempts treatment consistent with these hypotheses. Often he makes many false starts. Frequently the teacher enlists the aid of other adults and specialists. The following are two brief case studies illustrating the use of this method in handling problems that arise in the classroom:

Tommy* first came to view as a problem in a third-term class in modified English. Most of the other boys in the group seemed pleased that the work was within their grasp. Tommy scorned the work. Most of the other boys were willing to attempt the jobs they were given. Tommy would have none of them. He jeered at the others for trying, kept up a running stream of heckling (of teacher and classmates), and when talk failed to halt the class proceedings, he tried more overt action. He mutinied against all regulations and began to incite the other boys to rebellion against the subject, teacher, program, and school.

When he was finally persuaded to verbalize his grievance, it was discovered that what rankled was his assignment to the General Industrial Program. This was a new curriculum in our school, for boys who could be classified as "slow learners." The academic work was modified and a special shop program was arranged. Tommy had been a contented member of his group during

*From M. C. Dolan. What made Tommy fight? *Personnel and Guidance Journal*, 1954, *32*, 357–358. With permission of the American Personnel and Guidance Association.

his first year in school when he had no label and was indistinguishable from others of his grade. But in third term, all others in the grade had been allowed to make a choice of vocational shop while the General Industrial boys found themselves assigned to a shop which was to offer work adapted to their ability. He felt a difference in not being permitted to make a choice. He had over-heard an ill-advised comment on the General Industrial group made by one of the teachers; he had been teased by other students who cruelly labeled the group "the dumb ones." Now he was fighting back.

Why was he in the Slow Learner course? His application for admission to high school indicated an IQ of 64 on a Pintner B [test] and a rating of *Slow*; this had been the chief basis for classification. Grades of 6.4 in arith-metic and 5.4 in reading (on a Stanford Advanced Test) had been recorded when he was in the first half of his eighth school year. . . . Further searching into his record (which had not been feasible before making program assign-ments) showed that he had achieved an IQ of 81 on a Binet L when in the fourth grade of elementary school. In the sixth grade he had been given a Pintner Nonlanguage Test and had scored an IQ of 92. Examination of an Otis answer sheet and observation during the administration of a reading test showed that his technique in taking any group test was to mark all the answers at random.

When he came to trust us sufficiently, we found that he was completely a non-reader. He could not recognize words in a second or even first grade vocabulary. Although his health was good, his attendance in elementary school had been very poor. His shame at not knowing how to read was so great that he had become extremely clever in disguising his deficiency, and he had used bad behavior as a camouflage. The combination of frequent absence, and troublesome behavior when present, had apparently kept him from learning. Tommy himself transferred the blame for his predicament to others. He was filled with a fierce resentment against his elementary school teachers. Several times he said, "One thing I'm going to do is go back and get even with all of them who should have taught me and didn't."

Questioning about his background revealed that he was the youngest of six children, with quite an age gap between him and the older brothers and sisters. His father suffered from high blood pressure and was excitable. His mother had been deaf from the time of Tommy's birth and no hearing aids had helped her condition although many had been tried. Tommy himself smarted at the fact that a younger niece could read although he couldn't and tried swagger and bluff to carry off the situation.

What could our school do to help Tommy? It was not possible for him to attend any sort of clinic or receive private instruction; he had to be aided within the framework of our regular school organization. The first step was to give him a change from the scheduled General Industrial to a regular Vocational course. He made an attempt at radio but was handicapped too much by his lack of reading ability. Then he shifted to woodworking, where the work seemed to have a therapeutic value for him. An understanding and supportive shop teacher, whom he came to respect and like, changed the attitude of the boy toward work, school, and teachers.

Assignment was also made to remedial reading classes with interested teachers who gave him as much individualized help as they could. Here he blossomed. Gone was the heckling, obstreperous, cynical Tommy of previous days. No longer did he voice the hope, "I'd like to kill a teacher or a Russian." Seriously and painstakingly he cooperated with all efforts to help him, showing a new side of his nature to the teacher whose class he had tried to sabotage the term before. He was impatient only with himself, as he worked on such materials as the Dolch Word Cards and the Disney Readers. He even worked harmoniously with a rather unattractive girl who was also a non-reader. It was really another boy!

A special program was worked out for him, with particular teachers wherever possible, so that he was able to meet graduation requirements. He continued to attend remedial reading classes instead of being forced to cope with regular English work which was beyond him, and with the help he received he was able to pass the reading requirements of the Driver Education course. His attendance remained rather poor—he had an out-of-school job which made many demands on him—but his effort when in school was excellent and his behavior almost exemplary.

By his last term in school he could read material on approximately the fifth-grade level. He was, and probably always will be, a slow reader, but he had acquired a good method of attack on new words and a large enough comprehension vocabulary to understand the words when he had figured them out. He was able to understand and enjoy the adapted text of *Sherlock Holmes*, a daily paper, and such magazines as *Look* and *Life* because the illustrations give enough clues to the text.

An indication of his changed feelings toward school was shown in his seventh term when he brought his father to Parents' Night. For the first time in years he knew that the comments of his teachers would be favorable and he basked in the atmosphere of approval. All through his senior year he remained fearful that the goal of a diploma would elude him. "I can't believe I'm going to get it. Every once in a while I get a bad feeling that I'm not going to graduate."

But graduate he did. Now he is working full time at the job he held while in school—helping an older man establish a milk delivery service. He is working hard and making quite a lot of money. He will never be a bookworm but now he can at least function in the essentials of his business, and can keep records and read the notes his customers leave him. Tommy is so far removed from the violent ambitions of his former days that he came back to school on his day off to see his favorite reading teacher.

Sometimes a problem arises in the classroom which can be approached more effectively by referral to specialized personnel such as the guidance counselor or school psychologist. The following case* is such an illustration:

*From B. B. Washington. Did counseling function here? *Personnel and Guidance Journal*, 1954, *32*, 489–491. With permission of the American Personnel and Guidance Association.

A pocketbook was missing in Miss Jones's class. This situation introduced
Mary to us, who was a ninth grade pupil enrolled in the shop curriculum, a
foods major. In attempting to locate the missing wallet, the foods teacher
sought to identify the pupils who were nearest the loser. The teacher reported
that when Mary was questioned as others of the group, she jumped up protest-
ing that no one was going to call her a thief and get away with it. Further, to
the delight of her classmates, she vehemently questioned the teacher's ancestral
derivation. Following the outburst, she ran from the class crying and slammed
the door.

  * So Mary came to the counselor's office—a diffident, untidy, slightly
over-weight girl of fifteen. Many indictments were born of her resentfulness:
everyone at school and home had it in for her. Her mother and father nagged
her. The teachers nagged her and she didn't have any friends. What's more, she
didn't take the old pocketbook, but nobody would believe her. Even her own
family was always accusing her of taking things.

  Her voice broke. Between sobs she rehearsed an incident of the past
year. Without an investigation, her father had beaten her severely on the
charge of stealing a purse. When the mistake in the situation was later discovered and the real culprit disclosed, there had been no apology or clearing of
Mary. In fact, she stated, her father, in spite of his knowing the truth, had
never mentioned either pocketbook or punishment again. "Yes," she muttered,
"I got a bad temper just like my father; and you would too if you had to look
after four sisters and a baby brother, clean house, do laundry, and never
allowed to go places with anyone. I just couldn't help myself this morning in
class. Miss Jones was the nicest teacher in the building to me until this morning. I've done my best work in her class. I liked her and now this had to
happen."

  Following routine procedure, the counselor had the mother in—a rather
pretentious woman, over-dressed, even to imitation jewels and furs, moreover,
incensed that anyone would implicate her daughter in a theft. However, the
picture of Mary's home life slowly evolved, for the mother's story was not
unlike the girl's version with, of course, added indictment of her daughter's
attitude. Mrs. Thomas complained, "Mary fusses constantly about her home-
made clothes and not being able to go to house-to-house parties and neighborhood centers." A supercilious tone crept into her voice when mentioning the
community activities. "Of course," she added emphatically, "we do not permit
our daughter to associate with children who stay out as long as they want and
do as they please. It is a real problem for us to feed and clothe six children on
her father's salary. She's not satisfied with the size of the house and the way it
looks, yet she never does her share around the house, nor does she spend the
time she ought to on her home work. She is just a lazy, irresponsible girl."

  Facts of the home background emerging from the conference were: that
the father was a custodial worker in the Federal government; that the family
lived in a four-room dwelling unit of a public housing project; that Mary
shared her room with two younger sisters.

  Mary's scholastic aptitude, as shown by an individual and several group
tests, was normal, each test placing her approximately at the 50th percentile.

On the individual test she showed a mental age of 15 years and 8 months and a chronological age of 14 years and 11 months. Her examiner believed that Mary had sufficient ability to do acceptable though not outstanding work. Her progress in elementary school was highly satisfactory up to grade three. At this point her school achievement was marked unsatisfactory. She repeated grade five and had considerable difficulty in the first year of junior high school. Achievement scores in reading and arithmetic indicated a two and one grade level retardation respectively in comparison with the norm for her class. From the achievement test scores, the only pattern revealed was a slightly stronger development in mathematics as compared with that in verbal subjects. Mary's junior high school grades indicated passing but uniformly below average work in everything but Home Economics and General Science.

Her interest pattern revealed strong interest in the social service, scientific, and computational activities; average interest in clerical, outdoor, and mechanical, and low in literary, musical, and artistic. In types of interests, her choices were high in the manipulative and computational. Her level of interest indicated a preference for activities of moderate difficulty.

In the area of personality appraisal her cumulative record gave the following picture. It depicted the counselee as noncooperative, argumentative, stubborn, sulky, in many instances highly suspicious and ready to blame others for her shortcomings.

Thus was drawn the profile. To the counselor there seemed to be two main objectives. One, to help Mary understand and accept her home situation in order to overcome a sense of insecurity. The other, to assist her in clarifying her educational objectives in a permissive and insight producing situation.

By the third interview it was evident that Mary was willing to cooperate. She had rid herself of some of the hostility toward the school, although her uneasiness about staying in the Home Economics group and adjusting to her home life remained. She still resented the discipline of her father, which to her seemed autocratic, and the lack of understanding on her mother's part. In her relations with the foods teacher there was a paradoxical reaction. Although still suspicious of the teacher, she continually expressed a devotion to her, and a desire to continue under her tutelage. To her, Miss Jones was unfortunately the only teacher she could recall who had accepted her and shown an interest in her progress. Further, the group, following the example of the teacher, had not ostracized Mary. In light of the indicated aptitudes and this situation, it was not surprising that Mary's curriculum choice and occupational interests were in the field of Home Economics.

Miss Jones cooperated and Mary returned to class with no upset of routine or emphasis on the cause of her absence. She was even being assigned to her former home management duties.

Mary began to realize that her temper was not a matter of inheritance but rather a poor environmental pattern established to dominate and draw attention; one which she was only imitating. Finally, she started to practice leaving the scene when she felt an outburst of temper threatening. When she stopped looking for accusations of dishonesty, she admitted that many of her previous grievances had been imaginary.

As the parents sensed that Mary was making a genuine effort, they became less demanding of her time in household tasks and more lenient toward her social activities. To the counselor, in a later conference, they expressed a recognition that children cannot develop in an atmosphere of physical violence and nagging; that perhaps Mary had been overburdened with the care of younger children, and possibly felt slighted. In Mary's presence they agreed upon an agenda of home tasks with time for study and recreation. Through the placement office, the girl secured for the after-school hours a job baby-sitting. This undertaking allowed her to earn money, as well as put into practice some of the theory of the home management class.

Mary has not achieved a perfect adjustment. She sometimes loses her temper. The home situation is not perfect. However, Mary no longer lives in an atmosphere of family friction and bitterness. To please her family she completes household chores before leaving for school, and attends her classes regularly. She has her own circle of friends, and the security of spending money of her own earning. . . .

Supplementing the Formal Testing Program

There are several types of useful information that the teacher can collect in the classroom without special materials or equipment. This information is often a valuable adjunct to that available from standardized achievement and aptitude tests now available in the majority of schools.

Appraising the social structure of the classroom

The ultimate aim in the measurement of social structure is to determine the person's social status or position and dynamic interactions within the group. Sociometric measures assess the attractions and repulsions existing within a group. This type of measurement usually involves each member of the group selecting a number of other persons in the group with whom he would like to engage in some particular activity. For example, children in a class may be asked to write down the names of classmates with whom they would like to eat lunch, play, or work. Infrequently it also requires each person to select those individuals with whom he would not like to participate in the activity.

Considerable research has been devoted to the obtaining and interpreting of sociometric data. Graphic methods and quantitative methods, including statistical and matrix methods, have been used. The pioneer work was done by Moreno (1953). His approach, leading to the presentation of the results as a sociogram, has had wide use.

A few pupils with the largest number of choices are designated as "stars." The reasons for their being selected are often hard to determine and may vary considerably from one pupil to another. One pupil may select Tom to sit beside him because Tom is his best friend. A second may choose Tom because he is a good student and will be helpful in doing classwork. A third may prefer Tom because he is a friendly, helpful person whom he can look up to and who makes him feel more secure. An individual who is never chosen is called an "isolate." The teacher should be very careful in his interpretation of pupils classified as isolates. The reasons for a pupil's receiving no nominations as a desired person may also be extremely varied. They range all the way from extreme shyness to excessive aggression. The isolate may be a new-comer who has not yet become well acquainted. A "mutual pair" is said to exist when two individuals choose each other. A "triangle" exists when three pupils choose each other.

Pupils are asked to "Put down the name of your classmate with whom you would most like to work on a project."

Their responses may be tabled on a matrix (chart) like this:

	Sam	John	Betty	Sue	Mary	Bob	Etc.
1. Sam		1					
2. John			1				
3. Betty		1					
4. Sue		1					
5. Mary			1				
6. Bob					1		
Etc.							
Total choices received	0	3	2	0	1	0	

And made into a sociogram like this:

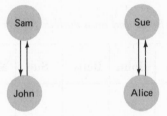

Figure 20-1. Simplified illustration of the construction of a sociogram from a table of choices made by pupils in a classroom.

Choices made and received within two mutual pairs or chums

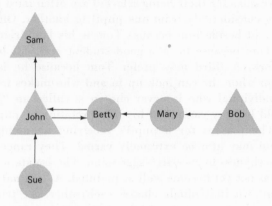

Choices made and received by three pupils in a triangle

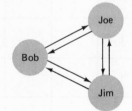

Choices received by a star and an isolate

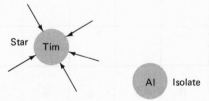

Figure 20-2. Diagram illustrating social status of some children.

The choices made in a classroom can be presented in a sociogram. Figure 20-2 shows the tabulation of the choices of a few pupils in a class and the sociogram depicting these choices. As can be seen, the teacher draws a chart in which he lists every pupil (triangles for boys and circles for girls), and draws arrows to show choices. The first sketch he makes is usually jumbled and confusing. However, the names can be arranged to put mutual friends together, and the lines shortened between choices. Figure 20-3 shows a sociogram for an entire class of 16 pupils.

From such a diagram the teacher can obtain much useful information. He can tell who are the stars and isolates, and the number and size of cliques. The pattern often comes as a surprise to the teacher. Because 30 pupils may be arranged in 435 *possible* pairs, he can rarely anticipate the detailed social structure. He may have noted certain friendships, rivalries, and groupings. He knows that Ellen has been going around with Sue's gang this fall. The sociogram, however, shows that Ellen is only a peripheral member of this clique. She is able to count on friendship from Sue only and is ignored by the other three members.

Since the information obtained from sociometric procedures is based upon judgments of one pupil by another, it is essential that the students know each other well enough to make the required selections. A sociometric device administered at the beginning of the year is not likely to be effective. If care is taken to explain and describe the procedure, the pupils are usually glad to participate. The teacher or counselor should explain why the questions are being asked. With older pupils one can explain that this information will be used in guidance. One can also explain that if the teacher knows their friends he can try to plan activities where they will work together. The teacher must convince the pupils that the sociometric approach is being used to help them rather than to pry into their private affairs. The procedure may backfire unless the pupils like the teacher and welcome his interest in them.

As an illustration of the contribution such information about social relations makes to other knowledge about the child and his environment (i.e., intelligence, achievement, home, community, etc.) let us consider Jane, who tested high in intelligence but low in academic achievement. When administered a sociometric test she was found to be an isolate in all the situations presented to the class. Here was an intelligent girl who was not achieving a reasonable amount academically and who was rejected by her classmates. Her definite dissatisfaction with her school environment was investigated as a possible reason for her academic failure.

Through a series of conferences the teacher found out that Jane felt that her classmates disliked and "were against" her. Hence she wasn't trying to do well in school. The teacher tried to help her become

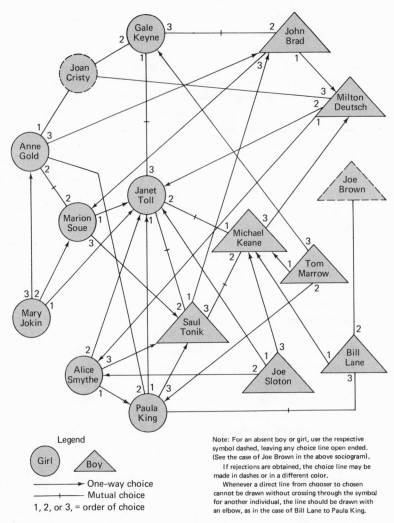

Figure 20-3. The social structure of one classroom. The data for this sociogram were obtained by asking each child in the class to make first, second, and third choices among his classmates for a particular social activity. (From H. H. Jennings. Sociometry in group relations: A manual for teachers. 2nd ed. Washington, D.C.: American Council on Education, 1958. P. 26. With permission.)

better adjusted and made a point of assigning Jane to work with groups containing pupils who were very friendly outgoing people. After a period of time Jane responded to their friendly acceptance and became an enthusiastic worker. She became especially friendly with one of her classmates and started to show some improvement in her academic work.

As a complementary example, let us consider Sam, who was high both in intelligence and achievement. However, the teacher regarded him as something of a lone wolf, a boy whom he felt should be "pushed" into more social activities. Upon administering a sociometric instrument he found that Sam was highly regarded by his classmates and that he liked them. This evidence combined with the observations of his characteristic behavior probably indicates that his social needs were minimal and were being adequately satisfied by the group. He was apparently accepted and liked by the group, and he felt the group was able to satisfy adequately his psychological needs. An attempt by the teacher to insist on a large amount of social activity might result in unhappiness for Sam and lower academic achievement. Sam may turn out to be one of those people who will make a substantial contribution to knowledge in research or some other such activity. Society could well lose by attempting to change his interests and activity preferences.

An important function of the school is to maintain adequate public relations. Teacher-pupil, pupil-pupil, and teacher-parent social relations are extremely important. Information of the type provided by a sociometric questionnaire is often useful in understanding and influencing pupil-pupil relations.

A number of research studies indicate that teachers generally do not know their students as well as they believe they do. Usually teachers find substantial differences between the view they hold and the one the pupils hold of the same boy or girl. Teachers, naming class leaders, may give undue attention to brighter or more verbal pupils, only to find that the pupils themselves name a quieter, less conspicuous pupil who is more effective in getting things done. Teachers are often very wrong when they try to name the most popular pupils. Bonney (1947) in checking teacher estimates of popularity against sociometric data found that the average teacher was 45 percent accurate in estimates for students of high and average popularity, but only 28 percent accurate for students of low popularity. Gronlund (1951) obtained similar findings in studying sixth-grade classes in Flint, Michigan. He reported a tendency of teachers to overjudge the acceptance of children they personally most preferred and to underjudge the status of those they least preferred. One of the difficulties is that teachers are unable to put themselves in the same frame of reference as the pupils. They are not fully aware of the bases that pupils use to make choices and are not able to see things as pupils see them. The use of a sociometric instrument can give the teacher objective information which will enable him to understand better the dynamics within his class.

Pupil appraisals of other pupils' behavior tendencies

Pupil ratings of other pupils are usually collected by *indirect* methods. For obvious reasons it seems undesirable to influence or crystallize a pupil's evaluations of his classmates' personality traits or adjustment problems.

One of the most widely used methods of soliciting pupils' appraisals of other pupils takes the form of "reputation ratings" or "Guess Who?" nominations. Each pupil is presented with a list of personal or behavioral descriptions and is asked to nominate one or more of his classmates as best fitting the description. For example, "Here is someone who is always friendly, has a smile for everybody, and is always willing to do you a favor. Guess who this person is." Each pupil selects one or more of his classmates as fitting the description. (See Table 20-1 for typical items.)

This technique has been employed in a number of interesting research studies (Kuhlen & Lee, 1943; Meyer & Thompson, 1956; Tryon, 1939) and has much to commend it. It is a highly flexible approach in that it can be easily modified to solicit selected kinds of peer evaluations. The teacher can write his own descriptions or construct them from the essays of his pupils on topics like "The person I like best," "The kind of person I would like to be," "Somebody I admire very much," and so on. If the procedure is coordinated with an academic assignment, pupils tend to accept it as a regular classroom routine and enjoy the experience. The teacher secures valuable information on each pupil's characteristics as viewed by one of his most important audiences. It is recommended that the beginning teacher try out one of the many variations of this popular approach to personality assessment. With experience the teacher will hit upon the most usable variation for his particular interest and needs as a counselor of boys and girls.

Table 20-1. Typical items and general format of a "reputation" rating schedule, or "Guess Who" inventory. The teacher may find it desirable to construct his own items for this kind of inventory.

Here is someone who is always happy and a lot of fun.

    1st choice   _____

    2nd choice _____

    3rd choice _____

Here is someone who is always fighting or quarreling with others.

    1st choice   _____

    2nd choice _____

    3rd choice _____

Here is someone who is always willing to help you with your problems.

    1st choice   _____

    2nd choice _____

    3rd choice _____

Observation and recording of pupils' "everyday" behavior

The teacher has an opportunity to observe his pupils as they respond to a wide range of adjustment situations. He cannot fail to note instances of personal and social growth, leadership, social rejection, dependency, aggression, withdrawal and depression, and so on. With experience he can become skillful in anticipating what types of social setting permit a particular pupil to forge ahead and the conditions that lead to unresolvable frustration and failure.

Information from the instruments previously discussed in this chapter will get the teacher off to an early start as an alert and insightful observer. However, in the last analysis he must be able to coordinate each pupil's successes and failures with identifiable goal strivings. These identifications will be the first steps toward a behavioral analysis of the antecedent and consequent conditions—the causes and effects. Why is Mary sometimes so depressed and unhappy? Why did Bill start the fight with Dick today—when usually they are such close friends? Is there anything I can do to encourage Virgil in his reading? Why does Alice refuse to pay attention on Monday mornings?

These are significant problems for the conscientious teacher. In order to solve them he must first understand the significant factors and their dynamic interrelationships. Then he can work toward changes in some of the most important conditions in an attempt to alter pupil behavior and adjustment. These efforts will be experimental, for even the most highly trained observer of human behavior will come up with *several* alternative hypotheses, equally plausible as to what can be done to help a given pupil in a particular adjustment situation.

The fact that the teacher must be an experimenter makes it desirable that he keep a set of records for his own guidance and for the other later teachers of the same pupils. Every careful experimenter has his laboratory manual. Although the teacher of many years of experience may feel that he can remember the necessary details, it seems likely that even his memories become fragmentary and distorted with the passage of time. There is an abundance of psychological evidence to document the existence of this human frailty.

What kind of records should the teacher keep? Brief and objective anecdotes will probably prove adequate for his needs. Most behavioral settings can be succinctly described on a 3″ x 5″ card which can be conveniently filed in the pupil's folder. It seems better to *keep* only moderately detailed records than to *plan* for longer reports which the teacher's busy schedule will not permit.

The content of the anecdotal records will of course vary from situation to situation. However, there are several rules which need to be followed if they are to serve a useful purpose in pupil guidance. The anecdotes should always point toward positive action by the teacher.

They may record courses of teacher action that don't prove successful with particular pupils, but even these anecdotes should indicate "next steps" in the guidance procedures. Negatively toned anecdotes are of little value to the teacher and may be injurious to a pupil's relationships with later teachers. For example, "Johnny and Eddie had a nasty quarrel this morning. I made them stay after school and told both of them to do their fighting away from school." In contrast, "Johnny and Eddie have both been making up some back work which they missed during the recent 'flu' epidemic. They got into a severe argument over who was going to use the classroom dictionary. The quarrel came to blows. I separated them and worked out a schedule of 'taking turns.' Maybe they are overtired from their recent illness. Perhaps I should have waited a while before asking them to do previous assignments. Note: this is not the first quarrel over the dictionary—Mary and Beth argued about its use last week. I will request another dictionary for the classroom." The latter anecdote does not malign the pupils and points toward reasonable next steps. It searches for possible causes and illustrates the fact that the difficulties of a pupil may have their origin in an unfavorable social situation.

Not all records should be devoted to "behavior problems." The modern teacher is just as concerned about the things that pupils can't or won't do as he is about their behavior transgressions. For example, "I have been trying for a long time to get Jimmy interested in our science collection. Every effort has failed. Today I think I may have stumbled onto a successful way. He was watching a tumble bug on the playground and I asked him what kind of bug it was. He gave me a long story about the bug and its habits, and then looked shy and embarrassed about his long speech. I think he may be afraid of showing his deep interest in science. I am going to try to organize an exhibit committee on insects of which he can be a member without taking the center of the stage. I wonder what things can be done to help him relate better to the other pupils?"

Now for a few additional rules. The anecdote should present the behavioral setting as well as the behavior. It should be couched in objective terms with a minimum of emotionally toned adjectives like "mean," "lazy," "willful," "neurotic," and so on. It seems doubtful that the latter type of labeling serves any useful purpose, and may do much harm.

And as previously mentioned, the anecdote should suggest desirable goals for further action on the part of the teacher, or present plausible hypotheses about next steps that may be taken in helping the pupil. Although other rules of lesser importance might be mentioned, the rules presented should help the teacher in his first efforts to make meaningful anecdotal records.

Summary

One of the teacher's most difficult and demanding assignments is the diagnosis of pupils with severe learning and adjustment difficulties. After the antecedents and surrounding conditions of a given difficulty are identified, it is still hard to carry through on a relevant program of remediation. Referral to other specialized school personnel is not always possible because of their unavailability in some of the smaller school districts and their typical large backlog of referrals in the larger schools. The classroom teacher is often forced to solve his own problems as best he can with no assistance. This chapter was written for teachers who must go it alone.

The case study is emphasized as the teacher's best aid in attempts to understand and help pupils with chronic or severe learning or adjustment difficulties. The teacher's role as an experimenter, a hypothesis-maker-and-tester, is discussed. Techniques for gathering important information by relatively simple procedures applied within the classroom are outlined. Approaches to the diagnosis of learning difficulties are suggested. The teacher is not an expert in all phases of the behavioral sciences or the healing arts, but he is often the only person in the community with sufficient background to note that certain pupils are in desperate need of special assistance. If the teacher cannot give help in a direct way through classroom procedures, he may be able to see that the troubled pupil is taken to specialists who may be of assistance.

Part VI

Appendices, Bibliography, and Index

Appendix A

Some descriptive statistics and derived scores used in tests and measurements

Some knowledge of elementary statistical definitions will be of help to the student in reading supplementary material in the psychological and educational literature related to the contents of the book. In addition, these ideas will be useful in working with tests.

Scores

Raw scores

Most readers of this book are familiar with *raw scores* from their earliest educational experiences. Such scores are ordinarily expressed in terms of the number of questions the pupil answers correctly on a test. For example, a raw score of 80 in Educational Psychology 100 means that the student answered 80 items correctly and nothing more. Notice that the example says nothing about whether the score is good, average, or poor. Even if it were known that there were 107 items in the test, we still would not know how the person stands with reference to the rest of his class. From this definition you can see that the raw score is *not* a percentage score.

Ranks

An informal method of describing a person's performance is simply by assigning a number to his position in the class according to the magnitude of his raw score. The person with the highest score receives a rank of 1, the person with the second highest score a rank of 2, and so on until all scores are accounted for. This permits the teacher to say the student ranks third (or whatever) in a class of 27.

Percentiles or percentile rank

The percentile rank is a third kind of score similar to a rank score because it tells us about the pupil's rank in relation to some reference group. For example, if you were to inquire about a pupil's standing on the Otis–Quick Scoring Intelligence Test you might be told he was in the 70th percentile with reference to a group of high school seniors. This would mean that his raw score was as high or higher than scores made by 70 percent of the high school seniors to whom the test had been given (that is, the norm group).

Working with Scores from Achievement and Other Tests

Teachers soon come to realize that dealing with raw scores singly is cumbersome when they try to describe the performance of even a small class. When the number gets beyond a certain limit, the task is downright impossible. The teacher then seeks more parsimonious ways of summarizing the information he obtains.

Table A-1.

Name	Raw Score	Rank	Percentile	Deviation	Deviation Squared
Agnes	40	1	100*	+9.5	90.25
Barbara	39	2	95	+8.5	72.25
Cathy	38	3	90	+7.5	56.25
Doug	37	4	85	+6.5	42.25
Edward	36	5	80	+5.5	30.25
Frank	35	6	75	+4.5	20.25
George	34	7	70	+3.5	12.25
Helen	33	8	65	+2.5	6.25
Ida	32	9	60	+1.5	2.25
James	31	10	55	+0.5	.25
Kenneth	30	11	50	−0.5	.25
Lillian	29	12	45	−1.5	2.25
Marion	28	13	40	−2.5	6.25
Nancy	27	14	35	−3.5	12.25
Oscar	26	15	30	−4.5	20.25
Peter	25	16	25	−5.5	30.25
Richard	24	17	20	−6.5	42.25
Steven	23	18	15	−7.5	56.25
Timothy	22	19	10	−8.5	72.25
Victor	21	20	5	−9.5	90.25
	610			100.0	665.00

*The percentile of 100 is employed to facilitate calculations. In principle, a percentile of either 0 or 100 cannot be assigned since these are the two limiting points of the scale.

An Example.   As a typical example, assume that a teacher gave a test of 64 items. (The total number of items is really incidental to our present purposes—it might have been 34 or 134 just as easily since the concern in most scores and measures is with the number correct.) The students in the class attained the raw scores, ranks, and percentiles as shown in Table A-1. The use of the *deviation* and *deviation squared* will be discussed later.

Measures of central tendency

One way of describing a class on the basis of raw scores is to obtain a measure of central tendency. The teacher would compute some one value that is typical of the class as a whole, i.e., a single value that is most typical or characteristic of all scores attained by the class. The measures that provide such descriptions are the *mean, median,* and *mode.*

Mean.   The reader already knows the statistical *mean* as the familiar "average" used in a variety of contexts. Most recently he probably used it for computing grade-point averages. When there are sufficient cases that the mean is not distorted by extreme scores, it is preferred to other measures of central tendency. In the example above, there are 20 raw scores whose sum equals 610. The formula for the mean is shown below with the symbolic substitutions to help you become familiar with statistical notation.

The *Mean* $(\overline{X})$ equals the *Sum* (Σ) of all *Scores* (X) divided by the *Number* (N) of *Scores;*

or,

$$\overline{X} = \frac{\Sigma X}{N}.$$

Thus, for the example in Table A-1:

$$\overline{X} = \frac{610}{20}$$

$$\overline{X} = 30.5$$

Median.   The median is that point of the distribution of scores, above and below which 50 percent of the cases fall, that is, it is at the 50th percentile point. Accordingly, when percentiles are used, the central tendency is expressed in terms of the median. In addition, when there is reason to believe that the mean will be distorted (pulled too high or too low) because of extreme scores and too few cases, then the median provides a more representative description of the group of scores. Suppose, for example, it was necessary to describe the amount of insurance held by three men, two of whom held ten thousand dollars worth each and the third had one million dollars worth. The average would be a third of a million dollars. Obviously, this figure represents neither the extreme holding nor the "majority" holding very well. The one exceedingly high "score" threw the average off balance. The median, however, of ten thousand dollars better describes the group.

Mode. This is simply the score which occurs with the greatest frequency. Since each score in the distribution shown in the example has a frequency of one, the mode is indeterminable. However, *assume*, for purposes of illustration, that a score of 30 had been obtained by any number of pupils greater than one, then the mode would be 30. Some distributions have two modes (bimodal distributions) especially where two distinct groups (e.g., heights of girls and boys) are represented.

Frequency distribution

When tests are administered to large groups of people the resulting scores may be graphed with the scores indicated from high to low on the horizontal axis (abscissa) and the number of persons receiving each score indicated on the vertical axis (ordinate). When the test is of average difficulty, is reliable, and is administered to a representative group, the scores, plotted in this way, will be distributed normally, that is in the shape of the *normal curve*. As shown in Figure 19-9 on page 570 the curve is symmetrical (bell-shaped) with many cases at the center region and few extreme scores at either end.

Measures of variability

In addition to measures of central tendency it is useful to know the spread of scores. That is, we can ask, "What is the range of scores from the highest to the lowest scores?" "How much do the scores deviate from the mean?" or, "How variable or scattered are the scores?"

Range

The range is the difference between the highest and lowest scores. In the numerical example given above, the range of scores is found by subtracting 21 from 40 and adding one which yields a range of 20 points. This simple measure, however, can be deceptively unstable because, like the mean, it can be affected by a single extreme score. Accordingly, other measures of variability are used.

The Interquartile Range. A more stable measure of dispersion or variability is obtained by the *semi-interquartile range*. It is the difference in the range of *raw scores* that falls between the first quartile point (i.e., the 25th percentile) and the third quartile point (i.e., the 75th percentile). Thus, it is the range of the *raw scores* in the middle 50 percent of all scores.

The Average Deviation.   The average deviation is only rarely used today. Once you recognize that we are speaking of deviation from the mean this statistic defines itself. It is the average of the deviations of all scores from the mean. If you turn to the example, you will see that the deviations are already figured out for you. In order to compute the average deviation the same formula is followed as was used for computing the mean; i.e., add the absolute value of the deviations and divide by the number of scores.

The formula is:

$$\text{Average Deviation} = \frac{\Sigma |X - \overline{X}|}{N}$$

$$\frac{100}{20} = 5.0$$

where:

Σ = sum

$|X - \overline{X}|$ = deviation of a single score from the average of all scores in the class

N = number of scores

The average deviation for the scores in the example is then 5.0.

Standard Deviation.   The remaining measure of variability to be discussed has much in common with the average deviation. The primary difference, computationally, is that the deviation scores are squared before entering them in the formula and the square root of the quotient is taken after dividing by N. The formula, then, is as follows:

$$\sigma = \sqrt{\frac{\Sigma(X - \overline{X})^2}{N}}$$

where:

Σ = sum

$(X - \overline{X})^2$ = the deviation of a score from the mean, squared

σ = standard deviation

$\sqrt{}$ = square root

The squared deviations $[(X - \overline{X})^2]$ have been figured out for you in the example. Substituting these values in the formula, the following solution is obtained:

$$\sigma = \sqrt{\frac{665}{20}}$$
$$= \sqrt{33.25}$$
$$= 5.8$$

The standard deviation is a useful device because the difference between scores can be expressed in terms of standard deviation units. In the example, a score of 36.3 would be exactly one standard deviation above the mean ($+1.0\sigma$) and a score of 24.7 would be exactly one standard deviation below the mean (-1.0σ). (Note that the standard deviation is not really a good measure of variability for the scores in the example since the distribution of scores is obviously not normal.) If the distribution of scores is normal, 34.13 percent of the area of the curve (or 34.13 percent of all scores) lies between the mean and one standard deviation from it (either above or below). There will then be 68.26 percent of the area always enclosed between the points of one standard deviation above the mean ($+1.0\sigma$) and one standard deviation below the mean (-1.0σ). There will always be 95.44 percent of all scores between the points of two standard deviations above the mean ($+2.0\sigma$) and two standard deviations below the mean (-2.0σ). These and other subdivisions of the normal curve are shown graphically in Figure 19-9 on page 570. If the distribution is not normal, these percentages will be distorted according to the degree that the distribution departs from normality.

Standard Scores. Standard scores are often used in the interpretation of individual test scores relative to the standard deviation. The basic standard score is called the z-score. It simply indicates the distance a given score is from the mean in terms of standard deviation units. The formula for finding z for a given raw score in any distribution is as follows:

$$z = \frac{X - \overline{X}}{\sigma}$$

where:

$X =$ the score for a single pupil

$\overline{X} =$ the mean score for the class or other group

$\sigma =$ standard deviation of the scores for the same class or group

Turning to the example, note that

X = 23 for Steven

$\overline{X}$ = 30.5 for the class

σ = 5.8 for all scores for that class

Steven's z-score is found by substitution. Thus,

$$z = \frac{23 - 30.5}{5.8} = \frac{-7.5}{5.8} = -1.29$$

which means that Steven's score is 1.29 standard deviations *below* the mean. (The mean z-score is 0.00). A positive z-score would indicate that the score is so many units above the mean. Note from Figure 19-9 the relation between z-scores and percentiles. The person, for example, with a z-score of +2.0 would surpass 97.7 percent of the reference group whereas one with a z-score of −2.0 would surpass only 2.3 percent.

T-Score. This score is much like the z-score, with the exception that signs are removed, the mean is 50 (rather than zero), the standard deviation is set at 10, and the scores are not expressed in decimals. These changes are accomplished by the following formula:

T-score = $10z + 50$

where:

10 (as the σ of the new distribution) is a multiplying constant and 50 (the new mean) is always added to the product of $10z$ (where z is the number of standard deviation units of the score in the original distribution).

Thus, the z-score is first computed as shown above, then it is multiplied by 10, and then 50 is added to the product. Using Steven's score as an example, recall that his z-score was −1.29. By substitution of that figure in the formula, we obtain a *T*-score for Steven as follows:

$$\begin{aligned} T\text{-score} &= (10)\ (-1.29) + 50 \\ &= -12.90 + 50 \\ &= 37.1 \end{aligned}$$

Other Standard Scores. Standard scores for other tests are often slight modifications of the procedure used for calculating *T*-scores. Thus, for example, note in Figure 19-9 the scores for the CEEB (College Entrance Examination Board Tests). These are computed in the same way as the *T*-score described above except that the multiplying constant for z is 100 (the standard deviation) and the additive constant is 500 (the new mean).

The deviation IQ for the WAIS is determined by the formula IQ

$= 15z + 100$ (because Wechsler wanted the mean set at 100 with a standard deviation of 15).

The deviation IQ for the 1960 revision of the Stanford-Binet is calculated by the formula $IQ = 16z + 100$ and, as with any z-score, is interpreted in terms of a norm group (usually an age group). These groups differ for the two tests so the IQ scores are not necessarily comparable.

Correlation.   The correlation coefficient is an index indicating the degree of relationship between two variables. It can be either positive $(+)$ or negative $(-)$. If it is positive it means the two variables vary directly, i.e., when the score is high on one it is also high on the other; if the coefficient is negative, it means the variables vary inversely, i.e., high scores on one are associated with low scores on the other and vice versa. Correlations (whether positive or negative) are never greater than 1.00 which value means the two variables are perfectly associated. A coefficient of correlation does not show a cause and effect relationship. It only indicates that there is an association. However, a coefficient of correlation does permit prediction. Thus, high correlations between intelligence test scores and college achievement can be used to predict (within the limits imposed by error of measurement, degree of correlation, etc.) which students will earn high grades and which will earn low grades. The prediction will be more accurate than it would be if the test scores were not available. Such predictions can be made equally well on the basis of correlations of equal magnitude regardless of the sign of the correlation.

Appendix B

Tom: A gifted underachieving child*

A frequently mentioned, but grossly underrated, force which helps forge the child's adaptive techniques is the school. Although the child spends as much or more time in school than he does with his parents, most therapists fail to utilize the school's influence in planning a psychotherapeutic treatment program.

When the school is merely seen as a stage upon which the child duplicates his familial behavior its dynamic influence is minimized. In the process of treating Tom D., a child with a learning problem, the impact of the school was found to extend beyond the confines of the learning area. It aided the further development and consolidation of important ego functions, and proved to be a useful adjunct in both the understanding and modification of the child's adaptive techniques.

Our conceptualization of the child-family unit encompasses more than the traditional family and includes all significant interpersonal transactions wherever their locus. The case of Tom D. is presented within this theoretical frame of reference.

History of the Problem

The school's intention of failing Tom in the fourth grade prompted his father to seek psychiatric evaluation. Tom was 9 yr, 6 mth old at the time of referral. There had been a history of poor school

---

*In slightly abridged form from Radin & Masling, 1963. With permission of authors and Pergamon Press Ltd.

work, particularly in arithmetic. He had difficulty not only in learning but also in relating to others and was frequently described as appearing dazed and apathetic. His papers were consistently messy and incomplete; he appeared uninterested and indifferent to his teachers, his classmates and his work. His teachers tried without success to make school interesting for him.

Tom's kindergarten and first grade experiences were unremarkable, although his teachers in both these grades commented on his seriousness and tendency to withdraw. The kindergarten teacher had some appreciation that Tom was unusually gifted, since she entered the following comment on his school record: "I think he is going to be an exceptional student as he has outstanding ability. Deep thinker."

Shortly after Tom had finished the first grade his father, Dr. D., took the family south, because of military service. There Tom experienced difficulty in completing the second and third grades. His second grade teacher suggested that Tom might be retarded. Prompted by this discussion, Dr. D. had Tom tested by a psychologist stationed at the base; this test revealed superior intelligence.

When Dr. D. completed his military duties the family returned home. Tom's learning problems continued in the fourth grade and he was then referred for psychiatric evaluation and treatment.

Pertinent developmental history

Tom was born on July 24, 1948, the 2nd of 4 children, all delivered by Caesarian section. He was full term and weighed 7 lb 14 oz at birth. A "section" was performed following prolonged labor, despite Mrs. D's wishes to have a normal delivery. During the first 2 mth, while on breast feeding, he was subject to occasional episodes of pseudo-projectile vomiting. He was abruptly weaned at 4 mth due to a breast abscess. Concurrent with this event severe intermittent diarrhea developed which persisted for a year and a half and caused frequent dietary adjustments. To this day he favors meat and potatoes and continues to dislike fruits, vegetables and juices.

Gross motor development was normal. He crept at 6 mth, sat at 7 mth and walked at 14 mth. He could write his name at 3½ yr but only backwards. His play activities at this time showed a vivid imagination and long attention span. Until the age of 2 yr his speech was limited to repetition of single words, except for one occasion at 1½ years when he spontaneously said "Daddy" and "bye bye." His parents were concerned that his speech was delayed but were reassured by the pediatrician. At 2 he began putting words together, e.g., "railroad track," and then speech progressed rapidly. At 22 mth he told a number of destructive and sad stories, one of them about a dirigible that crashed with a dog in it.

Adults were amazed at this ability. Even his earliest drawings, done at
3½ yr, portrayed destructive themes, e.g., houses on fire. His voice was
flat, drawn-out and monotonous. He appeared wistful, sad and melan-
choly and when rebuked might cry quietly or become angry and remain
under his bed. His parents perceived him to be affectionate, but he
never was physically demonstrative. Tom was terrified by inoculations,
given by his father—a physician—and needed to be restrained.

Toilet training was started at 1½ yr and completed at 2½ yr,
except for occasional daytime bowel and bladder accidents until the age
of 5 yr. Enuresis, however, was frequent until age 7 and occurred sporadically until the second year of his psychotherapy (age 11).

Family background

Tom's father (Wesley D.), age 38, is a successful physician, as
was his father. Marked feelings of anxiety and preoccupation with death
prompted him to enter psychoanalysis when Tom was 7:6. The analysis
was successfully completed after approximately four years. Although
highly regarded by others in his field, he was constantly dissatisfied and
unable to achieve the standards he set for himself. In regarding himself
as a failure he was internalizing his parents' absolute standards:
ninety-nine percent was not enough. His self-depreciation was prevalent
in many diverse roles. He frequently identified with his children's problems, his sense of self-esteem rising and falling with their successes and
failures. Dr. D's relationship with his parents was decidedly ambivalent.
He unconsciously resented the persons on whom he was dependent.

The unconscious attitudes of both Tom and his father were
remarkably similar and portrayed by heroic Oedipal dreams and daydreams. Their school performances, however, differed drastically. Dr.
D. was an excellent student, striving to comply with parental demands.
He was able to sublimate murderous, aggressive impulses by productive,
successful, competitive performance.

Tom's mother, age 35, was interviewed regularly in coordination
with Tom's therapy. When she was 2 months of age, an older sister, aged
16 months, died of meningitis. Mrs. D. always felt guilty and responsible
for this death because she, as an infant, required care and removed her
mother's attention from the sick child. Mrs. D. felt it her duty to care
for her two younger sisters after the death of their mother which
occurred when Mrs. D. was 12.

Mrs. D. has always been intellectually oriented and was enrolled
in a graduate program in English literature. She strived to treat her
children equally, and experienced guilt feelings when she or her husband showed preference. Despite this, she seemed to favor Tom's older
brother, Walter, and his sister, Margaret Louise. Her ability to assert

herself or express aggression was limited; her need for emotional control was excessive. She wanted her children to succeed academically and was at Tom every day, overseeing his school assignments and study habits.

Mrs. D.'s constant prodding of Tom raised a conflict within Dr. D. He would occasionally sit down and talk to Tom, stressing the importance of school, "and then for two or three days I would pay no attention to this and would even say, 'let's play ball, let's fish.' " Dr. D.'s inconsistent attitude represented an unconscious retaliation against academic pressure similar to that which he himself experienced as a child. As a result of the parents' therapy the interference patterns were replaced by more helpful, understanding attitudes.

Walter, age 12, intensely resented Tom's birth. His frequent physical assaults upon Tom, $2\frac{1}{2}$ yr his junior, provoked Dr. D. to such a degree that he severely punished Walter and rejected him. Mrs. D., in attempting to compensate for this rejection, sympathized with and overprotected Walter, while at the same time feeling guilty that she could not show more love for Tom. At age 7 Tom's rapid growth enabled him to protect himself against Walter's onslaughts. Dr. D.'s identification with Tom shifted from the role of defender to that of companion, with sharing of intellectual and outdoor interests. Dr. D. was involved with Walter in similar activities, but to a lesser degree. Many projects were initiated by Tom, who was the "brains of the outfit," according to Mrs. D. Walter would follow Tom's lead but would then take over, while Tom accepted the submissive role without overt objection.

When Margaret Louise, age 8, was born, Dr. D.'s positive relationship with Tom and Mrs. D.'s rejection of him were intensified. Margaret had colic during her first two months of life and her parents were frequently kept awake. Dr. D. gave this as the reason for rejecting her while Mrs. D. felt compelled to over-protect and identify with her daughter. Tom resented the monopolizing of his mother's time and affection by Walter and Margaret Louise. His envy of his sister's close relationship with their mother was reflected in his desire to share in their domestic duties. She was regarded as more subdued than the other siblings, particularly when Dr. D. was home.

Frank, age 6, resulted from the only unplanned pregnancy. He was colicky for the first 2 mth of life, was breast-fed for 8 mth and subsequently was weaned to the cup. He was the most independent of the siblings, had many friends and his emotional relationships with the members of his family had always been positive. His excellent academic achievement was a source of pride to his parents. He was the one child unequivocally accepted by both parents.

The family's wide variety of interests created an unusually stimulating milieu. Such pursuits as reading, archeology, bird-watching, rais-

ing animals, constructing radio equipment, camping, skiing, were
encouraged. (By the time he was 13 Tom had completed a University
summer demonstration course in mathematical logic which involved the
use of hieroglyphics and had conducted independent study of Greek
mythology). The home literally served as a laboratory for the expression
of the children's interests. This generally permissive attitude extended
into child-rearing practices, although Mrs. D. was more demanding than
her husband in the usual child routine areas.

Psychological Test Results

Intelligence tests

While the family had been in the South, at age 8:3, Tom had
been administered Form L of the 1937 Binet. The resulting I.Q. was at

Table B-1.   Tom's intelligence testing

	Date Administered	Score	Standard Deviation Scores $\times \dfrac{}{\sigma}$
Stanford-Binet, Form L	1956	173	4.62
California Test of Mental Maturity	1957	110	.62
Stanford-Binet, Form M	1958	196	6.04

least 173. (An exact I.Q. could not be determined because he was still
successfully passing items at the completion of the test.) In a personal
communication to the authors, the examiner commented on the exceptional memory for digits which Tom displayed, as well as memory for
words; in Year X, item 3, where the examiner reads a 53-word paragraph to the subject and later asks questions about its content, Tom was
able to repeat the paragraph almost *verbatim*, making mistakes on only
three words.

At the beginning of his fourth grade work, at age 9:2, Tom and
his class were given a group intelligence test, the California Test of
Mental Maturity. Tom scored 110, compared with the mean score of 100.
This was the only "objective" evidence of Tom's ability available to the
school.

At the request of the therapist at age 9:11, he was administered
Form M of the 1937 Binet. As with his earlier Form L performance, he
came to the end of the test still passing items. It was not possible to
determine how high a score he could have earned if the test had been
longer or more difficult, but based on this performance a Mental Age of
19 yr 5 mth was earned, yielding an I.Q. by extrapolation of 196.

The report of this testing indicated that carelessness produced most of Tom's errors: "In only three or four items did he show genuine lack of knowledge. He showed little that could be termed spontaneous or brilliant because his style appeared plodding rather than insightful. What is impressive is his breadth of knowledge, his ability to deal with abstract problems, his recognition (but not his use) of vocabulary, and his completely retentive memory."

Rorschach test

This test was administered at age 9:7. Excerpts are given below:

The most outstanding feature of Tom's Rorschach performance was that it looked so much like the typical record of a nine year old, despite his unusually high intellectual endowment. The formal characteristics of the performance—number of responses, use of color, number of content categories, form level, were compatible with the record of a child with an I.Q. of 100.

His approach to the test was as important as his responses. He was curious about the way in which the cards were manufactured, and he seemed highly interested in what was being written about him. He appeared calm and very matter-of-fact, betraying no indication of fearfulness. Since the testing situation does impose a mild degree of threat to most children, it can be assumed that Tom's objective, intellectual approach had at least some defensive features that enabled him to ward off anxiety.

There was an absence of signs of overt anxiety on the test record itself. Instead, the over-all impression was that of a well-organized, considerably defensive performance. The quality of his responses was more impoverished and superficial than would be expected of a child as bright as he. There was an obsessional-like quality to his behavior as he proceeded with the test. He would ruminate about what the blot could be, generally deciding in favor of a good, "safe" percept, one that did not contain any aggressive or hostile overtones. He tended to avoid dealing with affect in his responses. He dealt with objects or animals rather than people. Even when he saw people, it was in a detached, intellectualized form, e.g., "It is a face that looks like a mask," "This reminds me of a clown." By holding the world off at arm's length he is enabled to deal with it in a manner so controlled that his impulses are rigidly checked.

His defenses, mainly denial, displacement and intellectualization, are part of a mild obsessive-compulsive pattern. They are flexible enough to permit him to function effectively with ideas and concepts but seem too rigid to allow free expression of feelings.

Family testing

To obtain a complete record of the intellectual potential of the D. family, both parents and Walter were tested; the test records of Margaret Louise and Frank were available from the school. These results, excluding those from Tom, are summarized in Table B-2.

Table B-2.   D. family test results

Name	Age at date of testing	Test	Date of testing	Score	Standard deviation scores $\times \overline{\sigma}$
Dr. D.	38	WAIS	August, 1960	Verbal I.Q. 150	3.37
				Performance I.Q. 125	1.66
				Full Scale I.Q. 141	2.21
Mrs. D.	35	WAIS	October, 1960	Verbal I.Q. 141	2.76
				Performance I.Q. 110	.88
				Full Scale I.Q. 130	1.21
Walter	13	Wechsler-Bellevue	February, 1960	Verbal I.Q. 117	1.15
				Performance I.Q. 115	1.05
				Full Scale I.Q. 118	1.27
Margaret Louise	8	Binet, Form L 1937	January, 1959	169	4.36
Frank	6	Binet, Form L 1937	January, 1959	160	4.80

It is apparent from this table that this is a family of unusual intellectual endowment. While it is difficult to describe precisely a familial test performance pattern, some tendencies can be noted. The abilities found most strongly in all members of the family are rote memory and abstract verbal skills; by far the weakest areas are timed tests. Their slow, deliberate quality in the test approach penalizes them where speed counts. It should be noted that Dr. D.'s verbal I.Q. of 150 on the WAIS is just shy of the maximum score for his age group.

The school setting

The school was five years old and had 29 teachers and 658 pupils from kindergarten through the fifth grade. It was part of a suburban consolidated school district that consisted of two other elementary schools, a junior high school and a senior high school. Casual observation suggested that the faculty morale in Tom's school was good and professional involvement high. The community itself was rather homogeneous; the majority of the families were well educated and represented professional and business interests.

Although Tom's school offered as enlightened, interested and stimulating a climate as one could expect in public school education, his academic potential was completely unsuspected. From the point of view of the school Tom was an overly quiet, moderately under-achieving boy who expressed aggression through caustic remarks, wit and passive resistance. The concern for his under-achievement, while genuine, was misdirected because the only estimate of Tom's intelligence available to the school was the 110 score on the California Test of Mental Maturity. He was perceived as a child whose intelligence was close to the school mean, who did not do his lessons as directed and was learning somewhat less than he seemed capable of. When his classroom performance declined he was removed from the class of advanced readers. His difficulty with fourth grade work was interpreted as resulting primarily from mediocre intellectual capacity. The school authorities were not aware that Tom and his teacher were in conflict. Tom did not complete his homework or classroom assignments and appeared completely indifferent to school. Mr. W., his teacher, was annoyed and critical. The interaction between Tom's overt school behavior and Mr. W.'s response to this behavior resulted in an exacerbation of the neurotic conflict and the maladaptive attempts of the ego to cope with it. Mr. W.'s solution to the impasse was to recommend that Tom repeat the fourth grade.

At this point Dr. D. sought psychiatric consultation, psychological testing was performed and for the first time a realistic estimation of Tom's ability (Binet score of 196) was revealed to the school authorities. A conference subsequently held between the therapist and the principal produced immediate changes. Tom was promoted and assigned to the home-room of a firm, but warm, female teacher. She possessed the necessary skill and patience to establish a meaningful relationship with him. He was placed in special tutorial sections of bright children for intensive instruction. While he was still expected to do all his work, originality and interest were emphasized more than errors in promptness and neatness. In a sense, Tom became a special school project, and with practically no urging from the therapist a "total push" program developed. Impressed by their professional responsibility to Tom, the principal and teachers sought guidance and information, and enrolled in a University course on the Gifted Child. They were fearful of continuing a damaging situation for him and were most anxious to be of help.

Tom's sixth grade was held in another school. Again he experienced difficulty with his male teacher, this time because the teacher expected him to know all the answers and ridiculed him in front of the class when he did not. Tom frequently felt picked on and humiliated and his work suffered. The therapist interrupted this sado-masochistic relationship by having Tom transferred to another class.

a. School achievement tests

Tom's class was administered the Iowa Tests of Basic Skills in November, 1957, during the fourth grade, and again in October, 1958, in the fifth grade. His scores on these tests, all expressed in terms of grade placement, are shown in Table B-3.

It was clear from these achievement test results that he was much more competent in fourth and fifth grade skills than was evident in day-to-day classroom performance. Several classmates scored as well as Tom on the Iowa, but in contrast to him their classroom performances were brilliant.

Table B-3. Tom's Iowa Basic Skills results (expressed in grade placement)

	Reading		Language skills				Work study				Arithmetic		Total
	Vocab.	Compre-hension	Spell.	Capit.	Punct.	Usage	Total	Map Read.	Graphs	Reference Maps	Total	Concept.	Problems	Total	Total
November, 1957 (Fourth Grade)	7.3	8.4	4.4	4.4	5.3	4.9	4.8	5.8	3.3	4.0	4.4	4.9	3.5	4.2	5.8
October, 1958 (Fifth Grade)	9.6	9.0	7.6	5.3	9.0	9.2	7.8	6.8	4.7	6.2	5.9	6.2	4.3	5.3	7.5

b. Sociometric tests

In order to obtain information about Tom's status with his peers, sociometric tests were administered to his fifth grade home-room and advanced reading class. Table B-4 summarizes these results.

Table B-4. Sociometric test results

Question	Home-room Class (N = 25)			Advanced Reading Class (N = 23)		
	Total number of nominations	Nominations Tom received	Tom's Rank	Total number of nominations	Nominations Tom received	Tom's Rank
1. Who is the best reader?	49	7	7.5	41	3	5
2. Who has the best sense of humor?	36	2	7.5	32	1	12.5
3. Who can get the others to do what he wants them to do?	37	0		40	2	8
4. Who daydreams the most?	26	15	1	21	18	1
5. Who always does what the teacher wants?	50	0		43	0	
6. Who is the smartest pupil in the class?	50	5	4	39	3	6
7. Who do you like the best?	55	2	12.5	44	4	2.5
8. Who never seems to have a good time?	17	4	1	22	4	3
9. Who doesn't seem to care if the others like him or not?	26	5	2	24	10	1

It would appear from these data that the children perceived Tom as essentially aloof and withdrawn. Although he was by no means rejected or even isolated (notice that he was accepted more by the students in the advanced reading class than in his home-room), his behavior evidently indicated to his peers that he was not oriented toward interpersonal relationships. While he was considered bright his peers did not fully recognize his intellectual status. It should be noted that the child who received the greatest number of nominations (20) for question 6, "Who is the smartest pupil in this class?", was reported by the school to have an I.Q. of 173.

c. Classroom observations

Several visits to Tom's classes were made in January 1959, when he was aged 10:6, to observe him in the school setting. Excerpts from these reports are given so that the quality of his behavior in school can be appreciated:

In the advanced reading class of 19 children, Tom and three other boys form a sub-group. Tom is the tallest boy in the class and is the second tallest child. Mrs. L., the reading teacher, asks if the children had read any of the "Dr. Seuss" books. All the children wave their hands enthusiastically and seem interested and animated; Tom plays quietly with a date stamp he found on the desk. Mrs. L. asks the children to take paper and pencil and take notes of their reading on Hawaii; Tom continues to play with the stamp. While the rest of the class works, Tom aimlessly handles a pencil and paper bag, occasionally sniffling. After the class has finished reading the selection, Mrs. L. asks, "How many of you watch 'Meet the Press?'" All hands go up in the air except Tom's, who leans over and looks at a boy's paper. The children turn to watch the teacher who is walking around the room; Tom stares straight ahead. A question and answer period follows. The children appear to show what they have learned; Tom remains calm and removed from the excitement and enthusiasm around him. He never volunteers but answers correctly when called on. He duels briefly with pencils with the boy next to him while Mrs. L. conducts the class.

The class prepares for a "Meet the Press" forum to debate the issue of admission of Hawaii to statehood. After the children have read the assigned article Mrs. L. asks, "Who would like to be a United States Senator?" Tom is silent. She then asks, "Who would like to be a citizen of Hawaii?"; for the first time that morning Tom raises his hand and is selected for this role. During the ensuing debate Tom speaks with interest, but with more deliberation and less obvious glee than the others. He has not taken notes on the reading, but managed to borrow the notes compiled by some of the boys who sit next to him: his passivity seems to call forth succorance from his peers. Even without referring to notes, Tom's answers are accurate and concise. A boy who represents the anti-statehood argument claims that "2400 miles from California to Hawaii is too far for easy transportation." Tom comments in his slow, deliberate way that "Good transportation is already available and making Hawaii a state doesn't make the distance any farther."

In the home-room the children are doing arithmetic problems. All seem engrossed in work, except for Tom who cups his face with his hands, for 35 sec, with no change in posture. Suddenly he straightens up and starts to work. During the question and answer period midst waving hands and excited voices Tom sits silent as the sphinx.

In the library everyone except Tom listens while the teacher discusses a book; Tom is busy reading it. Aware of his behavior, Mrs. L. interrupts the discussion and asks the class, "Do you think Tom would like this book?" The class laughs. . . . A girl says, "Tom is already reading it, and is halfway through." Tom's boy friend says with pride, "He's on page 36 and he just picked up the book a second ago." Evidently the others know Tom's reading habits and seem protective of him. Mrs. L. and Tom are engaged in a mild struggle: she obviously wants him to participate freely in the discussion but his almost abrupt answers convey lack of interest. Once while a girl is reciting, Tom whispers, but the class shushes him immediately and he stops. After the recitation every child but Tom goes to the bookshelves to select books. He remains seated and when a girl approaches him with several books, he thanks her, and she leaves.

In the home-room citizenship education class the children are taking a test. Many pupils ask for help in spelling, but Tom does not. Some children get up and wander about, but Tom remains seated; he appears vacant, as he toys with a pencil.

The children line up to go to the gymnasium. There is considerable noise and milling about, but Tom and a friend seem oblivious to the confusion as they show each other a number of words in Indian sign language.

Summary of Psychotherapy of Patient

From the age of 9:6, Tom was treated in intensive psychotherapy for 2 yr, 9 mth. During the first year he was seen three times a week. This was reduced to twice a week for the second year and once a week for the remaining period. The presenting problem was the learning inhibition, but in addition, Tom had difficulty in making friends and was frequently enuretic.

The therapist's initial impression was that of a somewhat shy, retiring youngster. He was tall, lumbering and ungainly and created a disheveled appearance. His slow speech and poker face accompanied a generalized guarded attitude. These defenses imperfectly concealed an exceedingly agile mind that delved deftly among a multitude of subjects.

When questioned about school, Tom stated that it was boring and that he preferred to daydream and look out the window. He did not feel the need to repeat procedures once learned. The result was a series of unfinished assignments and poor grades. He much preferred to read, raise laboratory animals, perform chemical experiments and daydream. He was chronically bored with school and the usual interests of other children.

It became clear that Tom had difficulty competing actively against his older brother and his father. His aggressive and libidinal strivings were displaced and portrayed vividly in dreams and daydreams or subtly expressed in wit. He could not expose himself to the real or imagined dangers of aggressively dealing with real life situations. His difficulty in solving the Oedipal conflict was reflected by vacillation between a passive, feminine and an active, masculine identification. His attempts to achieve a masculine identification resulted in a lively phantasy life, predominantly centering around hero themes, and avid consumption of adventure stories. In his daydreams Tom's father and siblings were either assistants, or disguised rivals, in his pursuit of his mother's affection and acclaim. In dreams his father was frequently portrayed as a dangerous castrating and rejecting figure.

An early dream: Tom is lost in the woods with his sister and brothers, and wanders into a creepy place where a man is sitting cutting wallpaper. He has a beard and a moustache and is dressed in a red checkered shirt and blue jeans with patched knees. His wife is in a quilt-like dress, patchy with different colors and designs. There is a pile of scissors. The man says, "Don't touch or you'll get cut." Tom touches the blunt part of one and is cut on his left index finger. The man says, "What are you doing here?" and Tom replied, "We are lost and would like to know the way home." The man says, "Twenty miles down the road," and refuses to put the boys up for the night, although he has a great big house. They start to go away and then two apes covered with hair run out. They try to drag them into the house. When the boys draw their jack-knives the apes run. Before they chase the apes Tom says, "My knife is dull, can I use yours?" and Walter says, "No, mine is dull, too." Then the house, man and woman disappear and the children walk into the deep woods into some caves and go to sleep.

The mean man with the scissors cutting the wallpaper, as well as the apes, were identified as the castrating father. The blunt knives reflected problems of adequacy and development of masculine identification. Retreat to a safe cave to sleep was an escape from the castration threat. The Oedipal incestual theme was not interpreted at this time.

His initial behavior in treatment accented obedience and submission. His role of social outcast at school and at home was projected in the playroom. While his classmates were interested in rocket ships, space ships and television, Tom would have preferred the good old days of woodsmanship where he could make a living with his hands. This was one way he rationalized his feelings of being different.

His jealousy and rivalry with his sister for their mother's affection was expressed by symbolic destruction of his sister in the play room as well as by the overt desire to replace her as mother's helper. Accompanying this attempted identification with mother was his unconscious desire for passive possession by his father. While through such feminine identification Tom would have avoided the combat and possible destruction resulting from active competition with the stronger male authority, he would simultaneously have exposed himself to the danger of passive homosexual submission. This adaptive maneuver was too threatening and was, therefore, discarded.

Tom was able to express aggression in the play room only after a period of testing. However, this was anxiety provoking and the therapist appeared menacing; under these conditions Tom resorted to his old behavior of withdrawal and passive resistance. He avoided conversation and indulged in solitary play with clay and pick-up sticks. The therapist interpreted how dangerous it was to express aggressive feelings directly, and that it was safer to play alone and thus avoid the therapist. At this time Tom had a number of dreams of combat with monsters and sharks, and experienced difficulty with his male teacher.

This material can be more thoroughly understood when the sequence of significant developmental events is recalled: pseudo-projectile vomiting for the first two months, abrupt weaning at 4 mth, severe diarrhea from 4 mth to $1\frac{1}{2}$ yr, accompanied by frequent dietary changes and a subsequent history of food idiosyncrasies, all indicated early frustration of oral dependency needs. The pattern of family inter-actions continued to perpetuate and exaggerate these frustrations. Dr. D.'s identification with Tom, and rejection of both Walter and Margaret Louise, contributed to Mrs. D.'s preference for these two siblings and her relative neglect of Tom. Tom initially submitted to Walter's physi-cal attacks and then passively observed Dr. D.'s severe retaliation and rejection of Walter. This passivity was reinforced by the desire for the nurturance Margaret Louise received from the mother. If he were ren-dered helpless by Dr. D., as was Walter, or was a helpless girl, like Mar-garet Louise, then perhaps mother would feel sorry for him and join father in ministering to him.

Dr. D.'s giving inoculations (probably experienced as a sexual aggressive assault) in addition to his possession of Mrs. D., and his fond-ness for Frank, the younger brother, provoked rage and resentment in Tom. However, these aggressive impulses had to be repressed because of his intense fear of retaliation by father, his need for father's protection to insure his survival, and because of his identification with, and intense love for, his father.

The conflicts culminated in an adaptive, pervasive inhibition as expressed in passivity, social withdrawal, enuresis and learning difficul-ties. The dynamics of the learning block had several underlying aspects: (1) with the repression of aggressive impulses there was accompanying inhibition and impairment of normal assertiveness and of executive ego functioning;* (2) it expressed through Tom his father's wish to rebel against his own parents' unattainable academic standards; (3) it served as a retaliation against mother's rejection, by failure in an area where

---

*Plank and Plank (1954) relate the impairment of mathematical ability to strong pre-oedipal ties and to the inability to express aggressive impulses.

success was so important to her, while simultaneously deriving secondary gains provided by her extreme concern and prodding; (4) it was an
expression, as was his enuresis, of deep-seated passive, feminine strivings.

The repressed, but overflowing, aggressive and libidinal impulses
were indirectly portrayed in dreams, daydreams, drawings and stories.
In the dreams Tom was the hero, finding buried treasure,* overcoming
the enemy and winning mother's approval and acceptance. His real life
rivals, father and older brother, were placed in the roles of underlings
or disguised, threatening figures.

With the gaining of insight and subsequent diminution in anxiety, Tom began to view the therapist as an ally rather than a threatening enemy. He wrote a play at the beginning of the second year of treatment in which the therapist was portrayed as the good doctor who aided
Tom and his friends in out-witting mean assailants. The overpowering
of evil was also expressed in "good guys vs. bad guys" dreams. His
school performance improved dramatically and he overcame his conflict
with male teachers.

During the second and third years of therapy Tom grappled
more directly with his problems of sexual identification and castration
anxiety. He denied the difference between boys and girls. "Many boys
who are afraid of mice and don't play football might as well be girls.
Except for the hair there is little difference." Boys and girls being alike,
there need be no fear of castration. The following dream is typical of
those which occurred during this period and expresses symbolically his
difficulty in achieving masculine identification.

Dream: Walter came down and wanted to go for a hike in the woods. I
had to find my jack-knife with the tools in the cellar. I had to find my knife
sheath. I couldn't, then I could. I tried to put the knife in, and it wouldn't fit. I
tried it all ways.

Gradually he resolved the Oedipal conflict. Following this, he
began to explore his ideas of conception and birth. His heroic and
destructive phantasies markedly diminished, and he showed appropriate
interest in girls. His dreams became less threatening and violent and
were characterized by themes of cooperation and mastery.

Dream: I was rowing in a large boat with other children. We were
trying to overcome high waves and we succeeded.

Tom's behavior at the termination of therapy showed increasing
maturity, greater awareness of responsibility and a relinquishing of

*Dr. Selma Fraiberg (1954) has presented a detailed interpretation of the
significance of the discovery of buried treasure.

infantile and passive feminine behavior, as indicated by complete cessation of enuresis. His school performance improved and he accepted a newspaper route. His relationship with the therapist was frank and open. He was able to initiate and develop new friendships and became interested and aware of girls as objects of sexual interest. These gains were consolidated and extended in the several years that have passed since the termination of therapy.

Discussion

The psychological evaluation and therapeutic management of a child is advanced by considering more than him alone, or even the child-family unit, and extending the focus to include significant extrafamilial transactions. There are theoretical as well as therapeutic implications to such a view.

The comprehension of an individual's psychodynamics requires more than the knowledge of his internal psychic structure; it is essential to grasp the complex demands and responses of the one member of a group to the other members, particularly in the case of a child, whose ability to dictate his coming and going and to shape his own destiny is quite limited. His growth, development and maturational status, are profoundly affected by those environmental sources with which he sustains a reasonably continuous relationship.

As the child ages, environmental sources other than the home, particularly the school, consume an increasing amount of his time, energy and involvement. Sigmund Freud (1949, p. 17) recognized the significant figures in the mental development of the child: "The parents' influence naturally includes not merely the personalities of the parents themselves but also the racial, national and family traditions handed on through them as well as the demands of the immediate social *milieu* which they represent. In the same way, an individual's superego in the course of his development takes over contributions from later successors and substitutes of his parents, such as teachers, admired figures in public life, or high social ideals." The influences of the school program and the variety of inter-personal relationships not only affect superego development but also modify growth and development of ego functioning. An enumeration of the varied effects upon specific ego functions is beyond the scope of this paper.

Academic difficulty in childhood emphasizes the impact of the school. This influence is particularly striking in the case presented, because of the unusual presence of a profound school problem in a child of superior intellectual endowment. School personnel reacted to this child, once they had been told of his ability, as though they had a sacred mission. The energy and activity which characterized his teachers' and principal's interest in Tom seemed to be derived from several sources: (1) the guilt aroused by the discrepancy between his scholastic achievement and his incredible potential; (2) the need to redeem their professional competence and adequacy from the embarrassing situation caused by this school failure as shown in their need for obtaining reassurance from the child's therapist for a job well done; (3) departing further from observable data it is conceivable that Tom's enormous intellectual power reawakened in those responsible for educating him omnipotent fantasies characteristic of the stage of primary narcissism. Through identification with the child the possibility of control and modification of one's weltanschauung was within reach.

The child's parents were also highly involved in his treatment. They felt extremely guilty and did everything within their power to help their child. They were frightened by the thought that such potential might not be utilized.

After consideration of the motivations of the principal, teachers and parents, one wonders whether such cooperation would have been obtained in the case of an average child. The intense interest, enthusiasm and personal involvement of the important identification models were undoubtedly related to this child's genius. If less well endowed disturbed children evoked similar reactions and attitudes, the resolution of their emotional problems through psychotherapy might be facilitated.

The psychoanalytic treatment process of this child was aided by the utilization of those major environmental forces—school and family—which influenced him. Therapeutic progress was hastened by technical manoeuvres which included direct observation in school, advice, guidance and individual psychotherapy of both parents and conferences with school personnel concerning the formal academic program and teacher demands, expectations and attitudes toward the patient.

Appendix C

The science
of psychology

It may be helpful to consider what psychologists have attempted to accomplish in their role as scientists, by way of background for a consideration of how psychological knowledge can be used to improve educational practices. At the same time it may be instructive to review how the psychologist, as a scientist, goes about his work, because the skillful teacher frequently functions in an analogous fashion.

Why a Science of Psychology?

According to its Greek etymological origin, *psychology* is a discourse, or reasoning, about the human *soul*. For many centuries it remained an area of metaphysical speculation and conjecture, and was used as such in a supporting role to the world's religions. Then, in the nineteenth century *psycho* was redefined as "mind" in an effort to make it more tractable to scientific inquiry according to the methods developed by the psychophysicists and introspectionists. At the turn of the twentieth century, these methods were challenged and eventually replaced by the more objectively communicable procedures of scientists who were content to define *psycho* as "behavior"; at first only behavior that could be directly observed, later and currently extended to behavior with only an inferential basis (for example, phase sequences, mediation processes, and many other *constructed* models of what might be going on within the human organism).* This behavioristic approach to

*For representative interpretations of the origins of psychology as a science, see Boring (1942, 1957), and Miller (1962).

psychology has proved to be unusually successful in meeting the needs of twentieth century man. It has cast its long shadow over educational procedures in all civilized cultures of the world.

Thus, psychology, which was first needed to serve as a vehicle for one area of philosophical discourse, is currently needed to help modern man cope with environmental changes that his other scientific and technological achievements have so vastly accelerated that some wonder if man will be able to survive. Certainly, it seems most probable that psychology and the other behavioral sciences (anthropology, sociology, political science) will be needed to solve some of man's problems of adjusting to and mastering newly emerging dimensions of his natural and social environments. And a large part of the achievements that man may be able to claim by the close of the twentieth century will be based on the applications of psychological principles in education, in commerce, and in political affairs.

The Goals of Psychology as a Science

In order to qualify as a science, psychology has concerned itself with the principal goals of the older, well-established, physical sciences: description, prediction, and control. In the same manner as for all of the empirical sciences, the science of psychology is constructed from observations and the logic of induction. Consistently observed and consensually validated covariations gradually are accepted as the empirical relationships on which first approximations to explanatory models and theories can be constructed. Deductive logic is then used to apply the principles of the prototheories to nature, test their adequacy and validity for predicting previously established empirical relationships, and their fruitfulness for suggesting the possibility of phenomena and

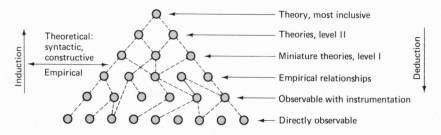

The scientist's nomological net and related observations

Figure C-1. A schematic representation of the multiple relationships that lead to theory construction and theory usage. Fruitful theories help to integrate known empirical relationships and to direct the scientist to new observations and further theoretical elaborations. (From Thompson, 1962. With permission.)

empirical relationships that have not hitherto been observed, or even imagined. The continuous interplay between inductive and deductive procedures in the construction and further elaboration of a science is schematically illustrated in Figure C-1.

When empirical relationships have become firmly established, scientists often speak of them as laws, however the more philosophically knowledgeable scientists continuously remind themselves that all empirical relationships must remain hypothetical for all time because of their inductive origin and because of the consensual basis of validating scientific phenomena.

The basic procedure of empirical science is observation. Scientific description starts with observation; confirmation of the hypotheses of a theory is attained when phenomena predicted on the theory are observed. The term "observation" has a meaning which is relative to a scientific situation. For example, observation of micro-physical entities requires the explicit use of physical principles as instruments of interpretation, but all observation involves more or less explicitly the element of hypothesis.

The truth of a perception is confirmed or disconfirmed by testing the predictions derivable from it. The development of the concept of an object is completed by the hypothesis of the identity of the perceptible object of a society of observers. Thus the concept of the objective thing is social; science is tested by social procedure. The scientific criterion of objectivity ultimately rests upon the possibility of occurrence of predicted perceptions to a society of observers. (From Lenzen, 1955, pp. 284–285. With permission.)

Psychological Theorizing as a Language Game

The making of science has been called a language game by some philosophers of science, because this enterprise always aspires toward the highest possible level of generality in description-explanation, a level that is made possible only through the use of linguistic notations like symbolic logic and mathematics.* The importance of the abstract notational forms of language to scientific theory cannot be overestimated, as may be inferred from the following succinct description of scientific theorizing.

A theory logically binds laws together under the heritage of a common set of postulates and definitions. Thus the theorems of the theory comprise the family of the derivable laws. And it is deductibility of a law within the theory that constitutes the formal requirement of scientific explanation. (From Turner, 1965, p. 252. With permission of author and publisher.)

*For extensive discussions of the philosophy of science, see Feigl & Brodbeck, 1953; Feigl & Maxwell, 1961; Hesse, 1963; Nagel, 1961. For various approaches to theorizing in psychology, see Koch, 1959; Marx, 1963; Turner, 1965.

The *game* aspect of "theorizing as a language game" has many connotations to people who utilize scientific procedures, whether they be formal scientists, parents, classroom teachers, or others who may try to infer antecedent-consequent relationships and make predictions therefrom. The game has rules that cannot be violated without destroying the very essence of the activity. All who play the game must therefore know the basic rules and try to follow them. The game is always something of an exciting adventure, because like all games its ending is uncertain. There is always an element of pleasurable suspense in seeing whether or not one is clever enough to predict the outcome. Can we predict the future course of events in a given situation? If so, then there is the equally exciting game of seeing whether or not the predicted outcome can be controlled by skillful manipulation of the preceding conditions.

> Today we smile a bit about the great controversy over description versus explanation. We can see that there was something to be said for both sides, but that their way of debating the question was futile. There is no real opposition between explanation and description. Of course, if description is taken in the narrowest sense, as merely describing what a certain scientist did on a certain day with certain materials, then the opponents of mere description were quite right in asking for more, for a real explanation. But today we see that description in the broader sense, that of placing phenomena in the context of more general laws, provides the only type of explanation that can be given for phenomena. Similarly, if the proponents of explanation mean a metaphysical explanation, not grounded in empirical procedures, then their opponents were correct in insisting that science should be concerned only with description. Each side had a valid point. Both description and explanation, rightly understood, are essential aspects of science. (From Carnap, 1966, p. 244. With permission of author and publisher.)

Perhaps the most exciting and personally rewarding possibility in the language game of science is the chance that one may be ingenious and creative enough to extend the conditions of play in such a way that the alteration will be meaningful and acceptable to others participating in the game. This extension might involve a new series of permitted activities (additional observations, experimental procedures, operational definitions), a new rule (hypothesis, syntactic definition), a more general interpretation of an old rule (newer, more abstract theory from which old theorems can be logically derived), or some combination of these possibilities. These contributions may have major influence on the future course of the scientific game, or they may be a long series of minor suggestions that finally summate in a major change. In psychology, scientists like Pavlov, Freud, Binet, and Thorndike had a major influence on the game, while many other contributors have made minor but substantial extensions of the rules for extending and refining the play. Then, of course, there are others whose work has been equally important socially but of a somewhat different type. The latter adapt the conditions of play to various locations and players; these are the technicians and artisans, the applied arm of the scientific enterprise. It is hoped that the contents of the present book, which is a selection and a distillation of scientific findings and theories in psychology, will be useful to all who attempt to guide the learning activities of pupils.

It is interesting to note in passing that some individuals are interested only in abstractions of the language game of science. They are not interested in any possible applications to the solution of human problems; indeed, a few are even repelled by the approximations and compromises in rules that are typically necessary in applying general rules to specific cases. Still others simply don't see any reasonable applications of their theories (Spence, 1959). Fortunately for the arts and the technologies on which so much of modern civilization is based, a great many imaginative and creative individuals *do* see how the language game of scientific psychology can be used to social advantage in solving some of the educational problems of our time (Skinner, 1953; Gagné, 1962).

To a philosopher with a somewhat open mind all intelligent acquisition of knowledge should appear sometimes as a guessing game, I think. In science as in everyday life, when faced by a new situation, we start out with some guess. Our first guess may fall wide of the mark, but we try it and, according to the degree of success, we modify it more or less. Eventually, after several trials and severe modifications, pushed by observations and led by analogy, we may arrive at a more satisfactory guess. The layman does not find it surprising that the naturalist works in this way. The knowledge of the naturalist may be better ordered with a view to selecting the appropriate analogies, his observations may be more purposeful and more careful, he may give more funny names to his guesses and call them "tentative generalizations," but the naturalist adapts his mind to a new situation by guessing like the common man. And the layman is not surprised to hear that the naturalist is guessing like himself. (From Polya, 1954, p. 158. With permission.)

Science, Technology, and the Applied Arts

Since science deals with the general and the abstract under carefully designated, "ideal" conditions, technical and artistic talents are needed for the application of scientific findings to everyday problems.

The outcome, or consequence, of an individual case is usually partially determined by antecedent variables whose approximate influence is known as a result of laboratory and field research; however, it is also usually influenced by antecedent variables whose effects are not as yet known. Furthermore, the identification and assessment of all the variables in the individual case is usually not possible, or at least not expedient. Someone must be able and willing: (1) to size up the problem situation in the best way that available knowledge and current conditions permit, (2) to select one or more hypotheses as to how one might alter the antecedent variables, and thereby produce the desired outcome, (3) to test the most promising hypothesis by appropriate intervention, (4) to evaluate the outcome, (5) to test another promising hypothesis, and still another and another, if the desired effects are not obtained, (6) if still not successful, look for new information or obtain expert opinion on which additional hypotheses might be based. This is the formidable task which the engineer, the artisan, and the specialized technician faces again and again, day after day, as he solves the recurring problems of modern civilization.

At first glance it may appear that the artisan-engineer-technician is proceeding in the same way as a scientist. This is an accurate and valid impression, to some extent, in many situations. Although the artisan's duties may usually consist of a routine following of directions and prescribed procedures, he will inevitably encounter the case where these conventional routines don't produce the anticipated and desired outcome. When this happens the technologist may have several alternative courses of action available to him: (1) he can often throw the product away as a valueless reject, (2) he can put the product through an alternative routine that has been prescribed for such cases, (3) he can try the first routine again on the possibility that he failed to follow its directions accurately, or (4) he can construct a promising hypothesis of the reasons for the failure on the basis of his knowledge, experience, and creativity, test the hypothesis by making relevant corrections in the usually followed procedures, and possibly thereby effect a successful outcome. In the latter case the artisan or engineer is functioning like a scientist, although not completely so in most instances. Unlike the careful scientist, the typical technician doesn't keep a record of what he does to solve various kinds of individual problems, because he doesn't have time to do so, doesn't have the necessary language skills (scientific vocabulary or symbolic-mathematical background) to describe what he does, or doesn't really know how he solved the problem (has only an artistic impression of what he did which, if repeated time and again, might result in an unverbalizable artistic skill that an apprentice might be able to imitate).

Common errors in science and in its application

There are some well-known pitfalls in scientific research and the application of its findings. The conscientious scientist continually reminds himself of the existence of these hazards, but the practitioner is not always aware of their existence. Although the following is certainly not an exhaustive listing of such errors, it does encompass some of the most troublesome.

A common mistake in science making or its application is the tendency to become stereotyped, routine, and unimaginative with repeated experiences of a similar nature. Self-corrections and admonitions are needed to avoid sloppy hypothesizing and a routinized approach to the procedures of science without much regard for their relevance or adequacy. It is very easy for an individual to substitute the satisfaction that comes from "acting like a scientist," within a culture that generally approves and rewards such actions, for the more enduring pleasure that comes from discovering new findings or applying old findings in new ways to solve important problems. It is also easy to fall in love with the precision and complexity of the conceptual and metric tools of science, and forget their true value for creating or applying scientific knowledge. One must be careful not to mistake the shadow for the substance. Scientific rituals practiced in the laboratory, the classroom, or wherever can become as empty and ridiculous as the annual weighing of pigs in ancient Abyssinia. According to legend, the priests tied the squealing animal on one end of a balance, then added carefully selected and polished stones to the other end of the beam until it was *precisely* balanced at its *exact* center, then the priest *guessed* at the weight of the stones! Efforts routinely directed toward the construction of science and its application can become a similar farce unless the scientist and practitioner guard against such debasing possibilities.

Another common error stems from the scientist's or the practitioner's being human, and thereby subject on occasion to the often unconscious vices of wishful thinking, pride, prejudice, and self-deception. Perhaps only time and social criticism are effective safeguards against such subtle errors, as suggested in the following appraisal.

Although the recommendation that social scientists make fully explicit their value commitments is undoubtedly salutary, and can produce excellent fruit, it verges on being a counsel of perfection. For the most part we are unaware of many assumptions that enter into our analyses and actions, so that despite resolute efforts to make our preconceptions explicit some decisive ones may not even occur to us. But in any event, the difficulties generated for scientific inquiry by unconscious bias and tacit value orientations are rarely overcome by devout resolutions to eliminate bias. They are usually overcome, often only gradually, through the self-corrective mechanisms of science as a social enterprise. For modern science encourages the invention, the mutual exchange, and the free but responsible criticism of ideas; it welcomes competition in the quest for knowledge between independent investigators, even when their intellectual orientations are different; and it progressively diminishes the effects of bias by retaining only those proposed conclusions of its inquiries that survive critical examination by an indefinitely large community of students, whatever be their value preferences or doctrinal commitments. (From Nagel, 1961, pp. 489–490. With permission of author and publisher.)

Another common error is based on misconception or faulty appraisal of what antecedents are associated with what consequents. This may perhaps be best explicated by illustration. The "halo effect" and the "situational demand" are good examples. One does certain things by explicit intention (for instance, a teacher may use a new method for teaching algebra), and notices certain desirable consequences. From this experience one is tempted to conclude uncritically that his intended actions "caused" the effects. Further experience, especially well-designed research studies, may show that the planned actions had little or nothing to do with the effects; rather the unplanned, accompanying conditions of the planned actions caused the desired effects (in our example, perhaps the teacher spends more time with individual pupils in the new method). Recent studies in psychology have shown that the relevant antecedent variables may be nothing more than the attitude of the practitioner or his being what he stands for in the culture (Orne, 1962; Rosenthal, 1968). Many studies have shown, for example, that when the patient believes he is going to be helped by a certain medical agent or procedure, its therapeutic effectiveness is greatly enhanced. Comparably, if the pupil believes he is going to learn certain things or acquire certain skills by going to school, it may be easy for the teacher to conclude erroneously that his particular actions were relevant and be surprised in later situations when they are ineffective.

Relating Psychological
Findings to Education

Psychology has a number of important things to contribute to education: (1) how to design effective and efficient learning situations, (2) how to analyze learning into its several dimensions and with this knowledge design learning situations so that gains in one area do not lead to losses in another, (3) how to assess the learning abilities of the individual pupil so that curricula can be designed that will challenge but not demoralize him, (4) how to design instructional methods so that they capitalize most fully on the talents, background, and needs of the pupil at different levels of maturity and at the same time prepare him best for future learning assignments, (5) how to diagnose learning difficulties that may be experienced by different pupils and measure their aptitudes for different kinds of learning.

Although the foregoing listing is not exhaustive by any means, it does encompass some of the more obvious kinds of knowledge that may be used to advantage by teachers and other educational personnel. As is well documented in this volume, the scientific study of *learning* in its broadest sense lies within the domain of psychology. Psychologists' laboratory and field studies of the learning process and attributes of learners have yielded many findings that can be profitably related to educational programs. Teaching the young how to acquire new skills, how to solve problems, how to be an independent learner, how to be individually resourceful and creative, and how to relate meaningfully, productively, and harmoniously to others lies at the very heart of what we attempt to accomplish in the modern school. Psychological research and theory are certainly not definitive guides to these teaching activities at the present time, but they are usually highly relevant and always provocative as to what might be accomplished in education under ideal conditions of knowledge and its application.

Since the individual learner's formal education is typically attempted during the time that he is growing toward maturity, teachers can profit from knowledge related to the receptivity and responsivity of boys and girls of different levels of physical and psychological growth. Developmental psychologists have focused on the emergence of cognitive skills, on defining the limits of behavioral change at different levels or stages of psychological growth (Bloom, 1964), on early experiences as they may be critical for later development (Hebb, 1949), on inventing and refining methods for assessing the status of developing interests, abilities, and styles of living (Meyers, 1960), and so on. These types of information can be used to advantage to help set the stage for efficient learning in the classroom, in the tutorial session, or during self-instructional exercises. The developmental psychologist's knowledge and sensitivities appear to be especially valuable guides to educational programs that are currently being developed for the three- and four-year-old children of economically underprivileged parents (Hess & Baer, 1968).

The emphasis in the present book is consistently on what scientific psychology can contribute to educational processes and programs. This should not be interpreted to mean that psychology is the only one of the behavioral sciences that has something potentially useful for the educational practitioners. Sociology and cultural anthropology can also help the educator to understand something of the scope and grandeur of his undertaking. It should also be noted that the educator often solves his day-to-day problems by conducting his own research and elaborating his own theory (Gage, 1964). In other words, it should be understood that teachers and other educational personnel need a great deal more than a knowledge of psychology to be effective in their professions.

Another word of caution may be in order during this discussion. As previously noted, all of science is based on man's conceptual constructions, and is regarded by contributors to it as being always hypothetical and forever subject to revision and reinterpretation. There are no irrevocable laws in science. There are only observations and inferential statements in which scientists may have come to place a very high degree of confidence, but even these are sometimes subject to revision and reinterpretation, as the history of science has repeatedly shown.

The tentativeness of scientific generalizations means that scientists can, and do, change their minds. This may be extremely annoying and disconcerting to the artisan, technician, and practitioner who may have been trying to apply a principle that is suddenly no longer tenable. For example, during Thorndike's early reign of influence on education, teachers were encouraged to use the repetitiveness of drill as an effective instructional device (Thorndike, 1932). Later psychological research demonstrated that drilling poorly motivated pupils often leads to boredom, a compounding of errors, stereotypy, and other equally undesirable outcomes (Lewin, 1935). After a reasonable period of social lag and considerable grumbling, the drill books were scrapped. These changes in principle as a natural accompaniment of continuing research and theory construction are inevitable in science; furthermore they seem especially frequent in the more recently developed life and behavioral sciences. The only safeguard that comes to mind for the teacher is to adopt an experimental attitude toward his work; to keep up with expanding psychological knowledge as best he can, to attempt application in a tentative fashion, to revise and vary his approach as appears needed in order to obtain desirable effects, and to regard his approach and methods at any one time as only the best he has been able to accomplish as yet. This is a quasi-scientific procedure in its lack of rigor and demand for social consensus, but it has served post-Renaissance man extremely well in his search for greater and greater control over natural and social events. It is empirical, inductive, and tentatively hypothetical—all hallmarks of the scientific approach to psychological inquiry.

Appendix D

Principles of learning in three theoretical positions as they are related to educational instruction

*Stimulus-Response Theory**

Education consists of changing *behaviors*. Teachers provide learning settings; they provide opportunities for practice; they administer reinforcements; and they expect the pupil to transfer what he has learned to new situations. In these respects, the S-R theory of learning has much to say, although it is not a complete theory of learning. Some important principles from this theory as they apply to classroom situations are as follows:

1. Pupils learn associations between stimuli (events, objects, or situations), between stimuli and responses, and between responses and their consequences.

2. Learning is produced strictly by the contiguity of the environmental and/or behavioral features to be associated.

3. Practice, rehearsal, repetition, recitation, or similar activity is essential for the development of an association. Repeated exposure to the material to be learned strengthens the association in cumulative fashion.

4. Responses that repeatedly follow a stimulus move increasingly forward in time. On later occasions the response may follow the stimulus immediately. Eventually, these responses may be implicit, fractional anticipatory representations of the original responses.

*Abridged from Logan, 1968. With permission.

5. Motivation is comprised of drives and incentives. Rewards reduce drives and their value depends upon the magnitude of drive-reduction. Incentive refers to the attractiveness of a reward and the extent to which it is related to repetition of a behavioral pattern. Typically, behaviors are selected which have been associated with most reward and least punishment.

6. Some drives such as the learning (competence, or effectance) drive appear to be unlearned or intrinsic. However, it is also likely that they are learned at a very early age. Along with other personal-social motives the intrinsic drives do not appear to conform to the drive-reduction principle.

7. All behavior produces internal feedback in the form of kinesthetic and proprioceptive cues as in the learning of motor skills. In addition, most responses produce changes in the environment and in the pupil's relation to his environment that also function as feedback stimuli. Pupils use these cues to distinguish the correct from the incorrect responses or just to distinguish differences among responses.

8. Performance is dependent upon learning, drive motivation, and incentive motivation. The pupil will perform a given behavior to the extent that he has learned it, and that he is motivated to do so by virtue of his motives and the expected return. Performance is inhibited by fatigue, pain, and other temporary conditions.

9. Motivation is required if the pupil is to experience stimuli, perform the responses, and react to the reward or punishment. Thus, indirectly motivation may result in learning but it is not an effector of learning. Learning of associations occurs entirely by contiguous experience.

10. Teachers (and learning aids in general) facilitate learning by arranging knowledge according to some reasonable hypotheses such as simple to complex, or putting related ideas together. Individual differences among pupils are considered since these affect what can be learned and the rate of learning. Situations are arranged to control exposure to stimuli, to assure that certain responses are made, e.g., in the form of assignments, practice periods, and pretests, and to provide opportunity for administering rewards and punishments; more generally, to learn requires activity. The sequence of activities is arranged with some view of the desired terminal performance, which may be reproduction of knowledge communicated by the teacher, transfer to reasoning and other creative uses (so learning must occur in varied contexts), or change in the free behavior of the pupil.

Cognitive Theory

Education is directed toward the changing of behavior and consists in large part of acquiring knowledge and ideas. Teachers often employ problem-solving techniques and inquiry as bases for instructional methods. They also point out new ways of perceiving a common phenomenon as a means of helping pupils to achieve new insights about the world around them. The cognitive theorists have attempted to deal with the principles governing such learning. These principles are presented below and can be compared with corresponding points of the behaviorists' theory. However, as a teacher you will want to develop your own theory of instruction based on what you eventually consider to be the best parts of the many theories.

1. Pupils learn to identify new perceptual features, means-ends relationships, and structural relationships among stimuli or events, and to reconstruct existing ideas into new organizations.

2. Learning is produced by experience with stimuli that develop cognitions of responses (paths) that will lead to rewards (goals). Learning is also produced by restructuring or reorganizing learning tasks to identify different ways the material can be viewed (structured) or arranged.

3. Rote learning can be accomplished by repetitive practice or drill. However, even the simplest of learning situations can be coded, that is, some meaning or structure can be imposed on the material. Meaning is accomplished by relating the subject matter to previous experience, thereby enhancing understanding, making the material more meaningful, and facilitating transfer. Structuring the material by ordering it from simple to complex or by some other hierarchical arrangement makes it an integrated single unit rather than several isolated units, thereby facilitating recall. (The importance of stimulus configurations, coding processes, and effective stimuli is also recognized by the neo-behaviorists.)

4. An important feature of all learning is that pupils learn cognitions related to directional signs, about what leads to what, about how different aspects of the world are laid out. These are called expectancies, cognitive maps, or codes.

5. Motivation is necessary to put acquired cognitions to use. Performance is maintained when the pupil's ideas about his present state are incongruous (different) or conflict with ideas about the desired state. Cognitive conflict, cognitive dissonance, or incongruity is an important motivational factor. Thus, knowing something about the goal (goal-setting) is essential if the pupil is to compare where he is at present and where he will be later.

6. Cognitions, whether concepts, interpretations, expectancies, or structured relationships, are provisionally tried as bases for accomplishing the end result—for reaching the goal. If the achieved goal does not live up to expectations, is not realized, or is only inadequately achieved, the interpretation is rejected, is either modified or substituted by

another, and the cycle may be repeated. Cognitive feedback involves the
testing of the validity of inferences. One's knowledge is confirmed if correct and contradicted if the learning is faulty leading to the necessity
for a change.

7. Creativity is characterized by the formation of restructured
situations so that novel relationships are seen, leading to original
hypotheses that effectively solve problems or lead to new discoveries.

*Personality and Motivational Theories**

Several general conditions affect the efficiency of learning and
further modify the effects of variables described by the behaviorist and
cognitive theorists. Among them are the differences in pupil abilities,
differences in developmental and cultural history, and differences in
motivation. The social atmosphere of the classroom can be added to
these as part of another class of variables. Contributions to our knowledge about these variables, from studies and theories concerning individual differences, motivation, and personality, have been summarized
by Hilgard and Bower (1966) as presented below, with but slight modification. In many respects these points provide an overview of a number
of sections of this book.

1. The pupil's abilities, including his intellectual ability, place a
limit on his learning *rate*. Grouping practices, team teaching, and individual methods of teaching such as tutorial, programmed instruction, and
computer-assisted instruction are among the provisions for accommodating fast and slow learners, as well as learners with special abilities.

2. All experiences in the pupil's postnatal developmental history
affect his confidence, his motivation, and his abilities. These factors may
be as important as hereditary and congenital factors in his readiness to
profit from learning situations.

3. Relative to all cultures, both the wider culture and the subculture limit the nature of the pupil's opportunities. Cultural limitations
restrict learning to the extent that they fail to coincide with requirements for scholastic success. Growing up in an impoverished subculture
can be particularly debilitating since the consequent learning deficits
appear to be cumulative.

4. Developmental histories also influence the pupil's tendency to
be anxious. Whether a teacher's comment is beneficial or detrimental to
learning sometimes depends on this acquired disposition. The highly
anxious pupils may, for example, make better progress at a task if they
are not continually reminded of the adequacy of their performance,

*Based on *Theories of Learning*, 3rd ed., by Ernest R. Hilgard and Gordon H.
Bower. Copyright © 1966. Reprinted by permission of authors and Appleton-Century-
Crofts, Division of Meredith Corporation.

while less anxious pupils are stimulated by continuing evaluations of their progress.

5. Any given situation (e.g., one which is intellectually competitive) may be effective for pupils in which one motive (e.g., the achievement motive) is dominant but simultaneously may be quite ineffective for pupils in which another motive (e.g., the affiliation motive) is dominant.

6. Goals are hierarchically arranged. The uppermost ones are the more general long-range goals under which the short-range activities are subsumed. Degree of pupil interest, participation, and achievement, given pupils of equal ability, is often determined by the relevancy of an assignment to his long-range goals.

7. Classroom climate is the outcome of all social and verbal interaction with peers and teachers. The consequent impression may be described along such dimensions as cold-warm; personal-impersonal; authoritarian-democratic; group-individual; competitive-cooperative; acceptant-rejectant; permissive-restrictive; and the like. The idiosyncratic atmosphere of a given class, with its unique combination of teacher and pupils, becomes quickly established and thereafter continues to influence the degree of satisfaction with school and learning, and to affect the learning product.

Bibliography

AAAS Commission on Science Education. *Science—A process approach.: Purposes, accomplishments, expectations.* Washington, D.C.: American Association for the Advancement of Science, 1967.

Adamson, R. E., Taylor, D. W. Functional fixedness as related to elapsed time and to set. *Journal of Experimental Psychology*, 1954, *47*, 122–126.

Adorno, T. W., *et al. The authoritarian personality.* New York: Harper, 1950.

Ahmann, J. S., & Glock, M. D. *Evaluating pupil growth: Principles of tests and measurements.* (3rd ed.) Boston: Allyn & Bacon, 1967.

Ainsworth, M. D., *et al. Deprivation of maternal care: A reassessment of its effects.* New York: Shocken Books, 1966.

Allport, G. W. *The nature of prejudice.* Reading, Mass.: Addison-Wesley, 1954.

Allport, G. W. On learning tolerance. In J. M. Seidman (Ed.), *Readings in educational psychology.* Boston: Houghton Mifflin. Cambridge: Riverside Press, 1955. Pp. 252–254.

Allport, G. W. *Personality and social encounter: Selected essays.* Boston: Beacon, 1960.

Allport, G. W. *Pattern and growth in personality.* New York: Holt, Rinehart, and Winston, 1961.

Allport, G. W., & Postman, L. *The psychology of rumor.* New York: Holt, 1947.

Anastasi, A. Heredity, environment and the question "How?" *Psychological Review*, 1958, *65*, 196–208.

Anderson, J. E. *A survey of children's adjustment over time: A report to the people of Nobles County.* Minneapolis, Minn.: Institute of Child Welfare and Development, University of Minnesota, 1959.

Archer, E. J. Concept identification as a function of obviousness of relevant and irrelevant information. *Journal of Experimental Psychology*, 1962, *63*, 616–620.

Arnoult, M. D. Stimulus predifferentiation: Some generalizations and hypotheses. *Psychological Bulletin*, 1957, *54*, 339–350.

Aronfreed, J. *Conduct and conscience: The socialization of internal control over behavior.* New York: Academic Press, 1968.

Aschner, M. J., & Bish, C. E. (Eds.) *Productive thinking in education.* Washington, D.C.: National Education Association, Carnegie Corporation of New York, 1965, 1968.

Atkinson, J. W. The mainsprings of achievement-oriented activity. In J. D. Krumboltz (Ed.), *Learning and the educational process.* Chicago: Rand-McNally, 1965.

Atkinson, J. W., & Litwin, G. H. Achievement motive and test anxiety conceived as motive to approach success and motive to avoid failure. *Journal of Abnormal and Social Psychology,* 1960, *60,* 52–63.

Atkinson, R. C. *Computerized instruction and the learning process.* Technical Report No. 122. Stanford: Institute for Mathematical Studies in the Social Sciences, 1967.

Ausubel, D. P. In defense of verbal learning. *Educational Theory,* 1961, *11,* 15–25. (a)

Ausubel, D. P. Learning by discovery: Rationale and mystique. *Bulletin of the National Association of Secondary School Principals,* 1961, *45,* 18–58. (b)

Ausubel, D. P. Cognitive structure and the facilitation of meaningful learning. *Journal of Teacher Education,* 1963, *14,* 217–222.

Ausubel, D. P. Meaningful reception learning and the acquisition of concepts. In H. J. Klausmeier & C. W. Harris (Eds.), *Analyses of concept learning.* New York: Academic Press, 1966. Pp. 157–175.

Ausubel, D. P. *Learning theory and classroom practice.* (Bulletin No. 1.) Toronto: Ontario Institute for Studies in Education, 1967.

Ausubel, D. P., & Fitzgerald, D. The role of discriminability in meaningful verbal learning and retention. *Journal of Educational Psychology,* 1961, *52,* 266–274.

Ausubel, D. P., & Fitzgerald, D. Organizer, general background and antecedent learning variables in sequential verbal learning. *Journal of Educational Psychology,* 1962, *53,* 243–249.

Ausubel, D. P., & Youssef, M. Role of discriminability in meaningful parallel learning. *Journal of Educational Psychology,* 1963, *54,* 331–336.

Baer, D. M., & Wolf, M. M. The reinforcement contingency in pre-school and remedial education. In R. D. Hess & R. M. Bear (Eds.), *Early Education.* Chicago: Aldine, 1968.

Bahrick, H. P. An analysis of stimulus variables influencing the proprioceptive control of movements. *Psychological Review,* 1957, *64,* 324–328.

Baldwin, A. L. *Behavior and development in childhood.* New York: Dryden, 1955.

Baldwin, A. L. *Theories of child development.* New York: Wiley, 1967.

Baller, W. R. Mid-life attainment of the mentally retarded: A longitudinal study. *Genetic Psychology Monographs,* 1967, *75,* 235–329.

Bandura, A. Social learning through imitation. In M. R. Jones (Ed.), *Nebraska symposium on motivation.* Lincoln, Nebraska: University of Nebraska Press, 1962. Pp. 211–269.

Bandura, A. Influence of models' reinforcement contingencies on the acquisition of imitative responses. *Journal of Personality and Social Psychology*, 1965, *1*, 589–595.

Bandura, A., & Kupers, C. J. Transmission of self-reinforcement through modeling. *Journal of Abnormal and Social Psychology*, 1964, *69*, 1–9.

Bandura, A., & Walters, R. H. *Social learning and personality development*. New York: Holt, Rinehart, and Winston, 1963.

Bandura, A., & Whalen, C. K. The influence of antecedent reinforcement and divergent modeling cues on patterns of self-reward. *Journal of Personality and Social Psychology*, 1966, *3*, 373–382.

Baratz, J. C., & Shuy, R. W. (Eds.) *Teaching black children to read*. Urban Language Series, Vol. 4. Washington, D.C.: Center for Applied Linguistics, 1969.

Barber, T. X., & Silver, M. J. Fact, fiction, and the experimenter bias effect. *Psychological Bulletin Monograph*, 1968, *70*, No. 6, Part 2, 1–29.

Bartlett, F. C. *Remembering: A study in experimental and social psychology*. New York: Macmillan, 1932.

Bartlett, F. C. *Thinking: An experimental and social study*. New York: Basic Books, 1958.

Bayley, N. On the growth of intelligence. *American Psychologist*, 1955, *10*, 805–818.

Bayley, N. Learning in adulthood: The role of intelligence. In H. J. Klausmeier & C. W. Harris (Eds.), *Analyses of concept learning*. New York: Academic Press, 1966.

Beach, F. A. The descent of instinct. *Psychological Review*, 1955, *62*, 401–410.

Beberman, M. *An emerging program of secondary school mathematics*. Cambridge, Mass.: Harvard University Press, 1958.

Beberman, M. An emerging program of secondary school mathematics. In R. W. Heath (Ed.), *New curricula*. New York: Harper & Row, 1964. Pp. 9–34.

Beilin, H. Teachers' and clinicians' attitudes toward the behavior problems of children: A reappraisal. *Child Development*, 1959, *30*, 9–25.

Benedict, R. Continuities and discontinuities in cultural conditioning. *Psychiatry*, 1938, Vol. 1.

Bennett, E. L., Diamond, M. C., Krech, D., & Rosenzweig, M. R. Chemical and anatomical plasticity of the brain. *Science*, 1964, *146*, 610–619.

Bennett, G. K. *Hand-tool dexterity test*. New York: Psychological Corporation, 1946.

Bennett, G. K., Seashore, H. G., & Wesman, A. G. *Differential aptitude tests*. (Grades 8–13 and adults.) New York: Psychological Corporation, 1947–1963.

Berdie, R. F. Scores on the Strong Vocational Interest Blank and the Kuder Preference Record in relation to self ratings. *Journal of Applied Psychology*, 1950, *34*, 42–49.

Berdie, R. F. Aptitude, achievement, interest, and personality tests: A longitudinal comparison. *Journal of Applied Psychology*, 1955, *39*, 103–114.

Bereiter, C., & Engelmann, S. *Teaching disadvantaged children in pre-school*. Englewood Cliffs, N.J.: Prentice-Hall, 1966.

Berg, H. D. The objective test item. In H. D. Berg (Ed.), *Evaluation in social studies*. 35th Yearbook of the National Council for the Social Studies. Washington, D.C.: National Education Association, 1965.

Berger, S. M. Conditioning through vicarious instigation. *Psychological Review*, 1962, *69*, 450–466.

Berlyne, D. E. Attention to change. *British Journal of Psychology*, 1951, *42*, 269–278.

Berlyne, D. E. Attention to change, conditioned inhibition (sIr) and stimulus satiation. *British Journal of Psychology*, 1957, *48*, 138–140.

Berlyne, D. E. *Conflict, arousal, and curiosity*. New York: McGraw-Hill, 1960.

Berlyne, D. E. *Structure and direction in thinking*. New York: Wiley, 1965.

Berlyne, D. E., & McDonnell, P. Effect of stimulus complexity and incongruity on duration of EEG desynchronization. *Electroencephalography and Clinical Neurology*, 1965, *18*, 156–161.

Bernstein, B. The role of speech in the development and transmission of culture. In G. J. Klopf & W. A. Hohman (Eds.), *Perspectives on learning*. New York: Published for Bank Street College of Education by Mental Health Materials Center, Inc., 1967. Pp. 15–45.

Bertocci, P. A. A critique of G. W. Allport's theory of motivation. *Psychological Review*, 1940, 47, 501–532.

Biggs, J. B. *Information and human learning*. North Melbourne, Victoria, Australia: Cassell Australia Ltd., 1968.

Bijou, S. W., & Baer, D. M. *Child development. Vol. 1: A systematic and empirical theory*. New York: Appleton-Century-Crofts, 1961.

Binder, A. Process of component and pattern learning. *Psychonomic Science*, 1966, *4*, 415–416.

Birch, H. G. Sources of order in maternal behavior of animals. *American Journal of Orthopsychiatry*, 1956, *26*, 279–284.

Bloom, B. S. *Stability and change in human characteristics*. New York: Wiley, 1964.

Bloom, B. S. Learning for mastery. In UCLA Center for the Study of Evaluation of Instructional Programs, *Evaluation Comment*, 1968, *1*, No. 2.

Bloom, B. S., Davis, A., & Hess, R. D. *Compensatory education for cultural deprivation*. New York: Holt, Rinehart, and Winston, 1965.

Bloom, B. S., Englehart, M. D., Furst, E. J., Hill, W. H., & Krathwohl, D. R. (Eds.) *Taxonomy of educational objectives: The classification of educational goals. Handbook I: Cognitive domain*. New York: David McKay, 1956.

Blum, G. S. *Psychoanalytic theories of personality*. New York: McGraw-Hill, 1953.

Bonney, M. E. Popular and unpopular children: A sociometric study. *Sociometry Monographs*, 1947, No. 9.

Bordin, E. S. A theory of vocational interests as dynamic phenomena. *Educational and Psychological Measurement*, 1943, *3*, 49–65.

Boring, E. G. *Sensation and perception in the history of experimental psychology*. New York: Appleton Century, 1942.

Boring, E. G. *A history of experimental psychology*. New York: Appleton-Century-Crofts, 1957.

Bossart, P., & Di Vesta, F. J. Effects of context, frequency, and order of presentation of evaluative assertions on impression formation. *Journal of Personality and Social Psychology*, 1966, *4*, 538–544.

Bourne, L. E., Jr. *Human conceptual behavior.* Boston: Allyn & Bacon, 1966.

Bourne, L. E., Jr. Learning and the utilization of conceptual rules. In B. Kleinmuntz (Ed.), *Concepts and the structure of memory.* New York: Wiley, 1967. Pp. 1–32.

Bourne, L. E., Jr., & Bunderson, C. V. Effects of delay of informative feedback and length of postfeedback interval on concept identification. *Journal of Experimental Psychology*, 1963, *65*, 1–5.

Bourne, L. E., Jr., & Restle, F. Mathematical theory of concept identification. *Psychological Review*, 1959, *66*, 278–296.

Bousfield, W. A. The occurrence of clustering in the recall of randomly arranged associates. *Journal of General Psychology*, 1953, *49*, 229–240.

Bower, B. D., & Jeavons, P. M. Phenylketonuria presenting as infantile spasms with sudden mental deterioration. *Developmental Medicine and Child Neurology*, 1963, *5*, 557–585.

Bower, G. H., Clark, M. C., Lesgold, A. M., & Winzenz, D. Hierarchical retrieval schemes in recall of categorized word lists. *Journal of Verbal Learning and Verbal Behavior*, 1969, *8*, 323–343.

Bower, G. H., & Winzenz, D. Group structure and memory for digit series. *Journal of Experimental Psychology Monograph*, 1969, *80*, 2, Part 2.

Bowlby, J. Maternal care and mental health. In *Deprivation of maternal care.* New York: Shocken Books, 1966.

Brandt, R. M. Self: Missing link for understanding behavior. *Mental Hygiene*, 1957, *41*, 24–33.

Bridgman, C. S., & Hollenbeck, G. P. Effect of simulated applicant status on Kuder Form D occupational interest scores. *Journal of Applied Psychology*, 1961, *45*, 237–239.

Broadhurst, P. L. Emotionality and the Yerkes-Dodson law. *Journal of Experimental Psychology*, 1957, *54*, 345–352.

Brown, R. W. How shall a thing be called? *Psychological Review*, 1958, *65*, 14–21.

Brown, R. W. *Social psychology.* New York: Free Press, 1965.

Broyler, C. R., Thorndike, E. L., & Woodyard, E. A second study of mental discipline in high school studies. *Journal of Educational Psychology*, 1927, *18*, 377–404.

Brueckner, L. J. *Diagnostic tests and self-helps in arithmetic.* Los Angeles: California Test Bureau, 1955.

Bruner, J. S. *The process of education.* Cambridge, Mass.: Harvard University Press, 1960.

Bruner, J. S. The cognitive consequences of early sensory deprivation. In P. Solomon, *et al.* (Eds.), *Sensory deprivation: A symposium held at Harvard Medical School.* Cambridge, Mass.: Harvard University Press, 1961. Pp. 195–207.

Bruner, J. S. The course of cognitive growth. *American Psychologist*, 1964, *19*, 1–15.

Bruner, J. S. Education as social invention. *Saturday Review*, 1966, February, *19*, 70–72, 102–103. (a)

Bruner, J. S. Some elements of discovery. In L. S. Shulman & E. R. Keislar (Eds.), *Learning by discovery*. Chicago: Rand McNally, 1966. Pp. 101–114. (b)

Bruner, J. S., Goodnow, J. J., & Austin, G. A. *A study of thinking*. New York: Wiley, 1956.

Bruner, J. S., Matter, J., & Papanek, M. L. Breadth of learning as a function of drive level and mechanization. *Psychological Review*, 1955, *62*, 1–10.

Bruner, J. S., & Olver, R. R. Development of equivalence transformations in children. In J. C. Wright & J. Kagan (Eds.), Basic cognitive processes in children. *Society for Research in Child Development Monographs*, 1963, *28*, No. 2, Serial No. 86.

Bruner, J. S., & Postman, L. Emotional selectivity in perception and reaction. *Journal of Personality*, 1947, *16*, 69–77.

Bugelski, B. R. *The psychology of learning applied to teaching*. New York: Bobbs-Merrill, 1964.

Bulgarella, R. G., & Archer, E. J. Concept identification of auditory stimuli as a function of amount of relevant and irrelevant information. *Journal of Experimental Psychology*, 1962, *63*, 254–257.

Buros, O. K. *The fourth mental measurements yearbook*. Highland Park, N.J.: Gryphon, 1953.

Buros, O. K. *The fifth mental measurements yearbook*. Highland Park, N.J.: Gryphon, 1959.

Buros, O. K. *The sixth mental measurements yearbook*. Highland Park, N.J.: Gryphon, 1965.

Burton, W. H. *The Guidance of Learning Activities*. New York: Appleton-Century-Crofts, 1960.

Buswell, G. T. Educational theory and the psychology of learning. *Journal of Educational Psychology*, 1956, *47*, 175–184.

Butler, R. A. Discrimination learning by rhesus monkeys to visual-exploration motivation. *Journal of Comparative and Physiological Psychology*, 1953, *46*, 95–98.

Byrne, D. Interpersonal attraction and attitude similarity. *Journal of Abnormal and Social Psychology*, 1961, *62*, 713–715.

Calvin, A. D., & Holtzman, W. H. Adjustment and discrepancy between self concept and inferred self. *Journal of Consulting Psychology*, 1953, *17*, 39–44.

Cameron, N. A. *Personality development and psychopathology: A dynamic approach*. Boston: Houghton Mifflin, 1963.

Campbell, D. P. The stability of vocational interests within occupations over long time spans. *Personnel and Guidance Journal*, 1966, *44*, 1012–1015.

Cannon, W. B. *Bodily changes in pain, hunger, fear and rage: An account of recent researches into the function of emotional excitement*. New York: D. Appleton and Co., 1923.

Cantor, G. N. The effects of three types of pretraining on discrimination learning in preschool children. *Journal of Experimental Psychology*, 1955, *49*, 339–342.

Cantor, J. H. Amount of pretraining as a factor in stimulus predifferentiation and performance set. *Journal of Experimental Psychology*, 1955, *50*, 180–184.

Cantor, J. H., & Cantor, G. N. Observing behavior in children as a function of stimulus novelty. *Child Development*, 1964, *35*, 119–128.

Cantor, N. *The teaching-learning process.* New York: Dryden, 1953.

Carkhuff, R. R., & Drasgow, J. The confusing literature on the OL scale of the SVIB. *Journal of Counseling Psychology*, 1963, *10*, 283–288.

Carlson, J. B., & Duncan, C. P. A study of autonomous change in the memory trace by the method of recognition. *American Journal of Psychology*, 1955 *68*, 280–284.

Carlson, R. Identification and personality structure in preadolescents. *Journal of Abnormal and Social Psychology*, 1963, *67*, 566–573.

Carmichael, L. (Ed.) *Manual of child psychology.* (2nd ed.) New York: Wiley, 1954.

Carmichael, L., Hogan, H. P., & Walter, A. A. An experimental study of the effect of language on the reproduction of visually perceived form. *Journal of Experimental Psychology*, 1932, *15*, 73–86.

Carnap, R. *Philosophical foundations of physics: An introduction to the philosophy of science.* (Ed. by Martin Gardner.) New York: Basic Books, 1966.

Carroll, J. B. A model of school learning. *Teachers College Record*, 1963, *64*, 723–733.

Carroll, J. B. *Language and thought.* Englewood Cliffs, N.J.: Prentice-Hall, 1964. (a)

Carroll, J. B. Words, meanings, and concepts. *Harvard Educational Review*, 1964, *34*, 178–202. (b)

Carroll, J. B. On learning from being told. *Educational Psychologist*, 1968, *5*, 1–10.

Carson, A. S., & Rabin, A. J. Verbal comprehension and communication in Negro and white children. *Journal of Educational Psychology*, 1960, *51*, 47–51.

Cattell, J. McK. A statistical study of eminent men. *Popular Science Monthly*, 1903, *62*, 359–377.

Cattell, R. B. *Prediction and understanding of the effect of children's interest upon school performance.* Urbana, Ill.: University of Illinois Press, 1961.

Cattell, R. B. Anxiety and motivation: Theory and crucial experiments. In C. B. Spielberger (Ed.), *Anxiety and behavior.* New York: Academic Press, 1966. Pp. 23–62.

Chan, A., & Travers, R. M. W. Effect on retention of labeling visual displays. *American Educational Research Journal*, 1966, *3*, 55–68.

Chapanis, N. P., & Chapanis, A. Cognitive dissonance: Five years later. *Psychological Bulletin*, 1964, *61*, 1–22.

Chauncey, H., & Dobbin, J. E. *Testing: Its place in education today.* New York: Harper & Row, 1963.

Child, I. L. Children's preference for goals easy or difficult to obtain. *Psychological Monographs*, 1946, *60*, No. 4.

Child, I. L., Potter, E. H., & Levine, E. M. Children's textbooks and personality development: An exploration in the social psychology of education. *Psychological Monographs*, 1946, *60*, No. 3.

Chomsky, N. *Syntactic structures.* The Hague, The Netherlands: Mouton, 1957.

Chomsky, N. *Aspects of the theory of syntax.* Cambridge, Mass.: MIT Press, 1965.

Chomsky, N. Language and the mind. *Psychology Today,* 1968, *1,* No. 9, February, 48–51, 66–69.

Chown, S. M. Rigidity: A flexible concept. *Psychological Bulletin,* 1959, *56,* 195–223.

Christie, R., & Jahoda, M. (Eds.) *Studies in the scope and method of "The authoritarian personality."* Glencoe, Ill.: Free Press, 1954.

Chu, Don-Chean. How can teachers' prestige be raised? *Journal of Experimental Education,* 1964, *32,* 333–346.

Churchill, W. D., & Smith, S. E. The relationship of the 1960 Stanford-Binet Intelligence Scale to intelligence and achievement test scores over a three-year period. *Educational and Psychological Measurement,* 1966, *26,* 1015–1020.

Clark, K. B. *Dark ghetto: Dilemmas of social power.* New York: Harper & Row, 1965.

Cofer, C. N. Reasoning as an associative process: III. The role of verbal responses in problem solving. *Journal of General Psychology,* 1957, *57,* 55–68.

Cofer, C. N. On some factors in the organizational characteristics of free recall. *American Psychologist,* 1965, *20,* 261–272.

Cohen, A. K. *Delinquent boys: The culture of the gang.* Glencoe, Ill.: Free Press, 1955.

Cohen, Y. A. *The transition from childhood to adolescence: Cross-cultural studies of initiation ceremonies, legal systems, and incest taboos.* Chicago: Aldine, 1964.

Coleman, A. L. Social scientists' predictions about desegregation: 1950–1955. *Social Forces,* 1960, *38,* 258–262.

Coleman, J. S. *The adolescent society.* Glencoe, Ill.: Free Press, 1961. (a)

Coleman, J. S. Social climates in high schools. *Cooperative Research Monograph No. 4.* Washington, D.C.: U.S. Dept. of Health, Education, and Welfare, Office of Education, 1961. (b)

Coleman, J. S., et al. *Equality of educational opportunity.* U.S. Department of Health, Education, and Welfare, Office of Education. Washington, D.C.: Government Printing Office, 1966.

Conry, R., & Plant, W. T. WAIS and group test predictions of an academic success criterion: High school and college. *Educational and Psychological Measurement,* 1965, *25,* 493–500.

Cook, W. W., Leeds, C. H., & Callis, R. *Minnesota Teacher Attitude Inventory.* New York: Psychological Corporation, 1951.

Cooperative English Test: Manual. Princeton, N.J.: Cooperative Test Division, Educational Testing Service, 1960.

Coopersmith, S. A method for determining types of self-esteem. *Journal of Abnormal and Social Psychology,* 1959, *59,* 87–94.

Coopersmith, S. *The antecedents of self-esteem.* San Francisco: W. H. Freeman, 1967.

Coopersmith, S. Studies in self-esteem. *Scientific American,* 1968, *218,* 96–107.

Cox, C. M. *Genetic studies of genius. Volume II. The early mental traits of three hundred geniuses.* Stanford, Calif.: Stanford University Press, 1926.

Crawford, J. E., & Crawford, D. M. *Small parts dexterity test.* New York: Psychological Corporation, 1946–1956.

Dabbs, J. M., Jr. Self-esteem, communicator characteristics, and attitude change. *Journal of Abnormal and Social Psychology,* 1964, *69,* 173–181.

Davis, A., & Eells, K. *Davis-Eells Games: Davis-Eells Test of General Intelligence or Problem-solving Ability: Manual.* Yonkers-on-the-Hudson, N.Y.: World, 1953.

Davis, D. M. Speech patterns of young children. In R. G. Kuhlen & G. G. Thompson (Eds.), *Psychological studies of human development.* New York: Appleton-Century-Crofts, 1952. Pp. 230–236.

Davis, G. A. Current status of research and theory in human problem solving. *Psychological Bulletin,* 1966, *66,* 36–54.

Davis, K. Extreme isolation of a child. *American Journal of Sociology,* 1940, *45,* 554–565.

Davis, K. Final note on a case of extreme isolation. *American Journal of Sociology,* 1947, *52,* 432–437.

Davis, R. B. Discovery in the teaching of mathematics. In L. S. Shulman & E. R. Kieslar (Eds.), *Learning by discovery: A critical appraisal.* Chicago: Rand McNally, 1966. Chapter VIII.

Deese, J. *General psychology.* Boston: Allyn & Bacon, 1967.

deGroat, A. F., & Thompson, G. G. A study of the distribution of teacher approval and disapproval among sixth-grade pupils. *Journal of Experimental Education,* 1949, *18,* 57–75.

deGroat, A. F., & Thompson, G. G. Teachers' responses to individual children. In R. G. Kuhlen & G. G. Thompson (Eds.), *Psychological studies of human development.* New York: Appleton-Century-Crofts, 1952. Pp. 429–436.

Dennis, W., & Najarian, P. Infant development under environmental handicap. *Psychological Monographs,* 1957, *71,* No. 1.

Deutsch, C. Learning in the disadvantaged. In H. J. Klausmeier & C. W. Harris (Eds.), *Analyses of concept learning.* New York: Academic Press, 1966. Pp. 189–206.

Deutsch, M. Early social environment: Its influence on school adaptation. In D. Schreiber (Ed.), *The school dropout.* Washington, D.C.: National Education Association, 1964. Pp. 89–100. (a)

Deutsch, M. Facilitating development in the preschool child: Social and psychological perspectives. *Merrill-Palmer Quarterly,* 1964, *10,* 249–264. (b)

Deutsch, M. Some psychosocial aspects of learning in the disadvantaged. *Teachers College Record,* 1966, *67,* 4, 260–265.

Deutsch, M., & Solomon, L. Reactions to evaluations by others as influenced by self-evaluations. *Sociometry,* 1959, *22,* 93–112.

Dewey, J. *Moral principles in education.* Boston: Houghton Mifflin, 1909.

Dewey, J. *How we think.* Boston: Heath, 1910.

Diggory, J. C. *Self-evaluation: Concepts and studies.* New York: Wiley, 1966.

Di Vesta, F. J. Effects of mediated generalization on the development of children's preferences for figures. *Child Development,* 1962, *33,* 209–222.

Di Vesta, F. J. The measurement of children's meaning. *Pedagogisk Forskning,* 1966, 150–168.

Di Vesta, F. J., & Stover, D. O. The semantic mediation of evaluative meaning. *Journal of Experimental Psychology*, 1962, *64*, 467–475.

Di Vesta, F. J., & Walls, R. T. Transfer of object-function in problem-solving. *American Educational Research Journal*, 1967, *4*, 207–216.

Dolan, M. C. What made Tommy fight? *Personnel and Guidance Journal*, 1954, *32*, 357–358.

Doll, E. A. *Your child grows up.* (Booklet) Boston: John Hancock Mutual Life Insurance Co., 1939.

Dollard, J., Doob, L. W., Miller, N. E., Mowrer, O. H., Sears, R. R., Ford, C. S., Hovland, C. I., & Sollenberger, R. T. *Frustration and aggression.* New Haven: Yale University Press, 1939.

Dollard, J., & Miller, N. E. *Personality and psychotherapy.* New York: McGraw-Hill, 1950.

Dorwart, W., Ezerman, R., Lewis, M., & Rosenhan, D. The effect of brief social deprivation on social and nonsocial reinforcement. *Journal of Personality and Social Psychology*, 1965, *2*, 111–115.

Dressel, P. L. (Ed.) *Evaluation in general education.* Dubuque, Iowa: W. C. Brown, 1954.

Duncker, K. Experimental modification of children's food preferences through social suggestion. *Journal of Abnormal and Social Psychology*, 1938, *33*, 489–507.

Duncker, K. (Lynne S. Lees, trans.) On problem-solving. *Psychological Monographs*, 1945, *58* (Whole No. 270).

Dunkleberger, C. J., & Tyler, L. E. Interest, stability and personality traits. *Journal of Counseling Psychology*, 1961, *8*, 70–74.

Ebel, R. L. Some empirical data on three points in test theory. *The 12th Yearbook of the National Council on Measurements Used in Education.* The Council, 1955. Pp. 30–34.

Ebel, R. L. Relation of the testing program to educational goals. In "The impact and improvement of school testing programs." Part 2. *The 62nd Yearbook of the NSSE*, 1963. Pp. 28–44.

Ebel, R. L. *Measuring educational achievement.* Englewood Cliffs, N.J.: Prentice-Hall, 1965.

Eckstrand, G. A., & Morgan, R. L. *A study of verbal mediation as a factor in transfer of training.* WADC Technical Report 53–34. Wright Patterson Air Force Base, Ohio: Wright Air Development Center, 1953.

Eisman, B. S. Attitude formation: The development of a color-preference response through mediated generalization. *Journal of Abnormal and Social Psychology*, 1955, *50*, 321–326.

Elkind, D. Giant in the nursery: Jean Piaget. *The New York Times Magazine*, May 26, 1968, Section 6. Pp. 25–27, 50, 52, 54, 59, and 77–80.

Ellis, W. *A source book of Gestalt psychology.* New York: Harcourt Brace, 1939.

Endler, N. S., Boulter, L. R., & Osser, H. (Eds.) *Contemporary issues in developmental psychology.* New York: Holt, Rinehart, and Winston, 1968.

English, H. B., & English, A. C. *A comprehensive dictionary of psychological and psychoanalytical terms.* New York: David McKay, 1958.

Entwistle, D. R. Evaluations of study-skill courses: A review. *Journal of Educational Research*, 1960, *53*, 243–251.

Erikson, E. H. *Childhood and society*. (2nd ed.) New York: W. W. Norton, 1963. (a)

Erikson, E. H. (Ed.) *Youth: Change and challenge*. New York: Basic Books, 1963. (b)

Erlenmeyer-Kimling, L., & Jarvik, L. F. Genetics and intelligence: A review. *Science*, 1963, *142*, 1477–1479.

Estes, W. K. The statistical approach to learning theory. In S. Koch (Ed.), *Psychology: A study of a science*. Vol. 2. *General systematic formulations, learning and special processes*. New York: McGraw-Hill, 1959. Pp. 380–491.

Eysenck, H. J. New ways in psychotherapy. *Psychology Today*, 1967, *1*, 39–47.

Fallon, D., & Battig, W. F. Role of difficulty in rote and concept learning. *Journal of Experimental Psychology*, 1964, *68*, 85–88.

Feather, N. T. Level of aspiration and performance variability. *Journal of Personality and Social Psychology*, 1967, *6*, 37–46.

Feifel, H., & Lorge, I. Qualitative differences in the vocabulary responses of children. *Journal of Educational Psychology*, 1950, *41*, 1–18.

Feigl, H., & Brodbeck, M. (Eds.) *Reading in the philosophy of science*. New York: Appleton-Century-Crofts, 1953.

Feigl, H., & Maxwell, G. (Eds.) *Current issues in the philosophy of science*. New York: Holt, Rinehart, and Winston, 1961.

Festinger, L. The psychological effects of insufficient rewards. *American Psychologist*, 1961, *16*, 1–11.

Festinger, L. Cognitive dissonance. *Scientific American*, 1962, *207*, 94–102.

Festinger, L. *Conflict, decision, and dissonance*. Stanford, Calif.: Stanford University Press, 1964.

Festinger, L., Schachter, S., & Back, K. *Social pressures in informal groups*. New York: Harper, 1950.

Fitts, P. M. Perceptual-motor skill learning. In A. W. Melton (Ed.), *Categories of human learning*. New York: Academic Press, 1964. Pp. 243–285.

Fitts, P. M. Factors in complex skill training. In R. Glaser (Ed.), *Training research and education*. New York: Wiley, 1965. Pp. 175–197.

Fitts, P. M., & Posner, M. I. *Human performance*. Belmont, Calif.: Brooks/Cole, 1967.

Flanagan, J. C., Davis, F. B., Dailey, J. T., Shaycroft, M. F., Orr, D. B., Goldberg, I., & Neyman, C. A., Jr. *The American high-school student*. Pittsburgh: University of Pittsburgh, 1964.

Flanders, N. A. Personal-social anxiety as a factor in experimental learning situations. *Journal of Educational Research*, 1951, *45*, 100–110.

Flavell, J. H. *The developmental psychology of Jean Piaget*. Princeton, N.J.: Van Nostrand, 1963.

Fleishman, E. A. Individual differences and motor learning. In R. M. Gagné (Ed.), *Learning and individual differences*. Columbus, Ohio: Charles E. Merrill, 1967. Pp. 165–191.

Fleishman, E. A., & Hempel, W. E., Jr. Changes in factor structure of a complex psycho-motor test as a function of practice. *Psychometrika*, 1954, 239–252.

Forgus, R. H. The effect of early perceptual learning on the behavioral organization of adult rats. *Journal of Comparative and Physiological Psychology*, 1954, *47*, 331–336.

Fraiberg, S. Tales of the discovery of the secret treasure. *Psychoanalytic Study of the Child*, 1954, *9*, 218–241.

Freedman, S. J., Grunebaum, H. U., & Greenblatt, M. Perceptual and cognitive changes in sensory deprivation. In P. Solomon, *et al.* (Ed.), *Sensory deprivation*. Cambridge, Mass.: Harvard University Press, 1961.

French, E. G. Effects of the interaction of motivation and feedback on task performance. In J. W. Atkinson (Ed.), *Motives in fantasy, action, and society*. Princeton, N.J.: Van Nostrand, 1958. Pp. 400–408.

French, J. R. P. Experimental study of group panic. *Journal of the Elisha Mitchell Science Society*, 1941, *57*, 195–196.

Frenkel-Brunswik, E. Further explorations by a contributor to "The authoritarian personality." In R. Christie & M. Jahoda (Eds.), *Studies in the scope and method of "The authoritarian personality."* Glencoe, Ill.: Free Press, 1954. Pp. 226–275.

Freud, Anna. *The psycho-analytic treatment of children*. London: Imago Publishing Co., 1946.

Freud, S. *The basic writings of Sigmund Freud*. New York: Modern Library, 1938.

Freud, S. *Group psychology and the analysis of the ego*. New York: Hogarth, 1948.

Freud, S. *An outline of psychoanalysis*. New York: Norton, 1949.

Freud, S. The unconscious. In J. Strachey (Ed.), *The standard edition of the complete psychological works of Sigmund Freud*. London: The Hogarth Press, 1957.

Friedman, M. S. Public school: Melting pot or what? *The Teachers College Record*, 1969, *70*, 347–351.

Fromm, E. *The sane society*. New York: Rinehart, 1955.

Furst, B. *The practical way to a better memory*. New York: Fawcett World Library, 1957.

Gage, N. Theories of teaching. In E. R. Hilgard (Ed.), *Theories of learning and instruction*. The 63rd Yearbook of the National Society for the Study of Education. Chicago: University of Chicago Press, 1964. Pp. 268–285.

Gagné, R. M. Military training and principles of learning. *American Psychologist*, 1962, *17*, 83–91.

Gagné, R. M. *The conditions of learning*. New York: Holt, Rinehart and Winston, 1965. (a)

Gagné, R. M. Educational objectives and human performance. In J. D. Krumboltz (Ed.), *Learning and the educational process*. Chicago: Rand McNally, 1965. (b)

Gagné, R. M. Human problem-solving: Internal and external events. In B. Kleinmuntz (Ed.), *Problem-solving: Research, method and theory*. New York: Wiley, 1966. Pp. 128–148.

Gagné, R. M. (Ed.) *Learning and individual differences*. Columbus, Ohio: Charles E. Merrill, 1967.

Gagné, R. M. Contributions of learning to human development. *Psychological Review*, 1968, *75*, 177–191. (a)

Gagné, R. M. Learning hierarchies. *Educational Psychologist*, 1968, *6*, 1–9. (b)

Gagné, R. M., & Brown, L. T. Some factors in the programming of conceptual learning. *Journal of Experimental Psychology*, 1961, *62*, 313–321.

Gallagher, J. J. *Research summary on gifted child education.* Illinois: Office of the Superintendent of Public Instruction, 1966.

Galton, F. *Hereditary genius: An inquiry into its laws and consequences.* London: Macmillan, 1869.

Gardner, E. F., Merwin, J. C., Callis, R., & Madden, R. *Stanford Achievement Test,* Form X, High School Battery. New York: Harcourt, Brace and World, 1965

Gerbner, G. Images across cultures: Teachers in mass media fiction and drama. *School Review,* 1966, 74, 212–230.

Gesell, A. *Infancy and human growth.* New York: Macmillan, 1928.

Gesell, A. Maturation and the patterning of behavior. In C. Murchison (Ed.), *A handbook of child psychology.* (2nd ed.) Worcester, Mass.: Clark University Press, 1933. Pp. 209–235.

Gesell, A. Some observations of developmental stability. *Psychological Monographs,* 1936, 47, No. 212.

Getzels, J. W. Creative thinking, problem-solving and instruction. In E. R. Hilgard (Ed.), *Theories of learning and instruction.* The 63rd Yearbook of the National Society for the Study of Education. Part I. Chicago: 1964. Pp. 240–267.

Getzels, J. W., & Jackson, P. W. *Creativity and intelligence: Explorations with gifted children.* New York: Wiley, 1962.

Getzels, J. W., & Walsh, J. J. The method of paired direct and projective questionnaires in the study of attitude structure and socialization. *Psychological Monographs,* 1958, 72 (1, Whole No. 454).

Gewirtz, J. L., & Baer, D. M. The effect of brief social deprivation on behaviors for a social reinforcer. *Journal of Abnormal and Social Psychology,* 1958, 56, 49–56.

Ghiselin, B. *The creative process.* Berkeley: University of California Press, 1952.

Gibson, E. J. A systematic application of the concepts of generalization and differentiation to verbal learning. *Psychological Review,* 1940, 47, 196–229.

Gibson, E. J., & Walk, R. D. The effect of prolonged exposure to visually presented patterns on learning to discriminate them. *Journal of Comparative and Physiological Psychology,* 1956, 49, 239–242.

Gibson, E. J., Walk, R. D., Pick, H. L., Jr., & Tighe, T. J. The effect of prolonged exposure to visual patterns on learning to discriminate similar and different patterns. *Journal of Comparative and Physiological Psychology,* 1958, 51, 584–587.

Gibson, J. J. *The senses considered as perceptual systems* Boston: Houghton Mifflin, 1966.

Glaser, R. Adapting the elementary curriculum to individual performance. *Proceedings of the 1967 invitational conference on testing problems.* Princeton N.J.: Educational Testing Service, 1968. (a)

Glaser, R. Concept learning and concept teaching. In R. M. Gagné and W. J. Gephart (Eds.), *Learning research and school subjects.* Itasca, Ill.: F. G. Peacock, 1968. Pp. 1–36. (b)

Glennon, V. J., & Hunnicutt, C. W. *What does research say about arithmetic?* Washington, D.C.: Association for Supervision and Curriculum Development, National Education Association, 1952.

Glucksberg, S. Problem solving: Response competition and the influence of drive. *Psychological Reports*, 1964, *15*, 939–942.

Glucksberg, S., & Weisberg, R. W. Verbal behavior and problem solving: Some effects of labeling in a functional fixedness problem. *Journal of Experimental Psychology*, 1966, *71*, 659–664.

Glueck, E. T. Distinguishing delinquents from pseudodelinquents. *Harvard Educational Review*, 1966, *36*, 119–130.

Glueck, S., & Glueck, E. *Predicting delinquency and crime*. Cambridge, Mass.: Harvard University Press, 1959.

Golden, R. I. *Improving English skills of culturally different youths*. Washington, D.C.: United States Government Printing Office, 1964.

Goldfarb, W. Infant rearing as a factor in foster home replacement. *American Journal of Orthopsychiatry*, 1944, *14*, 162–166.

Gollin, E. S. A developmental approach to learning and cognition. In L. P. Lipsitt & C. C. Spiker (Eds.), *Advances in child development and behavior*. Vol. 2. New York: Academic Press, 1965. Pp. 159–184.

Goodlad, J. I., & Anderson, R. H. *The nongraded elementary school*. (Rev. ed.) New York: Harcourt, Brace and World, 1963.

Goodlad, J. I., von Stoephasius, R., & Klein, M. F. *The changing school curriculum*. New York: The Fund for the Advancement of Education, 1966.

Gorow, F. F. *Better classroom testing*. San Francisco: Chandler, 1966.

Goslin, D. A., Epstein, R. R., & Hallock, B. A. *The use of standardized tests in elementary schools*. Technical Report No. 2 on the social consequences of testing. New York: Russell Sage Foundation, 1965.

Goss, A. E. Verbal mediating responses and concept formation. *Psychological Review*, 1961, *68*, 248–274.

Grambs, J. D. The self-concept: Basis for reeducation of Negro youth. In W. C. Kvaraceus (Ed.), *Negro self-concept: Implications for school and citizenship*. New York: McGraw-Hill, 1965. Pp. 11–51.

Grant, N., & Levine, S. (Eds.) *Early experience and behavior: The psychobiology of development*. Springfield, Ill.: Charles C Thomas, 1968.

Gray, S. W., & Klaus, R. A. The early training project and its general rationale. In R. D. Hess & R. Meyer Bear (Eds.), *Early education*. Chicago: Aldine, 1968. Pp. 63–70.

Griffiths, W. *Behavioral difficulties of children as perceived and judged by parents, teachers, and children themselves*. Minneapolis: University of Minnesota Press, 1952.

Grimes, J. W., & Allinsmith, W. Compulsivity, anxiety, and school achievement. *Merrill-Palmer Quarterly*, 1961, *7*, 248–271.

Grissom, R. J. Facilitation of memory by experimental restriction after learning. *American Journal of Psychology*, 1966, *79*, 613–617.

Gronlund, N. E. The accuracy of teachers' judgments concerning the sociometric status of sixth-grade pupils. *Sociometry*, 1950, *13*, (Part I) 197–225, (Part II) 320–357.

Gronlund, N. E. *Measurement and evaluation in teaching*. New York: Macmillan, 1965.

Gronlund, N. E. *Constructing achievement tests*. Englewood Cliffs, N.J.: Prentice-Hall, 1968.

Guide to the use of the General Aptitude Test Battery. Section III: Development. Washington, D.C.: Government Printing Office, 1952–1958.

Guilford, J. P. Three faces of intellect. *American Psychologist*, 1959, *14*, 469–479.

Guilford, J. P. Intelligence: 1965 model. *American Psychologist*, 1966, *21*, 20–26.

Guilford, J. P., Kettner, N. W., & Christensen, P. R. The nature of the general reasoning factor. *Psychological Review*, 1956, *63*, 169–172.

Gulliksen, H. O. The relation of item difficulty and inter-item correlation to test variance and reliability. *Psychometrika*, 1945, *10*, 79–91.

Guthrie, E. R. *The psychology of learning.* (Rev. ed.) New York: Harper, 1952.

Haan, N. Proposed model of ego functioning: Coping and defense mechanism in relationship to IQ change. *Psychological Monographs*, 1963, 77, No. 8.

Haber, R. N. A replication of selective attention and coding in visual perception. *Journal of Experimental Psychology*, 1964, *67*, 402–404.

Hagen, D. Careers and family atmospheres: An empirical test of Roe's theory. *Journal of Counseling Psychology*, 1960, 7, 251–256.

Hall, C. S. *A primer of Freudian psychology.* Cleveland, Ohio: World Publication Co., 1954.

Hall, C. S., & Lindzey, G. *Theories of personality.* New York: Wiley, 1957.

Hall, G. S. *Adolescence: Its psychology, and its relations to physiology, anthropology, sociology, sex, crime, religion, and education.* New York: D. Appleton, 1904. (2 vols.)

Hamachek, D. (Ed.) *The self in growth, teaching, and learning.* Englewood Cliffs, N.J.: Prentice-Hall, 1965.

Harlow, H. F. The formation of learning sets. *Psychological Review*, 1949, *56*, 51–65.

Harlow, H. F. Learning and satiation of response in intrinsically motivated complex puzzle performance by monkeys. *Journal of Comparative and Physiological Psychology*, 1950, *43*, 289–294.

Harlow, H. F., & Harlow, M. K. The affectional systems. In A. M. Schries, *et al.* (Eds.), *Behavior of non-human primates: Modern research trends.* Vol. II. New York: Academic Press, 1965.

Harter, S. Discrimination learning set in children as a function of IQ and MA. *Journal of Experimental Child Psychology*, 1965, *2*, 31–43.

Haugen, E. Bilingualism and bidialectalism. In R. Shuy (Ed.), *Social dialects and language learning.* Champaign, Ill.: National Council of Teachers of English, 1964.

Havighurst, R. J., Robinson, M. Z., & Dorr, M. The development of the ideal self in childhood and adolescence. *Journal of Educational Research*, 1946, *40*, 241–257.

Havighurst, R. J. *Human development and education.* New York: Longmans, Green, 1953.

Healy, W., Bronner, A., & Bowers, A. M. *The structure and meaning of psycho-analysis, as related to personality and behavior.* London: Knopf, 1930.

Hebb, D. O. The forms and conditions of chimpanzee anger. *Bulletin of Canadian Psychological Association*, 1945, *5*, 32–35.

Hebb, D. O. *The organization of behavior: A neuropsychological theory.* New York: Wiley, 1949.

Hebb, D. O. A neuropsychological theory. In S. Koch (Ed.), *Psychology: A study of a science.* Vol. I. *Sensory, perceptual, and physiological formulations.* New York: McGraw-Hill, 1959. Pp. 622–643.

Hebb, D. O. *A textbook of psychology.* (2nd ed.) Philadelphia: W. B. Saunders, 1966.

Hebb, D. O., & Foord, E. N. Errors of visual recognition and the nature of the trace. *Journal of Experimental Psychology,* 1945, *35,* 335–348.

Hechinger, F. M. (Ed.) *Pre-school education today.* Garden City, N.Y.: Doubleday, 1966.

Heidbreder, E. The attainment of concepts: I. Terminology and methodology. *Journal of General Psychology,* 1946, *35,* 173–189.

Heintz, E. His father is only the janitor! *The Phi Delta Kappan,* 1954, *35,* 265–270.

Held, R., & White, B. L. Competence and sensory motor development. Paper presented to Committee on Socialization and Social Structure, Social Science Research Councils, April 30, 1965.

Helson, H. *Adaptation-level theory.* New York: Harper & Row, 1964.

Helson, H. Some problems in motivation from the point of view of the theory of adaptation level. In D. Levine (Ed.), *Nebraska Symposium on Motivation.* Lincoln: University of Nebraska Press, 1966. Pp. 137–182.

Henry, J. *Culture against man.* New York: Random House, 1963.

Hess, E. H. Imprinting: An effect of early experience, imprinting determines later social behavior in animals. *Science,* 1959, *130,* 133–141.

Hess, R. D., & Bear, R. M. *Early education.* Chicago: Aldine, 1968.

Hess, R. D., & Shipman, V. C. Early experience and the socialization of cognitive modes in children. *Child Development,* 1965, *36,* 869–886. (a)

Hess, R. D., & Shipman, V. C. Early blocks to children's learning. *Children,* 1965, *12,* 189–194. (b)

Hess, R. D., & Shipman, V. C. Cognitive elements in maternal behavior. In J. P. Hill (Ed.), *Minnesota symposium on child psychology.* Minneapolis: University of Minnesota Press, 1967.

Hesse, M. B. *Models and analogies in science.* London: Sheed, 1963.

Hildreth, G. The difficulty reduction tendency in perception and problem-solving. *Journal of Educational Psychology,* 1941, *32,* 305–313.

Hilgard, E. R. The nature of the conditioned response: I. The case for and against stimulus-substitution. *Psychological Review,* 1936, *43,* 366–385.

Hilgard, E. R. *Introduction to psychology.* (3rd ed.) New York: Harcourt, Brace and World, Inc., 1962.

Hilgard, E. (Ed.) *Theories of learning and instruction.* 63rd Yearbook of the National Society for the Study of Education, Part I. Chicago: University of Chicago Press, 1964.

Hilgard, E. R., & Bower, G. H. *Theories of learning.* (3rd ed.) New York: Appleton-Century-Crofts, 1966.

Hilgard, E. R., Irvine, R. P., & Whipple, J. E. Rote memorization, understanding, and transfer: An extension of Katona's card-trick experiments. *Journal of Experimental Psychology,* 1953, *46,* 288–292.

Hill, W. F. Comments on Taylor's "drive theory and manifest anxiety." *Psychological Bulletin*, 1957, *54*, 490–493.

Hill, W. F. *Learning: A survey of psychological interpretations.* San Francisco: Chandler, 1963.

Hillson, J. S., & Worchel, P. Self concept and defensive behavior in the maladjusted. *Journal of Consulting Psychology*, 1957, *21*, 83–88.

Hively, W. Implications for the classroom of B. F. Skinner's analysis of behavior. *Harvard Educational Review*, 1959, *29*, 37–42.

Hoffman, L. H., & Hoffman, M. L. (Eds.) *Review of child development research.* New York: Russell Sage Foundation, (Vol. I) 1964, (Vol. 2) 1966.

Holland, J. G., & Skinner, B. F. *The analysis of behavior: A program for self-instruction.* New York: McGraw Hill, 1961.

Holland, J. L. *Manual for the Vocational Preference Inventory.* Palo Alto: Consulting Psychologists Press, 1958. (Now published by Educational Research Associates, Iowa City, Iowa.)

Holland, J. L. Some explorations of a theory of vocational choice: I. One- and two-year longitudinal studies. *Psychological Monographs*, 1962, *76* (26, Whole No. 545).

Holland, J. L. *The psychology of vocational choice.* Waltham, Mass.: Blaisdell, 1966.

Hollingworth, L. S. *Children above 180 IQ.* Yonkers-on-the-Hudson, N.Y.: World, 1942.

Horn, C. A., & Smith, L. F. The Horn Art Aptitude Inventory. *Journal of Applied Psychology*, 1945, *29*, 350–355.

Horn, J. L., & Morrison, W. L. Dimensions of teacher attitudes. *Journal of Educational Psychology*, 1965, *56*, 118–125.

Horney, K. *Neurosis and human growth.* New York: W. W. Norton, 1950.

Horrocks, J. E. *The psychology of adolescence: Behavior and development.* (3rd ed.) Boston: Houghton Mifflin, 1969.

Horrocks, J. E. *Assessment of behavior: The methodology and content of psychological measurement.* Columbus, Ohio: C. E. Merrill Books, 1964.

Hovland, C. I., & Janis, I. L. (Eds.) *Personality and persuasibility.* New Haven: Yale University Press, 1959.

Hull, C. L. Quantitative aspects of the evolution of concepts: An experimental study. *Psychological Monographs*, 1920, *28*, Whole No. 123.

Hull, C. L. *Principles of behavior.* New York: Appleton-Century, 1943.

Hull, C. L. *Essentials of behavior.* New Haven: Yale University Press, 1951.

Hull, C. L. *A behavior system.* New Haven: Yale University Press, 1952.

Hunt, J. McV. *Intelligence and experience.* New York: Ronald, 1961.

Ingersoll, R. W., & Peters, H. J. Predictive indices of the GATB. *Personnel and Guidance Journal*, 1966, *44*, 931–937.

Isaacson, R. L. Relation between n achievement, test anxiety, and curricular choices. *Journal of Abnormal and Social Psychology*, 1964, *68*, 447–452.

Jackson, P. W., & Getzels, J. W. Psychological health and classroom functioning: A study of dissatisfaction with school among adolescents. *Journal of Educational Psychology*, 1959, *50*, 295–300.

Jahoda, M. *Current concepts of positive mental health.* New York: Basic Books, 1958.

James, W. *The principles of psychology.* Vol. 1. New York: Henry Holt, 1918.

Jennings, H. H. *Sociometry in group relations: A manual for teachers.* Washington, D.C.: American Council on Education, 1958.

Jensen, A. R. Learning ability in retarded, average, and gifted children. *Merrill-Palmer Quarterly,* 1963, *9,* 123–140. (a)

Jensen, A. R. Learning in the preschool years. *Journal of Nursery Education,* 1963, *18,* 133–138. (b)

Jensen, A. R. Social class and verbal learning. In M. Deutsch and T. Pettigrew (Eds.), *Social class, race, and psychological development.* Society for the Study of Psychological Issues, 1965.

Jensen, A. R. Learning ability, intelligence, and educability. In V. L. Allen (Ed.), *Psychological factors in poverty.* Glencoe, Ill.: Free Press, 1968. (a)

Jensen, A. R. Social class and verbal learning. In M. Deutsch, I. Katz, and A. Jensen (Eds.), *Social class, race, and psychological development.* New York: Holt, Rinehart, and Winston, 1968. Pp. 115–174. (b)

Jersild, A. T. *In search of self: An exploration of the role of the school in promoting self-understanding.* New York: Bureau of Publications, Teachers College, Columbia University, 1952.

Jersild, A. T. *When teachers face themselves.* New York: Bureau of Publications, Teachers College, Columbia University, 1955.

Jersild, A. T., & Tasch, R. J. *Children's interests and what they suggest for education.* New York: Bureau of Publications, Teachers College, Columbia University, 1949.

John, V. P. The intellectual development of slum children: Some preliminary findings. *American Journal of Orthopsychiatry,* 1963, *33,* 813–822.

Johnson, D. M. *The psychology of thought and judgment.* New York: Harper, 1955.

Johnson, W. (Ed.) *Stuttering in children and adults.* Minneapolis: University of Minnesota Press, 1955.

Jones, E. E. *Ingratiation: A social psychological analysis.* New York: Appleton-Century-Crofts, 1964.

Jones, M. C. A report on three growth studies at the University of California. *Gerontologist,* 1967, *7,* 49–54.

Jordaan, J. P. Exploratory behavior: The formation of self and occupational concepts. In D. E. Super, R. Starishevsky, N. Matlin, & J. P. Jordaan (Eds.), *Career development: Self-concept theory.* New York: College Entrance Examination Board, 1963. Pp. 42–78.

Joy, E. S. *A book about me.* Chicago: Science Research Associates, 1952.

Kagan, J. A developmental approach to conceptual growth. In H. J. Klausmeier and C. W. Harris (Eds.), *Analyses of concept learning.* New York: Academic Press, 1966. Pp. 97–115.

Kagan, J., and Moss, H. A. *Birth to maturity: A study in psychological development.* New York: Wiley, 1962.

Katona, G. *Organizing and memorizing; studies in the psychology of learning and teaching.* New York: Columbia University Press, 1940.

Katz, M. *Decisions and values: A rationale for secondary school guidance.* New York: College Entrance Examination Board, 1963.

Katz, M. *The name and nature of vocational guidance.* Princeton, N.J.: Educational Testing Service, 1966.

Kausler, D. H. Aspiration level as a determinant of performance. *Journal of Personality,* 1959, *27,* 346–351.

Keach, E. T., Fulton, R., and Gardner, W. E. (Eds.) *Education and social crisis: Perspectives on teaching disadvantaged youth.* New York: Wiley, 1967.

Keliher, Alice V. *Life and growth.* New York: Appleton-Century-Crofts, 1938.

Kelley, T. L., Madden, R., Gardner, E. F., & Rudman, H. C. *Stanford Achievement Test,* Form W. Intermediate II, Complete Battery. New York: Harcourt, Brace, and World, 1964.

Kellogg, C. E., & Morton, N. W. *Revised Beta Examination.* New York: Psychological Corporation, 1957.

Kendler, H. H. The concept of the concept. In A. W. Melton (Ed.), *Categories of human learning.* New York: Academic Press, 1964. Pp. 211–236.

Kendler, H. H. *Basic psychology.* (2nd ed.) New York: Appleton-Century-Crofts, 1968.

Kendler, H. H., Greenberg, A., & Richman, H. The influence of massed and distributed practice on the development of mental set. *Journal of Experimental Psychology,* 1952, *43,* 21–25.

Kendler, H. H., & Kendler, T. S. Vertical and horizontal processes in problem solving. *Psychological Review,* 1962, *69,* 1–16.

Kennedy, W. A., & Willcutt, H. C. Praise and blame as incentives. *Psychological Bulletin,* 1964, *62,* 323–332.

Keppel, G. Facilitation in short- and long-term retention of paired associates following distributed practice in learning. *Journal of Verbal Learning and Verbal Behavior,* 1964, *3,* 91–111. (a)

Keppel, G. Verbal learning in children. *Psychological Bulletin,* 1964, *61,* 63–80. (b)

Keppel, G., & Underwood, B. J. Proactive inhibition in short-term retention of single items. *Journal of Verbal Learning and Verbal Behavior,* 1962, *1,* 153–161.

Kersh, B. Y. The motivating effect of learning by directed discovery. *Journal of Educational Psychology,* 1962, *53,* 65–71.

Kersh, B. Y. Programing classroom instruction. In R. Glaser (Ed.), *Teaching machines and programed learning, II: Data and directions.* Washington, D.C.: National Education Association, 1965.

Kersh, B. Y., & Wittrock, M. C. Learning by discovery: An interpretation of recent research. *Journal of Teacher Education,* 1962, *13,* 461–468.

Kessen, W. *The child.* New York: Wiley, 1965.

Kimble, G. A. *Hilgard and Marquis' conditioning and learning.* (2nd ed.) New York: Appleton-Century-Crofts, 1961.

Kimble, G. A., & Garmezy, N. *Principles of general psychology.* New York: Ronald, 1968.

King, P., Norrell, G., & Powers, G. P. Relationships between twin scales on the SVIB and the Kuder. *Journal of Counseling Psychology,* 1963, *10,* 395–401.

Kirchner, W. K. "Real-life" faking on the Strong Vocational Interest Blank by sales applicants. *Journal of Applied Psychology,* 1961, *45,* 273–276.

Kluckhohn, F. R., & Strodtbeck, F. L. *Variations in value orientations*. Evanston, Ill.: Row, Peterson, and Co., 1961.

Koch, S. (Ed.) *Psychology: A study of a science*. Vol. I. New York: McGraw-Hill, 1959.

Koffka, K. *Principles of Gestalt psychology*. New York: Harcourt, Brace, 1935.

Kogan, N., & Wallach, M. A. *Risk taking: A study in cognition and thinking*. New York: Holt, Rinehart, and Winston, 1964.

Kohlberg, L. Moral development and identification. In H. Stevenson (Ed.), *Child psychology*. Chicago: National Society for the Study of Education, 1963.

Kohlberg, L. Montessori with the culturally disadvantaged: A cognitive-developmental interpretation and some research findings. In R. D. Hess & R. M. Bear (Eds.), *Early education*. Chicago: Aldine, 1968. Pp. 105–118.

Kohn, M. L. Social class and parental values. *American Journal of Sociology*, 1959, *64*, 337–351.

Kohnstamm, G. A. An evaluation of part of Piaget's theory. In I. E. Sigel & F. H. Hooper (Eds.), *Logical thinking in children*. New York: Holt, Rinehart, and Winston, 1968. Pp. 394–423.

Kolb, D. A. Achievement motivation training for underachieving high school boys. *Journal of Personality and Social Psychology*, 1965, *2*, 783–792.

Kounin, J. S., Gump, P. V., & Ryan, J. J. Explorations in classroom management. *Journal of Teacher Education*, 1961, *12*, 235–246.

Krathwohl, D. R., Bloom, B. S., & Masia, B. B. (Eds.) *Taxonomy of educational objectives. Handbook II: Affective domain*. New York: David McKay, 1964.

Krech, D., Rosenzweig, M. R., & Bennett, E. L. Effects of environmental complexity and training on brain chemistry. *Journal of Comparative and Physiological Psychology*, 1960, *53*, 509–519.

Krueger, W. C. F. The effect of overlearning on retention. *Journal of Experimental Psychology*, 1929, *12*, 71–78.

Kuder, G. F. *Kuder Preference Record: Vocational: Form CH*. Chicago: Science Research Associates, 1948.

Kuder, G. F. *Kuder Preference Record: Vocational: Manual*. Chicago: Science Research Associates, 1956.

Kuder, G. F. Administrator's manual. *Kuder Preference Record: Vocational: Form C*. Chicago: Science Research Associates, 1960.

Kuder, G. F. A rationale for evaluating interests. *Educational and Psychological Measurement*, 1963, *23*, 3–12.

Kuenne, M. R. Experimental investigation of the relation of language behavior to transposition behavior in young children. *Journal of Experimental Psychology*, 1946, *36*, 471–490.

Kuhlen, R. G., & Lee, B. J. Personality characteristics and social acceptability in adolescence. *Journal of Educational Psychology*, 1943, *34*, 321–340.

Kuhlmann, C. K. *Visual imagery in children*. Unpublished doctoral dissertation, Radcliffe College, 1960.

Kvaraceus, W. C. *The community and the delinquent: Co-operative approaches to preventing and controlling delinquency*. Yonkers-on-the-Hudson, N.Y.: World, 1954.

Labov, W. Stages in the acquisition of Standard English. In R. Shuy (Ed.), *Social dialects and language learning.* Champaign, Ill.: National Council of Teachers of English, 1964. Pp. 77–103.

Lazarus, A. L. Grouping based on high interest versus general ability: A senior high school teacher's viewpoint. *California Journal of Secondary Education,* 1955, *30,* 38–41.

Lazarus, R. S. *Psychological stress and the coping process.* New York: McGraw-Hill, 1966.

Lazarus, R. S., Deese, J., & Osler, S. F. The effects of psychological stress upon performance. *Psychological Bulletin,* 1952, *49,* 293–317.

Lee, D. Being and value in a primitive culture. In C. E. Moustakas (Ed.) *The self: Explorations in personal growth.* New York: Harper, 1956.

Lees, R. B. The promise of transformational grammar. *English Journal,* 1963, *52,* 327–330.

Lefcourt, H. M. Internal versus external control of reinforcement: A review. *Psychological Bulletin,* 1966, *65,* 206–220.

Lenneberg, E. H. *Biological foundations of language.* New York: Wiley, 1967.

Lenzen, V. F. Procedures of empirical science. In O. Neurath, R. Carnap, & C. Morris (Eds.), *International encyclopedia of unified science.* Vol. I, Part 1. Chicago, Ill.: University of Chicago Press, 1955.

Lester, O. P. Mental set in relation to retroactive inhibition. *Journal of Experimental Psychology,* 1932, *15,* 681–699.

Leventhal, H., & Perloe, S. I. A relationship between self-esteem and persuasibility. *Journal of Abnormal and Social Psychology,* 1962, *64,* 385–388.

Lévi-Strauss, C. *Structural anthropology.* New York: Basic Books, 1963.

Levin, H. M. What difference do schools make? *Saturday Review,* 1968, *60,* 57–58.

Levin, H. M., Watson, J. S., & Feldman, M. Writing as pretraining for association learning. *Journal of Educational Psychology,* 1964, *55,* 181–184.

Levine, S., & Otis, L. The effect of handling before and after weaning on the resistance of albino rats to later deprivation. *Canadian Journal of Psychology,* 1958, *12,* 103–108.

Levitt, E. E. Effect of a "causal" teacher training program on authoritarianism and responsibility in grade school children. *Psychological Reports,* 1955, *1,* 449–458.

Levitt, E. E. *The psychology of anxiety.* Indianapolis: Bobbs-Merrill, 1967.

Levitt, E. E., & Ojemann, R. H. The aims of preventive psychiatry and "causality" as a personality pattern. *Journal of Psychology,* 1953, *36,* 393–400.

Lewin, K. *A dynamic theory of personality.* New York: McGraw-Hill, 1935.

Lewin, K. Group decision and social change. In G. Swanson, T. M. Newcomb, & E. L. Hartley (Eds.), *Readings in social psychology.* (Rev. ed.) New York: Holt, 1952. Pp. 459–473.

Lewin, K., Dembo, T., Festinger, L., & Sears, P. S. Level of aspiration. In J. McV. Hunt (Ed.), *Personality and behavior disorders.* New York: Ronald, 1944. Pp. 333–378.

Lindell, E. *The Swedish handwriting method.* Copenhagen, Denmark: Ejnar Munksgaard, 1964.

Lindeman, R. H. *Educational measurement.* Chicago: Scott, Foresman, 1967.

Lindquist, E. F., & Hieronymus, A. N. *Iowa Tests of Basic Skills (Multi-level edition for grades 3–9)*. Boston: Houghton Mifflin, 1964.

Lindsley, O. R. Direct measurement and prosthesis of retarded behavior. *Journal of Education*, 1964, *147*, 62–81.

Locke, J. *An essay concerning human understanding*. London: E. Holt for T. Basset, 1690.

Logan, F. A. Elements of a theory for educational psychology. Unpublished dittoed report, 1968.

Lohnes, P. *Measuring adolescent personality*. Pittsburgh: University of Pittsburgh Press, 1966.

Lorenz, C. Comments on Professor Piaget's paper. In J. M. Tanner & B. Inhelder (Eds.), *Discussions on child development*. Vol. 4. London: Tavistock, 1960. Pp. 28–29, 31.

Lorge, I., & Thorndike, R. L. *Lorge-Thorndike Intelligence Tests Manual*. Boston: Houghton Mifflin, 1954–1957.

Lorge, I., Thorndike, R. L., & Hagen, E. The *Lorge-Thorndike Intelligence Tests*, Verbal and Nonverbal Batteries. Form 1, Levels A-H. Boston: Houghton Mifflin, 1964.

Luchins, A. S. Mechanization in problem solving: The effect of *Einstellung*. *Psychological Monographs*, 1942, *54*, (6, Whole No. 248).

Luh, C. W. The conditions of retention. *Psychological Monographs*, 1922, *31*, No. 142.

Luria, A. R. *The role of speech in the regulation of normal and abnormal behavior*. (Edited by J. Tizard.) New York: Liverwright, 1961.

Mager, R. F. *Preparing instruction objectives*. Palo Alto, Calif.: Fearon, 1962.

Maier, N. R. F. Reasoning in humans. I. On direction. *Journal of Comparative Psychology*, 1930, *10*, 115–143.

Maier, N. R. F. An aspect of human reasoning. *British Journal of Psychology*, 1933, *24*, 144–155.

Maier, N. R. F. Reasoning in children. *Journal of Comparative Psychology*, 1936, *21*, 357–366.

Maltzman, I. Thinking: From a behavioristic point of view. *Psychological Review*, 1955, *62*, 275–286.

Maltzman, I. On the training of originality. *Psychological Review*, 1960, *67*, 229–242.

Maltzman, I. Individual differences in "attention": The orienting reflex. In R. M. Gagné (Ed.), *Learning and individual differences*. Columbus: Charles E. Merrill, 1967. Pp. 94–116.

Maltzman, I., Fox., J., & Morrisett, L., Jr. Some effects of manifest anxiety on mental set. *Journal of Experimental Psychology*, 1953, *46*, 50–54.

Mandler, G. Verbal learning. *New directions in psychology* III. New York: Holt, Rinehart, and Winston, 1966.

Mandler, G., & Sarason, S. B. A study of anxiety and learning. *Journal of Abnormal and Social Psychology*, 1952, *47*, 166–173.

Mannheim, B. F. Reference groups, membership groups and the self image. *Sociometry*, 1966, *29*, 265–279.

Marshall, J. C. Composition errors and essay examination grades re-examined. *American Educational Research Journal*, 1967, *4*, 375–385.

Marx, M. (Ed.) *Theories in contemporary psychology*. New York: Macmillan, 1963.

Maslow, A. H. *Motivation and personality*. New York: Harper, 1954.

Maslow, A. H. Self-actualizing people: A study of psychological health. In C. E. Moustakas (Ed.), *The self: Explorations in personal growth*. New York: Harper, 1956. Pp. 169–194.

Maslow, A. H. *Toward a psychology of being*. Princeton, N.J.: Van Nostrand, 1962.

Maslow, A. H. *Religions, values, and peak-experiences*. Columbus, Ohio: Ohio State University Press, 1964.

Maslow, A. H. A theory of metamotivation: The biological rooting of the value life. *Journal of Humanistic Psychology*, 1967, 7, 93–127.

McAllister, D. E. The effects of various kinds of relevant verbal pretraining on subsequent motor performance. *Journal of Experimental Psychology*, 1953, 46, 329–336.

McCarthy, D. Language development of the preschool child. *Institute of Child Welfare Monographs*, No. 4. Minneapolis: University of Minnesota Press, 1930.

McClelland, D., Atkinson, J. W., Clark, R. A., & Lowell, E. L. *The achievement motive*. New York: Appleton-Century-Crofts, 1953.

McClelland, D. C. (Ed.) *Studies in motivation*. New York: Appleton-Century-Crofts, 1955.

McClelland, D. C. *The achieving society*. Princeton, N.J.: Van Nostrand, 1961.

McClelland, D. C. Toward a theory of motive acquisition. *American Psychologist*, 1965, 20, 321–333.

McDavid, R. I., Jr. Social dialects: Cause or symptom of social maladjustment. In R. Shuy (Ed.), *Social dialects and language learning*: Proceedings of the Bloomington, Indiana conference. Champaign, Ill.: National Council of Teachers of English, 1964. Pp. 3–7.

McGaugh, J. L., & Hostetter, R. C. *Retention as a function of the temporal position of sleep and activity following waking*. 1961. Unpublished manuscript. (Reported in E. R. Hilgard, *Introduction to Psychology*. New York: Harcourt, Brace, and World, 1962.)

McGraw, M. B. *The neuromuscular maturation of the human infant*. New York: Columbia University Press, 1943. (Reprinted in 1962 by Hafner Publishing Co.)

McNeill, D. M. Developmental linguistics. In F. Smith & G. A. Miller (Eds.), *The genesis of language: A psycholinguistics approach*. Cambridge: MIT Press, 1966. Pp. 15–84.

McNemar, Q. Lost: Our intelligence? Why? *American Psychologist*, 1964, 19, 871–882.

Mech, E. V., Hurst, F. M., Auble, J. D., & Fattu, N. A. *An experimental analysis of patterns of differential verbal reinforcement in classroom situations*. School of Education Bulletins, Vol. 29, No. 5. Bloomington, Ind.: Indiana University, Division of Research and Field Service, 1953.

Mechanic, D. *Students under stress: A study of the social psychology of adaptation*. New York: Free Press, 1962.

Medley, D. M., & Mitzel, H. E. Some behavioral correlates of teacher effective-ness. *Journal of Educational Psychology*, 1959, *50*, 239–246.

Mednick, S. A. The associative basis of the creative process. *Psychological Review*, 1962, *69*, 220–232.

Mehler, J., Bever, T. G. Cognitive capacity of very young children. *Science*, 1967, *158*, 141–142.

Melton, A. W. Learning. In W. S. Monroe (Ed.), *Encyclopedia of educational research*. New York: Macmillan, 1950. Pp. 668–690.

Mendel, G. Choice of play objects as a function of their degree of novelty. Unpublished doctoral dissertation, University of Chicago, 1962.

Menninger, W. C. Self-understanding for teachers. *National Education Association Journal*, 1953, *42*, 331–333.

Meyer, W. J., & Thompson, G. G. Sex differences in the distribution of teacher approval and disapproval among sixth-grade children. *Journal of Educational Psychology*, 1956, *47*, 385–396.

Meyers, C. E., & Dingman, H. F. The structure of abilities at preschool ages: Hypothesized domains. *Psychological Bulletin*, 1960, *57*, 514–532.

Miles, C. C. Gifted children. In L. Carmichael (Ed.), *Manual of child psychology*. New York: Wiley, 1954. Pp. 984–1063.

Milholland, J. E., & Womer, F. B. The relation of ninth and tenth grade Differential Aptitude Test scores to choices of academic majors at the University of Michigan. *Journal of Educational Measurement*, 1965, *2*, 65–68.

Miller, D. R., & Swanson, G. *The changing American parent: A study in the Detroit area*. New York: Wiley, 1958.

Miller, G. A. The magical number seven, plus or minus two: Some limits on our capacity for processing information. *Psychological Review*, 1965, *63*, 81–97.

Miller, G. A. *Psychology: The science of mental life*. New York: Harper & Row, 1962.

Miller, G. A., Galanter, E., & Pribram, K. H. *Plans and the structure of behavior*. New York: Henry Holt, 1960.

Miller, N. E. Theory and experiment relating psychoanalytic displacement to stimulus-response generalization. *Journal of Abnormal and Social Psychology*, 1948, *43*, 155–178. (a)

Miller, N. E. Studies of fear as an acquirable drive: I. Fear as motivation and fear-reduction as reinforcement in the learning of new responses. *Journal of Experimental Psychology*, 1948, *38*, 89–101. (b)

Miller, N. E. Liberalization of basic S-R concepts: Extensions to conflict behavior, motivation, and social learning. In S. Koch (Ed.), *Psychology: A study of a science*. Vol. 2. New York: McGraw-Hill, 1959. Pp. 92–157.

Miller, N. E. Learning of visceral and glandular responses. *Science*, 1969, *163*, 434–445.

Miller, W. B. Lower-class culture as a generating milieu of gang delinquency. *Journal of Social Issues*, 1958, *14*, 3.

Milton, O. Two-year follow-up: Objective data after learning without class attendance. *Psychological Reports*, 1962, *11*, 833–836.

Mittman, L. R., & Terrell, G. An experimental study of curiosity in children. *Child Development*, 1964, *35*, 851–855.

Moore, O. K. Autotelic responsive environments and exceptional children. In O. J. Harvey (Ed.), *Experience, structure, and adaptability.* New York: Springer Publishing Co., 1966. Chapter 9.

Moreno, J. L. *Who shall survive? Foundations of sociometry, group psychotherapy and sociodrama.* (2nd ed.) Beacon, N.Y.: Beacon House, 1953.

Morgan, C. *Introduction to psychology.* New York: McGraw-Hill, 1961.

Mori, T. Structure of motivations for becoming a teacher. *Journal of Educational Psychology,* 1965, *56,* 175–183.

Morphett, M. V., & Washburne, C. When should children learn to read? *Elementary School Journal,* 1931, *31,* 496–503.

Morris, C. *Signs, language, and behavior.* New York: Prentice-Hall, 1946.

Morrisett, L., Jr., & Hovland, C. I. A comparison of three varieties of training in human problem solving. *Journal of Experimental Psychology,* 1959, *58,* 52–55.

Moustakas, C. E. *The teacher and the child: Personal interaction in the classroom.* New York: McGraw-Hill, 1956.

Mowrer, O. H *Learning theory and personality dynamics.* New York: Ronald, 1950.

Mowrer, O. H. *Learning theory and behavior.* New York: Wiley, 1960. (a)

Mowrer, O. H. *Learning theory and the symbolic processes.* New York: Wiley, 1960. (b)

Mullahy, P. *A study of interpersonal relations: New contributions to psychiatry.* (1st ed.) New York: Hermitage Press, 1949.

Murdock, B. B., Jr. The retention of individual items. *Journal of Experimental Psychology.* 1961, *62,* 618–625.

Murray, E. J. *Motivation and emotion.* Englewood Cliffs, N.J.: Prentice-Hall, 1964.

Murray, H. A. *Explorations in personality.* New York: Oxford University Press, 1938.

Mussen, P. H., Conger, J. J., & Kagan, J. *Child development and personality.* (2nd ed.) New York: Harper & Row, 1963.

Mussen, P. H., & Porter, L. W. Personal motivations and self-conceptions associated with effectiveness and ineffectiveness in emergent groups. *Journal of Abnormal and Social Psychology,* 1959, *59,* 23–27.

Nagel, E. *The structure of science: Problems in the logic of scientific explanation.* New York: Harcourt, Brace, and World, 1961.

Neubauer, Peter B. (Ed.) *Children in collectives: Childrearing aims and practices in the Kibbutz.* Springfield, Ill.: Charles C Thomas, 1965.

Newman, H. H., Freeman, F. N., & Holzinger, K. J. *Twins: A study of heredity and environment.* Chicago: University of Chicago Press, 1937.

Niemeyer, J. Some guidelines to desirable elementary school reorganization. *Programs for the educationally disadvantaged.* Washington, D.C.: U.S. Office of Education Bulletin, 1963, No. 17. P. 81.

Noble, C. E. Meaningfulness and familiarity. In C. N. Cofer & B. S. Musgrave (Eds.), *Verbal behavior and learning: Problems and processes.* New York: McGraw-Hill, 1963. Pp. 76–119.

Noll, V. H. *Introduction to educational measurement.* (2nd ed.) Boston: Houghton Mifflin, 1965.

Nunnally, J. C., Duchnowski, A. J., & Parker, R. K. Association of neutral objects with rewards: Effect on verbal evaluation, reward expectancy, and selective attention. *Journal of Personality and Social Psychology*, 1965, *1*, 270–273.

Nunnally, J. C., & Faw, T. T. The acquisition of conditioned reward value in discrimination learning. *Child Development*, 1968, *39*, 159–166.

Ojemann, R. H., Levitt, E. E., Lyle, W. H., Jr., & Whiteside, M. F. The effects of a "causal" teacher-training program and certain curricular changes on grade school children. *Journal of Experimental Education*, 1955, *24*, 95–114.

Orne, M. T. On the social psychology of the psychological experiment: With particular reference to demand characteristics and their implications. *American Psychologist*, 1962, *17*, 776–783.

Osborn, A. F. *Applied imagination: Principles and procedures of creative thinking*. New York: Charles Scribner's Sons, 1953. (Rev. ed., 1962.)

Osgood, C. E. The similarity paradox in human learning: A resolution. *Psychological Review*, 1949, *56*, 132–143.

Osgood C. E. The nature and measurement of meaning. *Psychological Bulletin*, 1952, *49*, 197–237.

Osgood, C. E. *Method and theory in experimental psychology*. New York: Oxford University Press, 1953.

Osgood, C. E., & Miron, M. S. Language behavior: The multivariate structure of qualification. In R. B. Cattell (Ed.), *Handbook of multivariate experimental psychology*. Chicago: Rand McNally, 1966. Pp. 790–819.

Osgood, C. E., Suci, G. J., & Tannenbaum, P. H. *The measurement of meaning*. Urbana, Ill.: University of Illinois Press, 1957.

Otis, A. S., & Lennon, R. T. *Otis-Lennon Mental Ability Test. Form Jr. Elementary II Level and Intermediate Level*. New York: Harcourt, Brace, and World, 1966.

Overing, R. L., & Travers, R. M. W. Effect upon transfer of variations in training conditions. *Journal of Educational Psychology*, 1966, *57*, 179–188.

Overing, R. L., & Travers, R. M. W. Variation in the amount of irrelevant cues in training and test conditions and the effect upon transfer. *Journal of Educational Psychology*, 1967, *58*, 62–68.

Overmier, J. B., & Seligman, M. E. P. Effects of inescapable shock on subsequent escape and avoidance responding. *Journal of Comparative and Physiological Psychology*, 1967, *63*, 28–33.

Page, E. B. Teacher comments and student performance: A seventy-four classroom experiment in school motivation. *Journal of Educational Psychology*, 1958, *49*, 173–181.

Paivio, A., Yuille, J. C., & Madigan, S. A. Concreteness, imagery, and meaningfulness: Values for 925 nouns. *Journal of Experimental Psychology Monograph Supplement*, 1968, *76*, No. 1, Part 2.

Parnes, S. J. Effects of extended efforts in creative problem solving. *Journal of Educational Psychology*, 1961, *52*, 117–122.

Parnes, S. J., & Meadow, A. Effects of "brainstorming" instructions on creative problem solving by trained and untrained subjects. *Journal of Educational Psychology*, 1959, *50*, 171–176.

Patrick, J. R. Studies in rational behavior and emotional excitement: II. The effect of emotional excitement on rational behavior in human subjects. *Journal of Comparative Psychology*, 1934, *18*, 153–195.

Patterson, G. R. Parents as dispensers of aversive stimuli. *Journal of Personality and Social Psychology*, 1965, *2*, 844–851.

Pavlov, I. P. (Trans. and edited by G. V. Anrep.) *Conditioned reflexes: An investigation of the physiological activity of the cerebral cortex.* London: Oxford University Press, 1927.

Pavlov, I. P. *Experimental psychology and other essays.* New York: Philosophical Library, 1957.

Peck, R. F., & Havighurst, R. J. *The psychology of character development.* New York: Wiley, 1960.

Peiper, A. *Cerebral function in infancy and childhood.* (Trans. of 3rd ed. by B. & H. Nagler.) New York: Consultants Bureau Enterprises, 1963.

Peterson, L. R., & Peterson. M. J. Short-term retention of individual verbal items. *Journal of Experimental Psychology*, 1959, *58*, 193–198.

Pettigrew, T. F. Social evaluation theory: Convergences and applications. In D. Levine (Ed.), *Nebraska Symposium on Motivation*, 1967. Pp. 241–311.

Pettigrew, T. F. Race and equal educational opportunity. *Harvard Educational Review*, 1968, *38*, 66–76.

Physical Science Study Committee. *Physics.* (2nd ed.) Boston: D. C. Heath, 1965.

Piaget, J. *The moral judgment of the child.* London: Kegan Paul, 1932.

Piaget, J. *The child's conception of number.* London: Routledge and Kegan Paul Ltd., 1952. (a)

Piaget, J. *The origins of intelligence in children.* New York: International Universities Press, 1952. (b)

Piaget, J. (Trans. J. & A. Tomlinson.) *The child's conception of the world.* Paterson, N.J.: Littlefield, Adams, 1960.

Pinneau, S. R. Changes in the intelligence quotient with age. *Testing today.* No. 6. Boston: Houghton Mifflin, 1962.

Pintner General Ability Tests, Non-language Series: Intermediate Test. Manual of directions. Yonkers-on-the-Hudson, N.Y.: World, 1945.

Plank, E., & Plank, R. Emotional components in arithmetical learning as seen through autobiographies. *Psychoanalytic Study of the Child*, 1954, *9*, 274–296.

Polya, G. *How to solve it.* Princeton, N.J.: Princeton University Press, 1945.

Polya, G. *Patterns of plausible inference. Vol. II of mathematics and plausible reasoning.* Princeton, N.J.: Princeton University Press, 1954.

Porter, A. Effect of organization size on validity of occupation-level score. *Personnel and Guidance Journal*, 1963, *41*, 547–548.

Postman, L. Recent developments in the experimental analysis of learning and concept formation. In W. B. Waetjen (Ed.), *New dimensions in learning: A multidisciplinary approach.* Washington, D.C.: Association for Supervision and Curriculum Development, National Education Association, 1961. Pp. 46–65.

Postman, L. Short-term memory and incidental learning. In A. W. Melton (Ed.), *Categories of human learning.* New York: Academic Press, 1964.

Postman, L., & Phillips, L. W. Studies in incidental learning: IX. A comparison of the methods of successive and single recalls. *Journal of Experimental Psychology*, 1961, *61*, 236–241.

Powell, M. *The psychology of adolescence.* Indianapolis: Bobbs-Merrill, 1963.

Prescott, D. (Ed.) *Helping teachers understand children.* Washington, D.C.: American Council on Education, 1945.

Pressey, S. L. A third and fourth contribution toward the coming "Industrial Revolution" in education. *School and Society*, 1932, *36*, 668–672.

Pressey, S. L. Two basic neglected psychoeducational problems. *American Psychologist*, 1965, *20*, 391–395.

Rabin, A. I. *Growing up in the Kibbutz.* New York: Springer, 1965.

Radin, S. S., & Masling, J. Tom: A gifted under-achieving child. *Journal of Child Psychology and Psychiatry*, 1963, *4*, 183–196.

Radke, M., Trager, H. G., & Davis, H. Social perceptions and attitudes of children. *Genetic Psychology Monographs*, 1949, *40*, 327–447.

Rapier, J. L. Learning abilities of normal and retarded children as a function of social class. *Journal of Educational Psychology*, 1968, *59*, 102–110.

Redl, F., & Wineman, D. *The aggressive child.* Glencoe, Ill.: Free Press, 1957.

Reese, H. Discrimination learning set and perceptual set in young children. *Child Development*, 1965, *36*, 153–161.

Reid, J. W. An experimental study of "analysis of the goal" in problem-solving. *Journal of General Psychology*, 1951, *4*, 51–69.

Restle, F., Andrews, M., & Rokeach, M. Differences between open- and closed-minded subjects on learning-set and oddity problems. *Journal of Abnormal and Social Psychology*, 1964, *68*, 648–654.

Reynolds, G. S. *A primer of operant conditioning.* Glenview, Ill.: Scott, Foresman, 1968.

Rheingold, H. L. The modification of social responsiveness in institutional babies. *Monograph of Society for Research in Child Development*, 1956, *21*, No. 2.

Riesman, D. *The lonely crowd: A study of the changing American character.* New Haven: Yale University Press, 1950.

Riessman, F. *The culturally deprived child.* New York: Harper & Row, 1962.

Ripple, R. E., & Rockcastle, V. N. (Eds.) *Piaget rediscovered.* Ithaca, N.Y.: School of Education, Cornell University, 1964.

Risley, T. Learning and lollipops. *Psychology Today*, 1968, *1* (8), 28–31, 62–65.

Robinson, E. S. The similarity factor in retroaction. *American Journal of Psychology*, 1927, *39*, 297–312.

Robinson, H. B., & Robinson, N. M. *The mentally retarded child: A psychological approach.* New York: McGraw-Hill, 1965.

Roe, A. *The making of a scientist.* New York: Dodd, Mead, 1953.

Roe, A. *The psychology of occupations.* New York: Wiley, 1956.

Roe, A., & Siegelman, M. *A study of the origin of interests.* APGA Inquiry Studies—No. 1. Washington, D.C.: American Personnel and Guidance Association, 1964.

Roff, M., Mink, W., & Hinrichs, G. *Developmental abnormal psychology.* New York: Holt, Rinehart, and Winston, 1966.

Rogers, C. R. Some issues concerning the control of human behavior. Part II. *Science*, 1956, *124*, 1060–1066.

Rogers, C. R. Toward a modern approach to values: The valuing process in the mature person. *Journal of Abnormal and Social Psychology*, 1964, *68*, 160–167.

Rogers, C. R. The interpersonal relationship in the facilitation of learning. In R. R. Leeper (Ed.), *Humanizing education: The person in the process.* Washington, D.C.: Association for Supervision and Curriculum Development, National Education Association, 1967. Pp. 1–18.

Rogers, C. R., & Dymond, R. F. *Psychotherapy and personality change: Co-ordinated research studies in the client-centered approach.* Chicago: University of Chicago Press, 1954.

Rokeach, M. *The open and closed mind: Investigations into the nature of belief systems and personality systems.* New York: Basic Books, 1960.

Rosekrans, M. A. Imitation in children as a function of perceived similarity to a social model and vicarious reinforcement. *Journal of Personality and Social Psychology*, 1967, 7, 307–315.

Rosen, B. C., & D'Andrade, R. The psychosocial origins of achievement motivation. *Sociometry*, 1959, *22*, 185–218.

Rosenbaum, M. E., & deCharms, R. Direct and vicarious reduction of hostility. *Journal of Abnormal and Social Psychology*, 1960, *60*, 105–112.

Rosenberg, M. *Society and the adolescent self-image.* Princeton, N.J.: Princeton University Press, 1965.

Rosenhan, D. L. Effects of social class and race on responsiveness to approval and disapproval. *Journal of Personality and Social Psychology*, 1966, *4*, 253–259.

Rosenthal, R. Experimenter expectancy and the reassuring nature of the null hypothesis decision procedure. *Psychological Bulletin Monograph*, 1968, *70*, No. 6, Part 2, 30–48.

Rosenthal, R. Empirical versus decreed validation of clocks and tests. *American Educational Research Journal*, 1969, *6*, 689–691.

Rosenthal, R., & Jacobson, L. *Pygmalion in the classroom: Teacher expectation and pupils' intellectual development.* New York: Holt, Rinehart, and Winston, 1968.

Roth, D. M. *Roth memory course.* Santa Monica: Motivation, 1961.

Rotter, J. B. Some implications of a social learning theory for the prediction of goal directed behavior from testing procedures. *Psychological Review*, 1960, *67*, 301–316.

Rotter, J. B. Generalized expectancies for internal versus external control of reinforcement. *Psychological Monographs*, 1966, *80* (1, Whole Number 609).

Russell, D. H. *Children's thinking.* Boston: Ginn and Co., 1956.

Russell, W. A., & Storms, L. H. Implicit verbal chaining in paired-associate learning. *Journal of Experimental Psychology*, 1955, *49*, 287–293.

Salomon, G., & Sieber, J. G. Relevant subjective response uncertainty as a function of stimulus-task interaction. *Research and Development Memorandum*, No. 3. Bloomington, Ind.: Indiana University, 1969.

Sanford, N. *Self and society: Social change and individual development.* New York: Atherton Press, 1966.

Sarason, S. B., Davidson, K. S., Lighthall, F. F., Waite, R. R., & Ruebush, B. K. *Anxiety in elementary school children.* New York: Wiley, 1960.

Sarason, S. B., Mandler, G., & Craighill, P. G. The effect of differential instructions on anxiety and learning. *Journal of Abnormal and Social Psychology,* 1952, *47,* 561–565.

Sarnoff, I., & Katz, D. The motivational bases of attitude change. *Journal of Abnormal and Social Psychology,* 1954, *49,* 115–124.

Sax, G., & Cromach, T. R. The effects of various forms of item arrangements on test performance. *Journal of Educational Measurement,* 1966, *3,* 309–311.

Sax, G., & Reade, M. Achievement as a function of test difficulty level. *American Educational Research Journal,* 1964, *1,* 22–25.

Scannell, D. P. *Tests of Academic Progress Multi-level Test Booklet for Grades 9–12.* Boston: Houghton Mifflin Co., 1964.

Scannell, D. P., & Marshall, J. C. The effect of selected composition errors on grades assigned to essay examinations. *American Educational Research Journal,* 1966, *3,* 125–130.

Schachter, S. *The psychology of affiliation.* Palo Alto, Calif.: Stanford University Press, 1959.

Schaffer, H. R. Objective observations of personality development in early infancy. *British Journal of Medical Psychology,* 1958, *31,* 174–183.

School Mathematics Study Group. *Description of SMSG Titles.* New Haven: Yale University Press, 1966.

Schreider, E. Possible selective mechanism of social differentiation in biological traits. *Human biology: An international record of research,* 1967, *39,* 14–20.

Schroder, H. M. Development and maintenance of the preference value of an object. *Journal of Experimental Psychology,* 1956, *51,* 139–141.

Schroder, H. M., & Rotter, J. B. Rigidity as learned behavior. *Journal of Experimental Psychology,* 1952, *44,* 141–150.

Schuldt, W. J., & Truax, C. B. Client awareness of adjustment in self- and ideal-self-concepts. *Journal of Counseling Psychology,* 1968, *15,* 158–159.

Schulz, R. W. Problem-solving behavior and transfer. *Harvard Educational Review,* 1960, *30,* 61–77.

Schumacher, A. S., Wright, J. M., & Wiesen, A. E. The self as a source of anxiety. *Journal of Consulting and Clinical Psychology,* 1968, *32,* 33–34.

Schrupp, M. H., Manfred, H., & Gjerde, C. M. Teacher growth and attitudes toward behavior problems of children. *Journal of Educational Psychology,* 1953, *44,* 203–214.

Scott, J. P. *Aggression.* Chicago: University of Chicago Press, 1958.

Scott, W. A. Attitude change by response reinforcement: Replication and extension. *Sociometry,* 1959, *22,* 328–335.

Sears, P. Levels of aspiration in academically successful and unsuccessful children. *Journal of Abnormal and Social Psychology,* 1940, *35,* 498–536.

Sears, P. *The effect of classroom conditions on the strength of achievement motive and work output of elementary school children.* U.S. Office of Education Cooperative Research Project No. 873. Palo Alto, Calif.: Stanford University Press, 1963.

Sears, P. S., & Sherman, V. S. *In pursuit of self-esteem: Case studies of eight elementary school children.* Belmont, Calif.: Wadsworth, 1964.

Sears, R. R., Maccoby, E. E., & Levin, H., in collaboration with Lowell, E. L., Sears, P. S., & Whiting, J. W. M. *Patterns of child rearing.* Evanston, Ill.: Row, Peterson, 1957.

Seashore, H. G. *Methods of expressing test scores.* Test Service Bulletin No. 48. New York: Psychological Corporation, 1955.

Seibel, R. Discrimination reaction time for a 1023-alternative task. *Journal of Experimental Psychology,* 1963, 66, 215–226.

Seibel, R. *Organization in human verbal learning.* Paper presented at the meeting of the Psychonomic Society, Chicago, October, 1965.

Seibel, R. *Organization in human learning: Some more on the study sheet paradigm and an experiment with "exhaustive" categories.* Paper delivered at the meeting of the Psychonomic Society, St. Louis, Missouri, October, 1966.

Sells, S. B. The atmosphere effect: An experimental study of reasoning. *Archives of Psychology,* 1936, Whole No. 200.

Shaffer, L. F., & Shoben, E. J., Jr. *The psychology of adjustment: A dynamic and experimental approach to personality and mental hygiene.* (2nd ed.) Boston: Houghton Mifflin, 1956.

Sheerer, E. T. An analysis of the relationship between acceptance of and respect for self and acceptance of and respect for others in ten counseling cases. *Journal of Consulting Psychology,* 1949, 13, 169–175.

Sherriffs, A. C., & Boomer, D. S. Who is penalized by the penalty for guessing? *Journal of Educational Psychology,* 1954, 45, 81–90.

Shiffrin, R. M. & Atkinson, R. C. Storage and retrieval processes in long term memory. *Psychological Review,* 1969, 76, 179–193.

Sieber, J. E., & Salomon, G. *Relevant subjective response uncertainty as a function of stimulus-task interaction.* Bloomington: Indiana University School of Education, Division of Instructional Media, Research and Development Memorandum No. 3, January, 1969.

Sigel, I. E. Developmental trends in the abstraction ability of children. *Child Development,* 1953, 24, 131–144.

Silberman, C. E. *Crisis in black and white.* New York: Random House, 1964.

Silberman, C. E. The schools and the fight against prejudice. In C. Y. Glock & E. Siegelman (Eds.), *Prejudice U. S. A.* New York: Frederick A. Praeger, 1969. Pp. 136–149.

Silverman, I. Self-esteem and differential responsiveness to success and failure. *Journal of Abnormal and Social Psychology,* 1964, 69, 115–119.

Simon, B. (Ed.) *Psychology in the Soviet Union.* Palo Alto, Calif.: Stanford University Press, 1957.

Simon, H. A., & Newell, A. Information processing in computer and man. *American Scientist,* 1964, 52, 281–300.

Skeels, H. M. Adult status of children with contrasting early life experiences: A follow-up study. *Monographs of the Society for Research in Child Development,* 1966, 31 (3, Serial No. 105).

Skinner, B. F. *Science and human behavior.* New York: Macmillan, 1953.

Skinner, B. F. Some issues concerning the control of human behavior. Part I. *Science,* 1956, 124, 1057–1060.

Skinner, B. F. *Verbal behavior.* New York: Appleton-Century-Crofts, 1957.

Skinner, B. F. *Cumulative record.* (Enlarged ed.) New York: Appleton-Century-Crofts, 1961.

Smedslund, J. The acquisition of conservation of substance and weight in children. V. Practice in conflict situations without external reinforcement. *The Scandinavian Journal of Psychology*, 1961, *2*, 156–160.

Smedslund, J. Patterns of experience and the acquisition of concrete transitivity of weight in eight-year-old children. *The Scandinavian Journal of Psychology*, 1963, *4*, 251–256.

Smith, D. E. P. (Ed.) *Learning to learn.* New York: Harcourt, Brace, and World, 1961.

Smith, M. B., Bruner, J. S., & White, R. W. *Opinions and personality.* New York: Wiley, 1956.

Smith, M. K. Measurement of the size of general English vocabulary through the elementary grades and high school. *Genetic Psychology Monographs*, 1941, *24*, 311–345.

Smith, R. K., & Noble, C. E. Effects of a mnemonic technique applied to verbal learning and memory. *Perceptual and Motor Skills*, 1965, *21*, 123–134.

Snow, R. E. Review of R. Rosenthal & L. Jacobson, Pygmalion in the classroom: Teacher expectation and pupils' intellectual development. *Contemporary Psychology*, 1969, *14*, 197–199.

Solomon, P., *et al.* (Eds.) *Sensory deprivation: A symposium held at Harvard Medical School.* Cambridge, Mass.: Harvard University Press, 1961.

Solomon, R. L. Punishment. *American Psychologist*, 1964, *19*, 239–253.

Solomon, R. J. Improving the essay test in the social studies. In H. D. Berg (Ed.), *Evaluation in social studies.* 35th Yearbook of the National Council for the Social Studies. Washington, D.C.; National Education Association, 1965. Pp. 137–153.

Sontag, L. W. Psychodynamics of child delinquency: Further contributions. *American Journal of Orthopsychiatry*, 1955, *25*, 254–261.

Sontag, L. W., & Kagan, J. The emergence of intellectual achievement motives. *American Journal of Orthopsychiatry*, 1963, *33*, 532–535.

Sorenson, A. G., Husek, T. R., & Yu, C. Divergent concepts of teacher role: An approach to the measurement of teacher effectiveness. *Journal of Educational Psychology*, 1963, *54*, 287–294.

Spence, K. W. Theoretical interpretations of learning. In S. S. Stevens (Ed.), *Handbook of experimental psychology.* New York: Wiley, 1951. Pp. 690–729.

Spence, K. W. *Behavior theory and conditioning.* New Haven: Yale University Press, 1956.

Spence, K. W. The relation of learning theory to the technology of education. *Harvard Educational Review*, 1959, *29*, 84–95.

Spence, K. W. Anxiety (drive) level and performance in eyelid conditioning. *Psychological Bulletin*, 1964, *61*, 129–139.

Spielberger, C. D. The effects of anxiety on complex learning and academic achievement. In C. D. Spielberger (Ed.), *Anxiety and behavior.* New York: Academic Press, 1966. Pp. 361–398.

Spielberger, C. D., & Lushene, R. E. Theory and measurement of anxiety states. In R. B. Cattell (Ed.), *Handbook of modern personality theory.* Chicago: Aldine, 1969.

Spiker, C. C. Experiments with children on the hypotheses of acquired distinctiveness and equivalence of cues. *Child Development*, 1956, *27*, 253–263. (a)

Spiker, C. C. The stimulus generalization gradient as a function of the intensity of stimulus lights. *Child Development*, 1956, *27*, 85–98. (b)

Spiro, M. E. *Kibbutz: Venture in Utopia*. New York: Schocken Books, 1963.

Spiro, M. E. *Children of the Kibbutz*. New York: Schocken Books, 1965.

Spitz, R. A. The smiling response: A contribution to the ontogenesis of social relations. *Genetic Psychology Monographs*, 1946, *34*, 57–125.

Staats, A. W. *Learning, language, and cognition*. New York: Holt, Rinehart, and Winston, 1968.

Staats, A. W., & Staats, C. K. *Complex human behavior: A systematic extension of learning principles*. New York: Holt, Rinehart, and Winston, 1963.

Staines, J. W. The self-picture as a factor in the classroom. *British Journal of Educational Psychology*, 1958, *28*, 97–111.

Starbuck, W. H. Level of aspiration. *Psychological Review*, 1963, *70*, 51–60.

Starch, D., and Elliott, E. C. Reliability of grading high-school work in English. *School Review*, 1912, *20*, 442–457.

Starch, D., & Elliott, E. C. Reliability of grading work in mathematics. *School Review*, 1913, *21*, 254–259.

Stefflre, B. The reading difficulty of interest inventories. *Occupations*, 1947, *26*, 95–96.

Stendler, C. B. Aspects of Piaget's theory that have implications for teacher education. *Journal of Teacher Education*, 1965. *16*, 329–335.

Stevenson, H. W., & Allen, S. Adult performance as a function of sex of experimenter and sex of subject. *Journal of Abnormal and Social Psychology*, 1964, *68*, 214–216.

Stewart, J. C. An experimental investigation of imagery. Toronto: University of Toronto, unpublished doctoral dissertation, 1965.

Stewart, W. A. Urban Negro speech: Sociolinguistic factors affecting English teaching. In R. Shuy (Ed.), *Social dialects and language learning*. Champaign, Ill.: National Council of Teachers of English, 1964. Pp. 10–18.

Stodolsky, S. S., & Lesser, G. Learning patterns in the disadvantaged. *Harvard Educational Review*, 1967, *37*, 546–593.

Stolurow, L. Computer assisted instruction. In A. Ellis, J. Weizenbaum, L. Stolurow, & E. Mesthene, *Cybernetics and education: A colloquium*. Cambridge: The New England Education Data Systems, 1968. Pp. 32–50.

Stone, L. J. A critique of studies of infant isolation. *Child Development*, 1954, *25*, 9–20.

Stotland, E., & Dunn, R. E. Empathy, self-esteem and birth order. *Journal of Abnormal and Social Psychology*, 1963, *66*, 532–540.

Stotland, E., & Hillmer, M. L., Jr. Identification, authoritarian defensiveness, and self-esteem. *Journal of Abnormal and Social Psychology*, 1962, *64*, 334–342.

Stouffer, G. A. W., Jr. Behavior problems of children as viewed by teachers and mental hygienists. *Mental Hygiene*, 1952, *36*, 271–285.

Stromberg, E. L. *Stromberg Dexterity Test*. New York: Psychological Corporation, 1947–1951.

Strong, E. K., Jr. *Vocational interests 18 years after college*. Minneapolis: University of Minnesota Press, 1955.

Strong, E. K., Jr. Good and poor interest items. *Journal of Applied Psychology*, 1962, *46*, 269–275.

Strong, E. K., Jr. Reworded versus new interest items. *Journal of Applied Psychology*, 1963, 47, 111–116.

Strong, E. K., Jr. *Strong Vocational Interest Blank for Men*, Form T399. Revised by E. K. Strong, Jr., D. P. Campbell, R. F. Berdie, & K. E Clark. Palo Alto, Calif.: Stanford University Press, 1966.

Strong, E. K., Jr., Berdie, R. F., Campbell, D. P., & Clark, K. E. Proposed scoring changes for the Strong Vocational Interest Blank. *Journal of Applied Psychology*, 1964, 48, 75–80.

Stroud, J. B. Experiments on learning in school situations. *Psychological Bulletin*, 1940, 37, 777–807.

Suchman, J. R. Inquiry training in the elementary school. *Science Teacher*, 1960, 27, 42–47.

Suchman, J. R. *Inquiry development program: Idea book*. Chicago: Science Research Associates, 1966. (a)

Suchman, J. R. A model for the analysis of inquiry. In H. J. Klausmeier & C. W. Harris (Eds.), *Analyses of concept learning*. New York: Academic Press, 1966. Pp. 177–187. (b)

Super, D. E. *Appraising vocational fitness by means of psychological tests*. New York: Harper & Brothers, 1949.

Super, D. E., & Crites, J. O. *Appraising vocational fitness by means of psychological tests*. (Rev. ed.) New York: Harper & Row, 1962.

Super, D. E., & Overstreet, P. L., in collaboration with C. N. Morris, W. Dubin, & M. B. Heyde. *The vocational maturity of ninth-grade boys*. New York: Bureau of Publications, Teachers College, Columbia University Press, 1960.

Super, D. E., Starishevsky, R., Matlin, N., & Jordaan, J. P. *Career development: Self-concept theory*. New York: College Entrance Examination Board, 1963.

Super, D. E., et al. *Vocational development: A framework for research*. New York: Bureau of Publications, Teachers College, Columbia University Press, 1957.

Suppes, P. Modern learning theory and the elementary-school curriculum. *American Educational Research Journal*, 1964, 1, 79–93.

Suziedelis, A., & Steimel, R. The relationship of need hierarchies to inventoried interests. *Personnel and Guidance Journal*, 1963, 42, 393–396.

Symonds, P. M. *The ego and the self*. New York: Appleton-Century-Crofts, 1951.

Tanner, J. M., & Inhelder, B. (Eds.) *Discussions on child development*. Vol. II. New York: International Universities Press, 1957.

Taylor, J. A. A personality scale of manifest anxiety. *Journal of Abnormal and Social Psychology*, 1953, 48, 285–290.

Taylor, J. Drive theory and manifest anxiety. *Psychological Bulletin*, 1956, 53, 303–320.

Terman, L. M. *The measurement of intelligence: An explanation of and a complete guide for the use of the Stanford-revision and extension of the Binet-Simon intelligence scale*. Boston: Houghton Mifflin, 1916.

Terman, L. M., & Merrill, M. A. *Measuring intelligence: A guide to the administration of the new revised Stanford-Binet tests of intelligence*. Boston: Houghton Mifflin, 1937.

Terman, L. M., & Merrill, M. A. *Stanford-Binet Intelligence Scale*. Boston: Houghton Mifflin, 1960.

Terman, L. M., & Oden, M. H. *The gifted child grows up: Twenty-five years' follow-up of a superior group.* Palo Alto, Calif.: Stanford University Press, 1947.

Terman, L. M., & Oden, M. H. *The gifted group at midlife.* Palo Alto, Calif.: Stanford University Press, 1959.

Terman, L. M., et al. *Genetic studies of genius:* I. *Mental and physical traits of a thousand gifted children.* Palo Alto, Calif.: Stanford University Press, 1925.

Thelen, H. A. Education dynamics: Theory and research. *Journal of Social Issues,* 1950, *6,* No. 2.

Thistlethwaite, D. Attitude and structure as factors in the distortion of reasoning. *Journal of Abnormal and Social Psychology,* 1950, *45,* 442–458.

Thomas, O. *Transformational grammar and the teacher of English.* New York: Holt, Rinehart, and Winston, 1965.

Thompson, G. G. *Child psychology: Growth trends in psychological adjustment.* (2nd ed.) Boston: Houghton Mifflin, 1962.

Thompson, G. G., & Witryol, S. L. Adult recall of unpleasant experiences during three periods of childhood. *Journal of Genetic Psychology,* 1948, *72,* 111–123.

Thompson, G. G., & Witryol, S. L. Unpleasant experiences during childhood. In R. G. Kuhlen & G. G. Thompson (Eds.), *Psychological studies of human development.* New York: Appleton-Century-Crofts, 1952.

Thorndike, E. L. *Educational psychology:* Vol. II. *The psychology of learning.* New York: Bureau of Publications, Teachers College, Columbia University Press, 1913.

Thorndike, E. L. Intelligence and its measurement: A symposium. *Journal of Educational Psychology,* 1921, *12,* 124–127.

Thorndike, E. L. Mental discipline in high school studies. *Journal of Educational Psychology,* 1924, *15,* 83–98.

Thorndike, E. L. *The fundamentals of learning.* New York: Teachers College, Columbia University, 1932.

Thorndike, E. L. *Selected writings from a connectionist's psychology.* New York: Appleton-Century-Crofts, 1949.

Thorndike, R. L. Review of R. Rosenthal & L. Jacobson. Pygmalion in the classroom: Teacher expectation and pupils' intellectual development. *American Educational Research Journal,* 1968, *5,* 708–711.

Thorndike, R. L. But you have to know how to tell time. *American Educational Research Journal,* 1969, *6,* 692.

Thorndike, R. L., & Hagen, E. *Ten Thousand Careers.* New York: Wiley, 1959.

Thurstone, L. L. *Multiple factor analysis: A development and expansion of the vectors of the mind.* Chicago: University of Chicago Press, 1947.

Thurstone, L. L. Psychological implications of factor analysis. *American Psychologist,* 1948, *3,* 402–408.

Thurstone, L. L., & Thurstone, T. G. *Primary mental abilities. Psychometric Monographs,* No. 1. Chicago: University of Chicago Press, 1938.

Thurstone, L. L., & Thurstone, T. G. Factorial studies of intelligence. *Psychometric Monographs,* 1941, No. 2.

Thurstone, L. L., & Thurstone, T. G. *SRA primary mental abilities scales: Primary, ages 5 to 7; elementary, ages 7 to 11; and, intermediate, ages 11 to 17.* Chicago: Science Research Associates, 1946–1958.

Tiedeman, D. V., & O'Hara, R. P. *Career development: Choice and adjustment: Differentiation and integration in career development.* Princeton, N.J.: College Entrance Examination Board, 1963.

Tinkelman, S. N. *Improving the classroom test: A manual of test construction procedure for the classroom teacher.* Albany: University of the State of New York, 1957.

Tolman, E. C. There is more than one kind of learning. *Psychological Review,* 1949, *56,* 144–155. (a)

Tolman, E. C. The nature and functioning of wants. *Psychological Review,* 1949, *56,* 357–369. (b)

Tolman, E. C. *Behavior and psychological man: Essays in motivation and learning.* Berkeley: University of California Press, 1958. (Originally published as *Collected papers in psychology,* 1951.)

Tolman, E. C. Principles of purposive behavior. In S. Koch (Ed.), *Psychology: A study of a science.* Vol. 2. New York: McGraw-Hill, 1959. Pp. 92–157.

Tolman, E. C. A psychological model. In T. Parsons & E. A. Shils (Eds.), *Toward a general theory of action.* Cambridge, Mass.: Harvard University Press, 1951. (Reprinted in 1962.)

Tolor, A., Scarpetti, W. L., & Lane, P. A. Teachers' attitudes towards children's behavior revisited. *Journal of Educational Psychology,* 1967, *58,* 175–180.

Torrance, E. P. *Guiding creative talent.* Englewood Cliffs, N.J.: Prentice-Hall, 1962.

Trager, H. G., & Yarrow, M. R. *They learn what they live: Prejudice in young children.* New York: Harper and Row, 1952.

Travers, R. M. W., Van Wagenen, R. K., Haygood, D. H., & McCormick, M. Learning as a consequence of the learner's task involvement under different conditions of feedback. *Journal of Educational Psychology,* 1964, *55,* 167–173.

Tryon, C. M. Comparisons between self-estimates and classmates' estimates of personality during adolescence. *Psychological Bulletin,* 1939, *36,* 568.

Tulving, E. The effect of alphabetical subjective organization on memorizing unrelated words. *Canadian Journal of Psychology,* 1962, *16,* 185–191.

Turner, M. B. *Philosophy and the science of behavior.* New York: Appleton-Century-Crofts, 1965.

Turner, R. H. Dithering devices in the classroom: How to succeed in shaking up a campus by really trying. *American Psychologist,* 1966, *21,* 957–963.

Tyler, L. E. The relationship of interests to abilities and reputation among first-grade children. *Educational and Psychological Measurement,* 1951, *11,* 255–264.

Tyler, L. E. The development of "Vocational Interests": I. The organization of likes and dislikes in ten-year-old children. *Journal of Genetic Psychology,* 1955, *86,* 33–44.

Tyler, L. E. *Tests and measurements.* Englewood Cliffs, N.J.: Prentice-Hall, 1963.

Tyler, L. E. *The psychology of human differences.* New York: Appleton-Century-Crofts, 1965.

Ulmer, G. Teaching geometry to cultivate reflective thinking: An experimental study with 1239 high school pupils. *Journal of Experimental Education,* 1939, *8,* 18–25.

Underwood, B. J. Interference and forgetting. *Psychological Review*, 1957, *64*, 49–60.

Underwood, B. J. *Experimental psychology*. New York: Appleton-Century-Crofts, 1966.

Updegraff, R., Keister, M. E., *et al.* Studies in preschool education I. *University of Iowa Studies in Child Welfare*, 1937, *14*, No. 346.

Vacchiano, R. B., Strauss, P. S., and Hochman, L. The open and closed mind: A review of dogmatism. *Psychological Bulletin*, 1969, *71*, 261–273.

Van De Riet, H. Effects of praise and reproof on paired-associate learning in educationally retarded children. *Journal of Educational Psychology*, 1964, *55*, 139–143.

Van Wagenen, R. K., & Travers, R. M. W. Learning under conditions of direct and vicarious reinforcement. *Journal of Educational Psychology*, 1963, *54*, 356–362.

Vernon, J. A., McGill, T. E., Gulick, W. L., & Candland, D. K. The effect of human isolation upon some perceptual and motor skills. In P. Solomon, *et al.* (Eds), *Sensory deprivation: A symposium held at Harvard Medical School.* Cambridge, Mass.: Harvard University Press, 1961. Pp. 41–57.

Vogel, W., Raymond, S., & Lazarus, R. S. Intrinsic motivation and psychological stress. *Journal of Abnormal and Social Psychology*, 1959, *58*, 225–233.

Walker, E. L. Psychological complexity as a basis for a theory of motivation and choice. In D. Levine (Ed.), *Nebraska symposium on motivation.* Lincoln, Neb.: University of Nebraska Press, 1964. Pp. 47–95.

Wallach, M. A., & Kogan, N. *Modes of thinking in young children.* New York: Holt, Rinehart, and Winston, 1965.

Walters, R. H., Leat, M., & Mezei, L. Inhibition and disinhibition of responses through empathetic learning. *Canadian Journal of Psychology*, 1963, *17*, 235–243.

Washington, B. B. Did counseling function here? *Personnel and Guidance Journal*, 1954, 489–491.

Weber, C. A. Do teachers understand learning theory? *Phi Delta Kappan*, 1965, *46*, 433–435.

Wechsler, D. *Wechsler Intelligence Scale for Children: Manual.* New York: Psychological Corporation, 1949.

Wechsler, D. *Wechsler Adult Intelligence Scale.* New York: Psychological Corporation, 1955.

Wechsler, D. *Wechsler Preschool and Primary Scale of Intelligence.* New York: Psychological Corporation, 1967.

Wertheimer, M. *Productive thinking.* (Enlarged ed. edited by M. Wertheimer.) New York: Harper & Row, 1959.

Wesman, A. G. *A study of transfer of training from high school subjects to intelligence.* Teachers College, Columbia University, Contributions to Education, No. 909. New York: Teachers College, Columbia University, 1945.

White, R. W. Motivation reconsidered: The concept of competence. *Psychological Review*, 1959, *66*, 297–333.

White, R. W. *Lives in progress: A study of the natural growth of personality.* (2nd ed.) New York: Holt, Rinehart, and Winston, 1966.

Whitehead, A. N. *The aims of education and other essays.* London: Williams and Northgate, 1950.

Whiteman, M., & Deutsch, M. Social disadvantage as related to intellective and language development. In M. Deutsch, I. Katz, & A. R. Jensen (Eds.), *Social class, race, and psychological development.* New York: Holt, Rinehart, and Winston, 1968.

Whiting, B. (Ed.) *Six cultures: Studies of child rearing.* New York: Wiley, 1963.

Whiting, J. W. M., & Child, I. L. *Child training and personality: A cross-cultural study.* New Haven: Yale University Press, 1953.

Wickman, E. K. *Children's behavior and teachers' attitudes.* New York: Commonwealth Fund, 1928.

Wilson, A. B. Residential segregation of social classes and aspirations of high school boys. *American Sociological Review,* 1959, *24,* 836–845.

Wilson, R. The structure of the intellect. In M. J. Aschner & C. E. Bish (Eds.), *Productive thinking in education.* (Rev. ed.) Washington, D.C.: Project on the academically talented students, National Education Association, 1968.

Winterbottom, M. R. The sources of achievement motivation in mothers' attitudes toward independence training. In D. C. McClelland, *et al.* (Eds.), *The achievement motive.* New York: Appleton-Century-Crofts, 1953. Pp. 297–306.

Witryol, S. L., Tyrrell, D. J., & Lowden, L. M. Development of incentive values in childhood. *Genetic Psychology Monographs,* 1965, *72,* 201–246.

Wittrock, M. C., Keislar, E. R., & Stern, C. Verbal cues in concept identification. *Journal of Educational Psychology,* 1964, *55,* 195–200.

Wolfe, J. B. Effectiveness of token rewards for chimpanzees. *Comparative Psychological Monographs,* 1932, *12,* 72.

Wolpe, J. *Psychotherapy by reciprocal inhibition.* Palo Alto, Calif.: Stanford University Press, 1958.

Wood, D. A. *Test construction: Development and interpretation of achievement tests.* Columbus, Ohio: Charles E. Merrill, 1960.

Wood, G. Mnemonic systems in recall. *Journal of Educational Psychology Monograph,* 1967, *58,* 6, Part 2. Whole No. 645.

Woodrow, H. The effect of type of training upon transference. *Journal of Educational Psychology,* 1927, *18,* 159–172.

Wright, H. F. How the psychology of motivation is related to curriculum development. *Journal of Educational Psychology,* 1948, *39,* 149–156.

Wright, J. C., & Kagan, J. (Eds.) Basic cognitive processes in children. *Society for Research in Child Development Monographs,* 1963, *28,* No. 2.

Wyckoff, L. B., Jr. The role of observing responses in discrimination learning: Part I. *Psychological Review,* 1952, *59,* 431–442.

Yavuz, H. S. The retention of incidentally learned connotative responses. *Journal of Psychology,* 1963, *55,* 409–418.

Yavuz, H. S., & Bousfield, W. A. Recall of connotative meaning. *Psychological Reports,* 1959, *5,* 319–320.

Yerkes, R. M., & Dodson, J. D. The relation of strength of stimulus to rapidity of habit formation. *Journal of Comparative Neurological Psychology,* 1908, *18,* 459–482.

Young, L. R. Delinquency from the child's viewpoint. *Focus*, May 1951, *30*, 69–74. Also in C. B. Vedder (Ed.), *The juvenile offender*. New York: Doubleday, 1954.

Youtz, A. C. An experimental evaluation of Jost's Laws. *Psychological Monographs*, 1941, *53*, Whole No. 238.

Zeiler, M. D. The ratio theory of intermediate size discrimination. *Psychological Review*, 1963, *70*, 516–533.

Zigler, E., & Kanzer, P. The effectiveness of two classes of verbal reinforcers on the performance of middle- and lower-class children. *Journal of Personality*, 1962, *30*, 157–163.

Subject index

Ability level, and programmed instruction, 30

Ability patterns of ethnic groups, 437

Abstract reasoning, in DAT, 592

Abstraction: and association, 56; in concept learning, 139, 307-308; object-based *vs* action-based, 56-57; and problem-solving, 373

Acceptance: learning of, 138; in self-actualization, 456

Accommodation: in adaptation, 99; and psychological growth, 54

Achievement: and aptitude scores, 566-557; factors influencing, 472-473; and interest, 230-231; as motive, 166, 167-168; and praise, 179, 180-181; and school quality, 81; and self-concept, 431, 479; and socioeconomic status, 472; tests of, 507-554. *See also* Success

Achievement demands in elementary schools, 484-485

Achievement ethic, and coping behavior, 409

Achievement motive, 194, 234, 663; development of, 208-214; and family atmosphere, 200-201; and socioeconomic status, 201; and success orientation, 189; and threat to goals, 198

Achievement need, 90; and effective stimuli, 107; and family, 72

Acrolect, 352

Activity, in stimulus-response theory, 660

Activity dimension of connotative meaning, 329

Adaptability, and verbal ability, 248

Adaptation, 98-100; *vs* adjustment, 86, 100; as goal of education, 103; and intense motivation, 175; in operant learning, 119; Piaget's concept, 54; problem-solving as, 143; psychological, ii; quantitative *vs* qualitative, 98; and readiness, 121

Adaptation level, and motivation, 232-233

Adaptive striving, 199-202

Adjustment, 86-98; and adaptation, 54, 100; of gifted children, 588; strategies of, 452; and striving, 199

Adjustment mechanisms, 404-414

Advertising, and attitude learning, 497; and self-esteem, 451

Advisor, teacher as, 77

Affection: in child raising, 74-75; as goal, 157; in self-actualization, 457; in teacher, 75

Affective attributes of concepts, 329

Affective components in attitude learning, 146

Affective reactions, and attitude learning, 138-139

Affiliation ethic, and coping behavior, 409

Affiliation motive, 194, 663; and threat to goals, 198

Affiliation need, and family, 72; as motive, 166, 168-169

AGCT, 578

Age: and achievement motivation, 200-201; chronological, and psychological development, 46; and cognitive development, 299; and cognitive process, 345-346; and concept formation, 338-